As more countries look to follow evidence-based policies on drug law reform, this book is a welcome addition to the literature on this subject. The "war on drugs" has been a failure. Policymakers need to know what the alternatives to futile attempts to prohibit drugs are. This book draws on the work of international experts to explore such options.

Rt Hon Helen Clark, former Prime Minister of New Zealand and member of the Global Commission on Drug Policy

This is a comprehensive account of the diverse forms that cannabis legalization has taken in recent years, with a separate chapter telling the story and considering the lessons for each case, ranging from Uruguay to Spain to Canada, with US states, Jamaica, the Netherlands and other places in between. Other chapters consider lessons for cannabis control from regulation of alcohol and of tobacco, and from New Zealand's attempts to regulate "legal highs". It's a "must read" for anyone interested in drug policy: its histories are memorable, its interpretations thought-provoking. It's worthwhile reading too for anyone interested in market regulation, in public health policy, or in law reform.

Prof. Robin Room, Centre for Alcohol Policy Research, La Trobe University

Professors Decorte, Lenton, and Wilkins have assembled a global all-star team of drug policy researchers for this excellent book. It's a must read for those seeking new insights about the past, present, and future of cannabis legalization.

Dr. Beau Kilmer, coauthor of Marijuana Legalization: What Everyone Needs to Know *and Director of the RAND Drug Policy Research Center*

Legalizing Cannabis

Marijuana is the most widely used illegal drug in the world. Over the past couple of decades, several Western jurisdictions have seen reforms in, or changes to, the way cannabis use is being controlled, departing from traditional approaches of criminal prohibition that have dominated cannabis use control regimes for most of the twentieth century. While reform is stalled at the international level, the last decade has seen an acceleration of legislative and regulatory reforms at the local and national levels, with countries no longer willing to bear the human and financial costs of prohibitive policies. Furthermore, legalization models have been implemented in US states, Canada and Uruguay, and are being debated in a number of other countries. These models are providing the world with unique pilot programs from which to study and learn.

This book assembles an international who's who of cannabis scholars who bring together the best available evidence and expertise to address questions such as: How should we evaluate the models of cannabis legalization as they have been implemented in several jurisdictions in the past few years? Which scenarios for future cannabis legalization have been developed elsewhere, and how similar/different are they from the models already implemented? What lessons from the successes and failures experienced with the regulation of other psychoactive substances (such as alcohol, tobacco, pharmaceuticals and "legal highs") can be translated to the effective regulation of cannabis markets?

This book may appeal to anyone interested in public health policies and drug policy reform and offers relevant insights for stakeholders in any other country where academic, societal or political evaluations of current cannabis policies (and even broader: current drug policies) are a subject of debate.

Tom Decorte is Professor of Criminology and Director of the Institute for Social Drug Research (ISD) at Ghent University (Belgium). He is co-founder of the Global Cannabis Cultivation Research Consortium (GCCRC). He has been advisor to a range of organizations on policies to improve public health relating to the use of drugs around the world.

Simon Lenton is a Professor and the Director of the National Drug Research Institute at Curtin University, Australia, and works part time as a clinical psychologist. He has published widely on drugs, health and the law and provided advice to a range of government and private organizations on evidence-based drug policy and other drug issues.

Chris Wilkins is Associate Professor and is the leader of the drug research team at SHORE & Whāriki Research Centre, Massey University, New Zealand. He has researched drug trends, drug markets and drug policy change. Dr Wilkins has been an invited speaker at international meetings in Europe, the United States and Australia.

Routledge Studies in Crime and Society

Changing Narratives of Youth Crime
From Social Causes to Threats to the Social
Bernd Dollinger

Human Enhancement Drugs
Edited by Katinka van de Ven, Kyle J.D. Mulrooney and Jim McVeigh

Organized Crime and Terrorist Networks
Edited by Vincenzo Ruggiero

Private Security and Domestic Violence
The Risks and Benefits of Private Security Companies Working with Victims of Domestic Violence
Diarmaid Harkin

The Human Factor of Cybercrime
Edited by Rutger Leukfeldt and Thomas J. Holt

Medical Misinformation and Social Harm in Non-Science Based Health Practices
A Multidisciplinary Perspective
Edited by Anita Lavorgna and Anna Di Ronco

Crime, Harm and Consumer Culture
Edited by Steve Hall, Tereza Kuldova and Mark Horsley

Legalizing Cannabis
Experiences, Lessons and Scenarios
Edited by Tom Decorte, Simon Lenton and Chris Wilkins

For more information about this series, please visit: www.routledge.com/Routledge-Studies-in-Crime-and-Society/book-series/RSCS

Legalizing Cannabis

Experiences, Lessons and Scenarios

Edited by Tom Decorte, Simon Lenton and Chris Wilkins

Routledge
Taylor & Francis Group
LONDON AND NEW YORK

First published 2020 by Routledge

2 Park Square, Milton Park, Abingdon, Oxon OX14 4RN
605 Third Avenue, New York, NY 10017

Routledge is an imprint of the Taylor & Francis Group, an informa business

First issued in paperback 2021

Publisher's Note

The publisher has gone to great lengths to ensure the quality of this reprint but points out that some imperfections in the original copies may be apparent.

British Library Cataloguing-in-Publication Data
A catalogue record for this book is available from the British Library

Library of Congress Cataloging-in-Publication Data
Names: Decorte, Tom, editor. | Lenton, Simon, 1961- editor. | Wilkins, Chris, editor.
Title: Legalizing cannabis : experiences, lessons and scenarios / Tom Decorte, Simon Lenton, Chris Wilkins.
Description: Abingdon, Oxon; New York, NY: Routledge, 2020. | Series: Routledge studies in crime and society | Includes bibliographical references and index. | Identifiers: LCCN 2019048744 | ISBN 9781138370906 (hardback) | ISBN 9780429427794 (ebook)
Subjects: LCSH: Drug legalization. | Cannabis–Law and legislation | Marijuana industry–Law and legislation
Classification: LCC K3641 .L44 2020 | DDC 344.05/4–dc23
LC record available at https://lccn.loc.gov/2019048744

ISBN: 978-1-138-37090-6 (hbk)
ISBN: 978-1-03-217404-4 (pbk)
DOI: 10.4324/9780429427794

Typeset in Bembo
by Wearset Ltd, Boldon, Tyne and Wear

Contents

Figures

Tables

Contributors

Scott Akins is Full Professor of Sociology in the School of Public Policy at Oregon State University. His research interests include the causes and correlates of drug use, drug policy and structural criminology. Scott Akins came to Oregon State University in 2004, where he teaches classes both on campus and online through OSU e-campus. Scott earned a bachelor's degree in criminal justice from Northern Arizona University, and a master's degree and PhD in sociology from Washington State University.

Simon Anderfuhren-Biget is Associate Researcher at the Department of Sociology at Geneva University. A doctor in political science, specialist in public organizations and employee behaviors, he shifted his research attention towards cannabis public policy reforms in 2014 with the opening of the first legal cannabis markets in the Americas. Since then, he has worked on the topic with academic institutions, NGOs and other interested stakeholders.

Xabier Araña is Professor in Criminal Law and Criminology in the Faculty of Law at the University of the Basque Country (UPV/EHU) (Spain). He has worked as a researcher in the Basque Institute of Criminology at the UPV/EHU since 2002, conducting research related to the social phenomenon of drugs and periodically organizing international symposia, congresses and workshops related to the drugs issue. His areas of interest include alternative drug policies, analysis of drugs legislation and the rights of drug users. He is a member of the UPV/EHU Consolidated Group of Researchers.

Vendula Belackova has conducted interdisciplinary research into drug policy. She is currently Senior Project Officer at the Uniting Medically Supervised Injecting Centre in Sydney, Australia and Adjunct Senior Lecturer at the Social Policy Research Centre, Faculty of Arts and Social Sciences, University of New South Wales. In her previous role as a lecturer at Charles University in Prague, she coordinated work streams on projects involving multiple European countries. Vendula completed a Fulbright post-graduate fellowship at the College of Social Sciences at the Florida

State University and Endeavour Visiting Research fellowship at the National Drug and Alcohol Research Centre in Sydney.

Tom Blickman is Senior Project Officer at the Transnational Institute (TNI), based in Amsterdam. Since 1997, he has been working for TNI's Drugs & Democracy Programme, specializing in international drug control policy and the UN conventions, drug markets, alternative development, money laundering and organized crime. Tom is a regular speaker at international policy conferences and advises on developments in the drugs field. He is co-editor of the TNI Drug Policy Briefing series.

Neil Boyd is Professor in the School of Criminology at Simon Fraser University, Vancouver, Canada, educated in psychology at the University of Western Ontario and in law at Osgoode Hall Law School, Toronto. He is a previous director of SFU's School of Criminology and the author of seven books and many academic articles, focused largely on drug policy and homicide. Professor Boyd is currently the Chair of the Board of Directors of the International Centre for Criminal Law Reform and Criminal Justice Policy at UBC Law and has been a member of the board since the 1990s.

Tom Decorte is Professor of Criminology and Director of the Institute for Social Drug Research (ISD) at Ghent University, Belgium. He has co-founded the Global Cannabis Cultivation Research Consortium (GCCRC) and is trustee of the board of the European Society for Social Drug Research (ESSD) and of the International Society for the Study of Drug Policy (ISSDP). His research interests include patterns of substance use, on the supply side of cannabis markets and on the implementation of local drug monitoring systems. He has been advisor to a range of organizations on policies to improve public health relating to the use of drugs around the world.

Niamh Eastwood is Executive Director of Release, the UK's center of expertise on drugs and drugs law. Niamh has co-authored a number of Release's policy papers including *A Quiet Revolution: Drug Decriminalization Across the Globe*. Niamh is an associate of The London School of Economics IDEAS International Drug Policy Project, a member of the Expert Steering Group for the Global Drug Survey and is a visiting lecturer at Liverpool John Moores University and at Middlesex University. She is also a committee member for DrugScience and has been a technical advisor to the Global Commission on Drug Policy.

Benedikt Fischer is the inaugural Hugh Green Foundation chair in addiction research at the Faculty of Medicine & Health Sciences, University of Auckland, New Zealand. Prior to that, he held senior academic research positions at the University of Toronto and Simon Fraser University, Vancouver, Canada. Professor Fischer's scientific work focuses primarily on psychoactive substance use, health outcomes and evidence-based interventions. He has worked on topics related to cannabis use, control and public health for two decades. He acted as a senior scientific advisor to the federal government of Canada towards developing their regulatory framework for legalization of non-medical cannabis use and supply.

Coral Gartner is Associate Professor at the University of Queensland's School of Public Health and the Queensland Alliance for Environmental Health Sciences. She holds a Bachelor of Applied Science (Environmental Health), Bachelor of Health Science (Hons) and a PhD in Environmental Epidemiology. She has held two NHMRC research fellowships. Coral was awarded the National Drug and Alcohol Award for Research in 2011. She has published over 120 peer-reviewed journal articles and her research focus since 2006 has been on policies to reduce the harm from tobacco use, including demand, supply and harm-reduction strategies.

Norman Giesbrecht PhD is Emeritus Scientist at the Institute for Mental Health Policy Research Department, Centre for Addiction and Mental Health, Toronto, and an Adjunct Professor at Dalla Lana School of Public Health, University of Toronto. He has served on numerous national and international research teams. His publications have focused on evaluation of the impacts of alcohol policies, assessments of the policy development process, impacts of drinking patterns on trauma and chronic disease, acute alcohol and suicide, community-based prevention strategies and harm to others from alcohol.

Wayne Hall is Professor at the Centre for Youth Substance Abuse Research at the University of Queensland and a Visiting Professor at the National Addiction Centre, Kings College London and the London School of Hygiene and Tropical Medicine. He was an NHMRC Australia Fellow at the University of Queensland Centre for Clinical Research and the University of Queensland Brain Institute (2009–2014). Wayne has advised the World Health Organization on the health effects of cannabis use, the contribution of illicit drug use to the global burden of disease and the ethical implications of genetic and neuroscience research on addiction.

Vicki J. Hanson is M.Phil./PhD Candidate in Public Policy at the Department of Government, University of the West Indies (Mona). Her research work involves exploring the public policy issues to be resolved in a regulated cannabis (ganja) industry in the Caribbean, using Jamaica as the case study. Vicki is the Director of Special Projects and Corporate Planner at the Cannabis Licensing Authority (CLA) and a committee member of the Ganja Growers & Producers Association Jamaica (GGPAJ). She is also a member of the board of directors for the International Drug Policy Consortium (IDPC) based in the UK.

Cédric Heeb is a board member of the IG Hanf, the Swiss hemp professional association, responsible for public policy, coalition building and advocacy on cannabis regulation matters. Currently an entrepreneur in the

Swiss Cannabis industry, he holds his main degree in business administration. With various experiences in multiple fields, he brings an organizational approach to the cannabis regulation topic as well as background on economic and environmental drivers.

Caitlin Elizabeth Hughes is Associate Professor in criminology and drug policy at the Centre for Crime Policy and Research, Flinders University, Visiting Fellow at the National Drug and Alcohol Research Centre and Vice President of the International Society for the Study of Drug Policy. She has published widely on the roles of different legislative regimes and law enforcement approaches to drug use and supply, outlining what laws and policies are deployed, assessing criminal justice, health and social impacts and identifying avenues for more effective responses. Caitlin works extensively with policymakers and police and has a track record of evidence-informed reform.

Dirk J. Korf is Professor in Criminology at the University of Amsterdam. He specializes in empirical research on hard to reach groups. His research is focused on the investigation of developments and patterns in recreational drug use and drug trafficking in the context of drug policy and from an international perspective. He has published widely on the demand and supply side of the cannabis market. He is chairman of the European Society for Social Drug Research and a member of the Scientific Committee of the European Centre for Drugs and Drug Addiction (EMCDDA) in Lisbon.

Simon Lenton is Professor and Director of the National Drug Research Institute at Curtin University (Australia) and works part-time as a clinical psychologist in private practice. His research interests include bridging the gap between drug policy research and drug policy practice, illicit drug use and harm reduction and impact of legislative options for drugs. He has published widely on drugs, health and the law and provided advice to a range of government and private organizations on evidence-based drug policy and other drug issues.

Clayton Mosher is Professor in the Department of Sociology at Washington State University. His research focuses on drugs and drug policies and racial and ethnic disparities in criminal and juvenile justice system processing. He has published five books and his work has appeared in both generalist and specialty sociology and criminology journals. With Scott Akins, he is author of *In the Weeds – Demonization, Legalization, and the Evolution of U.S. Marijuana Policy* (Temple University Press, 2019).

Mafalda Pardal is a postdoctoral researcher at the Institute for Social Drug Research at Ghent University, Belgium, and has been a visiting researcher at Universidad Católica del Uruguay. Previously she was a policy analyst at RAND Europe. Her research focuses on drug markets and policies and their media representations. Her latest work examines a non-profit model for the supply of cannabis: the Cannabis Social Club, which she has studied in both unregulated contexts (e.g. Belgium, Spain) and within the legal framework established for that model in Uruguay. She holds a PhD in criminology from Ghent University.

Bryce Pardo is a policy researcher at RAND, focusing on cannabis policy and regulation, opioid control and New Psychoactive Substances. He has over ten years of experience working with national, state and local governments in drug policy. He served five years as an official at the Inter-American Drug Abuse Control Commission (CICAD) within the Organization of American States (OAS) and has consulted with multilateral institutions. He holds a PhD in public policy from the University of Maryland. Bryce's research and academic work has been published in the *International Journal of Drug Policy*, *Addiction*, *Lancet Psychology* and *Criminology and Public Policy*.

Òscar Parés has an undergraduate degree in philosophy and anthropology and a master's degree in drug addiction from the Universidad de Barcelona. He worked for the Government of Catalonia's Program on Substance Abuse, coordinating nightlife risk-reduction programs and the regulation of Cannabis Social Clubs. Òscar is a founding member of the Drug Policy Unit of the Universitat Autònoma de Bellaterra (UAB). Currently, in his role as Deputy Director of the ICEERS Foundation, Òscar promotes educational, drug reform and research projects on Cannabis Social Clubs and is the lead organizer of the World Ayahuasca Conference.

Simone Pettigrew is a Program Head at The George Institute for Global Health in Sydney, Australia. Her work focuses on encouraging people to modify their lifestyle behaviors to improve individual and societal-level health outcomes, particularly in terms of reducing cancer risk. Her research also addresses structural and environmental factors that influence individuals' health-related behaviors. Primary areas of focus include smoking, alcohol consumption, physical activity, nutrition and mental health. Simone is a member of numerous international, national and state-based advisory committees for government and non-government organizations working in these areas.

Rosario Queirolo is Associate Professor in the Department of Social Sciences at Universidad Católica del Uruguay. She obtained her PhD in Political Science at the University of Pittsburgh. Her research interests are comparative politics and drugs policies. On the comparative politics field, she focuses on electoral behavior and public opinion. Since 2013, Queirolo has been working in the drug policy field studying the process and effects of marijuana regulation in Uruguay and the region, and publishing articles in *Addiction*, *International Journal of Drug Policy*, *Drug and Alcohol Review*, *Journal of Drug Issues and Drugs: Education, Prevention & Policy*, among others.

Michaela Roubalova, formerly Stefunkova, is a researcher at the Institute of Criminology and Social Prevention in Prague. Previously she worked at the Department of Addictology at the First Faculty of Medicine, Charles University, Prague. She obtained her PhD in criminal law and criminology at the Bratislava School of Law, Faculty of Law, Slovakia. Her research interests focus on drug-related crime, drug policy and other drug use-related topics, and victimology.

Cayley Russell is Research Coordinator/Analyst at the Institute for Mental Health Policy Research (IMHPR), based at the Centre for Addiction and Mental Health (CAMH). She has a combined master's degree in criminology and addiction studies from the University of Toronto, as well as an addiction medicine diploma. Her research interests largely focus on the intersection of mental health and addictions among vulnerable populations. She has published numerous articles, primarily examining opioid and cannabis-related health harms.

Marta Rychert is Drug Policy Researcher at the SHORE & Whāriki Research Centre, Massey University and Health Law Lecturer at Auckland University of Technology, Auckland, New Zealand. Her research interests focus on legal aspects of regulating alcohol and other drugs, including regulatory frameworks for cannabis, new psychoactive substances and e-cigarettes. Her doctoral work analyzed the implementation of New Zealand's Psychoactive Substances Act 2013. Prior to moving to New Zealand, she worked in the European Monitoring Centre for Drugs and Drug Addiction (EMCDDA) in Portugal. She holds a master's degree in law from the University of Warsaw and a PhD in public health from Massey University.

Catherine Sandwell is a researcher at the Transnational Institute (TNI) in Amsterdam. She holds an undergraduate degree in philosophy and religious studies and a master's degree in environmental studies from York University, Canada. Her work with TNI's Drugs & Democracy and Economic Justice Programmes focuses on cannabis policy, human rights and the rights of small farmers, among other topics.

Jean-Félix Savary is the general secretary of the French-speaking association of addiction professionals (GREA). As such, he is deeply involved in the political process in Switzerland concerning regulation and addiction management. He contributes regularly to the public debate and in the various political processes in Switzerland. He is specialized in public policy, coalition building and advocacy.

Adam Sherk, PhD, is a postdoctoral fellow at the Canadian Institute for Substance Use Research at the University of Victoria, Canada. His doctoral research focused on alcohol-related harms and substance use policy studies. His current program of research focuses on substance use epidemiology and policy research, including contributions at the global, national and subnational levels. He has contributed to studies regarding the health impacts of removing alcohol retail monopolies in Sweden and Finland and currently holds research funding to investigate the impact of cannabis legalization in Canada on cannabis and alcohol use and related clinical substance use disorders.

Tim Stockwell, PhD, is Director of the Canadian Institute for Substance Use Research and Professor of psychology at the University of Victoria. He has published over 400 research papers, book chapters, monographs and books on prevention and treatment issues. His research interests include the prevention of alcohol and other drug-related harm, alcohol and other drug policy, measurement of alcohol consumption and related harms, public health and safety impacts of substance use, alcohol harm reduction and policies to reduce alcohol-related harm. He was elected a Fellow of the Royal Society of Canada in 2018 and received the 2013 E.M. Jellinek Memorial Award.

Todd Subritzky is in the process of completing his PhD with the National Drug Research Institute at Curtin University. His thesis examines the legalization of cannabis in Colorado and his findings have been reported in multiple international journals and drug policy conferences. Todd also runs the website www.marijuanasurveys.org, which conducts independent cannabis research. He is also a lecturer at La Trobe University (Sydney campus) on the Health Information Management (HIM) program where he teaches data analytics in health care and other evidence-based research subjects. Todd is an advocate for reforming policy to end the criminalization of cannabis consumption.

Gerald Thomas is Director of Legal Substances & Problem Gambling Policy & Prevention at the British Columbia Ministry of Health, a collaborating scientist at the Canadian Institute for Substance Use Research at the University of Victoria, and Adjunct Professor in psychology at the University of British Columbia. His work applies a population and public health lens to substance use and gambling issues with a focus on policy and health promotion/prevention. Among other things, he represented the Ministry of Health in the BC Government during the recent legalization of non-medical cannabis in Canada.

Kate Vallance is a research associate at the Canadian Institute for Substance Use Research (CISUR) at the University of Victoria. Over the past ten years she has been involved in coordination and management of numerous research projects examining substance use and related harms. Most recently, she has been working on the Canadian Alcohol Policy Evaluation (CAPE) project assessing implementation of alcohol policies across federal, provincial and territorial jurisdictions as well as the Northern Territories Alcohol Labels Study testing the effectiveness of enhanced warning labels in Yukon, Canada. She holds a master's degree in sociology from the University of Victoria.

Katinka van de Ven, PhD, is a research fellow with the Drug Policy Modelling Program (DPMP) at the Social Policy Research Centre (SPRC), University of New South Wales. Her research interests focus on the alcohol and other drug treatment systems, the use and supply of performance and image-enhancing drugs, drugs policy (including cannabis regulation), consumer participation, harm reduction and translational research. She is an honorary research fellow at the Public Health Institute, Liverpool John Moores University. Katinka is editor-in-chief of *Performance Enhancement & Health* and the director of the Human Enhancement Drug Network (HEDN) (www.humanenhancementdrugs.com).

Ashley Wettlaufer is a research coordinator with the Institute for Mental Health Policy Research and World Health Organization Collaborating Centre at the Centre for Addiction and Mental Health (CAMH) and a research affiliate with the Canadian Institute for Substance Use Research (CISUR) at the University of Victoria. Most recently, she has been working on the Canadian Alcohol Policy Evaluation (CAPE) Project assessing implementation of effective alcohol policies across Canada. Her other work includes collaborating with the WHO to calculate global alcohol consumption in order to monitor implementation progress of the Global Strategy to Reduce the Harmful Use of Alcohol.

Chris Wilkins, Associate Professor, is the leader of the drug research team at SHORE & Whāriki Research Centre, Massey University, New Zealand. He has researched drug trends, drug markets and drug policy change. Most recently he has published on "not-for-profit" approaches to cannabis regulation, medicinal cannabis regimes, illegal cannabis markets, new psychoactive substances, organized crime and drug use in rural communities. Dr Wilkins has been an invited speaker at international meetings in Europe, the United States and Australia. He regularly presents papers at the annual meetings of the International Society for the Study of Drug Policy (ISSDP).

Frank Zobel is Deputy Director of Addiction Switzerland and a researcher in the drugs field. His areas of expertise are drug policy and drug markets analysis as well as the epidemiology of drug use. His previous positions were with the European Monitoring Centre for Drugs and Drug Addiction (EMCDDA) and with the University Institute for Social and Preventive Medicine (IUMSP) of Lausanne. He is a member of the federal advisory board on addiction issues (EKSF) of Switzerland.

Foreword

Ruth Dreifuss

According to the Single Convention on Narcotic Drugs, the non-medical use of all cannabis ingredients was destined to be eliminated from our planet between 1964 and 1989. Since then, the number of its consumers has increased massively and represented in 2017 a clear majority among the 271 million people reported to have used illicit drugs: 188 million. It is unclear how many of the 35 million people suffering from problematic drug use have a problem specifically with cannabis, but the probability is high that they represent a clear minority.

Drug dependence, social marginalization and possible consequences of early and massive cannabis consumption on cognitive functions, are not to be neglected. They are largely overestimated, however, and some of the other sources of these problems are too often denied. There is evidence that the illegal cannabis market, flourishing under prohibitive legislations, has increased the potency of its products, added dangerous pesticides and other chemical additives, and has intensified its aggressive marketing, particularly targeting kids and teens. The repression and criminalization of people who use cannabis intensify these harms by building obstacles to individually tailored treatment and by disrupting lives with harsh punishment, incarceration and loss of professional opportunities.

The first step in overcoming these negative consequences is to deepen our knowledge of cannabis – the various active substances that the plant possesses, and the real harms and benefits resulting from diverse forms and frequencies of consumption. Indeed, despite this lack of research, and as discussed in length in the Global Commission on Drug Policy's 2019 report *Classification of Drugs: When Science Was Left Behind*, cannabis has been classified in the schedules of the drug control conventions, without any evidence to back up this decision, as one of the most dangerous and addictive substances, without therapeutic benefits.

This classification error, which few governments are willing to question at the multilateral level, is a source of decades of failed efforts to ban a substance that people around the world want to use despite the legal risks. Classifying cannabis according to the scientific outcomes of research is pivotal to ending the current situation, where science is disregarded to the benefit of ideologically driven perceptions. Robust research on the effects of cannabis use will most probably confirm, as different studies now show, that the risks are not as severe as those of alcohol and tobacco – both legal psychoactive substances – and that there are benefits with regard to the therapeutic uses of the substance.

While reform is stalled at the international level, the last decade has seen an acceleration of legislative and regulatory reforms at the local and national levels, with countries no longer willing to bear the human and financial costs of prohibitive policies. This is one of the main reasons why some countries have decided to implement decriminalization policies and allow alternatives to incarceration for people who use cannabis. Beyond the famous models of the Czech Republic and Portugal, such schemes are being developed in a variety of countries such as Colombia, Ghana, some US states, Tunisia, France, Israel and Malaysia.

Furthermore, the current legalization models that have been implemented in US states, Canada and Uruguay, and that are being debated in Mexico, New Zealand and Luxembourg, are born of a simple conclusion: why leave the market for a product that presents only a mild risk to a person's health and with a large number of customers, in the hands of criminal organizations, thereby empowering them and strengthening their grip on neighborhoods and neglected communities? These states are also aware that public health issues need controls and limitation, learning from the successes and weaknesses of control frameworks that exist for potentially harmful substances that are legal (e.g. alcohol, tobacco, chemicals, isotopes, medicines).

These authorities and their legalization models are providing the world with unique pilot programs from which to study and learn. They offer examples of how to build new legal frameworks that reduce drug-related harms to consumers and society, without the toxic straitjacket of prohibition – and without providing fertile ground for a powerful cannabis industry and lobby, which could be hostile to restrictive measures taken by states to preserve public health. Indeed, it is necessary for drug policy scholars and professionals, as well as communities most affected by the drug trade, to prevent commercial interests from trumping societal wellbeing when pursuing cannabis policy reform.

The editors of this book have assembled an international who's who of cannabis scholars who bring together the best available evidence and expertise drawing together what is known from the existing evidence on this important topic. The five sections of the book and the chapters that comprise them provide us with: a clear and comprehensive view of the first outcomes of current cannabis legalization models; an analysis of the increasing trend towards the decriminalization and depenalization of cannabis use around the world; how different countries, regions or even cities are gaining ownership of their control policies; lessons learned from experiences of regulating alcohol, tobacco and legal highs; and finally considering new "middle-ground" legalization models for cannabis. This book is timely and helpful, arriving at a moment when we urgently need to reform drug policies that have only increased the problems they were supposed to solve.

Ruth Dreifuss is a former President of Switzerland (1999), Federal Councillor in charge of the Federal Department of Home Affairs (1993–2002), and the Chair of the Global Commission on Drug Policy (2016-current).

Acknowledgments

The editors and staff of Routledge Publishers thank the many scholars who have contributed their time and expertise to review manuscripts for this book project. The following individuals served as external ad hoc reviewers:

Professor Peter Adams (University of Auckland, NEW ZEALAND)
Associate Professor Robert Ali (University of Adelaide, AUSTRALIA)
Professor Daniel Bear (Humber College, Toronto, CANADA)
Dr. Vendula Belackova (University of New South Wales, AUSTRALIA)
Professor David Bewley-Taylor (Swansea University, UNITED KINGDOM)
Professor Martin Bouchard (Simon Fraser University, CANADA)
Professor Neil Boyd (Simon Fraser University, CANADA)
Professor Barbara Broers (University of Geneva, SWITZERLAND)
Professor Frank Chaloupka (University of Illinois at Chicago, UNITED STATES OF AMERICA)
Professor Daniel Ciccarone (University of California, UNITED STATES OF AMERICA)
Dr. Caroline Chatwin (University of Kent, UNITED KINGDOM)
Professor Tanya Chikritzhs (National Drug Research Institute, Curtin University, AUSTRALIA)
Emeritus Professor Mike Daube (Curtin University, AUSTRALIA)
Dr. Julia Dilley (University of Washington, UNITED STATES OF AMERICA)
Professor Patricia Erickson (University of Toronto, CANADA)
Professor Vibeke Asmussen Frank (Aarhus University, DENMARK)
Professor Pekka Hakkarainen (Finnish Institute for Health and Welfare, FINLAND)
Professor Wayne Hall (University of Queensland, AUSTRALIA)
Associate Professor Caitlin Hughes (Flinders University, AUSTRALIA)
Mrs. Rebecca Jesseman (Director of Policy, Canadian Centre on Substance Use and Addiction, CANADA)
Professor Mark Kleiman (New York University, UNITED STATES OF AMERICA) (†)
Dr. Axel Klein (Global Drug Policy Observatory, Swansea University, UNITED KINGDOM)

Pien Metaal (Transnational Institute, THE NETHERLANDS)
Mr. David McDonald (Australian National University, AUSTRALIA)
Dr. Clara Musto (University of the Republic, URUGUAY)
Dr. Mafalda Pardal (Ghent University, BELGIUM)
Dr. Bryce Pardo (RAND Corporation, UNITED STATES OF AMERICA)
Dr. Gary Potter (Lancaster University, UNITED KINGDOM)
Professor Peter Reuter (University of Maryland, UNITED STATES OF AMERICA)
Professor Robin Room (La Trobe University, AUSTRALIA)
Dr. Marta Rychert (Massey University, NEW ZEALAND)
Dr. Eric L. Sevigny (Georgia State University, UNITED STATES OF AMERICA)
Dr. Sharon Sznitman (University of Haifa, ISRAEL)
Dr. Margriet van Laar (Trimbos Institute, THE NETHERLANDS)
Dr. Bernd Werse (Goethe University Frankfurt, GERMANY)

Abbreviations

AAA	American Automobile Association
ACLU	American Civil Liberties Union
ACMPR	Access to Cannabis for Medical Purposes Regulations
ACT	Australian Capital Territory
AHOJ	Affichering, Harddrugs, Overlast, Jongeren (No advertising, No hard drugs, No nuisance, No minors)
AHOJ-G	Affichering, Harddrugs, Overlast, Jongeren, Grote hoeveelheden (No advertising, No hard drugs, No nuisance, No minors, No large quantities)
AIDS	Acquired Immune Deficiency Syndrome
AUD	Australian Dollar
AUMA	Adult Use of Marijuana Act
BEST	Building Excellent Schools Today
BfArM	Bundesinstitut für Arzneimittel und Medizinprodukte (Federal Institute for Pharmaceuticals and Medical Products)
BOTEC	Back-Of-The-Envelope Calculation
BZP	Benzylpiperazines
CAMH	Centre for Addiction and Mental Health
CARICOM	Caribbean Community and Common Market
CBD	Cannabidiol
CC	Constitutional Court
CCMRT	Cannabis Commercial and Medicinal Research Task Force
CCSA	Canadian Centre on Substance Abuse
CDOR	Colorado Department of Revenue
CDPHE	Colorado Department of Public Health and Environment
CDSA	Controlled Drugs and Substances Act
CDU	Christlich Demokratische Union (Christian Democratic Union of Germany)
CEN	Cannabis Expiation Notice
CEO	Chief Executive Officer
CFLD	Commission Fédérale pour les questions Liées aux Drogues (Federal Commission for Drug Issues)
CHF	Swiss Franc

CLA	Cannabis Licensing Authority
CONFAC	Confederación de Asociaciones Cannábicas (Confederation of Cannabis Associations)
CoR	Committee of the Regions
CRCM	Colorado Recreational Cannabis Market
CSA	Controlled Substance Act
CSC	Cannabis Social Club
DARE	Drug Abuse Resistance Education
DD(A)A	Dangerous Drug (Amendment) Act
DEA	Drug Enforcement Administration
DPA	Drug Policy Alliance
DUI	Driving Under the Influence
EACD	Expert Advisory Committee on Drugs
ECDP	European Cities on Drug Policy
EMCDDA	European Monitoring Centre for Drugs and Drug Addiction
ENCOD	European Coalition for Just and Effective Drug Policies
EU	European Union
FAAAT	For Alternative Approaches to Addiction, Think & Do Tank
FAC	Federación de Asociaciones Cannábicas (Federation of Cannabis Associations)
FARS	Fatal Analysis Reporting System
FCTC	Framework Convention on Tobacco Control
FDP	Freisinnig-Demokratische Partei (Liberal Democratic Party)
FOPH	Federal Office of Public Health
FY	Fiscal Year
GEPCA	Grupo de Estudio de Políticas Sobre el Cannabis (Policy Study Group on Cannabis)
GGPA	Ganja Growers and Producers Association
GREA	Groupement Romand d'Études des Addictions (Romand Group of Studies of Addictions)
HIV	Human Immunodeficiency Virus
HYS	Healthy Youth Survey
I	Initiative
ICD	International System of Classification of Diseases
ICH	International Council for Harmonization
IDDI	Illicit Drug Diversion Initiative
IIHS	Insurance Institute for Highway Safety
INCB	International Narcotics Control Board
IRCCA	Instituto de Regulación y Control del Cannabis (The Cannabis Regulation and Control Institute)
JLP	Jamaica Labour Party
KIs	Key Informants
KPI	Key Performance Indicator
LAPP	Local Approved Product Policies

LCB	Liquor Control Board or the Liquor and Cannabis Board
LPs	Licensed Producers
Lt.	Lieutenant
LTab	Tobacco Law
MAUCRSA	Medicinal and Adult-Use Cannabis Regulation and Safety Act
MCRSA	Medical Cannabis Regulatory and Safety Act
MED	Marijuana Enforcement Division
MICAF	Ministry of Industry, Commerce, Agriculture and Fisheries
MLG	Multi-Level Governance
MMAR	Marihuana Medical Access Regulations
MMPR	Marihuana for Medical Purposes Regulations
MOH	Ministry of Health
MP	Member of Parliament
MSA	Masters Settlement Agreement
NCA	Narcotic Control Act
NGO	Non-Governmental Organization
NHTSA	National Highway Traffic and Safety Administration
NIMBY	Not in My Back Yard
NORML	National Organization for Reform of Marijuana Laws
NPS	New Psychoactive Substances
NT	Northern Territory
N-VA	Nieuw-Vlaamse Alliantie (New Flemish Alliance)
NWHIDTA	Northwest High Intensity Drug Trafficking Area
NZD	New Zealand Dollars
NZLC	New Zealand Law Commission
NZZ	Neue Zürcher Zeitung (The New Zurich Times)
OCSetup	Drugs Control Ordinance
OECD	Organisation for Economic Co-operation and Development
OLCC	Oregon Liquor Control Commission
PNP	People's National Party
Project SAM	Project Smart Approaches to Marijuana
PSA	Psychoactive Substances Act
PSRA	Psychoactive Substances Regulatory Authority
PWUD	People Who Use Drugs
RCMP	Royal Canadian Mounted Police
RCN-NOK	Representación Cannábica de Navarra (Cannabis Representation of Navarre)
RMC	Retail Marijuana Code
RSR	Restricted Substances Regime
SA	South Australia
SC	Supreme Court
SCON	Simple Cannabis Offence Notice
SDGs	Sustainable Development Goals

SNV	Swiss Association for Normalization
SPD	Sozialdemokratische Partei Deutschlands (Social Democratic Party of Germany)
SQDC	Société Québécoise Du Cannabis (Quebec Cannabis Society)
STANZ	Social Tonics Association of New Zealand
STAR	Social Tonics Advocacy and Research
TEQ	Toxic Equivalency Factor
TFMPP	Trifluoromethylphenylpiperazine
TGA	Therapeutic Goods Authority
THC	Tetrahydrocannabinol
TNI	Transnational Institute
TobReg	Tobacco Product Regulation
UK	United Kingdom
UN	United Nations
UNDP	United Nations Development Programme
UNGASS	United Nations General Assembly Special Session on Drugs
UNHRC	United Nations Human Rights Council
UNODC	UN Office on Drugs and Crime
US	United States
VLNC	Very Low Nicotine Content
VNG	Vereniging Nederlandse Gemeenten (Association of Dutch Municipalities)
WA	Western Australia
WBO	Women Business Owners
WHO	World Health Organization

Introduction

Tom Decorte, Simon Lenton and Chris Wilkins

A new era in cannabis policy

Clearly, the cannabis policy landscape is undergoing a process of profound change. There is increasing appetite around the world for policy approaches to cannabis other than the long-standing prohibition with criminal penalties. Despite the proscriptions of the international drug control conventions of 1961, 1971 and 1988, regulated legal markets for cannabis in the United States of America, Uruguay and Canada are already taking shape. These recent legalizations have been preceded by moves, over four decades, by a number of countries to de-penalize and de-criminalize cannabis use and small-scale cultivation under various de facto and *de jure* policies. More recently, the widespread establishment of medicinal cannabis regimes has also provided greater legal access to cannabis, albeit under a medical framework, and challenged the underlying ideology of cannabis prohibition (i.e. that all cannabis use is high-risk). However, it has been the legalization of cannabis use and supply in parts of the Americas that has fundamentally changed the policy landscape.

Uruguay became the first country in the modern era to legalize cannabis in December 2013, when President José Alberto "El Pepe" Mujica signed a law to regulate recreational cannabis. The Uruguayan legislation (Law 19.172) allowed up to six cannabis plants to be grown at home, as well as making provision for the formation of cannabis-growing clubs and a state-controlled cannabis supply retail network via pharmacies, and establishing a cannabis regulatory institute (IRCCA in Spanish) (Bewley-Taylor, Blickman and Jelsma, 2014; Albrecht, 2014; Pardo, 2014).

In the US, over half the states now have provisions for medical cannabis use for a range of medical conditions. Further, since 2012, 11 US states (i.e.Alaska, California, Colorado, Illinois, Maine, Massachusetts, Michigan, Nevada, Oregon, Vermont and Washington), the District of Columbia at the federal level, and the Northern Mariana Islands have legalized the use and supply of cannabis for non-medical purposes, despite the fact that cannabis remains illegal under US federal law. In January 2018, Vermont became the first US state to legalize cannabis use for adults through the legislature (rather than via ballot initiative, as was done in the previous states that have legalized). The 11 states where cannabis is now legal are home to more than one in five American adults (Pardo, this volume).

In Canada, Prime Minister Justin Trudeau's government introduced legislation in April 2017 to regulate recreational cannabis use and supply, making Canada the first G7 country to legalize cannabis, and consequently putting it in direct contravention of the three UN drug treaties and conventions that have been in place since the 1961 Single Convention. The resulting Cannabis Act came into force on October 17, 2018. Under the legislation, persons aged 18 or older can possess up to 30 grams of dried cannabis or "equivalent non-dried form" in public. The provinces and territories of Canada have the power to develop their own regulations regarding retail distribution. These powers extend to determining the ownership model of retail outlets (i.e. provincial government or private stores and enterprises) but all include an option for online sales.

Legalization reforms are stimulating policy debates

The cannabis legalization reforms underway in the US, Canada and Uruguay, barely imaginable a mere decade ago, have renewed debate about appropriate policy settings for cannabis elsewhere, and the legalization of recreational cannabis use and supply is being seriously debated in a number of other countries. This constitutes a major change in policy focus that requires new thinking concerning alternative regulatory frameworks and empirical research investigating the outcomes of the reforms currently being implemented. The legalization of cannabis *potentially* creates opportunities to regulate some of the characteristics of the drug responsible for health risks, impose more nuanced control over production and sale, reduce the stigma associated with seeking help for drug problems, and remove the harmful consequences associated with arrest and conviction, particularly for ethnic and other minorities who have been disproportionately adversely impacted by law enforcement associated with cannabis. However, a profit-driven commercial cannabis market may promote heavier use and more harm by increasing physical availability, lowering prices, normalizing use through advertising and marketing, and creating a powerful industry focused on lobbying for weaker regulatory controls and expanding sales and profits (Adams, 2013; Caulkins, 2016; Hall, 2016). Ideally, policy ought to capture the benefits of a legal regulated market for cannabis while avoiding the harms of over-commercialization. However, this is proving to be difficult to achieve in practice at this early stage of implementation, and many of us are eagerly waiting for data to emerge from the case examples of legalization in the Americas.

Local and regional authorities in several countries in Europe are looking at regulation, either pressured by grassroots movements – in particular, the Cannabis Social Clubs (CSCs) – or in an attempt to reduce the involvement of criminal groups and improve public order. In the Netherlands, municipalities signed a Joint Manifest in which they asked the government to regulate the supply of cannabis to coffeeshops and address the long-standing "backdoor" problem. In late 2017, the newly formed coalition announced they would seek to implement an experimental new system in certain cities, whereby coffeeshops could legally acquire cannabis from a state-appointed producer. In Copenhagen (Denmark), Mons (Belgium) and Berlin, Frankfurt-am-Main, Hamburg and Cologne (Germany), local authorities have proposed coffeeshop-like cannabis dispensaries with a regulated supply. In Spain and Switzerland, regional and local authorities want to allow CSCs, while in Belgium, Portugal, France and the UK, campaigns for CSCs are gaining momentum.

Until very recently, the national governments of Europe seemed to be either inert or in denial about the changing policy landscape, while in the Americas, cannabis policy reform was taking off. Cannabis policy reform in Europe falls under the remit of European Union member states, not under the jurisdiction of the European Union (EU) itself. However, European law builds on the three UN drug control conventions that oblige member states to adopt measures to establish recreational cannabis use as a punishable (penal or administrative) offense, leaving very few options for reform other than non-enforcement of infractions. Moreover, EU member states have agreed to cooperate and to take the most appropriate measures against cannabis cultivation for recreational use. However, quite unexpectedly in December 2018, the new government coalition in Luxembourg – home to only 600,000 people – released a recreational cannabis proposal "for residents only" (Boffey, 2019). The coalition have agreed to implement this in the next legislative period, within five years. In doing so, Luxembourg will become the first country in Europe to permit and regulate adult cannabis use – a significant milestone for a continent that has thus far authorized only medicinal cannabis.

Looking at Oceania, in New Zealand, the coalition government has announced there will be a national referendum at the next general election in 2020 on whether to legalize cannabis for personal use. The government has released a general framework for their preferred option, which includes a retail cannabis market and home cultivation options, and invited feedback on the new approach (Ministry of Justice, 2019). A legislative bill outlining the details of the proposed reforms will be made public in early 2020 and will be the subject of the national referendum vote by November 2020. Greater legal access to medicinal cannabis has already been enacted via passage of the Misuse of Drugs (Medicinal Cannabis) Amendment Act in December 2018, and a new medicinal cannabis regulatory regime, including commercial supply, will be established by the end of 2019.

In Australia, since 2016, the Federal Parliament and many states and territories have passed laws allowing for medicinal cannabis. But unlike in other countries, the laws are very restrictive with strict controls over cultivation, product manufacture, product range and patient access. As of May 2019, there were only 56 medical practitioners authorized to prescribe medicinal cannabis products, and only 7,700 applications to prescribe to patients had been approved under the Special Access Scheme, although numbers are growing. With regard to recreational cannabis, most of the legislative moves over the last ten or so years have been toward restricting, or in one case completely overturning, the civil penalty schemes in the four states and territories which had them. The exception is the Australian Capital Territory (ACT), which in 2014 increased the amount eligible for an expiation from 25 to 50 grams. Most recently, a bill has been put before the ACT Assembly to legalize cannabis for personal use and allow home growing, which in June 2019 was supported by a parliamentary enquiry subject to some amendments. It will be interesting to see whether this bill progresses into law in the ACT.

In a number of other countries, recent court rulings have paved the way for cannabis policy reform. In December 2016, the Constitutional Court of Georgia declared that imprisonment for use of small amounts of cannabis, as well as its purchase, retention and production for personal use, was unconstitutional (Roberts, 2018). On July 30, 2018, the court made legal the use and possession of cannabis in Georgia but kept in place penalties for cultivation and sale of the drug. South Africa's Constitutional Court has passed down a judgement that makes it legal for adults to cultivate and smoke cannabis in their homes (Clarke, 2019). In September 2018, the country's highest court ruled that the right to privacy was violated by prohibiting the possession, purchase or cultivation of cannabis for personal consumption by an adult in a private dwelling. On October 31, 2018, the Mexican Supreme Court ruled that the prohibition of cannabis is unconstitutional as it violates the "fundamental right to the free development of the personality" (Transform, 2018). As the fifth such judgement, under Mexican law, this now means that it is binding on all judges nationally – effectively (de facto) legalizing the personal use, possession, private cultivation, and sharing of cannabis amongst adults. The judgement does *not* cover commercial production and sale. The Supreme Court decision means that the Mexican Congress has 90 days to repeal and reform the law judged to be unconstitutional – at which point the reform will assume *de jure* status.

What this book is about

Drug policy researchers are increasingly raising concerns about the profit-driven legal cannabis regimes established in Colorado and other US states. Scholars have pointed to declining prices, high-potency products (e.g. edibles, vaping and dabbing), accidental poisonings, use of unregulated pesticides by growers, aggressive marketing, high numbers of retail outlets, and industry influence over regulation making (Caulkins and Kilmer, 2016; Hasin, 2018; Hall and Lynskey, 2016; Hunt and Pacula, 2017; Subritzky, Lenton and Pettigrew, 2016; Orens, Light, Lewandowski, Rowberry and Saloga, 2018). Findings concerning the impact of commercial legal cannabis regimes on rates of youth cannabis use have been mixed to date, with rates of youth use increasing in Washington State, while apparently remaining fairly stable in Colorado (Cerdá et al., 2017). The retail price of cannabis in

Washington State has declined by 25 percent each year since legal retail outlets were opened in 2014 (Caulkins, 2017).

The unfolding concerns with the profit-driven cannabis law reforms established in US states has led health experts to call for a public health approach to further cannabis law reform (Pacula, Kilmer, Wagenaar, Chaloupka and Caulkins, 2014; Wilkins, 2018; Rolles and Murkin, 2016). However, it is not clear how existing public health learnings from decades of experience with tobacco and alcohol regulation can be applied to cannabis law reform. While there is likely to be broad commonality between alcohol/tobacco and cannabis in a number of regulatory areas, such as pricing, licensing, age restrictions, marketing, public consumption and impaired driving, these insights need to be adapted to the unique health, cultural, economic and horticultural aspects of cannabis use and production under different regulatory approaches. For example, if people are permitted to grow cannabis for personal use, how do we prevent these provisions being exploited to provide cannabis for sale to others for profit, perhaps even by organized criminal groups? If a commercial market for cannabis is permitted, who should be able to sell cannabis and where, what types of cannabis products should be sold (e.g. herbal plant, edibles, oils, shards, vapes), what types of marketing should be permitted (e.g. online, traditional media, onsite only, none), how will the different compounds of cannabis be regulated and taxed, what input should the community have over the number and location of retail outlets, and how should additional cannabis treatment and prevention be funded?

A number of drug policy scholars have pointed out there are actually a range of policy options for cannabis law reform between strict prohibition on one extreme and a profit-driven commercial market on the other. However, these "middle ground" options receive much less media and research attention than the recent commercial market approaches, and consequently, are less likely to be taken seriously by politicians, policymakers and the public when considering future options for cannabis law reform (Decorte and Pardal, 2017). There are currently a number of these "middle ground" options to cannabis reform operating around the world that could potentially provide important learnings for the reform debate. They include but are not limited to: prohibition with reduced penalties, allowing home growing, government involvement in at least a part of the supply chain, the Dutch coffeeshop model, the CSCs model, involvement of not-for profits and limited for-profit licenses.

How this book is organized

This book draws on a range of case studies of cannabis policy reforms and the experiences of scholars from the alcohol and tobacco research fields to inform this unfolding process of cannabis reform. It is organized into five parts.

Part I goes to the heart of the matter by attempting to answer what can be learned from jurisdictions that have already legalized cannabis. These chapters focus on the implementation of these legal cannabis models and the intended and unintended outcomes of these reforms. In this volume, Pardo (Chapter 1) describes the uneven repeal of cannabis prohibition across US states. Subritzky and colleagues (Chapter 2) discuss the practical lessons that can be gleaned from the Colorado legal cannabis scheme as the earliest implemented legal recreational market. Mosher and Akins (Chapter 3) explore the benefits and harms of the legalization of recreational marijuana in Washington State. Fischer and colleagues (Chapter 4) detail the Canadian experience of cannabis law reform and most recently, full cannabis legalization. Finally, in this part, Queirolo (Chapter 5) discusses the unique approach to legal cannabis taken in Uruguay, which was the first country to legalize cannabis.

Part II situates these recent developments in a broader conceptual context and pulls the focus back to the more macro issues of reform, beginning with a comprehensive discussion of cannabis decriminalization by Eastwood (Chapter 6). Belackova and colleagues (Chapter 7) reflect on the impact of different home cannabis cultivation policies and how they can be evaluated. Finally, Blickman and Sandwell (Chapter 8) investigate examples of city-level cannabis reform policies in Europe, which show how local policy levers can be used to address cannabis use and harm.

Part III shines a light on experiences with regulating alcohol, tobacco and other legal highs to divine insights for future cannabis legalization. Stockwell and colleagues (Chapter 9) discuss key regulatory lessons drawn from research on alcohol regulation that can be applied to cannabis markets with regard to availability, pricing, taxation, product labelling and point-of-sale. Similarly, Gartner and Hall (Chapter 10) identify key lessons from the history of the regulation of tobacco for legal cannabis markets, including health warnings, controls on advertising and promotion, taxation, retail licensing, product regulation and smoke-free laws and policies. Finally, Rychert and Wilkins (Chapter 11) draw on the failed attempt to regulate legal highs in New Zealand to identify key implementation lessons for cannabis law reform.

Part IV looks at some of the earlier examples of cannabis law reform, again drawing on this experience to identify lessons for current and future cannabis law reform. This includes a comprehensive retelling of the famous cannabis coffeeshop model in the Netherlands by Korf (Chapter 12). This is followed by a detailed history by Araña and Parés (Chapter 13) of CSCs in Spain. Anderfuhren-Biget and colleagues (Chapter 14) recount the twisted path to cannabis reform in Switzerland. Hughes (Chapter 15) describes the early ground-breaking enactment of cannabis decriminalization across Australian states, and the possibilities for further reform. Finally, Hanson (Chapter 16), describes the unique cultural and religious drivers of cannabis policy reform in Jamaica.

In Part V we conclude by looking at two recent proposals for new models of cannabis legalization. Wilkins and Rychert (Chapter 17) outline a community trust model for legal cannabis based on previous experience of this approach for retail alcohol and gaming machine gambling. Decorte and Pardal (Chapter 18) outline a detailed proposal for the development and regulation of the CSC model.

The book concludes with an attempt to distill some of the key messages from this rich and diverse collection of scholarly works as they relate to the challenges and opportunities of cannabis legalization going forward.

References

Adams, P.J. (2013). Addiction industry studies: Understanding how proconsumption influences block effective interventions. *American Journal of Public Health*, 103(4), 35–38.

Albrecht, L. (2014). Uruguay's drug policy reform: At the cutting edge of alternative policy. *Journal of Peace and Conflict Studies*, 1(1), 39–49.

Bewley-Taylor, D., Blickman, T. and Jelsma, M. (2014). *The rise and decline of cannabis prohibition - The history of cannabis in the UN drug control system and options for reform*. Amsterdam/Swansea: Transnational Institute/Global Drug Policy Observatory.

Boffey, D. (2019). Luxembourg to be first European country to legalise cannabis. *The Guardian*. Retrieved from www.theguardian.com/world/2019/aug/07/luxembourg-to-be-first-european-country-to-legalise-cannabis

Caulkins, J. (2016). Legalising drugs prudently: The importance of incentives and values. In J. Collins and A. Soderholm (Eds.), *After the drug wars: Report of the LSE expert group on the economics of drug policy* (pp. 40–50). London: London School of Economics and Political Science.

Caulkins, J.P. (2017). Recognizing and regulating cannabis as a temptation good. *International Journal of Drug Policy*, 42, 50–56.

Caulkins, J. and Kilmer, B. (2016). The US as an example of how *not* to legalize marijuana? *Addiction*, 111(12), 2095–2096.

Cerdá, M., Wall, M., Feng, T., Keyes, K.M., Sarvet, A., Schulenberg, J., O'Malley, P.M., Pacula, R.L., Galea, S. and Hasin, D.S. (2017). Association of state recreational marijuana laws with adolescent marijuana use. *JAMA Pediatrics*, 171, 142–149.

Clarke, M. (2019). *The Constitutional Court of South Africa's ruling on cannabis – A tipping point on the tip of Africa*. Retrieved from https://idpc.net/blog/2019/01/tipping-point-on-the-tip-of-africa

Decorte, T. and Pardal, M. (2017). Cannabis Social Clubs in Europe: Prospects and limits. In R. Colson and H. Bergeron (Eds.), *European drug policies: The ways of reform* (pp. 285–299). New York, NY: Routledge.

Hall, W. (2016). Alcohol and cannabis: Comparing their adverse health effects and regulatory regimes. *International Journal of Drug Policy*, 42, 57–62.

Hall, W. and Lynskey, M. (2016). Evaluating the public health impacts of legalizing recreational cannabis use in the United States. *Addiction*, 111(10), 1764–1773.

Hasin, D.S. (2018). US epidemiology of cannabis use and associated problems. *Neuropsychopharmacology Reviews*, 43, 195–212.

Hunt, P. and Pacula, R.L. (2017). Early impacts of marijuana legalization: An evaluation of prices in Colorado and Washington. *The Journal of Primary Prevention*, 38(3), 221–48.

Ministry of Justice (2019). *Cannabis Referendum – Legislative process and overarching policy settings for the regulatory model*. Cabinet paper. Considered by Cabinet on May 6, 2019. Released May 7, 2019. Retrieved from www.beehive.govt.nz/sites/default/files/2019-05/Proactive%20release%20-%20Cabinet%20paper%20-%202020%20Cannabis%20Referendum%20-%207%20May%202019.pdf

Orens, A., Light, M., Lewandowski, B., Rowberry, J. and Saloga, C. (2018). *Market size and demand for marijuana in Colorado: 2017 market update*. Colorado: Marijuana Policy Group LLC (MPG). Retrieved from www.colorado.gov/pacific/sites/default/files/MED%20Demand%20and%20Market%20%20Study%20%20082018.pdf

Pacula, R.L., Kilmer, B., Wagenaar, A.C., Chaloupka, F.J. and Caulkins, J.P. (2014). Developing public health regulations for marijuana: Lessons from alcohol and tobacco. *American Journal of Public Health,* 104(6), 1021–1028.

Pardo, B. (2014). Cannabis policy reforms in the Americas: A comparative analysis of Colorado, Washington, and Uruguay. *International Journal of Drug Policy,* 25(4), 727–735.

Roberts, C. (2018). Georgia's High Court removes marijuana possession penalties. *Marijuana Moment*. Retrieved from www.marijuanamoment.net/georgias-high-court-removes-marijuana-possession-penalties/.

Rolles, S. and Murkin, G. (2016). The commercial focus of US cannabis regulation models should not close our eyes to other options. *Addiction,* 111(12), 2092–2094.

Subritzky, T., Lenton, S., Pettigrew, S. (2016). Legal cannabis industry adopting strategies of the tobacco industry [Editorial]. *Drug and Alcohol Review,* 35(5), 511–513.

Transform. (2018). *Mexican Supreme Court ruling means recreational cannabis is now legal for adults*. Press release November 1, 2018. Retrieved from https://transformdrugs.org/press-release-mexican-supreme-court-ruling-means-recreational-cannabis-is-now-legal-for-adults/

Wilkins, C. (2018). A "not-for-profit" regulatory model for legal recreational cannabis: Insights from the regulation of gaming machine gambling in New Zealand. *International Journal of Drug Policy,* 53, 115–122.

Part I

The new legal cannabis markets

1 The uneven repeal of cannabis prohibition in the United States

Bryce Pardo

Introduction

Cannabis policy in the United States continues to change. However, unlike Canada and Uruguay, which have amended national laws, policy change in the US has occurred almost entirely at the sub-national level. The cannabis plant and most of its derivatives remain prohibited under federal law. However, since the mid-1990s states have moved to relax prohibition, permitting cultivation and use for various purposes. Initially, states began to amend their drug control and penal statutes to allow qualifying patients to obtain or possess cannabis to treat certain medical conditions. Though such state-level reforms for medical access conflict with federal drug laws, repeal has continued apace. In the last six years, states have taken additional steps to permit adults to use the drug for non-medical (i.e. recreational) purposes. In 2012, Colorado and Washington State were the first two jurisdictions of the modern era to vote in favor of regulating the supply and distribution of cannabis for anyone over the age of 21. Federal prohibition remains in place, though efforts have been made across levels of government to approach such legal conflicts pragmatically. Nevertheless, cannabis policy in the United States remains unguided, with states continuing to drive changes that favor private, for-profit commercialization.

After Colorado and Washington repealed prohibition in 2012 and replaced it with an alternative regulated system of supply, an additional nine jurisdictions now allow or will allow for non-medical supply and use by adults. Today, about one in five adults over the age of 21 in the United States live somewhere that permits them to legally obtain and use cannabis for mere recreation. Public opinion continues to favor ending prohibition on cannabis use. As trends continue, the federal government's cannabis policy appears increasingly out of step with developments in the various states and shifting national attitudes. Without robust policy guidance from federal authorities, states are stitching their own legal and regulatory patchwork for the supply and use of non-medical cannabis within the remaining legal bounds imposed by federal law (e.g. interstate sale and transport remain illegal and firms that cultivate or distribute the drug cannot engage legally with the federally-regulated banking system).

Most states that have repealed prohibition have adopted a commercial model, allowing licensed for-profit firms to produce, process and distribute cannabis for adult consumers in the state. The goals of these reforms are to reduce the costs and problems associated with the illicit market and traditional responses to it (e.g. excessive policing of minority communities that infringes on civil liberties) as well as generate tax revenues through the sale of cannabis (Hall and Lynskey, 2016). Within that vein, the policy and regulatory design across states with burgeoning commercial cannabis markets differs slightly. This is unlike the regulatory variation in states that permit medical cannabis (now 34 in number), which may restrict who can access and supply the market.

In terms of non-medical cannabis, some states limit the scope and quality of products available, tax product at different rates, or restrict where individuals can consume. Nevertheless, 9 of the 11 jurisdictions that have repealed prohibition on non-medical adult use license for-profit firms to participate in the cannabis trade. Only two jurisdictions have – at least for the time being – adopted a non-commercial model restricted to home cultivation and supply of cannabis for adults. We should note that some of these design choices are, in part, due to federal prohibition, which continues to indirectly shape state-level reforms.

It is too early to evaluate the impacts of these new laws. Instead, this chapter provides a broad overview of the changing dynamic of cannabis repeal efforts in the United States. In section two, we first provide a short descriptive history of repeal efforts in the United States since the 1990s, starting with medical cannabis in California in 1996 and continuing on through to the present day. By 2006, ten states had passed laws permitting patients to obtain medical cannabis that included some appreciable amount of tetrahydrocannabinol (THC), the principal intoxicative agent in cannabis.[1] By 2016, that number had risen to 28. Changing medical access laws and the permission of commercial retail establishments provided a framework with which to extend repeal to non-medical use. Advocacy groups have argued that cannabis should be regulated like alcohol.[2] The suggestion offers a common and familiar example to voters (Hickenlooper, 2014), helping to reframe commercial legalization of non-medical use.

We then describe the ongoing policy impasse between state and federal laws and policy surrounding cannabis and how the executive branch of the federal government has, at first, limited its response to state repeal efforts for non-medical use. Though rhetoric and actions at the highest levels of the current federal government have recently pivoted in favor of prohibition (Sessions, 2018), efforts to enforce federal cannabis prohibition or pre-empt state laws remain stymied given existing levels of support for repeal within states, limited federal enforcement capacity and shifting policy priorities amidst an ongoing opioid epidemic.

The third section goes into state repeal efforts as they pertain to non-medical use by adults. These follow in chronological order, with the first serious attempt starting with California's Proposition 19 in 2010. We then examine the two pioneer cases of Colorado and Washington, describing the immediate history and run-up to repeal, before describing some details of their regulatory framework. We then discuss the second wave of repeal efforts, two years later in Alaska, Oregon and Washington, DC and the third wave of voter-led repeal efforts, not all of which succeeded, in Arizona, California, Maine, Massachusetts, Nevada and Ohio. We note the one successful legislative repeal measure by Vermont and discuss some of the ongoing efforts of voter-led initiatives and bills in state legislatures.

The last section provides a brief comparative overview among the various regulatory frameworks across the states. Perhaps most useful is Table 1.3, which compares some regulatory design elements across nine jurisdictions. We note that most states have adopted a commercial model, though there are minor variations among them. There is more variation between commercial and non-commercial models, yet only two jurisdictions have adopted a non-commercial framework. It is possible that these jurisdictions will adopt a commercial framework in the near future.

Background

Medical cannabis

The establishment of regulated markets for adult non-medical use has its roots in the passage of voter initiatives that allow for medical access. Indeed, some note the concern that such medical access laws were intended to open the door to recreational reforms (Kilmer and MacCoun, 2017; MacCoun and Reuter, 2001). Starting with California's Proposition 215 in 1996, medical cannabis has expanded across the United States either through voter initiatives or legislative action. There are variations among medical cannabis laws. Today, 34 jurisdictions[3] allow for patients to obtain some form of cannabis or cannabis-derived product that contains appreciable amounts of THC. Another 13 states allow individuals to obtain oils derived from the plant that contain little or negligible amounts of THC.

California's referendum, which passed with 56 percent approval, carved out a legal exemption from criminal prosecution for patients and caregivers who possess or cultivate cannabis recommended by a physician. The initiative permitted doctors to recommend cannabis for conditions such as AIDS, cancer, glaucoma, chronic pain or "any other illness for which marijuana provides relief" (Proposition 215, 1996). This last provision granted broad access to medical cannabis for undiagnosable and nebulous conditions, which may have legitimate benefits for those suffering from some form of discomfort or pain. However, the open set of conditions, coupled with a lack of regulatory oversight, created a loose access scheme in California, allowing adults over 18 an easy means to obtain the drug (Kilmer and MacCoun, 2017). Such loose medical access regimes were adopted by states in the Western US during the late 1990s and early 2000s. Under these designs, an adult over 18 can access medical cannabis whenever deemed necessary by a physician, amounting to little more than a de facto recreational regime (National Academies of Sciences, Engineering, and Medicine, 2017).

After California passed Proposition 215 in 1996, Alaska, Oregon, Washington State and the District of Columbia[4] passed similar initiatives two years later to allow patients to access cannabis for qualifying conditions, which included several hard to diagnose ailments. Voters in Maine were the first state east of the Mississippi River to approve of medical cannabis, doing so in 1999. In 2000, voters in Colorado, Hawaii and Nevada approved medical cannabis. Of these, Nevada and Colorado amended these changes into their state constitutions, rather than laws. Enacting such a legal change into state constitutions requires a higher threshold of support and is thus harder to amend (or possibly strike down under a federal challenge). Also notable, Hawaii was the first state to adopt medical cannabis through the legislative process, rather than allow the voters to decide. States continued to adopt such laws over the years, with some like Florida, Missouri, Oklahoma and Utah loosening their medical laws from low-THC/high-CBD laws to allow greater access to THC (see Figure 1.1).

These laws vary across states in terms of qualifying conditions, patient registry, home cultivation, permission of caregivers and what products are available to patients. In Table 1.1 we provide a selection of such details for a handful of medical cannabis states when they adopted such laws. Some details have changed over time, as is the case with California which now requires a patient registry and permits licensed dispensaries.

Though states had started amending their laws to permit medical access to cannabis, initial efforts perhaps did not envision the commercial, for-profit model of private companies promoting brand-name strains of cannabis. Early laws were often vague and limited, given federal prohibition (Pacula, Powell,

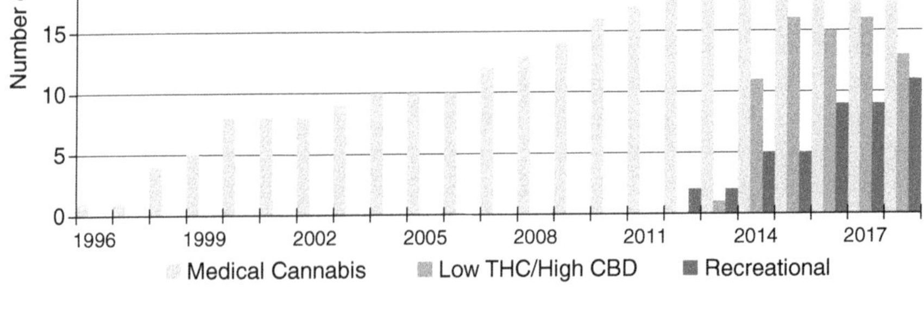

Figure 1.1 Number of state marijuana laws.

Table 1.1 Details of selected state medical cannabis laws at time of adoption

State (year adopted)	*Mandatory patient registry*	*Home cultivation*	*Dispensaries*	*Limits on qualifying conditions or use*
California (1996)	No	Yes	No	No
Alaska (1998)	No	Yes	No	No
Washington (1998)	No	No	No	No
Colorado (2000)	Yes	Yes	Yes	Qualifying conditions
New Mexico (2007)	Yes	Yes	Yes	Qualifying conditions
New York (2014)	Yes	No	Yes	Qualifying conditions and limited to non-smokeable forms
West Virginia (2017)	Yes	No	Yes	Qualifying conditions and limited to non-smokeable forms

Heaton and Sevigny, 2015). However, by the late 2000s, commercialization was becoming a reality in many pioneer medical cannabis states. The development of dispensaries coincided with lax medical cannabis laws in loose access states. In California, Washington and Colorado, private operators began to exploit broad access provisions written into statutes. Patient caregivers or collectives began to pool their authorized patient or plant counts, evolving into the brick and mortar dispensaries that are well known today. States that adopted medical access laws later were often doing so through legislative bodies that accounted for federal law enforcement and sometimes restricted access to a narrower set of conditions.

The federal government enforced the Controlled Substances Act of 1973 (CSA), raiding such dispensaries and cultivation operations during the Clinton and George W. Bush Administrations. However, by 2009, the Obama Administration, facing a shifting public attitude toward medical cannabis, issued what is now known as the Ogden Memorandum, written by Deputy Attorney General David Ogden. The policy memorandum directed federal authorities to focus on high-level targets, such as traffickers and organized criminal groups, and not individuals complying with state law. The memorandum did not offer legal protection to increasingly commercial firms that supplied cannabis to patients, yet, the directive was interpreted as such (Kamin, 2014; Kilmer and MacCoun, 2017). The memorandum is generally considered the starting point for the legitimization of commercial dispensaries. After its dissemination, states began to pass laws to offer legal protection for commercial operators, signaling that such firms were compliant with state law in an attempt to shield them from federal authorities (Pacula et al., 2015). These developments were seen in state medical markets. Colorado's medical cannabis system, which had existed since 2001, had less than 5,000 registered patients in 2008. That number jumped to over 40,000 in 2009, the first year of systematic registry recording, and reached nearly 120,000 in 2010 (Colorado Department of Public Health and Environment, 2018).

Evolving public opinion and policy impasse

Except for the opioid crisis, the most widely discussed issue involving drug policy in the United States today is shifting attitudes and laws on cannabis. The public debate arises between proponents of repeal, pointing to a range of perceived or actual benefits (e.g. enhancing civil liberties, generating tax revenues, etc.) and opponents, wanting to avoid health and social harms (e.g. drugged driving, the development of a large and powerful industry that promotes intemperate use, etc.). There is an additional level of political and legal complexity between state and federal law that touches upon states' rights embedded in the Constitution and the federal government's international treaty obligations, which require it to prohibit the non-authorized supply and use of cannabis in the United States.

Federal cannabis laws have largely gone unchanged since the passage of the CSA. Much of the federal drug law is derived from the United States' international treaty obligations which prohibit activities outside of sanctioned medical and scientific purposes. The Ogden Memorandum was interpreted as a concession, when in fact it merely redirected federal enforcement resources to high-level targets. State and federal conflicts remained, even as states continued to adopt medical access laws or formalize commercial dispensaries. These efforts continued until 2012 when voters of Colorado and Washington passed initiatives to regulate for-profit commercial cannabis in a fashion similar to alcohol – in clear violation of federal law, which supersedes state law under the supremacy clause of the US Constitution.[5]

A year after voters in Colorado and Washington repealed cannabis prohibition, the US Department of Justice issued another policy memorandum to guide federal enforcement efforts. The Cole Memorandum, issued by Deputy Attorney General James Cole, outlined eight priority areas for federal law enforcement, stipulating that states could implement their adult-use access laws if they adhered to guidelines and fashioned a strict regulatory system (Kamin, 2014; Pardo, 2014).

Voter initiatives in favor of repeal were driven by shifts in public attitudes. Since California first moved to allow for medical cannabis, underlying trends in public opinion have slowly moved away from support of prohibition. Public opinion polls have shown a steady increase in support for repeal since the early 2000s, reaching a tipping point in 2013 when a majority of respondents supported legalizing use of cannabis for non-medical purposes (McCarthy, 2017). Figures for support of medical cannabis are higher, though surveys gauge public attitudes on this matter with less frequency. According to Kilmer and MacCoun (2017), support for medical cannabis has ranged from 70–85 percent from 2000–2015. We note that growing favorability toward repeal for non-medical use in the last 15 years has coincided with the adoption and expansion of commercial medical cannabis.

The advent of commercial markets and the opening of retail outlets in early medical cannabis states, along with the absence of any immediate or obvious harms, demonstrated the feasibility of repeal to the average voter (Kilmer and MacCoun, 2017). This is important since voters are often passing these initiatives; as is the case for many of the commercial medical and recreational markets. State legislatures, on the other hand, have passed more restrictive medical cannabis laws. Vermont, the first state to legalize recreational cannabis through the state legislature, adopted a non-commercial model that prohibits retail sales.

State repeal efforts of non-medical cannabis

Prohibition, like repeal, was led by states that wanted to restrict access to drugs like cannabis. In fact, California was the first state to prohibit cannabis in 1913 (Gieringer, 2006). Likewise, states have begun to abolish such long-standing prohibitions. Repeal of cannabis prohibition began in earnest in the 2000s with failed voter initiatives in Alaska in 2000 and 2004 and Nevada in 2006 (Kilmer, Caulkins, Pacula, MacCoun and Reuter, 2010). However, in 2010, Proposition 19 in California, by far the most populous state in the country, opened up the debate to a wider policy and political discussion. The initiative failed, with 47 percent favoring the referendum that would have removed state-level criminal offenses involving cannabis and allowed municipal and county governments to regulate and tax cannabis-related activities as they sought fit. Proposition 19 would have created a regulatory patchwork, complicating the state's efforts to regulate its medical market. Though it failed, the vote and discussion had an impact on referenda in other states.

In Figure 1.2 below, we show the current panorama of state repeal efforts across the United States for non-medical cannabis. Most states have yet to consider, either by letting voters decide or through legislative debate, the question of repeal of cannabis prohibition. There have been two failed voter initiatives for non-medical cannabis repeal. Additionally, we map the four jurisdictions considering some form of repeal of prohibition for non-medical purposes in the coming election and legislative cycles.

Pioneer states

In 2012, Colorado, Oregon and Washington followed California's lead, submitting the question of repeal to voters. All three had robust and loosely regulated commercial medical cannabis markets with product often sold in brick and mortar stores. Oregon voters rejected Measure 80 with 53 percent opposed. Voters in Colorado and Washington voted in favor of their repeal measures with 55 and 56 percent, respectively. Though each had allowed the commercial medical cannabis trade to exist prior to repeal, these were the first jurisdictions in the modern era to vote to regulate the cultivation, processing, distribution and use of a plant that had been prohibited for generations. Further, each had proposed doing so under a for-profit commercial model, building

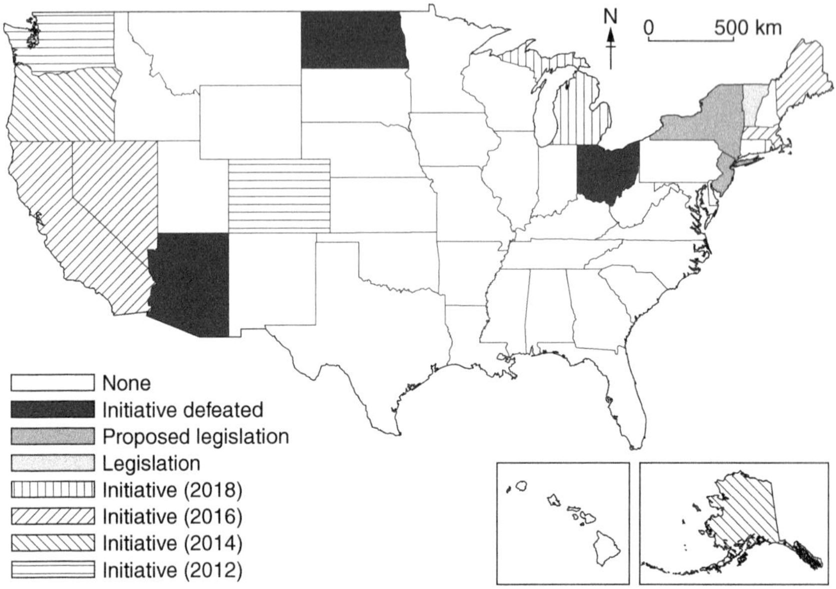

Figure 1.2 Non-medical cannabis repeal efforts by jurisdiction.

off their medical markets. At the time, it was unclear how the federal government would respond. As discussed, many interpreted the Ogden Memorandum as a signal of a move away from prohibition under newly elected President Obama, but these repeal efforts moved policy discussions further still.

Colorado

Amendment 64 to the Colorado State Constitution was approved by voters in November 2012. It was championed by advocates, civil society groups and the state's medical cannabis industry. The new language of the state constitution legalized the production, distribution and sale of cannabis, requiring further statutory changes by the State Assembly. Additionally, it established restrictions and taxes, requiring the Colorado Department of Revenue to license and regulate actors in the for-profit commercial industry. As one of the first jurisdictions to permit such activity, Governor John Hickenlooper took a cautious approach and formed a task force made up of a broad set of stakeholders (from public health authorities, criminal justice functionaries, researchers, industry representatives and others) to study requisite legal changes and the processes for developing effective laws and regulations that allow for adult access to cannabis, monitoring the impacts and designing new methodologies for cannabis-specific prevention programs.

The Colorado Department of Revenue (CDOR), the principal authority for regulating all aspects of the soon-to-be legal cannabis trade, drafted initial rules in July 2013, building off its three years' experience regulating the medical cannabis trade and from inputs of the Governor's Task Force (Pardo, 2014). This knowledge was adapted and expanded to suit a legal, non-medical cannabis industry. Initial rules were further amended after public input over the summer of 2013, and final rules were adopted in September. Starting in November 2013, the CDOR began accepting applications for producer, processor and distributor licenses. Licenses were issued and the legal, non-medical cannabis system began distribution in January 2014. It took Colorado approximately 14 months to develop regulations. Many of these regulations continued to undergo adjustments in response to several concerns over accidental ingestion and lack of consumer safety information. Emergency regulations were promulgated over the coming years, aimed at improving labeling, potency tests and serving sizes.

In the initial year, medical cannabis licensees were favored to obtain licenses to produce and distribute non-medical cannabis under Colorado's new law. This and other efforts by the state have aimed to bring both medical and recreational markets under a similar regulatory system and push adult medical patients toward recreational markets. Such trends have been reported. The number of registered medical cannabis patients hit nearly 115,000 in 2014. After three years of non-medical access, patient counts have continued to trend downward, reaching 88,000 in 2017 (Colorado Department of Public Health and Environment, 2018). Sales of non-medical cannabis show an upward trend over time since stores opened for business; however, medical cannabis sales have remained flat since January 2014. Non-medical cannabis sales totaled just over $300 million in 2014, compared to $380 million for medical sales. By 2017, non-medical sales were just over $1 billion, with medical sales reaching $417 million (Colorado Department of Revenue, 2018).

Washington

Much like Colorado, voters of Washington approved Initiative 502 (I-502) to amend existing statutes (rather than necessitate additional laws, as was the case in Colorado) and direct state agencies to draft regulations relevant to the cultivation, processing, distribution and use of non-medical cannabis by adults. I-502 directed the state Liquor Control Board (LCB, which later became the Liquor and Cannabis Board) to design a regulatory scheme to license private firms to supply the state's cannabis market. Coincidentally, the board had just finalized efforts to privatize the state's alcohol distribution system, allowing it to build off similar thematic areas of knowledge. As one of the first jurisdictions to repeal cannabis prohibition, state regulators sought to craft comprehensive regulations (Pardo, 2014). Like Colorado, authorities recognized the need for a comprehensive approach. The LCB hired BOTEC Analysis to advise the state on implementation, market sizing, and rule-making.

By July 2013, draft regulations were issued. Over the next two months, the board conducted a series of public hearings across the state, meeting with citizens and groups. After taking into account public input, new rules were filed in September 2013 and adopted a month later. The LCB began to accept applications for producer, processor and distributor licenses in December 2013. The board issued licenses in the beginning of 2014. Stores opened in July 2014, a full 20 months after the passage of the law. In mid-2015, the state legislature passed a new tax structure, moving from a three-tiered system, taxing cannabis at 25 percent at each point along the supply chain, to a 37 percent excise tax at retail (Cambron, Guttmannova and Fleming, 2017). The law also clarified that localities could prohibit licensed establishments.

Unlike Colorado, Washington State did not attempt to integrate its unregulated medical cannabis market into the newly regulated non-medical system. In fact, the state's medical cannabis industry opposed I-502 (Martin, 2012). Whereas Colorado sought buy-in from existing businesses with regulations that eased their transition into a new market, Washington prohibited vertical integration of cultivation and distribution and limited the number of retail stores across the state. Eventually in 2015, the legislature passed laws to bring its medical system under similar regulations, allowing some existing dispensaries the ability to obtain local endorsements that would allow them to become licensed with the state to sell regulated product to medical patients (Cambron et al., 2017). Sales of non-medical cannabis for fiscal year 2015 reached $790 million, doubling to $1.4 billion by fiscal year 2017 (Liquor and Cannabis Board, 2018).

Second wave of voter initiatives

Two years later, citizens in three more jurisdictions voted to repeal cannabis prohibition. In 2014, Alaska, Oregon and Washington, DC joined Colorado and Washington in allowing adults to obtain or use cannabis for non-medical purposes. Each had had medical access markets in place for some time. Oregon's Measure 91 was different to the failed Measure 80 of two years prior. Measure 91, which passed with 56 percent of the vote, limited the total amount of cannabis that adults could have in their home and, unlike Measure 80 which would have created a regulatory agency comprised of industry interests, directed the Oregon Liquor Control Commission to develop regulations. Alaska, which had a long history of medical cannabis and legal protections surrounding home cultivation, adopted its Measure 2 with 53 percent approval. Unlike Oregon and Alaska, which proposed commercially regulated cannabis markets, Initiative 71 in the District of Columbia amended the penal code to permit adults to possess up to an ounce and grow up to six plants. The Initiative, which passed with 70 percent of the vote, was the first non-commercial repeal effort in the country.

Between the first and second waves, Ohio put forward a proposal to repeal prohibition in 2015. Issue 3 overwhelmingly failed with 64 percent of voters opposed. The initiative was sponsored by business interests, which drafted the language to allow exclusive commercial rights to cultivate and process cannabis to the ten licensees. The funders behind the initiative were criticized for designing a favorable monopoly system, guaranteeing their ownership over the state industry. At the time, Ohio did not have medical access, making it the first state to vote on repealing cannabis prohibition for non-medical purposes prior to medical access (Smith and Stolberg, 2015). Surprisingly, national cannabis repeal advocates opposed or did not support the monopoly initiative (Ingraham, 2015).

Alaska

The status of cannabis in Alaska, unlike most other states, has gone through various periods of relaxation and re-prohibition since the 1970s. Because of several complicating and competing legal decisions, Alaska had permitted periods of home cultivation for a small number of plants under privacy protections (MacCoun, 2010). In 1998, Alaska had joined other states in adopting medical cannabis and the state had witnessed two failed repeal initiatives, one in 2000 and another in 2004 (Kilmer et al., 2010). By 2014, Colorado and Washington had cleared the way for Alaska's Measure 2 to win voters' support.

The initiative was similar to those of other states, allowing adults over 21 to obtain cannabis from licensed producers. The initiative's provisions allowing adults to possess or cultivate went into effect in February of 2015, but it would take the state several months to craft regulations that permitted regulated retail sale. Like Colorado, Alaska's legislature passed several pieces of legislation to establish the legal and regulatory environment wherein private firms could obtain licenses to cultivate, process and distribute cannabis for non-medical purposes. In April 2015, the legislature passed legislation to create a five-member Marijuana Control Board within the Alcoholic Beverage Control Board (Andrews, 2016a). This was signed into law in May 2015 and the governor began making appointments to the board in July of that year. Eventually the Marijuana Control Board and the Alcoholic Beverage Control Board would become separate boards within the Alcohol and Marijuana Control Office of the Department of Commerce.

The board began drafting regulations similar to those found in other commercial states. There are a few exceptions, taxation being the most noticeable. Unlike other states that adopted an ad valorem (i.e. on price) tax on cannabis, Alaska was the only state to statutorily adopt a per unit weight tax of $50 an ounce on bud and flower. Regulations were finalized and promulgated in February 2016. The board began accepting and reviewing applications in June, issuing the first licenses in August of that year (Alcohol and Marijuana Control Office, 2018a). By late October, Alaska's first non-medical dispensary opened its doors for sales (Andrews, 2016b).

Alaska is currently taking public input as to regulating on-site consumption (which is allowed under statute but currently banned until rules are in place) (Alcohol and Marijuana Control Office, 2018b). The board has continued to approve applications. As of 2017, the board reported that it had approved 113 licenses for various businesses operating in the cannabis supply chain. By 2018, this number had jumped to 219 (Alcohol and Marijuana Control Office, 2018a). In fiscal year 2017, the state had taken in a total of $1.7 million in tax revenue (Alaska Department of Revenue, 2018).

Oregon

In an effort to comply with the federal guidelines issued from the Cole Memorandum, Oregon's Measure 91 provided a broad framework for regulating the commercial market for non-medical cannabis (Helm and Leichtman, 2015). Like Colorado, the Measure necessitated statutory changes to Oregon's laws. To that end, the state legislature convened a task force to help define areas of consideration and amendment (Helm and Leichtman, 2015). In some cases, the draft laws required modifying certain components of Oregon's medical marijuana program, bringing that market under closer regulatory scrutiny. For example, it made changes to the producer registration and tracking systems, as well as added processor licenses, which were not regulated at the time, to the regulatory system (Helm and Leichtman, 2015).

The legislature made some amendments to the voter-approved initiative. For one, the initiative had placed a weight-based tax on cannabis ($35 per ounce). This was amended by the legislature to an ad valorem excise tax rate of 17 percent on the retail price of cannabis (Helm and Leichtman, 2015). Oregon's statutes granted broad authority to the Oregon Liquor Control Commission to incorporate rules from inputs from the community, the Oregon Health Authority, and the Department of Agriculture. Though aspects of the regulated market would not be operational until January 2016, non-medical use and possession of cannabis went into effect in July 2015. Given the lack of access, the OLCC and the Oregon Health Authority allowed non-medical sales to be conducted through registered medical dispensaries as a stopgap measure starting on October 1, 2015. During that phase-in period, adults over 21 were allowed to purchase up to a quarter ounce of cannabis (Helm and Leichtman, 2015). Non-medical retail dispensaries opened to consumers on October 1, 2016 (Associated Press, 2016). The state received over $20 million in tax receipts in fiscal year 2016, growing to over $70 million in fiscal year 2017 (Oregon Department of Revenue, 2018).

Washington, DC

Washington, DC, though not opting for a commercial cannabis system, followed other states along its trajectory toward repeal. Like many other states, the district has also decriminalized possession of small amounts of cannabis. In March 2014, the Marijuana Decriminalization Bill was approved by the city council. It reduced the maximum penalty for possession of an ounce of cannabis from six months in jail and a $1,000 fine to a civil infraction of

$25. Public use is now a misdemeanor offense, subject to up to 60 days in jail and/or a $500 fine.

Within a year, decriminalization was superseded by legalization of possession. In November 2014, district residents overwhelmingly voted in favor of Initiative 71, which removed criminal penalties for adults over 21 from the penal code for growing, possessing and gifting cannabis under certain limits. I71 was supposed to be the first step in a two-step process. After the initiative passed, the council began considering draft legislation to create a regulated commercial market, much like those seen in other states (Davis, 2017). However, Congress quickly prohibited the district from using appropriated funds to effect any legislation that would establish a regulated commercial market (Davis, 2017).

Initiative 71 became law in February of 2015, creating a non-commercial environment described as "home grow, home use" (Marijuana Private Club Task Force, 2016). Adults over 21 are allowed to grow up to six plants (no more than three in flower) at their place of residence, may possess up to two ounces and may gift up to an ounce to another adult without remuneration. The council did effect legislation to ban smoking in bars and clubs as well as to prohibit the formation of private marijuana clubs that would allow guests to use on-site until regulations are promulgated. At this time, there are no licensed producers, processors or distributors for non-medical cannabis in the district. Public consumption is a misdemeanor and individuals are still subject to criminal penalties under federal law.

Third wave of voter initiatives

In November 2016, voters in five states decided whether to repeal cannabis prohibition. Voters in California, Maine, Massachusetts and Nevada decided to join the five early cannabis repeal adopters. Voters in Arizona narrowly rejected repeal by a vote of 49 to 51 percent. Like their predecessors, medical cannabis preceded non-medical repeal efforts. In some instances, state legislatures undertook modifications of the voter-approved initiatives. Regulatory efforts in these states are still developing, and some have yet to allow for retail sales.

California

In anticipation of the state adopting repeal, the Lt. Governor, Gavin Newsom, convened a Blue Ribbon Commission on Marijuana Policy. The Commission started operating in 2013 and was made up of public health experts, policymakers and researchers with the goal of providing information on regulatory design and developments in other states (Newsom, Humphreys and Soltani, 2015). After failing six years earlier, voters in California approved Proposition 64, or the Adult Use of Marijuana Act (AUMA), by 57 percent. Much like the preceding commercial non-adult cannabis regimes established in other states, California's initiative created a framework from which to guide regulatory efforts while also allowing adults over 21 to cultivate and possess cannabis for personal use. Adult possession and cultivation provisions went into effect in November 2016, while the Proposition required the state to issue licenses for commercial operations by January 1, 2018. In 2015, the California State Assembly had passed a series of statutes to bring the state's medical cannabis market and regulatory structure into order after nearly 20 years of minimal oversight and control. The regulatory scheme, known as the Medical Cannabis Regulatory and Safety Act (MCRSA) aimed to ensure environmental safeguards and the development of a regulated medical system (Bureau of Cannabis Control, 2018a).

After passage of AUMA, lawmakers repealed the MCRSA and incorporated many of its provisions in AUMA, creating a single regulatory system for both medical and non-medical cannabis under the Medicinal and Adult-Use Cannabis Regulation and Safety Act (MAUCRSA) (Bureau of Cannabis Control, 2018a). The superseding legislation created the Bureau of Cannabis Control within the Department of Consumer Affairs to develop regulations and oversee the licensing and enforcement of businesses. Starting January 1, 2018, non-medical cannabis retailers began selling cannabis in 90 stores throughout the state (Atagi, 2018). With less than a year of operating sales, regulators continue to develop new rules (Bureau of Cannabis Control, 2018b). Nonetheless, California's regulated cannabis regime differs from other states. It imposes both an ad valorem (15 percent of retail price) and specific tax ($9.25/ounce of flower) on cannabis. Under regulations, licensed retailers are permitted to deliver cannabis to consumers at their home.

Maine

Similar to other states that have adopted non-medical cannabis repeal, Maine also has maintained medical cannabis access for years. Voters narrowly approved Question 1 in November 2016. Just over half of the voters approved the initiative. The vote was split by fewer than 4,000 votes and officials initiated a recount of ballots (Thistle, 2016). Initial recount efforts suggested no change in the outcome in favor of repeal and opponents to Question 1 requested an end to the recount efforts, essentially conceding defeat (Quimby, 2016). The initiative was broadly similar to other commercial initiatives in other states. It would direct the Department of Agriculture, Conservation and Forestry to create a licensing authority to regulate the cannabis industry and allow adults to grow and possess cannabis for personal use. The initiative's provisions on personal use took effect in late January 2017, allowing those over 21 to cultivate six plants and possess 2.5 ounces. Though Measure 1 directed the state to begin issuing licenses nine months after certification (about September 2017), the state legislature passed a law to delay implementation until February 2018, giving the state more time to craft regulations (Miller, 2017).

Repeal efforts were stymied by Governor Paul LePage, who issued an executive order moving regulatory oversight and rule-making to the Department of Administrative and Financial Services and prohibiting the state government from implementing legislation passed by the legislature (LePage, 2017a). Over the course of 2017, Maine's legislature crafted a bill to amend the voter-approved initiative. The bill provided the framework for non-medical adult use of cannabis and directed the Department of Administrative and Financial Services to draft rules and license operators. The bill, passed by the legislature in late October 2017, was vetoed by Governor LePage, citing federal prohibition and negative consequences of cannabis use (Cousins, 2017; LePage, 2017b). The legislature was unable to override the governor's veto (Thistle, 2017).

The legislature would deliberate for another five months, working out a veto-proof compromise. In April 2018, lawmakers passed a new law that banned on-site consumption at social clubs, required an excise fee of $335 per pound of cannabis – in addition to the 10 percent retail tax – and reduced home cultivation plant counts from six to three. Governor LePage vetoed the law on May 2, 2018, but was overridden by lawmakers (Maine State Legislature, 2018). The new law came into effect, ending the 18-month standoff since voters approved the initiative in November of 2016. Officials expect that the law's implementation will take no less than nine months to finalize for future approval (Shepherd, 2018). To date, only the law's provisions on personal use and home cultivation are in effect; there are currently no regulated commercial sales.

Massachusetts

Medical cannabis was approved by voters in Massachusetts in 2012. However, it took the state almost three years to finalize implementation of medical cannabis regulations; the first dispensary opened in June 2015. Not a year and half after implementation of medical cannabis, voters approved Question 4, allowing adult non-medical access, by 54 percent. The measure was broadly similar to those of other states, allowing adults over 21 to grow six plants in their home, possess up to an ounce on their person and craft a regulatory scheme to allow for the supply and distribution of cannabis in stores. Provisions related to personal possession and home grow went into effect in December 2016. The legislature passed a law that modified several provisions of the voter-approved initiative, including extending the initial deadline of implementation from January 2018 to July 2018, increasing the excise tax from 3.75 percent to 10.75 percent, allowing for local municipalities to hold local referenda on banning or permitting cannabis businesses, and increasing the number of members of the state's new Cannabis Control Commission from three to five (Commonwealth of Massachusetts, 2017; Wilson, 2017).

The Commission promulgated regulations in March of 2018 and has been reviewing applications and issuing provisional licenses. Similar to its slow rollout of its medical cannabis regime, the state missed the July 2018 implementation deadline. As of September 2018, 30 provisional non-medical licenses have been issued to existing medical facilities, including retailers and cultivators; however, the Commission has yet to issue a license for a testing lab (Adams, 2018). Without an approved testing facility, licensees cannot sell non-medical cannabis to consumers. Dispensaries finally opened on November 20, 2018 to great anticipation (Held, 2018).

Nevada

Though Nevada had made medical cannabis permissible under state law in 2000, it had not permitted commercial retail dispensaries until 2013. However, medical cannabis dispensaries did not open until July 2015 (Chereb, 2015). Though it took several years before medical cannabis dispensaries were operating, in November 2016, voters approved Question 2 with 55 percent. The initiative directed the Department of Taxation to draft and implement regulations, though it required an 18-month moratorium on granting licenses to applicants that were not already operating in the state's medical cannabis market and capped the total number of stores state-wide. These elements, similar to provisions in Colorado and Washington, would aid in the promulgation of regulations for the non-medical market.

The initiative's provisions relevant to possession and home cultivation by adults over 21 took effect on January 1, 2017. State authorities set an ambitious deadline to draft and approve regulations with the aim of allowing non-medical sales to begin by July 2017. In February, Department of Taxation Executive Director Deonne Contine stated that she expected to start accepting license applications in May, with the intention of seeing businesses open public sales by July 1 (Noon, 2017). Stores opened in July 2017 and have generated nearly $70 million in tax revenue in the first 12 months (Nevada Department of Taxation, 2018).

Legislative efforts

To date, Vermont is the only state to have adopted repeal by means of the legislative process. It too had an existing medical cannabis system and had made possession of up to an ounce a civil infraction in 2013 (Office of the Governor of Vermont, 2013). By 2014, then-Governor Peter Shumlin had indicated his support for a regulated non-medical system (Hirschfeld, 2015). In order to better understand the implications of state-wide repeal, the legislature passed Act 155, requiring the Secretary of Administration to produce a report on the consequences of repeal (Caulkins et al., 2015). Authorities contracted with the RAND Corporation's Drug Policy Research Center to evaluate the details and potential impacts of a regulatory system in that state. The report was delivered in early 2015 (Caulkins et al., 2015).

During the 2015–2016 legislative session, the General Assembly considered several pieces of legislation to repeal cannabis prohibition and to create a regulated market. However, none of them gained approval. It seemed that repeal, though favored by many elected officials, would languish in the legislature as few could agree on the various provisions and details required to establish a working regulatory system (Burlington Free Press, 2015). By January 2018, after the ascension of Governor Phil Scott and the seating of a new legislature, officials agreed to a non-commercial repeal. House Bill 511 was passed on January 4, 2018. Much like the law in DC, the text of Vermont's bill removed penalties for possession of up to one ounce of cannabis for those over 21 and allowed for cultivation of up to six plants (two flowering) in one's home. The bill was signed by incoming Governor Scott on January 22, making Vermont the first state to adopt cannabis repeal through the legislature.

Nevertheless, Vermont may eventually adopt a commercial system, much like those found in other states. The state senate had passed a commercial model in 2016, which would have allowed adults to purchase regulated product from commercial establishments (Hirschfeld, 2016). More recently, lawmakers in the state legislature have proposed similar commercial legislation this session (Hirschfeld, 2018).

Recent and future repeal

In late 2018, there were a handful of states looking to repeal cannabis prohibition, allowing adults to obtain and use it for non-medical purposes. In November 2018, voters in Michigan and North Dakota voted on repeal. Proposal 1 in Michigan passed with 56 percent in favor and will create a commercial system for taxed and regulated cannabis, much like those seen in other states (Board of State Canvassers, 2018). In North Dakota, voters rejected Measure 3 by almost 60 percent. The initiative was different to those presented to voters in other states. Measure 3 would have removed criminal penalties for adults over 21 for cannabis-related activity (including growing, selling, distributing or use) and expunge the criminal records of those who have been convicted of an offense (Measure 3, 2018). The initiative would have left it to the legislature to consider any future regulatory framework. The language of the text did not detail supply modes, let alone a regulated system; it merely repealed state prohibition and replaced it with no alternative. Of the 12 supply policies identified by Caulkins et al. (2015), this is considered one of two extreme options.

Additionally, there are currently ongoing discussions in the state legislatures of New York and New Jersey. The governor of New York, Andrew Cuomo, has put together a working group to draft legislation for a regulated adult-use cannabis system after the state Department of Health issued findings recommending such a task earlier this year (Office of the Governor of New York, 2018). Details have yet to be agreed, but the state is taking this endeavor seriously. Similarly, Governor Phil Murphy of New Jersey has been working with the state assembly to craft a commercial regime for non-medical cannabis. Under the current draft legislation, the state will adopt a similar commercial approach, including provisions for approved on-site consumption.

The law would also impose a 10 percent tax and conform a Cannabis Regulatory Commission to draft and implement rules governing the commercial trade (Guion, 2018).

It remains to be seen if future repeal efforts will pass either voter approval or legislative deliberation. Nonetheless, the fact remains that states are continuing to adopt repeal. Developments in pioneer states have provided some framework to voters and legislatures who are considering repealing cannabis prohibition. Yet, states are continuing to adopt legal changes amidst a backdrop of federal prohibition.

The ongoing impasse with federal law remains a barrier for some states that may want to repeal cannabis prohibition. At the same time, federal prohibition limits the growth of the commercial industry as it prevents interstate trade and limits economic efficiency.[6] However, federal lawmakers are starting to recognize the need for national reform (Kennedy, 2018). It is unclear when or if federal law will be amended to reflect the legal changes that are increasingly adopted by states.

Comparative analysis of regulations

There are now ten jurisdictions in the United States that have repealed cannabis prohibition. Most have adopted a for-profit, commercial model. Under this legal and regulatory framework, states have licensed private individuals and businesses to cultivate, process and distribute cannabis to adults over the age of 21. Much of this commercial design follows the existing medical cannabis regulatory frameworks in these states. Only two jurisdictions, Washington, DC and Vermont, have put forward non-commercial models of home cultivation and cannabis gifting. It is unclear at this time if a non-commercial model will survive an encroaching and unregulated "grey market" trade where buyers and sellers utilize a gifting loophole to exchange cannabis for remuneration.

In Table 1.2 below we provide some additional information, comparing the regulatory regimes found in all jurisdictions, except Vermont. We have omitted Vermont, given that it is much like Washington, DC, except for having a lower quantity threshold of one ounce instead of two. Examining the table, most jurisdictions have similar regulatory schemes that license cultivators, processors and retailers. Most have designated regulatory authority to a specific agency, tasked with writing and enforcing the rules. The minimum age, 21, is the same for all states. Most adopt a maximum personal possession limit of an ounce, except Maine and Washington, DC, which allow adults to possess 2.5 and 2 ounces, respectively. All jurisdictions, except the state of Washington, allow adults to grow several plants at home. Most prohibit public consumption, though a few allow for private establishments and waivers for events, allowing adults to consume cannabis in public. Nevertheless, using cannabis in public is a minor offense, resulting in a fine, much like drinking alcohol in public.

Table 1.2 Cross-state comparison of regulated cannabis in the United States

	Alaska	*California*	*Colorado*	*Maine*	*Massachusetts*	*Nevada*	*Oregon*	*Washington*	*District of Columbia*
Legal and regulatory background									
Legal process	Voter initiative, state statute	Voter initiative, state statute	Voter initiative, amendment to state constitution	Voter initiative, state statute	Voter initiative, state statute	Voter initiative, state statute	Voter initiative, state statute	Voter initiative, state statute	Voter initiative
Title of referendum	Ballot Measure 2	Proposition 64	Amendment 64	Question 1	Question 4	Question 2	Measure 91	Initiative 502	Initiative 71
Statute and regulatory code	AS 17.38 3 ACC 306	Medicinal and Adult-Use Cannabis Regulation and Safety Act CA Code Title 16 Division 42	12-43.4-101 eq. seq. C.R.S. 1 CCR 212-2	Marijuana Legalization Act Pending regulations	Chapter 55 935 CMR: Cannabis Control Commission	Chapter 453D R092-17	Chapter 845 Division 25 ORS Chapter 475B	Title 314 Washington Administrative Code	Not applicable
Date passed	November, 2014	November, 2016	November, 2012	November, 2016	November, 2016	November, 2016	November, 2014	November, 2012	November, 2014
Date implemented	February 2015: Personal possession and consumption. October 2016: Cultivation, processing and retail sales	December 2016: Personal possession, consumption, home cultivation January 2018: Cultivation, processing and retail sales	December 2012: Personal possession, consumption, home cultivation January 2014: Cultivation, processing and retail sales	January 2017: Personal possession, consumption, home cultivation Early 2020 (expected): Cultivation, processing, and retail sales pending regulations	December 2016: Personal possession, consumption, home cultivation February 2019 (expected): Cultivation, processing and retail sales	December 2016: Personal possession, consumption, home cultivation July 2017: Cultivation, processing and retail sales	July 2015: Personal possession, consumption, home cultivation October 1 2015: Retail sales via medical dispensaries October 2016: Retail sales through licensed retailers	December 2012: Personal possession, consumption July 2014: Cultivation, processing and retail sales	February 2015: Personal possession, consumption, home cultivation
Regulatory authority	Marijuana Control Board (Department of Commerce, Community and Economic Development)	Bureau of Cannabis Control (Department of Consumer Affairs)	Marijuana Enforcement Division (Department of Revenue)	Department of Administrative and Financial Services	Cannabis Control Commission	Department of Taxation	Oregon Liquor Control Commission	Liquor and Cannabis Board	Not applicable
Personal use									
Minimum age	21	21	21	21	21	21	21	21	21
Residency requirement	None	None	None	None	None	None	None	None	None

(continued)

Table 1.2 continued

	Alaska	*California*	*Colorado*	*Maine*	*Massachusetts*	*Nevada*	*Oregon*	*Washington*	*District of Columbia*
Personal possession quantity	28.5 g flower or equivalent	28.5 g flower 8 g concentrate	28.5 g flower or equivalent	71.25 g flower5 g concentrate	28.5 g flower5 g concentrate	28.5 g flower3.5 g concentrate	In public: 28.5 g flower453 g solid form (e.g. edibles) 5 g concentrate 2.1 liters in liquid form	28.5 g flower7 g concentrate	57 g flower or equivalent
Home cultivation	6 plants, 3 of which can be flowering	6 plants	6 plants, 3 of which can be flowering	3 mature plants 12 immature plants Localities can allow more	6 mature plants, 12 in a residence At home: 285 g flower	6 plants, no more than 12 on property and must be 25 miles away from retail marijuana store	4 plants in flower At home: 228 g flower	Not allowed	6 plants per person, 12 plants per household, 3 of which can be flowering
Interpersonal sharing and gifting	Permitted, up to personal possession quantity	Permitted, up to personal possession quantity	Permitted, up to personal possession quantity	Permitted for home grow, up to personal possession quantity	Permitted, up to personal possession quantity	Permitted, up to personal possession quantity	Permitted, up to personal possession quantity	Not allowed	Permitted, up to 28.5 g
Public consumption	Prohibited where not designated. Fine	Prohibited where not designated Fine	Prohibited Fine	Prohibited Fine	Prohibited Fine	Prohibited Fine	Prohibited Fine	Prohibited Fine	Prohibited, misdemeanor
Production, processing and retail									
Market structure	Commercially-regulated private firms Local governments can apply for distribution licenses Vertical integration permitted	Commercially-regulated private firms Vertical integration prohibited until 2023	Commercially-regulated private firms Vertical integration required during first year, now permitted Initial license allocation preference for medical firms	Commercially-regulated private firms Vertical integration permitted, but restrictions on size/number of licenses held by a single entity Localities prohibited from market activities	Commercially-regulated private firms Vertical integration required Initial license allocation preference for medical firms	Commercially-regulated private firms Vertical integration permitted Initial license allocation preference for medical firms Limits on the total number of licenses in a jurisdiction	Commercially-regulated private firms Vertical integration permitted Initial license allocation preference for medical firms	Commercially-regulated private firms Vertical integration prohibited	Only home grow and gifting by individuals

	Alaska	*California*	*Colorado*	*Maine*	*Massachusetts*	*Nevada*	*Oregon*	*Washington*	*District of Columbia*
Zoning and licensing restrictions	Licenses not permitted near schools, religious facilities and correctional facilities No co-location with alcohol licenses	Localities can impose additional zoning requirements	Localities can impose additional zoning requirements	Localities can impose additional zoning ordinances and permit individuals to cultivate more plants at home Licenses not permitted near schools	Localities can impose additional zoning requirements	Licenses not permitted near schools, religious facilities and correctional facilities No co-location with alcohol licenses	Licenses not permitted near schools Localities can impose additional zoning requirements	Licenses not permitted near schoolsLocalities can impose additional zoning requirements	Not applicable
Local restrictions and prohibitions	Localities can prohibit establishments through local bans and zoning	Localities can prohibit establishments	Localities can prohibit establishments	Localities can prohibit establishments through zoning restrictions	Localities can prohibit establishments through local bans	Localities can impose additional zoning requirements	Localities can prohibit establishments through local bans	Localities can prohibit establishments	
Retail transaction limit	28.5 g flower 7 g concentrates	28.5 g flower 8 g concentrates	Residents: 28.5 g Non-residents: 7 g	71.25 g flower 5 g concentrate	28.5 g flower 5 g concentrates	28.5 g flower 3.5 g concentrate	28.5 g flower 453 g solid form (e.g. edibles) 5 g concentrate 2.1 liters in liquid form	28.5 g flower 7 g concentrate	Not applicable
Maximum THC potency	Only for edibles: 50 mg per package, 5 mg per serving	Only for edibles: 10 mg per serving	Only for edibles: 100 mg per package, 10 mg per serving	Only for edibles: 100 mg per package, 10 mg per serving	Only for edibles: 100 mg per package, 5 mg per serving	Only for edibles: 100 mg per package, 10 mg per serving	Only for edibles: 50 mg per package, 5 mg per serving	Only for edibles: 100 mg per package, 10 mg per serving	Not applicable
Production	Licensed Marijuana Producers, licenses vary by size Caps on producer size.	Licensed Cultivator, licenses vary by size in canopy square feet and indoor vs outdoor Caps on producer size	Licensed Marijuana Cultivation Facilities, licenses vary by size by plant count Caps on producers	Licensed Marijuana Cultivation Facilities, licenses vary by canopy square feet Caps on producer size	Licensed Marijuana Cultivation Facilities, licenses vary by size in canopy square feet Caps on producer size	Licensed Cultivator No caps on producer size	Licensed Marijuana Producers, licenses vary by size Caps on producer size	Licensed Marijuana Producers, licenses vary by size in canopy square feet Caps on producer size	Home grow only
Distribution	Licensed Retail Marijuana Stores	Licensed Retailers, Distributors, and Microbusinesses	Licensed Retail Marijuana Stores	Licensed Retail Marijuana Stores	Licensed Marijuana Retailer	Licensed Distributor licenses separate from retail	Licensed Retail Marijuana Stores	Licensed Retailers	Interpersonal sharing/gifting only

(continued)

Table 1.2 continued

	Alaska	*California*	*Colorado*	*Maine*	*Massachusetts*	*Nevada*	*Oregon*	*Washington*	*District of Columbia*
Advertising	Retail establishments may not have more than 3 signs visible to general public and may not exceed a certain size Ads cannot promote excessive consumption, make false claims, or appeal to those under 21 Restrictions on where ads can be Ads must contain warnings.	Prohibits advertising that promotes excessive use, attractive to minors, contains false statements Limits advertising near highways or schools Prohibits ads directed at those under 18 or media markets where under 21 make up more than 30%	Restricted to media with no more than 30% of the audience under the age of 21 Cannot make false claims	Allowed, but restricted to those over 21 Restrictions on false advertisement or claims of untrue health benefits Products cannot appeal to children	Allowed, but restricted to those over 21 (media markets and events at least 85% over 21 years) Restrictions on false advertisement or claims of untrue health benefits Products cannot appeal to children	Restricted to media with no more than 30 percent of the audience under the age of 21 Prohibits ads near schools and other public spaces	Prohibits advertising that promotes excessive use, attractive to minors, contains false statements	Prohibits advertising that promotes excessive use, attractive to minors, contains false statements	Not applicable
Packaging and labeling	Quantity, serving size, ingredients, potency, warning labels, and child-proof containers	Quantity, serving size, ingredients, potency, warning labels, and child-proof containers	Quantity, serving size, ingredients, potency, warning labels, and child-proof containers	Not yet specified in regulations, statute requires child-proof packages, symbols, and warning labels and prohibits labeling that is attractive to youth or is deceptive	Quantity, serving size, ingredients, potency, warning labels, and child-proof containers Labeling and products require prior-approval Packaging cannot appeal to youth	Quantity, serving size, ingredients, potency, warning labels, and child-proof containers Labeling and products require prior-approval Packaging cannot appeal to youth	Quantity, serving size, ingredients, potency, warning labels, and child-proof containers	Quantity, serving size, ingredients, potency, warning labels, and child-proof containers Labeling and products require prior approval	Not applicable

	Alaska	*California*	*Colorado*	*Maine*	*Massachusetts*	*Nevada*	*Oregon*	*Washington*	*District of Columbia*
)n-site consumption	Permitted with approval of the Board	Localities can authorize on-site consumption. Authorities can waive on-site public consumption restrictions for certain events	Prohibited	Prohibited in public areas Private establishments may permit use	Prohibited at retail establishments Localities can vote to permit such establishments Commission allowing social consumption through pilot	Prohibited	Prohibited	Prohibited	Not applicable
'axation	$50 excise tax per ounce on sales or transfers from cultivation facility to retail store or product manufacturer; Additional local sales tax may apply	15% excise on retail $9.25 per dry-weight ounce (28.5 g) on flower after harvest $2.75 per dry-weight ounce (28.5 g) on leaves; Additional state and local sales tax	15% excise tax on cultivation; 15% Retail Marijuana Sales Tax (amended up from 10% in 2017); 2.9% additional state and local sales tax	Wholesale excise tax of $335 per pound of flower; $94 per pound of trim 10% retail excise tax	Retail excise sale tax 3.75% approved in initiative Raised by legislature to 10.75% Additional state sales tax 6.75% and local sales taxes	15% excise on wholesale 10% retail excise tax; Additional local sales tax	No tax on retail sales from October 2015–December 2015; 25% sales tax after January 5, 2016; 17% sales tax after January 1, 2017; Additional state and local sales tax	July 2014–June 2014: 25% tax at each stage (Production, Processing, Retail) Amended in July 2015 to 37% excise sales tax	Not applicable
1edical cannabis	Yes, since 2000	Yes, since 1996	Yes, since 2000	Yes, since 1999	Yes, since 2012	Yes, since 2000	Yes, since 1999	Yes, since 1999	Yes, since 2011

The market structures for commercial systems are mixed. Some states permit vertical integration, allowing individual firms to hold licenses for production and distribution. Others prohibit such market integration. All commercial markets impose a maximum plant or canopy cap for producers, except Nevada, though that state does cap the total number of licensed firms. All permit localities to further regulate licensees under local ordinances. Some jurisdictions allow for counties and cities to adopt bans on authorized cannabis firms. With the exception of Alaska and Oregon, which cap edibles at 5 mg THC, edibles in other commercial markets have a 10 mg THC serving size. Taxation varies across states, with most adopting an ad valorem tax on the wholesale or retail price. Some adopt a unit tax by weight, like Alaska. And California and Maine adopt a mixture of taxing by weight and value.

Given the novelty of repeal of cannabis prohibition, the outcomes of these varied regulatory approaches have yet to be measured in terms of their impacts on public health, safety and the economy. Most states in the US are adopting a commercial regulatory framework under the hanging cloud of federal prohibition. It is unclear how or when the federal government will repeal cannabis prohibition, let alone how these markets and state regulatory authorities will react. Nonetheless, in the coming years, additional states are likely to move forward with similar repeal efforts.

Notes

1 This is to differentiate from the 13 states that have also permitted the possession and use of cannabis oils that do not contain substantial amounts of THC (statutory limits range from 0.5 to 5 percent), but high concentrations of cannabidiol (CBD) to treat a narrow set of ailments, such as refractory epilepsy in young children.

2 See *The Case for Taxing and Regulating Marijuana like Alcohol* brochure from the Marijuana Policy Project. www.mpp.org/issues/legalization/tax-regulate-brochure/

3 We use the term "jurisdictions" to include the District of Columbia, which is not a state and thus is not afforded the same constitutional protections as other states in the Union. We exclude from this count the US territories that also permit or will establish a medical cannabis regime, such as Guam, Puerto Rico and the Northern Mariana Islands.

4 Due to Congressional oversight powers, the district was blocked from implementing its medical cannabis law until 2009 when Congress lifted its budgetary rider blocks (ACLU, n.d.; Kampia, 2009).

5 Under legal jurisprudence, the federal government cannot force states to criminally prohibit the supply or use of cannabis, though it could enjoin them from regulating the trade (Kamin, 2014). Therefore, any effort to maintain prohibition in Colorado and Washington would require federal law enforcement intervention – a politically unpalatable choice in a state that voted for repeal.

6 Certain climates are better suited to cultivating cannabis than others. In a future where cannabis is legal across the US, producers may eventually concentrate operations in regions with the ideal climate and resources to grow and process cannabis as efficiently as possible.

References

ACLU. (n.d.). *Democracy held hostage*. Retrieved from www.aclu.org/other/democracy-held-hostage.

Adams, D. (2018). *Marijuana shops could open in Mass*. Retrieved from www.bostonglobe.com/news/marijuana/2018/09/06/state-inches-closer-issuing-final-marijuana-licenses/7brSfcjY6XtOvHqH3xkOhK/story.html.

Alaska Department of Revenue. (2018). *Annual report for marijuana tax*. Tax Division. Retrieved from http://tax.alaska.gov/programs/programs/reports/Annual.aspx?60000&Year=2017.

Alcohol and Marijuana Control Office. (2018a). *History of marijuana control in Alaska*. Retrieved from www.commerce.alaska.gov/web/amco/MarijuanaHistory.aspx.

Alcohol and Marijuana Control Office. (2018b). *Notice of proposed changes to the regulations of the marijuana control board regarding the addition of an onsite marijuana consumption endorsement to the retail marijuana license*. Alaska online public notices. Retrieved from https://aws.state.ak.us/OnlinePublicNotices/Notices/View.aspx?id=191144.

Andrews, L. (2016a). *Mixed results for Alaska marijuana legislation as lawmakers wind down*. Retrieved from www.adn.com/cannabis-north/article/marijuana-control-board-bill-moves-forward-municipal-regulation-bill-returns/2015/04/20/.

Andrews, L. (2016b). *Marijuana milestone: Alaska's first pot shop opens to the public in Valdez*. Retrieved from www.adn.com/alaska-marijuana/2016/10/29/anticipation-builds-as-alaskas-first-marijuana-store-set-to-open-to-the-public/.

Associated Press. (2016). *This dispensary just became Oregon's first licensed recreational pot retailer*. Retrieved from http://katu.com/news/local/this-dispensary-just-became-oregons-first-licensed-recreational-pot-retailer.

Atagi, C. (2018). Pot sales now legal in California, but you can't find it everywhere yet. *USA TODAY*. Retrieved from www.usatoday.com/story/money/nation-now/2018/01/01/legal-california-pot/994263001/.

Board of State Canvassers. (2018). *Proposal 18–1*. Retrieved from www.michigan.gov/documents/sos/Official_Ballot_Wording_Prop_18-1_632051_7.pdf.

Bureau of Cannabis Control. (2018a). *About us*. Retrieved from www.bcc.ca.gov/about_us/.

Bureau of Cannabis Control. (2018b). *Bureau of cannabis control announces readoption of emergency cannabis regulations*. Retrieved from www.bcc.ca.gov/about_us/documents/media_20180608b.pdf.

Burlington Free Press. (2015). Little chance seen for VT legalizing pot this year. *Burlington Free Press*. Retrieved from www.burlingtonfreepress.com/story/news/politics/2015/02/17/little-chance-vermont-legalize-marijuana/23570195/.

Cambron, C., Guttmannova, K. and Fleming, C.B. (2017). State and national contexts in evaluating cannabis laws: A case study of Washington State. *Journal of Drug Issues*, 47(1), 74–90.

Caulkins, J., Kilmer, B., Kleiman, M., MacCoun, R., Midgette, G., Oglesby, P. and Reuter, P. (2015). *Considering marijuana legalization*. RAND Corporation. Retrieved from www.rand.org/pubs/research_reports/RR864.html.

Chereb, S. (2015). Nevada's first medical pot dispensary opens in Sparks. *Las Vegas Review-Journal*. Retrieved from www.reviewjournal.com/news/pot-news/nevadas-first-medical-pot-dispensary-opens-in-sparks/.

Colorado Department of Public Health and Environment. (2018). *Medical marijuana registry patient count*. Medical Marijuana Registry. Retrieved from www.colorado.gov/pacific/sites/default/files/CHED_MMR_2001-2017-average-count-year.pdf.

Colorado Department of Revenue. (2018). *Marijuana sales reports*. Retrieved from www.colorado.gov/pacific/revenue/colorado-marijuana-sales-reports.

Commonwealth of Massachusetts. (2017). *An act to ensure safe access to medical and adult-use of marijuana in the Commonwealth*. Retrieved from https://malegislature.gov/Bills/190/H3818.pdf.

Cousins, C. (2017). LePage vetoes bill to regulate marijuana sales in Maine. *Bangor Daily News*. Retrieved from https://bangordailynews.com/2017/11/03/politics/lepage-vetoes-bill-to-regulate-marijuana-sales-in-maine/.

Davis, A.C. (2017). Gunmen try, and fail, to rob a D.C. medical marijuana dispensary. *Washington Post*. Retrieved from www.washingtonpost.com/local/gunmen-try-and-fail-to-rob-a-dc-medical-marijuana-dispensary/2017/05/21/a6c9235c-3e48-11e7-adba-394ee67a7582_story.html.

Gieringer, D. (2006). *The origins of cannabis prohibition in California*. Federal Legal Publications. Retrieved from www.canorml.org/background/caloriginsmjproh.pdf.

Guion, P. (2018). Here are the details of N.J.'s new legal weed bill, including delivery and smoking lounges. Retrieved from www.nj.com/marijuana/2018/09/legal_weed_delivery_lounges.html.

Hall, W. and Lynskey, M. (2016). Evaluating the public health impacts of legalizing recreational cannabis use in the United States. *Addiction*, 111(10), 1764–1773.

Held, A. (2018). *Recreational pot shops now open for business in Massachusetts*. Retrieved from www.npr.org/2018/11/20/669519282/recreational-pot-shops-now-open-for-business-in-massachusetts.

Helm, K. and Leichtman, L. (2015). Implementation of Oregon's Measure 91 in the state legislature. *Willamette Law Review*, 52, 1–60.

Hickenlooper, G.J.W. (2014). Experimenting with pot: The state of Colorado's legalization of marijuana. *The Milbank Quarterly*, 92(2), 243–249.

Hirschfeld, P. (2015). *With Shumlin's time short, legalization proponents look to move quickly*. Retrieved from http://digital.vpr.net/post/shumlins-time-short-legalization-proponents-look-move-quickly.

Hirschfeld, P. (2016). *Vermont senate advances marijuana legalization*. Retrieved from http://digital.vpr.net/post/vermont-senate-advances-marijuana-legalization.

Hirschfeld, P. (2018). *House lawmakers spring late-session push for commercial cannabis market*. Retrieved from http://digital.vpr.net/post/house-lawmakers-spring-late-session-push-commercial-cannabis-market.

Ingraham, C. (2015). Why Ohio voted against legal marijuana — and what it means for the future of the pot debate. *Washington Post*. Retrieved from www.washingtonpost.com/news/wonk/wp/2015/11/03/ohio-rejected-legalizing-marijuana-what-that-means-for-the-future-of-pot/.

Kamin, S. (2014). Cooperative federalism and state marijuana regulation essays & speeches. *University of Colorado Law Review*, 85, 1105–1122.

Kampia, R. (2009). *Victory! Congress lifts ban on Washington, D.C.'s medical marijuana law*. Retrieved from https://stopthedrugwar.org/trenches/2009/dec/14/victory_congress_lifts_ban_washi.

Kennedy, J. (2018). *Time to legalize marijuana at the federal level.* Retrieved from www.statnews.com/2018/11/20/joe-kennedy-legalize-marijuana-federal-level/.

Kilmer, B., Caulkins, J., Pacula, R.L., MacCoun, R.J. and Reuter, P.H. (2010). *Altered state? Assessing how marijuana legalization in California could influence marijuana consumption and public budgets* (Product Page). Retrieved from www.rand.org/pubs/occasional_papers/OP315.html.

Kilmer, B. and MacCoun, R.J. (2017). How medical marijuana smoothed the transition to marijuana legalization in the United States. *Annual Review of Law and Social Science*, 13(1), 181–202.

LePage, P. (2017a). *Executive order regarding executive branch implementation of the marijuana legalization act.* Retrieved from www.maine.gov/tools/whatsnew/attach.php?id=729531&an=1.

LePage, P. (2017b). *Governor LePage issues statement upon veto of L.D. 1650, 'an act to amend the marijuana legalization act.'* Retrieved from www.maine.gov/tools/whatsnew/index.php?topic=Gov+News&id=770856&v=article2011.

Liquor and Cannabis Board. (2018). *WSLCB marijuana dashboard.* Retrieved from https://data.lcb.wa.gov/stories/s/WSLCB-Marijuana-Dashboard/hbnp-ia6v/.

MacCoun, R.J. (2010). *Estimating the non-price effects of legalization on cannabis consumption* (Product Page). Retrieved from www.rand.org/pubs/working_papers/WR767.html.

MacCoun, R.J. and Reuter, P. (2001). *Drug war heresies: Learning from other vices, times, and places.* Cambridge, UK; New York: Cambridge University Press.

Maine State Legislature. (2018). *Recreational marijuana in Maine.* Retrieved from https://legislature.maine.gov/lawlibrary/recreational_marijuana_in_maine/9419.

Marijuana Private Club Task Force. (2016). *Marijuana private club task force report 2016.* Washington, D.C: DC Council. Retrieved from https://doh.dc.gov/sites/default/files/dc/sites/doh/publication/attachments/Marijuana%20Private%20Club%20Taskforce%20Report%20_0.pdf.

Martin, J. (2012). *Little organized opposition to marijuana-legalization initiative.* Retrieved from www.seattletimes.com/seattle-news/little-organized-opposition-to-marijuana-legalization-initiative/.

McCarthy, J. (2017). *Record-high support for legalizing marijuana use in U.S.* Retrieved from https://news.gallup.com/poll/221018/record-high-support-legalizing-marijuana.aspx.

Measure 3. (2018). *Initiative petition to the secretary of the State of North Dakota.* Retrieved from https://vip.sos.nd.gov/pdfs/Measures%20Info/Petitions%20Being%20Circulated/Legalization%20of%20Marijuana.pdf.

Miller, K. (2017). *Committee endorses bill to delay marijuana sales in Maine.* Retrieved from www.pressherald.com/2017/01/19/bill-to-delay-marijuana-sales-passes-committee/.

National Academies of Sciences, Engineering, and Medicine. (2017). *The health effects of cannabis and cannabinoids: The current state of evidence and recommendations for research.* National Academies Press.

Nevada Department of Taxation. (2018). *Marijuana tax revenue. Nevada.* Retrieved from https://tax.nv.gov/uploadedFiles/taxnvgov/Content/TaxLibrary/NV-Marijuana-Revenue.xlsx.

Newsom, G., Humphreys, K. and Soltani, A. (2015). *Pathways report: Policy options for regulating marijuana in California.* Retrieved from www.safeandsmartpolicy.org/wp-content/uploads/2015/07/BRCPathwaysReport.pdf.

Noon, A. (2017). Nevada recreational marijuana shops could offer weed for sale in early summer. *Associated Press*. Retrieved from www.thecannabist.co/2017/02/09/nevada-recreational-marijuana-start/73373/.

Office of the Governor of New York. (2018). *Governor Cuomo announces workgroup to draft legislation for regulated adult-use marijuana program*. Retrieved from www.governor.ny.gov/news/governor-cuomo-announces-workgroup-draft-legislation-regulated-adult-use-marijuana-program.

Office of the Governor of Vermont. (2013). *Gov. Shumlin signs bill decriminalizing possession of limited amounts of marijuana*. Retrieved from https://web.archive.org/web/20130610093111/http://governor.vermont.gov/gov-shumlin-signs-marijuana-decriminalization.

Oregon Department of Revenue. (2018). *Oregon marijuana tax statistics: Accounting information*. Retrieved from www.oregon.gov/DOR/programs/gov-research/Documents/Financial-reporting-receipts-public.pdf.

Pacula, R.L., Powell, D., Heaton, P. and Sevigny, E.L. (2015). Assessing the effects of medical marijuana laws on marijuana use: The devil is in the details. *Journal of Policy Analysis and Management*, 34(1), 7–31.

Pardo, B. (2014). Cannabis policy reforms in the Americas: A comparative analysis of Colorado, Washington, and Uruguay. *The International Journal on Drug Policy*, 25(4), 727–735.

Proposition 215. (1996). *Compassionate Use Act of 1996*. Retrieved from https://medicalmarijuana.procon.org/sourcefiles/california-proposition-215.pdf.

Quimby, B. (2016). Opponents drop recount effort, acknowledge that Maine voters approved legalized marijuana. *Press Herald*. Retrieved from www.pressherald.com/2016/12/17/no-on-1-withdraws-marijuana-legalization-recount-request/.

Sessions, J. (2018). *Memorandum for all United States attorneys*. Office of the Attorney General. Retrieved from www.justice.gov/opa/press-release/file/1022196/download.

Shepherd, M. (2018). LePage veto fails, clearing way for recreational pot sales in Maine. *Bangor Daily News*. Retrieved from https://bangordailynews.com/2018/05/02/politics/lepage-veto-fails-clearing-way-for-recreational-pot-sales-in-maine/.

Smith, M. and Stolberg, S.G. (2015). On ballot, Ohio grapples with specter of marijuana monopoly. *The New York Times*. Retrieved from www.nytimes.com/2015/11/02/us/on-ballot-ohio-grapples-with-specter-of-marijuana-monopoly.html.

Thistle, S. (2016). Outcome unchanged as recount on marijuana referendum is suspended until the new year. *Press Herald*. Retrieved from www.pressherald.com/2016/12/16/recount-on-marijuana-ballot-suspended-until-after-the-new-year/.

Thistle, S. (2017). Maine House upholds LePage's veto of recreational marijuana regulations. *Press Herald*. Retrieved from www.pressherald.com/2017/11/06/legislature-set-to-take-up-lepage-veto-of-recreational-marijuana/.

Wilson, R. (2017). *Massachusetts governor signs bill to allow recreational pot (Text)*. Retrieved from https://thehill.com/homenews/state-watch/344343-massachusetts-governor-signs-bill-to-allow-recreational-pot.

2 Practical lessons learned from the first years of the regulated recreational cannabis market in Colorado

Todd Subritzky, Simon Lenton and Simone Pettigrew

Introduction and background

Colorado has a long history of cannabis reform having first decriminalized possession in 1975, legalized medical cannabis in 2000, regulated and commercialized the medical market in 2009/2010, and, to much fanfare, implemented the world's first seed-to-sale cannabis market for pleasure in 2014. The so-called adult use, or recreational cannabis market, was legalized via A64 (Colorado Amendment 64, 2012), a citizen-initiated constitutional amendment as opposed to government-led legislative change. It took place against a backdrop of federal prohibition in which cannabis remained a Schedule One drug under the Controlled Substances Act (Drug Enforcement Administration (DEA), 2018). The movement for legalization was backed by the Campaign to Regulate Marijuana Like Alcohol (2012), which is reflected in the Coloradan approach that is often described as the standard commercial model based on for-profit sales by licensed businesses, similar to alcohol bottle shops (Caulkins, Kilmer, Kleiman, MacCoun, Midgette, Oglesby and Reuter, 2015). The commercial model is concerning from a public health perspective as it incentivizes the sale of cannabis with profit, whereas a public health approach would seek to reduce cannabis consumption and associated harms, particularly among vulnerable populations such as youth and people with problematic use (Subritzky, 2018).

While the Colorado Recreational Cannabis Market (CRCM) can be considered from numerous perspectives, in this chapter we apply a public health lens and aim to document some of the practical issues associated with implementing the scheme. The chapter includes data reviewed and analyzed as part of a PhD study by the first author that investigated the first four years of the scheme's conception, implementation and evolution. Data sources included the Colorado Official State Web Portal and other government documents such as House and Senate Bills, Governor Executive Orders, state mandated impact and taskforce reports, Legislative Council records, industry notifications and work group meeting minutes. Additionally, the following were examined: the

Retail Marijuana Code (RMC); industry periodicals; emerging literature from noted cannabis scholars; media stories; interviews with senior regulators, industry executives and front-line public health officials; and field observations from tours of cultivation facilities, dispensaries, trade shows and policy symposiums (Subritzky, in preparation). This chapter is organized into three parts. Part 1 includes: (1) latest market insights around patterns of consumption in the state; (2) a brief review of the emerging literature on the CRCM; (3) the public health framework employed in Colorado; and (4) a summary of the RMC and its evolution. In Part 2, tensions between public health and commercial profit are explored with a focus on: (1) constitutional constraints on public health best practice; (2) marketing and advertising, most notably at the coal face of regulating controls by for-profit firms; (3) budtenders, the sales people in retail stores; and (4) the public health risks associated with the application of chemical pesticides for protection of commercial crops. Part 3 brings the material together to highlight important lessons learned from the CRCM for regulators in other jurisdictions considering the legalization of cannabis for adult use.

Market insights

Up until the implementation of the CRCM (and other US state schemes that have subsequently been implemented), evidence on legal commercial cannabis markets comprised hypothetical modelling based on extrapolating from other legal substances and illegal cannabis markets. In the five years since the implementation of the CRCM, evidence has been accruing that indicates: (1) recreational sales and state revenues from taxes and fees have increased year on year; (2) the market share of high-potency products is increasing; (3) prices have decreased per gram; (4) a minority of people who use cannabis consume the majority of cannabis sold in the state; (5) there is no evidence that consumption has increased among youth or adult consumers, with latest data suggesting similar patterns to pre-legalization; and (6) increased driving fatalities associated with cannabis-impaired driving, although challenges remain around these data.

First, according to data from the Colorado Department of Revenue (CDOR) (2018a) total sales for both recreational and medical markets increased from approximately $US700 million in 2014 to over US$1.5 billion in 2017. In 2018, total sales since implementation passed US$5 billion. State revenue from related fees and taxes increased from almost US$70 million in 2014 to almost US$250 million in 2017 (CDOR, 2018b). Over 85 percent of this revenue comes from the recreational market, which reflects disparities in tax rates in the two markets. The CRCM applied a 15 percent excise tax, a 10 percent special marijuana sales tax, and a 2.9 percent state sales tax (changed in 2017 as noted below), while the medical market is subject to just the 2.9 percent state sales tax.

Second, data collated by the Marijuana Policy Group (2018) that compared product type (flower, concentrates, edibles, non-edibles, shake/trim and other cannabis products), showed that the market share of high-potency concentrates increased from 11.6 percent in 2014 to 23.4 percent in 2017 in the recreational market. In the same period, flower sales reduced by an approximately corresponding amount from 66 percent in 2014 to 54 percent in 2017.

Third, retail prices for cannabis have been dropping in both markets for concentrates and flower but less so for edibles. For example, in the recreational market, the retail cost per gram of concentrates dropped from US$43 in March 2014 to US$21 in November 2017 and the price of flower dropped from almost $15 per gram to $5 per gram over the same period (Marijuana Policy Group, 2018). Other data from the same group show that prices per gram tend to be lower in metropolitan areas with higher outlet density.

Fourth, using Colorado data on consumption from multiple federal and state data sources, the Marijuana Policy Group (2018) confirmed that the majority of cannabis is used by a relatively small proportion of heavy consumers. They estimated that people who use cannabis 26–31 days a month comprise 22.5 percent of consumers; however, this group is responsible for 71.1 percent of all cannabis consumed in the state (Marijuana Policy Group, 2018).

Fifth, multiple datasets have indicated that while perception of cannabis harmfulness has markedly decreased among adolescents in Colorado (for whom possession, purchase, consumption and cultivation of cannabis remains illegal), an associated effect of increased consumption has not been identified, with rates of use similar to pre-legalization in this important cohort (Brooks-Russell, Ma, Levinson, Kattari, Kirchner, Goodell and Johnson, 2018). Similarly, no significant increase in adult consumption was identified in the latest available data compared to pre-legalization, although Colorado remained above the national average by 8 percent in 2016 (Colorado Department of Public Health and Environment, 2017).

Sixth, there are reports of increased traffic fatalities in Colorado involving cannabis since the CRCM was implemented (Denver Post, 2017b). However, this increase cannot yet be conclusively linked to the legal adult use market given challenges with data collection for this issue (Colorado Department of Public Safety Division of Criminal Justice, 2018). For example, there are data indicating increased fatalities where the driver tested positive for cannabis from 55 in 2013 to 125 in 2016 (Rocky Mountain High Intensity Drug Trafficking Area, 2017).[1] Indeed, data from the Fatality Analysis Reporting System (FARS) indicated that 20 percent of total road fatalities were cannabis related in Colorado in 2016 compared to 6 percent in 2006 (National Highway Traffic Safety Administration, 2018). However, these data are problematic due to changes in data collection and reporting. As noted by the Colorado Department of Transportation (2018, p. 1), "only active forms of THC such as Delta 9 can cause impairment (and) Delta 9 level information was not available prior to 2014." Furthermore, increased rates of testing mean that higher fatalities linked to cannabis could be the result of improved data collection (Colorado Department of Transportation, 2018).

Additionally, there is evidence of a 30 percent increase in unintentional exposures to cannabis by children in Colorado from 2009 to 2015, which accounted for approximately 6 out of every 1000 accidental poisoning admissions (Wang, Le Lait, Deakyne, Bronstein, Bajaj and Roosevelt, 2016).

Notably, this increase has been linked to the commercialization of the medical market in 2009 and rates of increase since implementation of the recreational market are not statistically significant (Colorado Department of Public Health and Environment, 2016). No fatalities linked to this issue have been recorded in the state, and symptoms appear limited to an uncomfortable few hours but no long-term damage (Kleiman, 2018). Latest data indicate that 6 percent of pregnant women in Colorado consume cannabis during pregnancy (Colorado Department of Public Health and Environment, 2017).

Finally, data indicate that the ten largest operators controlled approximately 25 percent of the market (Marijuana Policy Group, 2018). However, it remained highly competitive in comparison to other industries based on the Herfindahl-Hirschman Index, indicating that a "big cannabis" style market consolidation is yet to establish itself in the state (Marijuana Policy Group, 2018).

The emerging literature

Several scholars have begun to make important observations regarding potential implications for regulators *implementing* cannabis policy (as opposed to policy outcomes) based on the Colorado model, with many highlighting the complexity of creating a commodities market for the legal sale of cannabis. Blake and Finlaw (2014) described the massive undertaking and urged policymakers to be cautious in legalizing distribution networks for the drug. Kleiman (2015) pointed out the multifaceted nature of the scheme and difficulties with measuring impacts. For example, variation in cannabis potency testing, which reflects differences in sampling, equipment, and procedural methodologies, was recognized in Colorado House Bill 15–1283 (2015), which stipulated an allowable variance of plus or minus 15 percent in potency results for flower and concentrated products (Lenton and Subritzky, 2017). The Blue Ribbon Commission on Marijuana Policy (2015), a cannabis policy advisory body, noted cannabis legalization is not a single event, but rather an evolving process that requires continuous attention over many years.

Subritzky (in preparation) identified approximately 20 issues with major challenges for regulators associated with the implementation of the CRCM, ranging from how to deal with public consumption of cannabis through to transitioning from a black to a regulated market, and concerns around environmental degradation and excessive energy consumption. Furthermore, Kleiman (2016) contended that voter-driven cannabis legalization initiatives hinder the ability of regulators to fully implement best practice public health policy. While it has been noted that creating a regulated market on an established medical cannabis model may expediate the process of implementation in recreational markets (Ghosh, Van Dyke, Maffey, Whitley, Erpelding and Wolk, 2015; Kamin, 2017; Kilmer and MacCoun, 2017), it has also been pointed out that a medical cannabis foundation can facilitate grey markets, particularly in Colorado where designated patient caregivers can grow hundreds of cannabis plants legally, yet outside the scope of the retail or medical marijuana codes (Blake and Finlaw, 2014).

Based on the Coloradan experience, and perhaps counterintuitively, Kamin (2015) observed that the potential for increased tax revenue and cost savings associated with enforcement can be easily overstated, and may not provide a compelling argument for legalization per se. Moreover, Subritzky, Lenton, and Pettigrew (2016) documented a cannabis industry publication, which, like the tobacco industry before it, targeted commercial activities at people who consume cannabis on a daily basis because of their status as "the backbone of the industry," thereby highlighting public health concerns of the commercial approach. Additionally, the increasing popularity and public health risks associated with edible cannabis products have been described, particularly in relation to slickly packaged products that resemble children's confectionaries, and difficulties associated with controlling or titrating the dose (MacCoun and Mello, 2015). Challenges to implementing and enforcing cultivation standards, predominantly around the application of pesticides, plant growth regulators, and other chemical additives have also been laid out (Subritzky, Pettigrew and Lenton, 2017), and are discussed in more detail below. Furthermore, complications relating to federal prohibition have been well documented, most notably around the associated lack of access to banking services that can create a public safety risk associated with hold-ups and related crime due to hundreds of millions of dollars in cash being transported and used to pay tax revenues and other business-related expenses (Blake and Finlaw, 2014; Subritzky, Pettigrew and Lenton, 2016).

While observing that it was too early to judge the success of the policy itself, Hudak (2015) contended that, by and large, regulators implemented the commercial framework successfully within tight deadlines stipulated by A64. The document specified that "Not later than July 1, 2013, the Department shall adopt regulations necessary for implementation [of the CRCM] [and] begin accepting and processing applications on October 1, 2013" (Colorado Amendment 64, 2012, pp. 6–9). Indeed, "in a mere three months, the A64 Task Force developed a comprehensive framework for the legislation and regulations needed to implement A64" (Blake and Finlaw, 2014, p. 366). Based on the Coloradan experience, Carnevale, Kagan, Murphy, and Esrick (2017) offered recommendations in five areas: production and cultivation, governance, public health and safety, taxation and possession and consumption. Most notably, they articulated the utilitarian value of unifying medical and recreational cannabis markets and recommended unification of the two markets to maximize regulatory efficiency and minimize associated costs (Carnevale et al., 2017). This recommendation is at the cutting edge of cannabis policy and remains controversial, with international controls stipulating the two markets should be kept completely separate (Mead, 2014), despite considerable ontological and regulatory similarities under the Marijuana Enforcement Division in Colorado (MED). Indeed, the 2018 Sunset Review in Colorado recommended unification of the codes, which has a number of implications for regulators, industry and academia alike (Colorado Department of Regulatory Agencies, 2018). This unified market plugs into therapeutic and/or wellness conceptions of cannabis consumption (Subritzky, 2018).

Another issue is whether the cannabis industry should be "inside or outside the tent" when regulations are being drafted and implemented. In Colorado, faced with a lack of knowledge about regulating recreational cannabis, the exclusion of federal regulatory agencies because of the federal prohibition, and a tight timeline stipulated in A64, bureaucrats adopted a "Collaborative Governance approach" (Ansell and Gash, 2008) based on "pragmatism and mutual respect" (State of Colorado, 2012). Although other jurisdictions including California and Canada have adopted a similar approach, there is evidence that the industry has unsurprisingly lobbied hard for regulations that maximize profits and minimize "unnecessarily burdensome" regulations (Subritzky, Lenton, Pettigrew, 2016).

Colorado public health framework

Policymakers in Colorado have stated that the CRCM is public health-driven (Hickenlooper, 2014). The Colorado Department of Public Health and Environment (CDPHE) stated their primary goal was to implement policy that protects vulnerable populations and collects data to measure the impact of the legal cannabis policy (Ghosh, Van Dyke, Maffey, Whitley, Gillim-Ross and Wolk, 2016). Accordingly, they conceptualized a public health framework that draws on the expertise of "second-hand smoke prevention specialists, … environmental health and food safety experts, acute and chronic disease epidemiologists, toxicologists, laboratorians, maternal–child health and health communications experts, and poisoning and injury prevention specialists" (Ghosh et al., 2016, p. 21). The framework included three main components: (1) assessment; (2) policy development; and (3) assurance (Ghosh et al., 2016). These are now briefly described.

First, the assessment aspect of the CDPHE framework relates to the monitoring of two issues, namely the prevalence of use and health effects. Regarding surveillance of prevalence, the addition of several cannabis-related questions to existing population-based surveys was undertaken. Issues of interest include cannabis preparation, dosage, frequency of use and methods of consumption (Ghosh et al., 2016). Concerning the monitoring of health effects, changes to data collection were made in terms of how cannabis data are recorded at hospitals and emergency departments. The CDPHE is also attempting to develop better data sources around the issue of cannabis-impaired driving (Ghosh et al., 2016). A notable aspect of this is the lack of baseline data available pre-legalization, which makes impact assessment difficult.

Second, according to Ghosh et al. (2016, p. 24), policy recommendations were developed based "on the successes of the past 50 years of public health progress to reduce the prevalence of tobacco use." Specifically, the CDPHE included recommendations by the Community Preventive Services Task Force (2014) and Pacula, Kilmer, Wagenaar, Chaloupka, and Caulkins (2014), such as increased unit price via taxes, and smoke-free policies including Colorado's Clean Indoor Air Act. In addition, public health lessons from alcohol include limitations on opening hours and outlet density of retail stores (Babor, 2010; Livingston, 2008). These aspects are regulated in the CRCM by local jurisdictions who were empowered by A64 to oversee the "time, place, manner, and number of marijuana establishment operations" (Colorado Amendment 64, 2012, pp. 8–9).

Ghosh et al. (2016) further contended that rules established for labeling and packaging of recreational cannabis products are equal to, or exceed requirements for tobacco, although this has been contested by Barry and Glantz (2016). By 2018, the RMC stipulated that labels should not: be designed to appeal to children; contain false or misleading statements; or make any health benefit claims (Colorado Secretary of State, 2019). In addition, the following text must be included on labels of retail cannabis products:

> This product was produced without regulatory oversight for health, safety, or efficacy. There may be long term physical or mental health risks from use of marijuana including additional risks for women who are or may become pregnant or are breastfeeding. Use of marijuana may impair your ability to drive a car or operate machinery.
>
> (Colorado Secretary of State, 2019, p. 194)

Education is specified within the policy development component of the Colorado public health framework. It is the responsibility of the CDPHE to implement mass-reach health communications that increase public awareness around cannabis laws and the responsible use of cannabis. While Barry and Glantz (2016) contended that the resulting Coloradan public health messaging is youth focused and does not extend to the adult population, this is open to debate. For example, the "Good to Know Colorado" campaign aimed to "educate all Colorado residents and visitors about safe, legal, and responsible use of marijuana" (Ghosh et al., 2016, p. 24). Additional campaigns and comprehensive information on the potential harms associated with cannabis consumption from risks to youth through to dependency by adults are listed on the Colorado Official State Web Portal (2018). Prevention messaging campaigns are an important intervention to reduce harms at the population level (Ghosh et al., 2016).

The third component relates to assurance and includes enforcement of regulations, ensuring a competent workforce, and evaluation. The task of ensuring compliance is generally overseen by MED, who operate directly under the Colorado Department of Revenue (CDOR). Regarding a competent workforce, the CDPHE had an initial focus to expand its network of public health professionals at the city and county levels and hosted educational conferences for cannabis policy regulators (Ghosh et al., 2016). The final aspect of assurance considered under the CDPHE framework is the evaluation of data collection and surveillance efforts, education campaigns and perceptions of risk associated with cannabis consumption (Ghosh et al., 2016).

In line with increasing revenues, appropriations from the Marijuana Tax Cash Fund have increased in a number of areas. For example, large increases in funding can be noted for the Department of Education, particularly with regard to the school health professionals grant program, and the Department of Human Services, including US$12 million for increasing access to effective substance disorder services. Substance abuse is also addressed via the CDPHE with US$9 million allocated for grants in the 2017/2018 financial year (Colorado Office of State Planning and Budgeting, 2017). Additionally, as stipulated in A64, the first US$40 million in excise tax revenue annually is deposited in the Building Excellent Schools Today (BEST) Fund that "prioritizes funding based on issues such as asbestos removal, building code violations, overcrowding, and poor indoor air quality" (Colorado Legislative Council Staff, 2015, p. 1).

Evolution of Retail Marijuana Code (RMC)

Many practical issues associated with the regulation of cannabis policy have previously been articulated (Caulkins et al., 2015; Rolles and Murkin, 2016; Room, Fischer, Hall, Lenton and Reuter, 2010). Pardo (2014) summarized the first iteration of the RMC including taxation, production and distribution limits, labeling and quality control requirements, and made comparisons with Washington and Uruguay regulations. Furthermore, in regard to overall production, it was clarified that in Colorado, the quantity and numbers of licensees are determined by the free market mechanism as opposed to pre-set limits used in other states (Kamin, 2017).

At the time of writing in mid-2018, the permanent version of the RMC was in its tenth iteration and consisted of 262 pages, which compares with 124 pages in the first iteration in 2013 (Colorado Secretary of State, 2019). This provides an indication of how the regulations have become more complex as the CRCM has matured. Indeed, the RMC can be considered a dynamic document that is continuously evolving (Blue Ribbon Commission on Marijuana Policy, 2015).

According to the RMC 2013:

> The rules accomplish the state of Colorado's guiding principle: to create a robust regulatory and enforcement environment that protects public safety and prevents diversion of Retail Marijuana to individuals under the age of 21 or to individuals outside the state of Colorado.
>
> (Colorado Secretary of State, 2013, p. 3)

The extent to which this has been achieved remains open to debate. An undoubted strength of the CRCM, however, is a well-established rule-making process in the state that allows for swift implementation of new rules as required

(Colorado Secretary of State, 2018b, 2018c). Since June 2013, there have been 15 emergency/temporary rule adoptions together with the 10 permanent rule iterations of the RMC (Colorado Secretary of State, 2019). In general, emergency rules may be introduced within the Administrative Procedure Act framework when "immediate adoption of the rule is imperatively necessary to comply with state or federal law or federal regulations or for the preservation of public health, safety, or welfare" (Colorado Secretary of State, 2018a, Section 24–4-103(6a)). Emergency rules allow for timely temporary adoption of regulations and add an important element of flexibility for cannabis regulators in Colorado, particularly given the potential for unexpected consequences of regulations in a pioneering jurisdiction. Emergency rules expire after a period of 120 days unless converted to permanent through the full regulatory process.

By 2018, the RMC consisted of 18 rule categories including: General applicability; Licensing; Licensed premises; Retail marijuana store; Retail marijuana cultivation facilities; Retail marijuana products manufacturing facilities; Retail marijuana testing facilities; Transportation and storage; Business records and reporting; Labeling, packaging and products safety; Signage, marketing and advertising; Enforcement; Discipline; Division, local jurisdiction and law enforcement procedures; Retail Marijuana Testing Program; Retail Marijuana Transporters; Retail Marijuana Establishment Operators; and Retail Marijuana Transfers to Unlicensed Medical Research Facilities and Pesticide Manufacturers.

Broadly, key changes to the market since implementation include: (1) ending the requirement for vertical integration and the introduction of mandatory potency testing in 2014; (2) removal of the statutory two-year resident rule for (up to 15) investors in 2016 (SB 16–040, 2016);[2] (3) standardized edible serving amounts of 10 mg THC per portion introduced in 2016; (4) the new tax structure in 2017 (whereby the state retail marijuana sales tax was increased from 10 percent to 15 percent while the standard 2.9 percent state sales tax was exempted); and (5) mandatory testing for pesticides in flower and trim products in August 2018 (Marijuana Policy Group, 2018).

Tension between commercialism and public health

Although regulators followed the public health framework described above, the commercial model of cannabis regulation remains a concern (Lenton, 2014). Indeed, respected scholar Kleiman described the for-profit model as the second worse outcome behind prohibition. He reportedly stated, as seems apparent in the data presented above, that "marijuana companies' best customers are the problem users" (Lopez, 2014, December 17). The following section of the chapter explores the tension between public health and private profit within the context of a commercial cannabis market, with a focus on the issues of constitutional constraints, marketing and advertising, budtenders and the application of pesticides for crop protection.

Constitutional constraints on public health best practice

According to Governor Hickenlooper (2014, p. 1), "[Colorado is] working as a convener for all interested parties and experts to shape public policy that utilizes the decades of public health lessons gained from regulating alcohol and tobacco." However, the requirements of A64 hindered the ability of regulators to implement public health best practice on several fronts including: tight deadlines for market implementation; installing the CDOR as overseeing regulator (as opposed to, for example, public health or human services departments); outlining a commercial market structure based on the licensing of for-profit businesses; and lack of constraints over product diversity (Subritzky, in preparation).

In terms of product diversity, it is useful to highlight public health limitations identified in A64 that came about due to a generous definition of cannabis. The broad definition of cannabis stipulated in A64 follows:

> Marijuana or Marihuana (or cannabis) means all parts of the plant of the genus cannabis whether growing or not, the seeds thereof, the resin extracted from any part of the plant, and every compound, manufacture, salt, derivative, mixture, or preparation of the plant, its seeds, or its resin, including marihuana concentrate. Marijuana or Marihuana does not include industrial hemp, nor does it include fiber produced from the stalks, oil, or cake made from the seeds of the plant, sterilized seed of the plant which is incapable of germination, or the weight of any other ingredient combined with marijuana to prepare topical or oral administrations, food, drink, or other product.
>
> (Colorado Amendment 64, 2012, p. 3)

It has been argued that cannabis policy with a public health focus should include regulatory control over product diversity that encourages production of less harmful product variations such as those with lower THC potency or more balanced THC: cannabidiol (CBD) profiles in standard preparations of cannabis flower (Borland, 2003; Fischer, Russell, Sabioni, van den Brink, Le Foll, Hall, and Room, 2017; Rolles and Murkin, 2016). In contrast to these public health recommendations, the constitutionally defined cannabis allows for limitless product innovation, which in addition to higher public health risks, is also vastly more complicated to regulate effectively.

As a direct result of this A64 definition, dispensaries in Colorado offer a wide range of cannabis products including flower, concentrates, topicals, tinctures and edibles. The lion's share of merchandise consists of three broad preparation types: flower, high-potency concentrates, and THC-infused edible confectionaries (Marijuana Policy Group, 2018).

Marketing and advertising

From a public health perspective, the recommended default position for advertising regulated cannabis products is a complete ban (Rolles and Murkin,

2016). In Colorado, regulators were restricted by A64, which stipulated that cannabis be regulated like alcohol (this issue is separated from the above section due to its importance). Advertising in the alcohol industry in Colorado is governed by a voluntary industry standard that *encourages* restraints on advertising when there is a greater than 30 percent likelihood of it reaching minors. As stated in the RMC 2013:

> Voluntary standards adopted by the alcohol industry direct the industry to refrain from advertising where more than approximately 30% of the audience is reasonably expected to be under the age of 21. After reviewing the rulemaking record, the CDOR has determined … it is appropriate to model the retail marijuana advertising restrictions on this voluntary standard used by the alcohol industry. This standard is consistent with the directive in the state constitution to regulate marijuana in a manner that is similar to alcohol.
>
> (Colorado Secretary of State, 2019, pp. 107–108)

Beyond the obvious issue that in Colorado the RMC appears to condone a 30 percent likelihood of children being exposed to cannabis advertising, on the face of it there does not appear to be any protection for adult populations, particularly those with heavy consumption patterns (and therefore higher risk). However, the process of devising advertising restrictions was considered at length, and included several phases and collaboration between multiple departments, most notably the CDPHE and the Colorado Department of Human Services (Subritzky, in preparation). In general, the restrictions are focused on youth protection and lessons from tobacco. For example, RMC advertising restrictions are modelled on the Framework Convention on Tobacco Control (FCTC) and the Masters Settlement Agreement (MSA). From stakeholder interviews, it is apparent that experience from tobacco was a central focus. The following extract is indicative:

> We took a very hard look at the (MSA) and the requirements of that with respect to advertising tobacco products and many of the concepts that are contained within our marijuana advertising restrictions are modelled after some of the requirements in the tobacco settlement agreement.
>
> Group Interview: Barbara Brohl – Executive Director CDOR, Ron Kammerzell – Senior Director of Marijuana Enforcement Division (speaker), Mathew Scott – Senior Director of Taxation, Heidi Humphreys – Deputy Director CDOR, May 2017.
> (Subritzky, in preparation)

While lessons from tobacco are certainly helpful for devising advertising restrictions on cannabis sales, it is important to note that cannabis is an intoxicant in a way that tobacco is not. In this sense, the public health risks differ in important ways, most obviously around the issue of driving. While the advertising restrictions in the RMC are reasonably comprehensive, notable gaps relate to: (1) strain reviews; (2) social media; and (3) celebrity branding. These are now discussed.

First, there are numerous websites that publish strain reviews under the guise of providing valuable consumer information (Leafly.com, 2018; The Cannabist, 2018). However, the utility of this information is increasingly contested, and it can be argued that the naming of cannabis strains by cultivators is driven more by strategic marketing than scientific evidence. A gap in the RMC relates to the genetic (in)consistency of cannabis varieties or strains (again this can be linked to how cannabis is defined in A64). Based on an exploratory study of samples from Coloradan dispensaries, Schwabe and McGlaughlin (2017) identified considerable genetic variation among strains with the same names. Indeed, Mowgli Holmes, a molecular and evolutionary biologist and CEO of an agricultural genomics company reportedly stated, "No one has any idea what they're smoking. Everything is name draw, so consumers and patients don't know what they're getting" (Rolling Stone, 2018). Furthermore, the names of award-winning strains are replicated by multiple dispensaries with diverse genetic lineage and cultivation techniques (observations from the field) (Subritzky, in preparation).

Second, social media is inundated with advertisements for cannabis products and stores, as can be found on any of the major platforms with a cursory search for hashtag phrases such as #cannabis or #marijuana. Studies examining the high prevalence of "dab tweets" are insightful in this regard (Cavazos-Rehg, Sowles, Krauss, Agbonavbare, Grucza and Bierut, 2016; Daniulaityte, Nahhas, Wijeratne, Carlson, Lamy, Martins and Sheth, 2015). Furthermore, in a study of almost 1,000 mass and niche media articles focused on the CRCM, several hundred contained text from which codes were derived for "social media," and/or "Twitter," "Facebook," or "YouTube" (Subritzky, in preparation). Articles offering advice on the "do's and don'ts" of social media marketing for cannabis stores were particularly notable (Ganjapreneur, 2016). These concerns relating to the proliferation of advertising cannabis products on social media were recognized in a stakeholder interview with a senior public health official in Colorado:

> It's definitely an area of concern. I think realistically when we're wanting to limit the amount of advertising that can be seen by youth, we have to look at wherever that's going to be available. So social media is always going to be something of concern.
>
> Interview: Heath Harmon, Director of Health Division for Boulder County Public Health, August 2017.
> (Subritzky, in preparation)

Third, celebrity branding of cannabis products could be a consequence of the recommendation in the A64 Task Force Report to allow branded products to be sold in the state. This is despite public health recommendations that stipulate plain packaging (Rolles and Murkin, 2016). Since the CRCM was implemented, numerous celebrities have entered or stated the intention to enter the industry as producers of branded cannabis products including Willie Nelson, Snoop Dogg, Whoopi Goldberg, Melissa Etheridge, the family of Bob Marley, Tommy Chong, Gene Simmons (of the band KISS) and Mike Tyson (CNN Money, 2018, April 10). These celebrities have been afforded significant free coverage, both in consumer-focused niche media and on mass market platforms (Subritzky, in preparation). In Coloradan retail cannabis stores, these branded products tend to be prominently positioned with high visibility (observations from the field) (Subritzky, in preparation). Regulating plain packaging of products may reduce this glorification of cannabis products.

Budtenders and the retail experience: observations from the field

Budtenders are salespeople employed to sell cannabis at both medical and recreational stores in Colorado. All employees of a retail cannabis store must hold an occupational license. There are two types of occupational license that relate to key and support employees, of which budtenders are considered the latter. The criteria for obtaining an occupational license include being at least 21 years of age, of good moral character, a resident of Colorado and payment of the relevant fee (at the time of writing this was US$75 for support staff) (Colorado Department of Revenue Enforcement Division, 2018a).

While budtenders often receive training on issues of legal compliance, it is not a requirement. The regulations for both medical and adult use cannabis dispensaries in Colorado do not stipulate any specific training that budtenders must undertake – this is left entirely at the discretion of business owners and/or marketing strategists. Similarly, they are not required to have knowledge of the pharmacology of the plant (which has over 100 different cannabinoids), numerous methods of consumption, multiple product types and the large variations in potencies and individual consumer tolerance. Informal discussions with budtenders indicated that larger chains tended to offer more comprehensive training in regard to product knowledge, compliance and the sales process (observations from the field) (Subritzky, in preparation). Little mention of public health considerations was made, with the exception of offering dosing advice for purchasers of edibles, particularly those from out of state (observations from the field) (Subritzky, in preparation).

Further insight is provided by a job advertisement for a budtender listed by Native Roots, one of the largest operators in the state with 19 outlets at the time of writing. From this text it appears that budtenders are expected both to have a high knowledge of products in advance, and to "care," however it is apparent that sales performance is the dominant Key Performance Indicator (KPI).

> A caring, considerate and enthusiastic attitude for the industry is a must. Working knowledge of cannabis products as well as all current rules regulating retail and medical marijuana are required.

> Budtenders will be challenged by sales goals set by management. We are looking for candidates that will creatively contribute to the success and expansion of our company. This position gives a self-driven and motivated candidate room for development and growth.
>
> Medical and recreational budtender – Denver, Co.
> (Native Roots, 2018)

An additional issue is in-store labelling as noted in field observations in 2017 (Subritzky, in preparation). In general, cannabis stores in Colorado offer pre-packaged goods such as edibles and concentrate cartridges, and fresh produce such as flower. The pre-packaged products are in branded packaging and include all product information on labels as required by the RMC. However, the label information for fresh produce such as flower placed in jars of displayed product is generally limited to strain name, THC percentage and species type, that is sativa, indica or hybrid (observations from the field) (Subritzky, in preparation). Budtenders, under consistent queue pressure, represent the only option for consumers to make enquiries regarding additives used during the cultivation process before purchase, and furthermore it is unrealistic that their training will extend to knowing what additives were applied during cultivation. This observation relates to the RMC 2018 rule 1002–1 concerning packaging and labeling prior to transfer to consumer, which distinguishes between in-store and exit label requirements (Colorado Secretary of State, 2019, pp. 189–195). It was observed that this situation hinders consumers' ability to identify cannabis grown without the addition of chemical additives. From a public health perspective, this impedes the ability of those in search of organically grown products to make informed decisions, which is a central tenet of A64 and a core justification for legalization (Subritzky, in preparation).

Pesticides

In a study that examined issues in the implementation and evolution of the CRCM, pesticide related codes were derived from multiple government documents, over 200 media articles and several transcripts of interviews with key stakeholders (Subritzky, in preparation). Problems associated with pesticide use and reporting was initially identified in the A64 Task Force Report, which noted there existed "no standards of practice for ensuring product safety in the marijuana industry" (Brohl and Finlaw, 2013, p. 66). Definitions of pesticides may include plant growth regulators and other chemical nutrients used during the cultivation process (Subritzky et al., 2017), however this section considers pesticides as primarily chemicals used as protection against insect infestations that can devastate crops. Farmers may have considerable financial exposure in an industry where cannabis plantations are not covered by insurance companies, so there is a reported temptation to resort to nefarious measures (Subritzky et al., 2017). After prominent media coverage of the issue, the public health threat of contaminated cannabis was officially recognized in an Executive Order by Governor Hickenlooper in November 2015, which required state agencies to focus on the problem (Colorado Department of Revenue, 2015). Examples of this threat were provided in an interview with Seth Wong, President of TEQ Labs in Denver, and included the possibility of pesticides being concentrated in toxicity along with other cannabinoids when concentrated products are manufactured (Subritzky et al., 2017). Additionally, as noted by Wong:

> We don't know the difference of what that pesticide does to you if it is just ingested or if it is smoked. Some of them have applicable uses and that's a direct application to a plant, but that plant is not necessarily smoked. So if you smoke it, and that's the case with myclobutanil [a chemical compound used in some pesticides] that converts to cyanide once it gets treated with a flame, you've got myclobutanil on your cannabis bud and someone goes to smoke it you have potentially converted that to cyanide and potentially inhaled it.
>
> (Subritzky et al., 2017, p. 91)

At the time of writing, over five years since the legal market was implemented, significant progress had been made on how to effectively regulate cultivation standards, and in particular the application of pesticides and other chemical additives such as plant growth regulators. For example, standardized sampling procedures have been developed for flower, edibles, and concentrated products (Colorado Department of Public Health and Environment, 2018b). Furthermore, requirements for the certification of cannabis testing facilities in Colorado have evolved considerably since the first iteration of the RMC in 2013 (Colorado Department of Public Health and Environment, 2018a). After multiple work group meetings among subject matter experts, the reference library for proficiency standards has expanded to cover pesticide residue testing as well as other forms of contamination, sampling procedures, and validation guidelines (Colorado Department of Public Health and Environment, 2018c). Importantly too, it should be noted that the issue is also enforced at the local level, which offers an additional layer of protection. For example, it was reported that the City of Denver had recalled over 28,000 products due to pesticide contamination (Denver Post, 2017a). Reflecting this evolution of pesticide regulations in the state, 17 industry bulletins notifying cannabis businesses of changes relating to testing requirements to be implemented were issued by the state from April 2014 to May 2018 (Colorado Department of Revenue Enforcement Division, 2018b). However, while progress has been made, the issue remains challenging, and development of new regulations is ongoing. Notably, mandatory testing for pesticides in flower and trim products across both medical and recreational markets was not implemented until August 2018.

Lessons learned

As a pioneering jurisdiction, Colorado has blazed a trail implementing a commercial approach to legalized cannabis. Regulators developed a comprehensive public health framework, drew on lessons from alcohol and tobacco and modified rules in a timely fashion as unexpected consequences arose. While regulators should be recognized for their ground-breaking efforts, the Coloradan approach has limitations from a public health perspective and efforts were hindered on a number of fronts. In particular, constitutional constraints of A64 ensured a for-profit model, as opposed to a non-commercial alternative, was implemented. A64 also broadly defined cannabis, which allowed for enormous product diversity. Furthermore, the involvement of the cannabis industry in crafting the regulations that apply to the scheme remains a concern – as was predicted by many, the commercial model has seen the proliferation of widespread advertising and marketing strategies that are excluded from the regulations. In addition, major challenges have arisen regarding cultivation standards, most notably the inability to effectively devise rules and regulate the emerging public health threat of the application of pesticides, particularly in initial years of the market roll out. Furthermore, as previously noted in regard to the accidental ingestion data, the fact there was a well-developed medicinal cannabis market with retail outlets in Colorado for a number of years before recreational cannabis use was legalized has implications when interpreting the impact of recreational cannabis per se.

The following section outlines some of the major challenges identified from the Coloradan experience and offers some suggestions for regulators in other jurisdictions intending to implement a regulated cannabis market. The list is not exhaustive; however, it draws on examples introduced in the chapter to highlight key practical difficulties encountered during the first five years of implementation.

First, while the citizen-driven approach to legalization solves the problem of inactivity at the federal level, it does not encourage public health best practice (Kleiman, 2018). In the CRCM, an additional complication is that the core market structure was enshrined within the State Constitution via A64. Most notable among these constitutional constraints are the stipulations that cannabis be regulated like alcohol (under a commercial model) and that cannabis is broadly defined, which allowed huge product diversity. Lessons that can be drawn from this seem to be that implementation of more public health focused legal cannabis models would require proactive legislation by the government and that the definition of cannabis should be strictly defined at the outset. A definition that limited cannabis products to flower only, for example, would potentially reduce risks associated with higher potency concentrates, together with streamlining the initial regulations considerably. The definition could be expanded to include more products at a later date if that was desirable.

Second, the evidence from the CRCM seems to confirm a number of anticipated issues including: that a minority of people with problematic use constitute a majority of total consumption; that these people furthermore are a prime target for cannabis businesses; and that commercial entities will exploit loopholes in the regulations with hopes of increasing opportunities to promote products. From an entrepreneurial perspective this is understandable, while from a public health view it is not. Although information on the risks associated with cannabis dependency are available on the Colorado State Web Portal, more could be done to protect the most vulnerable by: (1) adding explicit warning regarding this issue to cannabis product labels; (2) artificially increasing prices (as noted above, although this strategy has been suggested within the Coloradan public health framework, prices continue to fall);[3] (3) strengthening advertising restrictions, particularly around social media, product reviews, and celebrity branding; and (4) regulating plain packaging to hinder brand recognition and potentially reduce product appeal.

Third, local jurisdictions have emerged as entities that may provide extra protection around important public health issues such as external signage, opening hours, outlet density, and the application of chemical pesticides during the cultivation stage. This can potentially be seen as a strength of the Coloradan approach, if the various levels of government can work harmoniously towards stated goals.

Fourth, regulating cannabis is a complex matter that touches numerous government departments, and from the Coloradan experience it is apparent that this complexity increases in the first years after market implementation. Unexpected consequences will arise and having the ability to effectively deal with these issues in a timely manner is important. The established rule-making process in Colorado has been helpful in this regard. Lessons from this include to go slow with the initial rollout. In particular, it may be advisable to begin with limited products, such as cannabis flower. This could even be limited to a few well-defined genetic varieties with balanced THC:CBD ratios. Complexity also has implications relating to how long the critical preimplantation phase should be. In Colorado this was again limited by constitutional restraints in A64 with tight deadlines stipulated. While it is preferable to have sufficient time to develop effective rules, it is also clear that finding perfect policy could be an exercise in perpetuity, so a balance needs to be found. Perhaps an 18-month to two-year period would suffice.

Fifth, funds were not appropriated until after they were received via taxes and fees. This resulted in delays of at least two years after implementation for funding of key public health initiatives such as substance prevention grants, youth education campaigns, roadside driver impairment training, and relevant impact assessment surveys. For other jurisdictions, advanced funding for these issues before tax revenues are generated is recommended.

Sixth, the issue of quality control that allows buyers to make informed choices is more complex than anticipated, particularly around variability in potency testing due to different testing procedures, lack of proficiency standards for cannabis cultivation and difficulties in regulating and enforcing restrictions on chemical pesticides and other additives. Furthermore, in-store labelling, particularly for fresh produce, was observed to be insufficient. To resolve these issues, regulators in other jurisdictions need to be aware of the immense challenges and extensive resources required to implement this aspect of legalization effectively. Prefunding the agricultural component of regulations and authorizing state testing labs with standardized testing methodologies may help to resolve the issue. Additionally, more stringent in-store labelling would facilitate more informed purchasing.

Notes

1 Although data from the Rocky Mountain High Intensity Drug Trafficking Area (RMHIDTA) is official federal data and reportedly informed former US Attorney General Jeff Session's decision to revoke the Cole Memorandum that provided federal government guidelines for states with legal cannabis markets (Office of the Attorney General, 2017, 2018), some commentators and state governors have raised issues about how the RMHIDTA interpret and present data (e.g. State of Alaska, 2017; State of Colorado, 2017; State of Oregon, 2017; State of Washington, 2017).

2 HB 18–1011 (2018) would have further increased flexibility for out-of-state investors in 2018 by allowing an unlimited number of investors and removing background checks. However, after it was passed through the General Assembly, it was vetoed by Governor Hickenlooper due to concerns about federal restrictions (State of Colorado, 2018).

3 There are reports that increased requirements for product testing introduced in August 2018 will increase prices though the extent of this impact remains unclear (Denver Post, 2018, August 26).

References

Ansell, C. and Gash, A. (2008). Collaborative governance in theory and practice. *Journal of Public Administration Research and Theory,* 18(4), 543–571.

Babor, T. (2010). *Alcohol: No ordinary commodity: Research and public policy* (2nd ed.). Oxford: Oxford University Press.

Barry, R. and Glantz, S. (2016). A public health framework for legalized retail marijuana based on the US experience: Avoiding a new tobacco industry. *PLoS Medicine,* 13(9), e1002131.

Blake, D. and Finlaw, J. (2014). Marijuana legalization in Colorado: Learned lessons. *Harvard Law & Policy Review,* 8, 359–380.

Blue Ribbon Commission on Marijuana Policy. (2015). *Pathways report: Policy options for regulating marijuana in California.* Retrieved from www.safeandsmartpolicy.org/wp-content/uploads/2015/07/BRCPathwaysReport.pdf.

Borland, R. (2003). A strategy for controlling the marketing of tobacco products: A regulated market model. *Tobacco Control,* 12(4), 374–382.

Brohl, B. and Finlaw, J. (2013). *Task force report on the implementation of Amendment 64.* Retrieved from www.colorado.gov/pacific/sites/default/files/A64TaskForceFinalReport%5B1%5D_1.pdf.

Brooks-Russell, A., Ma, M., Levinson, A., Kattari, L., Kirchner, T., Goodell, E. and Johnson, R. (2018). Adolescent marijuana use, marijuana-related perceptions, and use of other substances before and after initiation of retail marijuana sales in Colorado (2013–2015). *Prevention Science*, 1–9.

Campaign to Regulate Marijuana Like Alcohol. (2012). *Endorsements and supporters*. Retrieved from https://web.archive.org/web/20120904012727/www.regulatemarijuana.org/endorsements.

Carnevale, J., Kagan, R., Murphy, P. and Esrick, J. (2017). A practical framework for regulating for-profit recreational marijuana in US states: Lessons from Colorado and Washington. *International Journal of Drug Policy*, 42, 71–85.

Caulkins, J., Kilmer, B., Kleiman, M., MacCoun, R., Midgette, G., Oglesby, P. and Reuter, P. (2015). *Considering marijuana legalization: Insights for Vermont and other jurisdictions*. Santa Monica, CA: Rand Corporation.

Cavazos-Rehg, P., Sowles, S.J., Krauss, M.J., Agbonavbare, V., Grucza, R. and Bierut, L. (2016). A content analysis of tweets about high-potency marijuana. *Drug and Alcohol Dependence*, 166, 100–108.

CNN Money. (2018). *Celebs are jumping on the marijuana brand wagon*. Retrieved from https://money.cnn.com/2018/04/10/news/celebrity-marijuana-brands/index.html.

Colorado Amendment 64. (2012). *The regulate marijuana like alcohol act*. Retrieved from www.fcgov.com/mmj/pdf/amendment64.pdf.

Colorado Department of Public Health and Environment. (2016). *Monitoring trends in marijuana use*. Retrieved from www.colorado.gov/pacific/cdphe/monitoring-trends-marijuana-use.

Colorado Department of Public Health and Environment. (2017). *Monitoring health concerns relating to marijuana: 2016*. Retrieved from www.colorado.gov/pacific/cdphe/marijuana-health-report.

Colorado Department of Public Health and Environment. (2018a). *Inspection of marijuana testing facilities*. Retrieved from www.colorado.gov/pacific/cdphe/inspection-retail-marijuana-testing-facilities.

Colorado Department of Public Health and Environment. (2018b). *Marijuana inspection: Sampling procedures*. Retrieved from www.colorado.gov/pacific/cdphe/marijuana-sampling-procedures.

Colorado Department of Public Health and Environment. (2018c). *Marijuana reference library*. Retrieved from www.colorado.gov/pacific/cdphe/marijuana-reference-library.

Colorado Department of Public Safety Division of Criminal Justice. (2018). *Driving under the influence of alcohol and drugs: A report pursuant to House Bill 17–1315*. Retrieved from http://cdpsdocs.state.co.us/ors/docs/reports/2018-DUI_HB17-1315.pdf.

Colorado Department of Regulatory Agencies. (2018). *2018 Sunset Reviews: Colorado medical marijuana code and Colorado retail marijuana code*. Retrieved from https://drive.google.com/file/d/1QeSxuD7cqil3L5mLuInWze2BsyYpCSQj/view.

Colorado Department of Revenue. (2015). *Industry-wide bulletin: 15–10. Executive order directing state agencies to address threats to public safety posed by marijuana contaminated by pesticide*. Retrieved from www.colorado.gov/pacific/sites/default/files/15-10_IB-MJ%20Pesticides_1.pdf.

Colorado Department of Revenue. (2018a). *Marijuana sales reports*. Retrieved from www.colorado.gov/pacific/revenue/colorado-marijuana-sales-reports.

Colorado Department of Revenue. (2018b). *Marijuana tax data*. Retrieved from www.colorado.gov/pacific/revenue/colorado-marijuana-tax-data.

Colorado Department of Revenue Enforcement Division. (2018a). *Marijuana Enforcement Division (MED) occupational licensing*. Retrieved from www.colorado.gov/pacific/enforcement/med-occupational-licensing.

Colorado Department of Revenue Enforcement Division. (2018b). *MED Industry Bulletins*. Retrieved from www.colorado.gov/pacific/enforcement/med-industry-bulletins-0.

Colorado Department of Transportation. (2018). *Drugged driving statistics*. Retrieved from www.codot.gov/safety/alcohol-and-impaired-driving/druggeddriving/safety/alcohol-and-impaired-driving/druggeddriving/statistics.

Colorado House Bill 15–1283. (2015). *Marijuana reference library and lab testing access*. Retrieved from https://openstates.org/co/bills/2015A/HB15-1283/.

Colorado Legislative Council Staff. (2015). *Distribution of marijuana tax revenue*. Retrieved from https://leg.colorado.gov/sites/default/files/15-10_distribution_of_marijuana_tax_revenue_issue_brief_1.pdf.

Colorado Office of State Planning and Budgeting. (2017). *State of Colorado marijuana tax cash fund appropriations and actual expenditures updated 26/9/2017*. Retrieved from https://indusdictum.com/wp-content/uploads/2018/01/Colorado-Marijuana-Tax-Cash-Fund-Appropriations-and-Expenditure-Report-09-26-2017-PUBLIC.pdf.

Colorado Official State Web Portal. (2018). *Official state information on the laws and health effects of retail marijuana*. Retrieved from www.colorado.gov/pacific/marijuana/.

Colorado Secretary of State. (2013). *1 CCR 212–2: Retail marijuana regulations*. Retrieved from www.sos.state.co.us/CCR/GenerateRulePdf.do?ruleVersionId=5402&fileName=1%20CCR%20212-2.

Colorado Secretary of State. (2018a). *Colorado revised statutes: Article 4 rule-making and licensing procedures by state agencies*. Retrieved from www.sos.state.co.us/pubs/info_center/laws/Title24/Title24Article4.html.

Colorado Secretary of State. (2018b). *Emergency rulemaking process*. Retrieved from www.sos.state.co.us/pubs/CCR/files/emer_rulemaking_process_flowchart.pdf.

Colorado Secretary of State. (2018c). *Permanent rulemaking process*. Retrieved from www.sos.state.co.us/pubs/CCR/files/perm_rulemaking_process_flowchart.pdf.

Colorado Secretary of State. (2019). *1 CCR 212–2: Retail marijuana regulations*. Retrieved from www.sos.state.co.us/CCR/DisplayRule.do?action=ruleinfo&ruleId=3175&deptID=19&agencyID=185&deptName=200&agencyName=212%20Marijuana%20Enforcement%20Division&seriesNum=1%20CCR%20212-2.

Community Preventive Services Task Force. (2014). *Reducing tobacco use and second-hand smoke*. Retrieved from www.thecommunityguide.org/tobacco/index.html.

Daniulaityte, R., Nahhas, R., Wijeratne, S., Carlson, R., Lamy, F., Martins, S. and Sheth, A. (2015). "Time for dabs": Analyzing Twitter data on marijuana concentrates across the US. *Drug and Alcohol Dependence,* 155, 307–311.

Denver Post. (2017a). Denver releases 28,000 marijuana products it had recalled for pesticides. *Denver Post*. Retrieved from www.denverpost.com/2016/02/02/denver-releases-28000-marijuana-products-it-had-recalled-for-pesticides/.

Denver Post. (2017b). Exclusive: Traffic fatalities linked to marijuana are up sharply in Colorado. Is legalization to blame? *Denver Post*. Retrieved from www.denver-post.com/2017/08/25/colorado-marijuana-traffic-fatalities/.

Denver Post. (2018). Mandatory testing costly for Colorado marijuana growers. *Denver Post*. Retrieved from www.denverpost.com/2018/08/26/colorado-marijuana-mandatory-pesticide-testing/.

Drug Enforcement Administration (DEA). (2018). *Controlled Substances Act*. Retrieved from www.dea.gov/druginfo/csa.shtml.

Fischer, B., Russell, C., Sabioni, P., Van Den Brink, W., Le Foll, B., Hall, W. and Room, R. (2017). Lower-risk cannabis use guidelines: A comprehensive update of evidence and recommendations. *American Journal of Public Health*, 107(8), e1-e12.

Ganjapreneur. (2016). *Crafting your dispensary's voice on social media: Do's and dont's*. Retrieved from www.ganjapreneur.com/crafting-dispensarys-voice-social-media-dos-donts/.

Ghosh, T., Van Dyke, M., Maffey, A., Whitley, E., Erpelding, D. and Wolk, L. (2015). Medical marijuana's public health lessons — Implications for retail marijuana in Colorado. *New England Journal of Medicine*, 372(11), 991–993.

Ghosh, T., Van Dyke, M., Maffey, A., Whitley, E., Gillim-Ross, L. and Wolk, L. (2016). The public health framework of legalized marijuana in Colorado. *American Journal of Public Health*, 106(1), 21–27.

HB 18–1011. (2018). *Concerning measures to allow greater investment flexibility in marijuana businesses, and, in connection therewith, making an appropriation*. Retrieved from http://leg.colorado.gov/sites/default/files/documents/2018A/bills/2018a_1011_signed.pdf.

Hickenlooper, J. (2014). Experimenting with pot: The state of Colorado's legalization of marijuana. *Milbank Quarterly*, 92(2), 243–249.

Hudak, J. (2015). Colorado's rollout of legal marijuana is succeeding. A report on the state's implementation of legalization. *Case Western Reserve Law Review*, 65(3), 649–687.

Kamin, S. (2015). Marijuana legalization in Colorado: Lessons for Colombia. *Journal Columbian Institute of Tax Law*, 75.

Kamin, S. (2017). What California can learn from Colorado's marijuana regulations. *McGeorge Law Review*, 49, 13.

Kilmer, B. and MacCoun, R. (2017). How medical marijuana smoothed the transition to marijuana legalization in the United States. *Annual Review of Law and Social Science*, 13(1), 181–202.

Kleiman, M. (2015). *Legal commercial cannabis sales in Colorado and Washington: What can we learn*. Brookings Institution.

Kleiman, M. (2016). *We're legalising weed wrong*. Retrieved from www.slate.com/articles/business/moneybox/2016/11/america_is_legalizing_marijuana_wrong.html.

Kleiman, M. (2018). *How to prevent casual pot smokers from slipping into abuse and dependence*. Retrieved from www.vox.com/the-big-idea/2018/4/20/17259032/marijuana-abuse-dependency-risk-policy-420-drug-addiction.

Leafly.com. (2018). *Explore marijuana strains and infused products*. Retrieved from www.leafly.com/start-exploring.

Lenton, S. (2014). New regulated markets for recreational cannabis: Public health or private profit? *Addiction*, 109(3), 354–355.

Lenton, S. and Subritzky, T. (2017). On Sentinel samples, sales data and potency. Commentary on Kilmer & Pacula: Greening the black market. *Addiction*, 112(7), 1137–1138.

Livingston, M. (2008). Alcohol outlet density and assault: A spatial analysis. *Addiction*, 103(4), 619–628.

Lopez, G. (2014). *What if big marijuana becomes big tobacco?* Retrieved from www.vox.com/2014/9/23/6218695/case-against-pot-legalization-big-marijuana.

MacCoun, R. and Mello, M. (2015). Half-baked – The retail promotion of marijuana edibles. *The New England Journal of Medicine*, 989–991.

Marijuana Policy Group. (2018). *Market size and demand for marijuana in Colorado 2017 market update (prepared for Colorado Department of Revenue)*. Retrieved from www.colorado.gov/pacific/sites/default/files/MED%20Demand%20and%20Market%20%20Study%20%20082018.pdf.

Mead, A. (2014). *International control of cannabis*. In R. Pertwee (Ed.), *Handbook of cannabis*. New York, NY: Oxford University Press.

National Highway Traffic Safety Administration. (2018). *National Highway Traffic Safety Administration*. Retrieved from www.nhtsa.gov/research-data/fatality-analysis-reporting-system-fars.

Native Roots. (2018). *Medical & recreational budtender needed – Denver, Co*. Retrieved from https://jobs.lever.co/nativeroots/e4b10217-f6b9-4e5f-8ae2-a7d50c181bf6.

Office of the Attorney General. (2017). *Sessions-hickenlooper-July-24–2017-letter*. Retrieved from https://assets.documentcloud.org/documents/3913305/Sessions-Hickenlooper-July-24-2017-Letter.pdf.

Office of the Attorney General. (2018). *Memorandum for all United States attorneys*. Retrieved from www.documentcloud.org/documents/4343688-AG-Marijuana-Enforcement-1-4-18.html#document/p1.

Pacula, R., Kilmer, B., Wagenaar, A., Chaloupka, F. and Caulkins, J. (2014). Developing public health regulations for marijuana: Lessons from alcohol and tobacco. *American Journal of Public Health*, 104(6), 1021–1028.

Pardo, B. (2014). Cannabis policy reforms in the Americas: A comparative analysis of Colorado, Washington, and Uruguay. *International Journal of Drug Policy*, 25(4), 727–735.

Rocky Mountain High Intensity Drug Trafficking Area. (2017). *The legalization of marijuana in Colorado: The Impact. Volume 5*. Retrieved from www.rmhidta.org/html/FINAL%202017%20Legalization%20of%20Marijuana%20in%20Colorado%20The%20Impact.pdf.

Rolles, S. and Murkin, G. (2016). *How to regulate cannabis: A practical guide* (2nd ed.). London: Transform Drug Policy Foundation.

Rolling Stone. (2018). *How mapping marijuana DNA could change the future of pot*. Retrieved from www.rollingstone.com/culture/culture-features/how-mapping-marijuana-dna-could-change-the-future-of-pot-629606/.

Room, R., Fischer, B., Hall, W., Lenton, S. and Reuter, P. (2010). *Cannabis policy: Moving beyond stalemate*. Oxford: Oxford University Press.

SB 16–040. (2016). *Concerning changes to the requirements for owners of a licensed marijuana business, and, in connection therewith, making an appropriation*. Retrieved from https://leg.colorado.gov/sites/default/files/documents/2016a/bills/2016A_040_rer.pdf.

Schwabe, A. and McGlaughlin, M. (2017). *Weeding out the truth behind cannabis strain names: Genetic analyses confirm cannabis strain names are inconsistent and need regulation*. Paper presented at the Institute of Cannabis Research conference (1st: 2017: Colorado State University-Pueblo). Pueblo, Colorado.

State of Alaska. (2017). *Marijuana regulation and criminal prosecutions in Alaska*. Retrieved from https://assets.documentcloud.org/documents/3933419/08-14-17-Jeff-Sessions-Marijuana-Regulation-and.pdf.

State of Colorado. (2012). *B 2012–004 executive order. Creating a task force on the implementation of Amendment 64*. Retrieved from www.colorado.gov/governor/sites/default/files/executive_orders/b_2012-004.pdf.

State of Colorado. (2017). *Hickenlooper-Coffman letter, August 24, 2017.* Retrieved from https://s3.amazonaws.com/big.assets.huffingtonpost.com/Hickenlooper-Coffmanletter.pdf.

State of Colorado. (2018). *Letter to members of the Colorado House of Representatives.* Retrieved from www.colorado.gov/governor/sites/default/files/1011_letter.pdf.

State of Oregon. (2017). *Oregon Governor Kate Brown letter to Jeff Sessions.* Retrieved from www.documentcloud.org/documents/3943774-8-22-17-Sessions.html.

State of Washington. (2017). *Inslee Fergusen letter to Sessions re marijuana.* Retrieved from https://assets.documentcloud.org/documents/3933420/Inslee-Ferguson-Ltr-to-Sessions-Re-Marijuana-Aug.pdf.

Subritzky, T. (2018). Beyond deficit and harm reduction: Incorporating the spectrum of wellness as an interpretive framework for cannabis consumption. *International Journal of Drug Policy,* 60(10), 18–23.

Subritzky, T. (in preparation). *A multi-source investigation of issues arising from the implementation and evolution of a commercial, non-medical cannabis market in Colorado.* (Doctoral thesis). Curtin University, Perth, Australia.

Subritzky, T., Lenton, S. and Pettigrew, S. (2016). Legal cannabis industry adopting strategies of the tobacco industry. *Drug and Alcohol Review,* 35(5), 511–513.

Subritzky, T., Pettigrew, S. and Lenton, S. (2016). Issues in the implementation and evolution of the commercial recreational cannabis market in Colorado. *International Journal of Drug Policy,* 27, 1–12.

Subritzky, T., Pettigrew, S. and Lenton, S. (2017). Into the void: Regulating pesticide use in Colorado's commercial cannabis markets. *International Journal of Drug Policy,* 42(4), 86–96.

The Cannabist. (2018). *Strain reviews archive – The Cannabist.* Retrieved from www.thecannabist.co/strains/.

Wang, G., Le Lait, M., Deakyne, S.J., Bronstein, A.C., Bajaj, L. and Roosevelt, G. (2016). Unintentional pediatric exposures to marijuana in Colorado, 2009–2015. *JAMA Pediatrics,* 170(9), e160971.

3 Recreational marijuana legalization in Washington State

Benefits and harms

Clayton Mosher and Scott Akins

Introduction

In 2012, Washington State and Colorado became the first two states in the US to legalize the use of recreational marijuana. In this chapter, we trace the path to marijuana legalization in Washington State, discuss marijuana policy heterogeneity within the state, and examine "outcomes" of legalization, framed in the context of three of the key priorities set out in a 2013 Department of Justice memorandum (known as the "Cole Memorandum") on marijuana enforcement. Approximately four years after sales of recreational marijuana began in Washington State (on July 8, 2014), there are certainly some areas of concern, but there is sufficient evidence across a variety of domains to suggest that the legalization of recreational marijuana in Washington State has not been associated with serious problems. More specifically, while there have been increases in adult use of marijuana in the state (as has happened across the United States in recent years), youth increases in use have not manifested. And while there has been some increase in traffic fatalities associated with marijuana use, a greater problem is related to poly-drug use. While diversion of marijuana from Washington State appears to be occurring, due to certain provisions in the state legislation, this has been less of a problem than in other states that have legalized recreational marijuana. Washington State has also achieved one of the primary goals of the legislation – there have been significant reductions in the number of people in the state arrested for marijuana offenses, and the state has also seen significant reductions in the costs associated with the enforcement of marijuana laws. Finally, the state has realized significant fiscal benefits through the taxation of marijuana sales.

The path to marijuana legalization in Washington State

Washington State first considered the legalization of marijuana in 1971, when a bill was introduced in the legislature. Although the bill did not pass, in the same year, possession of less than 40 grams of marijuana was downgraded to a misdemeanor offense (Roffman, 2014). Debates surrounding marijuana legalization continued in the state through the 1970s and into the 1980s, and in

1988, voters in Washington State approved Initiative 692 – The Medical Use of Marijuana Act," with 59 percent of voters in favor of the measure (Fleming, Guttmanova, Cambron, Rhew and Oesterle, 2016), and approval in 30 of the 39 counties in the state (McCarthy, 2016). The legislation permitted qualifying patients to have a 60-day supply of marijuana. However, somewhat ironically, the law did not specify the quantity of marijuana that would constitute a 60-day supply, and it was not until 2008, under House Bill 6032, that the amount allowed was specified as 24 ounces of usable marijuana and up to 15 plants for home cultivation (Northwest High Intensity Drug Trafficking Area, 2016). In addition, although I-692 allowed for the use of medical marijuana in Washington State, it did not provide for any regulation, and in contrast to medical marijuana legislation in other states, Washington did not set up a database of registered patients (Mkrtchyan, 2012; Wilson, 2014).

Additional laws relating to medical marijuana were passed in Washington State in 2007 and 2010, and in 2011, Senate Bill 5073 passed, which established a regulatory system to license the production and distribution of medical marijuana, allowed for patient home grows and collective gardens, and created a voluntary patient registry (Cambron, Guttmanova and Fleming, 2017; Mkrtchyan, 2012). However, the provisions of the bill relating to licensing and regulation were vetoed by Washington State Governor Christine Gregoire, due to concerns regarding the potential federal prosecution of state employees involved in the actions required to license cannabis production and medical dispensaries. In fact, it was not until 2015, some 17 years after the legalization of medical marijuana in Washington State, that the state legislature (while implementing regulation and licensing for recreational marijuana) enacted specific licensing requirements for medical marijuana. Among other provisions, this legislation required retailers selling recreational marijuana to obtain a medical endorsement to sell medical-grade marijuana and replaced collective gardens and medical marijuana dispensaries with small-scale patient cooperatives which were required to register with the state's liquor and cannabis board. The legislation also stipulated that stores seeking medical endorsements had to employ at least one "consultant" who would receive 20 hours of training from the Department of Health to advise patients in selecting products for medical use – these consultants are also responsible for enrolling medical users in a state database (Washington State Department of Health, 2018). Individuals who enrol in the medical marijuana patient database are exempt from paying sales tax (approximately 8.4 percent) on the products purchased and are also allowed to "grow six plants by default in the system," and up to 15 plants if authorized by their healthcare provider (Washington State Department of Health, 2018). While Washington State officials predicted that up to 90,000 people would register in the patient database, apparently due to concerns about having their names in the registry (Harshman, 2017) – as of December 10, 2018 only 36,925 patients were enrolled (Washington State Department of Health, 2018).

In November of 2012, Initiative 502 – "marijuana legalization and regulation" – appeared on the Washington State ballot. Among the supporters of the legislation were several prominent politicians, former federal prosecutor John McKay, Seattle City Attorney Pete Holmes, Seattle's Mayor Michael McGinn, and the city council (Garber and Miletich, 2011; Martin, 2012).

Additional supporters of the legislation included international travel guide Rick Steves (who also served on the board of the national organization for the reform of marijuana laws) (Shapiro, 2012), televangelist Pat Robertson, the National Association for the Advancement of Colored People, the American Civil Liberties Union of Western Washington, and the George Soros-funded Drug Policy Alliance. In total, supporters of I-502 raised $6.2 million (compared to only $16,000 by opposition groups) (Leon and Weitzer, 2014). King County Sheriff Steve Strachan, a former drug abuse resistance education (DARE) officer, also endorsed marijuana legalization, commenting "with alcohol being highly regulated, we're able to have a little more discussion about it" (Westneat, 2012). Strachan acknowledged that the DARE program had "overblown the dangers of pot," and that the mixing of messages about marijuana with "truly dangerous" hard drugs was "incredibly unhelpful" (Holden, 2012).

In their analysis of the factors influencing support for "vice legislation" (laws relating to prostitution, gambling and drugs), Leon and Weitzer (2014) note the importance of media influences. In the context of marijuana legalization in Washington State, several prominent newspapers came out in support of the legislation. The *Seattle Times* published an editorial supporting legalization, with the first line echoing the primary theme of the I-502 campaign – "The question for voters is not whether marijuana is good. It is whether prohibition is good." The piece went on to note, "If marijuana killed people, or smoking it made people commit violence and mayhem, prohibition might be worth all its bad effects. But marijuana does not kill people; there's no lethal dose" (*Seattle Times*, 2012). With respect to concerns about possible increases in youth use of marijuana under legalization, the editorial made the important point that marijuana prohibition had not resulted in youth being unable to access marijuana:

> Parents may ask whether I-502 will make marijuana more available to their teenage children. The answer is to compare marijuana with beer. For teenagers, both are illegal – and available. But which is more easily available, the one that is banned or the one that is regulated? For more than 40 years, the one more easily available to teenagers has been the one that is banned.
>
> (Ibid.)

The daily newspaper in Vancouver, Washington (the fourth largest city in the state) commented "Initiative 502 offers the chance to abandon prohibition as a lost cause" (Honig, 2012). The newspaper in the state capital of Olympia similarly supported the measure, noting that it represented a "step toward making sense of marijuana laws" (Honig, 2012). Even the relatively conservative Spokane *Spokesman-Review*, the largest circulation newspaper in eastern Washington, supported I-502.

In contrast to the 2010 California marijuana legalization campaign and the 2012 proposals in Colorado and Oregon, the pro I-502 campaign in Washington State primarily focused on social and racial justice issues (Collingwood et al., 2018), reporting that between 1986 and 2012, there had been more than 241,000 marijuana possession arrests in Washington State, with Blacks and Latinos being much more likely to be arrested for the offense. Marijuana enforcement efforts were said to have cost the state $306 million over this period (Leon and Weitzer, 2014).

The legalization campaign in Washington State and its emphasis on social and racial justice issues was influenced by Deputy Campaign Director and Outreach Manager for New Approach Washington (the official name of the campaign), Tonia Winchester. In her role as prosecutor in the central Washington city of Wenatchee, Winchester wondered why a large proportion of the individuals she was prosecuting on marijuana charges were Latino and African American, when the majority of those using the substance were White (Hari, 2015).

Alison Holcomb, the primary architect of the pro I-502 campaign, had previously worked with Washington State legislators on medical marijuana provisions, and had also represented medical marijuana patients, providers and others involved with the substance in federal, state and local courts, primarily in her role with the American Civil Liberties Union. Holcomb and her colleagues focused the campaign on mainstream voters in the state, so the initiative was relatively conservative and attempted to address the most salient voter concerns, such as restrictions on driving under the influence of marijuana, in-home cultivation and the prevention of youth use (Martin and Rashidian, 2014). In contrast to the Amendment 64 marijuana legalization campaign in Colorado, which emphasized the relative harms of alcohol versus marijuana, the New Approach Washington campaign did not stress that cannabis was good, but instead that current cannabis laws were creating several social harms. The supporters of I-502 argued that marijuana should be legal not because it is safe, but in fact because it is dangerous – "individuals who deal drugs in streets do not check id" (Hari, 2015).

Interestingly, (and as had happened with the 2010 marijuana legalization measure in California), medical marijuana providers, led by the group Sensible Washington," were opposed to I-502 (Collingwood, O'Brien and Dreier, 2018; Mkrtchyan, 2012). While the opposition of providers was likely partially related to beliefs that their sales might be compromised with the legalization of recreational marijuana, the group was also concerned about a clause in I-502 that addressed driving under the influence of marijuana. Under the policy, impairment would be defined as having five nanograms of THC per milliliter of blood (Johnson, 2011), which, the medical marijuana providers argued, would result in substantial numbers of medical marijuana patients being charged with driving under the influence. Alison Holcomb and others involved in the pro I-502 campaign were aware of these concerns, but they also knew from reviewing survey results of California's failed 2010 Proposition 19 that many voters who initially supported that measure changed their minds and voted against it, at least partially due to concerns about driving under the influence of marijuana (Shapiro, 2012). The pro I-502 group also conducted a survey in Washington State in which 62 percent of respondents indicated they would be more likely to vote for legalization if the measure included a DUI provision. Longtime Washington State marijuana activist and retired University of Washington Professor Roger Roffman, a sponsor of the I-502 campaign commented, "I wouldn't have wanted to be connected to an initiative that didn't take into account the dangers of driving while stoned" (Shapiro, 2012).

The 2012 Washington State voter's pamphlet listed arguments for and against Initiative 502. Among the arguments in support of the legislation was included the fact that legalization would provide "billions in new revenue" for the state, and that "almost all marijuana law enforcement is handled by state and local police – it's time for Washingtonians to decide Washington's laws, not the federal government" (Clark County, 2012).

I-502 was supported by 55.7 percent of Washington State voters,[1] and established a regulatory structure for the licensing and taxation of marijuana production and distribution, and authorized possession of up to one ounce of cannabis for individuals 21 years of age and older (Washington State Senate, n.d.). The legislation initially imposed a 25 percent tax on (each of) the producers, processors and retailers, but in 2015, under Senate Bill 5121, the taxation system was changed so that a single 37 percent tax was levied on marijuana purchases. It is also important to note that Washington State's legal marijuana industry is not vertically integrated, in that businesses holding retail licenses are prohibited from involvement in production and processing (Darnell and Bitney, 2017). The state also limited the number of recreational marijuana retail licenses to 334 (later increased to 556 in July of 2016 with the "merger" of the medical and recreational systems) – the cap on retail licenses was unique to Washington State, and likely limited the market for marijuana.

Policy heterogeneity and local variation

There is considerable variation in the specifics of recreational (and medical) marijuana laws across states that have passed such laws. And importantly, even in states where the legalization of marijuana is in place, reflecting continuing division over marijuana legalization, there is considerable local variation. There is of course precedent for local jurisdictions adopting their own approaches to regulating the sale of psychoactive substances, as was evidenced in the emergence of several "dry" towns in the post-prohibition era in the United States in response to the re-legalization of alcohol.

In Washington State, the language of I-502 did not prohibit local bans on marijuana sales. While, as noted above, 55.7 percent of voters in the state approved marijuana legalization, the majority of voters in 19 of Washington State's 39 counties voted against the measure (Dilley, Hitchcock, McGrader, Greto and Richardson, 2017), so it is perhaps not surprising that several local jurisdictions have implemented bans on marijuana businesses. In response to a query by Washington State Liquor and Cannabis Board chair Sharon Foster regarding whether local governments were prevented by state law from prohibiting state-licensed marijuana producers, processors, or retailers within their jurisdictions, Washington State Attorney General Bob Ferguson acknowledged that "We are mindful that if a large number of jurisdictions were to ban (marijuana) licenses, it could interfere with the [I-502] measure's intent to supplant the illegal market." However, Ferguson added, "Under Washington law, there is a strong presumption against finding that state law pre-empts local ordinances … Local governments have broad authority to regulate within their jurisdictions, and nothing in I-502 limits that authority with respect to marijuana businesses" (Ferguson, 2014). Confirming the Attorney General's interpretation, through 2015, all five Washington State courts that had heard challenges to local bans agreed that these can be imposed (Ferguson, 2015). As a result, as of June 2016, six of Washington State's 39 counties, and 54 of 152 cities with populations of 3,000 or more (covering approximately 30 percent of the state's population) had implemented local bans on retail cannabis sales (Dilley et al., 2017). More recent data from the Municipal Research and Services Center (2018) indicate that, as of December 2018, seven counties and 78 cities (out of a total of 585) prohibited marijuana sales.[2]

Although cities have allowed retail sales within their boundaries, large Washington State counties such as Pierce (the second largest county in the state, with a 2017 population of 876,764) and Clark (the fifth largest county in the state, with a 2017 population of 474,643) originally banned recreational marijuana sales. Clark County Commissioner Tom Mielke, while admitting that he had not read the I-502 rules (similar to other elected officials in other policy contexts), justified the county's moratorium on sales by claiming that he was concerned about (unspecified) unintended consequences of allowing marijuana stores in the county (Graf, 2014). However, in Clark County, the local newspaper of record, the *Columbian*, recommended that the county commissioners rescind the ban (2014). At the time of writing, the ban on marijuana sales in Clark County had not been rescinded, although there were 13 retail marijuana stores within the county's boundaries (Washington State Liquor and Cannabis Board, 2018a).

It is by no means clear what elected officials are trying to accomplish in enacting these local bans. Are they unaware of the fact that residents of their jurisdictions are able to travel (in many cases, short distances) to purchase marijuana if they choose to do so? So, while purchases and consumption are likely not significantly impacted by local prohibitions on sales, jurisdictions imposing moratoriums forfeit significant tax revenues under the bans.

While the ban on marijuana sales in Clark County is still in place, Pierce County Executive Pat McCarthy vetoed that county's ban in June of 2016, commenting, "I am vetoing this ordinance because my job as an elected official requires me to advance the will of the people who voted in 2012, in a comprehensive election, to legalize recreational marijuana" (54 percent of Pierce County voters approved I-502) (Grimley, 2016). McCarthy's comments were in response to an April 2016, advisory election in Pierce County (which cost $425,000) in which voters in unincorporated areas of the county were asked to reconsider the ban on recreational sales. Of the 65,000 people who voted in the advisory election, 34,000 (52 percent) supported retaining the ban. However, as McCarthy noted in a letter to Pierce County Council Chair Doug Richardson, the voter turnout in the election was low, and not representative of the entire county. In her letter, McCarthy also noted that banning the sale of marijuana

> piecemeal throughout the state defeats one of the most important goals of I-502: that is, the eradication of the black market. Effective regulation, licensing, and enforcement of marijuana is the best tool we have for keeping marijuana out of the hands of young people.
>
> (McCarthy, 2016)

In order to address some of this policy confusion and its possible contribution to the continuation of the black market in marijuana, legislation proposed in Washington State in early 2017 would penalize local governments that prohibit marijuana but had not enacted such bans through specific legislation by taking away 70 percent of their tax revenues from liquor sales (Santos, 2017). As Alison Holcomb told the King County Council:

> Every city and county that has put itself above the law, above the vote of the people (by prohibiting marijuana sales) has done nothing more than fuel money into the illicit market but also into the hands of the privileged few who have managed to secure a state license.
>
> (Young, 2016)

Outcomes

In 2013, the Federal Department of Justice issued the Cole Memorandum to provide guidance regarding marijuana regulation. The Cole Memorandum begins by noting that "Congress has determined that marijuana is a dangerous drug and that illegal distribution and sale of marijuana is a serious crime that provides a significant source of revenue to large scale criminal enterprises, gangs, and cartels" (Cole, 2013).

Eight "enforcement priorities" were listed in the Cole memorandum,[3] including: (1) preventing the distribution of marijuana to minors; (2) preventing revenue from the sale of marijuana going to criminal enterprises, gangs and cartels; (3) preventing the diversion of marijuana from states where it is legal under state law in some form to other states; (4) preventing state-authorized marijuana activity from being used as a cover or pretext for the trafficking of other legal drugs or illegal activity; (5) preventing violence and the use of firearms in the cultivation and distribution of marijuana; (6) preventing drugged driving and the exacerbation of other adverse health consequences associated with marijuana use; (7) preventing the growing of marijuana on public lands and attendant public safety and environmental dangers posed by marijuana production on public lands; and (8) preventing marijuana possession on federal property. As potential increases in adolescent marijuana use and the impact of marijuana legalization on the drugged driving have been the focus of much debate in assessing the outcomes of marijuana legalization, our discussion below focuses on these two priorities. Given that there is less evidence to make firm conclusions on the issue, we address the issue of priority 3 (diversion) more briefly.

Adolescent marijuana use

"We had predicted based on changes in legalization, culture in the U.S. as well as decreasing perceptions among teenagers that marijuana was harmful [and] that [accessibility and use] would go up. But it hasn't gone up" stated Nora Volkow, the Director of the National Institute on Drug Abuse; Ingraham, 2016).

There is fairly strong evidence that marijuana use by adults has increased in recent years, both across the US, as revealed in the national survey on drug use and health (Bose, Hedden, Lipari and Park-Lee, 2018), and in Washington State (Darnell and Bitney, 2017; Miller, Rosenman and Cowan, 2017). However, there is debate regarding whether and to what extent increased use of marijuana by adults is problematic, especially given emerging evidence that cannabis may be a substitute for opiate drugs (Bachhuber, Saloner, Cunningham and Barry, 2014; Bradford and Bradford, 2016; Bradford and Bradford, 2017; Bradford, Bradford, Abraham and Adams, 2018; Livingston, Barnett, Delcher and Wagenaar, 2017; Piper, De Keuster, Beals, Cobb, Buchman, Perkinson, Lynn, Nichols and Abess, 2017; Reiman, 2009; Shi, 2017; Wen and Hockenberry, 2018) and alcohol (Lucas, Reiman, Earleyewine, McGowan, Oleson, Coward and Thomas, 2013; Lucas, Walsh, Crosby, Callaway, Belle-Isle, Kay, Capler and Holtzman, 2016; Reiman, 2009).

However, most would agree that if marijuana legalization leads to increases in youth use, or results in other harms to youth, there is legitimate reason for concern. Although, as we discuss below, these claims have been overstated;[4] particularly relevant here is that early marijuana use can lead to cognitive deficits and declines in IQ (Gilman, Kusler, Lee, Lee, Kim, Makris, van der Kouwe, Blood and Breiter, 2014; Meier, Caspi, Ambler, Harrington, Houts, Keefe, McDonald, Ward, Poulton and Moffitt, 2012).

In considering the results of studies on increases in youth use that we review in this chapter, it is important to stress that far too many legalization opponents (including special interest groups such as Project SAM (Smart Approaches to Marijuana), federal and state government and criminal justice system officials, reporters/journalists and some academics, almost seem unaware that marijuana existed and has been consumed by people (including youth) well before medical and recreational legalization (Mosher and Akins, in press). Related, it is also important to stress that, while recreational marijuana was legalized in Colorado and Washington State in November of 2012, retail sales of the substance did not begin until January 1, 2014 in Colorado, and July 8, 2014 in Washington State. As such, the results of studies of trends in youth cannabis use must be treated with caution, as the effects of legalization on youth (and adult) use may not have had sufficient time to manifest.

In order to assess potential increases in youth use and threats to youth wellbeing in states with legal (both medical and recreational) marijuana, researchers have generally used data from emergency room visits and poison control centers[5] (Onders, Casavant, Spiller, Chounthriath and Smith, 2016; Wang, Narana, Wells and Chuang, 2011; Wang, Roosevelt and Heard, 2013; Wang, Le Lait, Deakyne, Bronstein, Bajal and Roosevelt, 2016), and data from self-report surveys. Given space considerations, we focus on results from self-report surveys.

In considering the results of self-report surveys on trends in youth use of marijuana, it is necessary to be cognizant of the inherent weaknesses in survey methodology (e.g. sampling error, response bias, etc.) more generally (Mosher, Miethe and Hart, 2011). In the specific case of marijuana consumption, legalization itself (which signals an increased social acceptability of the substance) may influence survey respondents' tendencies to more truthfully report their use of the drug. Given this, an increase in self-reported use of marijuana over time may merely reflect changes in respondents' reporting tendencies.

With respect to youth use of psychoactive substances, it is also important to distinguish between casual use/experimentation and heavy use. Some studies have suggested that experimentation with alcohol, marijuana and other drugs is in fact a normal part of adolescence (Englund, Siebenbruner, Oliva, Egeland, Chung and Long, 2013; Substance Abuse and Mental Health Services Administration, 1999).

Turning to the research on the relationship between marijuana legalization and changes in youth use of the substance, a widely-cited study regarding the impact of recreational marijuana legalization on youth use was published in *JAMA Pediatrics* (Cerdá, Wall, Fena, Keyes, Sarvet, Schulenberg, O'Malley, Pacula, Galea and Hasin, 2017). Using data from the *Monitoring the Future* survey, this study found that, while there was no change in marijuana consumption among youth in Colorado over the 2010–2014 period, youth in the 8th and 10th grades in Washington State were more likely to report use of the substance since legalization, and that there had been increases in the proportion of youth in the state who believed that marijuana did not pose a great health risk.

In considering the results of this study, it is important to stress that Cerdá et al. (2017) found no increase in marijuana consumption among 12th graders in Washington State, and the increases for 8th graders (2 percent) and 10th graders (4 percent), were relatively modest. But in interpreting these increases, while providing no data to support their claims, Cerdá et al. (2017) suggest that legalization may have increased the availability of marijuana – "increasing adolescent access to marijuana indirectly through third party purchases," and/or that "legalization could have decreased the price of marijuana in the black market."

Even leaving aside our previous point that sales of recreational marijuana did not commence in Colorado until January 1, 2014, and in Washington State until July 8, 2014, it is by no means clear why the same arguments did not apply to youth in Colorado (where there was no increase in use) and 12th graders in Washington State (who also had no increases in use). And while Cerdá and colleagues do not specifically address these problems with their argument, they suggest that the lack of an increase in marijuana consumption by youth in Colorado was due to the fact that several years of medical marijuana sales in the state had already led to changes in youth use. This argument is also rather curious, given that Washington State legalized medical marijuana in 1998, Colorado in 2000.

Additional studies examining the relationship between changes in marijuana policies and youth use have generally not found strong associations. For example, in a meta-analysis of 11 studies examining changes in youth use following the legalization of medical marijuana laws, Sarvet, Wall, Fink, Green, Le, Boustead, Pacula, Keyes, Cerdá, Galea and Hasin (2018) reported that none of the studies found significant increases in marijuana use prevalence among adolescents compared with states that had not legalized medical marijuana. Using data for 10th grade students from Washington State's Healthy Youth Survey (HYS) for the 2002–2014 period, Fleming et al. (2016) report that, while the proportion of youth who do not perceive marijuana use as harmful has increased, youth use of the substance remained stable.

In examining changes in youth marijuana use in Washington State, the most useful source of data is the state's HYS, which has been conducted since 2002. We are of course aware of the weaknesses of survey data in general, and school-based surveys in particular (because school-based surveys will not include youth who have dropped out or are otherwise absent on dates when the surveys are administered – one could reasonably argue that dropouts and truants are more likely to use marijuana and/or other drugs).[6] However, unless there have been significant increases in the percentage of students dropping out over time (in fact, dropout rates have declined in Washington State, see Morton, 2018), we can use school survey data to examine longer term trends in youth use.

Figure 3.1 shows trends in current, or past 30-day use of marijuana for youth in grades 8, 10, and 12 in Washington State over the 2002 to 2016 period. Current use among 12th graders began increasing in 2006 to reach a peak of 26.7 percent in 2012 and 2014 and was essentially unchanged in 2016. For 8th and 10th graders, use peaked in 2010, and has declined since.

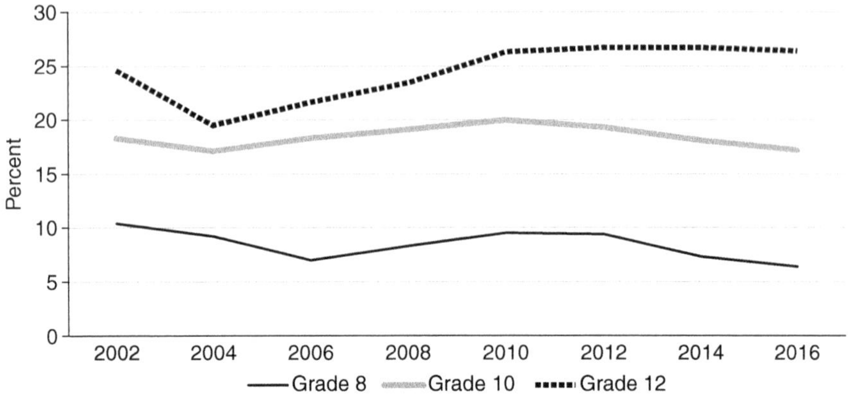

Figure 3.1 Current marijuana use by grade – Washington State, 2002–2016.

Figure 3.2 shows current use for Grade 10 students in 9 of the 10 largest counties in Washington State in 2010 and 2016,[7] while Figure 3.3 shows current use for Grade 10 students by race/ethnicity and suggests that these trends are fairly robust.

The lack of a significant increase in youth use of marijuana as revealed in the HYS has been mentioned in several media sources in Washington State and elsewhere. At the same time, however, commentators have expressed alarm over the decline in youth's perception of the harmfulness of marijuana.[8] But

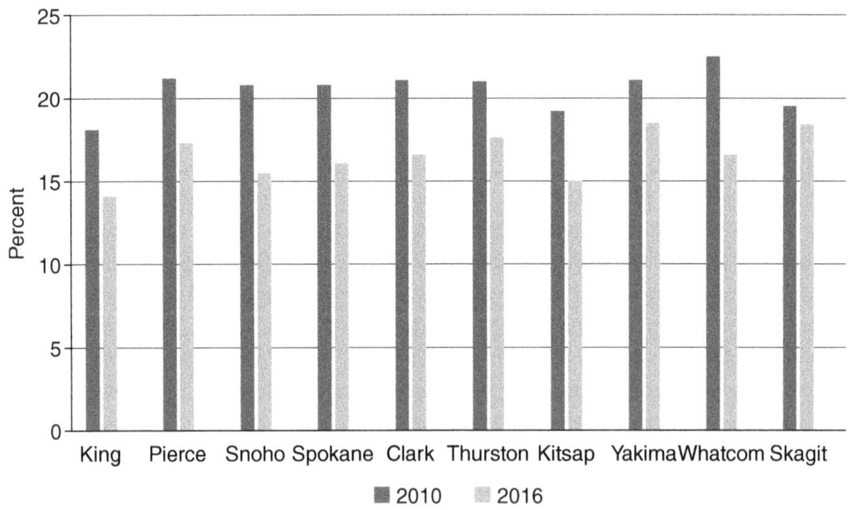

Figure 3.2 Current marijuana use by county – Washington State Grade 10 students, 2010 and 2016.

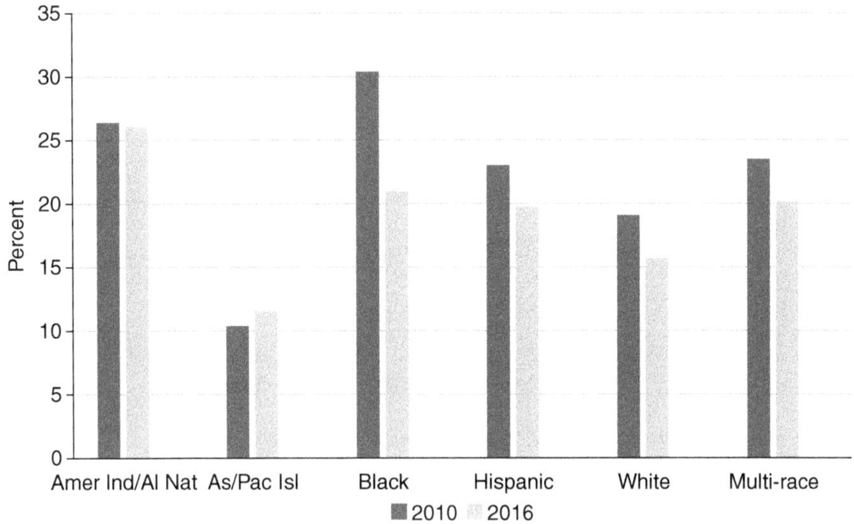

Figure 3.3 Current marijuana use – Washington State Grade 10 students by race/ethnicity, 2010 and 2016.

as Figure 3.4 shows, youth perceptions of the harm associated with marijuana use began declining well before legalization. Further, in responding to questions on the perceived harmfulness of marijuana, it seems reasonable to conclude that youth are simply being rational – the fact is, while marijuana certainly involves risks, especially for young people, in comparison to the harms associated with the use of other psychoactive substances, including alcohol and

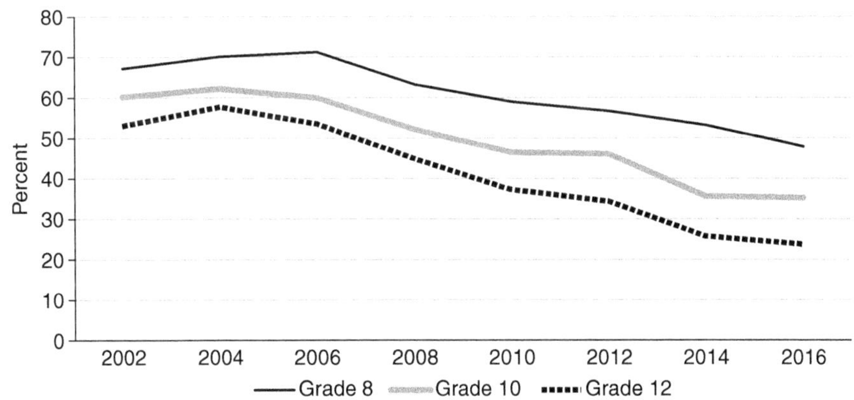

Figure 3.4 Perceived risk from regular marijuana use by grade – Washington State, 2002–2016.

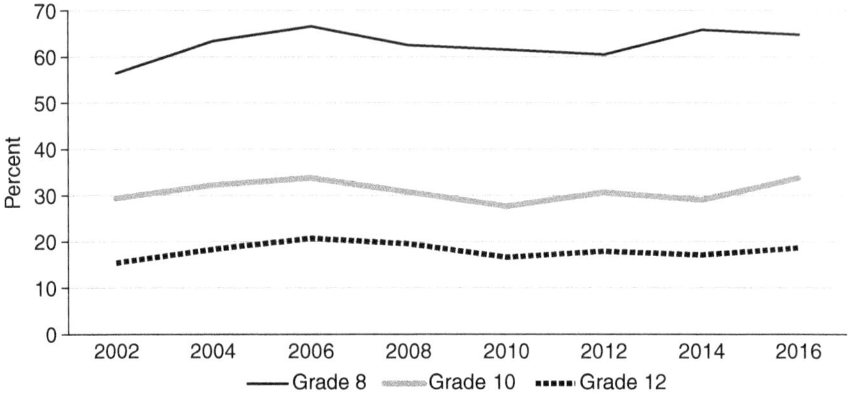

Figure 3.5 Access to marijuana ("Marijuana very hard to get") by grade – Washington State, 2002–2016.

several prescription drugs, marijuana is simply not that risky (Mosher and Akins, 2014; Nutt, King, Saulsbury and Blakemore, 2007). And of course, the normalization of marijuana through medical and recreational legalization has likely also contributed to these declines.

So, how do we explain the lack of significant increases in youth marijuana use in Washington State under legalization? We of course realize that more data are needed before reaching strong conclusions on this issue, but data from the Washington State HYS indicate that youth in all grades surveyed report that marijuana has become more difficult to obtain since legalization (see Figure 3.5). More specifically, among Grade 12 students in the state, in 2010, 16.5 percent said that marijuana would be very hard to obtain; by 2016, this percentage had increased to 18.6 percent. Among Grade 10 students, the percentage reporting that marijuana would be very hard to obtain increased from 27.8 percent in 2010 to 33.7 percent in 2016. As was the case with trends in youth use, these trends in access are robust with respect to county of residence and race/ethnicity of the youth (data not shown).

In this context, it is worth examining data from the Washington State Liquor and Cannabis Board's (LCB) compliance checks, in which an investigative aide aged 18–20 attempts to purchase cannabis to ensure that retail stores are not selling the substance to individuals under the age of 21. Of the 2,866 compliance checks conducted by the LCB between July of 2014 and April of 2018, 203, or 7.1 percent of marijuana retailers sold cannabis to underage people (Washington State Liquor and Cannabis Board, 2018b). While there is obviously still need for improvement, it is notable that compliance rates for retail marijuana stores in Washington State are in fact higher than for outlets selling alcohol and tobacco (Washington State Liquor and Cannabis Board, 2018). Collectively, these data suggest the possibility that the lack of significant increases (and in some groups, decreases) in youth marijuana use may be related to the fact that the substance has been more difficult for them to obtain under legalization.

To summarize the research on the effects of marijuana legalization and youth use of the substance, it is clear that there is little evidence of a strong relationship, if any at all. As *Washington Post* columnist Christopher Ingraham comments,

> There is a simple reason why legalization is not affecting teen use – adolescents already report that marijuana is widely available. The kids who want to smoke it are probably already doing so, and legalization will do little to change that.
>
> (Ingraham, 2016)

Marijuana-impaired driving

As noted above, an additional major concern of marijuana legalization opponents is that legalization of the substance will lead to increases in cannabis-impaired driving and related increases in collisions and traffic fatalities. Research on the relationship between marijuana consumption and driving performance generally involves two types of studies: "simulator" studies examining the effects of consumption on driving performance in laboratory-type situations, and aggregate-level epidemiological (sometimes referred to as "case-control") studies assessing the impact of changes in marijuana laws on automobile collisions and traffic fatalities.

With respect to the first types of studies, while there is a widespread belief that marijuana consumption has serious negative effects on driving performance, there is still considerable dispute in the scientific literature on this issue (Neavyn, Blohm, Babo and Bird, 2014; Sewell, Poling and Sofuoglo, 2009). In fact, even the National Highway Traffic and Safety Administration (NHTSA) has noted that "some (THC-intoxicated) drivers may actually be able to improve performance for brief periods by overcompensating for self-perceived impairment" (National Highway Traffic and Safety Administration, n.d.). A 2017 NHTSA report further noted that

> subjects dosed on marijuana showed reduced mean speed, increased time driving below the speed limit and increased following distance during a car following task. Alcohol, in contrast, was associated with higher mean speeds (over the speed limit) and greater variability in speed.
>
> (Compton, 2017)

Case-control studies on the influence of marijuana consumption on collisions and traffic fatalities have produced mixed results. A study by the American Automobile Association (AAA) examined the relationship between marijuana use and impaired driving using a census of all motor vehicle crashes on public roads in Washington State over the 2010–2014 period that resulted in a death within 30 days of the collision, focusing on the presence and concentration of THC in drivers involved in such collisions (Tefft, 2016). State-wide, 3,031 drivers were involved in fatal collisions over this period, an estimated 303 (10 percent) of whom had detectable levels of THC in their blood at or shortly after the time of the crash. Of the 303 drivers who tested positive for THC, only about one-third (34 percent) had neither alcohol or other drugs in their blood; 39 percent had detectable alcohol in addition to THC, 16.5 percent had other drugs in addition to THC, and 10.5 percent had both alcohol and other drugs in addition to THC in their blood (Tefft, 2016). Thus, in this study (as well as in several others examining the issue) it is difficult to disentangle the effects of marijuana, alcohol and other drugs on involvement in fatal crashes. And while some media and government officials have used this AAA study to claim that there is a strong relationship between marijuana consumption and involvement in fatal collisions, Tefft (2016) was much more cautious in his conclusions, noting "The results of this study do not indicate that drivers with detectable levels of THC in their blood at the time of the crash were necessarily impaired by THC or that they were at fault for the crash."

Two more recent studies on the relationship between marijuana consumption and involvement in collisions and fatalities, published in 2017, offered contrasting conclusions. The first, published in the *American Journal of Public Health*, used data from the NHTSA's fatal analysis reporting system (FARS) data to determine the annual number of fatal motor vehicle incidents over the 2009–2015 period in Colorado, Washington State, and eight comparison states (Aydelotte, Brown, Luftman, Mardock, Texeira, Coopwood and Brown, 2017). The authors compared yearly changes in crash fatality rates (per billion vehicle miles traveled) and found that, after the legalization of recreational marijuana, while the rates increased, they were not significantly different from those in the comparison states that had not legalized (there were 0.2 extra fatalities per billion miles traveled, equating to 77 additional traffic fatalities, or 2.7 percent of the 2,890 total fatalities). Aydelotte et al. (2017) concluded "Three years after recreational marijuana legalization, changes in motor vehicle crash fatality rates for Washington and Colorado are not significantly different from those in similar states without recreational marijuana legalization."

A second study, sponsored by the Insurance Institute for Highway Safety (IIHS) found that Colorado, Oregon and Washington State had insurance claims from collisions that were 2.7 percent higher than those in neighboring states (Idaho, Montana, Nevada, Utah and Wyoming) in the three years since legal sales of recreational marijuana began (Insurance Institute for Highway Safety, 2017). It is important to note that, in contrast to the Aydelotte et al. (2017) study, the IIHS study was not peer reviewed, and was unable to demonstrate that marijuana legalization was a direct cause of the increase in insurance claims. It is also important to note that the Aydelotte et al. (2017) study focused on collisions that resulted in fatalities, while the IIHS study examined collisions more generally (Ingraham, 2017b).

More recently, using FARS data for the 1993–2014 period, Sevigny (2018) found that medical marijuana laws in general had a null effect on "cannabis-positive" driving. However, Sevigny (2018) did report that in states that regulate the sale of cannabis through dispensaries, cannabis-positive driving increased by 0.011–0.014. He noted, however, that "this is a relatively small effect, representing an additional 87–113 cannabis-positive drivers in 2014 who were involved in fatal vehicle accidents who might not otherwise have been" (Sevigny, 2018).

Turning to more specific data from Washington State, in 2014, 72 drivers who were involved in fatal collisions tested positive for THC alone (or in combination with alcohol and/or other drugs) compared to 44 such cases in 2010. However, only 20 of the drivers testing positive in 2014 were positive for THC only (compared to 9 in 2010) (Drug Policy Alliance, 2016). While this increase is statistically significant, by itself it does not indicate that more people were driving while impaired by marijuana, nor that the fatalities that did occur were caused by marijuana-impaired drivers. Instead, the statistical increase may be related to changes in the screening and data-reporting methods and procedures after legalization in Washington State. Prior to the passage of I-502, law enforcement agencies in the state did not routinely conduct tests to determine whether THC was present in drivers involved in fatal crashes – such information had to be retroactively collected and manually obtained. Such methods are subject to high error rates and lead to problems in comparing "real-time" THC tests which were increasingly used after legalization (Drug Policy Alliance, 2016).

Despite limited (if any) evidence of substantial increases in traffic collisions and/or fatalities caused by marijuana consumption, organizations such as the federally funded Northwest High Intensity Drug Trafficking Area (NWHIDTA) have made claims that the problem has increased in Washington State. For example, a 2016 report by the NWHIDTA used the tactic of reporting large percentage increases in marijuana related DUIs to emphasize the alleged seriousness of the problem. It was noted that the Spokane Valley police department recorded eight marijuana related DUIs in 2012, compared to 40 in 2014, a "500% increase" (Northwest High Intensity Drug Trafficking Area, 2016). Also, in Spokane Valley, youth marijuana DUIs have been increasing exponentially. In 2012, Spokane Valley had one youth test confirmed for active THC. In 2014, the number was 18, a 1700 percent increase in three years. To further emphasize the extent of the marijuana DUI problem, the report included six anecdotes of "news articles related to Washington State roadways on marijuana use"– only one of which provided objective data (actual marijuana blood content) for the drivers involved (Northwest High Intensity Drug Trafficking Area, 2016).

A more recent report on the relationship between substance use and involvement in fatal crashes by the Washington State Traffic Safety Commission (2018) found a significant increase in the number of drivers involved in

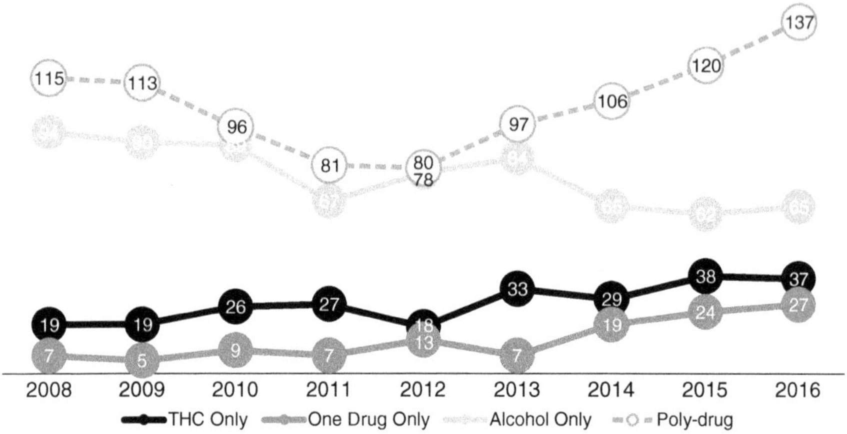

Figure 3.6 Drivers in fatal crashes testing positive for drugs – Washington State, 2008–2016.

Source: Adapted from Washington State Traffic Safety Commission (2018).

traffic fatalities in 2016 testing positive for two or more drugs – the number of poly-drug drivers was more than double the number of alcohol-only drivers and five times higher than the number of THC-only drivers involved in fatal collisions (see Figure 3.6). The report noted, "While the crash risk posed by alcohol is fairly well understood, it is critically important that we come to a better understanding of how THC and alcohol combine to increase crash risk in drivers" (Washington State Traffic Safety Commission, 2018).

To summarize the research on the relationship between cannabis consumption and involvement in collisions/traffic fatalities, it is safe to say that collectively, the results of both driving simulator-type studies and aggregate-level studies indicate some effects, although they are not inordinately large.[9] However, there are legitimate concerns regarding drivers who consume alcohol and cannabis (and other drugs). In a personal email correspondence with the senior author of this chapter, Staci Hoff,[10] research director for the Washington State Traffic Safety Commission noted that there was "obvious bias in the published research [on the relationship between marijuana consumption and involvement in collisions] offering erroneous conclusions while downplaying the significant study limitations" (Hoff, 2017). More importantly, Hoff noted that recent studies have demonstrated that the level of THC in the blood is not necessarily related to impairment:

> i.e. some subjects with greater than 15 ng/ml of THC in the blood exhibit no signs of driver impairment whereas a subject who has no

measurable THC but known to have recently used do exhibit signs of driver impairment. We must also consider and be honest regarding the frequent occurrence of other substances known to cause driver impairment, such as alcohol.

(Hoff, 2017)

Additional outcomes

Diversion

As noted above, one of the key provisions of the 2013 Cole Memorandum was that states with marijuana legalization policies needed to ensure that marijuana was not diverted to the black market and/or to other states – this has also been a major concern of (now former) Federal Attorney General Jeff Sessions. It is important to note that most legalization proponents did not claim that legalization would completely eliminate the black market in marijuana, but there is little doubt that diversion of cannabis from states with legalized marijuana is occurring, especially in Oregon (Oregon State Police, 2017) and perhaps to a somewhat lesser extent, Colorado (Rocky Mountain High Intensity Drug Trafficking Area, 2015).

However, in contrast to the situation in Oregon and Colorado, it appears that Washington State's comparatively strict monitoring of cannabis producers through site visits, the use of cameras, and a strong traceability system has led to considerably less "leakage" of cannabis across state lines (Coughlin-Bogue, 2017). Although the state's marijuana tracking system experienced problems in late 2017 into early 2018, as one commentator noted, "Whether marijuana from Washington State's legal market is being diverted to other states remains something of a mystery" (Bush, 2018). And in contrast to the other states that have legalized recreational marijuana, in Washington State, personal cultivation for those not registered in the medical marijuana system remains a felony offense,[11] which may also contribute to less diversion. Alison Holcomb explained that prohibiting home cultivation was a strategic decision on the part of the I-502 architects, who felt that adding a provision to allow for home growing would be risky, given that their polling data indicated that support for the measure was not robust (Kiley, 2015).

And despite claims to the contrary, it is not entirely clear that marijuana smuggling has become more of a problem under legalization in the past – although referring to the situation in Oregon, the comments of Oregon Democrat Representative Earl Blumenauer are relevant to the issue of diversion more generally, "Marijuana has left Oregon for decades. What's different is that now we have better mechanisms to try and control it" (Selsky, 2017). Similarly, the former Executive Director of the University of Washington's cannabis law and policy project, Sam Mendez, noted "there has always been diversion. There was plenty of cannabis being produced before legalization." Harvard economist Jeffrey Miron has suggested that the solution to the continued marijuana black market problem and diversion is "trivial: full legalization" (Miron, 2017). Here, the comments of Alison Holcomb are also worth considering – in reference to the fact that historically, much of the marijuana consumed in the United States came from Mexico, Holcomb stated – "If people are smoking Washington marijuana, isn't that better than smoking Mexican marijuana?" (Keefe, 2013).

Criminal justice system costs

As noted above, one of the primary foci of supporters of I-502 in Washington State was the criminal justice system costs associated with the enforcement of marijuana laws. Before the passage of I-502, a single arrest and prosecution for a possession of marijuana case in Washington State was estimated to cost between \$1,000 and \$2,000 (in police, prosecutor and court expenses), and it was estimated that the state had spent \$200 million on the enforcement of marijuana laws over the 2000–2010 period (Drug Policy Alliance, 2015). Data from Washington State's administrative office of the courts indicated that the law was having its intended effect with respect to this issue – in 2011, prior to the passage of I-502, there were 6,879 low-level court filings in the state, compared to only 120 in 2015 (Drug Policy Alliance, 2018), and the number of marijuana convictions in Washington decreased by 76 percent over the same period (7,303 to 1,723).

Although more current data on low-level marijuana court filings were not available at the time of writing, a report on trends in felony cannabis convictions in Washington State also showed significant declines. The report noted that between June 2008 and December 2009, there were 1,312 offenses that resulted in felony sentences for manufacture, delivery or possession with intent to deliver marijuana. However, during the 18-month period following the opening of recreational marijuana stores in the state, there were only 147 marijuana-related crimes that resulted in felony-level sentences (Jenkins, 2018). Related, although concerns that crime would increase under marijuana legalization was not a major theme of those opposed to legalization, it is notable that it was associated with a significant reduction of rape and theft arrests in Washington State (Dragone, Prarolo, Vanin and Zanella, 2018). In addition, Makin, Willits and Wu (2018) report that, post-legalization, for some types of crimes, clearance rates have improved.

Tax revenues

Another theme emphasized in the I-502 campaign was that Washington State would see significant tax revenues from marijuana legalization – and the revenues collected have exceeded initial projections. Since the commencement of recreational sales on July 8, 2014, the state has collected close to \$1 billion in tax revenues from marijuana sales – in fiscal year 2017, the state collected \$314.8 million, which was 26 percent more than predicted (Washington

State Liquor and Cannabis Board, 2018; Whittenberg, 2018). The state allocates these revenues to substance abuse education and treatment programs, and the largest proportion is allocated to the state's share of Medicaid. It is important to stress that Washington State collected zero tax revenue on marijuana sales prior to legalization.

Conclusion

Washington State's legalization of recreational marijuana, while not without problems, has largely been a success. Predictions regarding massive increases in youth marijuana use and significant increases in marijuana-related traffic collisions and fatalities have simply not manifested. While diversion of marijuana from the state's legal production facilities is likely occurring, there is no evidence to suggest that this is a huge problem. In addition, one of the primary goals of the legislation, a reduction in the number of arrests for marijuana offenses, with attendant social justice benefits, has largely been realized. Finally, the state has collected significant tax revenues from marijuana legalization – revenues that the state was unable to access when marijuana was prohibited. While we recognize that these legalization outcomes are specific to Washington State and are relatively short-term, we feel confident in concluding that "marijuana has been legalized, and the sky has not fallen."

Notes

1 Subbaraman and Kerr (2017) report that support for marijuana legalization has continued to increase in Washington State, reaching 78 percent as of April 2016.
2 In addition to outright bans on marijuana sales, several jurisdictions have implemented reduced buffer zones, enacted local zoning regulations, and/or limited the number of retail marijuana business/licenses/stores at a number below what the Liquor and Cannabis Board allows (Municipal Research and Services Center, 2018).
3 On January 4, 2018 (interestingly, only three days after sales of recreational marijuana in California commenced), (then) Attorney General Jeff Sessions rescinded the Cole Memorandum, stating "Given the Department's [of Justice] well-established general principles, previous nationwide specific guidance specific to marijuana enforcement is rescinded, effective immediately" (Sessions, 2018). At the time of writing, no large-scale federal actions had been initiated against marijuana in states where it is legal.
4 There is considerable disagreement regarding whether the cognitive deficits and IQ decline reported in studies on the issue is a direct result of marijuana use, or instead attributable to confounding factors and methodological problems (Rogeberg, 2013). In addition, several other studies on the issue have not reported similar results (Auer, Vittinghof, Kuzi, Kertesz, Levine, Albanese, Whitmer, Jacobs, Sidney, Glymour and Fletcher, 2016; Bava, Jacobus, Thayer and Tapert, 2013; Fried, Watkinson, James and Gray, 2002; Jackson, Isen, Khoddam, Irons, Tuublad, Iacono, McGue, Raine, and Baker, 2016; Mokrysz, Landy, Gage, Nuanto, Roiser and Curran, 2016).

5 In Washington State, there have been increases in "cannabis exposure" calls to poison control centers. In 2017, there were 378 such calls, an increase of 23 percent compared to 2016, with the largest increase for ages 0–5, which increased by 57.6 percent (from 52 to 82) (Segawa, 2018). However, Washington State's Liquor and Cannabis Board Public Health Education Liaison Mary Segawa's brief report on this issue was not as alarmist as many others – she noted that "overall [cannabis exposure] calls to the Poison Control Center are relatively low" (Segawa, 2018). Also, in considering data from emergency room visits and poison control centers, it is important to stress that these may simply be "reporting" increases – that is, parents may be more willing to take their children who have been exposed to marijuana products to emergency departments and/or poison control centers due to the fact that the normalization and legalization of marijuana may be leading to increases in people telling the truth. In addition, increases in reports may have been associated with the Liquor and Cannabis Board's decision to add the Washington State Poison Control Center number to edible packaging in 2017.

6 Coverage and participation rates in the Washington State Healthy Youth Survey are high. For example, in the 2016 survey, of the randomly selected schools asked to participate, about 94 percent of Grade 8 schools, 95 percent of Grade 10 schools, and 97 percent of Grade 12 schools took part in the survey. All students were eligible to participate in the survey, and an estimated 80 percent of Grade 8 students, 70 percent of Grade 10 students, and 49 percent of Grade 12 students took part. In total, 198 schools and 36,809 students participated in the statewide sample, and an additional 943 schools and 195,203 students participated as non-sampled schools in the 2016 survey (Washington State Healthy Youth Survey, 2017).

7 Due to a low number of students from certain racial/ethnic groups responding to the survey, data for Benton County, the tenth largest in Washington State, were suppressed.

8 In the Washington State Healthy Youth Survey, perceptions of harm from marijuana use was measured with the question "How much do you think people harm themselves if they use marijuana regularly (at least once or twice per week)?" The response options were "possibly not risky," and "great risk."

9 Analyses of data on the relationship between marijuana consumption and involvement in collisions/traffic fatalities also need to take into account the relationship between risky driving-related behaviors, marijuana consumption, gender and age. Compton and Benning (2015) note that in general, male drivers are more likely to be involved in collisions than female drivers, and younger drivers have higher crash risks than do older drivers. And given that males and younger people are more likely to consume both alcohol and marijuana, these demographic factors may explain some of the increased risk of collision associated with drug use (see also Johnson, 2017; Rogeberg and Elvik, 2016).

10 Dr. Hoff has generously provided permission for us to quote her; however, it is important to stress that this does not constitute an endorsement of our views on the relationship between cannabis consumption and driving.

11 Under a bill proposed in early 2017, Washington residents would be allowed to grow up to six plants. In addition, in revisions to Washington State's cannabis law passed in the spring of 2017, the Liquor and Cannabis Board was charged with conducting a study of options for "the legalization of marijuana plant possession and cultivation by recreational marijuana users" (Washburn, 2017). However, at the time of writing, no changes in the rules regarding cultivation had occurred.

References

Auer, R., Vittinghof, E., Kuzi, A., Kertesz, S., Levine, D., Albanese, E., Whitmer, B, Jacobs, D. Sidney, S., Glymour, N. and Fletcher, M. (2016). Association between lifetime marijuana use and cognitive function in middle age – The Coronary Artery Risk Development in Young Adults (CARDIA) study. *JAMA Internal Medicine*, 176, 352–361.

Aydelotte, J., Brown, L., Luftman, K., Mardock, A., Texeira, P, Coopwood, B. and Brown, C. (2017). Crash fatality rates after recreational marijuana legalization in Washington and Colorado. *American Journal of Public Health*, 107(8), 1329–1331.

Bachhuber, M., Saloner, B., Cunningham, C. and Barry, C. (2014). Medical cannabis laws and opioid analgesic overdose mortality in the United States, 1990–2010. *JAMA Internal Medicine*, 174, 1668–1673.

Bava, S., Jacobus, J., Thayer, R. and Tapert, S. (2013). Longitudinal changes in white matter integrity among adolescent substance users. *Alcoholism: Clinical and Experimental Research*, E181–189.

Bose, J., Hedden, S., Lipari, R. and Park-Lee, E. (2018). *Key substance use and mental health indicators in the United States: Results from the 2017 National Survey on Drug Use and Health*. Substance Abuse and Mental Health Services Administration. Retrieved from www.samhsa.gov/data/report/2017-nsduh-annual-national-report.

Bradford, A. and Bradford, D. (2016). Medical marijuana laws reduce prescription medication use in Medicare part d population. *Health Affairs*, 35, 1230–1236.

Bradford, A. and Bradford, D. (2017). Medical marijuana laws may be associated with a decline in the number of prescriptions for Medicaid enrollees. *Health Affairs*, 36, 945–951.

Bradford, A., Bradford, W., Abraham, A. and Adams, G. (2018). Association between US state medical cannabis laws and opioid prescribing in the Medicare part d population. *JAMA Internal Medicine*, 178, 667–672.

Bush, E. (2018). Is Washington marijuana ending up where it shouldn't? Industry ripe for 'diversion', some say. *Tacoma News Tribune*. Retrieved from www.thenewstribune.com.

Cambron, C., Guttmanova, K. and Fleming, C. (2017). State and national contexts in evaluating cannabis laws: A case study of Washington State. *Journal of Drug Issues*, 47, 74–90.

Cerdá, M., Wall, M., Fena, T., Keyes, K., Sarvet, A., Schulenberg, J., O'Malley, P., Pacula, R., Galea, S. and Hasin, D. (2017). Association of state recreational marijuana laws with adolescent marijuana use. *JAMA Pediatrics*, 171, 142–149.

Clark County. (2012). *State of Washington and Clark County voter's pamphlet*. Retrieved from www.clark.wa.gov.

Cole, J. (2013). *Memorandum for all United States attorneys: Guidance regarding marijuana enforcement*. Washington, D.C: Office of the Attorney General.

Collingwood, L., O'Brien, B. and Dreier, S. (2018). Evaluating ballot initiative support for legalized marijuana: The case of Washington. *International Journal of Drug Policy*, 56, 6–20.

Columbian. (2014). *Marijuana for sale*. Retrieved from www.columbian.com.

Compton, R. (2017). *Marijuana-impaired driving – A report to Congress*. Washington, D.C: US Department of Transportation.

Compton, R. and Benning, A. (2015). *Drugs and alcohol crash risk*. US Department of Transportation.

Coughlin-Bogue, T. (2017). Washington's legal pot experiment: Can it survive Trump? *Truthout*. Retrieved from www.truth-out.org.

Darnell, A. and Bitney, K. (2017). *I-502 evaluation and cost benefit analysis. Second required report*. Olympia, WA: Washington State Institute for Public Policy.

Dilley, J., Hitchcock, L., McGrader, N., Greto, L. and Richardson, S. (2017). Community-level responses to state marijuana legalization in Washington State. *International Journal of Drug Policy*, 42, 102–108.

Dragone, D., Prarolo, G., Vanin, P. and Zanella, G. (2018). Crime and the legalization of recreational marijuana. *Journal of Economic Behavior and Organization*. Retrieved from www.sciencedirect.com/science/article/pii/S0167268118300386.

Drug Policy Alliance. (2015). *Marijuana legalization in Washington after 1 year of retail sales and 2.5 years of legal possession*. Retrieved from www.drugpolicy.org.

Drug Policy Alliance. (2016). *So far, so good – What we know about marijuana legalization in Colorado, Washington, Alaska, Oregon, and Washington, D.C.* Retrieved from www.drugpolicy.org.

Drug Policy Alliance. (2018). *From prohibition to progress: A status report on marijuana legalization*. Retrieved from www.drugpolicy.org.

Englund, N.M., Siebenbruner, J., Oliva, M., Egeland, B., Chung, C. and Long, J. (2013). The developmental significance of late adolescent substance use for early adult functioning. *Developmental Psychology*, 49, 1554–1564.

Ferguson, B. (2014). *Whether statewide initiative establishing system for licensing marijuana producers, processors, and retailers preempts local ordinances*. Retrieved from www.atg.wa.gov.

Ferguson, B. (2015). Cities and counties have the right to ban the sale of marijuana. *Seattle Times*. Retrieved from www.seattletimes.com.

Fleming, C., Guttmanova, K., Cambron, C., Rhew, I. and Oesterle, S. (2016). Examination of the divergence in trends for adolescent marijuana use and marijuana-specific risk factors in Washington State. *Journal of Adolescent Health*, 59, 269–275.

Fried, P., Watkinson, B., James, D. and Gray, R. (2002). Current and former marijuana use: Preliminary findings of a longitudinal study of effects on IQ in young adults. *Canadian Medical Association Journal*, 167, 887–891.

Garber, A. and Miletich, S. (2011). Former U.S. Attorney McKay backs effort to legalize pot in Washington State. *Seattle Times*. Retrieved from www.seattletimes.com.

Gilman, J., Kusler, J., Lee, S., Lee, M., Kim, B., Makris, N., van der Kouwe, A., Blood, A. and Breiter, H. (2014). Cannabis use is quantitatively associated with nucleus accumbens and amygdala abnormalities in young adult recreational users. *The Journal of Neuroscience*, 34, 5529–5538.

Graf, T. (2014). Commissioners ban recreational marijuana facilities outside city limits. *Columbian*. Retrieved from www.columbian.com.

Grimley, B. (2016). Pierce county ban on pot businesses vetoed by county executive. *The News Tribune*. Retrieved from www.thenewstribune.com.

Hari, J. (2015). *Chasing the scream – The first and last days of the war on drugs*. New York: Bloomsbury.

Harshman, M. (2017). Pot merger gets mixed reviews. *Columbian*. Retrieved from www.columbian.com.

Hoff, S. (2017). Personal correspondence with C. Mosher.

Holden, D. (2012). The Sheriff and his opponent fight over who wants to legalize pot more. *The Stranger*. Retrieved from www.thestranger.com.

Honig, D. (2012). *Support for I-502 is bursting out all over*. American Civil Liberties Union of Washington. Retrieved from www.aclu-wa-org.

Ingraham, C. (2016). What happened in Washington State after voters legalized recreational marijuana. *The Washington Post*. Retrieved from https://washingtonpost.com/news/wonk/wp/2016/12/29/what-happened-in-washington-state-after-voters-legalized-recreational-weed/

Ingraham, C. (2017a). A big thing marijuana opponents warned you about is definitely not happening. *Washington Post*. Retrieved from www.washingtonpost.com.

Ingraham, C. (2017b). What marijuana legalization did to car accident rates. *Washington Post*. Retrieved from www.washingtonpost.com.

Insurance Institute for Highway Safety. (2017). *Legalizing recreational marijuana is linked to increased crashes*. Retrieved from www.iihs.org.

Jackson, N., Isen, J., Khoddam, R., Irons, D., Tuublad, C., Iacono, W., McGue, M., Raine, A. and Baker, L. (2016). Impact of adolescent marijuana use on intelligence: Results from two longitudinal twin studies. *Proceedings of the National Academy of Sciences*, 113, E500–508.

Jenkins, A. (2018). *Felony cannabis convictions in Washington down significantly since legalization*. Oregon Public Broadcasting. Retrieved from www.opb.org.

Johnson, G. (2011). States' effort to legalize pot faces legal pitfalls. *Associated Press*. Retrieved from www.ap.org.

Johnson, T. (2017). Young millennials to list of worst behaved drivers. *AAA Newsroom*. Retrieved from www.newsroom.aaa.com.

Keefe, P. (2013). Washington State discovers that it's not so easy to create a legal marijuana economy. *New Yorker*. Retrieved from www.newyorker.com.

Kiley, B. (2015). Washington is the only state with legal marijuana that doesn't allow home grows. *The Stranger*. Retrieved from www.thestranger.com.

Leon, K. and Weitzer, R. (2014). Legalizing recreational marijuana: Comparing ballot outcomes in four states. *Journal of Qualitative Criminal Justice and Criminology*, 2, 193–218.

Livingston, M., Barnett, T., Delcher, C. and Wagenaar, A. (2017). Recreational cannabis legalization and opioid-related deaths in Colorado, 2000–2015. *American Journal of Public Health*, 107, 1827–1829.

Lucas, P., Reiman, A., Earleyewine, M., McGowan, S., Oleson, M., Coward, M. and Thomas, B. (2013). Cannabis as a substitute for alcohol and other drugs: A dispensary-based survey of substitution effect in Canadian medical cannabis patients. *Addiction Research and Theory*, 21, 425–422.

Lucas, P., Walsh, Z., Crosby, K., Callaway, R., Belle-Isle, L., Kay, R., Capler, R. and Holtzman, S. (2016). Substituting cannabis for prescription drugs, alcohol, and other substances among medical cannabis patients: The impact of contextual factors. *Drug and Alcohol Review*, 25, 326–333.

Makin, D., Willits, D. and Wu, G. (2018). Marijuana legalization and crime clearance rates: Testing proponent assertions in Colorado and Washington State. *Police Quarterly*, 22(1), 31–55.

Martin, J. (2012). Children's alliance backs pot measure on ballot. *Seattle Times*. Retrieved from www.seattletimes.com.

Martin, A. and Rashidian, N. (2014). *A new leaf – The end of cannabis prohibition.* New York: The New Press.
McCarthy, P. (2016). *Dear Chair Richardson.* Retrieved from www.co.pierce,wa.us/DocumentCenter/View/42379.
Meier, M., Caspi, A., Ambler, A., Harrington, H., Houts, R., Keefe, R., McDonald, K., Ward, A., Poulton, R. and Moffitt, T. (2012). Persistent cannabis users show neuropsychological decline from childhood to midlife. *Proceedings of the National Academy of Sciences*, 109, E2657-E2664.
Miller, A., Rosenman, R. and Cowan, B. (2017). Recreational marijuana legalization and college student use: Early evidence. *SSM-Population Health*, 3, 649–657.
Miron, J. (2017). This economist has a strategy to kill the marijuana black market. *Denver Post.* Retrieved from www.denverpost.com.
Mkrtchyan, V. (2012). Initiative 692, now and then: The past, present, and future of medical marijuana in Washington State. *Gonzaga University Law Review*, 47, 839–876.
Mokrysz, C., Landy, R., Gage, S., Nuanto, M., Roiser, J. and Curran, H. (2016). Are IQ and educational outcomes in teenagers related to their cannabis use? A prospective cohort study. *Journal of Psychopharmacology*, 30, 159–168.
Morton, N. (2018). Washington State's high school graduation rate holds steady at 79%. *Seattle Times.* Retrieved from www.seattletimes.com.
Mosher, C. and Akins, S. (2014). *Drugs and drug policy – The control of consciousness alteration.* Thousand Oaks, CA: Sage Publications.
Mosher, C. and Akins, S. (In press). *In the weeds – Demonization, legalization, and the evolution of U.S. marijuana policy.* Philadelphia: Temple University Press.
Mosher, C., Miethe, T. and Hart, T. (2011). *The mismeasure of crime.* Thousand Oaks, CA: Sage Publications.
Municipal Research and Services Center. (2018). *Marijuana regulation in Washington State.* Retrieved from http://mrsc.org/Home/Explore-Topics/Legal/Regulation/Marijuana-Regulation-in-Washington-State.aspx.
National Highway Traffic Safety Administration. (n.d.). *Drug and human performance fact sheet – Cannabis.* Retrieved from www.nhtsa.gov.
Neavyn, M., Blohm, E., Babo, K. and Bird, S. (2014). Medical marijuana and driving: A review. *Journal of Medical Toxicology*, 10, 269–279.
Northwest High Intensity Drug Trafficking Area. (2016). *Washington State marijuana impact report.*
Nutt, D., King, L., Saulsbury, W. and Blakemore, C. (2007). Development of a rational scale to assess the harms of drugs. *The Lancet*, 369, 1047–1053.
Onders, B., Casavant, M., Spiller, H., Chounthriath, T. and Smith, G. (2016). Marijuana exposure among children younger than six years in the United States. *Clinical Pediatrics*, 55, 428–436.
Oregon State Police. (2017). *A baseline evaluation of cannabis enforcement priorities in Oregon.* Salem, OR: Oregon State Police.
Piper, B.J., De Keuster, R., Beals, M., Cobb, C., Buchman, C., Perkinson, L., Lynn, S., Nichols, S. and Abess, A. (2017). Substitution of medical cannabis for pharmaceutical agents for pain, anxiety, and sleep. *Journal of Psychopharmacology*, 31, 569–575.
Reiman, A. (2009). Cannabis as a substitute for alcohol and other drugs. *Harm Reduction Journal*, 6, 35.

Rocky Mountain High Intensity Drug Trafficking Area. (2015). *The legalization of marijuana in Colorado – The impact*. Rocky Mountain High Intensity Drug Trafficking Area.

Roffman, R. (2014). *Marijuana nation*. New York: Pegasus Books.

Rogeberg, O. (2013). Correlations between cannabis use and IQ change in the Dunedin cohort are consistent with confounding from socioeconomic status. *Proceedings of the National Academy of Sciences*, 110, 4251–4254.

Rogeberg, O. and Elvik, R. (2016). The effects of cannabis intoxication on motor vehicle collision revisited and revised. *Addiction*, 111, 1348–1359.

Santos, M. (2017). Plan would punish cities with unofficial pot bans by taking their liquor money. *The News Tribune*. Retrieved from www.thenewstribune.com.

Sarvet, A., Wall, M., Fink, D., Green, E., Le, A. Boustead, A., Pacula, R., Keyes, K., Cerda, M., Galea, S. and Hasin, D. (2018). Medical marijuana laws and adolescent marijuana use in the United States: A systematic review and meta-analysis. *Addiction*, 113, 1003–1016.

Seattle Times. (2012). Editorial: Approve Initiative 502 – It's time to legalize, regulate, and tax marijuana. *Seattle Times*. Retrieved from www.seattletimes.com.

Segawa, M. (2018). *Safeguarding others, safeguarding your business*. Washington State Liquor and Cannabis Board.

Selsky, A. (2017). Legal marijuana states try to curb interstate smuggling to fend off feds. *Associated Press*. Retrieved from www.ap.org.

Sessions, J. (2018). *Memorandum for all United States attorneys – Marijuana enforcement*. Washington, D.C: Office of the Attorney General.

Sevigny, E. (2018). The effects of medical marijuana laws on cannabis-involved driving. *Accident Analysis and Prevention*, 118, 57–65.

Sewell, A., Poling, J. and Sofuoglo, M. (2009). The effect of cannabis compared with alcohol on driving. *The American Journal on Addictions*, 18, 185–193.

Shapiro, N. (2012). Alison Holcomb – Pot mama. *Seattle Weekly*. Retrieved from www.seattleweekly.com.

Shi, Y. (2017). Medical marijuana policies and hospitalizations related to marijuana and opioid pan reliever. *Drug and Alcohol Dependence*, 173,144–150.

Subbaraman, M. and Kerr, W. (2017). Support for marijuana legalization in the U.S. state of Washington has continued to increase through 2016. *Drug and Alcohol Dependence*, 175, 205–209.

Substance Abuse and Mental Health Services Administration. (1999). *Treatment of adolescents with substance use disorders*. Retrieved from www.samhsa.gov.

Tefft, B. (2016). *Prevalence of marijuana involvement in fatal crashes, 2010–2014*. Washington, D.C: American Automobile Association.

Wang, G., Narana, S., Wells, K. and Chuang, R. (2011). A case series of marijuana exposures in pediatric patients less than 5 years of age. *Child Abuse and Neglect*, 35, 5563–5565.

Wang, G., Roosevelt, G. and Heard, K. (2013). Pediatric marijuana exposures in a medical marijuana state. *JAMA Pediatrics*, 167, 630–633.

Wang, G., Le Lait, M., Deakyne, S., Bronstein, A., Bajal, L. and Roosevelt, G. (2016). Unintentional pediatric exposures to marijuana in Colorado, 2009–2015. *JAMA Pediatrics*, 170.

Washburn, P. (2017). Here's what just changed in Washington State marijuana laws. *Denver Post*. Retrieved from www.denverpost.com.

Washington State Department of Health. (2018). *Medical marijuana*. Retrieved from www.doh.wa.gov.

Washington State Healthy Youth Survey. (2017). *2016 Analytic Report*. Retrieved from www.doh.wa.gov/Portals/1/Documents/Pubs/160-193-HYS-AnalyticReport 2016.pdf.

Washington State Liquor and Cannabis Board. (2018a). *Marijuana dashboard*. Retrieved from www.lcb.wa.gov.

Washington State Liquor and Cannabis Board. (2018b). *Annual report – Fiscal year 2017*. Retrieved from www.lcb.wa.gov.

Washington State Senate. (n.d.). *History of Washington State marijuana laws*. Retrieved from www.leg.wa.gov/senate.

Washington State Traffic Safety Commission. (2018). *Marijuana use, alcohol use, and driving in Washington State*. Retrieved from http://wtsc.wa.gov/wp-content/uploads/2018/04/Marijuana-and-Alcohol-Involvement-in-Fatal-Crashes-in-WA_FINAL.pdf.

Wen, H. and Hockenberry, J. (2018). Association of medical and adult-use marijuana laws with opioid prescribing for Medicaid enrollees. *JAMA Internal Medicine*, 178, 673–679.

Westneat, D. (2012). King County Sheriff makes case for pot. *Seattle Times*. Retrieved from www.seattletimes.com.

Whittenberg, J. (2018). *Where does Washington's marijuana tax money go?* Retrieved from www.king5news.com.

Wilson, R. (2014). Legal pot faces myriad obstacles. *Washington Post*. Retrieved from www.washingtonpost.com.

Young. B. (2016). Minorities, punished most by war on drugs, underrepresented in legal pot. *Seattle Times*. Retrieved from www.seattletimes.com.

4 A century of cannabis control in Canada

A brief overview of history, context and policy frameworks from prohibition to legalization

Benedikt Fischer, Cayley Russell and Neil Boyd

Introduction

Canada offers a notable global case study in the area of drug, and specifically cannabis, policy and control. While traditionally under strong influence from its immediate sole neighbor to the South, the United States, psychoactive substance control, including cannabis, in Canada has long been dominated by a paradigm of prohibition. However, this approach has gradually changed in recent decades, with incremental shifts towards more health and/or liberal policy approaches. While cannabis policy reform has been discussed for several decades in Canada, initial material changes came through the implementation of federal "medical cannabis" access provisions at the beginning of the twentieth century. These changes would gradually culminate in the seminal establishment of a national policy framework for the legalization of non-medical cannabis use and supply – the first in a G7 country – implemented in October 2018. In this chapter, we present key steps, context and parameters of Canadian cannabis control policy leading up to the legalization of non-medical cannabis use and supply in October 2018, in both a historical and contemporary perspective.

Cannabis control in Canada – early history

Cannabis control has been the subject of a turbulent, century-long history in Canada. This history begins with growing socio-political concern and attention related to – largely United States (US)-driven – "reefer madness" and corresponding anti-marijuana propaganda in the early 1900s (Giffen, Endicott and Boorman, 1991; Solomon, Single and Erickson, 1983). This occurred during a period which included both the proliferation and expansion of a domestic drug prohibition and enforcement apparatus (initially focused on opium), as well as the establishment of international drug control treaties (e.g. including the 1912 Hague International Opium and the 1925 Geneva Conventions which comprised the criminalization of cannabis in its scope) (Bewley-Taylor, Blickman and Jelsma, 2014; Carstairs, 2006). A crucial evolution amidst those developments in Canada was that – without much evidence of common cannabis-related problems or political debate – cannabis was included in the schedule of the then Canadian drug control law, the Opium and Other Drugs Act of 1923, next to various other drugs (Giffen et al., 1991; Solomon et al., 1983). The only mention the new law received in Canada's Parliament was the statement, "There is a new drug in the schedule." This law included severe penalties, including possible incarceration for simple possession offenses. However, in the decades immediately following, little, if any, attention was paid to cannabis-related policy or enforcement, while opium/opioids (e.g. heroin) and cocaine use and distribution were the primary focus (Giffen et al., 1991; Solomon and Green, 1988).

This picture changed, suddenly, in the mid-1960s. There and then, in the wider socio-political contexts of the "counterculture" (i.e. the popular anti-establishment movement in opposition of dominant power structures and ideologies, including those behind illicit drug laws), marijuana use became increasingly common in Canada, especially among young, educated and largely middle-class groups (including post-secondary students), while attention to other forms of illicit drug use diminished (Giffen et al., 1991; Solomon et al., 1983). Rising cannabis use was likely also spurred by developments of globalization in the 1960s, including increases in international travel and communication, and the consequent contact of youth with different cultures and lifestyles, including drug use.

The national drug enforcement system – now predominantly operated by the federal Royal Canadian Mounted Police (RCMP) for whom drug enforcement had become a main organizational *raison d'etre* – began to make quickly increasing numbers of cannabis-related arrests (mostly involving consumers) (Bryan, 1979; Carstairs, 2006). For example, arrests for simple cannabis possession increased from approximately 1,500 in 1969 to nearly 65,000 by the end of the following decade (Bryan, 1979; Dion, 1999; Statistics Canada, 2015). With most people being unaware of the drug control law's punitive provisions, and the potential legal consequences of a cannabis-related offense, tens of thousands of Canadians suddenly found themselves with either a conviction (e.g. typically including a fine as the penalty) or some form of discharge, both of which, however, resulted in a criminal record and thus rendered the convicted individual a "criminal" (Bryan, 1979; Giffen et al., 1991). Within a few years, cannabis had become Canada's predominant illicit drug both in terms of use and enforcement (Fischer, Ala-Leppilampi, Single and Robins, 2003).

Amidst wider challenges and questions about the actual harms associated with cannabis use arising in the 1960s, there was increasing socio-political controversy about the appropriateness, as well as the effectiveness and adverse consequences, of repressive cannabis control, including the broad-scale criminalization of primarily large numbers of young people (Giffen et al., 1991; Solomon and Green, 1988). This controversy reached and concerned highest political levels, including the federal government, catalyzing the establishment of the federal Commission of Inquiry into the Non-Medical Use of Drugs – or the Le Dain Commission for short, named after its Chairman, the Honorable Judge Gerald Le Dain – which began its work in 1969 (Erickson and Smart, 1988). The Le Dain Commission conducted a comprehensive, multi-year inquiry into the nature and harms of illegal substances and was to present the best options for interventions and policy alternatives going forward (Le Dain Commission, 1972). In its separate *Cannabis Report* (Le Dain Commission, 1972), the Commission essentially concluded that cannabis, compared to other prohibited drugs like heroin or cocaine, was a relatively innocuous substance, and that especially personal use should not be subject to criminal or other punitive consequences, which it considered more harmful than the direct risks of the drug (Le Dain Commission, 1972). Notably, the Le Dain Commission's recommendations concerning revised cannabis control can overall be read as a vision advocating for non-criminal and public health-oriented cannabis reform, although, one that evidently came far before its rightful time (Fischer et al., 2003).

Similar inquiries or commissions into cannabis use and control options were held in other Anglo-Saxon countries (e.g. the United Kingdom, US, Australia) around the same time, yet the tangible implications for the state of cannabis law and policy in Canada were virtually nil (European Monitoring Centre for Drugs and Drug Addiction (EMCDDA), 2008; Fischer et al., 2003). The drug law of the day (the Narcotic Control Act (NCA), established 1961) remained broad and punitive in scope, and drug-related arrests continued to increase, with cannabis-related "simple possession" (i.e. typically "use"-related) offenses consistently accounting for about half of annual NCA-based arrests reported in the years following (Fischer et al., 2003). The post-Le Dain Commission years saw numerous political declarations of intent (e.g. in the platforms of federal parties, but usually only when in opposition), as well as a Senate-sponsored bill (S-19; 1974) in favor of liberalization of cannabis use control (Fischer et al., 2003; Giffen et al., 1991). These efforts, however, largely subsided with the renewal of the "war on drugs" under the Reagan administration in the US in the 1980s, and the – supposedly "softer" – Canadian iteration or copy thereof under the federal Conservative Mulroney government (Fischer, 1999; Fischer et al., 2003). A select and minor exception came in the form of an "update" of the federal drug control law which would eventually culminate in Canada's current drug legislation, The Controlled Drugs and Substances Act (CDSA)," implemented in 1996 (Fischer, Erickson and Smart, 1996). The CDSA separated cannabis from other illicit drugs, placing "cannabis, its preparations and derivatives" in a separate schedule, with modest reductions in penalties for select offenses. This update concretely changed the way simple cannabis possession was controlled, where, under the CDSA, first-time offenses of small possession amounts would be handled as a "summary conviction" only, which restricted possible maximum sentences, yet implied no changes in terms of its criminal conviction or record consequences (Fischer et al., 2003).

Recent twenty-first century developments

The issue of possible cannabis control reform in Canada was revisited around the turn of the century. This happened, also, in the context of continuously rising cannabis use rates in the Canadian population. For example, the rate of current (past year) cannabis use almost doubled in the general population (e.g. from about 8 percent in 1994 to 15 percent in 2004) (Canadian Centre on Substance Abuse (CCSA) and Health Canada, 2004); similar or even more pronounced increases were observed for young adults, e.g. 18–29 years of age (Ialomiteanu, Hamilton, Adlaf and Mann, 2016). A couple of – parallel – federal parliamentary committee investigations based in the respective lower and upper chambers (the House of Commons and the Senate) of the Canadian parliament tabled tangible recommendations concerning cannabis control reform options (Fischer et al., 2003). Concretely, the House of Commons Special Committee on the Non-Medical Use of Drugs, in 2002, recommended that cannabis use remain illegal, yet that the possession or cultivation of small amounts be "decriminalized" by designation of a "contravention" (i.e. a "civil offense" provision within federal Canadian law) within the existent drug control law (House of Commons Special Committee on Non-Medical Use of Drugs, 2002). The Committee, hence, essentially recommended the establishment of a non-criminal type of control system for personal cannabis use and supply similar to an "expiation notice" (i.e. civil penalty-based frameworks recently implemented in select Australian states) (Christie, 1999; Sutton and McMillan, 2000). Notably, the "Senate Special Committee on Illegal Drugs," established in 2001, went considerably further in its recommendations for change. It characterized cannabis as a relatively innocuous substance and concluded that criminalization was ineffective, and therefore recommended the legalization of personal cannabis use as well as the establishment of a legal and regulated supply system positively supported by law (Nolin and Kenny, 2002). At around that same time, also amidst gradual liberalization of cannabis control practice primarily in Europe, several key socio-political entities or organizations, including the Canadian Medical Association, the Canadian Association of Chiefs of Police, and editorial boards of leading Canadian media outlets, explicitly called for liberalized cannabis control (Blickman, 2014; Canadian Association of Chiefs of Police, 2004; Haddad, 2002). Most of these recommended "decriminalization" for the control of personal cannabis use. However, it was not always clear what this meant for key features or consequences of the envisaged legal provisions or enforcement practice (Hyshka, 2009).

These various socio-political "winds of change" dynamics triggered a series of government-sponsored draft "decriminalization" bills – now under a Liberal, centrist federal government – beginning in 2003 (Hyshka, 2009). These decriminalization bills provided for initial "personal possession" offenses of up to 15 grams of marijuana and 1 gram of hashish to be punishable by various amounts of limited fines (between \$100 – \$400) by way of a non-criminal "contravention" in the federal drug law (Raaflaub, 2004). Subsequent offenses would incur higher fines or could result in criminal charges at law enforcement's discretion, whereas penalties involving larger amounts remained subject to strict and extensive criminal penalties. Select iterations of the draft bill also included reduced fine options for "personal production" of cannabis (i.e. a limited number of plants) (Raaflaub, 2004). The initial decriminalization draft bills were substantially informed by a "policy options" paper for cannabis control reform tabled by a national working group comprised of pan-Canadian addiction policy experts, as well as recent cannabis policy reform developments abroad, including the then "expiation notice" systems implemented in several Australian states, which included similar key features to the proposed reform legislation in Canada (Single, Christie and Ali, 2000; Single, Fischer, Room, Poulin, Sawka, Thompson and Topp, 1998; Sutton and McMillan, 2000). Although various draft iterations of the proposed decriminalization bills sat with the federal parliamentary committee for several years, they never made it to final reading (Fischer et al., 2003; Hyshka, 2009). Thus, these cannabis law reform efforts – likely the closest Canada had come to tangible cannabis law reform up until then – remained incomplete, and abruptly ended at the time the sponsoring Liberal government was defeated in the 2006 federal election (Hyshka, 2009). The incoming Conservative government under Prime Minister Stephen Harper made it categorically clear that they were not going to resume or continue these unfinished efforts, in that they considered cannabis a harmful drug and did "not intend to legalize or decriminalize" it (Bryden, 2014).

In the meantime, and despite these supposed liberalizing political intentions for cannabis policy, Canada saw persistent – and expanding – focus of law enforcement on cannabis-related behaviors. While the overall crime rate in Canada continuously declined, the rate for cannabis offenses almost doubled, from 119/100,000 population in 1991 to >220/100,000 in 2010 (Brennan and Dauvergne, 2011; Dauvergne, 2009). In 2013, about three-quarters of drug offenses processed under the federal drug law were cannabis-related, whereas the large majority (>80 percent) of enforced cannabis offenses were for personal possession (Cotter, Greenland and Karam, 2015). A review of processing data demonstrated that large numbers of cannabis possession offenses in Canada were either never formally charged, or were diverted out of the criminal justice system (including alternative measures like "Conditional Sentencing" possibly including treatment orders) which led to interpretations that prohibition of use de facto was largely suspended in practice; however, most offenses still resulted in criminal procedures and dispositions (including criminal records) (Pauls, Plecas, Cohen and Haarhoff, 2012).

Medical cannabis: plant-based therapy or "side-door legalization"?

In the context of rapidly expanding discussions about putative "medical benefits" of cannabis use for a variety of severe illnesses, a series of high-profile cases involving constitutional challenges were adjudicated by higher courts in

Canada at the turn of the century (Fischer, Kuganesan and Room, 2015; Lucas, 2008). The claimants were mostly individuals afflicted by chronic illness, claiming that their ability to access and use cannabis for medical benefit was unduly infringed by the existing categorical prohibition of cannabis in Canada, violating constitutional rights under the Canadian Charter of Rights and Freedoms, including Section 7 of "right to life, liberty and security of the person." These cases resulted in several seminal legal decisions, some repealing existing cannabis control provisions, which crucially forced the Canadian government to establish a medical cannabis access program to remedy these constitutional deficiencies (Belle-Isle, Walsh, Callaway, Lucas, Capler, Kay and Holtzman, 2014; Fischer et al., 2015). These developments – which various government officials would later frame as a progressive policy choice – led to the establishment of Canada's initial Marihuana Medical Access Regulations (MMAR) in 2001. The MMAR was to become the first iteration of numerous successive versions of the federal medical cannabis access program, many of which were triggered by legal challenges or court decisions (Belle-Isle et al., 2014; Fischer et al., 2015). Moreover, the Canadian medical cannabis access program and its evolution – most of which occurred, notably, under a Conservative government with a declared anti-cannabis stance – paved the way and pre-shaped key features of foundations towards the general legalization of non-medical cannabis use and supply to come (Fischer et al., 2015; Kilmer and MacCoun, 2017).

Survey data at the time of the MMAR's launch suggested that there were up to a million "medical users" of cannabis in Canada (Fischer et al., 2015; Walsh, Callaway, Belle-Isle, Capler, Kay, Lucas and Holtzman, 2013). Under the MMAR, any person applying for authorization from the federal government to become sanctioned as a medical cannabis user – which meant exemption from cannabis use and supply restrictions under the criminal drug control law – required a physician's endorsement for benefits from a list of eligible chronic/severe illnesses (Belle-Isle et al., 2014; Walsh et al., 2013). Medical cannabis supply could either be obtained directly from the federal government (Health Canada), which for some time produced – based on anecdotal user accounts, rather inferior – cannabis in an abandoned mine in Manitoba, from self-production or from approved designated "growers" (Belle-Isle et al., 2014; Fischer et al., 2015). However, the application requirements and process for MMAR approvals were highly complex and onerous, and only a few hundred individuals were effectively approved as medical cannabis users under the program in its initial years (Belle-Isle et al., 2014; Fischer et al., 2015).

While the MMAR was continuously revised (e.g. in regards to its medical cannabis supply provision), and there were about 28,000 medical cannabis users formally approved about a decade after its implementation (2012), it continued to face substantial criticism (Belle-Isle et al., 2014; Walsh et al., 2013). Consequently, the federal government fundamentally reframed its medical cannabis access program, which was officially re-launched in revised form as the Marihuana for Medical Purposes Regulations (MMPR) in 2013

(Belle-Isle et al., 2014). Among several significant changes from the MMAR, Health Canada, as the federal government agency responsible until then, removed itself as the "authorizer" from the actual approval process for legitimate medical cannabis use. This process and role were now shifted to eligible healthcare professionals including, primarily, but not limited to, physicians. From these, prospective patients were required to obtain an "endorsement" (or a quasi-prescription) for medical cannabis use – now possible for virtually any health condition where the medical endorser saw and confirmed potential benefits to the user – as the decisive step for approval (Belle-Isle et al., 2014; Fischer et al., 2015). These arrangements entailed considerable controversy among medical professionals which continued to be fundamentally divided on the benefits, and especially their role as a "gatekeeper" for access to cannabis as an alleged "medicine," and only a minority of physicians would provide medical cannabis endorsements (Kahan and Srivastava, 2014; Ziemianski, Capler, Tekanoff, Lacasse, Luconi and Ware, 2015). Doubts concerning this approach were compounded by the fact that such "endorsements" could easily be obtained from a rapidly increasing number of community-based, or even virtual, cannabis "clinics" or "dispensaries" which had proliferated across Canada, where assessments were conducted and endorsements typically issued "on the spot" (Capler, Walsh, Crosby, Belle-Isle, Holtzman, Lucas and Callaway, 2017; Walsh et al., 2013).

Another new provision of the MMPR was that medical cannabis supply was now primarily to be obtained – through mail order/delivery upon endorsed user registration – from an emerging industry of so-called "Licensed Producers" (LPs) of medical cannabis products, as regulated and approved by the federal government (Government of Canada, 2018b). This provision meant, in essence, the formal beginning and establishment of a legitimate, government-regulated – and quickly expanding – commercial cannabis industry in Canada, ironically introduced by the "anti-cannabis" (but pro-business) Conservative government. These sanctioned paths of medical cannabis supply were challenged by the widespread proliferation of growing numbers of community-level "cannabis dispensaries," mostly in urban centers, including Vancouver and Toronto, where some neighborhoods came to allegedly house more dispensaries than coffee shops (Capler et al., 2017; Friscolanti, 2016; Walsh et al., 2013). These "dispensaries" technically ran illegal operations and distributed illegal cannabis products, yet became a common source of cannabis supply for both approved "medical" and other cannabis users (Belle-Isle et al., 2014; Friscolanti, 2016). Law enforcement conducted highly publicized raids on several dispensary operations in Toronto and other jurisdictions, but largely failed to take them out of business. The city of Vancouver decided, as of 2015, to regulate and license a select number of these dispensaries (amounting to about 90 such outlets by 2018) as part of the overall cannabis retail scheme and operate in a fairly well-integrated way with other community-based business (City of Vancouver, 2018).

Meanwhile, in the first year of the MMPR (2014), there were 6 LPs federally approved to produce and distribute medical cannabis products in Canada (Government of Canada, 2018b). In 2015, the federal government endorsed LPs to produce additional (i.e. non-dried) forms – including oils, and fresh marijuana parts used to make edible or topical products – of cannabis for distribution to approved medical users (Government of Canada, 2016). Resistance to the requirement of obtaining medical cannabis products from an LP led to yet another key court ruling in early 2016 (*R v. Allard*), requiring options for "self-growing" by approved users, as subsequently enshrined in the revised Access to Cannabis for Medical Purposes Regulations (ACMPR), implemented in 2016 (Government of Canada, 2016). By mid-2018, the number of approved medical cannabis users in Canada had increased to more than 300,000 – or the equivalent of >1 percent of the Canadian adult population (Government of Canada, 2018b). In a series of self-report surveys based on convenience samples of medical cannabis users, cited reasons for use included a large variety of physical and mental health reasons (including pain, arthritis, sleep or mood problems), many of which, however, included symptoms for which little or no substantive supporting evidence for therapeutic benefits of cannabis currently exists (Belle-Isle et al., 2014; Walsh et al., 2013; Whiting, Wolff, Deshpande, Di Nisio, Duffy, Hernandez and Kleijnen, 2015). At the same time, economic projections estimated the size of the medical cannabis product market in Canada to exceed $1 billion by 2020 (Deloitte, 2018); projections for the size of a possible legal market for non-medical use were $5 – $9 billion, or substantially larger than the value of the market for alcoholic spirits in Canada, with a multifold possible economic value when considering future global trade opportunities for cannabis products in other jurisdictions with existing or prospective medical access provisions, including Europe and Latin America (Deloitte, 2018).

Within just about a decade, Canada had witnessed the establishment of both an extensive and rapidly expanding legal cannabis industry as well as an extensive population of legal cannabis users, facilitated by a rapidly expanding "medical access" umbrella of federal policy, while supposed "recreational" cannabis use and production remained criminally illegal and selectively enforced by federal law for most of this time.

The way to "non-medical" cannabis legalization

It is arguably difficult to isolate one single, exact "causal" factor that *sine qua non* brought about the legalization of non-medical cannabis use and supply in Canada. Rather, a number of important, catalytic forces contributed to this paradigm shift in Canadian cannabis policy. A first was that, since 2012, recreational cannabis legalization had been implemented in select US states (initially Colorado, and subsequently Washington and others) (Hall and Lynskey, 2016; Pardo, 2014; Room, 2014). This major departure from prohibitionist cannabis control in parts of the US, Canada's large and influential neighbor – albeit initially only in select jurisdictions – strongly shaped public discourse on cannabis control in Canada (Mosher, 2011; Room, Fischer, Hall, Lenton and Reuter, 2010). This included extensive mass media reporting on many facets of cannabis legalization especially in the "pioneer state" of Colorado, and its overall "normalization" as an increasingly realistic policy option (Fischer, Lomiteanu, Russell, Rehm and Mann, 2016; Martinez, 2014; Room, 2014). Notably, the implementation of cannabis legalization as a national policy in Uruguay – a member state of the Americas to the South – received minimal attention in comparison (Arie, 2013; Walsh and Ramsey, 2016).

A further circumstantial factor was that, in late 2014, the Centre for Addiction and Mental Health (CAMH), Canada's largest addiction and psychiatric hospital with active engagement in policy development, released a "Cannabis Policy Framework" in which it weighed the pros and cons of different reform options for cannabis policy (Centre for Addiction and Mental Health (CAMH), 2014). While giving "decriminalization" options serious consideration, the CAMH Framework essentially concluded that the limitations or possible unintended adverse consequences of "decriminalization" – for example, ambivalent messaging, "net widening" effects of enforcement focusing on users, or the absence of comprehensive supply regulation – substantially compromised its overall intended benefits for public welfare (Centre for Addiction and Mental Health (CAMH), 2014; Crépault, Rehm and Fischer, 2016). On this basis, the CAMH Framework argued that under current conditions of the Canadian context, including high use levels especially among young people, "legalization with strict regulation" of cannabis use and supply would be the overall preferred and recommended policy option (Centre for Addiction and Mental Health (CAMH), 2014; Crépault et al., 2016; Rehm and Fischer, 2015). This was, of course, a strong and unexpected position in favor of "legalization" coming specifically from an organization with a principal footing and constituency in psychiatry – i.e. a field that commonly equates substance, and specifically cannabis use with "addiction" and psychiatric disorders, and is typically cautious towards more "liberal" approaches to psychoactive drug use. The position added to a pertinent tension in ongoing discussions on cannabis use and "psychosis" as an allegedly common consequence of cannabis use among young people (Haney and Evins, 2016).

Third, and perhaps most crucial and central, was the fact that leading up to the impending federal election in October 2015, headed by its newly anointed leader, Justin Trudeau, the Liberal Party had included "cannabis legalization" in its election platform. This, at the time, was considered a rather risky position with the popular electorate by some but underscored especially Trudeau's image as a progressive leader "in touch" with key, and especially younger, segments of the Canadian population. According to survey data, popular opinion was definitely on Trudeau's side. While popular support for de-penalizing cannabis control had consistently increased in Canada for numerous years, by 2014, about seven in ten Canadians indicated support for cannabis law reform, whereas about half of those in favor supported a "decriminalization" option, with the other half (about one-third of the population) explicitly supporting "legalization" as their preference (Kennedy, 2014). The move to turn to legalization as the new policy in Canada is history: on October 19, 2015, Trudeau's Liberal Party won the federal election in Canada with a landslide victory, and the new government soon began to develop an implementation plan for legalization as one of its key election promises, initially aimed for implementation by summer 2018.

The Canadian cannabis legalization framework

Without question, the development and implementation of the Canadian cannabis legalization framework constituted both an exceptional task and challenge, yet also a major balancing act for the federal government within the distinct realities of Canadian policy formation. This was, for one, because of the government's self-imposed, extremely tight timelines to deliver on the legalization framework within a couple of years of the election, yet also other key socio-political sensitivities related to the issue. While "medical cannabis access" policy had enjoyed broad popular support and existed politically in rather undisputed fashion in Canada, non-medical cannabis legalization in no way constituted a socio-political "shoo-in" issue but remained politicized and controversial (Slaughter, 2017). In addition, the federal government needed to address the (sensitive and constitutionally relevant) challenges of Canadian federalism for policy implementation, and specifically how it would reconcile the often conflicting powers and interests of federal and provincial (as well as municipal) jurisdictions towards the development of the "legalization" framework (Menard and Hartery, 2016; Task Force on Cannabis Legalization and Regulation, 2016). At the same time, many key parameters of "legalization" were already pre-decided or shaped by de facto realities of the existing federal "medical cannabis" provisions, and so limited policymakers' degree of options on several fronts (Fischer et al., 2015). For example, it was clear that the large and quickly increasing numbers of federally approved commercial cannabis producers (LPs) would be the suppliers of what was going to become one of the largest legal cannabis markets in the Western world (Collier, 2016; Task Force on Cannabis Legalization and Regulation, 2016). This was in contrast to options where, for example, the federal government could have created a government-run cannabis production or distribution monopoly.

Throughout, and since the announcement of legalization as a coming policy reality, the Canadian government emphasized that its intention was to develop a legalization framework that was anchored in "public health" principles and safeguards, and focused on strict regulation towards this end (Task Force on Cannabis Legalization and Regulation, 2016); this mantra also implied that the intent was to create a distinctly "Canadian" model of legalization, especially in comparison to corresponding realities in US states (e.g. Colorado) viewed primarily as individual liberties- and commercially-driven regimes (Hall and Lynskey, 2016; Kilmer and Pacula, 2016; Pardo, 2014). As an elementary part of its legalization framework development efforts, the federal government established a "Legalization Taskforce" in June 2016, comprised of nine individuals from different key areas of expertise, and chaired by Anne McLellan, a former Liberal cabinet minister – who had overseen the failed "decriminalization" law reform efforts for cannabis in early 2000s – and co-chaired by Dr. Mark Ware, a renowned pain clinician and medical cannabinoid expert (Task Force on Cannabis Legalization and Regulation, 2016). The task force conducted comprehensive cross-Canada community and stakeholder consultations on key details of the legalization plan and presented its report in December 2016 (Task Force on Cannabis Legalization and Regulation, 2016). The Task Force's report outlined numerous parameters grounded in consultation-based input received towards the shaping of a framework of "legalization with strict regulation" in Canada, intended to deliver on the promise of increasing public health and safety. These parameters, for example, included recommendations on age of use, advertisement, product availability restrictions as well as pricing and taxation for cannabis; for regulated production, provincially organized retail distribution as well as personal cultivation; restrictions on personal possession amounts and public use; the maintenance of a separate medical cannabis access system; and a systematic evaluation of the legalization policy following implementation (Task Force on Cannabis Legalization and Regulation, 2016).

On April 13, 2017, the federal government introduced the initial draft of the Cannabis Act (Bill C-45), the "legalization bill," for first reading in parliament (Aiello, 2018b). Essentially, Bill C-45 was a piece of legislation creating a "shield provision" of legalization that – on the basis of federal jurisdiction – would legally define and facilitate key aspects of non-medical cannabis use, production and distribution. Other aspects of cannabis or other illicit drug use, production, distribution etc., would remain prohibited or become subject to even stricter punishments (e.g. as defined by the federal drug law). Specific details of legal cannabis use or availability would be rendered subject to subordinate – primarily – provincial jurisdictions (Canadian Centre for Substance Abuse (CCSA), 2018b; Fraser, 2018). As key hallmarks, Bill C-45: restricted legal non-medical cannabis use to individuals aged 18 and over; limited retail distribution to legally approved sources (details to be regulated provincially) and mail distribution (controlled federally); allowed for "personal production" of four cannabis plants per household; and restricted cannabis product advertising, specifically, allowing licensed producers to brand their products and requiring them to include product information for consumer choice-making, yet not promote the use of products, especially to youths. Available products were initially limited to dried cannabis products (e.g. for smoking) and oils (Canadian Centre for Substance Abuse (CCSA), 2018b; Fraser, 2018). Plans for "edible" cannabis product availability were subsequently tabled for implementation in 2019, essentially allowing for products with a maximum of 10mg THC content per discrete product unit (Government of Canada, 2018c). Importantly, and recognizing their jurisdictional powers, the provinces were empowered to discretionarily impose further limitations on use, possession and retail distribution.

Bill C-45 was accompanied by Bill C-46, the Impaired Driving Act," a draft bill including new and modernized "per se" provisions for drug (including cannabis) impaired driving, ranging from strict fines for lower-level cannabis impairment (between 2 ng – 5 ng THC/ml blood) to potential imprisonment for repeat offenses and/or higher impairment levels (5 ng or more THC/ml blood) based on defined limits (Canadian Centre for Substance Abuse (CCSA), 2018a). A key additional novelty was that the bill allowed for – in many circles rather controversial – oral fluid (saliva testing) for THC metabolites as a new testing method for cannabis-related driver impairment which spawned considerable controversy in the law enforcement community, mostly in favor of "Drug-Recognition-Expert"-based testing and apprehension (Platt, 2018). Based on the new law, cannabis-impaired driving could be punished with a prison sentence of up to ten years, and result in life imprisonment when resulting in bodily harm in Canada (Canadian Centre for Substance Abuse (CCSA), 2018a; Platt, 2018). Bill C-46 – which was passed on June 20, 2018 – constituted a key element in the government's plan to take a "tough line" on select cannabis-related harms to others, while rendering the use and supply of the drug legal for individual of-age adults.

Meanwhile, Bill C-45 had undergone extensive committee hearings in both the Canadian House of Commons and the Senate. In these hearings, a number of different issues were predominant in the debates between committee members from different parties and invited expert witnesses. For example, a commonly reoccurring topic was whether cannabis should be legally available to, or used by, persons under 25 years of age; this challenge was typically raised in reference to the popular claim that cannabis use harmed the developing brain of youth and young adults into their mid-twenties (Jacobus and Tapert, 2014; Volkow, Baler, Compton and Weiss, 2014). Categorical opposition to legalization came supported by persistent arguments that "cannabis use caused mental health problems," especially psychosis, among young people, and therefore was to be considered a dangerous drug (Marconi, Di Forti, Lewis, Murray and Vassos, 2016; Murray and Di Forti, 2016). Select submissions questioned whether or how the government would fulfil its promise to "keep cannabis out of the hands of young people" under its proposed legalization regime. There were diverse submissions as to the restrictions on cannabis promotion and advertising, or how such restrictions could work or be enforced in the context of a commercially produced and retailed product (Barry and Glantz, 2016; Pacula, Kilmer, Wagenaar, Chaloupka and Caulkins, 2014). Ample input indicated that cannabis should not be legally co-available with alcohol, as this would increase co-use and related harm, even though no concrete evidence for these concerns was presented. Other submissions questioned whether "home growing" provisions of cannabis could effectively be regulated and had a place in a public health-oriented cannabis framework. There was strong emphasis on the need for effective prevention of cannabis use, as well as enforcement of cannabis-impaired driving, even though there was major disagreement on how to effectively bring it about (Canadian Centre for Substance Abuse (CCSA), 2018a; Platt, 2018). Overall, notably, many of the committee discussions still appeared to imply a sense of anxiety about possible sudden realities of legally-sanctioned cannabis use and availability, and that cannabis and its use continued to be dangerous in ways that suggested it would be better to keep them prohibited.

Committee hearings on Bill C-45, especially in the senate, were rather intense, and it was speculated that its Conservative faction would seek to instrumentalize the hearing process for ways to stop the bill, and possibly the political project of "cannabis legalization" entirely, or at least delay it substantially (Tasker, 2018). In the end, Bill C-45 received final reading and approval by the senate on June 7, 2018, including a total of about 40 – mostly minor – amendments over the revised draft bill version it had received from the government. Major amendments included a provision for provinces to discretionarily opt out of the "home grow" option, also serving the aim to protect against possible constitutional challenges, and more stringent restrictions on advertisement, including a ban on cannabis "swag" (e.g. promotional materials, like clothing) and a "social sharing offense" provision for young adults sharing small amounts of cannabis with minors (Canadian Centre for Substance Abuse (CCSA), 2018b; Fraser, 2018). Bill C-45 was passed in the House of Commons the day following the senate vote, to become effective towards implementing non-medical cannabis legalization in Canada on October 17, 2018 (Aiello, 2018b). In parallel, the federal government had tabled regulations (June 28, 2018) in support of the Cannabis Act, including details for production, licensing and related security aspects of legal cannabis (Government of Canada, 2018a). A key provision therein was the creation of a "micro-cultivation license" for cannabis production that would serve to legalize many of the existent, but currently illegal, small-scale growers in the cannabis economy; these licenses would be available to cannabis grow operations with a limited number of employees and production space (<200 square meters) and an annual cannabis product yield under 600 kilograms (Government of Canada, 2018a).

The (heterogeneous) provincial regulation frameworks

While the federal cannabis legalization framework was shaped primarily through the committee hearings and subsequent revisions to Bill C-45, the provinces – rather frantically, given the tight timelines towards the planned launch of legalization – developed their respective regulatory schemes in parallel, primarily focusing on the regulations concerning cannabis use and retail distribution (Canadian Centre for Substance Abuse (CCSA), 2018b; Fraser, 2018). The key parameters of these provincial regulations starkly underscore how the practical realities of "cannabis legalization" in Canada

Table 4.1 Select details of regulations for cannabis use and retail in Canadian provinces/territories (as of January 9, 2019)

	British Columbia	Alberta	Saskatchewan	Manitoba	Ontario	Quebec	Newfoundland & Labrador	New Brunswick	Nova Scotia	Prince Edward Island	Yukon	Northwest Territories	Nunavut
Minimum use age (years)	19	18	19	19	19	21	19	19	19	19	19	19	19
Retail System*	Both public (govt. run) and private retail outlets; no cap on total licenses but individual maximum	Private retail outlets (65 stores	Private retail outlets (13 stores; 51 approved applicants)	Private retail outlets (16 stores)	Private retail outlets as of April 2019	Public (govt. run) retail outlets (12 stores)	Private retail outlets (25 stores)	Public (govt. run) retail outlets (20 stores)	Public (govt. run) retail outlets (12 stores)	Public (govt. run) retail outlets (4 stores)	Public (govt. run; 1 store) and private retail outlets (pending)	Public (govt. run) retail outlets (5 stores)	Public (govt. run) and private retail outlets (pending)
Personal Cultivation**	4 cannabis plants/ household max.; no publicly visible plants	4 cannabis plants/ household max.	4 cannabis plants/ household max.; can be restricted by landlord	Prohibited	4 cannabis plants/ household max.	Prohibited	4 cannabis plants/ Household max.; no publicly visible plants	4 cannabis plants/ household max.; must be secured & inaccessible to minors	4 cannabis plants/ household max.; can be restricted by landlord	4 cannabis plants/ household max.; no publicly visible plants; must be secured & inaccessible to minors	4 cannabis plants/ household max.	4 cannabis plants/ household max.; can be restricted by landlords	4 cannabis plants/ household max.
Use Restrictions***	Prohibited wherever tobacco smoking is prohibited, and around children	Prohibited wherever tobacco smoking is prohibited, and around children	Prohibited in public	Prohibited in public	Prohibited wherever smoking tobacco is prohibited, and around children and hospitals	Prohibited in public	Prohibited in public	Prohibited in public	Prohibited wherever smoking tobacco is prohibited	Prohibited in public	Prohibited in public	Prohibited in public	Prohibited wherever smoking tobacco is prohibited, and around children and hospitals

Reference/data source acknowledgments: This chart is, in part, based on Trina Fraser (Brazeau Seller Law): "Canadian Cannabis Legalization Highlights (by Province/Territory), version 18 Dec 2018", retrieved from https://dropbox.com/s/r7re1ewe94dxos8/Legalization_Chart%20-Dec.18.18.pdf?dl=0, and further informed by details from relevant government sources/websites.

Notes

* All provinces/territories provide access to federally regulated online sales (mail distribution) for legal cannabis products.

** The personal cultivation maximum of 4 cannabis plants/household is stipulated by the (federal) Cannabis Act but allows for provincial/territorial opt-out. All jurisdictions maintain the federally regulated personal possession limit of 30 grams for cannabis products.

*** All jurisdictions maintain federally stipulated prohibition of cannabis use in cars.

really do not consist of one coherent scheme or model, but are – like many public policy frameworks within the parameters of federalism – comprised of a heterogeneous multitude of individual regimes by province (see Table 4.1). Some of these inter-provincially different frameworks based on provincial regulations comprise the following issues and regulations.

Age restrictions: While most provinces allow legal cannabis use as of 19 years of age and up, others have set 18 years as the minimum; these regulations are mostly congruent with provincially applicable restrictions for legal alcohol use; a recent outlier is Quebec which restricted of-age use to 21 years or older.

Use restrictions: Most provinces stipulated use restrictions for non-medical cannabis use congruent with those applying to tobacco use, typically providing for the possibility of use in public spaces except where explicitly restricted (e.g. public buildings, restaurants, parks) and/or including other limitations (e.g. not where children are present, not in vehicles or boats). A couple of provinces (e.g. Saskatchewan, Newfoundland, New Brunswick and now also Quebec), however, categorically restricted cannabis use to private spaces or residences only (Canadian Centre for Substance Abuse (CCSA), 2018b; Fraser, 2018). This quickly raised the question of practical feasibility and public health implications, in that such restrictions would strongly limit cannabis use for social purposes; potentially lead to co-exposure of co-residents (including minors); as well as present obstacles for users living in rental or multi-unit dwellings, since many property owners quickly declared that they would not allow cannabis use in their dwellings based on applicable landlord and/or health and safety laws/regulations.

Distribution and retail regulations: While most provinces have rested control over cannabis distribution through a designated entity at arm's length to the government (e.g. by the – existent – provincial liquor control authority or a parallel cannabis control authority), the actual retail schemes differ considerably by province (Canadian Centre for Substance Abuse (CCSA), 2018b; Fraser, 2018). Concretely, in some provinces (e.g. Quebec), cannabis will be retailed only in public retail outlets, whereas in others (e.g. Alberta) this will happen exclusively in private (licensed) retail entities; other jurisdictions (e.g. British Columbia), again, will run a hybrid model of public and private retail outlets, also based on the fact that some of its municipalities had already begun to regulate and legalize (illegal) community storefront dispensaries for cannabis (City of Vancouver, 2018). A special case in this respect has been Ontario, where the provincial government had developed extensive plans, and infrastructure, for an exclusively public, i.e. government-operated, cannabis retail system; however, the newly elected (pro-business Conservative) provincial government fully reversed these plans at the last minute (August 2018) towards the creation of an exclusively private cannabis retail system to be implemented in 2019 (Government of Ontario, 2018). Most provincial regulations also stipulated details concerning the numbers, or locations (e.g. distance to schools), of retail outlets, as well as restricted co-availability with alcohol.

Home production: While most provinces allowed for home production of a limited number of cannabis plants as permitted by the federal Cannabis Act, others (e.g. Quebec, Manitoba) categorically opted out of, and did not permit, this source of personal supply in their jurisdictions. Questions remain as to the potential adverse consequences of these "home grow" provisions, and also how these home grow activities would be effectively monitored and enforced by relevant authorities.

Discussion and questions

Canada's recently implemented legalization of non-medical cannabis use and supply constitutes both an internationally unique paradigmatic reform, and a notable experiment in cannabis policy, the implementation and outcomes of which present open questions on many fronts for which the answers are uncertain at best, and will be so for some time. The Canadian approach chosen for non-medical cannabis legalization reflects Canada's comparably progressive stance on many controversial issues of social policy, for example, in the legalization of abortion, gay marriage and physician-assisted dying, as well as predominant values and practice of public health-oriented substance control, for example, Canada's public alcohol monopolies and restrictive tobacco control (Giesbrecht, Demers, Ogborne, Room, Stoduto and Lindquist, 2006; The Canada Guide, 2018; Wyckham, 1997). It is thus not a coincidence that in many – but not all – ways the Canadian legalization framework has been cast as an approach of "legalization with strict regulation for public health," emphasizing utilitarian benefits rather than individual freedoms (Rehm and Fischer, 2015). The Canadian cannabis legalization policy – given the country's respected status internationally, but also the continuously controversial state of cannabis legalization in a growing number of US states, and the relatively unnoticed legalization developments in Uruguay – will surely be closely watched and bear impacts on related plans or developments far beyond Canada's borders (Pardo, 2014; Room, 2014).

Numerous issues could be raised for discussion about the nature, virtues or likely impacts of cannabis legalization in Canada; a select few of primary pertinence are briefly considered in the following section.

What is the practical feasibility and uptake of the proposed legalization framework?

Many key aspects of the Canadian cannabis legalization framework are subject to tight regulations – including product availability, access and pricing, retail distribution and parameters of use. While these restrictions were developed in good faith with the primary interests of improving public health and safety, a key question is to which extent these are realistically feasible and will practically be embraced by, and work for consumers (Fischer, 2017; Rehm, Crépault and Fischer, 2017). Unquestionably, the realization of the intended public health benefit of cannabis legalization will crucially hinge on a large proportion of cannabis consumers effectively switching to legal cannabis products and supply sources. The tightly regulated legal cannabis retail distribution structures in Canada, however, will continue to compete with an existent vast "illegal" cannabis supply, currently including numerous storefront "dispensaries" not brought into the realm of regulation and legality, that may remain more appealing or convenient for many consumers. Here, much will depend on the extent to which unregulated cannabis retail operations are practically permitted to continue distribution activities. It will remain to be seen how successful the Canadian legalization scheme, and specifically its differential provincial retail regimes are in drawing cannabis consumers from illegal to legal markets and supply.

What will the public health effects of legalization be?

It has been noted widely for other jurisdictions of "cannabis legalization" (e.g. US states, Uruguay) that the public health consequences of these policy reforms remain mixed and unclear in their overall impact (Hall and Lynskey, 2016; Room, 2014; Walsh and Ramsey, 2016). These reforms appear to have been associated with select adverse developments, including increases in cannabis use as well as hospitalizations or injuries, for example from accidents (Hasin, 2018; Wang, Hall, Vigil, Banerji, Monte and VanDyke, 2017). In the interest of evidence-based cannabis policy-making both in Canada and other jurisdictions considering cannabis legalization, it will be critical to effectively monitor and evaluate the impact of Canadian legalization on public health; pertinent indicators and frameworks to do so have been proposed (Fischer, Russell, Rehm and Leece, 2018). It seems unlikely – given already existent high cannabis use levels among the Canadian population – for large additional numbers of Canadians to initiate cannabis use as a direct consequence of legalization or the "normalization" of cannabis in its wake. At the same time, however, increases in use and demand may occur, especially in current low-use sub-groups, based on the availability of an increasing range of new cannabis products and access. Regardless, a key question is whether there will be distinct legalization-attributable changes on key public health outcomes, e.g. cannabis use-related mental health problems, disorders, hospitalizations, driving/accidents; the same, of course, applies to and may include beneficial impacts (Fischer et al., 2018). It should be noted that increases for several key cannabis-related health problem indicators have been increasing in Canada for some time pre-legalization, yet also that cannabis use patterns have greatly fluctuated in the absence of legal control changes in the past decades.

What will happen to cannabis use among young people?

One of the political slogans used by the federal government to promote its cannabis legalization plan was that it would "keep cannabis out of the hands of young people" (Task Force on Cannabis Legalization and Regulation, 2016). This message appeared to imply that, given the legal availability of cannabis for adult users, illicit markets for cannabis would be dried out and cannabis use among minors would cease as a consequence of a lack of supply. This assumption likely constitutes naïve political opportunism at best, as the "why and how" for such a sudden demise of cannabis use to effectively happen in the (particularly vulnerable) group of underage users in Canada remains unclear (Fischer and Rehm, 2017; Watson and Erickson, 2018). Depending on the survey used, approximately 25–35 percent of adolescents/young adults ages 16–19 years currently use cannabis in Canada. It is rather unlikely that legalization will be effective in making interest in use or availability of cannabis disappear, or even substantially decrease, in this underage group – if anything, the opposite needs to be expected, based on experiences elsewhere (Cerdá, Wall, Feng, Keyes, Sarvet, Schulenberg and Hasin, 2017; Kerr, Bae, Phibbs and Kern, 2017). While diffusion of legal – and presumably safer, since quality-regulated – cannabis products may reach some young users, underage users will remain a highly vulnerable population unlikely to directly benefit from the provisions of legalization; on this basis, the effects of legalization on this particular risk group will need to be closely monitored.

How will the cannabis industry evolve and conduct itself?

The path to cannabis legalization in Canada, including its initial stepping stones of the medical cannabis access program, have created a massive "gold rush" type commercial industry, vying for a domestic economy and profits in the coming years estimated to be similar to that of alcohol and tobacco commerce; this is in addition to unfolding major international markets (Deloitte, 2018; Rosenthal, 2017). Many Canadian cannabis producer companies are now publicly listed and have experienced exorbitant market appreciation – dubbed as the "green bubble" – and multi-billion-dollar takeovers and mergers, including with tobacco or alcohol companies, have begun to take place (Rosenthal, 2017). The government's cannabis regulations have, on the one hand, actively created the grounds for this booming commercial industry, while at the same time attempting to regulate it more tightly than many other ordinary "consumer good" – including tobacco or alcohol industries, in certain respects (e.g. with highly restrictive advertisement bans, product and availability limitations). Unquestionably, in such an unusually lucrative but also vastly populated legal cannabis marketplace, competition will be intense. On this basis, it will be crucial to observe to what extent the present industry regulations will hold and work, or whether, or what, tools and tactics the cannabis industry may employ towards expanding its markets, sales and profits, and what efforts it will undertake to potentially adapt to or circumvent restrictive regulations – similar to what the alcohol and tobacco industries have successfully done, for example in regards to product tailoring and marketing to young consumers, which have worked against the interests of public health for decades (Barry, Hiilamo and Glantz, 2014; Richter and Levy, 2014). Notably, the cannabis industry in Canada has been actively presenting itself as "different" from the alcohol and tobacco industries, with claims of "true" interest in consumer wellbeing and selling a "healthy" or even "therapeutic" rather than just a recreational, and potentially hazardous, product (Crépault, 2018; Deloitte, 2018). A related question is to what extent the cannabis industry will be subject to multi-national and/or industry mergers (likely to undermine the potential of domestic regulation and governance), some of which are already occurring (Martin, 2018).

Will the heterogeneity of provincial regulation frameworks matter?

As described above, the provincial regulatory frameworks for key aspects of the Canadian legalization regime – for example, concerning retail distribution, use restrictions, etc., – differ considerably (Canadian Centre for Substance Abuse (CCSA), 2018b; Fraser, 2018). Such inter-jurisdictional differences for legal cannabis control have been associated with differential policy outcomes elsewhere, for example, between US states, as well as for provincial alcohol control regimes in Canada (Barry and Glantz, 2016; Giesbrecht, 2006; Pacula, Powell, Heaton and Sevigny, 2015). As part of the Canadian legalization policy "experiment," it will be key to ascertain to what extent the inter-provincial differences in regulatory parameters may translate into differential outcomes (e.g. use levels, legal supply access/utilization, health outcomes). As such, the Canadian legalization regimes present a – potentially valuable – series of "natural" comparison studies of different regulatory regimes towards evidence for future policy design.

How will Canada deal with the international treaties?

As the core components of the international drug control regime, a set of international treaties dictate fundamental parameters of requirements for its signatory states' efforts to limit and control the use and availability of psychoactive drugs, including cannabis (Jelsma and Armenta, 2015; Room and Reuter, 2012). While there have been numerous creative perspectives in regards to these obligations and specifically their implications for national law and policy reform, they essentially require signatory states to (criminally) prohibit the production and/or supply, as well as the use of these drugs, even while secondary or substitutive measures like "diversion" or "treatment-for-punishment" appear to be possible for the latter (Bewley-Taylor, Blickman and Jelsma, 2014; Bewley-Taylor, Jelsma, Rolles and Walsh, 2016; Room, 2012). It is, however, without doubt that a full-scale and explicit "legalization" of cannabis use and supply, as provided by the Canadian approach, contravenes the material requirements and spirit of the international drug conventions (Hoffman and Habibi, 2016; Walsh, Blickman, Jelsma and Bewley-Taylor,

2017). Given that Canada is a signatory state with high standing and reputation in the international community, it will be compelling to observe what – if anything – Canada will undertake to resolve these tensions concerning its international treaty obligations arising from legalization. Options for such resolution have been laid out elsewhere; for example, they may include secession from the treaties, or reaccession with reservations, or "inter se" modifications between like-minded reform signatories (Bewley-Taylor et al., 2014; Bewley-Taylor, Jelsma, Rolles and Walsh, 2016; Room, 2012). The possible path that Canada may choose is not only of relevance for Canadian cannabis policy reform nationally, but equally important for other jurisdictions – including those with lesser international clout, such as smaller countries in the Americas – possibly considering similar cannabis policy reforms (Fischer and Room, 2016).

Conclusion

Cannabis legalization is now unfolding – in the positive sense of innovative policymaking – as a major "social experiment" in Canada, the concrete outcomes and impacts of which will largely remain uncertain for some time. Comprehensive and detailed monitoring and evaluation over the coming years will provide empirical answers. It is noteworthy that the Canadian government, amidst its legalization plans, for a long time did not clarify their intent to address the harms of criminalization for cannabis users, as specifically voiced by demands for an amnesty for the several hundreds of thousands of Canadians burdened with a criminal record, and its substantial negative consequences for employment and travel, due to cannabis-related conviction over the past decades. On the day legalization came into force, the federal government announced plans for a "pardon" scheme for criminal records related to cannabis possession, although this proposal has been controversial, as the approach would not fully expunge or eliminate respective records and their detrimental consequences (Aiello, 2018a; Press and Kirkup, 2018). The government has instead, mostly, focused on the politically more opportune, but both practically questionable twin goals of eliminating the illicit market and reducing youth use. From a high-level and public health-oriented perspective, the Canadian legalization framework appears somewhat of a contradiction by design: it matches the element of a vast, commercial and quickly expanding psychoactive consumer goods industry – many facets of which are reminiscent of an alcohol or tobacco-like industry mammoth – yet with extremely tight restrictions in consumer-level availability and behavior; it is one of the essential questions of this policy reform experiment whether these countervailing features, eventually, will work for or against public health. For now, the great Canadian cannabis legalization project has become a reality – something most policy observers had not deemed a possibility even just a few years ago. If nothing else is certain, it will surely be a seminal and major experiment to watch unfold, nationally and internationally.

References

Aiello, R. (2018a). NDP MP makes last plea for feds to issue pot expungements, not pardons. *CTV News*. Retrieved from www.ctvnews.ca/politics/ndp-mp-makes-last-plea-for-feds-to-issue-pot-expungements-not-pardons-1.4208181.

Aiello, R. (2018b). Timeline of key events in marijuana bill's passage through parliament. *CTV News*. Retrieved from www.ctvnews.ca/politics/timeline-of-key-events-in-marijuana-bill-s-passage-through-parliament-1.3958662.

Arie, S. (2013). Uruguay legalises sale and production of marijuana. *British Medical Journal (Clinical Research Ed.),* 347, f7499.

Barry, R.A. and Glantz, S. (2016). A public health framework for legalized retail marijuana based on the US experience: Avoiding a new tobacco industry. *PLoS Medicine,* 13(9), e1002131.

Barry, R.A., Hiilamo, H. and Glantz, S.A. (2014). Waiting for the opportune moment: The tobacco industry and marijuana legalization. *The Milbank Quarterly,* 92(2), 207–242.

Belle-Isle, L., Walsh, Z., Callaway, R., Lucas, P., Capler, R., Kay, R. and Holtzman, S. (2014). Barriers to access for Canadians who use cannabis for therapeutic purposes. *International Journal of Drug Policy,* 25(4), 691–699.

Bewley-Taylor, D., Blickman, T. and Jelsma, M. (2014). *The rise and decline of cannabis prohibition*. Amsterdam, The Netherlands: Transnational Institute (TNI). Retrieved from www.tni.org/files/download/rise_and_decline_web.pdf.

Bewley-Taylor, D., Jelsma, M., Rolles, S. and Walsh, J. (2016). *Cannabis regulation and the UN drug treaties: Strategies for reform*. Amsterdam, The Netherlands: Transnational Institute (TNI). Retrieved from www.tni.org/files/publication-downloads/cannabis_regulation_and_the_un_drug_treaties_june_2016_web_0.pdf

Blickman, T. (2014). *Cannabis policy reform in Europe: Bottom up rather than top down*. Amsterdam, The Netherlands: Transnational Institute (TNI). Retrieved from www.tni.org/files/download/dlr28.pdf.

Brennan, S. and Dauvergne, M. (2011). *Police-reported crime statistics in Canada, 2010*. Ottawa, ON: Statistics Canada. Retrieved from www150.statcan.gc.ca/n1/en/pub/85–002-x/2011001/article/11523-eng.pdf?st=I5zTfYRs.

Bryan, M. (1979). Cannabis in Canada – A decade of indecision. *Contemporary Drug Problems*, 8, 169–192.

Bryden, J. (2014). Peter MacKay's marijuana legalization stance remains unchanged after addiction centre plea. *Huffington Post*. Retrieved from www.huffingtonpost.ca/entry/5961768.

Canadian Association of Chiefs of Police. (2004). *Cannabis reform legislation. Resolutions adopted at the 99th annual conference*. Vancouver, BC: Canadian Association of Chiefs of Police. Retrieved from www.cacp.ca/resolution.html?asst_id=318.

Canadian Centre for Substance Abuse (CCSA). (2018a). *Drug per se laws*. Ottawa, ON: Canadian Centre for Substance Abuse (CCSA). Retrieved from www.ccsa.ca/Resource%20Library/CCSA-Drug-per-Se-Laws-Policy-Brief-2018-en.pdf.

Canadian Centre for Substance Abuse (CCSA). (2018b). *Summary of provincial and territorial cannabis regulations*. Ottawa, ON: Canadian Centre for Substance Abuse (CCSA). Retrieved from www.ccdus.ca/Eng/topics/Cannabis/Legal-Status-of-Cannabis/Pages/default.aspx.

Canadian Centre on Substance Abuse (CCSA) and Health Canada. (2004). *Canadian Addiction Survey (CAS): A national survey of Canadians' use of alcohol and other drugs – Prevalence of use and related harm.* Ottawa, ON: Canadian Centre on Substance Abuse (CCSA). Retrieved from www.ccsa.ca/Resource%20Library/ccsa-004804-2004.pdf.

Capler, R., Walsh, Z., Crosby, K., Belle-Isle, L., Holtzman, S., Lucas, P. and Callaway, R. (2017). Are dispensaries indispensable? Patient experiences of access to cannabis from medical cannabis dispensaries in Canada. *International Journal of Drug Policy,* 47, 1–8.

Carstairs, C. (2006). *Jailed for possession: Illegal drug use, regulation, and power in Canada, 1920–1961.* Toronto, ON: University of Toronto Press.

Centre for Addiction and Mental Health (CAMH). (2014). *Cannabis policy framework.* Toronto, ON: Centre for Addiction and Mental Health (CAMH). Retrieved from www.camh.ca/en/hospital/about_camh/influencing_public_policy/Documents/CAMHCannabisPolicyFramework.pdf.

Cerdá, M., Wall, M., Feng, T., Keyes, K.M., Sarvet, A., Schulenberg, J. and Hasin, D.S. (2017). Association of state recreational marijuana laws with adolescent marijuana use. *JAMA Pediatrics,* 171(2), 142–149.

Christie, P. (1999). *Cannabis offences under the cannabis expiation notice scheme in South Australia.* Canberra, Australia: Commonwealth Department of Health and Aged Care.

City of Vancouver. (2018). *Cannabis retail stores.* Vancouver, BC: City of Vancouver. Retrieved from https://vancouver.ca/doing-business/cannabis-retail-dealer-business-licence.aspx.

Collier, R. (2016). How will pot legalization affect medical marijuana? *Canadian Medical Association Journal,* 188(11), 792–793.

Cotter, A., Greenland, J. and Karam, M. (2015). *Drug-related offences in Canada, 2013.* Ottawa, Ontario: Statistics Canada. Retrieved from www150.statcan.gc.ca/n1/en/pub/85–002-x/2015001/article/14201-eng.pdf?st=_gelv1Gz.

Crépault, J.F. (2018). Cannabis legalization in Canada: Reflections on public health and the governance of legal psychoactive substances. *Frontiers in Public Health,* 6, 220.

Crépault, J.F., Rehm, J. and Fischer, B. (2016). The cannabis policy framework by the centre for addiction and mental health: A proposal for a public health approach to cannabis policy in Canada. *The International Journal of Drug Policy,* 34, 1–4.

Dauvergne, M. (2009). *Trends in police-reported drug offences in Canada* (1209–6393). Ottawa, ON: Statistics Canada. Retrieved from www.statcan.gc.ca/pub/85-002-x/2009002/article/10847-eng.pdf.

Deloitte. (2018). *A society in transition, an industry ready to bloom: 2018 cannabis report.* Toronto, ON: Deloitte. Retrieved from www2.deloitte.com/content/dam/Deloitte/ca/Documents/consulting/ca-cannabis-2018-report-en.PDF.

Dion, G.A. (1999). *The structure of drug prohibition in international law and in Canadian law.* Ottawa, ON: Senate of Canada. Retrieved from https://sencanada.ca/content/sen/committee/371/ille/presentation/dion-e.htm#APPENDIX%204.

Erickson, P. and Smart, R. (1988). The Le Dain Commission recommendations. In J.C. Blackwell and P. Erickson (Eds.), *Illicit drugs in Canada: A risky business.* Ottawa, Canada: Nelson.

European Monitoring Centre for Drugs and Drug Addiction (EMCDDA). (2008). *A cannabis reader: Global issues and local experiences.* Lisbon, Portugal. European Monitoring Centre for Drugs and Drug Addiction. Retrieved from www.emcdda.europa.eu/publications/monographs/cannabis.

Fischer, B. (1999). Prohibition, public health and a window of opportunity: An analysis of Canadian drug policy, 1985–1997. *Policy Studies,* 20(3), 197–210.

Fischer, B. (2017). Legalisation of non-medical cannabis in Canada: Will supply regulations effectively serve public health? *The Lancet Public Health,* 2(12), e536-e537.

Fischer, B., Ala-Leppilampi, K., Single, E. and Robins, A. (2003). Cannabis law reform in Canada: Is the "saga of promise, hesitation and retreat" coming to an end? *Canadian Journal of Criminology and Criminal Justice,* 45(3), 265–298.

Fischer, B., Erickson, P. and Smart, R. (1996). The new Canadian drug law: One step forward, two steps backward. *The International Journal of Drug Policy,* 7(3), 172–179.

Fischer, B., Kuganesan, S. and Room, R. (2015). Medical marijuana programs: Implications for cannabis control policy – Observations from Canada. *International Journal of Drug Policy,* 26(1), 15–19.

Fischer, B., Lomiteanu, A.R., Russell, C., Rehm, J. and Mann, R.E. (2016). Public opinion towards cannabis control in Ontario: Strong but diversified support for reforming control of both use and supply. *Canadian Journal of Criminology and Criminal Justice,* 58(3), 443–459.

Fischer, B. and Rehm, J. (2017). Cannabis use, legalization and youth health. *Canadian Medical Association Journal,* 189(29), E971-E972.

Fischer, B. and Room, R. (2016). Cannabis legalization in Canada and the international conventions: Need for resolve and leadership. *Canadian Medical Association Journal,* 188(10).

Fischer, B., Russell, C., Rehm, J. and Leece, P. (2018). Assessing the public health impact of cannabis legalization in Canada: Core outcome indicators towards an "index" for monitoring and evaluation. *Journal of Public Health*, fdy090.

Fraser, T. (2018). *Canadian cannabis legalization highlights (by province/territory).* Retrieved from https://twitter.com/trinafraser/status/1046215626086322179.

Friscolanti, M. (2016). Why buying pot has never been easier: Inside Canada's completely out of control marijuana business. *Macleans.* Retrieved from www.macleans.ca/news/canada/canadas-completely-out-of-control-marijuana-business/.

Giesbrecht, N. (2006). Alcohol policy in Canada: Reflections on the role of the alcohol industry. *Nordic Studies on Alcohol and Drugs,* 23(6), 445–466.

Giesbrecht, N., Demers, A., Ogborne, A., Room, R., Stoduto, G. and Lindquist, E. (2006). *Sober reflections: Commerce, public health, and the evolution of alcohol policy in Canada, 1980–2000.* Montreal: McGill-Queen's University Press.

Giffen, P.J., Endicott, S.J. and Boorman, S. (1991). *Panic and indifference: The politics of Canada's drug laws: A study in the sociology of law.* Ottawa, ON: Canadian Centre on Substance Abuse.

Government of Canada. (2016). *Medical use of cannabis.* Ottawa, ON: Government of Canada. Retrieved from www.canada.ca/en/health-canada/services/drugs-medication/cannabis/medical-use-cannabis.html.

Government of Canada. (2018a). *Cannabis licensing application guide: Application requirements and process to become a licence holder under the Cannabis Act and its regulations.* Ottawa, ON: Government of Canada. Retrieved from www.canada.ca/en/health-canada/services/drugs-medication/cannabis/industry-licensees-applicants/licensing-summary/guide.html?_ga=2.249642959.819696592.1538503576-227924488.1538503576.

Government of Canada. (2018b). *Licensed producers of cannabis for medical purposes*. Ottawa, ON: Government of Canada. Retrieved from www.canada.ca/en/health-canada/services/drugs-medication/cannabis/licensed-producers/authorized-licensed-producers-medical-purposes.html.

Government of Canada. (2018c). *Proposed regulations for additional cannabis products*. Ottawa, ON: Government of Canada. Retrieved from www.canada.ca/content/dam/hc-sc/documents/services/drugs-medication/cannabis/resources/proposed-regulations-edible-cannabis-extracts-topical-eng.pdf.

Government of Ontario. (2018). *Cannabis legalization*. Ottawa, ON: Government of Ontario. Retrieved from www.ontario.ca/page/cannabis-legalization?gclid=Cj0KCQjwi8fdBRCVARIsAEkDvnLAzcX3S-rmyriIwd1pAEctRzkZ3DqlYqIHMR1NF_DkSmhgBidEQWgaAknbEALw_wcB.

Haddad, H. (2002). *A public health perspective on cannabis and other illegal drugs. CMA submission to the special senate committee on illegal drugs*. Ottawa, ON: Canadian Medical Association. Retrieved from http://policybase.cma.ca/dbtw-wpd/Brief-PDF/BR2002-08.pdf.

Hall, W. and Lynskey, M. (2016). Evaluating the public health impacts of legalizing recreational cannabis use in the United States. *Addiction*, 111(10), 1764–1773.

Haney, M. and Evins, A.E. (2016). Does cannabis cause, exacerbate or ameliorate psychiatric disorders? An oversimplified debate discussed. *Neuropsychopharmacology*, 41(2), 393.

Hasin, D.S. (2018). US epidemiology of cannabis use and associated problems. *Neuropsychopharmacology*, 43(1), 195.

Hoffman, S.J. and Habibi, R. (2016). International legal barriers to Canada's marijuana plans. *Canadian Medical Association Journal*, 188(10), E215-E216.

House of Commons Special Committee on Non-medical Use of Drugs. (2002). *Policy for the new millennium: Working together to redefine Canada's drug strategy: Report of the special committee on non-medical use of drugs*. Ottawa, Ontario: Government of Canada. Retrieved from www.ourcommons.ca/Content/Committee/372/SNUD/Reports/RP1032297/snudrp02/snudrp02-e.pdf.

Hyshka, E. (2009). The saga continues: Canadian legislative attempts to reform cannabis law in the twenty-first century. *Canadian Journal of Criminology and Criminal Justice*, 51(1), 73–91.

Ialomiteanu, A.R., Hamilton, H., Adlaf, E. and Mann, R. E. (2016). *CAMH Monitor eReport 2015: Substance use, mental health and well-being among Ontario adults*. Toronto, Ontario: Centre for Addiction and Mental Health. Retrieved from www.camh.ca/en/research/news_and_publications/CAMH%20Monitor/CAMH-Monitor-2015-eReport-Final-Web.pdf.

Jacobus, J. and Tapert, S.F. (2014). Effects of cannabis on the adolescent brain. *Current Pharmaceutical Design*, 20(13), 2186–2193.

Jelsma, M. and Armenta, A. (2015). *The UN drug control conventions: A primer*. Amsterdam, The Netherlands: Transnational Institute (TNI). Retrieved from www.tni.org/files/publication-downloads/primer_unconventions_24102015.pdf.

Kahan, M. and Srivastava, A. (2014). New medical marijuana regulations: The coming storm. *Canadian Medical Association Journal*, 186(12), 895–896.

Kennedy, M. (2014). Government's poll shows Canadians want marijuana laws changed. *Ottawa Citizen*. Retrieved from https://ottawacitizen.com/news/politics/conservative-governments-poll-shows-canadians-want-marijuana-laws-changed.

Kerr, D.C.R., Bae, H., Phibbs, S. and Kern, A.C. (2017). Changes in undergraduates' marijuana, heavy alcohol and cigarette use following legalization of recreational marijuana use in Oregon. *Addiction,* 112(11), 1992–2001.

Kilmer, B. and MacCoun, R.J. (2017). How medical marijuana smoothed the transition to marijuana legalization in the United States. *Annual Review of Law and Social Science,* 13, 181–202.

Kilmer, B. and Pacula, R.L. (2016). Understanding and learning from the diversification of cannabis supply laws. *Addiction,* 112(7), 1128–1135.

Le Dain Commission. (1972). *Cannabis: A report of the commission in the inquiry into the non-medical use of drugs*. Ottawa, Ontario: Information Canada. Retrieved from www.druglibrary.net/schaffer/Library/studies/ledain/ldctoc.html.

Lucas, P.G. (2008). Regulating compassion: An overview of Canada's federal medical cannabis policy and practice. *Harm Reduction Journal,* 5(5), 1–13.

Marconi, A., Di Forti, M., Lewis, C.M., Murray, R.M. and Vassos, E. (2016). Meta-analysis of the association between the level of cannabis use and risk of psychosis. *Schizophrenia Bulletin,* 42(5), 1262–1269.

Martin, T.J. (2018). Canadian cannabis stocks surge amid alcohol company deal speculation. *Financial Post.* Retrieved from https://business.financialpost.com/cannabis/canadian-cannabis-stocks-surge-amid-alcohol-company-deal-speculation.

Martinez, M. (2014). Colorado's recreational marijuana stores make history. *CNN News*. Retrieved from www.cnn.com/2013/12/31/us/colorado-recreational-marijuana/index.html.

Menard, X.F. and Hartery, J. (2016). Election promises and marijuana policy: What federalism has to offer. *Rule of Law*. Retrieved from www.ruleoflaw.ca/election-promises-and-marijuana-policy-what-federalism-has-to-offer/.

Mosher, C.J. (2011). Convergence or divergence? Recent developments in drug policies in Canada and the United States. *American Review of Canadian Studies,* 41(4), 370–386.

Murray, R.M. and Di Forti, M. (2016). Cannabis and psychosis: What degree of proof do we require? *Biological Psychiatry,* 79(7), 514–515.

Nolin, P.C. and Kenny, C. (2002). *Cannabis: Our position for a Canadian public policy. Report of the Senate Special Committee on illegal drugs*. Ottawa, Ontario: Senate Committee of Canada. Retrieved from https://sencanada.ca/content/sen/committee/371/ille/rep/summary-e.pdf.

Pacula, R.L., Kilmer, B., Wagenaar, A.C., Chaloupka, F.J. and Caulkins, J.P. (2014). Developing public health regulations for marijuana: Lessons from alcohol and tobacco. *American Journal of Public Health,* 104(6), 1021–1028.

Pacula, R.L., Powell, D., Heaton, P. and Sevigny, E.L. (2015). Assessing the effects of medical marijuana laws on marijuana use: The devil is in the details. *Journal of Policy Analysis and Management,* 34(1), 7–31.

Pardo, B. (2014). Cannabis policy reforms in the Americas: A comparative analysis of Colorado, Washington, and Uruguay. *International Journal of Drug Policy,* 25(4), 727–735.

Pauls, K., Plecas, D., Cohen, I.M. and Haarhoff, T. (2012). *The nature and extent of marihuana possession in British Columbia*. Abbotsford, British Columbia: University of the Fraser Valley. Retrieved from www.ufv.ca/media/assets/criminal-justice-research/The-Nature-and-Extent-of-Marijuana-Possession-in-BC.pdf.

Platt, B. (2018). Canada's impaired driving laws just got a huge and controversial overhaul — Here's what you should know. *National Post*. Retrieved from https://nationalpost.com/news/politics/canadas-impaired-driving-laws-just-got-a-huge-and-controversial-overhaul-heres-what-you-should-know.

Press, J. and Kirkup, K. (2018). Federal ministers to announce plan to expedite pardons for minor pot convictions. *CBC News*. Retrieved from www.cbc.ca/news/politics/pardons-pot-posession-expedite-1.4865291.

Raaflaub, W. (2004). *Bill C-17: An act to amend the Contraventions Act and the Controlled Drugs and Substances Act – Legislative summary*. Ottawa, ON: Library of Parliament. Retrieved from https://lop.parl.ca/sites/PublicWebsite/default/en_CA/ResearchPublications/LegislativeSummaries/381LS488E.

Rehm, J., Crépault, J.-F. and Fischer, B. (2017). The devil is in the details! On regulating cannabis use in Canada based on public health criteria: Comment on "Legalizing and regulating marijuana in Canada: Review of potential economic, social, and health impacts." *International Journal of Health Policy and Management,* 6(3), 173.

Rehm, J. and Fischer, B. (2015). Cannabis legalization with strict regulation, the overall superior policy option for public health. *Clinical Pharmacology and Therapeutics,* 97(6), 541–544.

Richter, K.P. and Levy, S. (2014). Big marijuana – Lessons from big tobacco. *The New England Journal of Medicine,* 371(5), 399–401.

Room, R. (2012). Reform by subtraction: The path of denunciation of international drug treaties and reaccession with reservations. *The International Journal on Drug Policy,* 23(5), 401–406.

Room, R. (2014). Legalising a market for cannabis for pleasure: Colorado, Washington, Uruguay and beyond. *Addiction,* 109(3), 345–351.

Room, R., Fischer, B., Hall, W., Lenton, S. and Reuter, P. (2010). *Cannabis policy: Moving beyond stalemate*. New York, NY: Oxford University Press.

Room, R. and Reuter, P. (2012). How well do international drug conventions protect public health? *The Lancet,* 379(9810), 84.

Rosenthal, J. (2017). Here's what you should know about Canada's emerging weed industry. *Huffington Post*. Retrieved from www.huffingtonpost.ca/jay-rosenthal/heres-what-you-should-know-about-canadas-emerging-weed-industry_a_23322152/.

Single, E., Christie, P. and Ali, R. (2000). The impact of cannabis decriminalisation in Australia and the United States. *Journal of Public Health Policy,* 21(2), 157–186.

Single, E., Fischer, B., Room, R., Poulin, C., Sawka, E., Thompson, H. and Topp, J. (1998). *Cannabis control in Canada: Options regarding possession: A Canadian Centre on Substance Abuse policy discussion document*. Ottawa, ON: Canadian Centre on Substance Abuse (CCSA) National Working Group on Addictions Policy.

Slaughter, G. (2017). Mixed reaction to marijuana legalization bill. *CTV News*. Retrieved from www.ctvnews.ca/politics/mixed-reaction-to-marijuana-legalization-bill-1.3368046.

Solomon, R. and Green, M. (1988). The first century: The history of non-medical opiate use and control policies in Canada, 1870–1970. In J.C. Blackwell and P.G. Erickson (Eds.), *Illicit drugs in Canada: A risky business* (pp. 88–116). Toronto: Nelson Canada.

Solomon, R., Single, E. and Erickson, P. (1983). Legal considerations in Canadian cannabis policy. *Canadian Public Policy,* 9(4), 419–433.

Statistics Canada. (2015). *Police-reported drug offences, by type of drug, Canada, 1977 to 2007.* Ottawa, ON: Statistics Canada. Retrieved from www150.statcan.gc.ca/n1/pub/85-002-x/2009002/article/10847/tbl/tbl1-eng.htm.

Sutton, A. and McMillan, E. (2000). Criminal justice perspectives on South Australia's cannabis expiation notice procedures. *Drug and Alcohol Review,* 19, 281–286.

Task Force on Cannabis Legalization and Regulation. (2016). *A framework for the legalization and regulation of cannabis in Canada: The final report of the Task Force on Cannabis Legalization and Regulation.* Ottawa, ON: Government of Canada. Retrieved from http://healthycanadians.gc.ca/task-force-marijuana-grope-etude/framework-cadre/alt/framework-cadre-eng.pdf.

Tasker, J.P. (2018). Government's cannabis bill faces live-or-die vote in Senate today. *CBC News.* Retrieved from www.cbc.ca/news/politics/government-cannabis-bill-live-die-vote-1.4586113.

The Canada Guide. (2018). *Social issues in Canada.* Retrieved from www.thecanadaguide.com/culture/social-issues/.

Volkow, N.D., Baler, R.D., Compton, W.M. and Weiss, S.R.B. (2014). Adverse health effects of marijuana use. *New England Journal of Medicine,* 370(23), 2219–2227.

Walsh, J., Blickman, T., Jelsma, M. and Bewley-Taylor, D. (2017). Yes, legalizing marijuana breaks treaties. We can deal with that. *ipolitics.* Retrieved from https://ipolitics.ca/2017/12/11/yes-legalizing-marijuana-breaks-treaties-not-problem/.

Walsh, J. and Ramsey, G. (2016). *Uruguay's drug policy: Major innovations, major challenges.* Washington, DC: Bookings: Center for 21st Century Security and Intelligence Latin America Initiative. Retrieved from www.brookings.edu/wp-content/uploads/2016/07/Walsh-Uruguay-final.pdf.

Walsh, Z., Callaway, R., Belle-Isle, L., Capler, R., Kay, R., Lucas, P. and Holtzman, S. (2013). Cannabis for therapeutic purposes: Patient characteristics, access, and reasons for use. *The International Journal on Drug Policy,* 24(6), 511–516.

Wang, G.S., Hall, K., Vigil, D., Banerji, S., Monte, A. and VanDyke, M. (2017). Marijuana and acute health care contacts in Colorado. *Preventive Medicine,* 104, 24–30.

Watson, T.M. and Erickson, P.G. (2018). Cannabis legalization in Canada: How might "strict" regulation impact youth? *Drugs: Education, Prevention and Policy,* 26(1), 1–5.

Whiting, P.F., Wolff, R.F., Deshpande, S., Di Nisio, M., Duffy, S., Hernandez, A.V. and Kleijnen, J. (2015). Cannabinoids for medical use: A systematic review and meta-analysis. *Journal of the American Medical Association,* 313(24), 2456–2473.

Wyckham, R.G. (1997). Regulating the marketing of tobacco products and controlling smoking in Canada. *Canadian Journal of Administrative Sciences,* 14(2), 141–164.

Ziemianski, D., Capler, R., Tekanoff, R., Lacasse, A., Luconi, F. and Ware, M.A. (2015). Cannabis in medicine: A national educational needs assessment among Canadian physicians. *BMC Medical Education,* 15(1), 52.

5 Uruguay

The first country to legalize cannabis

Rosario Queirolo

Why and how did Uruguay legalize recreational cannabis? Uruguay became the first country in the world to fully regulate its marijuana market, from production to consumption and distribution, and it did so in a highly state-oriented way using a top-down policy process. This chapter describes the reasons behind the passage of the marijuana regulation law in 2013, explains the main driving factors and actors behind the policy reform, and argues that a public insecurity window of opportunity was crucial for the regulatory model. The chapter provides a description of how the regulation was designed, particularly the three ways in which marijuana can be accessed: home cultivation, Cannabis Social Clubs (CSCs) and pharmacies and emphasizes how the state implements and enforces the law. Five years after being approved and implemented, it is possible to describe some of the main strengths and weaknesses of this state-oriented model, and departing from this first evaluation, draft some lessons for other countries pursuing legalization of recreational marijuana.

Uruguay: the first country to legalize recreational marijuana

In March 2010, when President José Mujica took office as the head of the second government of the Frente Amplio (a left-wing political party that has been in government since 2004), no one thought that recreational marijuana would be fully legal only three years later. Marijuana regulation was not in the public agenda, nor was it a key part of the electoral platform of the Frente Amplio. After Law 19,172 was passed in December 2013, Uruguay became the first country in the world to regulate consumption, production and distribution of cannabis (Hetzer and Walsh, 2014; Kilmer, Kruithof, Pardal, Caulkins and Rubin, 2013). The Uruguayan legislation stands out internationally because it was designed in a highly state-oriented way to ensure direct government involvement in the production, distribution and commercialization of marijuana (Pardo, 2014; Walsh and Ramsey, 2015). In addition, it is significant because it's a top-down policy in which neither activists, nor public opinion, nor a party's mandate towards its electorate played a decisive role in introducing the topic into the public agenda. Activists, national and international, became relevant only later, when they were able to influence the process that transform the single article proposed in the "strategy for life and coexistence" into Law 19,172 (Aguiar and Musto, 2015; von Hoffmann, 2016; Musto 2018).

Before 2013, marijuana consumption, as well as the consumption of other drugs, was legal in Uruguay. Since 1974, there has been a law stating that a minimum amount of the illegal substance, destined exclusively for personal consumption, was exempted from criminal penalty.[1] However, the "minimum amount for personal consumption" was too broad to constitute a clear definition and thus highly susceptible to police and judges' discretion, with the result that some users were criminalized (Bardazano, 2012).

Beginning in 2000, activists started to push for various initiatives to legalize access to recreational marijuana, mainly to address the contradiction that the law allowed marijuana use but banned any form of legal production or commercialization (Arrarás and Bello-Pardo, 2014; Garibotto, 2011). Most of the proposals that were raised in Congress were focused on allowing self-cultivation as a way to ensure legal access to marijuana (Garat, 2015). Several of these proposals were supported by groups of activists and young legislators from the three most important political parties in Uruguay: Partido Colorado, Partido Nacional and Frente Amplio (Garat, 2015; Repetto 2014). However, none of these initiatives was successful. Even the two parliamentary initiative projects proposing the regulation of marijuana self-cultivation, both of which were presented between 2010–2011 during the second Frente Amplio government under the presidency of Mujica, failed (Kilmer et al., 2013).

Uruguay's marijuana legalization law resulted from a strategy drawn up in the office of President Mujica (Garat, 2015; Muller and Draper, 2017; Queirolo, Rossel, Álvarez and Repetto, 2018). In other words, it was a top-down policy. In this respect it differed from other legalization processes described in this book, such as those in Colorado, Washington, and other United States jurisdictions, where there was a bottom-up process guided by activists who enabled legalization to be decided by a public referendum (Kilmer et al., 2013; Pardo, 2014; Room, 2014).

Despite the presence of social organizations mobilizing and lobbying in favor of marijuana legalization, the pressure created by these organizations was not strong enough to secure the inclusion of their proposals in the electoral programs of the political parties that competed in the 2009 election, or to have the issue placed on the government's agenda (Garat, 2015). In that sense, Uruguay's legalization process also differed from the Canadian one, in which the Liberal Party won the 2015 federal election based on a platform that included cannabis legalization.

Uruguay's cannabis regulation also contrasts with other cannabis legalization processes because public opinion in Uruguay was against the new law. Different surveys indicate that between 60 percent and 65 percent of the Uruguayan population was opposed to the regulation.[2] Support was greater among those who identified themselves as ideologically on the left, supported the government of the Frente Amplio and had more liberal social attitudes. Support was also stronger among those who have a greater social proximity to cannabis, either because they had used or use it, or had friends or relatives who used it. Conversely, rejection of marijuana regulation was greater among those with a more conservative belief system, who identified politically with opposition parties, and had never used marijuana (Cruz, Boidi and Queirolo, 2016; Cruz, Queirolo and Boidi, 2016). Since this initial disapproval, the number of citizens who disagreed with legalization has decreased: in March 2017, 54.1 percent were against (Cruz, Boidi and Queirolo 2018), and in December 2017 opposition diminished to 41.4 percent (Monitor Cannabis, 2017), but the population is still split on the form of cannabis regulation.

Given this context, it is puzzling why a government that was not compelled by an electoral mandate from voters to fight for this particular policy, and had no popular support for the policy, decided to embark on this drug policy change. The most plausible explanation is public insecurity: approval of this initiative occurred mainly because of an association between the legalization agenda and the public safety agenda that was fostered in the winter of 2012. This helped to generate the idea that cannabis legalization was a solution to the problem of public insecurity and drug-related crimes (Queirolo et al., 2018).

This chapter is organized using the following structure. The next section explains why Uruguay legalized recreational cannabis.[3] In the third section, the three ways of accessing marijuana are described and information on their functioning is provided. The fourth section states strengths and weaknesses of the regulation as it has been implemented. Finally, a group of lessons that can be learned from the Uruguayan regulation are stated.

Legalizing to increase public security

In addition to following a top-down policy process initiated by President José Mujica instead of the bottom-up process seen in other countries that have legalized cannabis, Uruguay's reasons for regulating were also partially different from those of the United States, Canada and Jamaica. Law 19,172 stated three main objectives. First, it aimed to decriminalize cannabis use by eliminating the legal inconsistency that had allowed marijuana possession and use (since 1974) but criminalized users for accessing cannabis. Second, it aimed to increase public security and reduce drug trafficking-related violence by taking cannabis supply out of the black market. Third, it aimed to improve public health through education and prevention campaigns that would minimize the risks and reduce the harms of cannabis consumption.

Among these objectives, cannabis legalization as a means of combating organized crime and drug trafficking was counterintuitive in the Latin American context where prohibitionist measures have been the traditional response to drug and crime problems. Even more striking is the fact that this objective is not emphasized in any other cannabis legalization in the world. The causal relationship between crime/violence and drugs is an open discussion in the literature (Brothers, 2003). While some scholars argue that there is strong evidence supporting the link between illicit drug use and crime (White and Gorman, 2000), others point to the complexity as well as the spurious and/or recursive nature of this relationship (Gottfredson and Hirschi, 1990; McBride and McCoy, 1993).

The causal connection between drugs and crime is more dubious when the drug is cannabis. Goldstein (1985) poses three different meanings that this association can entail. First, the "psychopharmacological violence" which comprises crimes that occur because of drug consumption. In the case of marijuana, the evidence linking marijuana use to violence is not conclusive (Schoeler, Theobald, Pingault, Farrington, Jennings, Piquero, Coid and Bhattacharyya, 2016). Moreover, experimental evidence suggests that THC, one of the main psychoactive components of marijuana, decreases aggressive behavior. The second form of association between drugs and violence is "economic compulsive violence," which involves crimes committed by drug-using individuals to fund their personal consumption. Third, "systemic violence" consists of crimes performed as part of drug trafficking activities. These last two types of violence are also easier to attribute to other types of drugs, such as cocaine, crack or heroin, than to cannabis. Taking this evidence into consideration, it seems highly implausible that legalizing marijuana will achieve the objective of reducing narcotrafficking and increasing public security.

Cannabis legalization in Uruguay had an initial goal of reducing the leverage of criminal organizations tied to drug trafficking, a strategy that has not been proven before and is quite counterintuitive for the region. Why did Uruguay legalize marijuana with the goal of increasing public security and reducing narcotrafficking? The main reason is a "window of opportunity" (Kingdon, 2011) that opened after a series of violent crimes that were linked with drugs (Repetto, 2014; Muller and Draper, 2017; Queirolo et al. 2018). This made it possible for some political actors, who were already convinced that cannabis legalization was the best way to undermine narcotrafficking, to propose and include legalization as one of the 15 measures in a document called the *Strategy for Life and Coexistence* designed to tackle the citizens' increasing perception of insecurity.

According to Kingdon, on some occasions, certain circumstances or junctures offer opportunities for public policy issues to enter the government's agenda. These unpredictable and unstructured scenarios allow changes in policies that otherwise would not succeed. These "windows of opportunity" form politically novel scenarios in which actors articulate problems and successfully connect them to public policy solutions.

That "window of opportunity" happened in 2012 with the occurrence of several notorious crimes that received extensive media coverage and were reported in the press as drug related. This led to a growing concern within Uruguayan society about the issue of security, and a march was organized against insecurity. The repercussions and media coverage of both the crimes and the march created a connection between concerns about security and concerns about drug consumption and trafficking. This view lined up with the idea, which was gaining international relevance, that the war on drug trafficking had failed (Henman, 2009; Tokatlian and Briscoe, 2010; Thoumi, 2009, 2010). This is the context that made President Mujica call for a Security Cabinet (which was officially created in February 2011).

In June 2012, the cabinet presented a "strategy for life and coexistence." Among the measures proposed in this strategy were the need to carry out a "comprehensive approach to the problem of people affected by a drug use problem and its environment, generating a comprehensive strategy to address the main consequences of drug use, mainly freebase cocaine" and the "creation of judicial mechanisms specialized in narcotrafficking." In addition, explicit reference was made to "legalization of marijuana, with a strong role from the State on the production" (Security Cabinet, 2012, p. 9).

A month after presenting the strategy, on August 8, 2012, the Executive sent a bill to Congress that would regulate the market for marijuana. The explanatory memorandum, which usually indicates why each project is presented, was an extensive document which provided detailed information on regulatory mechanisms, harm reduction and international experience. The project itself was a single article in which the state was given control over marijuana and its derivatives for importation, production, acquisition, storage, marketing and distribution. The project did not contain details about how and when the state would undertake these activities, nor were there any references to the three legal means of acquiring recreational marijuana that were subsequently adopted, namely, home growing, cannabis clubs or pharmacy sales.

Three means of acquisition: clubs, pharmacies and home growers

Uruguay's cannabis legalization involves state regulation and control of each of the three ways to access recreational marijuana: home cultivation, pharmacies and social cannabis clubs. No advertisement of any type is allowed, and it is forbidden to sell to tourists and Uruguayans under 18 years of age. These three ways to access marijuana require mandatory registration and people have to choose only one means of access. If they want to change to a different means of access, they have to wait three months.

Registered home growers can have up to 6 female flowering plants per household, with a production total of 480 grams per year. If they produce more, they must dispose of that surplus. Between the opening of the registry in August 2014 and August 2018, 9,711 persons have started the procedure to become home growers, 19.7 percent of those licenses have expired after 3 years because home growers didn't renew them, 4.4 percent were cancelled and

5.7 percent were denied, leaving 6,735 current registered growers (IRCCA, 2018).

Among those registered, 3 out of 4 are men and the mean age is 35, which is older than the mean consumer age of 28 reported in the VI national household survey on drug use.[4] Only one-third live in Montevideo, the capital city; the rest live in other regions of the country (mainly Canelones and Maldonado). Half of the home growers are owners of the place they use for cultivating (IRCCA, 2018).

Based on survey data, it is estimated that the number of non-registered growers is double that who have registered (Aguiar, 2018; Baudeau, 2018; Cruz, Boidi and Queirolo, 2018). But currently there is no information on how sociodemographic characteristics, attitudes or opinions may differ between registered and non-registered home growers. It is also unknown what incentives led some growers to register and others not to do so.

Cannabis Social Clubs (CSCs) are the second way to acquire legal recreational marijuana under the new regulations. A CSC is allowed to have up to 99 plants in the club, and it can distribute up to 480 grams per year per member. Surplus yield must be turned over to the authorities. Membership should be no fewer than 15 people and no more than 45. As with other means of access, registration is mandatory and only Uruguayan residents over 18 years old can be members (IRCCA, 2018).

The CSC registry opened in October 2014 as the second way to access cannabis implemented by the government. As of August 2018, there were 99 CSCs: 14 clubs applied in 2015, 35 in 2016, 41 in 2017 and 9 in 2018. Most of them are established in Montevideo (44.4 percent), followed by those located on the east coast of the country (Canelones, Maldonado and Rocha). In 11 out of the 19 regions of the country (known as "departments"), there are no CSCs. There are 2,517 registered people in the 99 CSCs, equating to a mean of 25 members per club. The majority of CSCs rent the space where they are located (63.6 percent) (IRCCA, 2018).

From the registry of the Instituto de Regulación y Control del Cannabis (IRCCA, 2018) we know that members of CSCs in Uruguay are mostly men (80 percent), with ages that vary from 18 to 88, and a mean age of 33 (older than persons who used in the previous year in the VI national household survey on drug use). Half of them have been members since the beginning of the club.

At the beginning, CSCs experienced financial, organizational, bureaucratic and collective action problems (Queirolo, Boidi, and Cruz, 2016; Decorte, Pardal, Queirolo, Boidi, Sánchez Avilés and Parés Franquero, 2017), but a learning process has taken place in which some of the first CSCs taught the new clubs how to successfully form a CSC (Pardal, Queirolo, Álvarez and Repetto, 2018). In terms of law enforcement, the IRCCA inspects CSCs several times per year, provides them feedback on their operations and asks CSCs for changes when necessary. There were a few cases in which the IRCCA inspections led to closure of CSCs (for example, a CSC with 900 plants that offered cannabis tours for tourists).

The third way to access legal recreational marijuana is through pharmacies. This was the last measure to be implemented in July 2017. The marijuana legalization law was an inheritance that President Tabaré Vázquez's government received from Mujica in 2015. Despite the fact that Vázquez was not very fond of this regulation, he ensured its complete implementation, including cannabis sales at pharmacies. Partly due to the lack of presidential support, however, the government carried out the implementation very slowly. After a months-long bidding process, two companies were selected to grow the cannabis that the government would sell at pharmacies;[5] both companies have a mix of Uruguayan and foreign capital (Hudak, Ramsey and Walsh, 2018).

Despite the process beginning in 2016, it was not until July 2017 that sales began in pharmacies. Because it is not mandatory for pharmacies to sell cannabis, it was difficult for the government to convince pharmacy owners to do so. Some argued that they would lose traditional clients if they started selling cannabis, others were afraid of experiencing robberies or problems with illegal drug dealers, and some simply didn't see cannabis as a profitable business. For that reason, only 16 pharmacies started selling in July 2017, and there were only 13 doing so as of September 2018 (IRCCA, 2018).

Users need to be registered to buy cannabis at pharmacies, and, as with the other two means of access, they are allowed up to 40 grams per month. By August 2018, there were 25,865 registered users, and 82 percent of them had bought marijuana at least once. The characteristics of buyers at pharmacies are not very different from users that prefer the other two means of acquisition. They are mostly male (70 percent), and half are between 18 and 29 years old, older than those who report marijuana consumption in the VI national household survey on drug use. One-third have at least some university education (making them less educated than consumers in the VI national household survey on drug use) (IRCCA, 2018).

Six out of ten registered buyers live in Montevideo, where most of the selling pharmacies are located, but the per capita rate of registrations is higher in other departments, such as Maldonado and Flores (20.66 and 18.46 out of 1000 respectively). As expected, accessibility matters: departments with pharmacies that sell cannabis have higher rates of registered buyers per capita (13.44 out of 1000) than departments that do not have pharmacies that sell cannabis (2.8 out of 1000) (IRCCA, 2018).

Strengths and weaknesses of the implementation

Almost five years after Law 19,172 was approved, there are several apparent strengths and weaknesses of the implementation process. Starting with the weaknesses, the law was implemented with extreme caution and slowly, particularly the sale of cannabis at pharmacies; however, caution was not enough to avoid problems, mainly related to supply.

As previously mentioned, IRCCA reports (IRCCA, 2018) that only 82 percent of registered individuals have purchased marijuana. There are multiple possible explanations for this phenomenon. One possibility is that individuals do not want to buy marijuana at a pharmacy despite having registered to do so. They might not buy because they do not use marijuana and have only registered to show support for the law, or they might not buy because they do not like the varieties or potency of the cannabis sold at pharmacies. But an alternative explanation focuses on the problems on the supply side.

First, there are not enough pharmacies selling to meet demand. As mentioned previously, many pharmacy owners didn't want to sell cannabis, and by August 2018 there were only 13 pharmacies among the more than 1,200 in the country that sell cannabis. There were initially 16 pharmacies but there was a problem with US banks that forbade marijuana-selling pharmacies to operate bank accounts, so some pharmacies dropped out. As a result, not all the Uruguayan territory is covered: there are 11 out of 19 departments without a pharmacy that sell cannabis and it is highly likely that at least part of the 18 percent of registered users who haven't bought marijuana do not have a pharmacy close by.

Second, the amount of marijuana authorized for production by the government and distributed to pharmacies has not been enough to meet demand. At the beginning of pharmacy sales, pharmacies ran out of marijuana after a few hours. As Hudak, et al. (2018), explain:

> Supply challenges in Uruguay arose because of a combination of typical economic forces and ones particular to the Uruguayan model. Uruguay faced the traditional information challenges regarding how much cannabis would be consumed, even as the law requires people to register to purchase at pharmacies and the law limits the monthly quantity that can be purchased. Growth in the number of registrants can happen quickly, while changes to cultivation (and consequently, output) take months to adjust.
>
> (p. 11)

Third, the approved cultivators had problems with production. Because the Uruguayan regulation implies heavy state control, all cannabis produced has to be tested and approved by IRCCA before it can be supplied to pharmacies. One of the cultivators was slow in getting the production ready and when they had produced cannabis, it did not pass the IRCCA tests. This event, in addition to the fact that during the first months a pharmacy could only receive two kilograms of cannabis monthly in deliveries every 14 days,[6] led to long lines of people waiting outside pharmacies for hours because pharmacies quickly ran out of marijuana.

Shortages and delays in sales at pharmacies created the problem that registered buyers were not able to buy legally and therefore had to use the illegal market. As one registered buyer at a pharmacy states clearly in a blog about Faso Map, an app that tells users which pharmacies have marijuana: "the government makes you register at pharmacy to finish with narcotrafficking and there is never stock. I have been waiting to buy for 20 days, and nothing, holy shit. So, I'll buy *prensado*."[7] These supply side problems arising from implementation have left the government in a weak position to enforce the law against illicit cultivation because there was not enough marijuana available through the three legal means of access.

Moving to the positive side of the regulation implementation, an important proportion of marijuana consumers are using legal marijuana, indicating that a market separation process is going on (Reinarman, 2009). Despite the difficulty of estimating that number with precision, IRCCA has 35,117 registered users, which accounts for almost a quarter of annual users (around 147,000 from the VI national household survey). However, we know that legal marijuana reaches more people because marijuana is shared with other users: home growers and members of CSCs share their marijuana with, on average, at least two more persons, while buyers at pharmacies share with one more (VI national household survey of drug use). Taking this sharing into account, around 54 percent of marijuana consumers in Uruguay are using legal marijuana.[8]

Having more than half of marijuana consumers accessing legal marijuana five years after passing the regulation is positive for two main reasons. First, those users are less exposed to illegal activities, places or networks. Data from a panel survey of frequent consumers indicate that exposure to illegal means of access to marijuana such a dealer or a "boca" has diminished. The comparison among those that buy marijuana, excluding those that buy at pharmacies, are members of CSCs or are home growers, shows that most of them buy from a friend, who can be a registered or non-registered user, but most likely is not someone who is involved in criminal activities (see Table 5.1). The rise in the number of users "buying from a friend" is an indicator of a grey marijuana market.

The second important benefit of access to legal marijuana is improved quality control. Users of legal marijuana are using flowers that, for the most part, have gone through quality tests. At least this is the case for flowers

Table 5.1 Most frequent way to buy marijuana (excluding pharmacies, home growing and cannabis clubs), %, 2014 and 2017

Way to buy marijuana	*2014*	*2017*
Regular dealer	34.3	26.8
A new dealer every time	10	10.7
Regular "boca"	14.3	10.7
Buys from a friend	30	50
Another	11.4	1.8
Total	100	100

Question: How do you usually get the marijuana (pressed or cogollo) that you buy or others buy for yourself? $N = 94$

Source: Panel survey with frequent consumers, LAMRI

Table 5.2 Most used mechanism to access marijuana in the last 6 months (in %), 2014 and 2017

Mechanism to access	*2014*	*2017*
Bought *prensado* directly	34.7	10.4
Bought flowers directly	5.3	19.8
A family member or friend bought *prensado* for her/him	23.2	2.1
A family member or friend bought flowers for her/him	2.1	7.3
Individual home growing	14.7	14.6
Group home growing	0	2.1
Someone gave her/him *prensado*	8.4	1
Someone gave her/him flowers	11.6	25
Bought at pharmacies or cannabis clubs (directly or through a friend or family member)*	0	17.6
Total	100	100

Source: Panel survey with frequent consumers, LAMRI

Note

* Buying at pharmacies and being a member of a cannabis social club were not available mechanisms in 2014

Question: Among these mechanisms of getting marijuana, which one did you use most frequently in the last 6 months? *N=94*

sold at pharmacies and cannabis clubs. On the other hand, "prensado" has almost disappeared. In 2014, 34.7 percent of frequent consumers had bought "prensado" directly, 23.2 percent had bought it through a friend or family member and 8.4 percent said that someone gave them "prensado." In 2017, those percentages were reduced to 10.4, 2.1 and 1 percent respectively (see Table 5.2). The flower market has also grown significantly: in 2014, 5.3 percent bought flowers directly, 2.1 percent bought flowers through a family member or a friend and 11.6 percent received flowers from someone. In 2017, those percentages had increased to 19.8, 7.3 and 25 percent respectively.

Lessons to be learned

Regardless of the weaknesses and strengths of the implementation of Uruguay's marijuana regulation, there have been positive and negative results. Among the positive is that cannabis use has been decriminalized in addition to more than half of annual users consuming legal marijuana, fewer people being exposed to the dealer or the "boca" and users having access to a better-quality marijuana (more flowers and less "prensado"). Since the legislation was passed, there were almost no reports on incidents among legal users and the police or the judicial system. Moreover, home growers and CSCs have experienced certainty and predictability about how the regulations work and what they must do in order to operate under the law. These positive results might partially explain why public opinion has become more favorable toward the law (Cruz, Boidi and Queirolo, 2018).

On the negative side, in addition to supply problems at pharmacies due to too few selling marijuana and the banking problems faced by pharmacies that do sell cannabis, there are other important issues that legalization has raised. There are some preliminary data indicating that the prevalence of annual and lifetime marijuana use has increased since legalization and is now a little bit over the average in Uruguay (Musto and Robaina, 2018).

Based on national household surveys of drug use that have been carried out since 2001, it is known that both annual and lifetime prevalence of marijuana use have increased. In 2001, lifetime marijuana use was 5.3 percent of the population; in 2006 it was 13.1 percent. This increased in 2011 to 20 percent, to 23.3 percent in 2014 and to 33.6 percent in 2017. The same trend occurred with past-year use, which went from 1.4 percent in 2001 to 5.5 percent in 2006, 8.3 percent in 2011, 9.3 percent in 2014 and 15.4 percent in 2017. The rise of the two prevalence rates from 2014 to 2017 looks impressive, and while the increases are significant, it is important to take into consideration that the 2014 values do not adjust to the increasing trend. Moreover, the same growth from 2014 to 2017 is found in the prevalence of cocaine use, which was not legalized (Musto and Robaina, 2018). In conclusion, more evidence is necessary to assess the effect that marijuana regulation has had on the prevalence of its use.

Although Law 19,172 was approved to reduce narcotrafficking and increase public security, crime and violence have not diminished. On the contrary, the homicide rate has increased, in particular among criminals (Ministerio del Interior, 2018). As mentioned previously, the causal link between marijuana legalization and increased public security was more a political than an evidence-based claim. This means that it makes little sense to judge this policy reform through the lens of increased public security, despite the fact that this was one of the law's main purposes.

There are several items on the "to do list" of Uruguay's legalization process which contain lessons for other countries considering similar policy changes. First, it is important to build the data infrastructure necessary to evaluate the impact of legalization. In the case of Uruguay, no relevant effort was made. Nor was an effort made to collect data on public health (no training for medical doctors or nurses to collect data on incidentals or intoxications). There are no data on rates of traffic accidents under the influence of marijuana.

Second, a grey market has flourished in a state-oriented form of cannabis regulation that requires mandatory consumer registration and has fixed limits on the amount of marijuana that a consumer can use. In Uruguay, those who are not registered but consume legal marijuana are part of this grey market which also includes illegal marijuana supplied by non-registered home growers. The size and characteristics of this market are still unknown.

The grey market brings up a third issue: the law enforcement dilemma. It is difficult to enforce the law that it is still being implemented. Consumers can complain that the regulation is not operating properly, for example, because of shortages at pharmacies so they have to buy cannabis illegally. However, once the implementation is fully achieved, the government will have to decide how and among whom it will enforce legalization.

Currently, marijuana legalization in Uruguay has the advantages that it has diminished criminalization of users, improved substance quality and decreased contact between cannabis users and illicit dealers. But there are several downsides that have to be followed closely and addressed. These include: the evolution of a grey market, the increased consumption (related to prevalence and age of initiation and the number of grams that are consumed and their potency) and the normalization of use.[9] Depending on how these evolve, public approval might keep rising or not, and greater support from citizens will work as a policy shield in the event of a change in the political context.

Notes

1 Law 14,294: https://legislativo.parlamento.gub.uy/temporales/leytemp5460733.htm#
2 Cifra consultores (2013): The Uruguayan and regulation of the production, sale and consumption of marijuana. Available in www.cifra.com. FACTUM. The doubts and contradictions of society about the legalization of marijuana. Available in: www.factum.edu.uy/node/1080
3 Law 19,172 also includes regulations for industrial hemp and medicinal cannabis, but this chapter is focused on the analysis of recreational marijuana.
4 Mean age of previous year's consumers.
5 ICC and Simbiosis are the two companies chosen among 20 that competed in the bidding. In September 2018, ICC was sold for $220 million to Aurora Cannabis.
6 This amount was increased to four kilograms in 2018.
7 Prensado is the name given to the marijuana that came from Paraguay in the form of a brick.
8 It is still to be estimated the proportion of total cannabis consumption that is now legal, because, due to the supply problems, it might be smaller than the proportion of legal users.
9 As the time of writing, IRCCA has delivered the "Pautas de reducción de riesgo en el uso de cannabis" which are an adaptation of the "Canada´s Lower Risk Cannabis Use Guidelines (LRCUG)," an evidence-based intervention initiative by the CIHR-funded CRISM. These are the first guidelines prepared by the IRCCA as educational and communication materials after the legalization has taken place.

References

Aguiar, S. (2018). *Cultivo en Uruguay: El patio trasero de la regulación*. Paper presented at Congreso cinco años de la regulación del cannabis, December 10–12, 2018, Montevideo, Uruguay.

Aguiar, S. and Musto, C. (2015). El rayo verde: Regulación de la marihuana en Uruguay. *Drogas, política y sociedad en América Latina y el Caribe*. México: CIDE, 297–316.

Arrarás, A. and Bello-Pardo, E.D. (2014). Inventando caminos – Cannabis regulation in Uruguay. In R. Zepeda and J.D.R. Rosen (Eds.), *Cooperation and drug policies in the Americas: Trends in the twenty-first century*. Lexington Books.

Bardazano, G. (2012). Sobre la justificación de las decisiones judiciales relativas a la interpretación del artículo 31 de Decreto Ley 14.294 en su redacción dada por la Ley 17.016: se presume culpable. *Revista de Derecho Penal*, 20, 93–110.

Baudeau, M. (2018). *Una primera lectura sobre los resultados de la regulación del cannabis en Uruguay a cinco años de promulgada la ley 19.172*. Paper presented at Congreso cinco años de la regulación del cannabis, December 10–12, 2018, Montevideo, Uruguay.

Brothers, D. (2003). Substance abuse and crime: An analysis of the relationship and its impact on Canadian drug policy. *Perspectives on Canadian Drug Policy*, 76–92. Kingston, ON: The John Howard Society of Canada.

Cruz, J.M., Boidi, M.F., Queirolo, R. (2016) Saying no to weed: Public opinion towards cannabis legalisation in Uruguay. *Drugs: Education, Prevention and Policy*, 25, 67–76.

Cruz, J.M., Boidi, M.F. and Queirolo, R. (2018). The status of support for cannabis regulation in Uruguay 4 years after reform: Evidence from public opinion surveys. *Drug and Alcohol Review*, 37, S429-S434.

Cruz, J.M., Queirolo, R. and Boidi, M.F. (2016) Determinants of public support for marijuana legalization in Uruguay, the United States, and El Salvador. *Journal of Drug Issues*, 46, 308–25.

Cruz, J.M., Queirolo, R. and Boidi, M.F. (2018). *El impacto de la regulación de la marihuana en los consumidores frecuentes en Uruguay*. Paper presented at Congreso cinco años de la regulación del cannabis, December 10–12, 2018, Montevideo, Uruguay.

Decorte, T., Pardal, M., Queirolo, R., Boidi, M. F., Sánchez Avilés, C. and Parés Franquero, Ò. (2017). Regulating cannabis social clubs: A comparative analysis of legal and self-regulatory practices in Spain, Belgium and Uruguay. *International Journal of Drug Policy*, 43, 44–56.

Garat, G. (2015). *El camino. Cómo se reguló el cannabis en Uruguay según sus actores políticos y sociales*. Friedrich Ebert Stiftung/junta nacional de drogas. Montevideo, Uruguay.

Garibotto, G. (2011). Prisons and drugs in Uruguay. In P. Metaal and C. Youngers (Eds.). *Systems overload, drug laws and prisons in Latin America* 7 (pp. 81–87). Washington, DC: Washington Office on Latin America.

Goldstein, P.J. (1985). The drugs/violence nexus: A tripartite conceptual framework. *Journal of Drug Issues*, 15(4), 493–506.

Gottfredson, M. and Hirschi, T. (1990). *A general theory of crime*. Stanford: Stanford University Press.

Henman, A. (2009). Efectos reales y alternativas a la prohibición: ¿Es posible aplicar políticas de reducción de riesgos y daños bajo las convenciones de la ONU? *Nueva Sociedad*, 222, 104–111.

Hetzer, H. and Walsh, J. (2014). Pioneering cannabis regulation in Uruguay. NACLA. *Report on the Americas*, 47(2), 33–35.

Hudak, J., Ramsey, G. and Walsh, J. (2018). *Uruguay's cannabis law: Pioneering a new paradigm*. WOLA.

Instituto de Regulación y Control del Cannabis IRCCA. (2018). *Mercado regulado de cannabis*. Informe al 05/04/2018. Montevideo.

Kilmer, B., Kruithof, K., Pardal, M., Caulkins, J.P. and Rubin, J. (2013). *Multinational overview of cannabis production regimes*. Brussels: Rand Europe.

Kingdon, J. (2011). *Agendas, alternatives and public policies* (2nd ed.). Longman Classics in Political Science.

McBride, D. and McCoy, C. (1993). The drugs-crime relationship: An analytical framework. *The Prison Journal,* 73(3), 257–278.

Ministerio del Interior (2018). Retrieved from: www.minterior.gub.uy/observatorio/images/pdf/homicidios.pdf.

Monitor Cannabis (2017). Retrieved from: http://monitorcannabis.uy/cambios-en-la-opinion-publica-sobre-la-regulacion-del-cannabis/.

Muller, C. and Draper, G. (2017). *Marihuana oficial: Crónica de un experimento uruguayo*. Sudamericana.

Musto, C. (2018). *Regulating cannabis markets: The construction of an innovative drug policy in Uruguay*. Doctoral dissertation. Utrecht: Utrecht University.

Musto, C. and Robaina, G. (2018). *Evolución del consumo de cannabis en Uruguay y mercados regulados*. Monitor Cannabis. Retrieved from: http://monitorcannabis.uy/evolucion-del-consumo-de-cannabis-en-uruguay-y-mercados-regulados/.

Pardal, M., Queirolo, R., Álvarez, E. and Repetto, L. (2019). Uruguayan Cannabis Social Clubs: From activism to dispensaries? *International Journal of Drug Policy,* 73, 49–57.

Pardo, B. (2014). Cannabis policy reforms in the Americas: A comparative analysis of Colorado, Washington, and Uruguay. *International Journal of Drug Policy,* 25(4), 727–735.

Queirolo, R., Boidi, M.F. and Cruz, J. M. (2016). Cannabis clubs in Uruguay: The challenges of regulation. *International Journal of Drug Policy,* 34, 41–48.

Queirolo, R., Rossel, C. Álvarez, E. and Repetto, L. (2018) Why Uruguay legalized marijuana? *Addiction,* 114(7), 1313–1321.

Reinarman, C. (2009). Cannabis policies and user practices: Market separation, price, potency, and accessibility in Amsterdam and San Francisco. *International Journal of Drug Policy*, 20(1), 28–37.

Repetto, L. (2014). Regulación del cannabis: ¿un asunto de seguridad? Entrada y mantenimiento en agenda de un problema de política pública. *Revista Uruguaya de Ciencia Política,* 23(1), 6–34.

Room, R. (2014). Legalizing a market for cannabis for pleasure: Colorado, Washington, Uruguay and beyond. *Addiction,* 109, 345–351.

Schoeler, T., Theobald, D., Pingault, J-B., Farrington, D.P., Jennings, W.G., Piquero, A.R., Coid, J.W. and Bhattacharyya, S. (2016). Continuity of cannabis use and violent offending over the life course. *Psychological Medicine,* 46, 1663–1.

Security Cabinet. (2012). *Strategy for life and coexistence*. Retrieved from: https://medios.presidencia.gub.uy/jm_portal/2012/noticias/NO_E582/Estrategia.pdf.

Thoumi, F.E. (2009). La normatividad internacional sobre drogas como camisa de fuerza. *Nueva Sociedad*, 222, 42–59.

Thoumi, F. (2010). Debates recientes de la Organización de las Naciones Unidas acerca del régimen internacional de drogas: Fundamentos, limitaciones e (im) posibles cambios. In J.G. Tokatlian (Ed.), *Drogas y prohibición. Una vieja guerra un nuevo debate* (pp. 27–56). Buenos Aires: Libros del Zorzal.

Tokatlian, J.G. and Briscoe, I. (2010). Drugs: Towards a post-prohibitionist paradigm. *Journal for International Relations and Global Trends,* 3, 102–110.

Von Hoffmann, J. (2016). The international dimension of drug policy reform in Uruguay. *International Journal of Drug Policy*, 34, 27–33.

Walsh, J. and Ramsey, G. (2015). *Uruguay's drug policy: Major innovations, major challenges*. Brookings Institute. Center for 21st Century Security and Intelligence Latin America Initiative. Retrieved from www.brookings.edu/wp-content/uploads/2016/07/Walsh-Uruguay-final.pdf.

White, H.R. and Gorman, D.M. (2000). Dynamics of the drug-crime relationship. *Criminal Justice*, 1(15), 1–218.

Part II

General models of reform

6 Cannabis decriminalization policies across the globe

Niamh Eastwood

Introduction

It is estimated that 83 per cent of all drug offenses globally are for personal possession of drugs (Economic and Social Council, 2013). The damage of criminalizing people caught in possession of drugs is well documented (Global Commission on Drug Policy, 2016). Cannabis, as the most widely consumed controlled drug (United Nations on Drugs and Crime, 2018), is a driver for many of these harms, as the vast majority of people criminalized will be so for the use or possession of this drug. In many parts of the world, people convicted for possession or use of cannabis will be imprisoned. This continues to occur in Russia, many South East Asian countries, in parts of Latin America and in African countries. Even where the criminal offense of cannabis use or possession carries a negligible risk of imprisonment, the damage done by a criminal record to an individual can be life-changing. The effect of criminalization can have a profound impact on employment and educational opportunities, access to state benefits and social housing, and can increase stigma and marginalization (Puras and Hannah, 2017). Criminalization can also contribute to an increased risk of reoffending.

The focus of drug law enforcement, in particular cannabis policing and prosecution, has a deleterious effect on certain communities who are over-policed on the basis of drug prohibition. In the United States (US), people of color are disproportionally policed for marijuana possession, with black people 3.73 times more likely to be arrested for the offense compared to white people, despite using cannabis at roughly the same rate as the white population (American Civil Liberties Union, 2013). In the UK, black people are sentenced at court at 11.8 times the rate of white people for the offense of cannabis possession, whilst government statistics estimate that black people use the drug at a lower rate than white people (Shiner, Carre, Delsol and Eastwood, 2018). These racial disparities, both in the UK and the US, are not limited to arrests or prosecutions, but are evident throughout policing, from stop and search through to prosecution (Shiner et al., 2018; Levine and Siegel, 2015). The racist nature of drug law enforcement is not new and was one of the drivers for originally prohibiting cannabis, at least in the US.

The criminalization of cannabis related activities – a relatively recent phenomenon

Cannabis prohibition is a relatively recent historical phenomenon with the first efforts to criminalize certain activities related to the substance emerging at the end of the nineteenth century. One of the first countries to prohibit access to cannabis was Egypt when, in 1884, it banned the cultivation and importation of the drug, and closed "mashhashas" (cannabis cafes), through national legislation. The early part of the twentieth century was marked by the widespread suppression of cannabis by countries across the globe, largely achieved through the use of criminal penalties. Many states enacted national legislation to prohibit the drug after it was controlled at the 1925 League of Nations' Second Opium Conference (Kendall, 2002).

In the first two decades of the twentieth century, the United States had already introduced federal legislation to control access to opium and cocaine. These actions were inextricably linked with racist overtures that sought to oppress and criminalize Chinese laborers[1] and African Americans, respectively (Nunn, 2002). Both groups were viewed as a threat to the white population. The non-medical use and supply of cocaine, opium and a number of other opiates, became illegal under the federal government's Harrison Act of 1914.

Cannabis possession and supply was not prohibited in the US federally until 1937, with the introduction of the Marijuana Tax Act. Prior to this, a number of US states had brought in legislation at a state level to prohibit possession, supply and production (Dills, Goffard and Miron, 2017). The use of cannabis was largely associated with the Hispanic community who, like the Chinese before them, were seen as an economic threat to labor and, like African Americans, were allegedly more likely to commit crime and become violent under the influence of the drug (Nunn, 2002). The racial prejudices that were evidently the foundation for the drug laws in the US would continue throughout the twentieth century and were one of the driving forces behind President Nixon's declaration of a "war on drugs."

A declaration of "war" and a partial retreat

The continued use of drug laws to control certain groups in society was central to Nixon's new "war" (Alexander, 2010). In fact, it has since been alleged that Nixon's decision to declare a "war on drugs" had little to do with the drugs themselves but rather was an excuse to target those opposing the war in Vietnam, and African Americans. In an interview, Nixon's domestic policy chief, John Ehrlichman stated:

> You understand what I'm saying? We knew we couldn't make it illegal to be either against the war or black, but by getting the public to associate the hippies with marijuana and blacks with heroin, and then criminalizing both heavily, we could disrupt those communities. We

> could arrest their leaders, raid their homes, break up their meetings, and vilify them night after night on the evening news. Did we know we were lying about the drugs? Of course we did.
>
> (Baum, 2016)

However, whilst in 1971 Nixon was declaring drugs as "public enemy number one," a number of US states were moving towards decriminalizing cannabis. Despite the risk of criminalization, cannabis use became more widespread in the US, resulting in significant increases in costs associated with enforcement and court proceedings. At the same time, there was greater public acceptance of use of the drug and, with it, growing support for reforming cannabis laws. In 1973, Oregon was the first US state to decriminalize possession of personal use of cannabis. Criminal penalties were replaced by a civil fine for those caught in possession of less than an ounce of cannabis; the fine was a maximum of $100 (Single, Christie and Ali, 2000). In 1975, California legislators moved cannabis possession from a felony to a misdemeanor offense. Possession of less than 28.5 grams resulted in a fine of up to $100 (Aldrich and Mikuriya, 1988). By 1978, 10 US states enacted legislation that saw cannabis possession dealt with through a system of fines (Single et al., 2000).

What is meant by decriminalization?

Decriminalization refers to the ending of criminal sanctions for possession of a controlled drug, including cannabis, and, in some cases, the cultivation of cannabis for a person's own use. In most jurisdictions, civil sanctions, such as fines or referral to treatment programs, will replace criminal penalties, although some systems have no penalty for personal possession or cultivation (Hughes and Stevens, 2010). Decriminalization of drug possession is largely achieved through *de jure* models, which means that a change in law was achieved either through legislative reform or on the basis of a Constitutional Court decision. In respect of the latter, the question the court has to consider is the compatibility of the criminal law to prohibit the private use of controlled drugs with the protection of fundamental constitutional rights, for example the right to privacy. Additionally, some countries have deprioritized the policing of drug possession through de facto decriminalization, which essentially means that the criminal offense of possession is still on the statute books, but the law is not enforced based on policing and/or prosecutorial guidance. Whilst this approach does not sit neatly within the definition above, there are some countries that are of note, in particular, the Netherlands, which has had such a policy in place since 1976.

Decriminalization models do not provide a system for the legal production and supply of controlled drugs, which are still treated as criminal offenses, although a limited number of jurisdictions do permit cultivation of cannabis for personal use, with a handful allowing social supply of cannabis. Generally, most models of decriminalization will be restrictive in the sense that possession of a controlled drug, and/or cannabis cultivation for personal use is still illegal but treated as a civil offense rather than a criminal one. Some systems could be perceived as more permissive where possession and/or cultivation is permitted for personal use in that there is simply no penalty. The term "decriminalization" is often unhelpfully conflated with the term "legalization." Legalization or regulation is the establishment of a legal framework for the lawful production, supply and possession of a controlled drug for non-medical purposes.

The different paths towards decriminalization – a global experience

It is estimated that in excess of 30 countries across the world have implemented some form of decriminalization of cannabis (Eastwood, Fox and Rosmarin, 2016). In the vast majority of countries, possession of all controlled drugs has been decriminalized. However, in several jurisdictions it is only cannabis possession, and in some cases cultivation of cannabis for personal use, where criminal penalties have been replaced by civil sanctions.

Countries that have decriminalized possession of all controlled drugs will be considered in this chapter, as their experiences are fundamental to understanding the processes by which the model is implemented and the impact decriminalization has on individuals and society, including in respect of cannabis. The different means of achieving decriminalization are explored with specific focus on the *de jure* models that are established through legislative reforms or constitutional court decisions and, finally, de facto decriminalization.

Drivers for legislative reforms leading to decriminalization of possession offenses

A number of countries have amended their drug laws or introduced new legislation ending the criminalization of drug possession, including cannabis, often replacing the criminal framework with an administrative or civil system for dealing with such activities. In fact, when we look at countries that have decriminalized personal use offenses, the vast majority have done so by amending legislation or introducing a new legislative framework. Considering how drug law reform is often seen as a risky or controversial issue for politicians (MacGregor, 2013), some exploration of the drivers for reform that led to governments taking steps towards ending the criminalization of people who use drugs are also explored.

As highlighted, many US states introduced or amended legislation throughout the 1970s as the use of cannabis amongst the American population increased significantly. Cannabis reforms in these states were driven by a number of factors including: increased prevalence resulting in a significant burden on criminal justice resources; greater public acceptance of cannabis use during that period; and concerns from politicians and opinion makers that middle-class kids were getting caught up in the criminal justice system as a result of being caught in possession of cannabis (Single et al., 2000). Whilst increased burden on criminal justice costs can be a driver towards decriminalization, there are other routes that have influenced drug law reform.

The influence of research on drug policy is unfortunately rare, however, the Czech Republic serves as an excellent example of a rational, evidence-based approach that led to legislative reform. The Czech authorities had actually decriminalized possession of drugs for personal use in 1990 (Act on Violations, Act No 200/1990). However, as a "moral panic" about drugs began to take hold in the media, there were demands from a number of political parties to criminalize drug possession. These demands were headed off by the government of the day by amending the penal code to criminalize possession of drugs where the amount involved was considered "greater than small" (Csete, 2012).

An evaluative study was subsequently commissioned by the National Drug Commission and set a number of propositions in relation to the amendment, namely, that "availability of illicit drugs will decrease" and that the "number of illicit drug users will decrease." In both cases, the research showed that despite the increased risk of criminalization, neither proposition was proven, the availability of controlled drugs had not been affected and prevalence had increased. Zabransky, Mravčík, Gajdosikova and Miovskù (2001) also found that the "social costs" of illegal drug use had significantly increased. The evaluative study, and efforts from experts and advocates, led to a revision of the drug laws in 2010 which introduced threshold amounts[2] in an attempt to define what constituted a "greater than small" amount (Csete, 2012). The revision of the law also introduced civil penalties for cultivation of cannabis for personal use (Belackova, Maalsté, Zabransky and Grund, 2015). In respect of cannabis possession, the threshold amount was 15 grams of herbal cannabis and 5 grams of resin; for cultivation it was up to 5 plants (Mravčík, 2015).[3] Whilst the Czech Republic is an excellent example of a rational approach to drug decriminalization, other countries have been less effective in their development of the law and policy in this area – the example of Mexico is a case in point.

Mexico has been ground zero for the war on drugs since 2006. To date, it is estimated that between 80,000 to 100,000 people have been murdered as a result of drug-related violence, with tens of thousands more disappeared or displaced (Council on Foreign Relations, 2018). In an attempt to refocus federal resources on drug trafficking and organized crime, the Mexican government introduced "narcomenudeo" law reforms in 2009. These reforms sought to decriminalize small amounts of drugs for personal use, to shift the policing and prosecution of low-level drug supply away from federal law enforcement to state-level enforcement and introduce mandatory treatment for "habitual" users (Arredondo, Gaines, Manian, Vilalta, Banuelos, Strathdee, and Beletsky, 2017).

The reforms around decriminalization of possession were largely meaningless. The threshold amounts that were introduced were nominal, with those caught in possession of less than 5 grams of cannabis, 0.5 grams of cocaine, 50 milligrams of heroin, or one ecstasy tablet, given encouragement to attend treatment in the first instance. If caught in possession of the threshold amount or less on three occasions, referral to treatment becomes mandatory (Artículos 478 and 479 "Narcomenudo Decree," 2009). The very low thresholds had a perverse effect, as the reforms to the 2009 law saw increased penalties for people caught in possession of drugs above the threshold amounts – even if possession is for personal use, people caught above the permitted amount face ten months to three years in prison (Russoniello, 2013). Mexico is an example of a system that fails to achieve what should be the primary purpose of decriminalization, that is, to divert anyone caught in possession for personal use away from the criminal justice system. Mexico is not the only country that has a weak model of decriminalization, which sees those caught above the threshold amount facing harsher sentences, including imprisonment for personal use offenses. A similar system works in Russia where the amounts specified to determine personal possession are extremely low, and those caught above the threshold level face lengthy prison sentences (Levison, 2008).

Constitutional Courts – developing a rights-based approach to drug use and possession

Beyond statutory reforms which seek to end criminal sanctions for possession of controlled drugs including cannabis, constitutional courts have played a vital role in balancing the rights of their citizens against interference by the state, who seek to use the criminal law to prohibit use of cannabis and other drugs. In the main, it has been European and Latin American constitutional courts that have ruled that the use of the criminal law to punish the private use of controlled drugs is unconstitutional or against legal norms within a country. Recently, South Africa's Constitutional Court ruled that cannabis possession and cultivation for personal use was protected under the Constitution (Constitutional Court of South Africa, Case CCT 108/17). In many instances, these decisions have paved the way for national legislation.

A number of courts have considered the issue of privacy and personal autonomy in respect of drug consumption and possession where it is for personal use and usually occurs in private settings. In addition, some courts have ruled against criminalization of possession of drugs on the grounds that it does not impede the health of anyone other than the person consuming the substance and it is therefore not proportional for the state to interfere with the individual's rights ("the proportionality test").

In 1994, the Colombian Constitutional Court ruled that the criminalization of possessing a small amount of drugs ("a personal dose") for personal use contravened Article 16 – the right to free personal development – and Article 49 – the right to affect one's health as long it does not interfere with the rights of third parties (Constitutional Court Gazette, 1994). The threshold amounts established by the court's decision were 20 grams of cannabis, 5 grams of hash, and 1 gram of cocaine (Guzmán and Yepes, 2010). This was the position in Colombia until 2009 when the then government introduced an amendment to restore a prohibitionist framework, albeit largely with administrative sanctions. However, the 1994 decision was reaffirmed by the Constitutional Court in 2012, which also confirmed the threshold amounts that had been previously established (Corte Constitucional de Colombia, 2012).

Similar decisions were made by constitutional courts in Argentina and Mexico. Argentina's Supreme Court ruled in 2009 that legislation that criminalized the possession of drugs for personal use was in violation of a person's constitutional right to privacy and their right to personal autonomy. Known as the *Arriola* decision, the case concerned possession of cannabis but has been interpreted as applying to all illicit drugs (Council of the European Union, 2014). More recently, the Mexican Supreme Court has considered a number of cases involving cannabis cultivation for personal use. The court considered two main questions: (1) what harm cannabis use posed to public health and public order and (2) did the relevant legislation minimize these harms? The court determined that the legislation had not reduced prevalence and, as such, had not reduced harms associated with use of cannabis. It also held that the legislation was disproportionate in its aims (Marks, 2018).

A number of European constitutional or supreme courts have also considered the application of the criminal law for possession of drugs, in particular, cannabis. In the early 1970s the Spanish Supreme Court held that possession of drugs for personal use was outside the scope of the criminal law. There were a number of grounds for their decision but one issue that was engaged was that of public health, where the court noted that the Criminal Code sought to protect public health. However, the court held that personal possession of drugs only created a risk to the health of the individual and that this was not the concern of the criminal law. The court's ruling was subsequently incorporated and reflected in criminal code reforms of the early 1980s (Marks, 2018).

Germany's Federal Constitutional Court (1994), was asked to consider the constitutionality of the criminal statute – the Intoxicating Substances Act 1992 – that prohibited activities related to cannabis. Whilst the court ruled that the use of the criminal statute to prohibited activities related to cannabis was proportional in its aim to protect public health and the reach of organized crime, the court was concerned that it would not be in the "public interest" to impose criminal penalties on a person who was in caught in possession of small quantities of cannabis for personal use. The judges in the case however identified that the Intoxicating Substances Act 1992, in conjunction with the Criminal Procedures Regulations, permitted prosecutors to discontinue a case against a defendant in circumstances where it was not in the public interest to bring a prosecution and that the drugs involved were for personal consumption. This included acts of cultivation, importation and exportation of a substance, as well as possession. The court highlighted that the application of the law to discontinue criminal prosecutions was not cohesive across German states ("landers") and that there was a "duty to ensure that the practice of the State Prosecution Services in respect of discontinuance of proceedings is substantially uniform" (German Federal Constitutional Court, 1994). This led to prosecutors in most landers establishing threshold amounts whereby criminal proceedings would be discontinued if the person caught in possession was below the level prescribed (Eastwood et al., 2016).

In 2018, Georgia's Constitutional Court abolished all sanctions for possession of cannabis, including administrative fines, on the basis that punishment of the activity contravenes Article 16 of the Georgian Constitution – "the right to a person's free development" (Constitution of Georgia, 1995). The court did say that if there was harm to a third party then it would be appropriate to impose sanctions, but in the absence of harm, it was not a punishable offense (OC Media, 2018).

There are some apparent weaknesses in the application of the legal rulings of constitutional or supreme courts. Where there has been a failure to implement the decisions of these higher courts into national law, police and prosecutors will continue to arrest and prosecute people for possession of drugs in spite of the rulings of the higher courts. For example, there are still high rates of arrest, and in some cases imprisonment, for possession of drugs for personal use in a number of countries highlighted above including Colombia and Argentina (Corda, 2015; Instituto Nacional Penitenciario y Carcelario, 2016). In Argentina, for example, Buenos Aires police arrested 2,093 people in the first three months of 2014; 98 percent of those arrests were for possession offenses (Council of the European Union, 2014).

De facto decriminalization – non-enforcement of the law

The Netherlands is an example of de facto decriminalization of possession of cannabis. In 1976, the Dutch Parliament amended the drug laws to create a legal distinction between "hard" and "soft" drugs. Hard drugs were considered to have "unacceptable risks" whilst "soft drugs," such as cannabis, were deemed to have "less severe risks" (Grund and Breeksema, 2013). Whilst legislation remained in place criminalizing possession and supply, the Ministry of Justice instructed law enforcement and prosecutors that cannabis offenses should be of the lowest priority (Stevens, 2010). Under this model, prosecutors were instructed not to prosecute those caught in possession of a certain amount of cannabis. Until 1996, the threshold was 30 grams, however, this was reduced to 5 grams (Reuter, 2010). The model also applies to "hard" drugs but the threshold in the case of these substances is 0.5 grams.

The Netherlands is the only example internationally of a national de facto *decriminalized* approach to possession of cannabis, although increasingly there is a trend, especially in the UK and Australia, for local police forces to implement diversion programs for people caught in possession of drugs. These programs result in no criminal record for the individuals diverted (Eastwood et al., 2016).

The impact of decriminalization policies

Considering that decriminalization of cannabis possession, and in some instances, cannabis cultivation for personal use, has been in operation in various jurisdictions for a number of decades, there is a wealth of evidence which considers the impact of these models. When decriminalization of personal use offenses is done well, the effects can be positive, such as in Portugal and some Australian states, especially in relation to the social impact of criminalization on individuals. Where the model has resulted in negative outcomes, these are arguably linked to implementation problems rather than the principle of decriminalization in itself.

Effects of cannabis decriminalization on levels of consumption

Politicians and policymakers often cite concerns about potential increases in consumption of controlled substances if there is a shift in the legal framework from criminalization to decriminalization. The question should be asked whether this metric is the most important in an effective drug policy, but in any event, the policy change itself has not led to significant increases – some jurisdictions that have decriminalized personal use offenses have experienced slight increases in consumption, whilst others have experienced slight decreases. Laquer (2014) notes that it is difficult to assess the genuine impact of such reforms on the basis that enforcement of the law was likely to be minimal prior to the implementation of the new legal framework. It is also worth considering the weaknesses of national prevalence estimates (Johnson, 2014) and the difficulty in assessing changes in drug use linked to policy reforms.

Australia has three states where possession of cannabis is decriminalized – South Australia (decriminalized in 1987), Australian Capital Territory (ACT) (decriminalized in 1993), and the Northern Territory (decriminalized in 1996) – all of these states deal with the offense through a system of civil fines. Both South Australia and ACT treat cultivation of cannabis for personal use as a civil offense. All three states rely on thresholds to determine whether a civil fine should be issued as an alternative to arrest. The threshold amounts vary, with changes to the levels over the years. Currently, South Australia treats possession of up to 100 grams, or one non-hydroponic plant, as punishable by way of a civil fine (maximum AUS $300). The threshold level in ACT is 50 grams of cannabis or cultivation of up to two hydroponic plants, with a civil fine of AUS $100. The Northern Territory's system excludes cultivation of cannabis for personal use, the state's threshold for cannabis possession is 50 grams and the fine is a maximum of AUS $200 (McLaren and Mattick, 2007).

Studies that look at the impact of decriminalization of cannabis offenses on prevalence in these states are mixed. Some studies have reported that the shift from criminal sanctions to civil penalties had little effect on rates of use compared to other Australian states, whilst others have pointed to an increase in the likelihood of use. One study considered the rates of cannabis consumption in South Australia from 1985–1995 and found that prevalence rose from 26 per cent to 36 percent in the 10-year period; however, similar patterns were observed in states that had continued to criminalize possession of cannabis (Donnelly, Hall and Christie, 1999). Studies considering the impact of decriminalization of cannabis possession on use amongst young people in South Australia and ACT found no statistically significant effect on lifetime or frequent use of cannabis (Neill, Christie and Cormack, 1991; McGeorge and Aitken, 1997). One study, however, did find that young people living in states where cannabis was decriminalized were more likely to use the drug (Williams and Bretteville-Jenson, 2014). Conversely, there is some evidence that suggests that decriminalization may lead to increased use amongst those over 25 years of age (Farrelly, Bray, Zarkin and Wendling, 2001). Overall, whilst the above trends have been identified, and the evidence from states that have decriminalized is varied, it is fair to say that any increase in prevalence is small and legislative change does not appear to correlate with an escalation in cannabis consumption. As we will explore below, the positive impact of decriminalization on social outcomes far outweighs perceived small increases in consumption.

Since the 1970s, 18 US states have decriminalized possession of cannabis for personal use – some of these states have gone on to regulate cannabis possession, supply and production for medical and/or recreational use. Another four US states have reclassified cannabis possession as a misdemeanor, which is still a criminal offense, but not punishable with imprisonment (NORML, 2018). Dills, Goffard and Miron (2017) considered the effect of cannabis decriminalization, legal access to medical cannabis and regulated models for cannabis in the US on teen drug use by analyzing prevalence data from 1977 to 2015. The results found that the legislative reforms had little to no impact on levels of use. Another recent paper looked at five US states that had decriminalized cannabis possession between 2008 and 2014 and the impact of the legal change on arrests and prevalence of cannabis use amongst teens. The study concluded that there had been large decreases in arrests for adults and young people and that there was no evidence of increased youth consumption of cannabis during the relevant period (Grucza, Vuolo, Krauss, Plunk, Agrawal, Chaloupka, and Beirut, 2018).

Some limitations in assessing the impact of decriminalization on prevalence have been cited in a number of studies. As discussed previously, the introduction of a decriminalized model for controlled substances does not necessarily mean a significant shift in law enforcement practices, where prior to the *de jure* model, police may have been effectively operating a de facto model of decriminalization (Laquer, 2014). In addition, MacCoun, Pacula, Chriqui, Harris, and Reuter (2009) have pointed to a lack of knowledge amongst the population of legislative reforms and so the introduction of decriminalization may have limited impact on prevalence.

Whilst it is difficult to assess the actual impact of decriminalization on consumption levels, largely because it is confounded by many factors, and drivers for cannabis use are multifaceted, it is reasonable to say that the ending of criminal sanctions for personal use offenses does not lead to an explosion in use. Where increases are observed, they are generally not significant. Many jurisdictions that adopt decriminalization can experience a decrease in prevalence after the change in law. Conversely, population estimates show that rates of drug consumption, including cannabis use, can be higher in states that adopt a criminal justice approach to possession offenses (Eastwood et al., 2016). It is probably safe to conclude that the legal framework for dealing with possession offenses has little impact on an individual's decision to use a drug; this is reflected in a study undertaken by Her Majesty's Home Office (2014) in the UK. That study compared the laws of 14 countries and determined that there was no "obvious relationship between the toughness of a country's enforcement against drug possession, and levels of drug use in that country" (Home Office, 2014). Beyond the issue of prevalence, decriminalization, when implemented effectively, is associated with positive social and economic outcomes.

Social outcomes associated with decriminalization

Whilst Portugal decriminalized possession of drugs in 2001, it is instructive to consider the impact of the policy, which was coupled with increased investment in treatment, harm reduction interventions and prevention. A 2015 study found that 11 years after implementation of the legal reform, there had been an 18 percent saving in social costs, largely driven by a reduction in health-related costs and costs associated with the legal system. In respect of the latter, the authors considered not only direct savings resulting from reduced burden on the criminal justice system, but also indirect savings resulting from loss of income due to criminalization – these savings were directly attributable to the decriminalization framework introduced in 2001 (Goncalves, Lourenc and Nogueira da Silva, 2015).

Whilst it is difficult to disentangle what savings would be related specifically to cannabis decriminalization, it is hard not to imagine that the ending of criminal sanctions for possession of cannabis would have a significant impact on the criminal justice system. As in the vast majority of countries across the globe, cannabis is the most widely used controlled substance, and hence, has the highest rates of prosecution for possession offenses related to the drug.

The social impact of decriminalizing personal use offenses related to cannabis has also been identified by Australian researchers. When comparing outcomes for first-time offenders in South Australia who had been subject to civil penalties for possession of cannabis against those who had been criminalized in Western Australia for the same offense, it was clear that those criminalized suffered more adverse social effects. Western Australian participants in the study reported that they suffered as a result of being criminalized. It resulted in: adverse impact on employment (32 percent versus 2 percent in South Australia); relationship problems (20 percent versus 5 percent); and accommodation complications (16 percent versus 0 percent). Furthermore, 32 percent of Western Australian respondents reported further contact with the criminal justice system compared to zero percent of respondents in South Australia (Ali, Christie, Lenton, Hawks, Sutton, Hall, and Allsop, 1999). The increased contact with the criminal justice system resulting from criminalization, is important not only for individuals but also for law enforcement, where reoffending is one of the metrics used to measure the efficacy of the system. Finally, respondents from Western Australia also reported they were less likely to trust the police and were more fearful of them as a result of being arrested for cannabis possession.

Similar findings on the social impact of criminalizing people caught in possession of cannabis were recently reported in a 2016 study. Again, the study focused on Australia, comparing the outcomes for people subject to diversion programs, specifically in respect of cannabis, and those who were charged for the offense. Interestingly, Shanahan, Hughes and McSweeney (2016) found that when comparing levels of reoffending for those criminalized to those who were subject to civil sanctions, there was a similar reduction in offending rates. The study did find that those who were subject to civil sanctions reported they experienced "fewer barriers in attaining or retaining employment, less conflict with family, partners and friends, and improved perceptions of legitimacy of the police."

Improved relationships between individuals, the community and police resulting from decriminalization has also been observed in other jurisdictions. Magson (2014) interviewed a number of key officials in respect of the Portuguese decriminalization model and found that police officials reported that they had been opposed to the legislative changes that decriminalized possession of drugs. In particular, police were concerned they would lose the ability to leverage information from arrestees about those higher up in the drugs trade. In practice, it is likely that information gained via this route was negligible, and therefore, the risk overstated. Whilst initially opposed to the reforms, police are now positive about the change in law, with some officials reporting an improved relationship between the police and the public and stronger community policing – this has in fact led to greater cooperation with the public, who are more likely to provide information as fear of criminalization has diminished.

Economic benefits of the approach

Criminalizing people for possession of cannabis is an expensive business, involving costs to the police, courts, probation and, potentially, the prison service. There are a number of research papers that have identified that diversion away from the criminal justice system can bring savings to the state and improve the economic opportunities for people who would have otherwise been criminalized – we have already touched on this in respect of the social costs saved as a result of decriminalization in Portugal.

Diversion costs associated with civil penalties for cannabis possession are invariably cheaper than charging and prosecuting someone for the offense. A comparison of the financial cost of possible outcomes for cannabis possession offenses in Australia found that the average cost of charging someone for possession of cannabis was AUS $1,918, compared to AUS $122 where someone is warned for the offense and AUS $264 for those given a civil fine. This study, as highlighted above, also found that the social outcomes for those charged were more deleterious than those who had received a non-criminal response, evidencing the cost-effectiveness of pursuing a model of decriminalization for cannabis possession (Shanahan et al., 2016).

California reduced cannabis possession from a felony offense to a misdemeanor in 1976, when possession of up to 28.5 grams was punishable with a $100 fine. It is estimated that the state saved $1 billon in policing, prosecution, and court costs in the first 10 years of the policy (Aldrich and Mikuriya, 1988).

In addition to the economic savings, many academic studies have reported a reduced burden on police officers' time when diverting people away from the criminal justice system (Magson, 2014; Shanahan et al., 2016).

Decriminalization of personal use offenses for cannabis is not a silver bullet

Decriminalization of personal use offenses only goes so far in addressing problems created by prohibitionist policies. Policy limitations are created when the policy is poorly implemented and fails in its aim to divert people away from the criminal justice system for the offenses discussed in this chapter. The ending of criminal sanctions for possession of cannabis and for cultivation of cannabis for a person's own consumption does not address the supply side of the market and the myriad of harms that can be associated with the illegal trade.

Implementation problems – thresholds, net-widening, sanctions and racial disparities

As discussed, threshold levels are invariably utilized to determine whether the offense of possession of controlled drugs should be treated as decriminalized. These threshold levels vary wildly, for example, Spain's threshold for herbal cannabis is 200 grams, compared to Mexico where it is 5 grams. If the threshold level is too low, the policy becomes unworkable and can lead to increased penalties if the amount of controlled drug possessed is above the stated level (Eastwood et al., 2016).

Another problem that has been experienced in terms of implementation is "net-widening." Jurisdictions that have introduced a policy of decriminalization, and have adopted civil fines as the sanction, will sometimes experience an increased level of policing as a result of the policy change. South Australia experienced "net-widening" on the introduction of the civil fine system for possession and personal cultivation of cannabis. It appears that the new system, which was introduced in 1987, was fully embraced by police who perceived the issuing of fines – known as Cannabis Expiation Notices (CEN) – as an easy disposal for the offense. In the first five years of the policy, the number of CENs issued increased by 180 percent (from 6000 CENs in 1987/88 to 17,000 in 1993/94) (Single et al., 2000). Compliance with the CEN system was low, with many failing to pay the fine within the prescribed period, leading to people being imprisoned for non-payment of the penalty; paradoxically this led to more people ending up in prison for the offense of cannabis possession. The South Australian Government adapted the scheme to make payments easier and more affordable (Christie and Ali, 2000). Net-widening occurs not as a result of increased cannabis use, but because a new formal system that is perceived as being easy to operate results in a greater number of people coming into contact with law enforcement (May, Warburton, Turnball and Hough, 2002; Stevens, 2010).

One of the most under-considered elements of an effective decriminalization model is the issue of sanctions; this includes whether there is a need to sanction and, if so, what type of sanctions should be available. The type of sanctions currently used range from a fine, to confiscation of passport or driving license, through to treatment referrals. In Portugal, for example, available administrative sanctions include: fines; community service; suspension of professional licenses and bans on attending designated places (Hughes and Stevens, 2010). The Portuguese legislation that introduced the new model of decriminalization requires that proceedings against a person be suspended if they are not drug dependent and have no previous record, which means that in practice the vast majority of cases are suspended.[4]

In a number of countries, there are no sanctions applied to possession offenses; this includes the Netherlands, Spain (although civil fines are issued for public possession) and Georgia (only in respect of cannabis).

Most countries will adopt administrative sanctions in lieu of criminal penalties. It is worth noting that a number of countries, for example Russia and Estonia, implement administrative detention for drug possession and, in some instances, drug use; that is, people are placed under house arrest or detained at a police station for a period of time. The European Court of Human Rights determined that this type of sanction is the deprivation of liberty and is considered equal to criminal liability (Merkinaite, 2012).

As highlighted above, there is very little research into the effect of sanctions and whether punishment as opposed to no punishment has any deterrent effect on initiation into drug use – although, this is not the most important metric in measuring an effective drug policy, and the pursuit of this goal arguably creates greater harms than focusing on policies that ensure a reduction in harms such as drug-related deaths and blood-borne viruses. In 2016, the Global Commission on Drug Policy[5] in their report, *Advancing Drug*

Policy Reform: A New Approach to Decriminalization, stated the Commission "believes that for the principle of human dignity and the rule of law to be firmly upheld there must be no penalty whatsoever imposed for low-level possession and/or consumption offences" (Global Commission on Drug Policy, 2016). Considering the inequitable application of the law – with largely people of color (Shiner et al., 2018) and people living in poverty targeted (Geller and Fagan, 2010) – and the failure of the law to generate widespread compliance in society, the recommendations of the Commission are to be welcomed.

What has been disappointing is the lack of analysis that exists in relation to the impact of decriminalization on people of color. There have been limited studies; all focus on the US and, despite removing possession offences from police powers, it seems law enforcement have been able to continue to use the drug laws that disproportionally target African Americans. Washington DC fully decriminalized cannabis in 2014. This is likely one of the most progressive models in the world, where it is legal to possess up to two ounces of cannabis for personal use or grow up to six plants; people can also "gift" up to one ounce on the basis there is no exchange of money. There are simply no penalties for these activities (Ballot Initiative 71). The reforms that took place in Washington DC were driven by a racial justice agenda, where too many young black and Hispanic people were being stopped and frisked for possession of cannabis. Whilst the absolute number of people being stopped and frisked and arrested for cannabis offenses has fallen dramatically since 2014, the reforms appear to have failed to truly address the racial disparity in drug offenses.

Data recently released by Washington DC's police department show that arrests for cannabis possession have fallen from 2,602 in 2012 to 19 in 2017 (Metropolitan Police Department, Washington DC, 2018). The reduction in possession arrests, which are a direct result of the 2014 reforms, certainly mean that fewer people, including African Americans, will come into contact with the police for this activity, so to some degree the change in law has been successful. However, the data shows that African Americans are still disproportionately targeted for other cannabis offenses – black people made up 86 percent of arrestees for all cannabis-related offenses in 2017 (black people make up 47 percent of Washington DC's population). Arrests for supply ("distribution") and public use of cannabis have increased significantly. In 2017, of the 403 people arrested for distribution, 92 percent were black, and of the 265 arrests for public consumption of cannabis, 75 percent of these arrests involved black people (Newman, 2018). There has been a woeful lack of developing drug policies that seek to reduce the harms for certain communities including people of color, and as such, it is imperative that models of legal reform seek to address these disparities.

We have only addressed some of the problems related to the implementation problems that exist in developing and enacting the model. Other issues include lengthy periods in prison as a result of pre-trial detention; this largely occurs in Latin American countries and involves issues of who should determine the offense – police, prosecutors or the judiciary – or the use of coercive treatment as an alternative sanction under a civil system and how this is compatible with a human rights perspective (Eastwood et al., 2016).

Beyond decriminalization – regulating the market

In conclusion, other chapters in this book explore the development of regulatory and quasi-regulatory models for the supply, sale and consumption of cannabis. One of the criticisms of decriminalization is that it essentially leaves the user no longer a criminal, but they are expected to engage with a criminal market, a market sometimes associated with violence, corruption and exploitation. Whilst this is certainly the case, the evolution of decriminalization has in many jurisdictions contributed to the development of regulatory markets for cannabis. The constitutional decision of the Spanish Supreme Court in the early 1970s underpinned the development of the Spanish Social Clubs; models of cannabis decriminalization were the experience of many US states that went on to regulate the cannabis market; and the 1976 law in the Netherlands paved the way for the cannabis coffee shops.

Decriminalization of personal use offenses is not a silver bullet for addressing the harms of drug prohibition. However, when implemented in a way that achieves its aim of diverting people away from the criminal justice system, and when coupled with investment in harm reduction and treatment services, decriminalization can have profound impacts on individuals and society. These impacts range from improved health outcomes to reductions in social problems related to housing, employment and relationships with others. Moreover, and importantly for decriminalization of cannabis, evidence shows that ending the criminalization of people caught in possession of the substance means they are less likely to reoffend or have further contact with the police. Considering the scale of law enforcement – especially at a community level – of cannabis possession offenses, the potential to reduce the risk of recidivism is significant. Finally, considering who is the focus of cannabis policing, decriminalization is an important legal reform for some of the most marginalized in society, many of whom are over-policed and unfairly targeted based on their economic or ethnic status.

The effectiveness of the model is ultimately reflected in how it is implemented, but if done well, decriminalization of personal use offenses can be the basis for policies that move towards a more human rights-based approach for those who use controlled drugs, including cannabis.

Notes

1 The Federal Government's Chinese Exclusion Act of 1892 allowed for the arrest and deportation of Chinese immigrants considered "opium addicts."

2 Threshold quantities are used in most jurisdictions as a way to determine whether an individual caught in possession of drugs should be subject to civil sanctions or receive no penalty, rather than being criminalized for being in possession of an

amount above the threshold. In some jurisdictions, the thresholds are strictly adhered to, whilst in others they are used as one factor in deciding whether a person is in possession of an amount of drugs for their own personal use. Threshold amounts vary wildly from jurisdiction to jurisdiction, as discussed.

3 A 2013 Supreme Court decision struck down the threshold amounts as they had been introduced by the government without the authority of parliament. The court ruled that the government was effectively operating outside its legal powers by independently introducing the threshold. This would have led to the law reverting back to the "greater than small" definition (Csete, 2012); however, the Supreme Court provided "tentative threshold quantities" with the amount of herbal cannabis reduced from 15 grams to 10 grams.

4 For example in 2013, 83 percent of all cases brought before the Dissuasion Commission for possession of drugs were suspended (EMCDDA, 2014).

5 The Global Commission was set up in 2011 and is comprised of political leaders, cultural figures, Nobel Prize laureates and former Presidents and Prime Ministers of Brazil, Chile, Colombia, East Timor, Greece, Malawi, Mexico, New Zealand, Nigeria, Poland, Portugal and Switzerland. The Commission acknowledges that the "war on drugs" has been an abject failure and advocates for alternative approaches, including decriminalization and regulation.

References

Aldrich, M.R. and Mikuriya, T. (1988). Savings in California marijuana law enforcement costs attributable to the Moscone Act of 1976: A summary. *Journal of Psychoactive Drugs*, 20(1), 75–81.

Alexander, M. (2010). *The new Jim Crow: Mass incarceration in the age of colorblindness.* New York: (Jackson, Tenn.): New Press.

Ali, R., Christie, P., Lenton, S., Hawks, D., Sutton, A., Hall, W. and Allsop, S. (1999). *The social impacts of the cannabis expiation notice scheme in South Australia.* Monograph no. 34. National Drug Strategy Committee. Retrieved from www.researchgate.net/publication/43493674_The_social_impacts_of_the_Cannabis_Expiation_Notice_Scheme_in_South_Australia_summary_report.

American Civil Liberties Union. (2013). *The war on marijuana in black and white.* New York: ACLU. Retrieved from www.aclu.org/report/report-war-marijuana-black-and-white.

Arredondo, J., Gaines, T., Manian, S., Vilalta, C., Banuelos, A., Strathdee, S.A. and Beletsky, L. (2017). The law on the streets: Evaluating the impact of Mexico's drug decriminalization reform on drug possession arrests in Tijuana, Mexico. *International Journal of Drug Policy,* 54, 1–8.

Artículos 478 and 479 of the "Narcomenudo Decree." (2009).

Baum, D. (2016). Legalize it all: How to win the war on drugs. *Harpers Magazine.* Retrieved from https://harpers.org/archive/2016/04/legalize-it-all/.

Belackova, V., Maalsté, N., Zabransky, T. and Grund, J.P. (2015). "Should I buy or should I grow?" How drug policy institutions and drug market transaction costs shape the decision to self-supply with cannabis in the Netherlands and the Czech Republic. *International Journal of Drug Policy,* 26(3), 296–310.

Christie, P. and Ali, R. (2000). Offences under the cannabis expiation notice scheme in South Australia. *Drug and Alcohol Review,* 19, 255.

Constitutional Court Gazette. (1994). Constitutional Court sentence No. C-221/94. Special edition.

Constitutional Court of South Africa. Case CCT 108/17. Retrieved from https://juta.co.za/media/filestore/2018/11/SALR_Minister_of_Justice_and_Constitutional_Development_v_Prince.pdf.

Constitution of Georgia. (1995). Article 16.

Corda, A. (2015). *Drug policy reform in Latin America: Discourse and reality*. Colectivo de Estudio Drogas y Derechos, 1–10. Retrieved from http://fileserver.idpc.net/library/CEDD_drug_policy_reform_latin_america%20(1).pdf.

Corte Constitucional de Colombia. Sentencia C-491/12, June 28, 2012. Retrieved from www.corteconstitucional.gov.co/relatoria/2012/c-491-12.htm.

Council of the European Union. (2014). *Regional report on South America (Dublin Group)*. Brussels: European Union, 13830/1/14REV1., 1–65. Retrieved from http://data.consilium.europa.eu/doc/document/ST-13830-2014-REV-1/en/pdf.

Council on Foreign Relations. (2018). *Global conflict tracker: Criminal violence in Mexico*. New York: CFR. Retrieved from www.cfr.org/interactives/global-conflict-tracker?marker=7#!/conflict/criminal-violence-in-mexico.

Csete, J. (2012). *A balancing act: Policymaking on illicit drugs in the Czech Republic*. Lessons for Drug Policy Series, New York: Open Society Foundations. Retrieved from www.opensocietyfoundations.org/sites/default/files/A_Balancing_Act-03-14-2012.pdf.

Dills, A., Goffard, S and Miron, J. (2017). *The effects of marijuana liberalizations: Evidence from monitoring the future*. Working paper 23779, National Bureau of Economic Research.

Donnelly, N., Hall, W. and Christie, P. (1999). *Effects of the cannabis expiation notice scheme on levels and patterns of cannabis use in South Australia: Evidence from the National Drug Strategy household surveys 1985–1995*. Canberra: Department of Health and Aged Care. Retrieved from http://nceta.flinders.edu.au/files/8912/5548/1112/EN3.pdf.

Eastwood, N., Fox, E. and Rosmarin, A. (2016). *A quiet revolution: Drug decriminalization across the globe*. London: Release. Retrieved from www.release.org.uk/sites/default/files/pdf/publications/A%20Quiet%20Revolution%20-%20Decriminalization%20Across%20the%20Globe.pdf.

Economic and Social Council. (2013). *World crime trends and emerging issues and responses in the field of crime prevention and criminal justice*. Vienna: United Nations. Retrieved from www.unodc.org/documents/data-and-analysis/statistics/crime/World_Crime_Trends_2013.pdf.

European Monitoring Centre for Drugs and Drug Addiction and SICAD. (2014). *2014 National Report (2013 data) to the EMCDDA by the Reitox National Focal Point "Portugal" New Developments, Trends*. Lisbon: EMCDDA. Retrieved from www.emcdda.europa.eu/system/files/publications/996/2014_NATIONAL_REPORT.pdf

Farrelly, M.C., Bray, J.W., Zarkin, G.A. and Wendling, B.W. (2001). The joint demand for cigarettes and marijuana. Evidence from the national household surveys on drug abuse. *Journal of Health Economics*, 20, 51–68.

Geller, A. and Fagan, J. (2010). Pot as pretext: Marijuana, race, and the new disorder in New York City street policing. *Journal of Empirical Legal Studies*, 7(4), 591–633.

German Federal Constitutional Court, Second Senate. (1994). BVerfGE 90, 145.

Global Commission on Drug Policy. (2016). *Advancing drug policy reform: A new approach to decriminalization*. Geneva: Global Commission on Drug Policy. Retrieved from www.globalcommissionondrugs.org/reports/advancing-drug-policy-reform/.

Goncalves, R., Lourenc, A. and Nogueira da Silva, S. (2015). A social cost perspective in the wake of the Portuguese strategy for the fight against drugs. *International Journal of Drug Policy*, 26, 199–209.

Grucza, R., Vuolo, M., Krauss, M., Plunk, A., Agrawal, A., Chaloupka, F. and Bierut, L. (2018). Cannabis decriminalization: A study of recent policy change in five US states. *International Journal of Drug Policy*, 59, 67–75.

Grund, J.P. and Breeksema J. (2013). *Coffee shops and compromise: Separated illicit drug markets in the Netherlands*. Lessons for Drug Policy Series, New York: Open Society Foundations. Retrieved from www.opensocietyfoundations.org/reports/coffee-shops-and-compromise-separated-illicit-drug-markets-netherlands.

Guzmán, D.E. and Yepes, R.U. (2010). *Prohibition, a backwards step: The personal dose in Colombia*. TNI and WOLA series on legislative reform on drug policies No. 4, 3. Retrieved from www.tni.org/en/briefing/prohibition-backwards-step.

Home Office. (2014). *Drugs international comparators*. London: Home Office. Retrieved from https://assets.publishing.service.gov.uk/government/uploads/system/uploads/attachment_data/file/368489/DrugsInternationalComparators.pdf.

Hughes, C. and Stevens, A. (2010). What can we learn from the Portuguese decriminalization of illicit drugs? *British Journal of Criminology*, 50(6), 999–1022.

Instituto Nacional Penitenciario y Carcelario. (2016). *Estadísticas enero de 2016 – modalidad delictiva población de internos en establecimientos de reclusión enero 31 de 2016*.

Johnson, T.P. (2014). Sources of error in substance use prevalence surveys. *International Scholarly Research Notices, 2014*, Article ID 923290, 21 pages.

Kendall, R. (2002). Cannabis condemned: The proscription of Indian hemp. *Addiction History*, 98, 143–151.

Laquer, H. (2014). Uses and abuses of drug decriminalization in Portugal. *Law and Social Inquiry*, 40(3), 746–781.

Levine, G.H. and Siegel, L. (2015). Marijuana madness: The scandal of New York City's racist marijuana possession arrests. In J.A. Eterno (Ed.) *The New York City Police Department: The impact of its policies and practices*. New York: CRC Press. Retrieved from https://qcpages.qc.cuny.edu/~hlevine/Marijuana_Madness__NYCs_Racist_Marijuana_Arrests.

Levison, L. (2008). Half a gram – A thousand lives. *Harm Reduction Journal*, 5(22), 1.

MacCoun, R., Pacula, R., Chriqui, J., Harris, K. and Reuter, P. (2009). Do citizens know whether their state has decriminalized marijuana? Assessing the perceptual component of deterrence theory. *Review of Law and Economics*, 5(1), 347—371.

MacGregor, S. (2013). Barriers to the influence of evidence on policy: Are politicians the problem? *Drugs: Education, Prevention and Policy*, 20(3), 225–233.

Magson, J. (2014). *Drugs, crime and decriminalization: Assessing the impact of drug decriminalization policies on the efficiency and integrity of the criminal justice system*. London: Winston Churchill Fellowship. Retrieved from www.wcmt.org.uk/fellows/reports/assessing-impact-drug-decriminalization-policies-efficiency-and-integrity-criminal.

Marks, A. (2018). Treating the "personal" as private in the absence of harm to others: A normative definition of "personal consumption" in legal instruments on drug control. *International & Comparative Law Quarterly*, (forthcoming) 68(1).

May, T., Warburton, H., Turnball, P. and Hough, M. (2002). *The times they are changing: Policing of cannabis*. London: Joseph Rowntree. Retrieved from www.jrf.org.uk/file/36657/download?token=W1s7o0Za&filetype=full-report.

McGeorge, J. and Aitken, C.K. (1997). Effects of cannabis decriminalization in the Australian capital territory on the university students' patterns of use. *Journal of Drug Issues*, 27, 785–793.

McLaren, J. and Mattick, R.P. (2007). *Cannabis in Australia: Use, supply, harms, and responses*. Sydney: National Drug and Alcohol Research Centre, University of New South Wales. Retrieved from www.nationaldrugstrategy.gov.au/internet/drugstrategy/publishing.nsf/Content/mono57.

Merkinaite, S. (2012). *A war against people who use drugs: The costs*. Vilnius: Eurasian Harm Reduction Network (EHRN). Retrieved from https://idhdp.com/mediaimport/15089/costs_report_final_eng.pdf.

Metropolitan Police Department. (2018). *Statistics and data, open data, marijuana arrests*. Washington, D.C. Retrieved from https://mpdc.dc.gov/publication/marijuana-arrest-data.

Mravčík, V. (2015). (De)criminalization of possession of drugs for personal use – A view from the Czech Republic. *International Journal of Drug Policy*, 26(7), 705–707.

Neill, M., Christie, P. and Cormack, S. (1991). *Trends in alcohol and other drug use by South Australian school children 1986–1989*. Adelaide: Drug and Alcohol Services Council South Australia. Retrieved from https://trove.nla.gov.au/work/153178181?q&versionId=217783746.

Newman, T. (2018). *Stark racial disparities and disturbing growth in Washington D.C. marijuana arrests despite legalization*. New York: Drug Policy Alliance. Retrieved from www.drugpolicy.org/press-release/2018/08/stark-racial-disparities-and-disturbing-growth-washington-dc-marijuana.

NORML. (2018). *States that have decriminalized*. Washington, D.C: NORML. Retrieved from https://norml.org/aboutmarijuana/item/states-that-have-decriminalized.

Nunn, K.B. (2002). Race, crime and the pool of surplus criminality or why the "war on drugs" was a "war on Blacks." *Gender, Race & Justice*, 6, 381–446. Retrieved from https://scholarship.law.ufl.edu/facultypub/107/.

OC Media. (2018). *Constitutional court outlaws all punishment for cannabis consumption in Georgia*. Retrieved from https://oc-media.org/constitutional-court-outlaws-all-punishment-for-cannabis-consumption-in-georgia/.

Puras, D. and Hannah, J. (2017). Reasons for drug policy reform: Prohibition enables systemic human rights abuses and undermines public health. *British Medical Journal, 358*.

Reuter, P. (2010). *Marijuana legalization: What can be learned from other countries?* Santa Monica, CA: Rand Drug Policy Research Center. Retrieved from www.rand.org/pubs/working_papers/WR771.html.

Russoniello, K. (2013). The devil (and drugs) in the details: Portugal's focus on public health as a model for decriminalization of drugs in Mexico. *Yale Journal of Health, Policy, Law and Ethics, 12*, 2(4). Retrieved from https://digitalcommons.law.yale.edu/yjhple/vol.12/iss2/4.

Shanahan, M., Hughes, C. and McSweeney, T. (2016). *Australian police diversion for cannabis offences: Assessing program outcomes and cost effectiveness.* Monograph Series 66, National Drug Law Enforcement Research Fund. Retrieved from https://aic.gov.au/file/6369/download?token=yB3KqkYQ.

Shiner, M., Carre, Z., Delsol, R. and Eastwood, N. (2018). *The color of injustice: "Race," drugs and law enforcement in England and Wales.* London: Release & StopWatch. Retrieved from www.release.org.uk/publications/ColourOfInjustice.

Single, E., Christie, P. and Ali R. (2000). The impact of cannabis decriminalization in Australia and the United States. *Journal of Public Health Policy*, 21(2), 157–186.

Stevens, A. (2010). *Drugs, crime and public health: The political economy of drug policy.* Abingdon: Routledge.

United Nations on Drugs and Crime. (2018). *The world drug report 2018.* Vienna: UNODC. Retrieved from www.unodc.org/wdr2018/.

Williams, J. and Bretteville-Jenson, A. (2014). Does liberalizing cannabis laws increase cannabis use? *Journal of Health Economics,* 36, 20–32.

Zabransky, T., Mravčík, V., Gajdosikova, H. and Miovskù, M. (2001). *Impact analysis project of new drugs legislation summary final report.* Prague: Secretariat of the National Drug Commission Office of the Czech government. Retrieved from www.adiktologie.cz/en/articles/detail/442/2205/PAD-Impact-Analysis-Project-of-New-Drugs-Legislation-Summary-Final-Report-.

7 "More than just counting the plants"

Different home cannabis cultivation policies, cannabis supply contexts and approaches to their evaluation

Vendula Belackova, Katinka van de Ven and Michaela Roubalova (Stefunkova)

Background

Home cannabis cultivation (referred to as small-scale or personal cultivation) for recreational use has been documented in different countries around the world. In the United States (US), where several policies pertaining to medicinal or recreational home cannabis cultivation were enacted, the number of people who report growing their own in the general population survey has more than doubled between 2002 and 2012 from an estimated 200,000 to 500,000 individuals (Caulkins, Kilmer, Kleiman, MacCoun, Midgette, Oglesby, Pacula and Reuter 2015; Gettman and Kennedy, 2014). A European drug market survey conducted in 2011 in the Netherlands, the Czech Republic, Portugal, Bulgaria, Sweden and the United Kingdom (UK) showed that between 1 percent and 10 percent of those who used cannabis in the past 12 months reported growing it (Caulkins and Pacula, 2006; Trautmann, Kilmer and Turnbull, 2013). An international survey of cannabis cultivators in Denmark, Finland, Australia, the UK and Germany reported that the reason why they grew cannabis was overwhelmingly (84 percent) to provide for their personal use (Potter, Barratt, Malm, Bouchard, Blok, Christensen, Decorte, Frank, Hakkarainen and Klein 2015). Home cultivation has been described as a relatively low-risk practice that yields several benefits to the consumers. Among these has been avoidance of an illegal market, low cost, high quality, knowledge about the contents and enjoyment of home growing as a leisure activity (Decorte, 2010; Potter et al., 2015).

This suggests that home cannabis cultivation is a practice highly relevant to people who use cannabis and should be considered when designing non-prohibitive cannabis policies. Yet, a systematic overview of home cultivation policies that could inform their design and suggest potential outcomes has been lacking. Exploring variations in policies surrounding cannabis home cultivation and understanding such variations will allow for better (and more realistic) assessment of home cultivation policies. Given that variations in said policies likely exist, this might have an impact on the possible outcomes to evaluate. The aim of this chapter has been to review home cultivation policies adopted around the world. As cannabis law reforms have been unfolding internationally and the evidence of their outcomes is growing (Hall and Weier, 2015; Hansen, Miller and Weber, 2018; Kerr, Bae and Koval, 2018), this chapter also aims to provide implications for evaluating outcomes of home cultivation policies.

Home cultivation and cannabis policy options

While in the majority of countries cannabis cultivation is illegal, a number of jurisdictions have amended their policies to account for this practice. For instance, several countries which have decriminalized cannabis possession have also decriminalized cultivation of a small number of plants, mainly for personal use (Eastwood, Fox and Rosmarin, 2016). While United Nations treaties require that cannabis (as well as other controlled drug) production is criminalized (UN, 1961, 1971, 1988), it has been suggested that decriminalizing personal cannabis cultivation is in line with these treaties, as it can be perceived as a form of personal drug possession where criminal sanctions are not necessary (Jelsma, 2011). Other jurisdictions have been referred to as having depenalized cannabis cultivation (MacCoun, 2010). For example, home cultivation has been included in cannabis legalization across several US states and in Uruguay (Pardo, 2014). While not a focus of this chapter, home cultivation has also been a component of many medicinal cannabis policies worldwide (Belackova, Shanahan and Ritter, 2017b; Pacula, Powell, Heaton and Sevigny, 2014b).

The concepts of decriminalization, depenalization and legalization require consideration before being applied to home cannabis cultivation. An earlier classification by the European Monitoring Centre for Drugs and Drug Addiction (EMCDDA) defines decriminalization as the absence of a criminal offense and/or presence of administrative sanctions with respect to an activity and depenalization as the relaxation of penal sanctions while the activity itself remains a criminal offense (EMCDDA, 2005). More recently, the EMCDDA has included a definition of legalization which refers to an activity that is no longer prohibited or is explicitly permitted (EMCDDA, 2016). Taking a slightly different approach, Hughes, Ritter, Chalmers, Lancaster, Barratt and Moxham-Hall (2016) distinguish between *de jure* and de facto decriminalization. *De jure* here means a change in the law, while de facto relates to non-enforcement of (criminal) laws. Importantly, both decriminalization and depenalization have been seen as referencing (personal) drug possession, while legalization pertains to production and supply (EMCDDA, 2016; Pacula, MacCoun, Reuter, Chriqui, Kilmer, Harris, Paoli and Schäfer, 2005). Yet, the classification of home cultivation policies is potentially more complex as home cultivation can be seen as a case of both possession and (self) supply – while it involves production, the quantities produced are seen to correspond with personal use.

Outcomes of home cultivation policies – analogies with medicinal marijuana

While this chapter (as well as this entire monograph) focuses on policies which are not restricted to medicinal use (i.e. "recreational" cannabis cultivation policies), the research evaluating population-level impact of home cultivation policies is scarce, and predominantly conducted in the context of medicinal marijuana laws.

Several studies which have assessed the impact of medicinal cannabis policies in the US have compared the outcomes in states that allowed for home cultivation (only) versus those where dispensaries were in place. A 2014 study, for instance, found that states which allowed for medicinal home cultivation were less likely to have increased marijuana use among youth or an increased demand for treatment than those where medicinal marijuana dispensaries were in place (Pacula et al., 2014b). However, a previous 2013 working paper by the same research team concluded quite the opposite – medicinal home cultivation was shown to be significantly associated with heavier youth cannabis use, not significantly associated with youth alcohol use, and negatively associated with fatal alcohol-involved accidents (Pacula, Powell, Heaton and Sevigny, 2013). Furthermore, a study that looked at different medicinal marijuana policies found that higher adolescent marijuana use rates (including heavy use) were associated with higher amounts of cannabis allowed for personal possession and with voluntary (as opposed to obligatory) registration schemes. However, there was no association with medicinal home cultivation laws, or the number of cannabis plants authorized under these laws (Johnson, Hodgkin and Harris, 2017).

Another study from the US assessed the impact of medicinal cannabis laws on cannabis potency. It concluded that potency was positively associated with the presence of dispensaries and overall decriminalization of marijuana possession for personal use (however, the latter was achieved by only two states in the sample), but not with not medical home cultivation policies (Sevigny, Pacula and Heaton, 2014). One study used an online survey among youth to indicate which policies contribute to cannabis vaping and use of edibles. Respondents from states with home cultivation laws (medicinal and recreational not distinguished) were more likely to try cannabis vaping and edibles and to try them at an earlier age (Borodovsky and Budney, 2017). However, the increased likelihood of vaping or eating cannabis was associated with other cannabis policy measures (e.g. the presence of dispensaries or recreational marijuana legalization as opposed to medicinal cannabis laws only).

The studies listed above generally found no specific association between medicinal home cultivation laws on cannabis or other substance use, although one study team published findings suggesting this could go both ways. Non-medicinal home cultivation policies were either not assessed in isolation or were found not to have any effect on the cannabis market (potency, vaping and/or edibles), at least not such that it would exceed the effects of other non-criminal policies.

Outcomes of home cultivation policies – studies of cultivation for recreational use

Evaluation of recreational (non-medicinal) home cultivation policies is limited in number and often includes broader cannabis policy reforms (e.g. decriminalization of cannabis possession for personal use). This restricts the possibilities to derive implications that are specific to home cultivation. For instance, two Australian states introduced a de facto decriminalization of small-scale cannabis cultivation, alongside the decriminalization of small-scale cannabis possession – South Australia (SA) in 1987 and Australian Capital Territory (ACT) in 1992 (Lenton, McDonald, Ali and Moore, 1999). No effect on rates of cannabis use were observed when it came to university students in ACT (McGeorge and Aitken, 1997) or to population-level cannabis use rates in SA (Donnelly, Hall and Christie, 2000), but the number of cannabis-related offenses increased in SA (Christie and Ali, 2000). None of these findings, however, can be specifically attributed to decriminalizing the home cultivation of cannabis, but rather to decriminalization overall.

In an overview of alternatives to prohibition and their impact, MacCoun (2010) assessed cannabis and other drug use data in Alaska which (re)decriminalized home cannabis cultivation in 2003 and found a drop in cannabis use rates occurred in 2006. While MacCoun stated that the drop was most likely unrelated to this policy, it seemed unparalleled in the rest of the US states (MacCoun, 2010). A more recent study looked at youth cannabis use rates in the Czech Republic before and after 2010, when the decriminalization of up to five plants for personal cultivation was introduced (Cerveny, Chomynová, Mravčík and van Ours, 2017). While the authors mistakenly refer to this period as pre- and post-decriminalization of the personal possession of cannabis, which has been in place since 1998 (Belackova and Stefunkova, 2018), they found no increase in use rates which could be interpreted to be related to home cannabis cultivation policy.

Two other studies aimed to assess the Czech cannabis home cultivation policy. One compared the Czech cannabis market to that in the Netherlands (Belackova, Maalsté, Zabransky and Grund, 2015). While both countries decriminalized drug possession and cannabis cultivation in small amounts, the enforcement priorities and the availability of commercial cannabis market (coffeeshops) made cannabis cultivation a less viable option for consumers in the Netherlands. The second study was of a qualitative nature and concluded that cannabis users in the Czech Republic had more access to information about the cannabis they used than those in New South Wales. While cannabis possession is (at least partially) decriminalized in both places, cultivation of up to five plants for personal use was decriminalized in the Czech Republic only (Belackova, Brandnerova and Vechet, 2018).

This research suggests that decriminalization of recreational home cultivation policies (when combined with decriminalization of personal possession) likely does not influence cannabis use rates. Additionally, other outcomes are possible, including changes in law enforcement indicators or better access to information about cannabis products. In any case, the level of law enforcement as well as alternative, non-criminal sources of cannabis might be important factors that influence whether consumers chose to cultivate their own cannabis. Home cultivation policies may take many forms, ranging from decriminalization to full legalization. In this analysis, we provide a detailed classification of home cannabis cultivation policies internationally and discuss the implications for further evaluation.

Methods

This analysis was conducted in several stages. First, we identified relevant jurisdictions that introduced non-prohibitive measures for recreational (non-medicinal) "home cannabis cultivation." In order to do that, we searched scientific and grey literature for a list of countries that introduced any cannabis law reform in the past. The sources included an overview of countries that decriminalized cannabis possession (Eastwood et al., 2016), a database of cannabis laws in the US administered by NORML.org (National Organization for Reform of Marijuana Laws) and a Wikipedia page "Legality of cannabis." We also searched relevant key words in Google, Google Scholar, EBSCO and ProQuest. The search terms included a combination of the terms "home," "personal," "small-scale," "cannabis," "cultivation," "policy," "law" and "regulation." A preliminary list was consulted with representatives of ENCOD (European Coalition for Just and Effective Drug Policies) and FAAAT (For Alternative Approaches to Addiction, Think and do tank) to include more candidate jurisdictions. This process resulted in a list of 51 jurisdictions that were further assessed (n = 28 that decriminalized cannabis possession, n = 10 that introduced cannabis legalization, and additional n = 13 where an unspecified cannabis law reform was presumed to take place). The initial search was conducted in April 2018; last updates were conducted in December 2018. All three authors assessed the 51 jurisdictions which was followed by a rigorous discussion between the authors to compare the results and discuss discrepancies. As such, the study has aimed to be a snapshot of laws and regulations at the time of the search, rather than to provide any insight into the evolution or duration of home cultivation policies.

Second, we reviewed the respective laws and regulations as well as other sources of information (e.g., reports, legal interpretations, media accounts) in these 51 jurisdictions in order to assess whether non-prohibitive measures towards home cannabis cultivation were in place. The aim was to identify jurisdictions with non-prohibitive measures towards non-medicinal (recreational) home cannabis cultivation and pertaining to psychoactive cannabis plants (not hemp). In assessing whether a particular jurisdiction had a non-prohibitive approach to home cultivation, we primarily regarded the respective laws and regulations and peer-reviewed literature. When the laws and regulations and/or peer-reviewed literature were not available in English or Spanish, and the remaining sources of information were ambiguous, we consulted national level experts (this was the case in Georgia and India). This process yielded a list of 27 jurisdictions with non-prohibitive approaches towards home cannabis cultivation.

Third, we classified the policies based on the type of law or regulation in place and examined the specific features of the home cultivation laws and policies (number of non-prohibited plants, approaches to sharing-gifting and quantity of cannabis allowed for personal possession after harvest). The categories of laws and regulations were based on the previously outlined classifications (EMCDDA, 2005, 2016; Hughes et al., 2016) and the specifics of home cannabis cultivation policies. We included each *de jure* and de facto options for *decriminalization, depenalization* and for *legalization* policies, yielding six basic policy categories. *Decriminalization* encompassed administrative sanctions for home cultivation, *depenalization* included policies where home cultivation remained a criminal offense but was not associated with custodial sanctions, and *legalization* was defined as authorizing/regulating a drug-related activity or absence of any sanctions pertaining to it (administrative or criminal/custodial). *De jure* policies were considered when the sanction (administrative for decriminalization, criminal but non-custodial for depenalization) or the authorized behavior were included in the law. De facto policies were all other mechanisms other than the law (e.g. police guideline or a court decision annulling or interpreting existing laws). Classifying court decisions was particularly challenging. When they had the nature of a Supreme Court decision (i.e. jurisprudence that instructed other courts not to prosecute a crime), we classified them as de facto *depenalization*. When they had the nature of a Constitutional Court decision (i.e. annulled a particular criminal provision), we considered them as de facto *legalization* (see Table 7.1).

Finally, we considered the context of home cultivation laws in terms of whether other non-criminal policies towards other supply options were in place ("home cultivation only" vs "home cultivation and other supply options"). This was to highlight the different context of home cultivation policies for further evaluations and has resulted in 12 policy categories (of which ten were populated with examples of different jurisdictions); see Table 7.2.

Table 7.1 Overview of regulations pertaining to small-scale/personal/home cannabis cultivation internationally

		Number of plants considered	*Cannabis possession quantity*	*Produce from plants authorized*	*Sharing/gifting / distribution*	*Laws/regulations*
DEPENALIZED de facto[1]	Colombia	20	20 g	-	–[f]	Art 375 of Penal Code, Supreme Court Resolution No. 44892/Act. No. 212
	Costa Rica	if not for sale	personal use[1]	-	–[f]	Resolution No 00481 – 2018 of the Third Chamber (Penal) of the Supreme Court
	Georgia[3]	151 g	70 g	-	–[f]	Constitutional Court's decision no 701,722,725 on the case *Citizens of Georgia Jambul Gvianidze, David Khomeriki and Lasha Gagishvili v. the Parliament of Georgia*, July 14, 2017
DEPENALIZED *de jure*[2]	Brazil	for personal use, determined by a judge		-	–[f]	Law No. 11,343 of August 23, 2006
	Chile	personal use in short term		-	–[f]	Law No. 20,000 that replaces Law No. 19,366 Penalising Illicit Trafficking of Narcotic Drugs and Psychotropic Substances
DECRIMINALIZED de facto	Belgium	1	3 g	-	–[f]	1921 Law on Narcotic Drugs; 2003 and 2005 Ministerial Guidelines
	The Netherlands	5	5 g	-	coffeeshops	Opium Act; Directive for the Prosecution of Opium Act Offenses

		Number of plants considered	Cannabis possession quantity	Produce from plants authorized	Sharing/gifting / distribution	Laws/regulations
DECRIMINALIZED *de jure*	South Australia (AU)[5]	1[d]	100 g	–	–[f]	South Australia's Controlled Substances Act 1984; 45A–Expiation of simple cannabis offenses)
	Australian Capital Territory (AU)[6]	2[c,d]	50 g	–	–[f]	Drugs of Dependence (Amendment) No. 52, 1992; Criminal Code (Serious Drug Offences) Amendment Act 2004; Simple Cannabis Offence Notice (SCON)
	Northern Territory (AU)[7]	2	50 g	–	–[f]	Misuse of Drugs Amendment Act 1996 (Act No. 4, 1996)
	Czech Republic	5[c]	10 g	–	–[f]	Section 39 of the Act No. 167/1998 Coll., on Addictive Substances (administrative offence); Section 285 and 284 of the Act No. 40/2009 Coll., Penal Code (criminal offence)
	Jamaica	5 or unlimited for religion 6 [a]	57 g 57 g	– YES	–[f] not for profit small-scale transactions	The Dangerous Drugs (Amendment) Act 2015 Initiative 502, 2015 Cannabis Patient Protection Act (SB 5052)
	Spain	not limited, fine if not in private[4]	private n/a., 100 g in public		de facto depenalized	Organic Law 4/2015 on the Protection of Public Security; Article 368 of the Criminal Code; Supreme Court's Interpretation- "closed-circle" doctrine
LEGALIZED de facto [3]	South Africa	in a private place [c]			–[f]	Constitutional Court Judgment 2018 (10) BCLR 1220 (CC) – Sections 4(b) and 5(b) of Drugs and Drug Trafficking Act 140 of 1992 ruled unconstitutional
	Mexico	personal use[c]		-	–[f]	Supreme Court of Justice of the Nation, Resolution 548/2018 and 547/2018

(continued)

Table 7.1 continued

		Number of plants considered	*Cannabis possession quantity*	*Produce from plants authorized*	*Sharing/gifting / distribution*	*Laws/regulations*
LEGALIZED *de jure* the only option	Antigua and Barbuda	4[a]	15 g	-	–[f]	The Misuse of Drugs (Amendment) Act, 2018
	Maine (US)	12 (3 mature)[b,e]	71 g	YES	–[f]	Maine Revised Statutes, Title 7, Chapter 417: CANNABIS LEGALIZATION ACT
	Vermont (US)	4 (2 mature)[a, b, e]	28 g (5 g hashish)	YES	–[f]	Act No. 86. An act relating to eliminating penalties for possession of limited amounts of marijuana by adults 21 years of age or older (H.511)
	Washington DC (US)	6 (3 mature); 12 (6 mature) per residence[a]	57 g	YES	not for profit small scale transactions	Initiative 71. District of Columbia Code Division VIII. General Laws. § 48-904.01
LEGALIZED *de jure* – alongside other supply options	Alaska (US)	6 (3 mature)	28 g (113 g in private)	YES	up to 28 g gifted	Alaska Statutes Title 17. Food and Drugs; Chapter 17.38 THE REGULATION OF CANNABIS
	California (US)	6 per residence[a,b,c]	28 g	YES	gift 28 g or less	Adult Use of Cannabis Act (AUMA) (Proposition 64)
	Colorado (US)	6 (3 mature)[b]	28 g	YES	–[f]	Colo. Const. Art. XVIII, Section 16 PERSONAL USE AND REGULATION OF CANNABIS
	Massachusetts (US)	6 (12 per residence)[c]	283 g	YES	–[f]	Massachusetts General Laws Part I. Administration of the Government (Ch. 1–182); Ch. 94G REGULATION OF THE USE AND DISTRIBUTION OF CANNABIS NOT MEDICALLY PRESCRIBED

	Number of plants considered	*Cannabis possession quantity*	*Produce from plants authorized*	*Sharing/gifting / distribution*	*Laws/regulations*
Nevada (US)	6 (12 per residence)[b, c, e]	28 g	YES	gifting up to 28 g	2017 Nevada Revised Statutes Chapter 453D – Regulation and Taxation of Cannabis Act
Oregon (US)	4 per residence	28 g	up to 227 g	–[f]	Measure 91 (Control, Regulation, and Taxation of Cannabis and Industrial Hemp Act)
Canada	4 per residence[c]	30 g	-	share up to 30 g with adults	The Cannabis Act (Bill C-45)
Uruguay	6 – has to register	480 g per year	-	–[f]	Law No. 19172 on December 20, 2013

Source: Eastwood et al (2016), Norml.org, state and national-level laws or regulations and other publicly available sources.

Notes

- no/not specified,

a in one's residence and/or owner's approval needed.

b enclosed space and/or not visible.

c for personal use.

d not hydroponic/artificially grown.

e other restrictions,

f more serious offence.

1 Criminal penalties should/can be dismissed by a judge according to Supreme Court rulings (providing guidance to other courts such that home cannabis cultivation shouldn't be prosecuted as a crime).

2 Criminal penalties should/can be dismissed by a judge according to the law.

3 Criminal provisions revoked as invalid by the Constitutional Court, but further laws not yet in place.

4 A law was passed in Catalonia such that 150 kg/year per CSC, could be distributed among the members (Law 13/2017, July 6, 2017, about associations of cannabis consumers; Bulletin of the State no. 187, Sec I., page 77,688; *not in line with federal regulations)* but was deemed unconstitutional by the Spanish Federal Court; CSC – Cannabis Social Clubs.

5 Police have the discretion to issue an on the spot fine or Cannabis Expiation Notice or charge with a criminal offence if not grown hydroponically; if a fine is not paid within 28 days, a person might be convicted of a "simple (criminal) cannabis offence".

6 Police have the discretion to apply offence notice or charge with a criminal offence if for personal use and not grown artificially (hydroponically); if a fine for an offence notice is paid within 60 days, will be convicted of a "simple (criminal) cannabis offence".

7 Police have the discretion to issue an infringement notice; if fine not paid within 28 days, further action may be pursued (e.g. community service or imprisonment).

Table 7.2 Overview of home cultivation policies

	De facto	*De jure*
DEPENALIZED		
Home cultivation only	Colombia, Costa Rica & Georgia	Brazil & Chile
Home cultivation & other supply options	Spain*	N/A
DECRIMINALIZED		
Home cultivation only	Belgium	South Australia, ACT, Northern Territory, Czech Republic & Jamaica
Home cultivation & other supply options	The Netherlands	Spain*
LEGALIZED		
Home cultivation only	Mexico & South Africa	3 US states (Maine, Vermont and Washington D.C) and Antigua & Barbuda
Home cultivation & other supply options	N/A	6 US states (Alaska, California, Colorado, Massachusetts, Nevada and Oregon), Canada and Uruguay

Note

* Drug sharing among habitual users has been de facto depenalized by the Spanish Supreme Court and together with home cannabis cultivation being *de jure* decriminalized, this has been interpreted that Cannabis Social Clubs are not prohibited.

Findings

We identified 27 jurisdictions where non-prohibitive measures to home cannabis cultivation have been adopted. These were six Latin American countries (Brazil, Chile, Colombia, Costa Rica, Mexico and Uruguay), three North American countries and nine states in the US (Antigua and Barbuda, Canada, Jamaica and the US states Alaska, California, Colorado, Nevada, Maine, Massachusetts, Oregon, Vermont and Washington, DC), five European countries (Czech Republic, Belgium, Georgia, the Netherlands and Spain), three Australian states (South Australia, Australian Capital Territory and Northern Territory), and one country in Africa (South Africa). The laws and policies pertaining to home cannabis cultivation in these places, however, differed significantly.

Depenalization of home cultivation

In two countries (Brazil and Chile) there were criminal provisions in the drug law which stated that the judge should decide whether the cultivation was for personal use and in that case, apply non-custodial sanctions (e.g. fine, education or community work). This adhered to the accepted definition of depenalization (decreasing or removing criminal penalties) and because this was stated in the actual law, we classified these provisions as *de jure depenalization*.

In three other countries (Colombia, Costa Rica and Georgia), criminal provisions pertaining to home cultivation were repealed by a decision of their respective Supreme Courts or, as in the case of Georgia, by Constitutional Court. These court decisions were classified as de facto *depenalization*, meaning that while the particular provisions pertaining to home cultivation remained a criminal offense in the law, the Supreme/Constitutional Court instructed lower courts that these criminal cases should be dismissed. In other words, according to these courts' interpretation, cannabis cultivation for personal use should not be considered a criminal offense. In the particular case of Georgia, the Constitutional Court decided that for home cultivation in an amount smaller than 151 grams, it was unconstitutional to apply jail (custodial) sentences (Human Rights Watch, 2018).

None of the countries above depenalized any provisions pertaining to cannabis supply, thus home cannabis cultivation remained the only (self) supply option aside from the illegal market. However, one example of drug supply de facto *depenalization* exists. In Spain, a Supreme Court ruling established that behaviors where drugs are shared among habitual or dependent users and that are not publicized and/or extended to a third party should not be punished (Muñoz and Soto, 2001). Taken together with the fact that home cannabis cultivation is *de jure* decriminalized in Spain (see the next section), this has established a legal interpretation that private, non-profit associations of cannabis users who cultivate cannabis on behalf of their members and fellow cannabis users, and can supply them with amounts of cannabis for their personal use, can be legally operated (Barriuso, 2011).

Decriminalization of home cultivation

Further on, we identified two jurisdictions where home cultivation was de facto *decriminalized* (Belgium and the Netherlands). This took the form of police guidelines that home cannabis cultivation should not be prosecuted (the Netherlands) or should have low prosecutorial priority (Belgium). In the Netherlands, this extended to de facto decriminalization of retail cannabis sales of less than 5 grams, providing the basis for the operation of retail coffeeshops.

We also identified six jurisdictions where home cultivation was *decriminalized de jure*; i.e. not a criminal offense by the law and/or referring to administrative offenses instead (three Australian states – South Australia, Australian Capital Territory, and Northern Territory, Czech Republic, Spain and Jamaica). In the three Australian states, decriminalization had a discretionary nature – the police could opt to issue an administrative notice consisting of a fine instead of charging the person with a criminal offense. In general, the offender had to pay the fine within a certain time frame in order to avoid criminal charges and/or custodial sentence (details are provided in Table 7.1). None of these jurisdictions decriminalized any other cannabis supply option, except for the de facto *depenalization* of supply among habitual users in Spain (see above).

Legalization of home cultivation

In two instances, a Constitutional Court (South Africa) and a Supreme Court (Mexico) introduced *jurisprudence* stating that the criminal provisions (together with all legal restrictions and punishments) related to home cannabis cultivation were unconstitutional. Such jurisprudence meant that criminal provisions pertaining to home cultivation policies were invalid and that legislators should amend the legislation further (e.g. replace the invalid paragraphs). Given that, in these two cases, no criminal and no administrative provisions regulating home cannabis cultivation were adopted (yet), we concluded that both countries were in a state of de facto *legalization*.

Finally, we found ten jurisdictions where home cannabis cultivation was *de jure legalized*. From those, regulation of home cannabis cultivation was introduced in parallel to regulating other cannabis supply options in seven jurisdictions. This was the case in six US states (Alaska, California, Colorado, Massachusetts, Nevada and Oregon), Canada and Uruguay. While in the US, these were state-level regulations, Canada introduced a federal policy in which provinces could limit the scope of legalization. In both instances, home cultivation was allowed alongside a retail market composed of licensed producers. In Uruguay, home cannabis cultivation was legal, as was supply via pharmacies and Cannabis Social Clubs (CSCs). In four countries/states (Antigua and Barbuda, Maine, Vermont, Washington, DC), home cannabis cultivation was *de jure legalized*, however no other cannabis supply options were made available.

Number of cannabis plants

The extent of cannabis cultivation exempted from prohibition differed by jurisdiction. In the case of all Latin American countries, except for Colombia and Uruguay, the number of cannabis plants was not specified, instead referring to "personal use" in Brazil (*de jure depenalized*) and Mexico (de facto *legalized*), "personal use in short term" in Chile (*de jure depenalized*) and "not for sale" in Costa Rica (de facto *depenalized*). Similarly, in South Africa, (de facto *legalized*), this was stated as cultivated "in a private place for personal consumption in private." Private space was the only limitation in the case of Spain as well (*de jure decriminalization*).

In the remaining jurisdictions, the number of plants was specified, but differed widely. Uruguay and all US states except for Oregon and Vermont set the limit at six plants (*de jure legalized*). A slightly lower limit of five plants was introduced in the Netherlands, the Czech Republic and Jamaica (de facto or *de jure decriminalized*) and four plants in Canada, Oregon, Vermont and Antigua and Barbuda (de facto or *de jure legalized*). The outliers were the two de facto *decriminalized* Australian states with one plant (South Australia) and two plants (Australian Capital Territory and Northern Territory) and Belgium with one plant. On the other hand, the court ruling in Colombia established that growing up to 20 plants should not be punished by the court (de facto *depenalization*). Overall, in jurisdictions that allowed other cannabis supply options (Canada, Netherlands, Spain, five US states and Uruguay), the limit was between four and six plants, avoiding the extremely low (one or two plants) or extremely high (20 plants) thresholds.

Other circumstances of cannabis cultivation

Beyond the mere number of plants, other restrictions were in place. For instance, in several US states, only half the plants were allowed to be mature (Alaska, Colorado, Vermont and Washington, DC), while in the case of Maine this number was less than 3 of 12 plants. The limit for personal cultivation was also to apply specifically per residence in certain jurisdictions (California, Oregon and Canada). In some jurisdictions, the limit per residence was set up as twice the threshold number of plants for personal cultivation; for instance, 6 plants were allowed per person, but only 12 in total per residence (Massachusetts, Nevada and Washington, DC). In a number of jurisdictions, home cannabis cultivation was only possible in one's residence and/or with approval of the property owner. In two Australian states (South Australia and Australian Capital Territory), only non-hydroponic cultivation was decriminalized. This was in contrast to several US states that required cultivation in an enclosed or non-visible place, potentially favoring indoor cultivation (Maine, Vermont, California, Colorado and Nevada). Other restrictions included, for instance, the requirement to tag each plant with the cultivator's details (Maine) or to cultivate only from seeds obtained via an authorized source (Canada). A number of additional restrictions can be expected across Canadian provinces which have the autonomy to further restrict the federal legalization policy.

Cannabis after harvest

In the US states that legalized home cultivation, the laws that were put in place clearly stated that all produce from the plants was authorized for possession. In other places, the situation was less clear. In all jurisdictions where non-prohibitive measures towards home cannabis cultivation were introduced, we identified that possession of a small amount of cannabis was also not prohibited. However, the quantities of non-prohibited cannabis possession in countries that introduced any form of depenalization or decriminalization of home cultivation were rather low compared to the potential dried harvest, notably in countries like the Czech Republic (10 g), Belgium/the Netherlands (3 g) or Costa Rica (20 g). One could hypothesize that, had the law enforcement discovered the produce of these plants (e.g. dried herbal cannabis), quantities allowed for personal possession of cannabis rather than the number of plants would be considered. One exception to this might be Georgia where the home cultivation limit was not stated in terms of the number of plants, but rather in grams (151 g).

Second, as pointed to in the previous section, the laws and policies were often exclusively limited to personal use rather than to the number of plants (Brazil, Chile and Spain), and sometimes both requirements were in place (Czech Republic). However, in several US states that legalized home cultivation, sharing of cannabis without remuneration was specifically authorized if not greater than 28 g (Alaska, California and Nevada), but not in others (Oregon, Colorado, Massachusetts and Maine). Similarly, it was allowed in Canada, but not in Uruguay. Paradoxically, in some US states, only cultivation for personal use was authorized, but gifting was allowed too (California and Nevada).

Discussion

Twenty-seven jurisdictions (states/countries) worldwide adopted non-prohibition approaches to home cannabis cultivation by the time of this analysis (December 2018). There were large differences in terms of whether this was simply the removal of certain penalties (*depenalization*), replacing criminal prosecutions with administrative offenses (*decriminalization*) or removing all prohibitive measures (*legalization*). We found several examples where such provisions were not written in the law (*de jure*), but rather introduced as a de facto measure (i.e. via police instructions or court decisions regarding criminal prosecution). Other variations in these policies included the number of "not prohibited" plants (all plants, mature plants and plants per residence), type of cultivation (non-hydroponic and enclosed space), or approaches to the produce of these plants and allowing for sharing of this produce with no monetary reward.

Importantly, in the majority of cases, no other cannabis supply option other than self-supply was authorized (and only small limits for personal possession of cannabis were tolerated). Two European countries (the Netherlands and Spain) had de facto provisions in place that allowed for the operation of coffee shops and CSCs respectively. Six US states, Canada and Uruguay legalized other cannabis supply options (pharmacies and CSCs in Uruguay and licensed producers in the remaining places). Three US states and Canada allowed sharing of up to 28–30 g of cannabis without monetary exchange.

Several criteria have been suggested for the evaluation of cannabis legalization policies. These pertain to public health outcomes, notably impact on adolescent cannabis use and cannabis use patterns overall (new users and intensity of use), effect on motor vehicle convictions, damage and fatalities, emergency room attendances, children treated for accidental ingestion of edibles or help-seeking among older cannabis users (Hall and Weier, 2015). The measures of interest provided in the literature also include impact on cannabis potency, and availability and prices (Pacula, Kilmer, Wagenaar, Chaloupka and Caulkins, 2014a). In addition, cost to the regulator, tax revenue and any impact on public expenditure should be included (Caulkins, Kilmer, MacCoun, Pacula and Reuter, 2012; Rogeberg, Bergsvik, Phillips, Van Amsterdam, Eastwood, Henderson, Lynskey, Measham, Ponton and Rolles, 2018). Other objectives could include prioritization of human rights (Hathaway, 2002), avoidance of social costs pertaining to law enforcement and to lost productivity due to criminal proceedings or incarceration (Collins, Lapsley, Brochu, Easton, Pérez-Gómez, Rehm and Single, 2006; Collins and Lapsley, 2002), or reduction of harms from prohibition, such as disrespect to laws or the black market and associated violence (Hall, 2001; Werb, Rowell, Guyatt, Kerr, Montaner and Wood, 2011). Yet, the wide variation in home cannabis cultivation policies will have an impact on whether and to what extent these outcomes can be observed.

The complexity of home cultivation policies and impact on policy outcomes

Variability in legal provisions as well as in supply alternatives may complicate evaluations of home cultivation policies. This is supported by a previous analysis of medicinal marijuana policies which concluded that when it comes to policy evaluation, "the devil is in the (policy) detail" (Pacula et al., 2014b). Whether non-prohibitive approaches to home cannabis cultivation will have any effect will likely depend on the type of policy as well as on the other cannabis supply options in place.

The mere depenalization or decriminalization of home cannabis cultivation may not be enough to result in any changes. While such policies may decrease the chance of criminal prosecution compared to prohibition, consumers still face the risk of their plants being seized and being subjected to large administrative fines (*decriminalization*) or prolonged administrative or criminal proceedings before the case is dismissed (*depenalization*). In addition, in jurisdictions where possession of the entire home cultivation crop is not specifically authorized, people who grow their own cannabis within the non-prohibited threshold number of plants could still face criminal sanctions if detected by law enforcement after harvest. Overall, a discrepancy between laws and their enforcement has been described (Belackova, Ritter, Shanahan and Hughes, 2017a), and decriminalization as well as depenalization policies might be prone to shifts in law enforcement priorities.

Legalization of home cultivation may have the strongest impact on consumer behavior out of the policy options outlined in this paper. However, when other supply options are readily available (retail stores or pharmacies) and when/if consumers have to register their home cultivation with the authorities, they might prefer to choose the easier alternative of buying cannabis rather than producing their own. Similarly, they might prefer to continue purchasing their cannabis from illegitimate sources if these are seen as superior to both the licensed market and home cultivation regulations. Thus, the effect of allowing home cultivation may have little impact when other cannabis supply alternatives are in place (Caulkins et al., 2015; Rolles, 2009). The low proportion of cannabis cultivators in the Netherlands where coffeeshops are in operation could be an example (Belackova et al., 2015).

Places that legalize home cannabis cultivation and no other cannabis supply option may provide the best avenue to observe substantial policy effects. Yet, accounts from people who cultivate cannabis show that the marginal cost of cannabis cultivation decreases as the size of the cultivation increases, suggesting that they might want to cultivate more plants than is legally allowed (Barratt, Chanteloup, Lenton and Marsh, 2005) or to pool their cultivation together with other consumers (Belackova and Zabransky, 2014). While solutions such as pooled cannabis cultivation within the Cannabis Social Clubs (CSCs) exist (Decorte, Pardal, Queirolo, Boidi, Avilés and Franquero, 2017), policymakers might be reluctant to set high cultivation limits and potentially facilitate that the produce is sold without tax revenue (Caulkins et al., 2015).

Evaluation of home cultivation policies – cost of law enforcement

We suggest that only some outcome types will be meaningful in evaluating home cannabis cultivation policies. First and foremost, the mere removal of criminal penalties or sanctions on the existing home cultivation behavior would likely yield savings in terms of law enforcement, an apparent advantage of any alternatives to drug prohibition (Miron and Zwiebel, 1995; Thornton, 2014). It could be expected that depenalization would reduce the cost of imprisonment for a proportion of cannabis cultivation offenses and that decriminalization would also reduce the cost of court proceedings and, potentially, the part of criminal prosecution conducted by police. Legalization in itself should reduce both, including all costs related to policing. Additionally, depenalization and decriminalization could yield revenues in the form of criminal or administrative fines respectively.

However, certain levels of law enforcement for cannabis cultivation offenses would likely remain in place given that cannabis cultivation exceeding the threshold limit of plants would be prosecuted. The impact on the number of criminal offenses associated with non-prohibitive approaches to home cultivation might not also be straightforward. We previously pointed out that the number of cannabis-related offenses increased in SA after home cannabis cultivation and personal cannabis possession were decriminalized (Christie and Ali, 2000). Similarly, in the Czech Republic, the number of criminal cannabis cultivation offenses (>5 decriminalized plants) increased from 145 in 2010 when decriminalization of home cultivation was introduced to 209 in 2014, settling at around 160 between 2015–2017. The criminal offense of drug production under which home cannabis cultivation would be classified, previously steeply increased as well, as did the proportion of small-scale plantations (6–49 plants) detected by the police, and recent data demonstrate an increase in administrative offenses pertaining to cannabis (Mravčík, Chomynová, Grohmannová, Janíková, Černíková, Rous, Tion Leštinová, Kiššová, Nechanská, Vlach, Fidesová and Vopravil, 2018). This suggests that the Czech policy change did not decrease law enforcement activity or costs and, as argued above, that drug laws may not correspond to their enforcement (Belackova et al., 2017a).

Evaluation of home cultivation policies – population-level outcomes

An important area of inquiry will be the extent to which home cultivation policies can alter the behavior of consumers and suppliers in the cannabis market. In this respect, the relevant questions for evaluation include whether when non-prohibitive measures to home cultivation measures are introduced: (1) more consumers will cultivate their own cannabis within the limitations of the law; (2) more people will cultivate cannabis irrespective of the legal limits; (3) fewer people will obtain some or all of their cannabis from illegitimate sources; (4) more people will use cannabis as a result of being able to cultivate it; (5) people who use cannabis will use more of it due to being able to cultivate it; (6) whether harms from cannabis use will increase.

The Czech case, outlined above, suggests that both decriminalized and criminal behaviors pertaining to cannabis cultivation, as noted in points (1) and (2), could increase with non-prohibitive measures and sourcing cannabis from illegitimate sources could decrease (3). Yet, the relatively high latency of home cannabis cultivation and other drug crimes makes it difficult to determine whether the increase can be attributed to any behavioral changes or, rather, to the apparent intensification of law enforcement activities (Zeman, Stefunkova and Travnickova, 2015). Therefore, representative surveys exploring the proportion of people who grow cannabis in a population (including the size of the cultivation site) should remain the primary source of information on home cultivation rates and other consumer behavior. These surveys could aim to estimate: (a) the proportion of cannabis users who obtain cannabis via home cultivation; (b) those who obtain cannabis from someone who grows it for free or (c) for money; (d) those who purchase cannabis from other non-legitimate sources; and (e) those who purchase cannabis legally – if applicable. This could involve estimating the volume of cannabis retrieved by those different means.

Discovering the increase in the volume of cannabis sourced via home cultivation can be a policy objective in itself. For instance, separation of the cannabis market from other illegal drugs, or the separation of cannabis users from the cannabis market overall, can be seen as a positive policy outcome

(Reinarman, 2009; Van Vliet, 1990). Several studies have also estimated the monetary value of cannabis markets (Caulkins and Kilmer, 2013; Giommoni, 2014; Legleye, Ben Lakhdar, Legleye, Ben Lakhdar, Spilka, Legleye, Ben Lakhdar and Spilka, 2008; Werb, Nosyk, Kerr, Fischer, Montaner and Wood 2012; Wilkins, Reilly, Pledger and Casswell, 2005); shifting a proportion of cannabis consumption away from the market to self-supply can potentially reduce the size of this (illicit) market (Belackova et al., 2018). Non-compliance with home cultivation policy could yield positive outcomes too. For instance, if a policy change made people who supply cannabis within their social network grow the cannabis they sell instead of buying it on the wholesale market, this could reduce the volume of cannabis that is produced by organized criminal groups.

When it comes to researching the impact on cannabis use patterns – (4) and (5) – the up-to-date research has shown no effect (Cerveny et al., 2017; Donnelly et al., 2000; Johnson et al., 2017; McGeorge and Aitken, 1997; Pacula et al., 2014b), some increase in youth cannabis use (Pacula et al., 2013), but also decrease in cannabis use rates (MacCoun, 2010). In terms of harms (6), home cultivation policies were potentially associated with fewer alcohol-involved accidents (Pacula et al., 2013) and with more vaping and use of edibles, but still comparable to other non-prohibitive measures (Borodovsky and Budney, 2017). These studies were predominantly limited by the inability to separate effect of home cultivation from overall cannabis decriminalization or were conducted in the context of medicinal cannabis laws.

An important question is whether cannabis quality will change (from indoor to outdoor or the other way around, if variability of cannabis strains will increase and if potency and prices of cannabis will increase or decrease), as this may have an impact on use patterns and harms. It has been previously pointed out that people who cultivate their cannabis are often motivated by the fact that they can produce cannabis which is of higher quality (Belackova, Tomkova and Zabransky, 2016; Potter et al., 2015). Regarding cannabis potency on the market, no effect was found in one study (Sevigny et al., 2014). Importantly, alterations in cannabis quality when produced in home conditions might involve lower presence of pesticides and other harmful adulterants, influencing the level of health harms from smoking cannabis (Hazekamp, 2006; Subritzky, Pettigrew and Lenton, 2017). Yet, the majority of samples included in those analyses has relied on police seizures. Pre- and post-assessments of cannabis potency and quality would require a more complex sampling design, given that legitimate home produce would likely consist in an insignificant proportion of cannabis seizures.

Operational-level assessments of home cultivation policies

Importantly, while the de facto measures introduced in this chapter provide less legal security than formal policies, several have been based on high-level court decisions that the laws prohibiting home cannabis cultivation are unconstitutional; i.e. not in line with basic legal principles and citizens' rights. This line of policy development might indicate that home cultivation policies should be, in the first place, respective of their constituents' needs and rights (Hathaway, 2002; Jürgens, 2008).

Not limited to this argument, operational-level questions will be important in evaluations in order to assess whether policies are designed in a way that respects the realm of consumer behavior and whether they are designed in a way that can be adhered to (Gettman and Kennedy, 2014). This could include assessment of whether the number of plants set up by the policy is enough to satisfy the consumer need. For example, in places where climatic conditions are not favorable to outdoor cannabis cultivation, the plant limit might be too low because indoor plants yield a substantially lower amount of cannabis (Caulkins, 2010). The other aspects might include the level of adherence to the provisions on cannabis sharing. For instance, it is plausible that people who cultivate their cannabis will not adhere to the policy if sharing with others is prohibited, as this behavior has been a well-documented social practice (Potter et al., 2015). Unintended consequences can take place, such as emerging businesses that provide "free" cannabis as a complement to otherwise overpriced petty goods (Martell, 2018). Overall, despite indications that people who cultivate cannabis are willing to participate in regulatory schemes (Lenton, Frank, Barratt, Dahl and Potter, 2015), it seems important to assess their willingness to, for example, register with authorities and gauge the overall perception of home cultivation policies that are in place. In particular, limitations to the number of mature plants, number of plants per residence or cultivation methods might not be seen as feasible from a cultivator's perspective.

Towards methodology of assessing home cultivation policies

Future evaluators could use the diversity of design features to inform best practice home cannabis laws and regulations. The outcome indicators we proposed above (cost of law enforcement, sources of cannabis, levels of cannabis use and harms, operational-level assessments) could be tested upon the various policy and market settings (see Table 7.2). Relevant research design could involve pre- and post-assessment, in particular on a locality that introduces a home cultivation policy. Comparison of localities with similar policy designs but varying features could also be performed (e.g. jurisdictions that legalized home cannabis cultivation only but differed in terms of number of cannabis plants, cannabis sharing policy), as well as comparison of localities with similar policies but different enforcement practice (e.g. discretional vs. full decriminalization). Comparisons could focus on jurisdictions which have similar policy contexts (e.g. licensed cannabis market), one with home cultivation policy in place and another one without. For instance, among the ten US states which legalized cannabis, only one (the state of Washington) did not allow for home cultivation (Pardo, 2014). Similarly, some Canadian provinces have opted out of home cannabis cultivation policies (Government of Manitoba, 2018; Government of Quebec, 2018).

Conclusions

Home cannabis cultivation is seen as a low-risk practice which seems to yield many individual-level benefits. Up-to-date evaluation of home cultivation policies, with some exceptions, has been limited to medicinal cannabis policies or to policies that were implemented together with the decriminalization of personal cannabis possession. Any evaluations should consider that home cultivation policies are highly variable, and consumers may not respond to the different models in equal ways. We identified 27 jurisdictions that have adopted non-prohibitive approaches to home cultivation and divided them into ten categories. These differed in terms of the level in which they remove the risk of criminal prosecution (de facto and *de jure depenalization, decriminalization* and *legalization*) and in terms of what cannabis supply options exist in parallel with home cultivation.

In theory, home cultivation policies should reduce the cost of law enforcement, yet some examples from practice suggest that this might not be the case if law enforcement remains a priority. There is also little indication that home cannabis policies can influence the rates of cannabis use and harms. Large spill-over effects of home cultivation would be needed to create any detectable changes. One way to approach evaluations of home cultivation policies could be to shift attention to representative surveys on how consumers obtain their cannabis (i.e. how many engage in low-risk practices such as home cultivation) and to operational-level assessments of how these policies fit the realm of cannabis acquisition behavior. Equally, several outcome indicators (cost of law enforcement, sources of cannabis, levels of cannabis use and harms and operational-level assessments) could be tested upon the various policy and market settings via, for example, pre- and post-study design or by comparison with similar policies which differ in their particular features.

Acknowledgments

The authors would like to thank Dr. Dato Otiashvili and Dr. Irma Kirtadze (Alternative Georgia), Mrs. Nivedita Bansal (Shah Hemp Inno-Ventures), Mr. Frantisek Pisarik (ENCOD) and Mr. Kenzi Riboulet Zemouli (FAAAT) who were consulted in the analysis of national legislations. We would also like to thank Dr. Kyle Mulrooney (University of New England) for proof-reading this manuscript and his valuable comments.

References

Barratt, M.J., Chanteloup, F., Lenton, S. and Marsh, A. (2005). Cannabis law reform in Western Australia: An opportunity to test theories of marginal deterrence and legitimacy. *Drug and Alcohol Review*, 24(4), 321–330.

Barriuso, M.A. (2011). Cannabis social clubs in Spain: A normalizing alternative underway. In *Series on legislative reform of drug policies* (Vol. 9). Amsterdam: Transnational Institute.

Belackova, V., Brandnerova, M. and Vechet, D. (2018). How close to the "honeypot?" A comparative analysis of cannabis markets under two different policies toward personal cultivation. *International Criminal Justice Review*, 28(3), 206–225.

Belackova, V., Maalsté, N., Zabransky, T. and Grund, J.P. (2015). "Should I buy or should I grow?" How drug policy institutions and drug market transaction costs shape the decision to self-supply with cannabis in the Netherlands and the Czech Republic. *International Journal of Drug Policy*, 26(3), 296–310.

Belackova, V., Ritter, A., Shanahan, M. and Hughes, C.E. (2017a). Assessing the concordance between illicit drug laws on the books and drug law enforcement: Comparison of three states on the continuum from "decriminalized" to "punitive." *International Journal of Drug Policy*, 41, 148–157.

Belackova, V., Shanahan, M. and Ritter, A. (2017b). Mapping regulatory models for medicinal cannabis: A matrix of options. *Australian Health Review*, 42(4), 403–411.

Belackova, V. and Stefunkova, M. (2018). Interpreting the Czech drug decriminalization: The glass is half full. Response to Cerveny, J., Chomynová, P., Mravčík, V. & van Ours, J.C. (2017). Cannabis decriminalization and the age of onset of cannabis use. *International Journal of Drug Policy*, 52, 102–105.

Belackova, V., Tomkova, A. and Zabransky, T. (2016). Qualitative research in Spanish cannabis social clubs: "The moment you enter the door, you are minimising the risks." *International Journal of Drug Policy*, 34, 49–57.

Belackova, V. and Zabransky, T. (2014). Assessing the users' risks in the shift towards indoor cannabis cultivation – The case of the Czech Republic. *Adiktologie*, 14(4), 410–418.

Borodovsky, J.T. and Budney, A.J. (2017). Legal cannabis laws, home cultivation, and use of edible cannabis products: A growing relationship? *International Journal of Drug Policy*, 50, 102–110.

Caulkins, J.P. (2010). *Estimated cost of production for legalized cannabis*. RAND, drug Policy Research Center. Retrieved from www.rand.org/content/dam/rand/pubs/working_papers/2010/RAND_WR764.pdf.

Caulkins, J.P. and Kilmer, B. (2013). *Estimating the size of the EU cannabis market*. Retrieved from www.rand.org/pubs/external_publications/EP50375.html.

Caulkins, J.P., Kilmer, B., Kleiman, M., MacCoun, R.J., Midgette, G., Oglesby, P., Pacula, R.L. and Reuter, P. (2015). *Considering marijuana legalization: Insights for Vermont and other jurisdictions*. Santa Monica: RAND Corporation.

Caulkins, J.P., Kilmer, B., MacCoun, R.J., Pacula, R.L. and Reuter, P. (2012). Design considerations for legalizing cannabis: Lessons inspired by analysis of California's Proposition 19. *Addiction*, 107(5), 865–871.

Caulkins, J.P. and Pacula, R. (2006). Marijuana markets: Inferences from reports by the household population. *Journal of Drug Issues*, 22(3), 16.

Cerveny, J., Chomynová, P., Mrav ík, V. and van Ours, J.C. (2017). Cannabis decriminalization and the age of onset of cannabis use. *International Journal of Drug Policy*, 43, 122–129.

Christie, P. and Ali, R. (2000). Offences under the cannabis expiation notice scheme in South Australia. *Drug and Alcohol Review*, 19(3), 251–256.

Collins, D.J. and Lapsley, H.M. (2002). *Counting the cost: Estimates of the social costs of drug abuse in Australia in 1998–9*. Retrieved from http://drogfokuszpont.hu/wp-content/uploads/kokk_social_cost_australia_99.pdf.

Collins, D.J., Lapsley, H., Brochu, S., Easton, B., Pérez-Gómez, A., Rehm, J. and Single, E. (2006). *International guidelines for the estimation of the avoidable costs of substance abuse*. Retrieved from https://oraprdnt.uqtr.uquebec.ca/pls/public/docs/FWG/GSC/Publication/4242/60/5333/1/61261/5/F1234461959_2006_Brochu_costs_SPA.pdf.

Decorte, T. (2010). The case for small-scale domestic cannabis cultivation. *International Journal of Drug Policy*, 21(4), 271–275.

Decorte, T., Pardal, M., Queirolo, R., Boidi, M.F., Avilés, C.S. and Franquero, Ò.P. (2017). Regulating cannabis social clubs: A comparative analysis of legal and self-regulatory practices in Spain, Belgium and Uruguay. *International Journal of Drug Policy*, 43, 44–56.

Donnelly, N., Hall, W. and Christie, P. (2000). The effects of the cannabis expiation notice system on the prevalence of cannabis use in South Australia: Evidence from the national drug strategy household surveys 1985–95. *Drug and Alcohol Review*, 19(3), 265–269.

Eastwood, N., Fox, E. and Rosmarin, A. (2016). *A quiet revolution: Drug decriminalization across the globe*. Retrieved from www.release.org.uk/sites/default/files/pdf/publications/A%20Quiet%20Revolution%20-%20Decriminalization%20Across%20the%20Globe.pdf.

EMCDDA. (2005). *EMCDDA thematic papers: Illicit drug use in the EU: Legislative approaches*. Lisbon: European Monitoring Centre for Drugs and Drug Addiction.

EMCDDA. (2016). *Models for the legal supply of cannabis: Recent developments*. Retrieved from emcdda.europa.eu/topics/pods/legal-supply-of-cannabis.

Gettman, J. and Kennedy, M. (2014). Let it grow – The open market solution to marijuana control. *Harm Reduction Journal*, 11(1), 32.

Giommoni, L. (2014). The retail value of the illicit drug market in Italy: A consumption-based approach. *Global Crime*, 15(1–2), 27–50.

Government of Manitoba. (2018). *Cannabis in Manitoba*. Retrieved from www.gov.mb.ca/cannabis/index.html.

Government of Quebec (Producer). (2018). *The legislation on cannabis in brief*. Retrieved from https://encadrementcannabis.gouv.qc.ca/en/loi/.

Hall, W. (2001). Reducing the harms caused by cannabis use: The policy debate in Australia. *Drug and Alcohol Dependence*, 62(3), 163–174.

Hall, W. and Weier, M. (2015). Assessing the public health impacts of legalizing recreational cannabis use in the USA. *Clinical Pharmacology & Therapeutics*, 97(6), 607–615.

Hansen, B., Miller, K. and Weber, C. (Producer). (2018). Early evidence on recreational marijuana legalization and traffic fatalities. *Economic Inquiry*. Retrieved from http://faculty.washington.edu/ceweber/HMW_marijuana_traffic.pdf.

Hathaway, A.D. (2002). From harm reduction to human rights: Bringing liberalism back into drug reform debates. *Drug and Alcohol Review*, 21(4), 397–404.

Hazekamp, A. (2006). An evaluation of the quality of medicinal grade cannabis in the Netherlands. *Cannabinoids*, 1(1), 1–9.

Hughes, C.E., Ritter, A., Chalmers, J., Lancaster, K., Barratt, M.J. and Moxham-Hall, V. (2016). *Decriminalization of drug use and possession in Australia – A briefing note*. Retrieved from https://ndarc.med.unsw.edu.au/resource/decriminalization-drug-use-and-possession-australia-briefing-note.

Human Rights Watch (Producer). (2018). *The human toll of Georgia's abusive drug policies*. Retrieved from www.hrw.org/report/2018/08/13/harsh-punishment/human-toll-georgias-abusive-drug-policies.

Jelsma, M. (2011). *The development of international drug control: Lessons learned and strategic challenges of the future*: International Drug Policy Consortium.

Johnson, J., Hodgkin, D. and Harris, S.K. (2017). The design of medical marijuana laws and adolescent use and heavy use of marijuana: Analysis of 45 states from 1991 to 2011. *Drug and Alcohol Dependence,* 170, 1–8.

Jürgens, R. (2008). *"Nothing about us without us": Greater, meaningful involvement of people who use illegal drugs, a public health, ethical and human rights imperative*. Retrieved from www.opensocietyfoundations.org/sites/default/files/Int%2520Nothing%2520About%2520Us%2520%2528May%25202008%2529.pdf.

Kerr, D.C., Bae, H. and Koval, A.L. (2018). Oregon recreational marijuana legalization: Changes in undergraduates' marijuana use rates from 2008 to 2016. *Psychology of Addictive Behaviors,* 32(6), 670.

Legleye, S., Ben Lakhdar, C., Legleye, S., Ben Lakhdar, C., Spilka, S., Legleye, S., Ben Lakhdar, C. and Spilka, S. (2008). Two ways of estimating the euro value of the illicit market for cannabis in France. *Drug and Alcohol Review,* 27(5), 466–472.

Lenton, S., Frank, V.A., Barratt, M.J., Dahl, H.V. and Potter, G.R. (2015). Attitudes of cannabis growers to regulation of cannabis cultivation under a non-prohibition cannabis model. *International Journal of Drug Policy,* 26(3), 257–266.

Lenton, S., McDonald, D., Ali, R. and Moore, T. (1999). Laws applying to minor cannabis offences in Australia and their evaluation. *International Journal of Drug Policy,* 10(4), 299–303.

MacCoun, R.J. (2010). *Estimating the non-price effects of legalization on cannabis consumption*. Retrieved from www.rand.org/content/dam/rand/pubs/working_papers/2010/RAND_WR767.pdf.

Martell, N. (2018). 3 delivery services that offer marijuana as a free gift. *DC Refined*. Retrieved from http://dcrefined.com/eat-drink/3-delivery-services-that-offer-marijuana-as-a-free-gift.

McGeorge, J. and Aitken, C.K. (1997). Effects of cannabis decriminalization in the Australian capital territory on university students' patterns of use. *Journal of Drug Issues,* 27(4), 785–794.

Miron, J.A. and Zwiebel, J. (1995). The economic case against drug prohibition. *The Journal of Economic Perspectives,* 9(4), 175–192.

Mrav ík, V., Chomynová, P., Grohmannová, K., Janíková, B., erníková, T., Rous, Z., Tion Leštinová, Z., Kiššová, L., Nechanská, B., Vlach, T., Fidesová, H. and Vopravil, J. (2018). *Výro ní zpráva o stavu ve v cech drog v eské republice v roce 2017 (Annual report on the drug situation in the Czech Republic in 2017)*. Retrieved from www.drogy-info.cz/data/obj_files/32962/837/VZdrogy2017_web181207.pdf.

Muñoz, J. and Soto, S. (2001). El uso terapéutico de cannabis y la creación de establecimientos para su adquisición y consumo. *Revista de Derecho Penal y Criminología,* 7, 49–94.

Pacula, R.L., Kilmer, B., Wagenaar, A.C., Chaloupka, F.J. and Caulkins, J.P. (2014). Developing public health regulations for marijuana: Lessons from alcohol and tobacco. *American Journal of Public Health,* 104(6), 1021–1028.

Pacula, R.L., MacCoun, R., Reuter, P., Chriqui, J., Kilmer, B., Harris, K., Paoli, L. and Schäfer, C. (2005). What does it mean to decriminalize marijuana? A cross-national empirical examination. *Advances in Health Economics and Health Services Research,* 16, 347–369.

Pacula, R.L., Powell, D., Heaton, P. and Sevigny, E.L. (2013). Assessing the effects of medical marijuana laws on marijuana and alcohol use: The devil is in the details. (No. w19302). National Bureau of Economic Research.

Pacula, R.L., Powell, D., Heaton, P. and Sevigny, E.L. (2015). Assessing the effects of medical marijuana laws on marijuana use: The devil is in the details. *Journal of Policy Analysis and Management,* 34(1), 7–31.

Pardo, B. (2014). Cannabis policy reforms in the Americas: A comparative analysis of Colorado, Washington, and Uruguay. *International Journal of Drug Policy,* 25(4), 727–735.

Potter, G.R., Barratt, M.J., Malm, A., Bouchard, M., Blok, T., Christensen, A.-S., Decorte, T., Frank, V.A., Hakkarainen, P. and Klein, A. (2015). Global patterns of domestic cannabis cultivation: Sample characteristics and patterns of growing across eleven countries. *International Journal of Drug Policy,* 26(3), 226–237.

Reinarman, C. (2009). Cannabis policies and user practices: Market separation, price, potency, and accessibility in Amsterdam and San Francisco. *International Journal of Drug Policy,* 20(1), 28–37.

Rogeberg, O., Bergsvik, D., Phillips, L.D., Van Amsterdam, J., Eastwood, N., Henderson, G., Lynskey, M., Measham, F., Ponton, R. and Rolles, S. (2018). A new approach to formulating and appraising drug policy: A multi-criterion decision analysis applied to alcohol and cannabis regulation. *International Journal of Drug Policy,* 56, 144–152.

Rolles, S. (2009). *After the war on drugs: Blueprint for regulation.* Retrieved from www.tdpf.org.uk/sites/default/files/Blueprint.pdf.

Sevigny, E.L., Pacula, R.L. and Heaton, P. (2014). The effects of medical marijuana laws on potency. *International Journal of Drug Policy,* 25(2), 308–319.

Subritzky, T., Pettigrew, S. and Lenton, S. (2017). Into the void: Regulating pesticide use in Colorado's commercial cannabis markets. *International Journal of Drug Policy,* 42, 86–96.

Thornton, M. (2014). *The economics of prohibition* (1610164652). Retrieved from https://mises.org/library/economics-prohibition-0.

Trautmann, F., Kilmer, B. and Turnbull, P. (2013). *Further insights into aspects of the EU illicit drugs market.* Luxembourg: Publications Office of the European Union.

U.N. (1961). *Single convention on narcotic drugs.* New York: United Nations.

U.N. (1971). *Convention on psychotropic substances.* Vienna: United Nations.

U.N. (1988). *Convention against illicit traffic in narcotic drugs and psychotropic substances.* Vienna: United Nations.

Van Vliet, H.J. (1990). Separation of drug markets and the normalization of drug problems in the Netherlands: An example for other nations? *Journal of Drug Issues,* 20(3), 463–471.

Werb, D., Nosyk, B., Kerr, T., Fischer, B., Montaner, J. and Wood, E. (2012). Estimating the economic value of British Columbia's domestic cannabis market: Implications for provincial cannabis policy. *International Journal of Drug Policy,* 23(6), 436–441.

Werb, D., Rowell, G., Guyatt, G., Kerr, T., Montaner, J. and Wood, E. (2011). Effect of drug law enforcement on drug market violence: A systematic review. *International Journal of Drug Policy,* 22(2), 87–94.

Wilkins, C., Reilly, J.L., Pledger, M. and Casswell, S. (2005). Estimating the dollar value of the illicit market for cannabis in New Zealand. *Drug and Alcohol Review,* 24(3), 227–234.

Zeman, P., Stefunkova, M. and Travnickova, I. (2015). *Drogova kriminalita a trestni zakonin (Drug offences and the penal code).* Retrieved from www.ok.cz/iksp/docs/426.pdf.

8 City-level policies of regulating recreational cannabis in Europe

From pilot projects to "local customization"?

Tom Blickman and Catherine Sandwell[1]

Introduction

Recently, there have been clear signs of a shift in governments' approaches to recreational cannabis markets. Countries like Uruguay in 2013 and Canada in 2018 – as well as a number of US states since 2012 – have moved to control cannabis through regulated markets from seed to sale, rather than prohibition. More recently, the newly elected president of Mexico also announced his intention to legalize and regulate the cannabis market (Reuters, 2018). Proponents of this approach argue that current prohibition policies, even where they are modulated by decriminalization of use or possession for personal use, have shown themselves to be largely ineffective at eliminating illicit recreational cannabis markets or reducing the harms associated with these markets. After decades of relatively progressive drug policies (European Monitoring Centre for Drugs and Drug Addiction, (EMCDDA) 2017), governments have seemingly been left behind by changes elsewhere in the world, operating in a state of denial about the changing policy landscape that is beginning to take shape worldwide, in particular, in North America. At the same time, however, calls for change from local authorities, who have to deal with the negative consequences of local illicit cannabis markets, are increasing (EMCDDA, 2017; Blickman, 2014).

Local authorities in several countries in Europe are searching for tools and mechanisms to regulate their recreational cannabis markets. However, EU-level consensus on national cannabis regulation by member states looks as unlikely as ever and, at the national level, many European governments are cautious about addressing the issue, if not outright dismissive (EMCDDA, 2017; Kilmer, Kruithof, Pardal, Caulkins and Rubin, 2013). Confronted with this reality, municipalities in the Netherlands and elsewhere in Europe, notably in Switzerland (where some cantonal governments have also played a role), Denmark and Germany, are increasingly advocating for some form of regulation of recreational cannabis markets, while Spain and Belgium have seen the emergence of Cannabis Social Clubs (CSCs) in which cannabis activists have begun cultivating cannabis for members in a "closed circuit" (Blickman, 2014; Kilmer et al., 2013). The expansion of CSCs has put pressure on regional and local authorities (particularly at the regional level in Spain, where some autonomous regions have broad competencies on social and health policies) to take clear stances on recreational cannabis regulation (Araña, 2019; Decorte, 2019).

With these developments in mind, a study was initiated looking at recent policy changes with respect to cannabis in six countries (Belgium, Denmark, Germany, the Netherlands, Spain and Switzerland) where local initiatives were having some impact on the policy debate at the time (2016), commissioning country studies from researchers in those countries. While examining the local contexts of national developments, it became increasingly clear that some local authorities (municipalities or regional authorities such as the cantons in Switzerland, the autonomous communities in Spain or states – Länder – in Germany) are looking for more room to maneuver in relation to recreational cannabis regulation. There are municipalities and regions in each country which are eager to move forward with innovative solutions to problems linked to unregulated illicit cannabis markets in their jurisdictions. As noted by the European Monitoring Centre for Drugs and Drug Addiction (EMCDDA), city-level drug policies are often overshadowed by developments at the national and international level, which obscures the origins of new problems and innovative responses at the local level (EMCDDA, 2015). In this chapter, we try to fill in this gap and will summarize the main developments in these six countries with a focus on local initiatives, looking for an overarching framework to discuss the conundrum.

We will identify the concept of "Multilevel Governance" (MLG) and "local customization" as two possible policy options arising from this research. The European MLG concept breaks down, to a certain degree, the distinction between national and local governance or competencies and its success, therefore requires a level of reciprocity between different levels of governance which national governments may perceive as a risk. Nonetheless, this approach to policymaking, which prioritizes the facilitation of creative solutions in local contexts and offers new pathways for bottom-up policymaking, may offer the best chance at a way out of the current impasse in European drug policy, providing the best hope of progress towards more effective and human- and health-centered cannabis policy, as well as instruments to tackle criminal involvement with illicit markets.

Multi-level governance and local customization

In the last 30 years, a substantial body of academic and policy literature has advocated for political and administrative decentralization (Pollit, 2005). A group of theorists and policymakers have argued that decentralized decision- and policymaking has the capacity to lead to more effective policies, adapted to local environments, needs, and interests (De Vries, 2000). At the same time, some advocates consider decentralized policymaking to be more democratic, offering opportunities for citizens to directly influence policies that impact their daily lives, and enhancing both engagement and buy-in for policies (Pollit, 2005). Although policymakers and scholars have cautioned against assuming that decentralization as such leads automatically to better governance or more locally-adapted policies (Jans, 2015; Purcell, 2006; Pollit, 2005; De Vries, 2000), decentralized governance has nonetheless gained significant, if cautious, support within the EU.

Decentralization has been endorsed by the European Union as a principle of good governance (Garcia, 2006), where it has been widely discussed in connection with MLG. The European Charter of Local Self-Government, introduced by the Council of Europe (1985), and ultimately ratified by all member states, introduced the principles of decentralization and affirmed the significance of local authorities. The Maastricht Treaty is widely interpreted to offer support for certain forms of decentralization (Pollit, 2005), and a 2001 White Paper on European Governance stated that "The quality, relevance and effectiveness of EU policies depend on ensuring wide participation throughout the policy chain – from conception to implementation." (Commission of the European Union, 2001, p. 10). Further, in 2009, the Committee of the Regions, a body of the EU charged with giving non-national authorities a voice in European policymaking, issued a white paper on the significance of multilevel governance in a wide range of European policy areas (Committee of the Regions, 2009), and the Lisbon Treaty incorporated some key principles of this approach.

In 2014, the Committee of the Regions (2014) launched the Charter for Multilevel Governance (MLG) in Europe which, as of February 2019, had been endorsed by 220 signatories across Europe. The charter argues for the key significance of this governance approach. Critically, the principles of MLG suggest that municipalities, regions, and other sub-national levels of government should be able to play a direct role in development, and not only implementation, of European-level policies, stating that: "In line with the subsidiarity principle which places decisions at the most effective level and as close as possible to the citizens, we attach great importance to co-creating policy solutions that reflect the needs of citizens" (Committee of the Regions, 2014).

Some analysts have suggested that greater reliance on the principles of MLG could provide a partial way out of the current impasse in European-level drug policy (Chatwin, 2007). In MLG, practical decisions are made at the local level, encouraging greater involvement from citizens – a guiding principle in the EU. "A system of multi-level governance would allow initiatives to develop at the local level with power following a bottom-up structure," as opposed to top-down solutions that do not fit local and regional needs (Chatwin, 2007). Given the already wide diversity of drug policies in Europe, different cannabis regulation regimes would then no longer be an arena of multilateral, or even national, contention, but could instead be judged on their effectiveness, leaving the desired room for maneuver for local authorities.

Drug policy which prioritized creating opportunities for the local adaptation might help to advance European cannabis policy without the need to achieve consensus on certain key points. While criminal law obviously remains a core competency of the nation state and subject to multilateral conventions and agreements, which cannot be devolved to the sub-national level, some aspects of its implementation could be tailored to fit local circumstances, and a variety of mechanisms are available for this. However, as Chatwin (2007) notes, the status of MLG in the EU today should not be overstated. Although a white paper on European Governance provides official support for the concept (Commission of the European Union, 2001), EU member states still scrupulously defend their gatekeeping role (Chatwin, 2007). Nevertheless, principles of MLG and decentralized policymaking have been implemented, to varying degrees, by a number of nations within Europe (and elsewhere).

The Netherlands, for instance, has embarked on a political project of devolving certain kinds of decision-making to the lowest possible level. In the coalition agreement of the Rutte II government (2012–2016) this decentralization was justified by the argument that:

> The transfer of a large number of tasks from the central government to municipalities allows for local tailoring and customization and allows for stronger citizen involvement. Municipalities can better coordinate the implementation of tasks, and thus do more with less money. To this end, the central government gives them wide discretion.
>
> (Jans, 2015, p. 9)

Although not specifically envisaged to include cannabis policies, this concept of "local customization" ("*lokaal maatwerk*" in Dutch) did enter the debate about cannabis policy in the Netherlands, allowing municipalities to diverge from national guidelines about the introduction of controversial residence and registration criteria for coffeeshops, intended to counter cannabis tourism. With the benefit of hindsight, one could argue that local customization was already being implemented since at least 1996, when the government decentralized aspects of its coffeeshop policy to municipalities, notably giving them the option to veto cannabis retailing in the municipality, and to set additional policies within the national laws and guidelines (Korf, 2019).

Local customization is used in international business strategy on issues relating to the dilemmas of global vis-a-vis local strategy, that is, the trade-off between global standardization and local customization in the marketing of products and the organization of business management. According to Begley and Boyd (2003), to achieve strategic objectives, a company's top management has to cope with the structural tension of global formalization versus local flexibility, the process tension of global standardization versus local customization, and the power tension of global dictate versus local delegation. These are closely analogous to the tensions that policymakers are facing regarding cannabis, which is formalized globally in the standards set by the three international drug control conventions, allowing for some flexibility at the national level in the implementation of global rule-setting in national law; this formalization is now increasingly challenged by local authorities that want more flexibility to cope with local circumstances.

In this chapter, we use the term local customization to encompass a possible response to these three tensions in policymaking. It could be loosely defined as a process of decentralization, in which the implementation of international obligations embedded in national laws and guidelines are tailored to address specific local circumstances in a reciprocal process of decision-making between different levels of governance, which will in turn require the adaptation of current international and national legal standards. While such an orientation may open new pathways to moving forward with regulation, it will not automatically resolve political conflicts about drug control within or between countries. Rather, it provides a policymaking framework, with both historical precedent and popular support, which different levels of government can use in order to negotiate more nuanced compromises and bypass some seemingly intractable roadblocks on the path to more effective drug policy. The results of our research in six European countries showed that the time for these kinds of compromises is ripe, and that some cities and regions are keen to take on a more active and creative role in policy development in this area.

Policy shifts regarding recreational cannabis

In Europe, a wide array of approaches have been employed to deal with a problem that suffers from a high level of "policy resistance": actors are pulling in different directions and everyone has to put great effort into keeping the situation where no one wants it to be (Meadows, 2009, pp. 113–14). On the one hand, national governments in Europe are bound by international obligations – the UN drug control conventions and EU legislation – which limit their room for maneuver, particularly regarding the cultivation and supply of cannabis, and they want to avoid the diplomatic repercussions of attempting to reform domestic cannabis control (Blickman, 2018). Local authorities, on the other hand, tend to look pragmatically at the issue from the perspective of addressing public disorder related to street dealing, and addressing the hazards of illegal cultivation in residential areas and involvement of organized criminal groups in the local market; they need policy instruments and legislation that national governments currently cannot or will not deliver, depending on the political constellation.

Until recently, all countries in Europe have interpreted their obligations under the UN drug control conventions and current EU legislation to mean that full legalization and regulation of a cannabis market for recreational use is impossible. This position is reflected in the European Union Drugs Strategy (2013–2020), (EU, 2012/C 402/01), which reiterates the fact that EU drug policy is based on the UN drug control conventions and relevant EU law. However, in November 2018, the new coalition government of Luxembourg announced its intention to legalize and regulate recreational cannabis, although when and how it will do so remains unclear (Luxembourg Times, 2018). Despite the obvious conflict with current EU policy regarding the recreational use of cannabis, the EU and member states have not yet publicly reacted to the news. Luxembourg is the first EU country to address its willingness to move on the issue, although most EU countries have implemented changes to policy and practice intended to reduce the harms associated with criminalization, prohibition and repression (EMCDDA, 2017). Thus, occasionally, arrangements are reached to at least try to manage part of the problem. Confronted with the fact that it is virtually impossible to eradicate the cannabis market – due to the substantive societal, public health and law enforcement costs that would be involved – and in the absence of a clear legalization and regulation at the national level, a certain leniency towards cannabis use and possession for personal use has developed since the 1970s, when cannabis use substantially increased in Europe as a result of the counter-cultural movements of the 1960s. In practice, it was often left to local authorities to manage the resulting "grey areas" deriving from ambiguities and loopholes in national drug legislation.

The result is indeed a situation that no one wants, and it leads to odd arrangements, but breakthroughs to definitively solve the problem are extremely difficult to reach. Perhaps the clearest example of the kind of "half-baked" arrangements present across the EU is the coffeeshop system in the Netherlands, where municipalities provide licenses to cannabis-selling dispensaries that are in fact prohibited to sell cannabis according to the law in the books. While this arrangement at what is popularly known as the "front door" of the coffeeshop resolves most problems of the retail distribution of cannabis, the supply at the "back door" remains fully illegal and everyone involved must pretend not to know where the cannabis is coming from. The toleration of retail sales and this "immaculate conception" of cannabis – a result of some 40 years of pushing and pulling by different stakeholders at national and local level – has had a remarkable life span, but it has reached its expiration date.

In 2015, a working group of mayors and aldermen of Dutch municipalities through the Association of Dutch Municipalities (*Vereniging Nederlandse Gemeenten* – VNG) published a report, *Het failliet van het gedogen* (Toleration: a bankrupt policy), which concluded that the policy of toleration was no longer adequate and had become untenable to effectively tackle the problems they faced, in particular, the grip of organized crime groups controlling the supply of cannabis (Meesters, 2015). The "verdict" of the report is worth quoting as it reflects the situation of local authorities in Europe more broadly:

> The discussion on cannabis policy has reached an impasse, between proponents and opponents of regulation. We cannot allow the various levels of administration to become bogged down in discussions, while organized crime profits and public health remains insufficiently protected. We

> call upon all parties to above all employ a pragmatic approach in searching for solutions. We have reached the conclusion that a system of rules for the entire cannabis supply chain offers the best possibilities. We call upon all parties to work in favor of this approach, and subsequently join forces in its further elaboration. This means making choices, further elaborating those choices in a system based on experimentation, and subsequently consistently implementing those choices. Only together can we arrive at a truly effective approach to the problems.
>
> (Meesters, 2015)

At the annual congress of the VNG in June 2016, 89 percent of municipalities overwhelmingly supported legal regulation of a transparent supply chain to coffeeshops. The constant pressure of Dutch municipalities to regulate the supply of cannabis – the mayors of 60 Dutch municipalities already proposed an experiment back in 1999 (Spapens, Müller and Van de Bunt, 2015) – was a decisive factor in the decision of the current coalition government, which was formed in October 2017, to conduct an experiment regulating a transparent supply chain for coffeeshops (see Chapter 12). At the time of writing, the government and local municipalities are still fighting over the details and the extent of the experiment, while a bill to regulate the supply of cannabis is left hanging in the upper house of parliament, after being approved in the lower house in February 2017.

Drug policy and local authorities in Europe

Historically, cities have been at the vanguard of developing new solutions to drug problems, as they are the first level of government, closest to citizens, and are thus the first to be confronted with drug-related problems and related public nuisance (EMCDDA, 2015). While cities have significant room for maneuver in shaping policies to the needs of local circumstances, in particular on social, economic and public health issues, they also bear the costs of existing drug policies, both financially and operationally, which are determined at the national and even international level, in particular regarding matters of criminal law that significantly shape drug policies. Cities often find themselves in an unenviable position between the hammer and the anvil; between top-down policies and national criminal law and bottom-up demands from citizens and civil society actors confronted with the negative consequences of a policy-resistant problem.

Municipalities often function as "laboratories" for policy experimentation. A good example of how local authorities can shape national and even international drug policies with their capacity to experiment is the experience of a network of European cities confronted with the heroin crisis of the 1980s. In 1990, Amsterdam, Frankfurt, Hamburg and Zürich initiated the network by signing the *Frankfurt Resolution*, which became the charter of the European Cities on Drug Policy (ECDP) (European Cities on Drug Policy, 1991).

Other cities joined, including Basel, Charleroi, Dortmund, Hamburg, Hanover, Rotterdam, Ljubljana and Zagreb amongst others. These cities joined forces to advocate a more pragmatic, less prohibitionist drug policy and initiated a set of innovative harm-reduction measures, such as heroin substitution programs, social inclusion through housing-and-work programs, drug-consumption rooms and heroin-assisted treatment (Boekhout van Solinge, 1999). It is interesting to read one of the network's statements of purpose:

> Drug problems are crystalizing, above all, in major cities, producing the whole pallet of subsequent problems to a specifically intensive extent. Approaching these problems solely by conventional strategies of repressive, therapeutic, or preventive measures have led us to borders that cannot be crossed without the development and implementation of innovative – and sometimes unconventional policies.
>
> Moreover, it happens rather frequently that national or international drug legislation and guidelines prove to be instruments unsuited for the development of pragmatic approaches at communal level. Therefore, we observe a clear discrepancy between international conventions, their realization at governmental level, and local solutions. In this respect, we had to recognize that we are unable to delegate the problem to the governments of the states. Instead, we are being called to develop local strategies in collaboration and exchange with other cities and regions.
>
> (ECDP, 2002)

Over the years, the full spectrum of harm reduction measures would increasingly be adopted in national policies, and, ever more, at the international level as well. The example of the ECDP shows that it is possible for municipalities to successfully initiate drug policy reform from the bottom up (Schardt, 2001). The implementation of harm reduction measures mainly happened through social and health policies – an area in which local authorities have more policy space and autonomy. The ECDP also included the decriminalization of cannabis in its goals but had lost its momentum by the time this became a major issue. Interestingly, some of the cities involved with the ECDP are now also in the vanguard of advocating for regulation of the cannabis market, such as Amsterdam, Frankfurt, Hanover, Basel and Zürich.

While harm reduction measures could be defended due to the urgent need to tackle a public health crisis, including the emerging HIV/AIDS crisis, and the public disorder of open drug scenes, the regulation of a cannabis market of recreational, non-medical and non-scientific use is a different matter. Nevertheless, progress was also made on that issue during those years. In 1994, for instance, the Federal Constitutional Court of Germany cleared the way to decriminalize the use of cannabis. The "hashish decision" questioned excessive criminal prosecution and suggested not pursuing minor infringements. The decision reflected a trend in many European countries engaged in what is labelled as "soft defection" from the prohibitive regime enshrined in the UN drug control conventions (Bewley-Taylor, Blickman and Jelsma, 2014). Over time, starting with the Netherlands in the mid-1970s, most countries in Europe gradually decriminalized possession for personal use through prosecutorial guidelines, giving cannabis a low law enforcement priority and establishing thresholds that indicated "tolerated" amounts of cannabis that could avoid criminal prosecution (Rosmarin and Eastwood, 2012/2016). Cannabis was seen as a less harmful substance in comparison with other recreational drugs, and the heroin crisis starting in the 1970s and 1980s shifted policy attention away from cannabis. At the time, policies on cannabis were mainly about health and social concerns – through a separation of the markets for drugs which are less hazardous (like cannabis) and the markets for more hazardous drugs (like heroin), for instance – and concerns about the adverse effect of over-criminalizing cannabis users and law enforcement capacity problems with tackling the increasing numbers of users.

While these concerns sometimes led to government proposals towards regulation of the cannabis market, notably in the Netherlands in 1996 and Switzerland in 2001, those proposals were nipped in the bud due to political opposition both at home and abroad, including from UN institutions, in particular the International Narcotics Control Board (INCB), the "independent and quasi-judicial expert body" tasked with monitoring compliance with the international drug control treaties. While more jurisdictions would eventually decriminalize cannabis use and possession for personal use, no one went as far as the Dutch in terms of allowing the sale of small amounts in licensed retail shops. It is important to note that the Dutch government never proposed the institution of coffeeshops. The policy was originally intended to allow "house dealers" in popular youth centers, but over the years, the criteria used to allow tolerated sale of cannabis extended to more commercial enterprises due to court rulings that favored the emerging coffeeshop system (Jansen, 1994).

Cannabis policy at the local level: the Dutch experience

In the Netherlands, a more tolerant attitude towards cannabis use emerged in the 1970s, culminating in the revised 1976 Opium Act, which distinguished between cannabis (soft drugs) and "drugs with unacceptable risks" (hard drugs). The revision was a response to developments at the local level, in particular in the larger urban centers in the country, while taking into account expert advice by national commissions that looked at the actual situation in society at the time (Korf, 2019). In Amsterdam, as in other large Dutch cities, coffeeshops already existed before the 1976 law change. Initially, numerous frictions existed between the operators of the coffeeshops and local authorities, but progressively, a policy of toleration developed, characterized by fairly strict conditions imposed on the operations of coffeeshops, sanctioned by prosecutorial guidelines (Jansen, 1994). The particulars of the policy were influenced by conflicts between authorities at the legislative and executive levels, and conflicts between national and local authorities. In addition, both cannabis dealers and consumers, through their method of "civil disobedience," constituted another important force in shaping the Dutch drug policy (Jansen, 1994).

In 1979, official national Guidelines for Investigation and Prosecution were introduced which laid the groundwork for the coffeeshop system. These guidelines established a clear set of conditions under which cannabis sales, while still illegal, would not be prosecuted. Known as AHOJ-G for their Dutch acronym – no overt advertising ("*Affichering*"), no Hard drugs," no public nuisance ("*Overlast*"), no underage clientele ("*Jongeren*") and no large quantities ("*Grote hoeveelheden*") – they were built on "house rules" that had already been introduced by the semi-legal coffeeshop entrepreneurs in Amsterdam, in particular the ones regarding hard drugs, age and nuisance. The coffeeshop owners never lost sight of their economic interests but have been important contributors to achieving one of the main aims of Dutch drug policy: a strict separation of the soft and hard drug markets (Jansen, 1994). Regular consultations between local authorities and coffeeshop owners remain a customary feature in many Dutch cities to avoid problems and public nuisance.

The development of the current coffeeshop system has been a haphazard and gradual process of dynamic interaction between national and local executive authorities, prosecutorial guidelines, policing and court decisions reacting to substantial societal change and democratic pressure for either stability or change. Laws and enforcement policies at the national level adapted in response to developments in society and local policy reforms in the larger cities, and to the need to provide tools for municipalities to manage and correct situations that had gotten out of control. These changes created new circumstances at the local level, which in turn again needed adjustments and corrections, leading to adaptations of the law. The system evolved from turning a blind eye to house dealers in youth centers to a system of licensing an illegal situation with administrative and law enforcement inspection. Nobody would have, or could have, predicted in the late 1960s that this would be the policy in the early 2000s, when the situation had more or less matured into the current system.

This process was facilitated by several factors. An important factor was the expediency principle in Dutch law, which allows discretion by prosecutor's offices not to prosecute if it is expedient or convenient, or otherwise serving the public interest. Prosecutorial decisions around cannabis were formalized through national guidelines. Another important factor was the rather decentralized governance structure in the Netherlands regarding public order, which at the municipal level was mainly administered by a "triangular consultation" between the public prosecutor, the mayor, and the chief of police, under secondary control by the city council. Jansen (1994) characterized Dutch cannabis policy at the time as a process of "muddling through," a process of trial and error, in which cities played a major role as "policy laboratories" and catalysts for reform.

In 1996, municipalities in the Netherlands were formally put in charge of local cannabis policies. In 1995, the Dutch government, in the white paper *Continuity and Change* (GON, 1995) raised both cannabis tourism and the increasing involvement of organized crime in cannabis supply chains as major issues. The Dutch government at the time was committed to ending the inconsistency between permitted sales at the coffeeshops' front door and the illegal supply at the back door. The proposed policy was, in fact, an extension of the expediency principle that allowed for regulated sales of cannabis in coffeeshops to the cultivation and supply of those products for the coffeeshops (Van Dijk, 1998). Municipalities wishing to experiment with the supply of locally cultivated cannabis to *bona fide* coffeeshops could do so if the local "triangular" body responsible for public order in the city agreed, and the prosecutor general at the national level gave consent. The idea was that a regulated supply could reduce the criminal opportunities that had emerged since the 1980s for large-scale illegal Dutch hash traders, who were not only supplying the domestic market, but were also responsible for a large proportion of the international cannabis trade.

Those intended reforms, however, stirred strong opposition amongst European partners, in particular, with French President Jacques Chirac. Chirac started a campaign against Dutch coffeeshops and mobilized political support in Brussels, where European cooperation had been extended to include law enforcement and justice. France threatened to refuse to follow the Schengen Agreement and open its borders with the Benelux countries (Belgium, Netherlands and Luxembourg) if the policy changes went ahead. The Dutch government, worried about the damage that unilateral steps could have on international relations, abandoned the idea of regulating cannabis supplies for coffeeshops, reduced the amount a person could purchase in a coffeeshop from 30 to 5 grams, and opted for stricter control of coffeeshops (Boekhout van Solinge, 2017).

The final result was an accommodation on the cannabis issue. The original intention to regulate the back door was abandoned, but the position of coffeeshops in the cannabis market was formally consolidated, and these became the only endorsed cannabis retail selling points, facing stricter municipal licensing requirements. While municipalities were always able to take measures against coffeeshops who violated the AHOJ-G criteria, legal changes after 1995 allowed them to veto coffeeshops in their municipality entirely (a choice taken by some 70 percent of municipalities in the country) and to impose a variety of licensing conditions, including limiting opening hours, requiring certain forms of security, introducing criminal screening of operators and imposing a minimum distance between coffeeshops and schools, among others. This marked a shift in public and official attitudes towards cannabis and began an era of increasing regulation of coffeeshops, including a number of amendments to both administrative and criminal law. While designed to control nuisance and organized crime, the measures had the intended or unintended consequence of dramatically reducing the number of coffeeshops in the Netherlands; an estimated 1,100–1,500 coffee shops were active in 1995 and by 2016 this number had decreased to 573 shops, operating in just 103 of the 390 Dutch municipalities (Bieleman, Mennes and Sijtstra,2017).

Cannabis supply to coffeeshops remained illegal, but new prosecution guidelines were issued to try to shape illegal supply. The intention was to reduce cannabis imports by large criminal networks (who mainly imported hash) in favor of small-scale home growing of cannabis. Small, non-professional home growers with five plants or less were considered a "low law enforcement priority," with the apparent intent that many of these small growers would supply coffeeshops. Allowing many of these small growers to supply coffeeshops was seen as the second-best option for reducing the opportunities for criminal cannabis suppliers and organized crime. However, subsequent governments would abandon the small-scale local supply option and, as a result of European "harmonization," more law enforcement emphasis was geared towards repressing local cannabis cultivation. The "low hanging fruit" of smaller local growers were the first to leave an increasingly violent and criminal domestic cannabis production market (Maalsté and Panhuysen, 2015).

At the retail distribution level, the shift in Dutch cannabis policy did not involve major top-down policy changes but the creation of new capabilities for Dutch municipalities to control coffeeshops within their locale. Municipalities were given more legal tools to regulate the front door of the coffeeshops. Over the years, a process of "local customization" led to policies that fit local circumstances under more general legislation and prosecutorial guidelines. The introduction of a residence criterion (the I-criterion) in 2012 to hamper cannabis tourism from abroad – which created public nuisance, particularly in southern border towns – was successfully countered by major cities in the western and northern part of the country, who argued that such a policy was unnecessary and even counterproductive in their local situation. The criterion became optional, and was largely ignored (Korf, 2019).

While municipalities got a better grip over the front door, they were increasingly confronted with the negative consequences of increasing repression of the back door. Since the late 1990s, more and more local authorities began advocating a transparent supply chain as a regulatory solution, which has recently been taken up in the form of an experiment to see if a regulated supply to the coffeeshops would lead to a decline in criminality around cannabis cultivation, and whether the crop could be monitored to have fewer harmful adulterants or contaminants. At the time of writing, serious disagreements still exist between the national government and the municipalities about the duration and the scale and size of the proposed experiment.

Over time, the pendulum in Dutch coffeeshop policy has been shifting between a stronger local and a stronger national orientation – and vice versa (Korf, 2019). In a dynamic process, coffeeshops became more and more regulated, while local policies towards coffeeshops became formalized, and national criteria governing them were defined – and enforced. The Dutch government provided legal instruments to create local customization for municipal coffeeshop policy, i.e. to define additional criteria for coffeeshops, as well as giving municipalities the opportunity to opt for a zero policy, and thereby not allow coffeeshops at all. Interestingly, the difference between supporters and opponents of regulating cannabis cultivation is not so much in the problem analysis. Both recognize the paradox in Dutch cannabis policy (tolerated sales through the front door, no supply via the back door) and are concerned about the role of organized crime in cannabis production. The crucial difference is in the advocated political solution: more enforcement in order to fight organized crime versus regulation to counter organized crime (Korf, 2019).

Repression and regulation in Denmark

Although the Netherlands is the only European country with a system of semi-legal toleration of cannabis, there are other countries where cannabis is sold relatively openly in somewhat comparable ways, such as "pusher street" in the Christiania commune, "hash clubs" in Copenhagen (Denmark) and "hemp shops" that were tolerated in the early 2000s in Switzerland (Wouters, Benschop and Korf, 2010). Starting in the 1990s, there was a shift towards public security concerns about the increasing involvement of criminal organizations in the domestic cultivation and distribution of cannabis, overlapping with an increased tendency towards a "culture of control" promoted by a rise of neoconservative politics in the Western world, whereby politicians across the board leaned more strongly towards repression (Nygaard-Christensen and Asmussen Frank, 2019; Garland, 2001).

A case in point is the development in Denmark, where from 1969 to 2004, possession of up to ten grams of cannabis for personal use was not prosecuted, with law enforcement turning a blind eye to small-scale cannabis sales, in particular in and around the Freetown Christiania, an abandoned military area in Denmark's capital Copenhagen, squatted in 1971. An alternative creative scene of the counter-cultural movement developed, which included a street-level cannabis market, known as "pusher street." Pusher street would become one of the largest street-level cannabis markets in Northern Europe (Møller, 2010, p. 135), which "included about 40 street stalls, attracting both a domestic clientele and cross-border drugs tourists, particularly from Sweden. Clients could openly buy drugs to take away or could smoke "in situ" in the street or in Christiania's bars and cafés" (Asmussen, 2008).

Because hard drugs have mostly been kept out of Christiania, the cannabis market was mainly tolerated until the early 2000s. This accommodation was disturbed when a liberal-conservative government came into power in 2001, tightening controls on cannabis. In its 2003 action plan, *The Fight against Drugs*, the distinction between seller and buyer was explicitly removed, and, a year later, possession of cannabis for personal use was "re-criminalized," with an obligatory fine of €70, which was quadrupled in 2007 (Asmussen, 2008). The new "zero tolerance" policy replaced passive policing of street-level retail sales and the reluctant acceptance of cannabis markets that had been part of an overall harm reduction strategy. The new law, intended to counter the "normalization" of cannabis with a stronger enforcement deterrent, was followed by a police crackdown on Christiania's open cannabis retail market and the approximately 100 "hash clubs" – clubs selling cannabis or Dutch-style coffeeshops providing a social space as well – in the rest of Copenhagen. The increasingly repressive drug policy and enforcement practices targeted not only sellers and distributors of cannabis, but also buyers and users (Nygaard-Christensen and Asmussen Frank, 2019).

Repeated police crackdowns on Christiania contributed to the opening of the cannabis market to a new set of criminal groupings and led to a restructuring of the cannabis market, allowing immigrant youth gangs to enter the market which had previously been dominated by outlaw motorcycle gangs such as the Hells Angels (Møller, 2009; Møller 2017). Market-related violence of criminal gangs disputing control over selling points increased, including fatal shootings. Disappointed with the outcome of the re-criminalization policies, the Copenhagen City Council in September 2009 approved a memorandum that proposed to run a three-year trial with cannabis stores staffed by healthcare professionals that would sell cannabis in small quantities at about 50 kroner (about 7 euro) per gram – similar to the current street price. The shops would be supplied by licensed growers. Only city residents would be able to buy the cannabis, thus preventing Dutch-style "cannabis tourism" – mostly coming from Sweden (Copenhagen Post, 2009; Københavns Kommune, 2009; Blickman, 2012a).

The proposal for the pilot project was rejected by the national government. However, the situation did not really change and in the subsequent years, crackdowns continued in Christiania, but the "pusher street" has continually re-emerged, even after residents of Christiania closed down the market. The City Council of Copenhagen again submitted cannabis regulation pilot project proposals to the government in 2012, 2014 and 2016, but these were all rejected, even by a center-left government, despite the fact that the Copenhagen City Council was of the similar center-left political composition. A proposal for a trial by a party in the national government in 2016, the *Radikale Venstre*, received a similar fate. It was tabled following a shootout at Christiania and several massive police raids to close down "pusher street." The proposals focused on reducing consumption and especially the abuse of cannabis; more effective public education about the effects and adverse effects of using cannabis; creating a better and earlier contact between cannabis addicts and treatment systems; separating the market of cannabis and hard drugs; and limiting organized crime, especially violent gang crime (Nygaard-Christensen and Asmussen Frank, 2019; Københavns Kommune, 2012; Blickman, 2012b).

Local authorities take the initiative

The current inaction at the national level in Europe regarding cannabis has led more and more local authorities to take the initiative. These interventions take place in different alliances and configurations, are based on diverse motives, and garner the support of a wide variety of groups and organizations. In northern countries in Europe, this often takes the form of proposals for experiments, trials or pilot projects, embedded in scientific research protocols. In Germany, Switzerland, Italy and the Netherlands, law proposals to regulate cannabis have further been introduced in the national parliaments. In the Netherlands, a bill to regulate the supply of cannabis to coffeeshops is currently hanging in the upper house of parliament, after being approved in the lower house in February 2017 (Korf, 2019).

Apart from the Netherlands, where a limited national experiment is currently being developed, and Denmark, where the situation is currently at a stalemate, municipalities in Switzerland and Germany are developing regulation proposals in the form of scientific experiments. In both countries, the national agencies that need to approve such proposals have so far rejected such proposals on procedural grounds, although the Swiss federal government is open to a change of the law that would permit scientific experiments of a non-medical character (Neue Zürcher Zeitung, 2019; Zobel, 2019). In Spain, a different dynamic is at play, due to the emergence of the Cannabis Social Club (CSC) model (see Chapter 13). Proposals to regulate CSCs were first initiated at the level of the most autonomous regions of Catalonia and the Basque Country, although some local authorities also used municipal administrative bylaws to regulate certain aspects (Araña, 2019).

The first municipal proposal was made in San Sebastian in the Basque Country in December 2014, which had 23 registered CSCs at the time, with some 10,000 cannabis users (Diario Vasco, 2014). The local bylaw aimed to regulate the setting up of associations by stipulating the distances that must exist between one association and the next, and between them and schools and health centers. These bylaws not only seek to ensure that these associations are properly registered in the public records, but also that the venues used by cannabis associations meet minimum conditions required to avoid disturbing the neighborhood and with regard to the safety, health and hygiene of the people who use them. The bylaw entailed a formal recognition of clubs. "We had two options," said a local councilor, critical of the current, restrictive national legislation on cannabis. "Ignore the existence of these clubs, or attempt to regulate to ensure the reduction of risks from consumption" (El País, 2014; El Diario, 2014; Blickman, 2014). The city of Bilbao adopted a similar bylaw in 2016 (El Diario, 2016) and in 2018, there were about 25 municipalities with such regulations (ICEERS, 2018).

Girona in Catalonia, another pioneering municipality in local regulation since 2014, adopted a new bylaw in February 2017, which also regulated certain aspects regarding the internal operation of CSCs, such as a daily restriction of cannabis use per member to 3 grams per day or 25 grams per week, up to a maximum of 90 grams per month. Clubs were also not allowed to cultivate plants inside (El Periódico, 2017). However, with the recent rulings of the Constitutional Court in December 2017, sub-national regulation legislation has been declared unconstitutional, while the Supreme Court severely limited the size and scope of clubs (Araña, 2019). Municipalities are now at the forefront of regulation attempts. The municipality of Barcelona, which is the city with most CSCs (there are about 250), is considering a more in-depth regulation. The city had already adopted a restrictive bylaw that provided for the closure of most of the then 150 clubs in the city and instated a moratorium on new clubs. However, a new city council headed by the activist party *Barcelona en Comú* revised and substantially softened the bylaw in 2016 (La Vanguardia, 2016). The municipality is now elaborating a new bylaw, which will also interfere with the internal operation of the clubs (ICEERS, 2018).

The CSC model was reproduced in Belgium (see Chapter 18). In 2003, possession of cannabis for personal use was differentiated in law from all other drug offenses, giving public prosecutors the option of declining to prosecute cannabis possession where there was no evidence of problematic drug use or public nuisance. A ministerial guideline issued in 2005 to clarify these terms established possession of under three grams or one female plant, in the absence of aggravating circumstances, as the lowest possible prosecutorial priority (Decorte, 2019). This provided social activists with the opportunity to set up CSCs. The first CSC was established in 2006 in Antwerp for both recreational and medical cannabis users. The club argued that imposing a limit of one plant per member in a collective growing arrangement would respect the threshold established by the ministerial guidelines and thus should also be considered a "low priority" for law enforcement. Other clubs followed, but many CSCs have been subject to police interventions, with their crops being confiscated by police, and members facing criminal proceedings, leaving Belgian CSCs in a vulnerable position (Decorte, 2019).

Within the scope of Belgian national drug laws and ministerial guidelines, judicial districts and local governments can apply individual accents in their drug policy, which results in a patchwork of different drug policies in Belgium, differing between judicial districts and local communities. This leads to unequal judicial or sanctioning practices and to uncertainty of rights among civilians. When a person undertakes a road trip through Belgium with some cannabis in their car, they can face dramatically different consequences depending on where they are caught (Decorte, 2019). In Antwerp (Flanders) under a national-conservative mayor (Flemish Nationalist NV-A) since 2013, policies have become stricter and a person "caught" in possession of cannabis gets a fine on the spot (an "immediate financial settlement") of 75 euro. The oldest and biggest CSC in Belgium, based in Antwerp, was subject to a new police intervention, with some of its representatives being held in custody for several weeks. In contrast, in Mons (Wallonia) there is a proposal, initiated by a Socialist mayor, to introduce a social-scientific experiment of legal regulation involving social clubs (Decorte, 2019).

Switzerland: towards local experiments

Switzerland has had its own history with cannabis regulation for recreational use (See Chapter 14). In 2001, the Federal Office of Public Health, after recommendations by the national advisory board on drugs, put forward a proposal for an in-depth revision of the law. The proposal institutionalized harm reduction but also provided the tools to decriminalize drug use, as suggested by the advisory board, and to develop a quasi-regulated cannabis market (Zobel, 2019). According to the proposal, federal authorities were allowed to set priorities for penal prosecution and thereby to limit the obligation to prosecute drug use in general, but also cannabis-related offenses. Cannabis supply and possession would remain illegal but not prosecuted under circumstances to be defined by the government. This approach was seen as being compatible with existing UN Conventions and partly copied the Dutch approach – the only "model" available at that time – but, in contrast with and learning from the Dutch approach, included cannabis production and distribution (Zobel, 2019).

The attempt met with strong opposition by the International Narcotics Control Board (INCB) (International Narcotics Control Board, 2001, pp. 222–225), and the lower house of the Swiss federal legislature rejected the proposal in 2004. Meanwhile, in the intervening three years, widespread experimentation with local-level cannabis regulation took place in a legal grey zone. Several cantons reduced their law enforcement efforts against the cannabis market, and this resulted, by 2002, in the presence of about 400 unregulated cannabis shops throughout the country (Leimlehner, 2004). Although those dispensaries were shut down after the 2004 rejection of the reform proposal, the issue remained on the agenda. Attempts to legalize cannabis through a referendum in 2008 failed and eventually a much less ambitious form of decriminalization was accepted in 2012. The change of law introduced a minimal penalty: a 100 CHF fine (about 85 euro) for under 10 grams by adults, not accompanied by criminal proceedings when aggravating factors were absent. Interpretation of this law has varied widely throughout the country and courts and prosecutors in several cantons seem to have interpreted the measure as amounting effectively to a full decriminalization of cannabis use and of possession. A series of Supreme Court decisions mean that those who are prosecuted have increasing grounds (and therefore motivation) to challenge charges in court (Zobel, 2019).

While opportunities for reform stalled at the federal level, at the subnational level several proposals were initiated in the past five years. In the past, city councils of the larger cities such as Zürich and Basel had advocated for controlled cannabis sales but had not advanced concrete proposals. The debate on regulation gained impetus when, in December 2013, an interparty working group in the Geneva canton advised starting a pilot project allowing cannabis clubs, following the Spanish model at least in name, to buy state-certified cannabis for personal use (Zobel, 2019). The clubs' membership would be restricted to adults and they would be called "cannabis users associations," because "social club" was considered too promotional. The proposal was supported by a majority of parties across the political spectrum in Geneva (Tribune de Genève, 2013). The interparty working group noted that the open drug market in Geneva was a cause of insecurity to many and had led to a loss of control over a part of the public space. Therefore, the group proposed a three-year pilot in Geneva to allow for the cultivation, distribution and consumption of cannabis – and derivatives such as hashish and oil – in regulated associations (Groupe de Réflexion Interpartis du Canton de Genève, 2013). The intention of the interparty working group was to de-politicize the issue.

In June 2014, the Geneva working group published a second report, saying that "rather than throwing taxpayers' money in a costly and ineffective war against the drug" it would be more effective to allow adult users to smoke in a secure and controlled environment (Groupe de Réflexion Interpartis du Canton de Genève, 2014). Although the report did not elaborate on details, which were left to a group of experts, it did set some general conditions: a minimum age of 18 years (following the minimum age in the law that decriminalized possession of cannabis). The cannabis should be consumed at home and not in the association. The report also endorsed Portuguese-style dissuasion commissions[2] for minors with problematic use who cannot be members, as well as the obligation to refer members that develop problematic use to those commissions. The group also considered a limit on THC content. The associations should be non-profit, and members are required to register, with due consideration for privacy. The cannabis should be free and the pilot project should be budget neutral – it should not cost the state anything, but it should also not generate revenue for the state – with costs covered by tax or membership fees. The anticipated benefits would be in improved conditions for users and the ability to identify problematic users, as well as the reduction of the black market and improvement of public security.

Other cities and cantons such as Zürich, Basel, Lausanne, Bern, Luzern and Bielle are looking at participating in experiments. After mutual consultations, they started to work on different proposals for cannabis production and distribution models (Zobel, 2019; Zobel and Marthaler, 2014). The best way to develop cannabis regulation at the local level was through scientific trials under Article 8 of the narcotics law, according to legal guidance, following the example used in the past to introduce medical heroin prescription. Two cities (Bern and Zürich) and two cantons (Basel and Geneva) were to be the first four attempting to implement the cannabis distribution trials (Zobel, 2019). Four types of target populations were identified: (1) existing adult users; (2) underage problem cannabis users; (3) adult problem cannabis users; and (4) medical cannabis users who self-medicate (Zobel, 2019). The city of

Bern developed a project mainly for the first group, and the canton of Basel only for the fourth, while the city of Zürich and the canton of Geneva initially planned projects for all four groups. The Federal Office of Public Health that needs to give approval for such projects has rejected the initial proposal of Bern, because recreational cannabis use, as provided for in the study, is excluded in accordance with the Narcotics Act, even in the context of scientific projects. However, the federal government did acknowledge the possible positive merits of such projects and is open to changing current laws in order to allow them. A new article in the narcotics law is intended to allow pilot tests for scientific purposes only with a maximum of five years' duration (Zobel, 2019; Neue Zürcher Zeitung, 2019).

Germany: the fight for pilot projects

In Germany, some 20 cities are interested in a regulated cannabis market, including Berlin, Bremen, Hamburg and Düsseldorf. The first local authority in Germany that proposed an experiment was the Berlin district of Friedrichshain-Kreuzberg. In September 2013, Mayor Monika Hermann of the Greens, announced a plan for a pilot project of city-run shops selling cannabis as a means of tackling the increasing open-air drug-dealing in the district's Görlitzer Park that caused substantial public disorder in the district (Deutsche Welle, 2013). Although the proposed dispensaries were dubbed coffeeshops by the media, Herrmann preferred to call them "selling points," with locally produced cannabis, medically trained workers, a minimum age for buyers and, if necessary, security guards (Blickman, 2014).

As in Switzerland, local authorities that want reform rely on an exemption under paragraph 3 of the German drug law: pilot experiments can be approved if they serve "scientific and other purposes of public interest." The drug law exemption was used in Frankfurt some 15 years ago to initiate a successful heroin prescription program for problematic users (Stöver, 2019). In order to go forward with a pilot project, an application to the Federal Institute for Medicine and Medicinal Produce (*Bundesinstitut für Arzneimittel und Medizinprodukte* – BfArM) which reports to the Federal Ministry of Health, must be prepared, preferably with the support of research centers, counselling centers, police representatives, politicians and residents. The BfArM must allow the controlled supply of cannabis and legal questions, such as potential operators and supply, must also be clarified. In 2015, Berlin's Kreuzberg-Friedrichshain district applied for an exemption and submitted plans for four "specialist cannabis shops" in the district (Bezirksamt Friedrichshain-Kreuzberg von Berlin, 2015). However, the proposal was rejected by the BfArM (Deutsche Welle, 2015). Kreuzberg-Friedrichshain launched legal action to contest the decision, but the appeal was rejected again on the grounds that recreational cannabis use is not allowed according to the Federal Narcotics Act (Die Welt, 2016).

The proposal of Friedrichshain-Kreuzberg was followed by others, often a declaration of intention, rather than a concrete proposal. A district assembly (of the *Bahnhofsviertel*) in Frankfurt-am-Main recommended "one or more legal outlets for cannabis products" (Frankfurter Rundschau, 2014a; Frankfurter Rundschau, 2014b). These were not intended to make cannabis readily available, but – as in Berlin – to control "the rampant black market" (Frankfurter Rundschau, 2014c). The city council of Frankfurt did accept the proposal, and the Health Department and Drug Unit organized an international expert meeting in November 2014 to discuss proposals, where many called for the liberalization of cannabis (Drogenreferat der Stadt Frankfurt, 2014; DPA/Die Welt, 2014). However, on the issue of cannabis, the CDU and the Greens currently form the governing parties in Frankfurt and an agreement needs to be reached on how to continue, since the CDU is less convinced of the need for regulation (Frankfurter Rundschau, 2015). In Hamburg, the district assembly of Altona also voted in favor of a pilot project to counter dealing in the Florapark area (Hamburger Morgenpost, 2013). The district council of the city center of Cologne also approved an initiative for a pilot project in 2014 (Kölnische Rundschau, 2014) and again in 2018 (Kölner Stadt-Anzeiger, 2018).

In 2015, Düsseldorf, the capital of Germany's most populous state – Nordrhein-Westphalen, bordering the Netherlands – announced a plan for a strictly-regulated trade that would provide cannabis to adults (The Local, 2015a). Hamburg and the town of Münster in Nordrhein-Westphalen followed (Zeit Online, 2015). Münster announced a controversial pilot project that would distribute cannabis to randomly selected citizens who would receive two grams of cannabis a week free of charge for one year. The project was rejected (Westfälische Nachrichten, 2017b; Frankfurter Allgemeine Zeitung, 2017). A Green-Red coalition in the city and state of Bremen also wanted to move forward on cannabis regulation (Weser Kurier, 2015a), but the plans were stalled by the social-democrat SPD, the junior partner in the German federal government, after the rejection of the Kreuzberg-Friedrichshain proposal (Weser Kurier, 2015b). Currently, the city of Düsseldorf is leading the way, learning from the failure of predecessors like Münster, Bremen and Kreuzberg-Friedrichshain and has opted for pharmacies instead of coffeeshops, and with a scientific approach that is not purely geared towards recreational consumption (Die Welt, 2017). A new left-leaning coalition in Berlin also agreed on developing a pilot project, and Hanover organized an expert meeting (*Fachtagung*) on the issue, usually a first step in the development of a project.

Nevertheless, in order to override the blockade to such scientific pilot projects by the BfArM, the federal states of Bremen and Thuringia, with the support of Berlin, submitted a proposal to the *Bundesrat*, the legislative body that represents the 16 *Länder* at the national level, calling on the federal government to initiate an amendment to the narcotics law in order to create a legal basis for scientifically-supported model projects. The proposal was rejected. The situation is currently at a stalemate, although there is a theoretical majority in parliament for full decriminalization since the social-democrat

SPD has become more open to the issue, joining the FDP, Grünen and Die Linke. The debate on decriminalization still lingers in the Bundestag with different proposals from different parties (Deutscher Bundestag, 2018). The Greens had already introduced a full regulation proposal in the *Bundestag* in 2015, allowing the possession of 30 grams of cannabis for personal use and the cultivation of three cannabis plants (Stöver, 2019; The Local, 2015b; Deutscher Bundestag, 2018).

However, proponents of proposals of pilot projects or experiments in several European countries are aware of the tensions between the scientific value and the practical impact of the experiments. The "scientific" pilot projects tend to focus on youth protection and problematic use and are likely to have less impact on criminal markets. Proponents are aware of this dilemma and the risk of "medicalization" of the experiments (Cannabis in the City, 2018). In many cases, municipalities would actually prefer a fully regulated market to pilot projects. However, under the current political conditions, regulation is still a bridge too far, despite growing support among the public and political parties in many countries. Initiating pilot projects are a kind of compromise, to keep the issue on the political agenda, while at the national level no decision is reached on regulation.

Towards "local customization"?

While historically liberal countries like the Netherlands and Denmark used to defend their cannabis policies with a public health argument based on the separation of markets for fewer and more hazardous drugs, the emphasis has shifted to a public security approach, to counter the public disorder of street dealing, and the involvement of organized crime groups in illicit cultivation and supply. The decriminalization of cannabis and semi-regulated compromises like the Dutch coffeeshop system, while useful to avoid unnecessary criminalization of users, and to limit the exposure of cannabis users to more harmful drugs, do not address the legal supply of cannabis. Local authorities today are confronted with a range of problems that, in the end, are impossible to solve without some kind of a regulated and transparent supply chain. Apart from addressing concerns around public security and public nuisance, regulation would also provide solutions for consumer protection issues, such as quality control of cannabis in terms of the use of fertilizers and pesticides, access barriers such as age limits and maximum amounts to be purchased per user per day, week or month, and controls on the THC and CBD contents of cannabis. Additional benefits are to be found in more targeted prevention and detection of problematic use, and improved referrals to treatment for problematic users.

As others have argued (Chatwin, 2007), European cannabis policy might best develop through a model of "multi-level governance," a style of governance with increasing traction within the EU, in particular regarding social policies. In this model, multiple actors at multiple levels are engaged, and specific details of governance are decentralized and may diversify under EU guidelines. Pragmatic policies are developed at the local level, encouraging greater involvement from citizens. Advocates hope that, "A system of multi-level governance would allow initiatives to develop at the local level with power following a bottom-up structure," as opposed to top-down solutions that do not fit local and regional needs (Committee of the Regions, 2014). Given the already wide diversity of drug policies in Europe, different local cannabis regulation regimes could then be judged on their effectiveness, leaving local authorities room to maneuver, develop innovative solutions adapted to local circumstances, and customize national policies to their particular circumstances. The principles of proportionality and subsidiarity within the EU, which respect the different approaches of European countries due to historical and cultural differences, seem to be gaining momentum (De Witte, 2013), although potential cross-border effects of changes to cannabis policy may continue to present an obstacle.

While the scientific experiments currently proposed in several European countries could be characterized as "policies of last resort" in the face of a deadlock at the level of national regulation, it is possible that this deadlock may be broken in the coming years and that national level policy change could follow. In that case, instead of opting for regulated local cannabis markets, local customization might entail that municipalities acquire the right to opt out of regulation, as is happening in US states like Washington and Colorado that legalized and regulated cannabis at the state level. In the Netherlands, "local customization" is already an established guiding principle, with most municipalities opting out of allowing coffeeshops, while in Germany, cannabis decriminalization policies at the state level differ significantly. In other European countries, policies also vary widely at the local or regional level. The future may well be in "local customization" of policies that fit particular circumstances under more general national legislation and prosecutorial guidelines. Local pilot projects might well develop into locally customized regulatory models, giving opponents of cannabis regulation the option of opting out or differentiating policies. This flexibility may soften opposition to more liberal cannabis policies, allowing for more nuanced accommodation to the different needs of cities, towns or regions with very different needs, demographics, histories and political visions.

Such an approach would require an international and national political consensus to adjust national laws and guidelines to give local authorities room for maneuver. In order to achieve a workable solution, the three levels of governance need to find a structure where the current top-down decision-making process (the dictate of multilateral rule-setting by UN conventions and EU legislation) is counterbalanced by a bottom-up "reality check" by local authorities and is able to take into account local experiences of what works and what does not work. Whether such a change would be possible at the international level is another question, given the current dynamics at the United Nations (Bewley-Taylor and Martin Jelsma, 2016). While a global consensus on cannabis policy reform is unimaginable at the moment, a group of like-minded states seriously considering legal regulation of the recreational cannabis market might be obliged to challenge the current status quo in the UN drug control system by modifying its obligations through a process known as inter se modification. Through an inter se modification of the UN drug control conventions, such a reform-minded group could conclude agreements among themselves that permit the production, trade and consumption of cannabis for non-medical and non-scientific purposes, while minimizing the impact on other states and on the goals of the drug conventions (Jelsma, Boister, Bewley-Taylor, Fitzmaurice and Walsh, 2018; Blickman, 2018).

The concept of local customization could be part of such an inter se agreement, to which it also has certain theoretical parallels. Although most scholars conclude that decentralization as such is not a panacea for effective policies, and although critics have identified important risks in relation to exacerbating regional inequalities, the experiences of cities in promoting harm reduction policies in the 1990s have shown the possibilities of this strategy. The organized action of a group of cities led to those policies being accepted at the national, and increasingly, at the international level. While contemplating steps towards local customization, policymakers could also take into account the experiences of international businesses, drawing on their strategic insights in order to achieve effective, efficient and fair policies. Some useful guiding questions are raised which, taking into account the fundamental differences between business and political governance, might nonetheless be useful in considering the question of what could be delegated to which level of governance and what could be customized locally. For effectiveness, the question revolves around the extent to which policies could be set as formal regulations or as flexible guidelines. For efficiency, the key question revolves around the extent to which policies could be universally standardized or locally customized. And, for the question of how to locate the power to develop policy at the suitable level, the question is whether policies should be centrally mandated or locally delegated (Begley and Boyd, 2003). The immense diversity of practical and political contexts at the local and regional level within Europe, and the demonstrated commitment of sub-national authorities to developing their own locally adapted solutions, speaks to an untapped resource for policy development. Better harnessing this knowledge, experience, and innovation and facilitating local customization – while not ignoring political contention between and within the levels of governance – may yet offer a promising path towards elegant compromises and, ultimately, a more effective and humane cannabis policy for Europe.

Notes

1 Tom Blickman and Catherine Sandwell are researchers at the Transnational Institute (TNI), based in Amsterdam. The research for this chapter is part of the project 'Comparative Analysis of Cannabis Regulation Models in Europe', made possible

through the grant 'New Approaches in Harm Reduction Policies and Practices' (NAHRPP), provided by the European Union (European Commission, DG Migration and Home Affairs) and co-funded by the Open Society Institute. Local research was conducted by Xabier Araña (Universidad del Pais Vasco), Heino Stöver (Frankfurt University of Applied Sciences), Dirk Korf (Bonger Institute, University of Amsterdam), Maj Nygaard-Christensen and Vibeke Asmussen Frank (Centre for Alcohol and Drug Research, Department of Psychology and Behavioural Sciences, Aarhus University) and Tom Decorte (Department of Criminology, Penal Law and Social Law, Ghent University). Any errors of fact or judgement remain those of the author.

2 Since 2001, all drugs, including cannabis, have been decriminalized in Portugal. It is no longer a crime to acquire, possess or use cannabis. The threshold for possession has been set to 10 days of personal use, or 25 grams, for cannabis. Administrative sanctions can still be applied by Commissions for Drug Addiction Dissuasion – often composed of a lawyer, a doctor and a social assistant. These commissions provide information, discourage people from using drugs and refer users to the most suitable options, including, if required, treatment.

References

Araña, X. (2019). *Cannabis regulation in Europe: Country report Spain.* Country report for Cannabis in the City project. Amsterdam: Transnational Institute.

Asmussen, V. (2008). Cannabis policy: Tightening the ties in Denmark. In *A cannabis reader: Global issues and local experiences* (Monograph series 8, Volume 1). Lisbon: European Monitoring Centre for Drugs and Drug Addiction.

Begley, T.M. and Boyd, D.P. (2003). The need for a corporate global mind-set. *MIT Sloan Management Review*, 44(2), 25 32.

Bewley-Taylor, D., Blickman, T. and Jelsma, M. (2014). *The rise and decline of cannabis prohibition: The history of cannabis in the UN drug control system and options for reform.* Amsterdam: Transnational Institute & Global Drug Policy Observatory.

Bewley-Taylor, D. and Jelsma, M. (2016). *UNGASS 2016: A broken or b-r-o-a-d consensus?* Drug policy briefing No 45. Amsterdam: Transnational Institute.

Bezirksamt Friedrichshain-Kreuzberg von Berlin (2015). *Regulierung von cannabis in Friedrichshain-Kreuzberg.* Retrieved from www.berlin.de/ba-friedrichshain-kreuzberg/politik-und-verwaltung/service-und-organisationseinheiten/bezirkliche-planung-und-koordinierung/planungs-und-koordinierungsstelle-gesundheit/aktuelles/artikel.158549.php).

Bieleman, B., Mennes, R. and Sijtstra, M. (2017). *Coffeeshops in Nederland 2016.* Groningen-Rotterdam: Intraval.

Blickman, T. (2012a). *Copenhagen wants controlled cannabis shops.* Amsterdam: Transnational Institute.

Blickman, T. (2012b). *Government opposes Copenhagen City Council on cannabis shops.* Amsterdam: Transnational Institute.

Blickman, T. (2014). Cannabis policy reform in Europe: Bottom up rather than top down. *TNI series on legislative reform of drug policies.* Amsterdam: Transnational Institute.

Blickman, T. (2018). The elephant in the room: Cannabis in the international drug control regime. In A. Klein and B. Stothard (Eds.), *Collapse of the global order on drugs: From UNGASS 2016 to Review 2019* (pp. 101–131). Bingley: Emerald Publishing.

Boekhout van Solinge, T. (1999). Dutch drug policy in a European context. *Journal of Drug Issues,* 29(3), 511–528.

Boekhout van Solinge, T. (2017). The Dutch model of cannabis decriminalization and tolerated retail. In E. Savona, M. Kleiman and F. Calderoni (Eds.), *Dual markets: Comparative approaches to regulation* (pp. 145–170). Cham (Switzerland): Springer.

Cannabis in the City. (2018). *Cannabis in the City: Regulation and local authorities in Europe.* Seminar, Brussels.

Chatwin, C. (2007). Multi-level governance: The way forward for European illicit drug policy? *International Journal of Drug Policy,* 18(6), 494–502.

Commission of the European Union. (2001). *European governance: A white paper.* COM2001(428): Brussels.

Committee of the Regions (CoR). (2009). *The Committee of the Regions' white paper on multilevel governance* (CONST-IV-020). 80th plenary session.

Committee of the Regions (CoR). (2014). A charter for multilevel governance in Europe. Retrieved from https://portal.cor.europa.eu/mlgcharter/Pages/default.aspx

Copenhagen Post. (2009). Council may enter drug trade.

Council of Europe. (1985). *European charter of local self-government.* European Treaty Series – No. 122, Strasbourg.

De Vries, M.S. (2000), The rise and fall of decentralization: A comparative analysis of arguments and practices in European countries. *European Journal of Political Research,* 38(2), 193–224.

De Witte, F. (2013) Sex, drugs and EU law: The recognition of moral and ethical diversity in EU law. *Common Market Law Review,* 50, 1545–1578.

Decorte, T. (2019). *Cannabis regulation in Europe: Country report Belgium.* Country report for Cannabis in the City project. Amsterdam: Transnational Institute.

Deutsche Welle. (2013). Cannabis cafes could set up shop in Berlin. *Deutsche Welle.* Retrieved from www.dw.de/cannabis-cafes-could-set-up-shop-in-berlin/a-17089498.

Deutsche Welle. (2015). Berlin district loses marijuana legalization bid.

Deutscher Bundestag. (2018). Neue vorstöße zum umgang mit cannabis beraten. *Deutscher Bundestag.* Retrieved from www.bundestag.de/dokumente/textarchiv/2018/kw08-de-cannabis/542302.

Diario Vasco. (2014). Donostia se convierte en la primera localidad en regular los clubes sociales de cannabis.

Die Welt. (2016). Aus für coffee-shop-idee? Kreuzberger pläne erneut abgelehnt.

Die Welt. (2017). Kiffen auf der kö: Düsseldorf will vorreiter-rolle bei cannabis-legalisierung.

DPA/Die Welt. (2014). Experten fordern cannabis-liberalisierung.

Drogenreferat der Stadt Frankfurt. (2014). *Erste Frankfurter fachtagung zu cannabis.* Retrieved from www.frankfurt.de/sixcms/detail.php?id=3003&_ffmpar[_id_inhalt]=26738041.

El Diario. (2014). Los clubes de cannabis ya son legales en Donostia.

El Diario. (2016). Bilbao se adelanta al parlamento y regulará la instalación de clubes de cannabis.

El Periódico. (2017). Girona limita el consumo en los clubs de cannabis a tres gramos diarios.

El País. (2014). Una ventana abierta a la marihuana.

European Cities on Drug Policy (ECDP). (1991). *1st conference: European cities at the centre of illegal trade in drugs.* Retrieved from www.realitaeten-bureau.de/en_news_04.html.

European Cities on Drug Policy. (2002). Who we are. Retrieved from http://ecdp.net/whoweare.htm. (June 5, 2002; Accessed December 9, 2019).

European Monitoring Centre for Drugs and Drug Addiction (EMCDDA). (2015). *Drugs policy and the city in Europe*. EMCDDA papers. Luxembourg: Publications Office of the European Union.

European Monitoring Centre for Drugs and Drug Addiction (EMCDDA). (2017). *Cannabis legislation in Europe: An overview*. Luxembourg: Publications Office of the European Union.

European Union. (2012/C 402/01). *EU drugs strategy (2013–20)*. Official Journal of the European Union.

Frankfurter Allgemeine Zeitung. (2017). So will Münster legales Kiffen testen.

Frankfurter Rundschau. (2014a). Kiffen für die Gesundheit.

Frankfurter Rundschau. (2014b). Cannabis auf dem Prüfstand.

Frankfurter Rundschau. (2014c). Ortsbeiräte fordern legale Verkaufsstellen.

Frankfurter Rundschau. (2015). CDU blockiert Cannabis-Versuch.

Garcia, M. (2006). Citizenship practices and urban governance in European cities. *Urban Studies*, 43(4), 745–765.

Garland, D. (2001). *The culture of control. Crime and social order in contemporary society*. Oxford: Oxford University Press.

GON. (1995). Ministerie van Binnenlandse Zaken, Ministerie van Justitie, Ministerie van Volksgezondheid, Welzijn en Sport (1995). *Het Nederlandse drugbeleid; Continuïteit en verandering*. Tweede Kamer, vergaderjaar 1994–1995, 24077, nrs. 2–3. [English version: Drugs policy in the Netherlands: Continuity and change.] Retrieved from www.emcdda.europa.eu/system/files/Ministerie%20VWS%20%281995%29%20Continuity%20and%20Change%2C%20Dutch%20drug%20policy.pdf.

Groupe de Réflexion Interpartis du Canton de Genève. (2013). *Pour plus de sécurité dans la ville. le cannabis social club: Un modèle efficace de réglementation de l'accès au cannabis*. Genève: Document de discussion.

Groupe de Réflexion Interpartis du Canton de Genève. (2014). *Addendum 1 au rapport* Pour plus de sécurité dans la ville. les associations de consommateurs de cannabis: Un modèle efficace de réglementation de l'accès au cannabis *du Groupe de Réflexion Interpartis du Canton de Genève*. Genève: Document de discussion.

Hamburger Morgenpost. (2013). Schanze: Mehrheit für den kiffer-laden!

ICEERS. (2018). *II foro de clubes y asociaciones de cannabis de cataluña*. Barcelona.

International Narcotics Control Board (INCB). (2001). *Report of the International Narcotics Control Board for 2001*. New York: United Nations.

Jans, W. (2015). *Policy innovation in Dutch municipalities*. Enschede: Institute for Innovation and Government Studies (IGS), University of Twente (dissertation).

Jansen, A.C.M. (1994). The development of a "legal" consumers' market for cannabis: The "coffee shop" phenomenon. In E. Leuw and I. Haen Marshall (Eds.), *Between prohibition and legalization: The Dutch experiment in drug policy*. Amsterdam/New York: Kugler Publications.

Jelsma, M., Boister, N., Bewley-Taylor, D., Fitzmaurice, M. and Walsh, J. (2018). *Balancing treaty stability and change; Inter se modification of the UN drug control conventions to facilitate cannabis regulation*. Global Drug Policy Observatory (GDPO). Washington Office on Latin America (WOLA). Transnational Institute (TNI).

Kilmer, B., Kruithof, K., Pardal, M., Caulkins, J.P. and Rubin, J. (2013). *Multi-national overview of cannabis production regimes*. Brussels: RAND Europe.

Københavns Kommune. (2009). Notat til indstilling, afkriminalisering af hashhandlen i København, socialforvaltningen, Sagsnr. 2009–66143.

Københavns Kommune. (2012). *Bilag til brev til justitsministeren: Komponenter i forslag til etablering af forsøgsordning for regulering af lovlig hashhandel i København*, Sagsnr. 2011–172010.

Kölner Stadt-Anzeiger. (2018). Modellversuch in Köln: Cannabis gibt es bald legal in Kölner apotheken.

Kölnische Rundschau. (2014). Stadt Köln prüft cannabis-vorstoß der bezirksvertretung innenstadt.

Korf, D.J. (2019). *Cannabis and coffeeshops in the Netherlands: Balancing between national and local policy*. Country report for Cannabis in the City project. Amsterdam: Transnational Institute.

La Vanguardia. (2016). *Barcelona indulta un centenar de clubs de fumadores de cannabis*.

Leimlehner, E. (2004). Der Cannabismarkt in der Schweiz. Strukturen, Veränderungen und Risiken. *Abhängigkeiten*, 2/2004, 1–8.

Luxembourg Times. (2018). Cannabis to be made legal for recreational use in Luxembourg.

Maalsté, N. and Panhuusen, M. (2015). *De wiet-industrie. De slag om de achterdeur*. Amsterdam: Nieuw Amsterdam.

Meadows, D.H. (2009). *Thinking in systems: A primer*. London/New York: Earthscan.

Meesters, M. (2015). *Het failliet van het gedogen. Op weg naar de cannabiswet*. VNG. Retrieved from https://vng.nl/files/vng/rapport_werkgroep_cannabisbeleid_engels.pdf).

Møller, K. (2009). Police crackdown on Christiania in Copenhagen. *Crime, Law and Social Change*, 52(4), 337–345.

Møller, K. (2010). Policy displacement and disparate sanctioning from policing cannabis in Denmark. *Journal of Scandinavian Studies in Criminology and Crime Prevention*, 11(2), 135–150.

Møller, K. (2017). Cannabis sales and immigrant youth gangs in Denmark: An exploratory study of market structure and youth gang evolution. *Journal of Scandinavian Studies in Criminology and Crime Prevention*, 18(1), 20–34.

Neue Zürcher Zeitung (NZZ). (2019). Kiffer in städten sollen legal cannabis konsumieren dürfen.

Nygaard-Christensen, M. and Asmussen Frank, V. (2019). *Comparative analysis of cannabis regulation models in Europe: Country report Denmark*. Country report for Cannabis in the City project. Amsterdam: Transnational Institute.

Pollit, C. (2005). Decentralization. A central concept in contemporary public management. *The Oxford Handbook of Public Management*, 371–397.

Purcell, M. (2006). Urban democracy and the local trap. *Urban Studies*, 43(11), 1921–1941.

Reuters. (2018). Mexico introduces bill to legalize medical and recreational cannabis use.

Rosmarin, A. and Eastwood, N. (2012/2016). *A quiet revolution: Drug decriminalisation policies in practice across the globe*. London: Release.

Schardt, S. (Ed.). (2001). *European Cities on Drug Policy. Cooperation and community consensus. The multi-agency approach to effective local drug policies*. Frankfurt am Main, Germany: European Cities on Drug Policy.

Spapens, T., Müller, T. and Van de Bunt, H. (2015). The Dutch drug policy from a regulatory perspective. *European Journal on Criminal Policy and Research*, 21(1), 191–205.

Stöver, H. (2019). *Comparative analysis of cannabis regulation models in Europe: Country report Germany*. Country report for Cannabis in the City project. Amsterdam: Transnational Institute.

The Local. (2015a). Düsseldorf moots cannabis legalization: Following Berlin's footsteps.

The Local. (2015b). Cannabis lovers greet green legalization plan.

Tribune de Genève. (2013). Des députés genevois favorables à une fumette légalisée.

Van Dijk, J.J.M. (1998). The narrow margins of the Dutch drug policy: A cost-benefit analysis. *European Journal on Criminal Policy and Research*, 6(3), 369–393.

Weser Kurier. (2015a). Bremen will cannabis freigeben.

Weser Kurier. (2015b). Bremer SPD bremst cannabis-pläne.

Westfälische Nachrichten. (2017b). Bundesinstitut stoppt cannabis-modellprojekt.

Wouters, M., Benschop, A. and Korf D.J. (2010). Local politics and retail cannabis markets: The case of the Dutch coffeeshops. *International Journal of Drug Policy*, 21, 315–320.

Zeit Online. (2015). Was wird aus der idee, gras legal zu verkaufen?

Zobel, F. (2019). *Comparative analysis of cannabis regulation models in Europe: Country report Switzerland*. Country report for Cannabis in the City project. Amsterdam: Transnational Institute.

Zobel, F. and Marthaler, M. (2014). *Du Río de la plata au Lac Léman. Nouveaux développements concernant la régulation du marché du cannabis*. Addiction Suisse.

Part III

Lessons from alcohol, tobacco and legal highs

9 Lessons learned from the alcohol regulation perspective

Tim Stockwell, Norman Giesbrecht, Adam Sherk, Gerald Thomas, Kate Vallance and Ashley Wettlaufer

Introduction

Perhaps appropriately (though doubtless later than our editors would have liked), we began writing this chapter on a momentous day for cannabis policy in Canada: Wednesday October 17, 2018, the day non-medical cannabis use and sale was legalized. It is certainly a time for reflection on what this means for the future of substance use patterns, benefits and harms; and we know that the world is watching. As municipal, provincial and federal regulators are scrambling to develop policy and practice, teething problems abound. In the city of Victoria, for example, it was impossible to buy cannabis at all as the "grey market" (i.e. previously illegal dispensaries previously tolerated) were initially encouraged to close until they could get an official license to sell cannabis for recreational purposes, a process estimated to take at least one month. There was only one government-owned store in the whole of British Columbia (in distant Kamloops) that was ready to sell product to the queues that started in the early hours of October 17th.

As a group of researchers who have been immersed in the world of alcohol policy and epidemiology for several decades, we have been suggesting that our provincial and territorial governments learn from the successes and failures now well documented with alcohol policies, both in Canada and in other countries. What we see, however, is an enthusiasm to allow the private sector to take the reins in many Canadian jurisdictions, with governments largely taking a backseat to enjoy the ride (and the revenues), albeit with some restrictions on packaging and requirements for health warnings.

In this chapter, we will reflect on some of the lessons that can be learned from international experiences with regulating alcohol distribution and sale. We will try to present the case that the private sector should not be entrusted with full responsibility for selling potentially hazardous products like alcohol, tobacco and cannabis – at least not for off-premise consumption (i.e. liquor store sales). In an ideal world, we suggest that the various public interests are best served and balanced by government-owned substance retailers with direct responsibility for sales and distribution, and which report to ministries concerned with health and social welfare, like, for example, the Finnish and

Swedish alcohol monopolies (Stockwell, Sherk, Norstrom, Angus, Ramstedt, Andreasson and Makela, 2018; Stockwell, Wettlaufer, Vallance, Chow, Giesbrecht, April and Thompson, 2018). We believe this could usefully incorporate responsibility for all the legal psychoactive drugs now used recreationally in Canada, i.e. alcohol, tobacco and cannabis.

Similarities and differences between alcohol and cannabis

Before embarking on the exercise of what cannabis policymakers might learn from alcohol, it is important to first reflect on some of the basic similarities and differences between these two popular psychoactive substances. There are many similarities. First, both are complex substances in which the psychoactive ingredients (mainly tetrahydrocannabinol, or THC, in cannabis and ethanol in alcohol) are present in varying concentrations. Both are claimed to have medicinal properties but are also known to place users at risk of both acute harm from impairment and also longer term risk of serious disease and dependence (Sherk, Stockwell, Chikritzhs, Andréasson, Angus, Gripenberg and Woods, 2018; National Academies of Sciences, Engineering, and Medicine, 2017). Many medicinal properties of cannabis are thought to be associated with another ingredient, cannabidiol or CBD, which has only mildly psychoactive properties. While there is some evidence to suggest that the effects of THC may be moderated by the presence of CBD, this evidence is at best mixed and the US Academy of Sciences' report on cannabis identifies THC as the major ingredient posing a risk to both health and safety (National Academies of Sciences, Engineering, and Medicine, 2017).

Undoubtedly, there is more complexity and variability in how different modes of administration result in different concentrations of THC blood versus alcohol. The standard drink method of recording alcohol intake in many countries takes account of different alcohol concentrations in different types of beverage, e.g. 0.5 percent in some low alcohol beers versus 99 percent in some illicit forms of alcohol. However, the speed with which THC enters the bloodstream variously from smoking or vaping versus eating cannabis and the duration of effects will vary. Rough conversion factors calculated for different forms of smoked cannabis equivalent to "standard joints" have been described (Zeisser, Thompson, Stockwell, Duff, Chow, Vallance and Lucas, 2012) and it may be possible to estimate approximate equivalents for edible sources. Of course, there are large individual differences due to body weight, tolerance and other factors determining blood alcohol concentrations as well, but to a lesser degree than applies for cannabis (Macdonald, 2018).

Both are also commonly used "recreationally" to experience social facilitation, relaxation and improved mood (Patrick, Schulenberg, O'Malley, Johnston and Bachman, 2011). There is also evidence that their use can be both relatively interchangeable (i.e. one substance can substitute for the other) and complementary (i.e. there may be synergistic effects from combined use) (Subbaraman, 2016).

While there is evidence that the combined use of alcohol and cannabis poses special risks, e.g. for impaired driving (Asbridge, Wickens, Mann and Cartwright, 2017), a key difference between the two substances is in the extent of their capacity to cause harm, both directly to consumers and to others. Expert opinion tends to rank alcohol far higher on a continuum of risk than cannabis. For example, Nutt et al. (Nutt, King and Phillips, 2010) used a Delphic method to compare the relative harmfulness of 20 psychoactive substances, ranking alcohol first (or in the top three) and cannabis was among the least hazardous, both to users and those around them. Using more precise, quantitative measures, a recent Canadian exercise estimated the harms and economic costs uniquely associated with eight categories of psychoactive substances (Canadian Substance Use Costs and Harms Scientific Working Group, 2018). The economic costs from alcohol at $14.6 billion in 2014 exceeded those of any other individual substance, including $2.8 billion estimated for cannabis. The harms contributing to these costs are also in stark contrast, with about 850 deaths attributed to cannabis use versus 14,800 for alcohol (Canadian Substance Use Costs and Harms Scientific Working Group, 2018). Of course, at a population level, alcohol use is more prevalent than cannabis use (by a factor of four or five) – but for an individual user, its potential for harm is still far greater than that for cannabis. Some 50 major categories of illness and injury are attributable to alcohol versus maybe four for cannabis: cannabis use disorders, impaired driving injuries, lung diseases and psychotic illness (Canadian Substance Use Costs and Harms Scientific Working Group, 2018; Fischer, Imtiaz, Rudzinski and Rehm, 2016; Sherk et al., and 2018; National Academies of Sciences, Engineering, and Medicine, 2017). Nonetheless, one commonality is that the risk of these potentially serious harms will follow a dose response relationship such that greater exposure to ethanol or THC leads to a higher risk of acute and chronic health and safety issues (Macdonald, 2018; Sherk et al., 2018; Zeisser et al., 2012). In the case of the risk for lung disease associated with cannabis use, however, it is not the presence of THC but a range of other carcinogens present in cannabis smoke that exposes the user to risk (Callaghan, Verdichevski, Fyfe and Gatley, 2017).

The availability and the single distribution theories of alcohol consumption: do they apply to cannabis?

Two key theoretical concepts underpinning modern understandings of the effects of alcohol policies on consumption and harm are the following:

1 Availability Theory: the greater the physical and economic availability of alcohol, the higher the per capita consumption (Babor, Caetano, Casswell, Edwards, Giesbrecht, Graham, and Rossow, 2010; Edwards, Anderson, Babor, Casswell, Ferrence, Giesbrecht and Skog, 1994);

2 Single Distribution Theory: the greater the per capita consumption in a population, the more heavy drinkers are in that population (Ledermann, 1956; Skog, 1985) and hence more alcohol-related harms (Sherk et al., 2018).

Together, these two foundational ideas contribute to what is sometimes referred to as the Total Consumption Model, or the idea that an effective and efficient way to reduce alcohol-related harms is to reduce the total per capita consumption in a given population. Over the past 50 plus years, evidence for these two core principles has accumulated and strengthened, albeit with some interesting and quite specific advances in understanding. "Availability Theory" was initially understood in very general terms, e.g. higher prices and fewer liquor outlets result in less consumption (Edwards and Oliphant, 1992). There is also now a more nuanced appreciation of the role of local contexts in determining precise impacts on local patterns of alcohol use and types of related harm (Stockwell and Gruenewald, 2001). As the published research evidence mounts on the outcomes of numerous natural policy experiments around the world, much greater resolution and specificity is possible regarding how best to implement such policies. For example, in terms of pricing strategies, we now know that setting a minimum price per standard drink indexed to the cost of living may be one of the most effective policies available for reducing alcohol-related harm (Bruun, Edwards, Lumio, Makela, Pan, Popham and Osterberg, 1975; Thomas and Wettlaufer, 2017). There is some evidence that government-owned liquor stores will mean less alcohol consumption and harm than will a similar number of privately-owned liquor stores in the same area (Stockwell, Wettlaufer, et al., 2018; Stockwell, Zhao, Macdonald, Vallance, Gruenewald, Ponicki and Treno, 2011), though this likely depends on the extent to which government-owned outlets are managed to maximize profits versus protecting health and safety.

There have also been significant advances in relation to the Single Distribution Theory of Alcohol Consumption linking the number of heavy users to the average consumption of a population. Initially proposed by Ledermann in 1956 (Ledermann, 1956), Single Distribution Theory was importantly extended by Ole-Jørgen Skog throughout the 1980s (Skog, 1985). Skog developed the "collectivity of drinking," a social extension of Ledermann's original theory, which posited that alcohol consumption occurs largely in groups and that the behavior of an individual within the group is very strongly influenced by the behavior of the group itself. Skog, like Ledermann, adopted the "laws of proportional effects" (Skog, 2006), which have the property of predicting a highly skewed drinking distribution (which, in practice, is always the observed shape). Mathematically, this was formalized by predicting that this distribution would follow the shape of a lognormal curve (Skog, 2006). More recently, pioneering work by Rehm and colleagues has developed and tested empirically a more precise formulation of this relationship using data from more than 60 countries (Kehoe, Gmel, Shield, Gmel and Rehm, 2012). This work shows that it is only necessary to know the number and average consumption of a population of drinkers to be able to accurately predict proportions of low, medium and high-volume consumers, with these proportions following a Gamma distribution; a curve in the log-normal family of distributions.

The Single Distribution Theory posits that an effective way to reduce the number of heavy drinkers and mitigate alcohol-related harms is to reduce total population alcohol consumption. Next, Availability Theory provides a series of policy pathways that policymakers may consider in order to achieve this goal, with pricing strategies (economic availability) and constraints on physical availability (such as outlet density and days and hours of sale) consistently ranking highly in terms of effectiveness (Babor et al., 2010).

So, will these principles also apply to cannabis consumption? There is already some early work indicating that Availability Theory may apply equally well to cannabis as to alcohol markets. For example, Freisthler and Gruenewald (and 2014) have found significant relationships between the density of cannabis outlets in a population and overall levels of use. There is every reason to believe that cannabis will behave like other commodities such that frequency and quantity of use in a population will be responsive to market prices (Caulkins, 2012). We do of course need further research on the intersections between cannabis policies, consumption and harm but it seems a reasonable starting place to assume the underlying relationships may closely resemble those that have been found to apply for alcohol policies (Babor et al., 2010). In the rest of this chapter, we will try to pursue the general idea that cannabis policymakers should look carefully at what has been learned in the general area of alcohol policy, with specific reference to four policy levers. Two of these have some of the most unambiguous evidence both of effectiveness and broad scope of public health and safety impact, namely, pricing/taxation and physical availability (Stockwell, Wettlaufer, et al., 2018). Two others, direct government market controls and health messaging, can be used to facilitate the implementation of other effective strategies (Stockwell, Wettlaufer, et al., 2018). There are other policy domains where learnings might be generalized from alcohol to cannabis, such as deterrence of impaired driving, restrictions on marketing and advertising, enforcement of laws regarding underage use and service to intoxicated customers and the value of a comprehensive government strategy straddling all of these domains (Giesbrecht, Wettlaufer, Simpson, Vallance, Stockwell, Asbridge and Thompson, 2015; Stockwell, Wettlaufer, et al., 2018). We suggest that the four domains selected are among those with the greatest evidence and have the greatest potential collectively for population-wide impact.

Policy domain 1: what can be learned from alcohol pricing and taxation strategies?

Of all the policy instruments available to governments to limit hazardous use of alcohol and related harms, those that directly influence prices are potentially the most powerful. In essence, alcohol is like nearly all consumer products in that its consumption is sensitive to price (Babor et al., 2010; Meier, Purshouse and Brennan, 2010; Sharma, Sinha and Vandenberg, 2017; Wagenaar, Tobler and Komro, 2010). Systematic reviews suggest that a 10 percent increase in alcohol prices will be associated with a 4 percent to 5 percent reduction in consumption (Gallet, 2007; Wagenaar, Salois and Komro, 2009; Wagenaar et al., 2010). However, beyond the very general and well-established principle that higher alcohol prices mean less consumption, there is much complexity and a myriad of choices to be made about how to best apply such policies to improve public health outcomes.

Alcohol is a complex commodity such that in most mature markets there are many thousands of products available, varying in price, strength, beverage type, container size and quality (Gruenewald, Ponicki, Holder and Romelsjo, 2006; Stockwell, Pakula, MacDonald, Buxton, Zhao, Tu and Duff, 2007). The main policy levers available in most countries are (1) excise taxes (usually set by national governments) which must be paid by retailers and distributors on purchases directly from manufacturers; (2) sales taxes paid by the consumer at point-of-sale and transferred by the retailer to a state/provincial or national government; and (3) minimum or "floor" prices which prohibit the sale of alcohol below a particular price for some kind of measure of product quantity, e.g. a "standard drink." Each of these types of pricing or taxation measure can be applied differently (separately or in combination) and with potentially quite different outcomes for consumption and related harms. As outlined by Thomas and Wettlaufer (2017) and Stockwell and colleagues (2007), the key issues to consider are as follows:

Excise and sales taxes: principles to consider

1 Are they calculated per liter of beverage, per liter of absolute alcohol (or per standard drink) or as a percentage of the value of the product concerned? From a public health and safety point of view, it is the amount of pure alcohol (i.e. ethanol) consumed which places drinkers at risk of disease and injury in a dose-dependent fashion (Rehm and Shield, 2014). Thus, it follows that directly taxing alcohol content provides a financial incentive for consumers to reduce their overall consumption of alcohol (Stockwell and Crosbie, 2001; Stockwell, Zhao, Giesbrecht, Macdonald, Thomas and Wettlaufer, 2012).
2 Are they applied comprehensively and equitably across all types of alcoholic product? It should not be cheaper, for example, to purchase a standard drink or unit of 8 per cent than 4 percent strength beer, as is often the case. Nor should a malt-based drink of 8 percent be cheaper than a wine or spirit-based drink of the same strength – which is also often the case.
3 Is the tax rate charged sufficient to give meaningful incentives for consumers to choose lower-strength varieties?

4 Is the price/tax charged indexed to the cost of living? Over time, excise taxes charged at a fixed rate per liter of ethanol will decline in real terms. In some US states, the failure to increase excise taxes has rendered them so low as to be meaningless, e.g. one penny per gallon.

Applying this analysis to cannabis, it follows that in the increasing number of legal cannabis markets, taxation rates should be based on the total volume of THC in the product, not just the percentage of THC or the weight of product alone. Again, understanding the rationale for this approach to cannabis taxation and its communication might be facilitated by the wide use and communication of a standard unit or "joint" of cannabis, e.g. 0.25 g containing 8 percent THC (Zeisser et al., 2012). Given the different routes of administering cannabis and their implications for the metabolization of THC, thought will be needed as to how best to apply such a system for edibles as well as smoked or inhaled varieties (National Academies of Sciences, Engineering, and Medicine, 2017). Cannabis taxes applied at a rate per standard unit or "joint" thereby incentivize consumers to both use modest amounts of THC overall and to select lower-strength varieties. Further, these "volumetric" cannabis taxes would need to be indexed to the cost of living to avoid losing their effectiveness over time. Consideration might also be given to having lower taxes paid to safer forms of administration of cannabis in terms of reduced risk of lung disease, e.g. via the use of vaporizers.

Minimum or "floor" prices

Following six years of legal battles through the highest courts in Europe and the UK, Scotland's government introduced a minimum price for alcohol of 50p for a UK "unit" (8 g ethanol) from May 1, 2018. Throughout this lengthy process, scientific evidence for the effectiveness of minimum pricing as a means of targeting regular heavy drinking and reducing alcohol-related harm received the highest possible levels of scrutiny. A recent comprehensive review of the evidence for minimum pricing concluded that there was strong evidence that many of the Bradford Hill criteria for causality have been met, although replication studies outside of Canada are required (Boniface, Scannell and Marlow, 2017).

In a landmark decision, the Scottish courts determined that "minimum unit pricing" (MUP) was a proportionate, targeted and effective public health strategy. Other jurisdictions in Europe, the UK and Australia are following Scotland's example to introduce MUPs, e.g. the Republic of Ireland, Australia's Northern Territory (Northern Territory Government, 2018), Wales and Northern Ireland. The evidence for the effectiveness of minimum pricing rests variously on formal evaluations of different minimum pricing policies that have been operating in Canada for several decades (Stockwell, Auld, Zhao and Martin, 2012; Stockwell, Zhao, Martin, Macdonald, Vallance, Treno and Buxton, 2013), survey data showing that heavier drinkers select the cheapest alcohol (Kerr and Greenfield, 2007) and modelling studies (Holmes, Meng, Meier, Brennan, Angus, Campbell-Burton and Purshouse, 2014) designed to estimate impacts of different rates of minimum pricing on consumption, harms and economic costs in particular jurisdictions.

Thomas and Wettlaufer (and 2017) outlined similar principles for the application of minimum pricing as for alcohol excise taxes listed above, i.e. that they are applied at a rate per standard drink (or "unit") of alcohol, they are applied comprehensively to all beverage types and at a significant level that is indexed to the cost of living. Exactly the same principles should be considered in the setting of minimum prices for standard units/joints of THC to limited availability and affordability of very cheap, high-strength THC cannabis.

It is frequently argued that when a cannabis market is legalized that it is necessary to keep legal prices low in order to compete with the black market. From a public health and safety point of view, it may be an error to take this idea to an extreme. Taken to its logical conclusion, it follows that prices of legal cannabis need to be as low as possible to extinguish the black market almost completely. Saturating the market with cheap legally-sourced cannabis will likely lead to greater overall consumption and uptake of cannabis use in the population – on the plausible assumption that market saturation has not already occurred with partial or full prohibition. At the other extreme, having a very restricted range of cannabis products at very high prices will severely limit the size of the legal market and the potential to regulate cannabis in the public interest. As with alcohol, there will be a sweet spot in every market where high-quality products of known quantity and THC/CBD content that do not risk criminal prosecution will be preferred to black market products of unknown quality. This will likely be at a higher price than some black-market supplies but will still offer the opportunity of a sizeable market capable of being regulated according to principles that advance public health and safety.

Of course, such specific policies as outlined above have little meaning in the great majority of jurisdictions that completely prohibit the sale and consumption of cannabis. These principles can, however, be applied to a limited degree in markets where cannabis is made available for supposedly "therapeutic" or "medicinal" purposes. Acknowledging that while there are likely some therapeutic benefits for some people from the use of cannabis, nonetheless medicinal sources often also supply substantial amounts of cannabis for recreational purposes (Cerdá, Wall, Keyes, Galea and Hasin, 2012). Product prices could be set by factoring in the number of standard units of THC. Beyond that, if the ultimate aim of law enforcement in illegal markets is to reduce harms from cannabis use, then there may be a case for targeting enforcement strategically towards certain products to influence prices so that (1) they are not too low and (2) prices of stronger and riskier products increase through reduced supply.

Policy domain 2: what can be learned from policies that influence the physical availability of alcohol?

The physical availability of alcohol is determined by the "density" of liquor outlets in a particular region and by the days and hours such outlets are allowed to trade. Many studies have documented strong associations between changes in the density of liquor outlets and changes in rates of alcohol consumption and related harm (Popova, Giesbrecht, Bekmuradov and Patra, 2009; Stockwell, Zhao, Macdonald, Pakula, Gruenewald and Holder, 2009; Stockwell et al., 2011; Stockwell et al., 2013; Zhao, Stockwell, Martin, Macdonald, Vallance, Treno and Buxton, 2013). Hahn, Middleton, Elder, Brewer, Fielding, Naimi and Campbell (2012), Popova et al. (2009) and Burton, Henn, Lavoie, O'Connor, Perkins, Sweeney and Sheron (2017) have each reviewed the large literature on alcohol availability and concluded there is good evidence that these relationships hold for both off-premise and on-premise liquor outlets. Specific alcohol-related harms found to be associated with the density of liquor outlets include fatal and non-fatal injuries from violence, road crashes and self-harm suicide (Giesbrecht et al., and 2015; Popova et al., 2009). Livingston (2008) studied the effect of outlet density on assault rates in Melbourne, Australia, concluding there may be a critical threshold of bar density above which risks of violence are especially likely to increase.

Policy experiments have also indicated that adding an extra day of trading (e.g. Saturday or Sunday) is usually associated with both increased per capita alcohol consumption (Sherk et al., 2018) and also increases in some acute forms of alcohol-related harm (Norstrom and Skog, 2005). An Organization for Economic Co-operation and Development (OECD) review concluded that reducing both off-premise and on-premise trading hours can be cost-effective strategies, especially in densely populated areas and if the trading hours are enforced (Sassi, 2015).

A detailed analysis of widely differing rates of outlet density in British Columbia has provided evidence of a decreasing marginal effect on levels of alcohol consumption such that each unit increase in density leads to increasingly small increases in consumption (Stockwell, Sherk, et al., 2018). Finally, it is also important to note related literature documenting the substantial problems that can occur in entertainment districts of medium or large cities. Some excellent case studies of this phenomenon have been conducted in Australia, e.g. in Surfers Paradise, Queensland (Andrade, Homel and Townsley, 2016). Extreme public health and safety issues can arise when a large number of bars and clubs compete for the custom of crowds of young people out on the town where drinking has a central role in their socializing. Fierce local competition for customers can drive down both prices and standards of service so that, in some instances, heavily discounted or even free alcohol is available in at least one outlet at almost any time of night or in the early hours of the morning. Furthermore, there can be strong pressure on managers and serving staff to encourage service to intoxicated customers and to turn a blind eye to aggressive or potentially aggressive behaviors from their highest-spending customers.

As mentioned above, there is already emerging evidence that the population density of cannabis outlets can be related to measures of cannabis consumption (Freisthler and Gruenewald, 2014). One consideration here is that specific relationships between types of alcohol outlet and types of alcohol-related harm should also be relevant for cannabis markets. The densities and hours of trading for on-premise liquor outlets (bars and restaurants) have been related to acute alcohol-related harms, namely violence and road crashes (Kypri, Jones, McElduff and Barker, 2011). The densities of off-premise liquor stores have been related to changes in general population consumption (Sherk et al., 2018) which in turn can be related to rates of chronic alcohol-related diseases (Stockwell, Sherk, et al., 2018). The dimension of acute versus chronic harm is also likely to be relevant for cannabis markets. Thus, population densities for on-premise cannabis consumption (e.g. cafés) are likely to be related to acute outcomes – in the case of cannabis this is unlikely to be related to rates of public violence but more likely to be related to rates of road crashes due to cannabis impairment. Population density rates of cannabis outlets for off-premise sales (likely the great majority of cannabis sold) will be most likely related to levels of population consumption and also rates of chronic disease associated with cannabis use, for example lung diseases (National Academies of Sciences, Engineering, and Medicine, 2017). The related issue of the extent to which cannabis might be sold in the same outlets as alcohol will be discussed below.

As discussed later, a larger question potentially overshadowing these considerations is the extent to which increased cannabis use arising from the above causes might substitute for alcohol, a more harmful substance.

Policy domain 3: what can be learned from government controls of alcohol markets?

Full or partial government monopolies on the sale and/or distribution of alcohol can still be found in 17 US, 13 Canadian, 5 Scandinavian and 1 Indian jurisdiction (Stockwell, Sherk, et al., 2018). Increasingly, there is political pressure in these regions to privatize existing alcohol monopolies and there is a trend towards permitting more alcohol and more beverage types for sale in private liquor stores and/or grocery stores (Holder, Kuhlhorn, Nordlund, Österberg, Romelsjo and Ugland, 1998; Stockwell, Sherk, et al., 2018).

The US and Canadian monopolies were mostly set up in the 1920s and 1930s after the repeal of alcohol prohibitions in various states and provinces. The idea originally was to tightly regulate sales in order to balance consumer demand for access against concerns about health and safety. At the present time, the overriding missions of these government alcohol monopolies appear to be protecting government revenues rather than the public's health and safety. This is indicated by the fact that nearly all North American monopolies report to ministries concerned with finance rather than health or safety (Giesbrecht, Wettlaufer, Walker, Ialomiteanu and Stockwell, 2012). Just two Scandinavian monopolies report to ministries of health and social affairs: Finland and Sweden (Stockwell, Sherk, et al., 2018).

Comprehensive and systematic reviews confirm that privatization of retail alcohol sales is usually associated with substantial increases in per capita alcohol consumption (Babor et al., 2010; Hahn et al., 2012). A study by Ramstedt (2002) examined the re-monopolization of medium-strength beer in Sweden and found evidence that reversing privatization led to reduced alcohol-related harm. In a detailed local area-level analysis of a Canadian province during a period of rapid privatization of government monopoly retail stores, it was found that greater increases in the density of privately owned stores were associated with significantly higher per capita alcohol consumption (Stockwell et al., 2009), alcohol-attributable mortality (Stockwell et al., 2011) and morbidity (Stockwell et al., 2013). There is also literature from a number of countries showing that retail staff in government monopoly liquor stores are more likely to check and are more efficient at checking for potentially underage customers (Harding, Hingson, Klitzner, Mosher, Brown, Vincent and Cannon, 2016).

A recent modelling study sought to estimate likely impact of privatizing the Swedish alcohol monopoly, Systembolaget, on per capita consumption (Stockwell, Sherk, et al., 2018). Table 9.1 below provides the resulting estimates of changes in per capita consumption that would occur in Sweden were key policies to change under two plausible privatization scenarios. In Scenario 1, government-run stores were replaced by an equal number of private stores resulting in a 20 percent increase in consumption. In Scenario 2, a 31 percent increase in consumption was estimated if alcohol was available for sale in all grocery stores.

The implications of such changes in consumption for tangible harms were estimated based on published meta-analyses of a range of alcohol consumption and disease risk relationships using the state-of-the-art International Model of Alcohol Harms and Policies (InterMAHP) platform (Sherk, Stockwell, Rehm, Dorocicz and Shield, 2017). For example, replacing government stores with grocery store alcohol sales was estimated to result in 76 percent more deaths and 42 percent more hospital stays per year, as a result of these estimated increases in total alcohol consumption.

The main reasons for these profound impacts on public health and safety estimated from monopolizing or privatizing alcohol markets is that government monopolies provide readily available and direct controls over the very policies which have most impact on consumption and related harm, i.e. pricing, availability and advertising/marketing (Giesbrecht, Wettlaufer, Simpson, April, Asbridge, Cukier and Vallance, 2013). In privatized systems, there are many more private commercial actors with the resources and

Table 9.1 Estimated changes in age 15+ per capita alcohol consumption for key policies and the overall change in consumption in two privatization scenarios

Policy lever	*Scenario 1:Specialty private liquor stores*	*Scenario 2:Alcohol sold in grocery stores*
Density of outlets	9.47% *(7.44%–11.58%)*	16.43% *(14.71%–18.19%)*
Sunday trading	1.01% *(–3.21%–5.27%)*	1.18% *(CI –3.70%–6.24%)*
Extended trading hours	3.83% *(3.31%–4.36%)*	4.82% *(CI 4.15%–5.48%)*
Average prices	–2.83% *(–3.91%––1.73%)*	–1.41% *(–1.96%––0.88%)*
Minimum prices	13.34% *(10.24%–16.44%)*	16.67% *(12.86%–20.55%)*
Advertising/ Promotion	2.50% *(0.27%–4.75%)*	5.00% *(0.58%–9.50%)*
Change in Total Consumption (including unrecorded)	19.99% *(15.34%–24.73%)*	31.23% *(25.12%–37.33%)*

Source: Stockwell, Sherk et al., 2018.

incentives to lobby governments to relax restrictions on alcohol sales and tone down health and safety messaging to the public, e.g. through using warning labels. There is even evidence that alcohol monopolies can help reduce the acceptability of alcohol use in the general population (Abbey, Scott and Smith, 1993).

Put simply, the evidence suggests that the more efficient and competitive an alcohol market, the higher the per capita alcohol consumption. This results in more heavy drinking occasions across the whole population, along with more harm and economic costs. Government intervention in the free market is generally associated with reduced affordability and convenience of access, and better implementation of controls (e.g. sales to minors). Government monopolies also allow ready access to critical policy levers that help directly reduce health and safety harms from the use of alcohol.

These conclusions are likely highly applicable to the increasing number of legal cannabis markets. In the next few years, the many natural policy experiments unfolding across North America will yield more definitive answers. Across Canada's 13 provinces and territories, a full range of regulatory models will be open for study, ranging from sales restrictions to government stores, mixed models allowing both government and private stores and fully privatized retail systems. Interestingly, while pharmacies will be increasingly involved in the prescription of cannabis for therapeutic purposes (e.g. Shoppers Drug Mart, see https://cannabis.shoppersdrugmart.ca/en_CA), some Canadian pharmacists are also moving to get permission to prescribe alcohol for similar purposes as a means of supporting alcohol-dependent patients on Managed Alcohol Programs (Crowe, 2018; Pauly, Vallance, Wettlaufer, Chow, Brown, Evans and Stockwell, 2018).

We suggest some of the main lessons to be drawn from experiences with government-controlled alcohol markets are as follows:

1 they will usually limit some of the excesses of private systems which sometimes encourage hazardous practices for health and safety as a result of competition between commercial rivals;
2 they provide easier access to the policy levers of pricing, outlet density/ trading hours, point-of-sale promotions and checks on sales to intoxicated and underage customers;
3 government-run monopolies can be extremely popular with the general public, for example Systembolaget has been regularly voted one of Sweden's most popular companies (Trolldal, 2015);
4 a government-run monopoly does not guarantee available policy mechanisms will be employed for public health and safety purposes. Public health and safety are more likely to be prioritized in the situation, like in Sweden or Finland, where the monopoly reports to a ministry directly concerned with health and social affairs. Further, in comparison with other European countries with fully privatized systems, these alcohol monopoly countries tend to have lower levels of alcohol consumption and related harm (World Health Organization, 2019).

In Canada, the new government-controlled cannabis sales and distribution systems are mostly being run by the same agencies that manage the government monopolies for alcohol. This raises interesting questions about the advisability of selling both cannabis and alcohol from the same locations. Most jurisdictions, but not all, will be establishing separate shopfronts for each substance, given evidence of the potential for additional hazards of combined use of alcohol and cannabis (Asbridge et al., 2017). Regardless of the precise combination of sales and distribution systems, these arrangements should move public health and safety regulators and policymakers towards a more rational, evidence-based approach which treats each substance in accordance with established evidence for harmfulness. Government-run systems responsible for balancing consumer access against potential for health and safety harms should be expected to take a more objective approach to the relative harmfulness of different products, according to their alcohol and THC strengths, for example, and evidence of relative harmfulness (Canadian Substance Use Costs and Harms Scientific Working Group, 2018; Nutt et al., 2010). The substantial additional government revenues, worth billions of dollars annually in developed countries, also raise realistic prospects of improved funding for prevention, treatment, health promotion and research to support better public health and safety outcomes. But again, the establishment of government control over the sale and distribution of psychoactive substances does not guarantee that revenue-raising will not take precedence over public health and safety objectives. Having such agencies report to ministries concerned with health and/or safety will be more likely to protect these broader objectives.

Policy domain 4: health messaging on product labels and at point-of-sale

The WHO Global Information System on Alcohol indicates that in early 2019, 47 countries mandate some kind of health warning out of the 194 countries included. Of these, 41 require warnings about underage drinking, 31 about impaired driving and 27 about drinking alcohol when pregnant (World Health Organization, 2019). Health messages on alcohol containers and at point of sale in retail stores have the potential to raise awareness of the health consequences of consumption. However, there is only limited evidence of effectiveness for warning labels, for example (Babor et al., 2010; Burton et al., 2017), if they are implemented in isolation from other more effective strategies, e.g. restrictions on marketing and promotions. Most of this evidence to date is based on US research regarding the introduction of hard to read warning labels on bottles and cans as well as some point-of-sale signs in bars. These variously advise about the risks of drinking during pregnancy, while driving, risks of alcohol-use disorders and alcohol-related diseases. Soon after their introduction, there was evidence that noticing the new labels prompted people to discuss health risks from drinking (Kaskutas and Greenfield, 1992) and may have led to some reduced inclinations to drink and drive (Greenfield, 1997). There was also evidence that health messages on containers have the special virtue of targeting heavier drinkers as they are more likely to see these labels (Greenfield, Graves and Kaskutas, 1999).

Petticrew, Shemilt, Lorenc, Marteau, Melendez-Torres, O'Mara-Eves and Thomas (2017) describe how alcohol labelling can influence alcohol consumption and related harms via influencing complex causal systems of interconnected psychological, behavioral, social, economic, legal and environmental factors. These factors are shaped by governments (e.g. licensing laws, container labelling and taxation), by consumers (e.g. patterns of alcohol consumption, perception of product risks) and by alcohol industry practices (e.g. advertising and promotions). As with tobacco control, it is insufficient to solely consider the potential for container labels to directly change population drinking behaviors and risks in isolation from other strategies and policies. It is relevant to also consider the potential impacts of labelled messages on more proximal indicators within the expected causal chain, e.g. the consumers' awareness of alcohol-related health risks and on intentions to quit or moderate alcohol use, both overall and in certain high-risk situations.

A new Canadian study examined the impact of the experimental introduction of health messages about cancer risks from drinking and low-risk drinking guidelines (Hobin, Vallance, Zuo, Stockwell, Rosella, Simniceanu and Hammond, 2018). Specially developed, visible and colorful health messages significantly increased the awareness of liquor store customers about these twin issues from quite low levels, with approximately 25 percent being aware of either the cancer risk or national risk guidelines prior to the intervention. There is also other evidence of limited public awareness of the strong scientific evidence for a connection between even low levels of alcohol consumption and increased risk of various cancers (American Society of Clinical Oncology, 2017). Experimental studies concerning possible warning label messages suggest that clear information about cancer risks result in a product being seen less positively (Kersbergen and Field, 2017). Messages regarding cancer risk have also been shown to increase drinkers' intentions to cut down on their consumption (Pettigrew, Jongenelis, Pratt, Liang, Slevin, Chikritzhs and Glance, 2016). A related point is that having higher awareness of cancer risks from drinking has been shown to be associated with greater support for more effective alcohol policies (Buykx, Li, Gavens, Hooper, Lovatt, Gomes de Matos and Holmes, 2016).

In addition to providing consumers with information about health risks and low-risk drinking guidelines, there is also a case for using messages on containers and at point of sale to improve knowledge of the alcohol content of beverages in terms of "standard drinks." There is evidence from Australia and Canada (Hobin et al., 2018; Kerr and Stockwell, 2012; Osiowy, Stockwell, Zhao, Thompson and Moore, 2015) that adding labels to alcohol containers, which accurately depict their precise number of standard drinks, helps consumers to understand how much they can drink while staying within low-risk drinking guidelines. Further, consumers participating in these studies expressed strong support for the idea of adding standard drink labels to alcohol containers. The problem at present is that in most countries it is only a requirement to state the size of the container and its percent alcohol content by volume. Because of the increasing variation in strengths of different types of alcohol (e.g. beer can now be found with alcohol contents below 1 percent and above 20 percent), it is hard for people to quickly do the mental arithmetic to estimate the number of standard drinks in a container that has an unusual strength or size (Osiowy et al., 2015).

Thus, such messages on alcohol containers and at point-of-sale signs can both be seen as serving a basic consumer right to know about health risks. They may also indirectly lead to greater public support for the introduction of more powerful, effective alcohol policies such as those that reduce convenience of access and affordability (Babor et al., 2010; Giesbrecht et al., 2015).

We suggest that some of the lessons about health messaging on alcohol containers and at point of sale are directly applicable to how these media can be exploited for the promotion of health and safety around cannabis use. Some specific examples are listed below.

1 While the evidence for effectiveness of health messaging as a means of changing behavior at the level of the whole population is relatively weak, there is stronger evidence in relation to influencing intervening variables such as awareness of health risks, awareness of low-risk drinking guidelines, intentions to use a product more safely and the likelihood of discussing these issues with friends or family. It is perhaps unrealistic to expect such

a restricted communication strategy in isolation to effect measurable population-wide behavior change. It is more realistic to expect specific benefits around particular types of risk that may result from use of the product, e.g. in relation to potential to impair driving.

2 Health messaging can help create a climate that supports the introduction and maintenance of more directly effective public health and safety-oriented policies.
3 Just as it has become necessary to develop the concept of a "standard drink" measurement to variously facilitate the conduct of self-report surveys, communicate low-risk drinking levels, depict the alcohol content of different brands and apply pricing or taxation strategies at a rate per "unit" of alcohol, it may also be essential to introduce the concept of a "standard joint" or "unit" of THC (Macdonald, Stockwell, Reist, Belle-Isle, Benoit, Callaghan and Zhao, 2016; Zeisser et al., 2012).
4 Container labelling and point-of-sale messages are ideal media for targeting heavier users as they are significantly more likely to be exposed to these messages and to remember them.

It is clear from public discussions both in the media and in informal settings that there is a wide range of beliefs about the safety or harmfulness of cannabis, just as there is for alcohol. These range from viewing cannabis as equivalent to a harmless herb with some potential medicinal properties to, at the other extreme, a distorted view that it is more harmful than alcohol, a gateway to the use of more harmful illicit drugs and a major source of mental health comorbidity (Hall and Lynskey, 2016). The precise range of physical and mental health issues potentially caused by cannabis is by no means certain and more research is required (Callaghan et al., 2017; Canadian Substance Use Costs and Harms Scientific Working Group, 2018). However, consumers have a right to the most balanced and accurate advice as is currently supported from expert reviewers of growing literature on this subject. Labelling and point-of-sale messaging can make valuable contributions to raising awareness and supporting evidence-based regulations aimed at protecting public health and safety around the use of cannabis.

Conclusions

There are some important commonalities around ways alcohol and cannabis can be used, while there are substantial differences in their relative degrees of harmfulness. In both cases, however, a careful government-regulated and controlled system of distributing and selling cannabis will likely produce better health and safety outcomes than will fully privatized systems where there will be incentives for encouraging high levels of use.

A well-regulated substance use authority responsible for the distribution and sale of psychoactive substances that are legally available for recreational use is an ideal that is, however, not in the least guaranteed by government ownership. It is essential that the mission of such authority is well articulated and explicitly grounded in public health and safety as well as evidence-based principles for achieving these broad social purposes. Having such an authority report to government ministries concerned with health and/or safety is more likely to guarantee the realization of such objectives than those reporting only to ministries of finance or business.

The achievement of public health and safety outcomes can also be supported by ongoing monitoring of policy implementation as well as health and safety outcomes against objective criteria informed by a population health perspective (Stockwell, Wettlaufer, et al., 2018). The monitoring and evaluation of health and safety outcomes should not be conducted one substance at a time in isolation but should examine outcomes across multiple substances, in particular those most commonly used such as alcohol, nicotine and cannabis with the goal of creating coherent policies.

The new wave of cannabis decriminalization and legalization, especially in North America, may herald an era in which the relative harmfulness of commonly used psychoactive substances can be viewed objectively and comparatively so that regulatory responses can be geared more precisely towards the most harmful products and patterns of use.

References

Abbey, A., Scott, R. and Smith, M. (1993). Physical, subjective, and social availability: Their relationship to alcohol consumption in rural and urban areas. *Addiction,* 88(4), 489–499.

American Society of Clinical Oncology. (2017). Alcohol and cancer. *The Lancet,* 390(10109), 2215.

Andrade, D., Homel, R. and Townsley, M. (2016). Trouble in paradise: The crime and health outcomes of the Surfers Paradise licensed venue lockout. *Drug and Alcohol Review,* 35(5), 564–572.

Asbridge, M., Wickens, C., Mann, R. and Cartwright, J. (2017). Alcohol, cannabis, and new drivers. *Handbook of teen and novice drivers: Research, practice, policy, and directions,* 191–210.

Babor, T., Caetano, R., Casswell, S., Edwards, G., Giesbrecht, N., Grube, J. & Rossow, I. (2010). *Alcohol: No ordinary commodity – research and public policy – Revised edition.* Oxford: Oxford University Press.

Boniface, S., Scannell, J.W. and Marlow, S. (2017). Evidence for the effectiveness of minimum pricing of alcohol: A systematic review and assessment using the Bradford Hill criteria for causality. *BMJ Open,* 7(5), e013497.

Bruun, K., Edwards, G., Lumio, M., Makela, K., Pan, L., Popham, R. and Osterberg, E. (1975). *Alcohol control policies in public health perspective.* Finland.

Burton, R., Henn, C., Lavoie, D., O'Connor, R., Perkins, C., Sweeney, K. and Sheron, N. (2017). A rapid evidence review of the effectiveness and cost-effectiveness of alcohol control policies: An English perspective. *The Lancet,* 389(10078), 1558–1580.

Buykx, P., Li, J., Gavens, L., Hooper, L., Lovatt, M., Gomes de Matos, E. and Holmes, J. (2016). Public awareness of the link between alcohol and cancer in England in 2015: A population-based survey. *BMC Public Health,* 16(1), 1194–1206.

Callaghan, R., Verdichevski, M., Fyfe, T. and Gatley, J. (2017). Chapter e9 – Does cannabis use increase the risk of developing cancer in humans? In V.R. Preedy (Ed.), *Handbook of cannabis and related pathologies biology, pharmacology, diagnosis, and treatment* (pp. e80–e100). Cambridge, MA: Academic Press.

Canadian Substance Use Costs and Harms Scientific Working Group. (2018). *Estimating Canadian substance use costs and harms (2007–2014).* Prepared by the Canadian Institute for Substance Use Research and the Canadian Centre on Substance Use and Addiction. Ottawa, Ont: Canadian Centre on Substance Use and Addiction.

Caulkins, J. (2012). A future of legalized marijuana? *World Futures Review,* 4.

Cerdá, M., Wall, M., Keyes, K. M., Galea, S. and Hasin, D. (2012). Medical marijuana laws in 50 states: Investigating the relationship between state legalization of medical marijuana and marijuana use, abuse and dependence. *Drug and Alcohol Dependence,* 120(1–3), 22–27.

Crowe, K. (2018). *Why is shoppers drug mart training doctors to prescribe medical cannabis?* Retrieved from www.cbc.ca/news/health/shoppers-drug-mart-medical-cannabis-marijuana-conflict-of-interest-pharmacist-dispensing-1.4900353.

Edwards, G., Anderson, P., Babor, T., Casswell, S., Ferrence, R., Giesbrecht, N. and Skog, O.-J. (1994). *Alcohol policy and the public good.* Oxford: Oxford University Press.

Edwards, R. and Oliphant, J. (1992). Paracetamol toxicity in chronic alcohol abusers – A plea for greater consumer awareness. *New Zealand Medical Journal,* 105(933), 174–175.

Fischer, B., Imtiaz, S., Rudzinski, K. and Rehm, J. (2016). Crude estimates of cannabis-attributable mortality and morbidity in Canada – Implications for public health focused intervention priorities. *Journal of Public health,* 38(1), 183–188.

Freisthler, B. and Gruenewald, P.J. (2014). Examining the relationship between the physical availability of medical marijuana and marijuana use across fifty California cities. *Drug and Alcohol Dependence,* 143, 244–250.

Gallet, C.A. (2007). The demand for alcohol: A meta-analysis of elasticities. *Australian Journal of Agricultural and Resource Economics,* 51(2), 121–135.

Giesbrecht, N., Wettlaufer, A., Simpson, S., April, N., Asbridge, M., Cukier, S. and Vallance, K. (2013). *Strategies to reduce alcohol-related harms and costs in Canada: A comparison of provincial policies.* Retrieved from http://ijadr.org/index.php/ijadr/article/view/221/396.

Giesbrecht, N., Wettlaufer, A., Simpson, S., Vallance, K., Stockwell, T., Asbridge, M. and Thompson, K. (2015). Strategies to reduce alcohol-related harms and costs in Canada: A comparison of provincial policies. *International Journal of Alcohol and Drug Research,* 5(2), 33–45.

Giesbrecht, N., Wettlaufer, A., Walker, E., Ialomiteanu, A. and Stockwell, T. (2012). Beer, wine and distilled spirits in Ontario: A comparison of recent policies, regulations and practices. *Nordic Studies on Alcohol and Drugs,* 29(1), 79–102.

Greenfield, T. (1997). Warning labels: Evidence on harm reduction from long-term American surveys. *Alcohol: Minimizing the harm*, 105–125.

Greenfield, T., Graves, K. and Kaskutas, L. (1999). Long-term effects of alcohol warning labels: Findings from a comparison of the United States and Ontario, Canada. *Psychology and Marketing,* 16(3), 261–282.

Gruenewald, P.J., Ponicki, W.R., Holder, H.D. and Romelsjo, A. (2006). Alcohol prices, beverage quality, and the demand for alcohol: Quality substitutions and price elasticities. *Alcoholism, Clinical and Experimental Research,* 30(1), 96–105.

Hahn, R.A., Middleton, J.C., Elder, R., Brewer, R., Fielding, J., Naimi, T.S. and Campbell, C.A. (2012). Effects of alcohol retail privatization on excessive alcohol consumption and related harms. *American Journal of Preventive Medicine,* 42(4), 418–427.

Hall, W. and Lynskey, M. (2016). Evaluating the public health impacts of legalizing recreational cannabis use in the United States. *Addiction,* 111(10), 1764–1773.

Harding, F.M., Hingson, R.W., Klitzner, M., Mosher, J.F., Brown, J., Vincent, R.M. and Cannon, C.L. (2016). Underage drinking: A review of trends and prevention strategies. *American Journal of Preventive Medicine,* 51(4/Supplement 2), S148-S157.

Hobin, E., Vallance, K., Zuo, F., Stockwell, T., Rosella, L., Simniceanu, A. and Hammond, D. (2018). Testing the efficacy of alcohol labels with standard drink information and national drinking guidelines on consumers' ability to estimate alcohol consumption. *Alcohol and Alcoholism,* 53(1), 3–11.

Holder, H., Kuhlhorn, E., Nordlund, S., Österberg, E., Romelsjo, A. and Ugland, T. (1998). *European integration and Nordic alcohol policies.* Aldershot, England: Ashgate Publishing Ltd.

Holmes, J., Meng, Y., Meier, P.S., Brennan, A., Angus, C., Campbell-Burton, A. and Purshouse, R. (2014). Effects of minimum unit pricing for alcohol on different income and socioeconomic groups: a modelling study. *The Lancet,* 383(9929), 1655–1664.

Kaskutas, L. and Greenfield, T.K. (1992). First effects of warning labels on alcoholic beverage containers. *Drug and Alcohol Dependence,* 31(1), 1–14.

Kehoe, T., Gmel, G., Shield, K.D., Gmel, G. and Rehm, J. (2012). Determining the best population-level alcohol consumption model and its impact on estimates of alcohol-attributable harms. *Population Health Metrics,* 10(1), 6.

Kerr, W.C. and Greenfield, T.K. (2007). Distribution of alcohol consumption and expenditures and the impact of improved measurement on coverage of alcohol sales in the 2000 National Alcohol Survey. *Alcoholism-Clinical and Experimental Research,* 31(10), 1714–1722.

Kerr, W.C. and Stockwell, T. (2012). Understanding standard drinks and drinking guidelines. *Drug and Alcohol Review,* 31(2), 200–205.

Kersbergen, I. and Field, M. (2017). Visual attention to alcohol cues and responsible drinking statements within alcohol advertisements and public health campaigns: Relationships with drinking intentions and alcohol consumption in the laboratory. *Psychology of Addictive Behaviors,* 31(4), 435–446.

Kypri, K., Jones, C., McElduff, P. and Barker, D. (2011). Effects of restricting pub closing times on night time assaults in an Australian city. *Addiction,* 106(2), 303–310.

Ledermann, S. (1956). *Alcool, alcoolisme, alcoolisation.* Paris, France: Presses Universitaires de France.

Livingston, M. (2008). Alcohol outlet density and assault: A spatial analysis. *Addiction,* 103(4), 619–628.

Macdonald, S. (2018). *Cannabis crashes myths and truths.* Victoria, BC: Scott Macdonald.

Macdonald, S., Stockwell, T., Reist, D., Belle-Isle, L., Benoit, C., Callaghan, R. and Zhao, J. (2016). *Legalization of cannabis in Canada: Implementation strategies and public health.* Victoria: University of Victoria, Centre for Addictions Research of BC.

Meier, P.S., Purshouse, R. and Brennan, A. (2010). Policy options for alcohol price regulation: Response to the commentaries. *Addiction,* 105(3), 400–401.

National Academies of Sciences, Engineering, and Medicine. (2017). *The health effects of cannabis and cannabinoids: Current state of evidence and recommendations for research.* Washington, D.C: The National Academies Press. Available at: www.nationalacademies.org/hmd/Reports/2017/health-effects-of-cannabis-and-cannabinoids.aspx

Norstrom, T. and Skog, O.J. (2005). Saturday opening of alcohol retail shops in Sweden: An experiment in two phases. *Addiction,* 100(6), 767–776.

Northern Territory Government. (2018). *Northern territory alcohol policies and legislation reform.* Retrieved from https://alcoholreform.nt.gov.au/floor-price.

Nutt, D.J., King, L.A. and Phillips, L.D. (2010). Drug harms in the UK: A multicriteria decision analysis. *The Lancet,* 376(9752), 1558–1565.

Osiowy, M., Stockwell, T., Zhao, J., Thompson, K. and Moore, S. (2015). How much did you actually drink last night? An evaluation of standard drink labels as an aid to monitoring personal consumption. *Addiction Research & Theory,* 23(2), 163–169.

Patrick, M.E., Schulenberg, J.E., O'Malley, P.M., Johnston, L.D. and Bachman, J.G. (2011). Adolescents' reported reasons for alcohol and marijuana use as predictors of substance use and problems in adulthood. *Journal of Studies on Alcohol and Drugs,* 72(1), 106–116.

Pauly, B., Vallance, K., Wettlaufer, A., Chow, C., Brown, R., Evans, J. and Stockwell, T. (2018). Community managed alcohol programs in Canada: Overview of key dimensions and implementation. *Drug and Alcohol Review,* 37(S1), S132-S139.

Petticrew, M., Shemilt, I., Lorenc, T., Marteau, T.M., Melendez-Torres, G.J., O'Mara-Eves, A. and Thomas, J. (2017). Alcohol advertising and public health: Systems perspectives versus narrow perspectives. *Journal of Epidemiology and Community Health,* 71(3), 308–312.

Pettigrew, S., Jongenelis, M., Pratt, I.S., Liang, W.B., Slevin, T., Chikritzhs, T. and Glance, D. (2016). Australian drinkers' perceptions of alcohol-related risk by consumption status. *Addiction Research & Theory,* 24(6), 507–513.

Popova, S., Giesbrecht, N., Bekmuradov, D. and Patra, J. (2009). Hours and days of sale and density of alcohol outlets: Impacts on alcohol consumption and damage: A systematic review. *Alcohol and Alcoholism,* 44(5), 500–516.

Ramstedt, M. (2002). The repeal of medium-strength beer in grocery stores in Sweden — The impact on alcohol-related hospitalisations in different age groups. In R. Room (Ed.), *The effects of Nordic alcohol policies. What happens to drinking and harm when alcohol controls change?* (pp. 117–132). NAD Publication No. 42. Helsinki: Nordic Council for Alcohol and Drug Research (NAD).

Rehm, J. and Shield, K.D. (2014). Alcohol and mortality: Global alcohol-attributable deaths from cancer, liver cirrhosis, and injury in 2010. *Alcohol Research: Current Reviews,* 35(2), 174–183.

Sassi, F. (Ed.) (2015). *Tackling harmful alcohol use: Economics and public health policy.* Paris: OECD Publishing.

Sharma, A., Sinha, K. and Vandenberg, B. (2017). Pricing as a means of controlling alcohol consumption. *British Medical Bulletin,* 123(1), 149–158.

Sherk, A., Stockwell, T., Chikritzhs, T., Andréasson, S., Angus, C., Gripenberg, J. and Woods, J. (2018). Alcohol consumption and the physical availability of take-away alcohol: Systematic reviews and meta-analyses of the days and hours of sale and outlet density. *Journal of Studies on Alcohol and Drugs,* 79(1), 58–67.

Sherk, A., Stockwell, T., Rehm, J., Dorocicz, J. and Shield, K. (2017). *The International Model of Alcohol Harms and Policies (InterMAHP): A comprehensive guide to the estimation of alcohol-attributable morbidity and mortality* (Version 1.0). December 2017. Canadian Institute for Substance Use Research, University of Victoria. Victoria, BC Canada. Retrieved from www.uvic.ca/research/centres/cisur/projects/intermahp/index.php.

Skog, O.J. (1985). The collectivity of drinking cultures: A theory of the distribution of alcohol consumption. *British Journal of Addiction,* 80(1), 83–99.

Skog, O.J. (2006). The historical roots of Ledermann's theory of the distribution of alcohol consumption. *Contemporary Drug Problems,* 33(1), 143–174.

Stockwell, T., Auld, M.C., Zhao, J.H. and Martin, G. (2012). Does minimum pricing reduce alcohol consumption? The experience of a Canadian province. *Addiction,* 107(5), 912–920.

Stockwell, T. and Crosbie, D. (2001). Supply and demand for alcohol in Australia: Relationships between industry structures, regulation and the marketplace. *International Journal of Drug Policy,* 12(2), 139–152.

Stockwell, T. and Gruenewald, P. (2001). Controls on the physical availability of alcohol. In T.P.N. Heather and T. Stockwell, (Eds.), *International handbook on alcohol dependence and problems* (pp. 699–720). West Sussex, England: John Wiley and Sons Ltd.

Stockwell, T., Pakula, B., MacDonald, S., Buxton, J., Zhao, J., Tu, A. and Duff, C. (2007). *Alcohol consumption in British Columbia Canada: A case for liquor taxes that reduce harm.* Bulletin 3, December 2007. Centre for Addictions Research of BC (CARBC).

Stockwell, T., Sherk, A., Norstrom, T., Angus, C., Ramstedt, M., Andreasson, S. and Makela, P. (2018). Estimating the public health impact of disbanding a government alcohol monopoly: Application of new methods to the case of Sweden. *BMC Public Health.*

Stockwell, T., Wettlaufer, A., Vallance, K., Chow, C., Giesbrecht, N., April, N. and Thompson, K. (2018). *Strategies to reduce alcohol-related harms and costs in Canada: A comparison of provincial and territorial policies.* Victoria, BC: Centre for Addictions Research of BC (CARBC).

Stockwell, T., Zhao, J., Giesbrecht, N., Macdonald, S., Thomas, G. and Wettlaufer, A. (2012). The raising of minimum alcohol prices in Saskatchewan, Canada: Impacts on consumption and implications for public health. *American Journal of Public Health,* 102(12), e103–110.

Stockwell, T., Zhao, J., Macdonald, S., Pakula, B., Gruenewald, P. and Holder, H. (2009). Changes in per capita alcohol sales during the partial privatization of British Columbia's retail alcohol monopoly 2003–2008: A multi-level local area analysis. *Addiction,* 104(11), 1827–1836.

Stockwell, T., Zhao, J.H., Macdonald, S., Vallance, K., Gruenewald, P., Ponicki, W. and Treno, A. (2011). Impact on alcohol-related mortality of a rapid rise in the density of private liquor outlets in British Columbia: A local area multi-level analysis. *Addiction,* 106(4), 768–776.

Stockwell, T., Zhao, J.H., Martin, G., Macdonald, S., Vallance, K., Treno, A. and Buxton, J. (2013). Minimum alcohol prices and outlet densities in British Columbia, Canada: Estimated impacts on alcohol-attributable hospital admissions. *American Journal of Public Health,* 103(11), 2014–2020.

Subbaraman, M.S. (2016). Substitution and complementarity of alcohol and cannabis: A review of the literature. *Substance Use and Misuse,* 51(11), 1399–1414.

Thomas, G.T.S. and Wettlaufer, A. (2017). The role of public health research and knowledge translation in advancing alcohol minimum pricing policy in Canada. In N.B. Giesbrecht and L. Editors (Eds.), *Preventing alcohol-related problems: Evidence and community-based initiatives.* Washington, D.C: American Public Health Association.

Trolldal, B. (2015). *Alcohol consumption in Sweden 2015.* Retrieved from www.can.se/contentassets/8a116b56043e49eab7f4128010a7f6b2/alkoholkonsumtionen-i-sverige-2015.pdf.

Wagenaar, A.C., Salois, M.J. and Komro, K.A. (2009). Effects of beverage alcohol price and tax levels on drinking: A meta-analysis of 1003 estimates from 112 studies. *Addiction,* 104(2), 179–190.

Wagenaar, A.C., Tobler, A.L. and Komro, K.A. (2010). Effects of alcohol tax and price policies on morbidity and mortality: A systematic review. *American Journal of Public Health,* 100(11), 2270–2278.

World Health Organization (2019). *Global Information System on Alcohol and Health (GISAH).* Retrieved from www.who.int/substance_abuse/activities/gisah/en/.

Zeisser, C., Thompson, K., Stockwell, T., Duff, C., Chow, C., Vallance, K. and Lucas, P. (2012). A "standard joint"? The role of quantity in predicting cannabis-related problems. *Addiction Research & Theory,* 20(1), 82–92.

Zhao, J.H., Stockwell, T., Martin, G., Macdonald, S., Vallance, K., Treno, A. and Buxton, J. (2013). The relationship between minimum alcohol prices, outlet densities and alcohol-attributable deaths in British Columbia, 2002–09. *Addiction,* 108(6), 1059–1069.

10 Lessons from tobacco regulation for cannabis product regulation

Coral Gartner and Wayne Hall

Background

As a legal commodity, tobacco cigarettes are unparalleled in the scale of disease and premature death they have caused on a global scale. Their status as a legal recreational substance is an anomaly of history and it is often acknowledged that if tobacco cigarettes were a new product, no country would allow them to be commercially marketed (Hall and West, 2008). Some governments prohibited the sale of non-smoked tobacco products, such as oral snuff and chewing tobacco (e.g. European Union, Australia) (Bates, Fagerström, Jarvis, Kunze, McNeill and Ramström 2003; Gartner and Hall, 2009), but there has been a strong reluctance to prohibit the sale of the product that causes most of the global tobacco disease burden: the cigarette. Initially, banning smoked tobacco was seen as impractical because the high prevalence of adult use would make it politically difficult to enact and impossible to enforce without generating a black market in tobacco. Even now in countries that have achieved (or are heading towards) a ten percent smoking prevalence, there is little discussion of banning cigarette sales (for exceptions, see examples in section *Potential lessons from tobacco endgame discussions*). Instead, a range of strategies have been used to encourage smokers to quit and non-smokers not to start smoking. This chapter will briefly describe the strategies that have been used to reduce tobacco smoking and discuss their potential relevance to the regulation of legalized recreational cannabis products.

Evolution of the "cigarette epidemic" and public health responses

Prior to the First World War, the majority of tobacco use was in the form of smokeless tobacco (snuff and chewing tobacco), pipe tobacco and cigars (Brandt, 2007). The invention of the Bonsack cigarette rolling machine made the mass production and marketing of tobacco cigarettes possible and ensured that after the First World War manufactured cigarettes quickly became the dominant tobacco product in most developed countries (Proctor, 2012). The aggressive marketing of this highly addictive, inexpensive and convenient product saw tobacco smoking reach peak prevalence in the 1950s in the UK, where 80 percent of men and 40 percent of women smoked (Peto, Darby, Deo, Silcocks, Whitley and Doll, 2000).

As evidence emerged that smoking caused serious diseases, particularly lung cancer, efforts commenced to discourage smoking. Initially, public health officials assumed that most smokers would simply quit once informed about the dangers of smoking (Berridge, 2007). This assumption underappreciated both the addictiveness of cigarette smoking and the tenacity of the tobacco industry in maintaining their market. The persistence of smoking in the population led to tobacco control strategies beyond early public education campaigns being slowly and incrementally introduced. Campaigns by advocacy organizations (e.g. the Non-smokers Rights Movement, Action on Smoking and Health and Campaign for Tobacco Free Kids), health charities and medical organizations, as well as major reports by health authorities, were instrumental in creating the political will to introduce new tobacco control policies in the face of industry opposition (Wolfson, 2017).

Tobacco control strategies can be categorized into demand reduction, supply reduction and harm reduction strategies, which form the basis for the World Health Organization's Framework Convention on Tobacco Control (FCTC) (World Health Organization, 2005). The FCTC is an international treaty that outlines a range of strategies to reduce tobacco use that parties to FCTC agree to implement. The vast majority of strategies outlined in the FCTC are demand and supply reduction strategies.

The idea of an international treaty for tobacco control was proposed in a 1979 report of the World Health Organization (WHO) Expert Committee on Smoking Control (Convention Secretariat WHO Framework Convention on Tobacco Control, 2009). Momentum for a treaty under the auspices of the WHO grew and eventually led to the adoption of the FCTC in 2003. By 2018, there were 181 parties to the FCTC at varying stages of implementation of the 17 articles.

Application to legal cannabis markets

There are a number of differences between the legal cannabis market and the tobacco cigarette market that need to be considered when seeking to draw lessons for cannabis regulation from tobacco control. Firstly, the tobacco cigarette market was well-established, and smoking was highly pervasive in high-income countries by the time their governments introduced strategies to reduce smoking. Hence, the policy challenge in tobacco control was to increase the number of smokers who stopped smoking, reduce smoking uptake among young non-smokers and limit the spread of the cigarette epidemic to low and middle-income countries. In contrast, the fact that cannabis has been an illicit substance since at least 1961 means that the starting place for regulation is to bring an illicit cannabis market under better regulatory control and to regulate an expanding legal market in ways that minimize harm to users and the broader public. This history potentially presents a unique opportunity to develop a more coherent and comprehensive regulatory framework in an earlier stage of a developing legal market than was the case for tobacco, where incremental increases in regulation have occurred over a long period since tobacco became a global industry.

The evidence that tobacco smoking causes a range of serious and fatal diseases such as lung cancer, cardiovascular disease and respiratory diseases is very strong. The evidence for adverse health outcomes from cannabis is more mixed for many reasons, such as compounding with tobacco exposure which is commonly used at the same time, and the fact that to date, few cannabis users have used cannabis daily for decades, as most tobacco smokers do. These factors have made studying potential health outcomes of long-term cannabis use difficult. The most probable health impacts "include a dependence syndrome, increased risk of motor vehicle crashes, impaired respiratory function, cardiovascular disease, and adverse effects of regular use on adolescent psychosocial development and mental health" (Hall and Degenhardt, 2009). There also appear to be adverse fetal effects, such as low birthweight (Gunn, Rosales, Center, Nuñez, Gibson, Christ and Ehiri, 2016).

The difference in the evidence on the health risks of tobacco and cannabis use has important policy implications. Implementing strong tobacco control policies has been justified by the overwhelming evidence of substantial harm to the majority of smokers. The lack of similar evidence for comparable harms from cannabis presents a major challenge in making the case for ensuring cannabis control policies are as restrictive as those on tobacco. Most jurisdictions that have legalized cannabis have chosen to adopt and adapt regulations used for alcohol rather than tobacco (Hall, 2017). This reflects the similarity in reasons for using alcohol and cannabis and the fact that, as with alcohol, the minority of heavy users of cannabis are most likely to experience its harms.

Another difference with implications for policy and regulation is the greater addictiveness of tobacco smoke than cannabis and the very different psychoactive effects of the two substances. Most tobacco smokers would like to stop smoking but find stopping difficult because of withdrawal effects and a habitual behavior that has become a part of their daily routine. Around 90 percent of tobacco smokers regret starting to smoke (Fong, Hammond, Laux, Zanna, Cummings, Borland and Ross, 2004) and a substantial proportion support strong tobacco control regulations, including highly restrictive policies which may assist them to stop smoking (Chung-Hall, Fong, Driezen and Craig, 2018; Edwards, Wilson, Peace, Weerasekera, Thomson, and Gifford, 2013). By contrast, the proportion of cannabis users who become long-term daily users and develop a dependence syndrome is much lower, in the order of 10–20 percent (Anthony, Warner and Kessler, 1994; Coffey and Patton, 2016). The following sections discuss specific examples of tobacco control strategies and their potential relevance to cannabis control.

Demand reduction strategies

Anti-smoking mass media campaigns

Mass media campaigns have been used extensively to educate smokers about the health risks of tobacco smoking and the benefits of quitting. Reviews suggest that mass media campaigns can be effective at encouraging adult smokers to make a quit attempt and in reducing smoking prevalence (Bala, Strzeszynski, Topor-Madry and Cahill, 2013; Durkin, Brennan and Wakefield, 2012). However, their effectiveness depends on campaign duration and intensity (Bala et al., 2013; Durkin et al., 2012). Mass media campaigns that focus on the negative health effects of smoking may be more effective than positively framed messages (Durkin et al., 2012). Fear-based appeals that graphically show the adverse health impacts of smoking have been widely employed in anti-smoking mass media campaigns (Lupton, 2015). These messages both educate the public of the potential risks of smoking and generate feelings of disgust toward the behavior (Lupton, 2015). While fear-based media campaigns for cigarette smoking are supported by extensive scientific evidence on the serious health consequences of smoking, fear-based anti-vaping campaigns have also been used despite the very limited evidence that vaping produces serious health risks (Sangalang, Volinsky, Liu, Yang, Lee, Gibson and Hornik, 2019; Zeller, 2019). Generating negative affect towards smoking via mass media campaigns has probably contributed to tobacco denormalization, which is both a product of and a contributor to reduced smoking prevalence (Chapman and Freeman, 2008).

The evidence for effectiveness of mass media campaigns for preventing uptake of smoking among youth is mixed (Carson, Ameer, Sayehmiri, Hnin, van Agteren, Sayehmiri and Smith, 2017). Some research suggests that mass media campaigns targeting adult smokers that feature the health effects of smoking may also be effective at increasing anti-smoking attitudes among youth (White, Tan, Wakefield and Hill, 2003). However, youth anti-smoking campaigns have often focused on messages other than health effects. For example, the "Truth Campaign" mobilized youth to oppose the tobacco industry (Hoffman, 2016). Other research has identified "smoking for mood, social acceptance and social popularity" as promising potential targets for youth smoking prevention campaigns (Brennan, Gibson, Kybert-Momjian, Liu and Hornik, 2017).

It is uncertain how effective negatively framed mass media campaigns with strong fear appeals would be for cannabis. Such messages may lack credibility with the public and be readily dismissed as examples of "Reefer Madness" propaganda. They will also be contested because evidence on the health risks of cannabis use is much weaker than that on smoking tobacco. Furthermore, some youth anti-drug campaigns may have increased cannabis use by developing curiosity about drug effects, suggesting that increased harms are also a possible outcome (Allara, Ferri, Bo, Gasparrini and Faggiano, 2015).

Another issue in judging the appropriateness of tobacco control-style mass media anti-cannabis campaigns is the potential to increase stigma experienced by users. While some have argued that shame-based appeals are a legitimate strategy for reducing smoking (Amonini, Pettigrew and Clayforth, 2015), others are concerned about the harmful consequences of stigmatizing smokers, particularly those from socially marginalized populations among whom smoking is increasingly concentrated (Bell, Salmon, Bowers, Bell and McCullough, 2010; Brown-Johnson and Prochaska, 2015; Hefler and Chapman, 2015; Lupton, 2015). Similar concerns are relevant to potential stigmatization of regular cannabis users who are increasingly found in more socially disadvantaged populations (Chan, Leung, Quinn, Weier and Hall, 2018).

As a relatively new industry, the legal cannabis industry has not yet had the time to generate a history of misconduct like that of the tobacco industry. This may make "anti-industry" campaigns less relevant for the cannabis industry at present. They may come to play a role if the cannabis industry begins to behave like the tobacco and alcohol industries, or if Big Tobacco and the alcohol industry invest heavily in cannabis companies and begin to use their skills in consumer marketing to expand the number of regular cannabis users. These are realistic concerns because internal tobacco industry documents show that tobacco companies have been interested in entering the cannabis market (Barry, Hiilamo and Glantz, 2014) and Altria (owner of Philip Morris) recently acquired a significant stake in a major Canadian cannabis producer (Brumpton and Sampath Kumar, 2018).

Taxation

High tobacco taxation is widely accepted as the most effective tobacco control strategy, despite the fact that demand for tobacco is "relatively inelastic" in economic terms (U.S. National Cancer Institute and World Health Organization, 2016). The WHO recommends that tobacco taxes should make up at least 70 percent of the retail price of tobacco products (World Health Organization, 2015). In addition to encouraging smokers to quit, high retail prices deter initiation among youth who have lower disposable incomes. As for tobacco (World Health Organization, 2010), a substantial level of tax on legal cannabis products would be expected to limit youth use and discourage heavy consumption among both youth and adult users (Amlung, Reed, Morris, Aston, Metrik and MacKillop, 2019). As for tobacco, cannabis taxation could also be an important source of government revenue, although on a much lower scale.

Hypothecation of a proportion of cannabis tax revenue to fund cannabis control activities including control of the illicit market, treatment programs for cannabis users who develop problematic use and research is recommended, as was done with tobacco taxes in California to fund a comprehensive tobacco control and research program (Doetinchem, 2010; Sweanor, Ballin, Corcoran, Davis, Deasy, Ferrence and Wasserman, 1992). This type of tax would increase public support for taxation of cannabis products and make funds available for programs to manage risks arising from the cannabis market. In US states that have legalized cannabis sales, the hypothecation of cannabis taxes to fund treatment and prevention and other worthy government functions, such as education has been common in early adopter states such as Colorado and Washington State. It probably played a role in securing public support for cannabis legalization in popular ballots (McGinty, Niederdeppe, Heley and Barry, 2017).

Careful consideration will need to be given to setting the appropriate level of tax and the type of tax structure for cannabis products. Keeping the tax structure simple (rather than multi-tiered) and using product-specific taxes rather than *ad valorem* taxes is recommended. Furthermore, taxes need to be regularly increased to avoid inflation eroding the effect of the tax (World Health Organization, 2010). As in the tobacco control field, high cannabis taxes will raise concerns about potential adverse impacts on low income populations. It is debated whether tobacco taxation is regressive and harms low income populations (Bader, Boisclair and Ferrence, 2011; U.S. National Cancer Institute and World Health Organization, 2016; Warner, 2000). Some authors point to the unintended impacts of high tobacco taxes on low income households, particularly those containing children, in which a large proportion of limited incomes is diverted from purchasing essentials to paying for tobacco (Thomson, Wilson, O'Dea, Reid and Howden-Chapman, 2002). Others cite a greater positive impact of tobacco taxation on quit rates in low income populations as evidence that tobacco taxes are progressive and reduce inequities (Warner, 2000). While tobacco use is increasingly concentrated among low income populations, evidence for the relationship between cannabis use and income and employment outcomes is mixed (Popovici and French, 2014; Stinson, Ruan, Pickering and Grant, 2006; Warner, 2000). Monitoring the impacts of cannabis taxation on low income populations will be important in determining whether cannabis taxation increases or reduces health disparities.

An important final issue in determining the optimal tax rate for cannabis products is the impact of cannabis prices on the size of the black market. The impact of tobacco tax rates on the illicit tobacco trade is debated. The tobacco industry has used the argument that high tobacco taxes stimulate the illicit tobacco market to discourage governments from raising tobacco taxes. It is notable that tobacco industry estimates of the size of the illicit tobacco market are generally higher than those made by independent sources (Gallagher, Evans-Reeves, Hatchard and Gilmore, 2018). Retailers and producers in a legal cannabis market also argue that cannabis taxes need to be low to reduce the size of the black market. It will be important for governments to invest in independent monitoring of the illicit cannabis market. However, if the price of licit cannabis products is very high some consumers will undoubtedly revert to the black market (Amlung et al., 2019). To limit the black market, regulators can limit the taxes applied to legal cannabis products to undermine the profit incentive of the illicit market. Alternatively, they can invest more in law enforcement activities against black market cannabis producers and sellers.

Controls on advertising and promotions

The WHO FCTC definition of tobacco advertising and promotion includes "any form of commercial communication, recommendation or action with the aim, effect or likely effect of promoting a tobacco product or tobacco use either directly or indirectly" (World Health Organization, 2005). Parties to the FCTC are required to "undertake a comprehensive ban on all tobacco advertising, promotion and sponsorship" (World Health Organization, 2005). In addition to advertising bans, other restrictions on promotional activities that have been enacted for tobacco products include: bans on sports sponsorship, bans on misleading descriptors, mandatory plain packaging, retail display bans, and bans on toys, confectionary and novelty items that feature tobacco brand names or are designed to resemble tobacco products (Henriksen, 2012).

A challenge for both the tobacco and cannabis control fields is the use of new media to promote products via both commercial advertisements and user-generated content (Freeman, 2012). Some popular platforms, such as Facebook and Twitter, have policies not to accept commercial advertising of tobacco on their sites, but it is less straightforward to censor non-commercial communications about tobacco or cannabis.

A controversial strategy that has been implemented in some countries is to require an adult rating on movies that feature smoking or to ban smoking in movies and television shows by "pixelating out" cigarettes (Chapman and Farrelly, 2011). Proponents of this policy cite evidence of a dose response association between youth smoking initiation and youth viewing content containing smoking (Leonardi Bee, Nderi and Britton, 2016). Similar associations have been reported between watching movies featuring cannabis use and cannabis smoking (American Academy of Pediatrics, 2010). Regulators will need to consider what classification is appropriate for media in an era of legal cannabis products, particularly because cannabis legalization will lead to more incidental depictions of cannabis in cinema and television and other media, such as video games.

Strong controls on cannabis promotions to youth and adults are needed, given that the goal of advertising and promotional activities is to increase consumer demand and grow the market and there is evidence that exposure to tobacco promotions increases youth smoking (Lovato, Watts and Stead, 2011). Some of these marketing and promotional restrictions from tobacco control have already been applied to cannabis regulations. Health Canada's Cannabis Regulations, for example, prohibit advertising of cannabis products and prevent packages containing cannabis products from displaying any brand elements or images ("Cannabis Regulations (SOR/2018–144)," 2018). Uruguay's legal cannabis scheme also prohibits advertising of cannabis products (Pardo, 2014). The advertising and promotion of cannabis products in the USA is banned because cannabis remains illegal under US federal law. If cannabis legalization were to become US national policy, there would probably be fewer restrictions on the promotion of cannabis products because of constitutional protection of freedom of speech (Pacula, Kilmer, Wagenaar, Chaloupka and Caulkins, 2014). Cannabis producers will no doubt argue that they should have the right to advertise their products if they are legal commodities. The advertising restrictions that are applied to tobacco, which is also a legal commodity, would provide a good example that could be followed.

Health warnings

Health warnings on tobacco products began with simple text-based messages. They have since evolved to include highly graphic photos of tobacco-related disease such as gangrenous toes, lung cancer and mouth cancer. These warnings not only educate about potential health effects of smoking but also "elicit strong feelings of disgust and revulsion" (Haines-Saah, Bell and Dennis, 2015). Research suggests that the effectiveness of pack health warnings is dependent on their size and style. Text warnings are least effective and graphic images that generate strong negative affect are the most effective (Hammond, 2011). Graphic pack health warnings may also be effective in reducing smoking initiation among youth (Hammond, 2011). Graphic pack warnings also contribute to the denormalization of tobacco products, particularly when combined with plain packaging (Haines-Saah et al., 2015).

The challenge in making the case for and designing appropriate pack health warnings for cannabis products is the greater uncertainty about (and likely contestation of) evidence on the adverse health impacts of long-term cannabis use.

While graphic health warnings are more effective than text warnings for tobacco products, we need research on whether these would work for cannabis warning labels. For example, while the gory images of tobacco-related diseases have featured strongly on cigarette pack warning labels in many countries, these would be inappropriate in portraying the risks of cannabis dependence or of serious mental illness, such as psychotic disorders, without risking further stigmatizing people with mental health conditions. Similar warning labels to tobacco could be appropriate for cannabis use in pregnancy.

The cannabis health warning labels implemented by Health Canada are text only, accompanied by a cannabis symbol. They include statements that: cannabis smoke is harmful, cannabis can be addictive (and adolescents are at greater risk), cannabis use increases the risk of psychosis and schizophrenia when used regularly, cannabis should not be used while pregnant or breastfeeding and cannabis should not be used when operating machinery or driving (Health Canada, 2018).

Product regulation to reduce the attractiveness and addictiveness of tobacco products

Article 9 of the FCTC requires parties to regulate the contents and emissions of tobacco products and Article 10 covers disclosure of tobacco product contents and emissions. Targets for tobacco product regulation include reducing the attractiveness of tobacco products, such as by prohibiting the addition of flavors to make tobacco products more palatable, or addictiveness by limiting their nicotine content (discussed further under "Potential lessons from tobacco endgame discussions"). Some jurisdictions have enacted bans on characterizing flavors, such as fruit and confectionary flavors, to reduce the attractiveness of tobacco products, particularly to youth (Courtemanche, Palmer and Pesko, 2017). The US FDA is currently considering banning menthol in cigarettes (FDA, 2018).

Regulation of the THC and CBD levels in legal cannabis is a possibility advocated by some researchers (Caulkins, Kilmer and Kleiman, 2016). It is likely to be resisted by the cannabis industry in the US on at least two grounds: that there is no evidence to justify this approach to cannabis; and that testing potency will greatly increase the price of legal cannabis and make it uncompetitive with black market products. Prohibiting the addition of flavorings to cannabis products that could increase their appeal to young people would be sensible policy. Producers of edible cannabis products (where these are permitted) have resisted regulations to make their products less palatable. Limits on the addition of sweetening and flavoring agents (e.g. chocolate) could reduce the attractiveness of edible products to youth and reduce the risk of accidental poisoning of children who unknowingly consume edible cannabis products. One can expect opposition from the cannabis industry in the US, given the substantial sales of edible products in states that have legalized cannabis (Smart, Caulkins, Kilmer, Davenport and Midgette, 2017).

Cessation treatment

While the majority of tobacco smokers quit without medical assistance, many require multiple quit attempts over a number of years to stop (Chaiton, Diemert, Cohen, Bondy, Selby, Philipneri, and Schwartz, 2016). A range of smoking cessation treatments are effective in increasing the success of a quit attempt, including pharmacotherapies (Cahill, Stevens, Perera and Lancaster, 2013) and counselling (Lancaster and Stead, 2017). Assisting smokers to quit smoking is covered in Article 14 of the FCTC. The guidelines for implementation of Article 14 covers a range of both individual-level and population-level strategies, including making health education, behavioral support and smoking cessation pharmacotherapy widely available and affordable (WHO FCTC Conference of the Parties, 2010). The level of smoking cessation support available varies between countries. For example, in the UK, smoking cessation clinics provide access to counselling programs and free cessation pharmacotherapy in addition to widespread availability to nicotine replacement therapy over the counter in pharmacies and general retailers. In Australia, smoking cessation counselling is available via a telephone quit line service and smoking cessation pharmacotherapy is sold over the counter in pharmacies and general retailers, and is available at a subsidized price when prescribed by a medical practitioner.

As with tobacco smoking, the majority of people who develop cannabis dependence cease their use without formal assistance (Coffey, Carlin, Lynskey, Li and Patton, 2003). However, an essential policy component of cannabis legalization should be to ensure that cannabis users who develop dependence or problematic use have ready access to treatment and assistance. Current treatments for cannabis use disorders rely on psychosocial interventions, such as motivational interviewing and cognitive behavioral therapy (EMCDDA, 2015). There are no approved or effective pharmacotherapies for treating cannabis use disorders (Marshall, Gowing, Ali and Le Foll, 2014). There is limited evidence that counselling delivered via a cannabis helpline can assist with reducing dependence symptoms and related problems (Gates, Norberg, Copeland and Digiusto, 2012). More research is needed on the effectiveness and cost-effectiveness of cannabis use helplines which may be a low-cost method of making treatment for cannabis problems more accessible.

Supply reduction strategies

Age restrictions

Restrictions on purchasing age, generally 18 years, is a widely adopted policy for tobacco products. Some jurisdictions only make sales to under-aged persons illegal, while others also make purchase, possession and use by underage persons illegal. Evidence suggests that achieving and maintaining compliance with these laws requires active enforcement (Stead and Lancaster, 2005). Penalizing youth for purchasing, possessing and using tobacco has been criticized as impractical because of difficulties in detecting and enforcing infringements and as distracting attention from the tobacco industry's role in promoting their products to young non-smokers (Wakefield and Giovino, 2003). A number of US jurisdictions (local and state) have raised the minimum purchase age to 21 years, with some evidence that this has led to greater declines in youth smoking than in jurisdictions that haven't adopted this policy (Morain, Winickoff and Mello, 2016).

Most jurisdictions that have legalized cannabis for adult use have set restrictions on minimum age of purchase. In US states, the minimum legal purchase age is the same as that for alcohol, namely, 21 years. In Canada, the federal government has set a minimum age of 19 years but it will allow provincial governments to set a higher age, if they wish to, which in most cases will also be the same age as for alcohol (Kilmer, 2017; Subritzky, Pettigrew and Lenton, 2016).

Retailer licenses

Licensing tobacco retailers controls who sells tobacco, where it is sold and under what conditions. Licenses can be cancelled for breaches (e.g. selling to underage people), and regulators can add license conditions that require the reporting of sales figures to allow close monitoring of sales and to match producer and wholesaler figures. While retailer licensing is recommended in the FCTC, some parties to the FCTC do not have comprehensive retailer licensing schemes. Implementing retailer licensing is more difficult for tobacco than cannabis because of the large number of general retailers who are able to sell tobacco products. High retailer density for tobacco has been linked to higher tobacco sales that may lower prices through greater competition. It also makes quitting more difficult because of the widespread access to tobacco. The policy of reducing the number of tobacco retailers in an area has been discussed in tobacco control but not widely implemented. Restricting the number of licenses issued per geographic area will be much easier for the legal cannabis market if done early during implementation. Some US jurisdictions allow local governments to ban cannabis retail outlets, others have implemented a cap on the number of retailers (Washington State Liquor and Cannabis Board, 2015). Others have not.

Overly strict regulations of legal cannabis outlets, including limiting their number, could encourage the persistence of the illicit cannabis trade and smuggling. However, given the potential difficulties in reducing the number of retailers in the market after licenses are issued, failing to place limits on the number of licenses would be a wasted opportunity to control the size of the legal cannabis market.

Illicit trade provisions

The illicit trade in tobacco products includes the sale of unbranded loose tobacco which is diverted from tobacco farms or grown in illegal plantations, counterfeit manufactured products, and smuggling of genuine tobacco products to avoid taxation. The tobacco industry has been implicated as a participant in the latter (Joossens and Raw, 2000). The FCTC Protocol to eliminate illicit trade in tobacco products (World Health Organization, 2013) outlines a number of strategies of possible relevance for cannabis products. All actors within the product supply chain should be licensed for activities including: importation, growing, manufacturing, wholesaling, transporting commercial quantities, warehousing and retailing of tobacco products or manufacturing equipment. Due diligence requirements specify actions such as monitoring sales. The protocol requires parties to the FCTC to implement a global tracking and tracing regime comprised of "national and/or regional tracking and tracing systems and a global information-sharing focal point" which enables all parties to access relevant information. All product packages must be affixed with "unique, secure and non-removable identification markings." Access to important information that clearly identifies the tobacco product's origin and point of departure from the official supply chain is required as part of the tracing system. Cooperation between parties, such as the sharing of relevant information related to cross-border movement of products is also outlined. Legal cannabis markets have implemented similar track and trace systems, such as the California Cannabis Track-and-Trace system. This maintains records of stock and movement of cannabis products through the supply chain based on a licensing system for growing, manufacturing, retailing, distributing, laboratory analysis and microbusinesses.

Harm reduction strategies

Smoke-free laws and policies

One successful and popular harm reduction strategy for tobacco smoking is public smoke-free policies and laws. This strategy primarily reduces harms that smoking may cause to others rather than the user, by preventing smoking in public spaces where non-smokers may be exposed to second-hand smoke (Gartner, Hall and McNeill, 2010). It has also contributed to denormalization of smoking and reduced opportunities to smoke (Gartner et al., 2010). As exposure to second-hand cannabis smoke is likely to also present risks to non-smoking by-standers, regulators should ensure that smoke-free policies and laws intended for tobacco smoking also apply to cannabis smoking. Cannabis use in the workplace is likely to already be covered by workplace drug and alcohol policies, but some jurisdictions have included public use bans in their cannabis regulations (Pardo, 2014).

Alternative nicotine products

People smoke tobacco for the effects of nicotine, but it is the toxic gases, particulate matter and carcinogenic tars that they inhale from the non-nicotine components of burnt tobacco that are responsible for the vast majority of tobacco-related harm (Russell, 1976). Hence, there is substantial potential for reducing the harm of nicotine use if smokers used cleaner delivery systems for nicotine. However, harm reduction strategies that involve encouraging tobacco smokers to switch to lower-risk nicotine products are one of the most underutilized approaches in tobacco control. They are strongly opposed by many in the tobacco control field because of concerns about youth uptake. However, proponents of tobacco harm reduction have pointed out that an increase in youth use of lower-risk nicotine products may also divert some youth from smoking. Time trend analyses demonstrate a faster decline in any recent smoking and more established smoking among youth in the US after 2014, when youth vaping prevalence increased substantially (Levy, Warner, Cummings, Hammond, Kuo, Fong, Borland, 2018). The history of opposition to tobacco harm reduction largely originates from experience with tobacco industry marketing of cigarette products that purported to reduce harm but were later found to be ineffective at reducing health risk (Gartner and Hall, 2010). The promotion of filter cigarettes and "light"/"low tar" cigarettes likely increased overall harm by discouraging health-conscious smokers from quitting (Kozlowski, Goldberg, Yost, White, Sweeney, and Pillitteri, 1998). These product innovations were initially supported by the public health community (Gartner and Hall, 2010), but once the fraud was discovered, tobacco control advocates focused their efforts on goals of: (1) ending tobacco-related death and disease; (2) ending nicotine addiction; and (3) destroying the tobacco industry (Arnott, 2013).

While cigarette filters and "light" cigarettes did not reduce harm to tobacco smokers, there is an increasing range of nicotine and tobacco products that are substantially less harmful than cigarettes. These lie on a spectrum of risk. Medicinal nicotine products, such as gum and lozenges are at the lowest end; cigarettes are at the highest level of risk; and products that deliver nicotine without burning tobacco, such as low nitrosamine smokeless tobacco (e.g. Swedish snus), electronic vapor products (e.g. e-cigarettes) and heated tobacco products, lie somewhere in between (McNeill and Munafò, 2013). Current evidence suggests these non-smoked alternative nicotine products could be substantially less harmful than cigarettes and in some cases may be closer in their risk profile to medicinal nicotine than that of smoked tobacco (Gartner, Hall, Vos, Bertram, Wallace and Lim, 2007; National Academies of Sciences and Medicine, 2018; Stephens, 2018; Tobacco Advisory Group of the Royal College of Physicians, 2016). A lack of conclusive evidence on the safety of long-term use of some of these non-medicinal products (e.g. nicotine-containing vapor products) has been used to justify a ban on their introduction into Australia (Department of Health, 2018). It is noteworthy that with the exception of New Zealand[1] (Department of Health, 2018), very few countries have reversed bans on the sale of Swedish snus, despite good evidence from long-term epidemiological studies that confirms its low-risk profile. This suggests that high-quality epidemiological evidence of lower risk may not be sufficient to overturn sales bans on vaporized nicotine.

Regulation of electronic vapor products, such as e-cigarettes, varies globally. Most Western democracies (Europe, UK, USA, Canada, New Zealand) allow these products to be sold with or without nicotine, either as consumer products or as therapeutic goods if there is evidence of safety and efficacy for use as cessation aids (Gartner and Bromberg, 2019). The EU Tobacco Products Directive specifies a range of requirements for nicotine vapor products such as limits on the size of bottles containing refill fluid (10 mL maximum) and maximum nicotine concentration (20 mg/mL). Sellers of these products need to notify the regulating authority prior to sale of their ingredients. Products that do not conform to these specifications (e.g. >20 mg/mL) can only be marketed if approved as a medicine. Canada and New Zealand are currently developing regulations for vaping products that are sold as consumer goods.

Countries with prohibitions on the sale or use of non-medicinal vaping products include Australia, Malaysia, Thailand, Singapore and Hong Kong. Malaysia and most states of Australia[2] allow the sale of nicotine-free vapor products but nicotine-containing products cannot be sold unless approved by the medicines regulators. Individuals have been prosecuted in Australia for possession of relatively small quantities of nicotine vaping liquid (<100 mL) (Gartner and Bromberg, 2019). Thailand and Singapore both ban the sale and use of vaping products regardless of whether or not they contain nicotine. There are reports of British nationals being arrested for possessing a vaporizer in Thailand (Gov.UK).

Cannabis regulators would be well-advised to avoid adopting the same perverse regulatory framework as some countries have adopted for nicotine and tobacco products. These bans arguably provide market protection and exemptions from product regulations for the most harmful nicotine products (cigarettes) and impose more severe restrictions including sales bans on some lower-risk nicotine products (e.g. Swedish snus, nicotine vapor products). As with tobacco, smoked cannabis products are likely to be the most risky because they expose users' lungs to the by-products of combustion, such as particulate matter. While evidence is still developing on the risks of non-smoked cannabis products, such as dry herb vaporizers, cannabis oil vaporizers and edible cannabis products, these would appear to be lower risk than smoked cannabis (Fischer, Russell, Sabioni, van den Brink, Le Foll, Hall, and Room, 2017; Hall and Fischer, 2010). Regulators might consider imposing higher taxes on cannabis products intended for smoking. Product warnings that emphasize combustion as the most harmful route of administration could also be helpful in steering consumers toward lower-risk delivery methods. At a minimum, it would be prudent not to limit the legal market to smoked cannabis products or to enact greater restrictions on potentially lower-risk cannabis products. Discouraging cannabis users from mixing their cannabis with tobacco is a harm reduction strategy that could encourage users to adopt non-smoked methods of using cannabis (Fischer et al., 2017; Gartner, 2015).

Edible cannabis products eliminate the respiratory risks of cannabis smoking but are not risk-free. Inexperienced cannabis users inadvertently overdosed on edible cannabis products in the early stage of cannabis legalization in Colorado (Monte, Zane, and Heard, 2015). More serious problems occur in children who accidentally ingest edible cannabis products that they assume to be confectionary (Richards, Smith and Moulin, 2017). Regulatory changes to the potency, packaging and labelling of edible cannabis products have been introduced in some US states to address these problems with as yet unknown success.

Product regulation

Regulating the constituents and emissions of tobacco products to reduce toxicity is included in the FCTC (Article 9). It has been the focus of the WHO Study Group on Tobacco Product Regulation (TobReg). However, there are few examples of the use of tobacco product regulations to reduce the harms of tobacco smoking. One harm reduction product standard that has been implemented is a Reduced Ignition Propensity standard to reduce cigarette-related fires (Saar, 2018). Sweden has an industry standard to limit the levels of tobacco specific nitrosamines in smokeless tobacco products (Stepanov and Hatsukami, 2016), but no country has enacted product standards to reduce the toxicity of cigarettes.

Potential targets for cannabis product standards include maximum permissible levels for contaminants, such as pesticides (Subritzky, Pettigrew and Lenton, 2017) and maximum THC content for smokeable, edible and extract forms. Many US states do require testing of cannabis products for heavy metals, pesticides and micro-organisms. The substantial failure rates of testing in some states has prompted complaints from the cannabis industry about forcing up their costs and reducing their ability to compete with illegally produced cannabis.

Potential lessons from tobacco endgame discussions

There is an increasing discussion within the tobacco control field about an "endgame" for tobacco smoking. These discussions aim to eliminate tobacco smoking as a major public health issue by setting a very low population smoking prevalence as a goal (typically 5 percent or less), setting a target date by which to achieve this and outlining a strategy to do so that goes beyond "business as usual" (McDaniel, Smith and Malone, 2016). Some of these proposals and their potential relevance to cannabis control are discussed below.

Abolition

Proctor has proposed abolishing legal tobacco sales (Proctor, 2013). He argues that abolition is different from prohibition because users would be permitted to grow and possess tobacco for their own personal use. This is similar to the decriminalization model used for cannabis in some Australian and US states. However, unlike the model proposed by Proctor for tobacco, criminal penalties have been retained under cannabis decriminalization for cannabis cultivation; only users found in possession are given fines or diverted to treatment programs (Hall and Fischer, 2010). While the Uruguay model of cannabis legalization includes the option to purchase cannabis products through licensed pharmacies, registered users may also grow their own. This model may offer an alternative to legalization of commercial cannabis cultivation and sales (Caulkins et al., 2016).

A regulated market model

Borland has proposed a regulated market model for tobacco (Borland, 2003). Under this proposal, a government-owned monopsonistic agency (the

Tobacco Products Agency) would license manufacturers to produce tobacco products that complied with their standards and then supply them to retailers. As the sole wholesaler of tobacco products, the Tobacco Products Agency would have control over the price, packaging and constituents of the products in the retail market. The most harmful tobacco products could be withdrawn from the market by phasing out their supply to retailers. This model was also used until very recently to regulate alcohol in Scandinavia and some Canadian provinces.

None of the jurisdictions with legalized cannabis markets have adopted this model. It is likely to face similar barriers to its adoption for tobacco, such as the reluctance of governments to become monopoly suppliers of a potentially harmful recreational drug. Moreover, most governments are privatizing state-owned enterprises, such as utility wholesalers and prisons, rather than setting up new state-owned businesses (Megginson and Netter, 2001). Nevertheless, if there were sufficient political support, a regulated market model for cannabis could be a viable way of better controlling and monitoring legal cannabis markets (Caulkins et al., 2016).

Restricting sales to non-profit enterprises with a health mandate

Callard and colleagues have proposed a regulatory model to remove the profit incentive from the tobacco market by transferring the manufacture and supply of tobacco products from commercial corporations to an enterprise "with the mandate to achieve a timetabled reduction in tobacco and the market power to innovate measures to meet these targets" by acquiring their operations through voluntary or legislated purchase (Callard, Thompson and Collishaw, 2005). Government-controlled monopolies already exist in some countries (e.g. China Tobacco Company), although run without an explicit health mandate. It could be argued that Compassion Clubs that were set up as non-profit user cooperatives are an example of a non-profit model that has been used in cannabis control. This proposal is very similar to the regulated market model; it would require governments to be the sole suppliers of cannabis products to the market.

Smoker licensing

Chapman has proposed a licensing scheme for tobacco smokers, whereby both suppliers and purchasers would require a license (Chapman, 2012). The scheme would allow close monitoring of tobacco use, limit the quantity that could be purchased and include financial incentives for users to surrender their license when they quit smoking to reduce their risk of relapse by preventing impulse purchasing of tobacco. Other features proposed include a license exam to ensure that those applying for licenses are aware of the risks of smoking. Cannabis legalization in Uruguay shares some features of the smoker's license proposal, such as the requirement for users to register with the state and the imposition of limits on the amount of cannabis that can be purchased (Pardo, 2014). A limitation of this model is that users may prefer to access cannabis from the black market if they are concerned about identifying themselves as cannabis users by applying for a license or registering as a user, or resist attempts to limit their cannabis consumption (Hudak, Ramsey and Walsh, 2018).

Sinking lid and cap-and-trade schemes

Wilson and colleagues have proposed a quota system to limit the quantity of tobacco that can be sold within a country and require suppliers to bid for the right to sell the tobacco (Wilson, Thomson, Edwards and Blakely, 2013). The amount of tobacco available for sale could be gradually reduced in order to drive up prices. The idea is similar to using carbon trading models to reduce carbon dioxide levels. The approach has not been implemented for tobacco in any jurisdiction and would require strong political will and large-scale compensation of commercial tobacco suppliers. Free trade agreements may also present a barrier.

An issue requiring careful consideration would be managing the demand for tobacco among addicted consumers who are unable to purchase tobacco if the lid sinks faster than the prevalence of smoking. Governments that set up a legal cannabis market could limit the amount of cannabis produced and released into the retail market in order to contain the growth of the market. This would allow governments to decide what would be an acceptable size for a legal cannabis market. The major downside of this approach would again be consumers turning to the black market if consumer demand exceeded the amount of cannabis available from the legal market.

Reducing the nicotine in smoked tobacco products to non-addictive levels

In 2017, the US FDA announced its intention to mandate the reduction of nicotine in smoked tobacco products to minimally or non-addictive levels (FDA News Release, 2017). The main aim of this policy, first proposed more than 20 years ago, is to protect new smokers from becoming addicted to smoking tobacco (Benowitz and Henningfield, 2013). Unlike ventilated cigarettes, which produce low nicotine readings by diluting the smoke with air drawn in from the side of the cigarette, the tobacco in Very Low Nicotine Content (VLNC) cigarettes has been grown or treated so that there is minimal nicotine in the plant material used to manufacture the cigarettes (Donny, Denlinger, Tidey, Koopmeiners, Benowitz, Vandrey, and Hatsukami, 2015). While smokers of "light" cigarettes can receive the same amount of nicotine by altering their puffing topography, smokers of VLNC cigarettes are not able to compensate for the lower nicotine delivery. Randomized trials of VLNC cigarettes have found that smokers assigned to use these cigarettes reduced their exposure to nicotine and report lower nicotine dependence scores at follow-up than smokers who continued to smoke the control cigarettes. Since nicotine is the main addictive component of tobacco and the main reason that people continue smoking when they no longer want to, a mandated VLNC standard for cigarettes would be expected to dramatically impact the current tobacco cigarette market.

This policy may be more acceptable and feasible if combined with tobacco harm reduction options. In announcing the intended policy, the then FDA commissioner, Scott Gottlieb, also announced that lower-risk alternative nicotine products would remain available so that "adults who still need or want nicotine can get it from an alternative and less harmful source" (FDA News Release, 2017).

A survey of smokers in Canada reported high public support for removing nicotine from cigarettes (Chung-Hall, Fong, Driezen and Craig, 2018). However, this strategy has not been implemented outside of controlled trials so there is substantial uncertainty about whether smokers would accept the policy if implemented. Possible impacts include substantial consumer pressure to reverse the ban, an increase in black market tobacco with high nicotine content, and consumers adding nicotine sourced from medicinal nicotine or alternative nicotine products to VLNC cigarettes.

An equivalent policy for cannabis would be a mandated limit on the THC content of cannabis. Similar concerns would apply to this policy as for VLNC tobacco cigarettes. The availability of lower-risk sources of THC would need to provide an alternative to consumers who could purchase high THC smoked cannabis products from the black market. This presents a major challenge to this policy because some lower-risk delivery methods, such as vaporization, use loose cannabis that can be smoked. Hence, there is no easy way to ensure smoked cannabis products have low THC content while providing access to higher THC cannabis for vaporization.

Conclusions

Tobacco smoking prevalence has been reduced substantially over the past 50 years thanks to a comprehensive set of strategies that have discouraged smoking. Some lessons from Tobacco Control policy are transferable and have already been transferred to Cannabis Control policy, e.g. use of taxation; age restrictions on sales; smoke-free policies; restrictions on promotional activities; track and trace programs and plain packaging. However, the transferability of other lessons is more uncertain. This includes mass media campaigns that use strong fear appeals and tobacco endgame policies that aim to remove or minimize levels of the main psychoactive component in cannabis. Cannabis regulators have a unique opportunity to set up a coherent framework that utilizes some of the innovative regulatory options that have been suggested for tobacco. These have proven difficult to implement for tobacco because of the challenges in radically changing how tobacco is marketed when large numbers of daily tobacco smokers will be affected, and highly profitable transnational tobacco companies can effectively oppose them. Even without these barriers, adoption of some proposed strategies, such as state-run cannabis monopolies, will be difficult to achieve politically. They would require strong advocacy campaigns from public health organizations to support their introduction.

Regulations should be developed in a way that allows lower-risk cannabis products to be sold. Elements of some policies that have only been discussed for tobacco have already been implemented for cannabis. However, some of these have not been in place long enough to evaluate (e.g. Uruguay's registered cannabis user program). Endgame discussions in the tobacco control field have identified smoking prevalence goals. Governments embarking on legalization of cannabis might consider setting a maximum cannabis use prevalence benchmark to prompt public discussions of the sort of restrictions that should be placed on cannabis sales.

Notes

1 The New Zealand *Smoke-free Environments Act 1990,* s 29(2) prohibits the commercial importation of tobacco products that are "labelled or otherwise described as suitable for chewing, or for any other oral use (other than smoking)" (Ministry of Health, 1990). However, in 2016, the New Zealand Ministry of Health announced it was "considering how best to apply risk-proportionate regulation across all tobacco products including smoked tobacco, smokeless tobacco and vaping products" (Ministry of Health, 2016).

2 Western Australia does not permit the sale of vaping devices, regardless of whether they contain nicotine or not.

References

Allara, E., Ferri, M., Bo, A., Gasparrini, A. and Faggiano, F. (2015). Are mass-media campaigns effective in preventing drug use? A Cochrane systematic review and meta-analysis. *BMJ Open,* 5(9).

American Academy of Pediatrics. (2010). Children, adolescents, substance abuse, and the media. *Pediatrics*, 126(4), 791.

Amlung, M., Reed, D.D., Morris, V., Aston, E.R., Metrik, J. and MacKillop, J. (2019). Price elasticity of illegal versus legal cannabis: A behavioral economic substitutability analysis. *Addiction,* 114(1), 112–118.

Amonini, C., Pettigrew, S. and Clayforth, C. (2015). The potential of shame as a message appeal in antismoking television advertisements. *Tobacco Control,* 24(5), 436.

Anthony, J.C., Warner, L.A. and Kessler, R.C. (1994). Comparative epidemiology of dependence on tobacco, alcohol, controlled substances, and inhalants: Basic findings from the National Comorbidity Survey. *Experimental and Clinical Psychopharmacology,* 2(3), 244.

Arnott, D. (2013). There's no single endgame. *Tobacco Control,* 22(Suppl. 1), i38.

Bader, P., Boisclair, D. and Ferrence, R. (2011). Effects of tobacco taxation and pricing on smoking behavior in high risk populations: A knowledge synthesis. *International Journal of Environmental Research and Public Health*, 8(11), 4118–4139.

Bala, M.M., Strzeszynski, L., Topor-Madry, R. and Cahill, K. (2013). Mass media interventions for smoking cessation in adults. *Cochrane Database of Systematic Reviews*, 6. doi:10.1002/14651858.CD004704.pub3.

Barry, R.A., Hiilamo, H. and Glantz, S.A. (2014). Waiting for the opportune moment: The tobacco industry and marijuana legalization. *The Milbank Quarterly*, 92(2), 207–242.

Bates, C., Fagerström, K., Jarvis, M.J., Kunze, M., McNeill, A. and Ramström, L. (2003). European Union policy on smokeless tobacco: A statement in favour of evidence based regulation for public health. *Tobacco Control*, 12(4), 360.

Bell, K., Salmon, A., Bowers, M., Bell, J. and McCullough, L. (2010). Smoking, stigma and tobacco "denormalization": Further reflections on the use of stigma as a public health tool. A commentary on Social Science & Medicine's stigma, prejudice, discrimination and health special issue. *Social Science & Medicine*, 70(6), 795–799.

Benowitz, N.L. and Henningfield, J.E. (2013). Reducing the nicotine content to make cigarettes less addictive. *Tobacco Control*, 22(Suppl. 1), i14–i17.

Berridge, V. (2007). *Marketing health: Smoking and the discourse of public health in Britain, 1945–2000*. Oxford: Oxford University Press on Demand.

Borland, R. (2003). A strategy for controlling the marketing of tobacco products: A regulated market model. *Tobacco Control*, 12(4), 374.

Brandt, A.M. (2007). *The cigarette century: The rise, fall, and deadly persistence of the product that defined America*. New York: Basic Books.

Brennan, E., Gibson, L.A., Kybert-Momjian, A., Liu, J. and Hornik, R.C. (2017). Promising themes for antismoking campaigns targeting youth and young adults. *Tobacco Regulatory Science*, 3(1), 29–46.

Brown-Johnson, C.G. and Prochaska, J.J. (2015). Shame-based appeals in a tobacco control public health campaign: Potential harms and benefits. *Tobacco Control*, 24(5), 419.

Brumpton, H. and Sampath Kumar, U. (2018). Altria to marry pot with big tobacco in $1.8 billion Cronos deal. *Reuters*. Retrieved from www.reuters.com/article/us-cronos-group-m-a-altria-group/altria-to-marry-pot-with-big-tobacco-in-1-8-billion-cronos-deal-idUSKBN1O61BS.

Cahill, K., Stevens, S., Perera, R. and Lancaster, T. (2013). Pharmacological interventions for smoking cessation: An overview and network meta-analysis. *Cochrane Database of Systematic Reviews*, 5. doi:10.1002/14651858.CD009329.pub2.

Callard, C., Thompson, D. and Collishaw, N. (2005). Transforming the tobacco market: Why the supply of cigarettes should be transferred from for-profit corporations to non-profit enterprises with a public health mandate. *Tobacco Control*, 14(4), 278.

Cannabis Regulations. (2018). (SOR/2018–144) (2018).

Carson, K.V., Ameer, F., Sayehmiri, K., Hnin, K., van Agteren, J.E., Sayehmiri, F. and Smith, B.J. (2017). Mass media interventions for preventing smoking in young people. *Cochrane Database of Systematic Reviews*, 6. doi:10.1002/14651858.CD001006.pub3.

Caulkins, J.P., Kilmer, B. and Kleiman, M.A.R. (2016). *Marijuana legalization: What everyone needs to know* (2nd ed.). Oxford: Oxford University Press.

Chaiton, M., Diemert, L., Cohen, J.E., Bondy, S.J., Selby, P., Philipneri, A. and Schwartz, R. (2016). Estimating the number of quit attempts it takes to quit smoking successfully in a longitudinal cohort of smokers. *BMJ Open*, 6(6).

Chan, G.C.K., Leung, J., Quinn, C., Weier, M. and Hall, W. (2018). Socio-economic differentials in cannabis use trends in Australia. *Addiction,* 113(3), 454–461.

Chapman, S. (2012). The case for a smoker's license. *PLoS Medicine*, 9(11), e1001342.

Chapman, S. and Farrelly, M.C. (2011). Four arguments against the adult-rating of movies with smoking scenes. *PLoS Medicine*, 8(8), e1001078.

Chapman, S. and Freeman, B. (2008). Markers of the denormalisation of smoking and the tobacco industry. *Tobacco Control,* 17(1), 25.

Chung-Hall, J., Fong, G.T., Driezen, P., and Craig, L. (2018). Smokers' support for tobacco endgame measures in Canada: Findings from the 2016 International Tobacco Control Smoking and Vaping Survey. *CMAJ Open*, 6(3), E412–E422.

Coffey, C., Carlin, J.B., Lynskey, M., Li, N. and Patton, G.C. (2003). Adolescent precursors of cannabis dependence: Findings from the Victorian adolescent health cohort study. *British Journal of Psychiatry,* 182, 330–336.

Coffey, C. and Patton, G.C. (2016). Cannabis use in adolescence and young adulthood: A review of findings from the Victorian Adolescent Health Cohort Study. *Canadian Journal of Psychiatry*, 61(6), 318–327.

Convention Secretariat, WHO Framework Convention on Tobacco Control. (2009). *History of the World Health Organization Framework Convention on Tobacco Control.* Geneva, Switzerland: World Health Organization.

Courtemanche, C.J., Palmer, M.K. and Pesko, M.F. (2017). Influence of the flavored cigarette ban on adolescent tobacco use. *American Journal of Preventive Medicine*, 52(5), e139-e146.

Department of Health. (2018). *Principles that underpin the current policy and regulatory approach to electronic cigarettes (E-Cigarettes) in Australia.* Retrieved from https://www.health.gov.au/sites/default/files/documents/2019/12/policy-and-regulatory-approach-to-electronic-cigarettes-e-cigarettes-in-australia-principles-that-underpin-the-current-policy-and-regulatory-approach-to-electronic-cigarettes-e-cigarettes-in-australia.pdf.

Doetinchem, O. (2010). *Hypothecation of tax revenue for health. World Health Report. Background Paper, No 51.* Retrieved from Geneva, Switzerland: World Health organization. Retrieved from https://www.who.int/healthsystems/topics/financing/healthreport/51Hypothecation.pdf.

Donny, E.C., Denlinger, R.L., Tidey, J.W., Koopmeiners, J.S., Benowitz, N.L., Vandrey, R.G., Hatsukami, D.K. (2015). Randomized trial of reduced-nicotine standards for cigarettes. *The New England Journal of Medicine*, 373(14), 1340–1349.

Durkin, S., Brennan, E. and Wakefield, M. (2012). Mass media campaigns to promote smoking cessation among adults: An integrative review. *Tobacco Control,* 21(2), 127.

Edwards, R., Wilson, N., Peace, J., Weerasekera, D., Thomson, G.W. and Gifford, H. (2013). Support for a tobacco endgame and increased regulation of the tobacco industry among New Zealand smokers: Results from a National Survey. *Tobacco Control*, 22(e1), e86-e93.

EMCDDA. (2015). *Prevention of addictive behaviours* (Updated and expanded edition). Luxembourg: Publication Office of the European Union.

FDA. (2018, July 20). *Menthol and other flavors in tobacco products.* Retrieved from www.fda.gov/tobaccoproducts/labeling/productsingredientscomponents/ucm2019416.htm.

FDA. (2017, July 27). *FDA announces comprehensive regulatory plan to shift trajectory of tobacco-related disease, death: Agency to pursue lowering nicotine in cigarettes to non-addictive levels and create more predictability in tobacco regulation* [Press release]. Retrieved from www.fda.gov/NewsEvents/Newsroom/PressAnnouncements/ucm568923.htm.

Fischer, B., Russell, C., Sabioni, P., van den Brink, W., Le Foll, B., Hall, W. and Room, R. (2017). Lower-risk cannabis use guidelines: A comprehensive update of evidence and recommendations. *American Journal of Public Health,* 107(8), e1-e12.

Fong, G.T., Hammond, D., Laux, F.L., Zanna, M.P., Cummings, K.M., Borland, R. and Ross, H. (2004). The near-universal experience of regret among smokers in four countries: Findings from the international tobacco control policy evaluation survey. *Nicotine & Tobacco Research*, 6(Suppl 3), S341–351.

Freeman, B. (2012). New media and tobacco control. *Tobacco Control,* 21(2), 139.

Gallagher, A.W.A., Evans-Reeves, K.A., Hatchard, J.L. and Gilmore, A.B. (2019). Tobacco industry data on illicit tobacco trade: A systematic review of existing assessments. *Tobacco Control,* 28(3), 334–345.

Gartner, C. (2015). Mull it over: Cannabis vaporizers and harm reduction. *Addiction,* 110(11), 1709–1710.

Gartner, C. and Bromberg, M. (2019). One does not simply sell e-cigarettes in Australia: An overview of Australian e-cigarette regulations. In L. Gruszczynski (Ed.), *The regulation of e-cigarettes: International, European and national challenges* (pp. 249–279). Elgar Studies in Health and the Law. Cheltenham: Edward Elgar.

Gartner, C. and Hall, W. (2009). Smokeless tobacco use in Australia. *Drug and Alcohol Review,* 28(3), 284–291.

Gartner, C. and Hall, W. (2010). Harm reduction policies for tobacco users. *International Journal of Drug Policy,* 21(2), 129–130.

Gartner, C., Hall, W. and McNeill, A. (2010). Chapter 9: Harm reduction policies for tobacco. In T. Rhodes and D. Hedrich (Eds.), *Harm reduction: Evidence, impacts and challenges* (pp. 255–273). Lisbon: European Monitoring Centre for Drugs and Drug Addiction.

Gartner, C., Hall, W., Vos, T., Bertram, M., Wallace, A. and Lim, S. (2007). Assessment of Swedish snus for tobacco harm reduction: An epidemiological modelling study. *The Lancet,* 369(9578), 2010–2014.

Gates, P.J., Norberg, M.M., Copeland, J. and Digiusto, E. (2012). Randomized controlled trial of a novel cannabis use intervention delivered by telephone. *Addiction,* 107(12), 2149–2158.

Gov.uk. *Foreign travel advice: Thailand.* Retrieved from https://www.gov.uk/foreign-travel-advice/thailand/local-laws-and-customs.

Gunn, J.K.L., Rosales, C.B., Center, K.E., Nuñez, A., Gibson, S.J., Christ, C. and Ehiri, J.E. (2016). Prenatal exposure to cannabis and maternal and child health outcomes: A systematic review and meta-analysis. *BMJ Open,* 6(4).

Haines-Saah, R.J., Bell, K. and Dennis, S. (2015). A qualitative content analysis of cigarette health warning labels in Australia, Canada, the United Kingdom, and the United States. *American Journal of Public Health,* 105(2), e61-e69.

Hall, W. (2017). Alcohol and cannabis: Comparing their adverse health effects and regulatory regimes. *International Journal of Drug Policy,* 42, 57–62.

Hall, W. and Degenhardt, L. (2009). Adverse health effects of non-medical cannabis use. *The Lancet,* 374(9698), 1383–1391.

Hall, W. and Fischer, B. (2010). Chapter 8: Harm reduction policies for cannabis. In T. Rhodes and D. Hedrich (Eds.), *Harm reduction: Evidence, impacts and challenges* (pp. 235–252). Lisbon: European Monitoring Centre for Drugs and Drug Addiction.

Hall, W. and West, R. (2008). Thinking about the unthinkable: A de facto prohibition on smoked tobacco products. *Addiction,* 103(6), 873–874.

Hammond, D. (2011). Health warning messages on tobacco products: A review. *Tobacco Control,* 20(5), 327.

Health Canada. (2018, October 17). *Cannabis health warning messages.* Retrieved from www.canada.ca/en/health-canada/services/drugs-medication/cannabis/laws-regulations/regulations-support-cannabis-act/health-warning-messages.html.

Hefler, M. and Chapman, S. (2015). Disadvantaged youth and smoking in mature tobacco control contexts: A systematic review and synthesis of qualitative research. *Tobacco Control,* 24(5), 429.

Henriksen, L. (2012). Comprehensive tobacco marketing restrictions: Promotion, packaging, price and place. *Tobacco Control,* 21(2), 147–153.

Hoffman, E.W. (2016). Improving the future by looking to the past: An examination of Florida's "truth" anti-smoking campaign. *Florida Communication Journal,* 44(1), 49–59.

Hudak, J., Ramsey, G. and Walsh, J. (2018). *Uruguay's cannabis law: Pioneering a new paradigm.* Washington, D.C: The Brookings Institution. Retrieved from www.brookings.edu/research/uruguays-cannabis-law-pioneering-a-new-paradigm/.

Joossens, L. and Raw, M. (2000). How can cigarette smuggling be reduced? *British Medical Journal,* 321(7266), 947–950.

Kozlowski, L.T., Goldberg, M.E., Yost, B.A., White, E.L., Sweeney, C.T. and Pillitteri, J.L. (1998). Smokers' misperceptions of light and ultra-light cigarettes may keep them smoking. *American Journal of Preventive Medicine,* 15(1), 9–16.

Lancaster, T. and Stead, L. F. (2017). Individual behavioural counselling for smoking cessation. *Cochrane Database of Systematic Reviews,* 3. doi:10.1002/14651858.CD001292.pub3.

Leonardi-Bee, J., Nderi, M. and Britton, J. (2016). Smoking in movies and smoking initiation in adolescents: Systematic review and meta-analysis. *Addiction,* 111(10), 1750–1763.

Kilmer, B. (2017). *New developments in cannabis regulation.* Background paper commissioned by the EMCDDA for *Health and social responses to drug problems: A European guide.* Luxembourg: Publications Office of the European Union. Retrieved from http://www.emcdda.europa.eu/system/files/attachments/6232/EuropeanResponsesGuide2017_BackgroundPaper-Cannabis-policy_0.pdf.

Levy, D.T., Warner, K.E., Cummings, K.M., Hammond, D., Kuo, C., Fong, G.T., Borland, R. (2019). Examining the relationship of vaping to smoking initiation among US youth and young adults: A reality check. *Tobacco Control,* 28:629–635.

Lovato, C., Watts, A. and Stead, L.F. (2011). Impact of tobacco advertising and promotion on increasing adolescent smoking behaviours. *Cochrane Database of Systematic Reviews,* 10. doi:10.1002/14651858.CD003439.pub2.

Lupton, D. (2015). The pedagogy of disgust: The ethical, moral and political implications of using disgust in public health campaigns. *Critical Public Health,* 25(1), 4–14.

Marshall, K., Gowing, L., Ali, R. and Le Foll, B. (2014). Pharmacotherapies for cannabis dependence. *Cochrane Database of Systematic Reviews,* 12. doi:10.1002/14651858.CD008940.pub2.

McDaniel, P.A., Smith, E.A. and Malone, R.E. (2016). The tobacco endgame: A qualitative review and synthesis. *Tobacco Control*, 25(5), 594.

McGinty, E.E., Niederdeppe, J., Heley, K. and Barry, C.L. (2017). Public perceptions of arguments supporting and opposing recreational marijuana legalization. *Preventive Medicine,* 99, 80–86.

McNeill, A. and Munafò, M.R. (2013). Reducing harm from tobacco use. *Journal of Psychopharmacology*, 27(1), 13–18.

Megginson, W.L. and Netter, J.M. (2001). From state to market: A survey of empirical studies on privatization. *Journal of Economic Literature*, 39(2), 321–389.

Ministry of Health. (2010). Smoke-free Environments Act 1990, Pub. L. No. 108. Retrieved from http://www.legislation.govt.nz/act/public/1990/0108/latest/whole.html.

Ministry of Health. (2016). *Vaping and smokeless tobacco*. Retrieved from www.health.govt.nz/our-work/preventative-health-wellness/tobacco-control/vaping-smokeless-including-heated-tobacco.

Monte, A.A., Zane, R.D. and Heard, K.J. (2015). The implications of marijuana legalization in Colorado. *JAMA*, 313(3), 241–242.

Morain, S.R., Winickoff, J.P. and Mello, M.M. (2016). Have tobacco 21 laws come of age? *New England Journal of Medicine,* 374(17), 1601–1604.

National Academies of Science, Engineering and Medicine. (2018). *Public health consequences of e-cigarettes*. Washington, DC: National Academies Press.

Pacula, R.L., Kilmer, B., Wagenaar, A.C., Chaloupka, F.J. and Caulkins, J.P. (2014). Developing public health regulations for marijuana: Lessons from alcohol and tobacco. *American Journal of Public Health*, 104(6), 1021–1028.

Pardo, B. (2014). Cannabis policy reforms in the Americas: A comparative analysis of Colorado, Washington, and Uruguay. *International Journal of Drug Policy*, 25(4), 727–735.

Peto, R., Darby, S., Deo, H., Silcocks, P., Whitley, E. and Doll, R. (2000). Smoking, smoking cessation, and lung cancer in the UK since 1950: Combination of national statistics with two case-control studies. *British Medical Journal,* 321(7257), 323–329.

Popovici, I. and French, M.T. (2014). Cannabis use, employment, and income: Fixed-effects analysis of panel data. *The Journal of Behavioral Health Services & Research,* 41(2), 185–202.

Proctor, R.N. (2012). The history of the discovery of the cigarette–lung cancer link: Evidentiary traditions, corporate denial, global toll. *Tobacco Control*, 21(2), 87.

Proctor, R.N. (2013). Why ban the sale of cigarettes? The case for abolition. *Tobacco Control*, 22(Suppl. 1), i27.

Richards, J.R., Smith, N.E. and Moulin, A.K. (2017). Unintentional cannabis ingestion in children: A systematic review. *The Journal of Pediatrics,* 190, 142–152.

Russell, M. (1976). Low-tar medium-nicotine cigarettes: A new approach to safer smoking. *British Medical Journal, 1(6023*), 1430–1433.

Saar, I. (2018). The effects of the lower ignition propensity cigarettes standard in Estonia: Time-series analysis. *Injury Prevention*, 24(1), 29.

Sangalang, A., Volinsky, A.C., Liu, J., Yang, Q., Lee, S.J., Gibson, L.A. and Hornik, R.C. (2019). Identifying potential campaign themes to prevent youth initiation of E-cigarettes. *American Journal of Preventive Medicine,* 56(2, Suppl. 1), S65-S75.

Smart, R., Caulkins, J.P., Kilmer, B., Davenport, S. and Midgette, G. (2017). Variation in cannabis potency and prices in a newly legal market: Evidence from 30 million cannabis sales in Washington State. *Addiction*, 112(12), 2167–2177.

Stead, L.F. and Lancaster, T. (2005). Interventions for preventing tobacco sales to minors. *Cochrane Database of Systematic Reviews*, 1. doi:10.1002/14651858.CD001497.pub2.

Stepanov, I. and Hatsukami, D. (2016). Call to establish constituent standards for smokeless tobacco products. *Tobacco Regulatory Science*, 2(1), 9–30.

Stephens, W.E. (2018). Comparing the cancer potencies of emissions from vapourised nicotine products including e-cigarettes with those of tobacco smoke. *Tobacco Control*, 27(1), 10–17.

Stinson, F.S., Ruan, W.J., Pickering, R. and Grant, B.F. (2006). Cannabis use disorders in the USA: Prevalence, correlates and co-morbidity. *Psychological Medicine,* 36(10), 1447–1460.

Subritzky, T., Pettigrew, S. and Lenton, S. (2016). Issues in the implementation and evolution of the commercial recreational cannabis market in Colorado. *International Journal of Drug Policy,* 27, 1–12.

Subritzky, T., Pettigrew, S. and Lenton, S. (2017). Into the void: Regulating pesticide use in Colorado's commercial cannabis markets. *International Journal of Drug Policy,* 42, 86–96.

Sweanor, D., Ballin, S., Corcoran, R.D., Davis, A., Deasy, K., Ferrence, R.G. and Wasserman, J. (1992). Report of the tobacco policy research study group on tobacco pricing and taxation in the United States. *Tobacco Control,* 1(Suppl. 1), S31.

Thomson, G.W., Wilson, N.A., O'Dea, D., Reid, P.J. and Howden-Chapman, P. (2002). Tobacco spending and children in low income households. *Tobacco Control,* 11(4), 372.

Tobacco Advisory Group of the Royal College of Physicians. (2016). *Nicotine without smoke – Tobacco harm reduction.* London: Royal College of Physicians.

U.S. National Cancer Institute and World Health Organization. (2016). *The economics of tobacco and tobacco control. National Cancer Institute Tobacco Control Monograph 21. NIH Publication No. 16-CA-8029A.* Bethesda, MD and Geneva, CH: US Department of Health and Human Services, National Institutes of Health, National Cancer Institute; World Health Organization.

Wakefield, M. and Giovino, G. (2003). Teen penalties for tobacco possession, use, and purchase: Evidence and issues. *Tobacco Control,* 12(Suppl. 1), i6.

Warner, K.E. (2000). The economics of tobacco: Myths and realities. *Tobacco Control,* 9(1), 78–89.

Washington State Liquor and Cannabis Board. (2015). *Board to increase number of retail marijuana stores following analysis of marketplace* (Press release). Retrieved from https://lcb.wa.gov/pressreleases/lcb-to-increase-number-of-retail-mj-stores.

White, V., Tan, N., Wakefield, M. and Hill, D. (2003). Do adult focused anti-smoking campaigns have an impact on adolescents? The case of the Australian National Tobacco Campaign. *Tobacco Control*, 12(Suppl. 2), ii23.

WHO FCTC Conference of the Parties. (2010). *Guidelines for implementation of Article 14: Guidelines on demand reduction measures concerning tobacco dependence and cessation.* Geneva: World Health Organization.

Wilson, N., Thomson, G.W., Edwards, R. and Blakely, T. (2013). Potential advantages and disadvantages of an endgame strategy: A "sinking lid" on tobacco supply. *Tobacco Control*, 22(Suppl. 1), i18.

Wolfson, M. (2017). *The fight against big tobacco: The movement, the state and the public's health*. London: Routledge.

World Health Organization. (2005). *Framework Convention on Tobacco Control*. Geneva: World Health Organization.

World Health Organization. (2010). *WHO technical manual on tobacco tax administration*. Geneva: World Health Organization.

World Health Organization. (2013). *Protocol to eliminate illicit trade in tobacco products*. Geneva: World Health Organization.

World Health Organization. (2015). *WHO report on the global tobacco epidemic, 2015: Raising taxes on tobacco*. Geneva, Switzerland: World Health Organization. Retrieved from: https://www.who.int/tobacco/global_report/2015/en/.

Zeller, M. (2019). Evolving "the real cost" campaign to address the rising epidemic of youth e-cigarette use. *American Journal of Preventive Medicine*, 56(2, Suppl. 1), S76-S78.

11 How *not* to legalize cannabis

Lessons from New Zealand's experiment with regulating "legal highs"

Marta Rychert and Chris Wilkins

Introduction

New Psychoactive Substances (NPS), sometimes also known as "legal highs," are recreational drugs *not* controlled under the international drug control system but which "*may* pose a public health threat" (UNODC, 2013). Since 2009, over 800 different NPS compounds have been reported internationally (UNODC, 2018), well surpassing the number of illegal drugs controlled under the United Nations drug conventions. NPS belong to diverse chemical families, including synthetic cannabinoids (e.g. JWH-200, AB-FUBINACA), synthetic cathinones (e.g. alpha-PVP), piperazines (e.g. mCPP) and synthetic opioids (e.g. acetylfentanyl). They are often manufactured in China and India and shipped to consumer countries where they are marketed as "legal alternatives" to illegal drugs. The emergence of NPS has challenged international and national drug control systems over the last decade (Brandt, King and Evans-Brown, 2014).

Overwhelmingly, the response to the influx of NPS has been to prohibit the sale of these compounds, either by adding them to the lists of prohibited substances in national drug laws, or by imposing bans on broad categories of substances defined by their similarity to already scheduled drugs (generic and analogue approaches) (King, 2013). However, scheduling requires time and financial resources as substances have to be assessed for harmfulness and prohibition orders need to pass through legislative assemblies. By the time a given compound is prohibited, a new synthetic substance will be developed and will appear on the market, illustrating the so-called "cat and mouse game" between NPS producers and national authorities (Brandt et al., 2014; Seddon, 2014). A number of countries, including Ireland, Poland, Romania, the United Kingdom and Australia, have responded by imposing so-called "blanket bans" on sale of any psychoactive products (Barratt, Seear and Lancaster, 2017; Hughes and Griffiths, 2014; Stevens, Fortson, Measham and Sumnall, 2015). These prohibitive responses have been criticized for restricting the use of NPS in legitimate industries and research (Kavanagh and Power, 2014), and for creating practical challenges with policing (Malczewski, 2015) and issues around the legal definition of "psychoactivity" (Reuter and Pardo, 2017; Stevens et al., 2015).

In contrast to the prohibitive approaches developed in other countries, the New Zealand Government decided to develop a regulatory approach to NPS (Wilkins, Sheridan, Adams, Russell, Ram and Newcombe, 2013). Between 2005 and 2008, so-called "party pills" containing benzylpiperazines (BZP) were allowed to be sold legally under the "Restricted Substances Regime" (RSR), a new drug classification established under the existing Misuse of Drugs Act 1975. In July 2013, five years after ending the regulated market for BZP, the New Zealand Parliament passed the Psychoactive Substances Act (PSA) 2013, the world's first comprehensive pre-market approval regime for NPS. Under the PSA, product sponsors can legally manufacture and sell recreational drugs containing NPS, provided they can prove through toxicology and clinical trials that the products pose no more than a "low risk" to consumers' health (New Zealand Parliament, 2013b). This novel approach received considerable international attention as a "long-term" (UN, 2013), balanced (EMCDDA, 2015), and "bold and innovative" response (UK NPS Expert Review Panel, 2014).

However, both the BZP "party pills" regime and the synthetic cannabinoid market, which operated under the interim PSA provisions, failed to endure. In May 2013, an amendment to the Psychoactive Substances Act prohibited the use of evidence from animal testing in product approval applications, setting a prohibitively high bar for approval of any "legal high" product in the foreseeable future. As a result, there are currently no NPS products on legal sale in New Zealand, and indeed no applications for approval of an NPS have ever been made. This chapter analyzes the New Zealand attempts to regulate the legal high market and discusses implications for emerging regimes for recreational cannabis.

Policy context: New Zealand drug market and the new drugs phenomenon

New Zealand, an island nation in the South Pacific populated by 4.5 million people, is separated from its neighbor Australia by some 1,500 km of the Tasman Sea. Its geographical isolation has long influenced the traditional illegal drug markets, with drugs that need to be smuggled from other countries, such as cocaine, MDMA and heroin, of uncertain quality and high price (Wilkins, Prasad, Wong and Rychert, 2015). Locally produced drugs, primarily cannabis and methamphetamine, are much more widely available. As in other Western countries, cannabis has been the most widely used illegal drug for many decades, with the latest general population survey reporting 11.6 percent of adults (defined as 15 and over) used cannabis in the last year (Ministry of Health, 2017). The use, possession and supply of cannabis is prohibited. The situation with methamphetamine is distinctive, with prevalence rates high by international standards (i.e. 0.8 percent last year use in the general population, see Ministry of Health, 2017). The scarcity and high price of drug types like MDMA contribute to the demand for alternative synthetic stimulants and hallucinogens.

Around 2000, New Zealand entrepreneur Matt Bowden developed a range of products containing the synthetic stimulants benzylpiperazine (BZP) and trifluoromethylphenylpiperazine (TFMPP) (Wilkins and Sweetsur, 2010). Bowden, previously addicted to methamphetamine, presented his product as a lower risk, safer alternative to methamphetamine (Kerr and Davis, 2011). His company and lobby group Stargate International (STAR standing for Social Tonics Advocacy and Research) started marketing BZP "party pills" on a commercial scale, with much of the manufacturing happening in India and China thanks to the unregulated status of BZP internationally (Szalavitz, 2015). BZP "party pills" rapidly grew in popularity as a new recreational "legal high" product. It is estimated that by 2004, approximately five million legal BZP/TFMPP party pills had been produced, generating sales of 24 million New Zealand Dollars (NZD) per year (Wilkins and Sweetsur, 2010). STANZ (Social Tonics Association of New Zealand), a new party pills industry association, developed a voluntary "Code of Practice" covering aspects such as the quality and dosages of BZP products (including maximum strength), labelling and packaging (including the warning "do not consume with alcohol") and retail sales, but attempts at industry self-regulation were not effective at reducing the potency of products and related harms (Wilkins and Sweetsur, 2010). Consequently, there were calls for a government response to address the growing popularity of BZP and uncertainties around potential health impacts.

Restricted Substances Regime (RSR): market regulation that didn't happen

In 2004, following an evaluation of BZP safety, the Expert Advisory Committee on Drugs (EACD) concluded that existing evidence of BZP-related health harms was insufficient to make an informed scheduling decision (EACD, 2004). While further government-commissioned research was being undertaken, the EACD recommended adoption of some form of government control over the existing BZP market.

In 2005, a new regime for substances assessed by the government to be "low risk" was established by an amendment to the Misuse of Drugs Act. The so-called "Restricted Substances Regime" (RSR) imposed broad market regulations, including an age limit on sales (i.e. 18 years or older), restrictions on advertising in major media, and bans on the giving away of free samples as part of promotional activities (Sheridan and Butler, 2010). BZP was immediately included in the new schedule (New Zealand Parliament, 2005). The BZP industry continued commercial sales of their products under this limited regulatory scheme. It is estimated that in 2007/2008, at the height of BZP's popularity, the industry was selling 200,000 party pills per month, with a product range of around 80 to 120 brands (Wilkins et al., 2013). More detailed government regulations for the RSR were intended, including product quality standards and maximum dose limits, but there were significant delays in their release. The industry responded to the lack of progress with regulation by commissioning a public law firm to draft regulations (STANZ, 2007b) and a *Code of Good Manufacturing Practice* (STANZ, 2007a), which were subsequently submitted to the government (STANZ, 2007c). In 2008, based on new evidence of BZP-related health harms, including from previously commissioned government research (Thompson, Williams, Aldington, Williams, Caldwell, Dickson, and Beasley, 2006), BZP was rescheduled as a Class C drug and prohibited under the Misuse of Drugs Act, thereby removing it from the RSR regime. No other substance was scheduled under the RSR and the regime was ultimately abandoned in 2013.

The industry responded to the ban on BZP by shifting production to non-BZP party pills and synthetic cannabinoids, which were not controlled by any legislation (Wilkins et al., 2013). Synthetic cannabinoids became increasingly popular after 2010 and, similarly to BZP products, were sold from convenience stores without any regulatory restrictions. Again, little was known about their health impacts and the speed of government response was limited due to the slowness of assessment and scheduling processes. Despite attempts to ban several synthetic cannabinoid compounds via temporary orders, the market continued to expand with replacement compounds. In early 2013, the Ministry of Health (MOH) estimated that approximately 200–300 psychoactive products were being sold from around 3,000–4,000 retail outlets in New Zealand (MOH, 2014e).

Psychoactive Substances Act (PSA): a promise of comprehensive legal control

The ongoing problems with controlling NPS came to the attention of the New Zealand Law Commission (NZLC) in 2011, as part of their independent review of the country's Misuse of Drugs Act. The Law Commission recommended the development of a new pre-market approval regulatory regime requiring producers of NPS products to demonstrate the safety of their products before they are permitted to be sold on the legal market (rather than the government having to prove that the products are unsafe in order to remove products from the market). Forty-five recommendations on how the new pre-market approval regime should operate were included in the final NZLC report, including restrictions on retail sale and advertising (NZLC, 2011).

The Psychoactive Substances Act (PSA) was passed in July 2013 with nearly unanimous cross-party support in parliament (119 in favor and 1 vote against the legislation) (New Zealand Parliament, 2013a). Under this regime, developers of NPS products can receive government approval to legally manufacture, import and sell their products, provided they can prove through pre-clinical and clinical trials that their products cause no more than a "low risk" of harm to their consumers (Wilkins, 2014a). The importation, manufacture, supply and possession of any other "unapproved" NPS is prohibited by default (Rychert and Wilkins, 2016b).

Requirements for testing the safety of psychoactive products resemble the pre-market approval regime for medicines and are modelled on pharmaceuticals standards developed by the International Council for Harmonization of Technical Requirements for Pharmaceuticals for Human Use (ICH). This means that scientific evidence from a series of toxicology and clinical trials are required for each product application (PSRA, 2014a). The approval is granted for each separate product *formulation* (not *substance*), and thus the strength of the product cannot be modified once approval is granted. The New Zealand Ministry of Health have estimated that the cost of testing is likely to be 1–2 million NZD per product (MOH, 2013a). The product application fee is set at 175,000 NZD per product. While this might seem like a lot of money, returns from the market are likely to compensate the initial expenses. Estimated annual retail sales from a regulated synthetic cannabis market during the "interim phase" of the PSA implementation reached 140 million NZD (MOH, 2014e).

The retail framework for the regime is broadly modelled on regulations for tobacco and alcohol. Approved recreational products are allowed to be legally sold from specialized licensed retail outlets. No food or alcohol can be sold from the same premises, and the PSA explicitly bans the sale of products from supermarkets, petrol stations, local convenience stores or alcohol retail outlets. Retail sales are only allowed to customers 18 years of age and over (which matches the legal drinking age in New Zealand). Further restrictions on location of licensed retailers, including minimum distance from "sensitive sites" such as schools, sports fields or churches, can be imposed by local councils. Advertising is limited to the "point of sale" only (i.e. no advertising in television, radio, or newspapers) and must be limited to objective information about the product, such as active ingredients and the price. The PSA specifically prohibits advertising which conveys a message that an approved product is "safe." While online sale of products is allowed, it can only be done through websites established specifically for this purpose (but not other internet platforms, including social media websites). Packaging for NPS products must include a list of ingredients, health warnings, contact details of the manufacturer and the telephone number of the National Poisons Centre (New Zealand Parliament, 2013b).

The Psychoactive Substances Regulatory Authority (PSRA), a new government agency established within the Ministry of Health, is tasked with overseeing implementation of the PSA. The PSRA has the ability to revoke any product approval if, after introducing the product to the market, reports about adverse effects emerge and the product is no longer considered to be "low risk."

Issues with implementing the PSA during the "interim regime"

When the PSA was passed in July 2013, much of the regulatory framework required for the regime to become fully operational had yet to be completed, including the required safety testing standards for product approval. While these regulations were being developed by the PSRA, the so-called "interim regime" was established as a transitional regime. This allowed a limited number of products available on the market before passage of the PSA to continue to be sold subject to new retail and advertising restrictions until the full regime and related regulations were finalized (which was projected to happen by the end of 2013). The interim regime was deemed necessary to avoid the creation of a black market, which could have emerged if all existing products had been immediately taken off the market (New Zealand Parliament, 2013a).

Forty-seven products received interim approvals, 40 of which were synthetic cannabinoid smoking blends containing compounds such as AB-FUBINACA, PB-22, CL-2201, or SGT-24 (Wilkins, 2014b). These products did not pass any safety tests but were deemed to be low risk as they complied with interim approval criteria, i.e. they had been on the market for at least three months before the PSA and there were no adverse effect notifications against them (New Zealand Parliament, 2013a, 2013b). One-hundred and fifty-two specialized retailers were licensed to sell the "interim approved" products, a 95 percent reduction in the number of outlets selling NPS products compared to pre-PSA when an estimated 3,000–4,000 unlicensed shops, mostly local convenience stores, sold NPS products.

Managing the market during the interim stage of PSA implementation proved challenging (see implementation timeline, Figure 11.1). The interim PSA regime operated for ten months until the Government brought it to an abrupt end in May 2014, following reports of social disruption around retail stores and health risks from products (MOH, 2014e). Research on the PSA legislation and interim regime identified a range of issues including with identifying and monitoring interim approved products (Rychert, Wilkins and Witten, 2017), regulating the retail environment (Rychert and Wilkins, 2016a; Rychert, Wilkins and Witten, 2018), developing detailed regulations for the full PSA regime, and communicating the policy to the public and key stakeholders (Rychert and Wilkins, 2018b).

Identifying and monitoring interim approved products

The products allowed to be sold on the interim PSA market turned out to be problematic, with ongoing reports of health harms and dependency issues (Rychert et al., 2017). Some of the compounds used in the interim approved products were particularly potent synthetic cannabinoids compared to THC in natural cannabis (Hermanns-Clausen, Kneisel, Szabo and Auwärter, 2013; Wilkins, 2014b), and have subsequently been banned in other countries (e.g. AB-FUBINACA, PB-22, PB-22–5F, 5F-ADBICA) (China Food and Drug Administration, 2015; Drug Enforcement Administration Department of Justice, 2014; German Federal Narcotics Act, 2014). A number of New Zealand studies have retrospectively identified serious health harms related to products approved for the interim regime (Glue, Courts, Gray and Patterson,

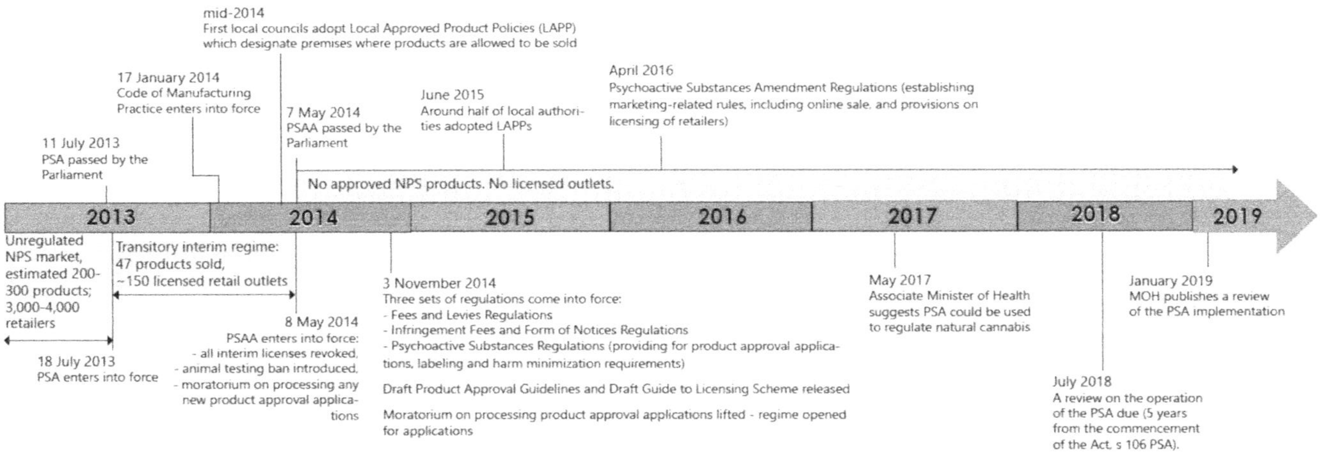

Figure 11.1 PSA implementation timeline (Update of the timeline originally published in Rychert and Wilkins (2015a)).

2016; Glue, Courts, MacDonald, Gale and Mason, 2015; Macfarlane and Christie, 2015; Wilkins, Prasad, Wong, Graydon-Guy and Rychert, 2016). The approval of high-potency synthetic cannabinoids in the interim market meant that lower-strength and potentially "safer" products were not commercially viable (Rychert et al., 2017). Some commentators have suggested that the legal criteria for interim approvals were too lenient and there were issues in applying the criteria in practice, i.e. interim approvals relied on data about adverse events from specific products, which was largely not available at the time the interim PSA regime was established (Rychert et al., 2017). Issues with harmfulness were exacerbated by the lack of manufacturing controls during the interim regime. The *Code of Manufacturing Practice* was finalized by the PSRA and came into force only in January 2014, i.e. six months into the interim regime (MOH, 2014d), meaning that for most of the interim regime, there was no specific mechanism for monitoring manufacturing standards. The introduction of the new standards in the *Manufacturing Code* resulted in the suspension of all ten interim licenses to manufacture products (MOH, 2014e).

The system for monitoring product safety was not fully developed at the time the interim regulated market was established, and hence the process for removing interim approved products that caused harms lacked speed and efficiency (Rychert et al., 2017). The framework to assess the risks of interim products was developed and released two months after the PSA was enacted (MOH, 2013b). The system relied on anonymous telephone calls from the public to the free "Drug and Alcohol Helpline" and National Poisons Centre, reports sent by medical professionals to the Pharmacovigilance Centre, and reports made by a subset of hospital emergency units (MOH, 2013b). However, health professionals appeared to be unaware of the reporting system, raising concerns about under-reporting of adverse events from the approved products (Rychert et al., 2017). The existing system for recording hospital admissions in New Zealand (International System of Classification of Diseases (ICD)) did not integrate well into the product monitoring system as it does not include codes specific to synthetic cannabinoids (let alone specific products) and the coding was not applied consistently across different district health boards (Rychert et al., 2017). In retrospect, drug community services and NGOs expressed concerns that the system was complex and confusing for consumers and their families. Eleven products were withdrawn from the market during the interim regime: five in January 2014 (Wilkins, 2014b) and six in May 2014 (MOH, 2014a) (i.e. a mere week before the interim regime was ended).

Controlling interim retail sales

Challenges were identified with monitoring the compliance of interim licensed retailers under the new PSA framework, including the age restrictions on purchase (i.e. 18 years+) (Rychert et al., 2018). Other problematic retail behaviors included the operation of shops during late night and early morning hours (as there are no legal rules on retail hours under the PSA), and the price discounting of products (driven by market competition). Some commentators claim that the reduction in the number of retail outlets under the interim regime (i.e. down from 3,000–4,000 convenience stores to 150 licensed outlets) concentrated a large number of customers at licensed shops (the so-called "bottleneck effect"), which then increased the visibility of outlets and related social nuisance such as queuing, begging and intoxication (Rychert et al., 2018). Targeting young and low-income customers was among the business strategies adopted by some industry actors in response to market competition (Rychert and Wilkins, 2016a). There have also been reports that some retailers used price-cutting as a strategy to attract customers (Rychert and Wilkins, 2016a) and offered to sell products on credit to customers awaiting social welfare payments (Rychert et al., 2018). The PSA does not include any special price control provisions (e.g. excise tax or minimum pricing). Although it was acknowledged that an excise tax should be applied, policymakers indicated they were reluctant to do so due to the technical difficulties of choosing an appropriate level of tax without knowledge of how the new market would develop, and agreed to revisit the issue in the future (New Zealand Parliament, 2013a).

Under the PSA, local government authorities are granted powers to limit the operation of retail outlets in their district via so-called Local Approved Product Policies (LAPP). LAPPs can include rules about the density of retail outlets and define a minimum distance that retail outlets are required to be from sensitive sites, such as schools, churches or drug treatment facilities (i.e. typically 500 meters). However, there were significant delays in developing these policies; by the end of the interim regime, only 5 out of 71 local councils had developed a LAPP (Anderson, 2014). Stakeholders from local councils explained that delays were caused by not having the financial resources to develop these policies and conduct related public consultations, and by general community opposition to the regime. They also expressed resentment about the lack of local body-specific consultation when the regime was being developed (Rychert et al., 2018). Some councils demonstrated their opposition by implementing LAPPs that severely restricted the operation of retail outlets in their districts. For example, the LAPP developed in Hamilton included bus stops as "sensitive sites," as they are places where children gather, and this severely reduced the number of places where retail outlets could be located. The industry lobby group challenged the Hamilton LAPP in court (*The Star Trust v Hamilton City Council*, 2016) but the case was dropped after the ending of the interim regime.

Public communications and regulatory workload

Increasing public opposition to the interim PSA regime emerged in response to the opening of retail outlets in local neighborhoods and the ongoing reports of adverse effects from products. Public opposition may have been exacerbated by a lack of clear communication about the aims of the PSA early in the policy process. For example, during parliamentary debates on the PSA, one politician *supported* the PSA in the hope "it will send them (the industry) out of business"

(New Zealand Parliament, 2013a). In public announcements, restrictive regulatory measures were emphasized, perhaps adding to the misunderstanding about the PSA among the general public (Rychert and Wilkins, 2018b). For example, 7 out of 72 written submissions from the general public expressed their support for the PSA under the mistaken understanding that it intended to impose a ban on all legal highs (Rychert and Wilkins, 2018a). Some commentators linked public opposition to the "bottleneck effect" which increased visibility of licensed retailers, and in turn, attracted negative media attention. Indeed, media reporting during the interim regime has been described as "biased" and "sensational," with a focus on negative stories featuring drug dependency and public nuisance (Rychert et al., 2018).

The public backlash and related media interest added to the workload of the PSRA. Stakeholders directly involved in the regulatory regime described how their day-to-day work focused on managing the regime, including responding to legal challenges from the industry (when an individual product or license was revoked) and responding to media queries, leaving little time to work on regulations for the full PSA framework (Rychert et al., 2018). Finalizing the product testing regime was originally projected to take no more than six months and be completed by the end of 2013 (MOH, 2014e). However, the *Draft Product Approval Guidelines* were not actually released until November 2014 (i.e. six months after the ending of the interim regime). The *Code of Manufacturing Practice* was the only regulatory instrument developed for the full PSA regime that entered into force during the interim regime (January 17, 2014) (MOH, 2014d). Stakeholders directly involved in the regime believed that resource limitations at the PSRA, and an underestimation of the scale of the regulatory work required, were the reasons for these delays (Rychert et al., 2018).

Psychoactive Substances Amendment Act 2014: policy U-turn

Issues with products, retail outlets and the public backlash, in combination with political pressure created by the impending general election (scheduled for September 2014), resulted in an abrupt end to the interim regime (Rychert and Wilkins, 2018b). In May 2014, the government passed an amendment to the PSA which revoked all interim product approvals and interim retail licenses. The amendment was passed under urgency, without public consultation or a Select Committee process.

While the ending of the interim regime has been widely viewed as a setback, a potentially more fatal impact of this amendment was the decision to ban the use of evidence from animal tests (including tests conducted overseas) (New Zealand Parliament, 2014a; PSRA, 2014a) in future product approval applications (Bell, 2015; Schep, Gee, Tingle, Galea and Newcombe, 2014). The animal testing ban followed public protests against the harming of animals for the purpose of testing products with no therapeutic effect (Ministry of Health, 2014; New Zealand Parliament, 2014a). The issue of testing psychoactive products on animals had been raised during the initial public consultation process in early 2013, but the Select

Committee considered it "not relevant to the purpose of the Bill" and oral submissions regarding animal testing were not heard (New Zealand Health Committee, 2013). As originally enacted, the PSA allowed animal testing only in instances where there was no *in vitro* alternative. The legislation did not contain any limitation on the animal species allowed to be used for product testing. This led to widespread concerns about the possibility of testing NPS products on companion animals, such as "beagle dogs," and this concern was manifested in public marches and petitions throughout 2013 and into 2014 (MOH, 2014e; New Zealand Anti-Vivisection Society, 2014; New Zealand Parliament, 2014a).

After the amendment, the work on regulations continued, and in November 2014, the regime was open to receive and assess product applications under the newly released Psychoactive Substances Regulations 2014 and related *Product Approval Testing Guidelines* (MOH, 2014c; PSRA, 2014a). No product applications have been received to date (as of February 2019), with the ban on the use of animals for the testing of products identified as a major challenge to obtaining the necessary evidence for regulatory approval (Rychert and Wilkins, 2015a, 2015b; Schep et al. and, 2014; Wilkins and Rychert, 2017). The Psychoactive Substances Regulatory Authority (PSRA) has gone so far as to state that "it is unlikely that a product can be shown to pose no more than a low risk of harm without the use of animal testing," suggesting the PSA is now unworkable (PSRA, 2014a).

Implications for other countries: how *not* to legalize cannabis?

Despite two attempts to regulate the market for "legal highs," there are currently no recreational NPS products allowed for sale in New Zealand. The troubled implementation of the Restricted Substances Regime and the Psychoactive Substances Act provides lessons for other countries which may be contemplating regulating recreational drugs, including natural cannabis. Indeed, there are many similarities to designing and implementing cannabis legislation as illustrated in Table 11.1.

Unrealistic time frames and insufficient planning

Perhaps the biggest lesson is that significant time and planning are required to develop a comprehensive and detailed regulatory framework for a recreational drug. The implementation of regulations on the quality and safety of BZP products under the Restricted Substances Regime took over two years (by which time BZP had already been prohibited under Schedule C of the Misuse of Drugs Act). Finalization of the product testing framework for the PSA took one and a half years, instead of the anticipated six months, by which time the PSA had effectively been made unworkable by an amendment to prohibit the use of evidence from animal testing. After the abrupt ending of the interim PSA regime in May 2014, one New Zealand official gave the advice to "keep

Table 11.1 Comparison of selected issues in the design and implementation of legal and regulatory responses to recreational drugs in NZ, Colorado, Washington and Uruguay

		"Low risk" psychoactive products regime	*Recreational cannabis regimes*		
		NZ	*Colorado*	*Washington*	*Uruguay*
Organizational and legal context	Level of law	National law PSA 2013	State constitution (art. 18, s. 16) (conflict with federal law)	State law (conflict with federal law)	National law Ley 19.172
	Government agency	PSRA (MOH)	Marijuana Enforcement Division (Department of Revenue)	State Liquor and Cannabis Board	Institute for the Control and Regulation of Cannabis (IRCA)
Policy content (from legal access channels)	Legal access channels	Licensed retailers	Licensed retailers, Home-growing for private use (up to 6 plants, 3 in flower)	Licensed retailers	Licensed pharmacies, Home growing for private use (up to 6 plants) Registered clubs
	Licensing	- Products - Retailers-Manufacturing-Import - Research	- Retailers - Cultivators - Manufacturers - Testing facilities	- Retailers - Producers and processors (i.e. cultivating and manufacturing)	- Retailers (i.e. pharmacies) - Cultivating - Manufacturing - Club members (users)
	Price control measures	GST only (general sales tax)	15% excise tax on sale from cultivator to retailer; 15% sales tax	37% cannabis excise tax	"Variable fee" (prices set by IRCA)
	Education and prevention provisions	No mention of prevention and education specific to the use of approved products in NZ laws	Colorado Revised Statute (§ 25-3.5-1001 through 25-3.5-1007) requires implementation of education, public awareness and prevention messages for retail cannabis	Initiative 502 (part 4, s. 28) and Revised Code of Washington (CW 69.50.540) require establishment of cannabis prevention and public health programs	Ley 19.172 (art. 9) requires cannabis education to be integrated into public education system

Table 11.1 continued

		"Low risk" psychoactive products regime	*Recreational cannabis regimes*		
		NZ	*Colorado*	*Washington*	*Uruguay*
Policy content	User and sale restrictions	R18, sale limits ("no more than 2 products at a time" – Psychoactive Substances Regulations 2014)	R21, purchase and possession limits (up to 1 oz (28.5 g))	R21, purchase and possession limits (up to 1 oz (28.5 g))	R18, registered in national database (must be citizen or resident for min. 2 years), monthly limits on purchase 1.4 oz (40 g)
	Delegation of power to local authorities	Yes – Local Approved Products Policies can restrict location of licensed retailers	Yes – local authorities may enact regulations on time, place, manner, number of retailers in their localities (s. 16, point 5)	Not in the main law But Attorney General Opinion confirmed cities and counties can ban retailers	No
	Advertising	Regulated, allowed at "point of sale" but prohibited in mainstream media	Regulated, e.g. no advertising on TV and radio unless reliable evidence that no more than 30% audience is under 21 (Permanent Rules Related to the Colorado Retail Marijuana Code)	Regulated, e.g. max. 2 signs identifying licensed retail outlet (Washington Administrative Code WAC 314-55-155)	All forms of advertising, direct and indirect, prohibited (art. 11 Ley 19.172)

continued

		"Low risk" psychoactive products regime	*Recreational cannabis regimes*		
		NZ	*Colorado*	*Washington*	*Uruguay*
Policy process	Who initiated policy change?	Parliament	Citizen initiative ("Amendment 64")	Citizen initiative ("Initiative 502")	Parliament
	Legislative process	Shorter Select Committee (May 2013)	Standard	Standard	Standard
	Public support at the time of change	Unknown (from analysis of public submissions from individual citizens: 50% support, 32% oppose)	55% support, 45% oppose	56% support, 44% oppose	Opinion polls: ~30% support, ~60% oppose, 5–10% don't know
	How long from the law to the first shop?	Same day (July 2013)	1 year 2 months (Nov 2012–Jan 2014)	1 year 8 months (Nov 2012–Jul 2014)	8 months – home growers; 10 months – clubs; pharmacies – 3 years 7 months (Dec 2013–July 2017)
	Major political changes during implementation?	Associate Minister of Health Peter Dunne out of office between June 2013 and January 2014	No mention in academic literature	No mention in academic literature	President José Mujica stepped down from office March 2015
	Major challenges	Animal testing ban	Product quality and testing (purity, potency), monitoring impacts, industry influence	Product quality and testing (purity, potency), monitoring impacts, industry influence	Supply at pharmacies; reluctance to register as a user; opposition from pharmacists

Compiled through legal research, review of academic literature and policy documents (Colorado Department of Revenue, 2013; Cruz, Queirolo and Boidi, 2016; EMCDDA, 2016; Hall and Lynskey, 2016; Roffman, 2016; Room, 2014; Rychert and Wilkins, 2015b; Subritzky, Pettigrew and Lenton, 2017; Walsh and Ramsey, 2015) transitional provisions short, if at all" (Hannah, 2014), illustrating the challenges with managing the market *and* developing regulations for the full regime at the same time. Investing time in planning and setting realistic implementation time frames *before* the cannabis law reform actually takes effect may help secure a more predictable and stable implementation process.

Inadequate financial and personnel resources

The design and implementation of a new regulated drug market requires significant resources, including financial, staff and organizational assets. Under the Psychoactive Substances Act, a range of fees and levies have been imposed on the legal high industry, including a product application fee of 175,000 NZD (MOH, 2014b), to cover the direct and indirect costs of managing the regime (s. 90–97 PSA) (PSRA, 2014b). However, these high fees were not required for interim product approvals, resulting in underfunding of the PSRA during the interim regime. The limited number of personnel and their relative lack of experience with drug policy issues were identified as challenges during the implementation of the PSA (Rychert et al., 2018).

One lesson for jurisdictions interested in regulating legal recreational cannabis is to secure a budget and people with relevant expertise to develop the required regulatory frameworks. Some commentators have suggested that effective health-focused regulation can be achieved by "choosing an aggressive regulatory agency" to manage the new cannabis markets (Caulkins, 2016); for example, an agency located within the portfolio of health rather than government revenue. While this may be true for some jurisdictions, based on the New Zealand experience, it is fair to conclude that relevant expertise and stringent regulations should not be taken for granted based only on the assumed culture of the government agency.

Not covering the basics: prices and availability

Evidence from tobacco and alcohol identifies price control (product taxes and minimum prices) and availability restrictions as some of the most powerful regulatory tools to control consumption and related harm (Babor, Caetano, Casswell, Edwards, Giesbrecht and Graham, 2010). Yet, there were no special price control mechanisms under the Restricted Substances Regime and the Psychoactive Substances Act (i.e. either excise tax or minimum pricing), which may have contributed to the declining prices of legal high products over the years, and the "price wars" between retailers. The lack of regulation of retail opening hours meant consumers were able to purchase legal highs when alcohol stores were required to close, an outcome described by communities as "ridiculous" (Rychert et al., 2018). On the other hand, restrictions on the number and location of retail outlets during the interim PSA regime meant large numbers of buyers were concentrated at each retail outlet (known as the "bottleneck effect"), increasing the visibility of the shops, related neighborhood disruption and ultimately attracting negative media attention.

In the context of cannabis regulation, there has been extensive policy debate about price control options, e.g. what tax rate to apply and what the tax base for these products should be (i.e. weight of a drug sold, value of a drug or a "unit of intoxication," such as THC) (Caulkins and Kilmer, 2016). Technical difficulties should not discourage regulators from imposing a price control mechanism which can be adjusted later if needed. With regard to controlling the number of retail outlets, the New Zealand experience shows that careful consideration needs to be given to meeting current demand with adequate supply, without encouraging an expansion of demand via a proliferation of outlets and availability.

Without risk management and a vigilance plan

While the Restricted Substances Regime simply allowed the legal sale of BZP products without detailed regulations on product safety, the Psychoactive Substances Act provided a much more sophisticated framework for assessment and monitoring of products, even during the interim stage of implementation. Under the interim PSA, regulation focused on specific products rather than generic substances, which improved regulatory control. Product formulations could not be changed once regulatory approval had been granted. The introduction of a new product with the same ingredients but higher potency would require a separate regulatory approval. If anything, the legal cannabis regimes to date have been less focused on the safety of product *types*, and consequently have been surprised by the emergence of cannabis-infused products and concentrates with high health risks (Subritzky, Pettigrew and Lenton, 2016). Adopting a product-based regulatory regime for cannabis, including maximum limits on THC content, could be one possible solution to addressing the proliferation of high-potency cannabis. An alternative approach might be to set a maximum potency limit for all cannabis products.

The New Zealand experience also highlights the need for an advanced system for monitoring adverse events from legal recreational products, including integration of existing data collection systems. The challenge is to set up a system that is highly responsive and able to remove unsafe products from the market as quickly as possible.

Without stakeholders and public on board

The New Zealand experience also highlights the importance of effective communication with the public and relevant stakeholders involved in the development and implementation of a new regulatory regime (including medical professionals, community representative groups, other government agencies, local government bodies and any other professional groups that may be relevant in cannabis law reform, e.g. pharmacists). Stakeholders should be informed about their potential role in the new regime and allowed time to provide feedback and disseminate knowledge among their peers.

The analysis of the PSA implementation process suggests that some aspects of the implementation process (e.g. monitoring harms from interim approved products; development of LAPPs) could have been improved with more extensive stakeholder consultation and communication. On the other hand, some issues raised in the consultation process (e.g. testing the products on animals; the need to control product price via a dedicated excise tax) were simply ignored by policymakers. The subsequent re-surfacing of these issues during the implementation process suggests that more careful consideration of stakeholder feedback may have improved the implementation process.

The extent of public support for the drug law reform is another important factor to consider (Cruz, Queirolo and Boidi, 2016). One lesson for emerging cannabis regimes is to probe public opinion about the proposed policy change and facilitate an honest debate about cannabis regulation in the media. In New Zealand, findings from media opinion polls indicate that public support for the PSA regime declined towards the end of the interim regime (Smith, 2014). This may reflect the potential for public revision of support for drug law reform once people are faced with the reality of retail outlets and legal products. This indicates a need for ongoing monitoring of public support as reforms are implemented.

With industry influence (versus input)

The role of the legal high industry in the process of developing the Restricted Substances Regime and the Psychoactive Substances Act was not always clear and transparent, leaving questions about their influence on the final shape of the laws and regulations. Given that the legal high industry freely admitted they were actively lobbying for policy change to a regulated market approach (Rychert and Wilkins, 2016a) and had a clear monetary interest in industry-friendly regulation, greater transparency in interactions with government officials would have been desirable.

In the context of emerging cannabis regimes, establishing clear rules around engagement and consultation between government officials and commercial cannabis industry actors could prevent problems with industry influence. One possible approach is to adopt rules similar to those set in the Framework Convention on Tobacco Control (Article 5.3), under which the industry is excluded from the policymaking processes (WHO, 2008). While input from the regulated industry cannot be avoided at times (especially when highly technical aspects of regulation are considered), legislation should guard against commercial influence on laws and regulations.

Without prevention and education campaigns

Neither the Restricted Substances Regime nor the Psychoactive Substances Act regime addressed the need to educate the public concerning the health risks of approved legal high products. Public health education was limited to the health warning on product packaging and advice volunteered by the retail staff.

Although existing evidence of the effectiveness of education and prevention campaigns in the area of alcohol and other drug use remains limited (with little overall effect of such campaigns on long-term patterns of use and harm, high costs compared to alternative policy interventions such as taxes and retail zoning and only a *modest* effect of some community-based interventions see Babor et al., 2010), we argue that public education alongside price control and other availability control strategies would be worthwhile in contributing to a wider public health approach. Education campaigns are also a useful mechanism for engaging with the public, something that was lacking during the legal high policy process in New Zealand. Public education may be particularly important for cannabis (as opposed to alcohol) because its newly legal status may mean that many new users are not familiar with likely effects. To secure effective implementation of such a campaign, the public agency and external partners responsible for education should be clearly identified and funding secured (e.g. as a percentage of product tax or other industry fees).

Without a "plan B"

With adequate planning, resourcing, stakeholder engagement and regulatory controls, the chances are that setbacks along the cannabis law reform pathway can be minimized. Yet, as the New Zealand experience with the regulation of "legal highs" shows, it is difficult to predict how the market, consumers and communities will respond to a new legal drug market. Consequently, devising contingency plans (e.g. imposing further restrictions on sales; removing suspicious products from the market; engaging in targeted media campaigns) may be needed if a "worst case" scenario materializes. From a policy perspective, measured responses are preferable to a complete overhaul of policy (such as happened with the PSA amendment in New Zealand), as the latter is likely to undermine the credibility of drug reform in general.

Concluding remarks

This chapter aimed to analyze the troubled implementation of regulatory regimes for "legal highs" in New Zealand and draw lessons for other countries considering regulatory approaches to cannabis. We have shown that both the Restricted Substances Regime and the interim Psychoactive Substances Act market suffered from insufficient regulation on pricing, availability and product safety. Insufficient planning, resourcing and limited engagement with key stakeholders during the policy development and implementation stages were identified as factors in the problems experienced during the implementation process. Industry influence on regulation-making was also identified as problematic, reflecting the need to establish clear legal rules for engagement between government and commercial actors during the drug law reform process.

Perhaps the biggest lesson for emerging cannabis regimes is to take a considered approach to drug law reform, both in terms of legislating adequate and detailed market controls and adopting a cautious policy process with wide stakeholder consultation, public communication and buy-in and adequate planning. Given the issues with managing numerous products and the potential for significant commercialization, a cautious approach to opening up a new recreational cannabis market is recommended. This could be achieved by regulating the number and types of different cannabis products allowed on the legal market, and their potency. A case-by-case approval process for products rather than generic compounds, modelled on the PSA provisions, could be adopted to provide greater regulatory control over retail markets.

The above suggestion illustrates that there were some positive elements in the way "legal highs" were regulated in New Zealand. Overall, the Restricted Substances Regime and subsequently the Psychoactive Substances Act moved towards more comprehensive regulation of the market. Some commentators even suggested that the interim regime was ended prematurely, as responsible officials were just starting to get control of the numerous challenges related to monitoring the products and enforcing the law around retailers (MOH, 2014e; Rychert et al., 2017).

As of early 2019, progress with the PSA has been stalled by the ban on animal testing included in the May 2014 amendment, which has effectively prohibited all existing products and prevented any new product applications. This has not escaped the attention of some commentators who argue the PSA is essentially "prohibition under the guise of reform" (Buchanan, 2016). This view illustrates how prohibitively high regulatory standards can undermine the credibility and legitimacy of drug reform laws. Meanwhile, a new coalition government in New Zealand has signaled its interest in drug policy reform, with a national referendum on cannabis law reform to be conducted at the next general election in 2020 (Walls and Cheng, 2018). Although some have previously suggested that the PSA could be used to regulate legal recreational cannabis products in New Zealand (New Zealand Herald, 2017), the government is now developing new cannabis-specific legislation. The learnings from the problematic implementation of RSR and PSA will continue to be relevant for this new process.

Acknowledgments

The analysis in this chapter was supported by the Marsden Fund Council managed by New Zealand Royal Society Te Apārangi (MFP-MAU1813).

References

Anderson, L. (2014, April 26). Opponents beg for ban on "legal poison". *Rotorua Daily Post*. Retrieved from www.nzherald.co.nz/rotorua-daily-post/news/article.cfm?c_id=1503438&objectid=11244489.

Babor, T., Caetano, R., Casswell, S., Edwards, G., Giesbrecht, N. and Graham, K. (2010). *Alcohol: No ordinary commodity – Research and public policy* (2nd ed). Oxford, UK: Oxford University Press.

Barratt, M.J., Seear, K. and Lancaster, K. (2017). A critical examination of the definition of "psychoactive effect" in Australian drug legislation. *International Journal of Drug Policy,* 40, 16–25.

Bell, R. (2015). War on drugs: The Kiwi comedown has lessons for all new scientist. *New Scientist (Vol. 3003).* Retrieved from www.newscientist.com/article/mg22530030.200-war-on-drugs-the-kiwi-comedown-has-lessons-for-all.html#.VLL3HtKUfAl.

Brandt, S., King, L. and Evans-Brown, M. (2014). The new drug phenomenon. *Drug Testing and Analysis,* 6(7–8), 587–597.

Buchanan, J. (2016, April 26). Whatever happened to New Zealand's lauded drug regulation? *Volteface.* Retrieved from http://volteface.me/features/what-ever-happened-to-new-zealands-much-hailed-drug-regulation/.

Caulkins, J. (2016). *Legalising drugs prudently: The importance of incentives and values.* Retrieved from www.lse.ac.uk/IDEAS/publications/reports/pdf/LSE-IDEAS-After-the-Drug-Wars.pdf.

Caulkins, J. and Kilmer, B. (2016). Considering marijuana legalization carefully: Insights for other jurisdictions from analysis for Vermont. *Addiction,* 111(12), 2082–2089.

China Food and Drug Administration. (2015). Retrieved from www.sfda.gov.cn/WS01/CL0056/130753.html.

Colorado Department of Revenue. (2013). *Permanent rules related to the Colorado retail marijuana code.* Retrieved from www.colorado.gov/pacific/sites/default/files/Retail%20Marijuana%20Rules,%20Adopted%20090913,%20Effective%20101513%5B1%5D_0.pdf.

Cruz, J. M., Queirolo, R. and Boidi, M. F. (2016). Determinants of public support for marijuana legalization in Uruguay, the United States, and El Salvador. *Journal of Drug Issues,* 46(4), 308–325.

Drug Enforcement Administration Department of Justice. (2014). Schedules of controlled substances: Temporary placement of four synthetic cannabinoids into Schedule I. Final order. *Federal Register,* 79(27), 7577–7582.

EACD. (2004). *The Expert Advisory Committee on Drugs (EACD) advice to the minister on: Benzylpiperazine (BZP).* Wellington.

EMCDDA. (2015). *Perspectives on drugs: Legal approaches to controlling New Psychoactive Substances.* Retrieved from www.emcdda.europa.eu/topics/pods/controlling-new-psychoactive-substances.

EMCDDA. (2016). *Models for the legal supply of cannabis: Recent developments. Perspectives on drugs.* Retrieved from www.emcdda.europa.eu/system/files/publications/2720/Legal%20supply%20cannabis_update%202016.pdf.

German Federal Narcotics Act. (2014). Retrieved from www.gesetze-im-internet.de/btmg_1981/anlage_ii.html.

Glue, P., Courts, J., Gray, A. and Patterson, T. (2016). Influence of law changes affecting synthetic cannabinoid availability and frequency of hospital presentations: 4-year national survey. *New Zealand Medical Journal,* 129(1433), 37–40.

Glue, P., Courts, J., MacDonald, M., Gale, C. and Mason, E. (2015). Implementation of the 2013 psychoactive substances act and mental health harms from synthetic cannabinoids. *New Zealand Medical Journal,* 128(1414), 15–18.

Hall, W. and Lynskey, M. (2016). Evaluating the public health impacts of legalizing recreational cannabis use in the United States. *Addiction,* 111(10), 1764–1773.

Hannah, D. (2014). *The new psychoactive substances regime in New Zealand: A different approach to regulation.* Retrieved from http://iport.dronet.org/com/filedownloadlink/allegatoQ.php?key=7329.

Hermanns-Clausen, M., Kneisel, S., Szabo, B. and Auwärter, V. (2013). Acute toxicity due to the confirmed consumption of synthetic cannabinoids: Clinical and laboratory findings. *Addiction,* 108(3), 534–544.

Hughes, B. and Griffiths, P. (2014). Regulatory approaches to New Psychoactive Substances (NPS) in the European Union (Commentary). *Addiction,* 109(10), 1591–1593.

Kavanagh, P. and Power, J. (2014). New psychoactive substances legislation in Ireland – Perspectives from academia. *Drug Testing and Analysis,* 6(7–8), 884–891.

Kerr, J.R. and Davis, L.S. (2011). Benzylpiperazine in New Zealand: Brief history and current implications. *Journal of the Royal Society of New Zealand,* 41(1), 155–164.

King, L.A. (2013). Legal classification of novel psychoactive substances: An international comparison. In P. Dargan and D. Wood (Eds.), *Novel psychoactive substances: Classification, pharmacology and toxicology* (pp. 3–27). London: Academic Press.

Macfarlane, V. and Christie, G. (2015). Synthetic cannabinoid withdrawal: A new demand on detoxification services. *Drug and Alcohol Review,* 34(2), 147–153.

Malczewski, A. (2015). "Doapalcze" A.D. 2014 – Nowe otwarcie. *Remedium,* 1(263), 24–25.

Ministry of Health. (2014). *Regulatory impact statement: Amendment to the Psychoactive Substances Act 2013.* Retrieved from www.health.govt.nz/about-ministry/legislation-and-regulation/regulatory-impact-statements/amendment-psychoactive-substance-act-2013.

Ministry of Health. (2017). *New Zealand health survey. Annual data explorer (updated December 2017).* Retrieved from www.health.govt.nz/publication/annual-update-key-results-2016-17-new-zealand-health-survey.

MOH. (2013a). *Regulatory impact statement – New regulatory regime for psychoactive substances.* Retrieved from www.health.govt.nz/about-ministry/legislation-and-regulation/regulatory-impact-statements/new-regulatory-regime-psychoactive-substances.

MOH. (2013b). *Safety assessment of psychoactive products.* Retrieved from www.health.govt.nz/system/files/documents/pages/safety-assessment-psychoactive-products-v3.pdf.

MOH. (2014a). *Interim approvals revoked* (recall notice). Retrieved from www.legal-highs.co.nz/synthetic-cannabis/six-synthetic-cannabis-products-removed-from-shelves-early/2014.

MOH. (2014b). *Psychoactive Substances (Fees and Levies) Regulations 2014.* Retrieved from www.legislation.govt.nz/regulation/public/2014/0244/latest/whole.html%20-%20contents.

MOH. (2014c). *Psychoactive Substances Regulations 2014.* Retrieved from www.legislation.govt.nz/regulation/public/2014/0243/latest/DLM6203143.html?search=qs_act%40bill%40regulation%40deemedreg_psychoactive+substances+regulations_resel_25_h&p=1&sr=1.

MOH. (2014d). *Psychoactive substances: Code of Manufacturing Practice.* Retrieved from www.health.govt.nz/system/files/documents/publications/psychoactive-substances-code-of-manufacturing-practice-nov14-v2.pdf.

MOH. (2014e). *Regulatory impact statement: Amendment to the Psychoactive Substances Act 2013.* Retrieved from www.health.govt.nz/about-ministry/legislation-and-regulation/regulatory-impact-statements/amendment-psychoactive-substance-act-2013.

New Zealand Anti-Vivisection Society. (2014). *No animal testing of legal highs allowed.* Retrieved from www.leaveanimalsout.org.nz.
New Zealand Health Committee. (2013). *Psychoactive Substances Bill as reported from the Health Committee.* Retrieved from www.parliament.nz/resource/en-nz/50DBSCH_SCR5885_1/4b810f91d964aa258387391f8a2ec84ab2d70092.
New Zealand Herald. (2017). Associate Health Minister Peter Dunne wants cannabis, other class C drugs tested and sold by licenced manufacturers. *New Zealand Herald.* Retrieved from www.nzherald.co.nz/nz/news/article.cfm?c_id=1&objectid=11864545.
New Zealand Parliament. (2005). *Misuse of Drugs Amendment Act 2005. Public Act 2005 No 81, date of assent 21 June 2005.* Retrieved from www.legislation.govt.nz/act/public/2005/0081/latest/DLM356224.html.
New Zealand Parliament. (2013a). *Psychoactive Substances Bill — First reading, second reading, in committee, third reading: Hansard (debates).* Retrieved from www.parliament.nz/en/pb/bills-and-laws/bills-proposed-laws/document/00DBHOH_BILL12021_1/psychoactive-substances-bill.
New Zealand Parliament. (2013b). *Psychoactive Substances Act 2013. Public Act 2013, No 53.* Retrieved from www.legislation.govt.nz/act/public/2013/0053/20.0/DLM5042921.html.
New Zealand Parliament. (2014a). *Psychoactive Substances Amendment Bill — First reading, second reading, in committee, third reading.* Retrieved from www.parliament.nz/en-nz/pb/debates/debates/50HansD_20140506_00000936/psychoactive-substances-amendment-bill-—-first-reading.
NZLC. (2011). *Controlling and regulating drugs. A review of the Misuse of Drugs Act 1975* (No. 122). Wellington, New Zealand: New Zealand Law Commission.
PSRA. (2014a). *Draft Psychoactive Substances Product Approval Guidelines (November 2014).* Retrieved from http://psychoactives.health.govt.nz/industry/guidelines-and-application-forms.
PSRA. (2014b). *Psychoactive Substances Regulations: A consultation document.* Wellington: Ministry of Health. Retrieved from www.health.govt.nz/system/files/documents/publications/psychoactive-substances-regulations-consultation-feb14-v2.pdf.
Reuter, P. and Pardo, B. (2017). Can new psychoactive substances be regulated effectively? An assessment of the British Psychoactive Substances Bill. *Addiction,* 112(1), 25–31.
Roffman, R. (2016). Legalization of cannabis in Washington State: How is it going? *Addiction,* 111(7), 1139–1140.
Room, R. (2014). Legalizing a market for cannabis for pleasure: Colorado, Washington, Uruguay and beyond. *Addiction,* 109(3), 345–351.
Rychert, M. and Wilkins, C. (2015a). The challenge of a ban on animal testing for the development of a regulated legal market for New Psychoactive Substances (NPS) ("legal highs") in New Zealand: Issues and options for resolution. *International Journal of Drug Policy,* 26(12), 1273–1278.
Rychert, M. and Wilkins, C. (2015b). Is the recent ban on animal testing of legal high products a fatal blow to the development of a legal market for "low-risk" psychoactive products in New Zealand? *Addiction,* 110(4), 713–714.
Rychert, M. and Wilkins, C. (2016a). Legal high industry business and lobbying strategies under a legal market for New Psychoactive Substances (NPS, "legal highs") in New Zealand. *International Journal of Drug Policy,* 37, 90–97.

Rychert, M. and Wilkins, C. (2016b). What products are considered psychoactive under New Zealand's legal market for New Psychoactive Substances (NPS, "legal highs")? Implications for law enforcement and penalties. *Drug Testing and Analysis,* 8(8), 768–778.

Rychert, M. and Wilkins, C. (2018a). A critical analysis of the implementation of a legal regulated market for new psychoactive substances ("legal highs") in New Zealand. *International Journal of Drug Policy,* 55, 88–94.

Rychert, M. and Wilkins, C. (2018b). Understanding the development of a regulated market approach to New Psychoactive Substances (NPS) in New Zealand using Punctuated Equilibrium Theory. *Addiction,* 113(11), 2132–2139.

Rychert, M., Wilkins, C. and Witten, K. (2017). Issues with monitoring the safety of psychoactive products under a legal regulated market for New Psychoactive Substances (NPS) ("legal highs") in New Zealand. *Drug and Alcohol Review,* 36(5), 589–596.

Rychert, M., Wilkins, C. and Witten, K. (2018). "Lost in translation": Issues with the establishment of a legal market for "low risk" psychoactive products ("legal highs") in New Zealand. *Drugs: Education, Prevention and Policy,* 25(3), 254–261.

Schep, L., Gee, P., Tingle, M., Galea, S. and Newcombe, D. (2014). Regulating new psychoactive drugs: Innovation leading to compromise. *British Medical Journal,* 349, g5085.

Seddon, T. (2014). Drug policy and global regulatory capitalism: The case of New Psychoactive Substances (NPS). *International Journal of Drug Policy,* 25(5), 1019–1024.

Sheridan, J. and Butler, R. (2010). "They're legal so they're safe, right?" What did the legal status of BZP-party pills mean to young people in New Zealand? *International Journal of Drug Policy,* 21(1), 77–81.

Smith, N. (2014). *Subscriber-only poll results: Is the government right to ban all legal highs?* Retrieved from www.nbr.co.nz/article/subscriber-only-poll-result-government-right-ban-all-legal-highs-ns-p-155379.

STANZ. (2007a). *Code of good manufacturing practice for restricted substances.* Retrieved from www.webcitation.org/6hyccRWIW.

STANZ. (2007b). *Proposed restricted substances regulations.* Retrieved from https://web.archive.org/web/20070716013451/www.stanz.org.nz/proposed%20regs_001.pdf.

STANZ. (2007c). *STANZ offers full safety code for party pills.* Retrieved from www.webcitation.org/6hyf5Pvpg.

Stevens, A., Fortson, R., Measham, F. and Sumnall, H. (2015). Legally flawed, scientifically problematic, potentially harmful: The UK psychoactive substances bill. *International Journal of Drug Policy,* 26, 1167–1170.

Subritzky, T., Pettigrew, S. and Lenton, S. (2016). Issues in the implementation and evolution of the commercial recreational cannabis market in Colorado. *International Journal of Drug Policy,* 27, 1–12.

Subritzky, T., Pettigrew, S. and Lenton, S. (2017). Into the void: Regulating pesticide use in Colorado's commercial cannabis markets. *International Journal of Drug Policy,* 42, 86–96.

Szalavitz, M. (2015). *The drug lord with a social mission.* Retrieved from www.psmag.com/health-and-behavior/the-drug-lord-with-a-social-mission-also-performs-under-the-alter-ego-starboy.

The Star Trust v Hamilton City Council. (2016). NZHC 821.

Thompson, I., Williams, G., Aldington, A., Williams, M., Caldwell, B., Dickson, S. and Beasley, R. (2006). *The benzylpiperazine (BZP)/trifluoromethylphenylpiperazine*

(TFMPP) and alcohol safety study. Report for the Ministry of Health. Retrieved from www.health.govt.nz/system/files/documents/publications/bzp-report-08.pdf.
UK NPS Expert Review Panel. (2014). *New psychoactive substances review. Report of the Expert Panel.* Retrieved from www.gov.uk/government/uploads/system/uploads/attachment_data/file/368583/NPSexpertReviewPanelReport.pdf. Archived by Web Cite® at www.webcitation.org/6VXQmAGNd.
UN. (2013). *Report from expert consultation on New Psychoactive Substances, Vienna.* Commission on Narcotic Drugs. Retrieved from www.unodc.org/documents/commissions/CND/CND_Sessions/CND_57/E-CN7-2014-CRP01_V1400178_E.pdf.
UNODC. (2013). *The challenge of new psychoactive substances. A report from the global SMART programme.* Retrieved from www.unodc.org/documents/scientific/NPS_2013_SMART.pdf.
UNODC. (2018). *World drug report 2018.* United Nations Office on Drugs and Crime. Retrieved from www.unodc.org/wdr2018/.
Walls, J. and Cheng, D. (2018). Justice Minister confirms recreational cannabis referendum at 2020 election. *New Zealand Herald.* Retrieved from www.nzherald.co.nz/nz/news/article.cfm?c_id=1&objectid=12178729.
Walsh, J. and Ramsey, G. (2015). *Uruguay's drug policy, major innovation, major challenges.* Retrieved from www.wola.org/publications/uruguay_s_drug_policy_major_innovations_major_challenges.
WHO. (2008). *Guidelines for implementation of Article 5.3 of the WHO Framework Convention on Tobacco Control.* Retrieved from www.who.int/fctc/guidelines/article_5_3.pdf.
Wilkins, C. (2014a). A critical first assessment of the new pre-market approval regime for New Psychoactive Substances (NPS) in New Zealand. *Addiction,* 109(10), 1580–1586.
Wilkins, C. (2014b). The interim regulated legal market for NPS ("legal high") products in New Zealand: The impact of new retail restrictions and product licensing. *Drug Testing and Analysis,* 6, 868–875.
Wilkins, C., Prasad, J., Wong, K., Graydon-Guy, T. and Rychert, M. (2016). An exploratory study of the health harms and utilisation of health services of frequent legal high users under the interim regulated legal high market in central Auckland. *New Zealand Medical Journal,* 129(1431), 51–58.
Wilkins, C., Prasad, J., Wong, K. and Rychert, M. (2015). *Recent trends in illegal drug use in New Zealand 2006–2013: Findings from the 2006, 2007, 2008, 2009, 2010, 2011, 2012 and 2013 Illegal Drug Monitoring System (IDMS).* Auckland: SHORE & Whāriki Research Centre, Massey University. Retrieved from www.massey.ac.nz/massey/learning/departments/centres-research/shore/projects/illicit-drug-monitoring-system.cfm.
Wilkins, C. and Rychert, M. (2017). Recent developments with the New Zealand regulated market approach to "low-risk" psychoactive products. *Addiction,* 112(1), 34–36.
Wilkins, C., Sheridan, J., Adams, P., Russell, B., Ram, S. and Newcombe, D. (2013). The new psychoactive substances regime in New Zealand: A different approach to regulation. *Journal of Psychopharmacology,* 27(7), 584–589.
Wilkins, C. and Sweetsur, P. (2010). Differences in harm from legal BZP/TFMPP party pills between North Island and South Island users in New Zealand: A case of effective industry self-regulation? *International Journal of Drug Policy,* 21(1), 86–90.

Part IV

Earlier innovations in cannabis law reform

12 Coffeeshops in the Netherlands

Regulating the front door and the back door

Dirk J. Korf

Introduction

Although cannabis is an illegal drug in the Netherlands, marijuana and hashish are openly sold in so-called "coffeeshops" – thereby probably representing the widest known example of Dutch drug policy. Originally, these coffeeshops were café-like places, where users could buy and use small amounts of cannabis. In general, this is still the case, although today some coffeeshops function more as a takeaway store where one can buy, but not use cannabis.

Selling cannabis in coffeeshops is condoned, but not without strict regulations. Coffeeshops sell cannabis to consumers from their "front door," but of course this is only possible when the shops are supplied. The supply of coffeeshops is commonly known in the Netherlands as the "back door," even though in reality, both suppliers and customers use the same door to enter the coffeeshop. While the Dutch policy of tolerance does not apply to the back door, this problem has been ignored for many years. In recent years however, fueled mainly by worries about organized crime and local order problems related to domestic cannabis cultivation, this inconsistency has become a major issue in the national debate on cannabis policy, not in the least because of pleas by local authorities for policy reform, in particular to regulate the back door and to establish a closed legal circuit from cannabis cultivation to selling to consumers in coffeeshops.

Cannabis criminalization and decriminalization

In the Netherlands, the first statutory provisions on illicit drugs were enacted in 1919, in the *Opiumwet* (Opium Act), but they were confined to opiates and cocaine. The import and export of cannabis was introduced into the Opium Act in 1928, because this had been made obligatory by the Geneva Convention of 1925.[1] Not until 1953 did hemp products come to receive the same treatment as opiates and cocaine; possession, manufacture and sale became criminal offenses. Additional changes made to the Opium Act in 1956 reduced the definition of hemp to include only the dried tops of the plant.[2] Statutory decriminalization of cannabis (i.e. use, possession for personal use and sale of up to 30 grams for personal use) took place in 1976. De facto decriminalization, however, set in somewhat earlier.

Prior to the Second World War, cannabis use had scarcely been heard of in the Netherlands, and this did not change much in the early post-war years. The 1950s can be seen as the introductory phase of cannabis in the Netherlands, when marihuana was used by small groups of jazz musicians and other artists who had learned to use it while abroad, as well as foreign seamen and German-based US military personnel, in particular in Amsterdam (Cohen, 1975; de Kort and Korf, 1992; de Kort, 1995). In the course of the 1960s, cannabis use in the Netherlands rapidly gained popularity. An increasing number of adolescents began smoking it, but not until the end of the decade was a users' subculture in evidence. Cannabis spread still further in the wake of the hippie movement. Smoking hash at the national monument in Dam Square or in the Vondelpark in Amsterdam became a must for a burgeoning international youth "counterculture" (Leuw, 1973).

In 1969, the Netherlands ratified the UN Single Convention of 1961. In the first debate in the Dutch Parliament in 1963 on ratification, it had been concluded that the Single Convention gave the national legislature every freedom to set only those punishments pertaining to narcotic drugs which it deemed appropriate.[3] During this parliamentary debate, a representative of the Social Democratic Party was already questioning whether cannabis should be defined as an illicit drug in all cases. Legalization of cannabis was frequently brought up during the parliamentary debates leading up to the revision of the Opium Act in 1976. As the Single Convention did not appear to allow legalization, a compromise between prohibition and legalization seemed the only available route. The revised Opium Act for the first time drew a distinction between "drugs presenting unacceptable risks," such as heroin, cocaine, amphetamines and LSD (Schedule I) and "hemp products" (Schedule II); moreover, it differentiated the related criminal offenses and the penalties they carried. The old law had provided only one general penalty for all intentional trafficking in, or possession of, any prohibited drug: up to four years imprisonment, or six months in jail for unintentional acts. In 1976, penalties relating to cannabis were reduced to a lower level than those for Schedule I drugs. The possession of hashish or marijuana up to 30 grams was reduced from a serious to a petty offense, carrying a maximum sentence of one month's imprisonment. This differentiation between "soft" and "hard" drugs was based on the concept that the use of different illicit drugs entails differential risks. It was believed that undifferentiated criminalization of all drug users and drug dealers would bring cannabis users into contact with hard drugs more readily. Differentiating between soft and hard drugs was intended to separate the respective drug markets and thus reduce this risk.

There were two major reasons for the statutory decriminalization of cannabis in 1976: the advent of heroin and the increasing use of cannabis, which brought with it a de-stigmatization of cannabis use. Although opiate addiction was not unknown prior to the early 1970s, it had been considered chiefly a problem of renegade doctors and nurses, other morphinists and a small group of elderly Chinese opium smokers. The introduction of heroin, and especially the use of it by young people taking it intravenously, confronted legal authorities, the medical profession and social workers with a wholly new phenomenon. Combating the further spread of heroin obviously demanded a much higher priority than concerns about drugs which were far less dangerous – as seen by members of these various professions – such as hashish and marijuana. Initially, hashish and marijuana had been rated as extremely dangerous. After many years of defining users as criminals, authorities began redefining the use of these substances as a symptom of psychiatric or psychological pathology. Gradually, they were further destigmatized to a symptom of social pathology. The focus began shifting away from the individual user as a delinquent or patient. Cannabis use came to be perceived as nonconformist behavior, a collective protest of a new subculture against dominant social structures. The final step was the redefinition of cannabis use as recreational behavior (Leuw, 1972).

From underground market to coffeeshops

With regard to the cannabis retail market in the Netherlands until the mid-1990s, three phases can be distinguished (Korf, 1995; Korf, 2002). During the first stage (1960s and early 1970s) the Dutch cannabis retail market was a predominantly *underground* market. Cannabis was bought and consumed in a subcultural environment, which became known as a youth counterculture.

The second stage was ushered in when Dutch authorities began to tolerate so-called *house dealers* in youth centers. Experiments with this approach were formalized in the statutory decriminalization in the revised Opium Act of 1976. Official national *Guidelines for Investigation and Prosecution* came into force in 1979.[4] A general prosecution of cannabis offenses was believed to not serve the public interest, but to stigmatize many young people and socially isolate them from society. According to the national guidelines, the retail sale of cannabis to consumers was tolerated when the house dealer met the so-called AHOJ criteria: no overt advertising (*Affichering*), no Hard drugs, no nuisance (*Overlast*), no underage clientele (*Jongeren*); and later AHOJ-G criteria, no large quantities (*Grote hoeveelheden*). The small-scale dealing of cannabis was thus an offense from a legal viewpoint, but under certain conditions it was not prosecuted. It is important to acknowledge that the second stage was initiated *before* and became most visible *after* the Opium Act was revised in 1976 (the AHOJ criteria were made official in 1979). By the end of the 1970s, the house dealer had become a formidable competitor of the street dealer.

In the third stage, hashish and marijuana were sold predominantly in *coffeeshops*.[5] Although the Dutch government never intended this development, through case law it was decided that coffeeshops were to be tolerated according to the same criteria as house dealers. During the 1980s, coffeeshops captured a bigger and bigger share of the Dutch retail cannabis market (Jansen, 1991).

Rethinking the "Dutch model"

The revised Opium Act of 1976 – and more generally Dutch drug policy since the 1970s – was based on the central notion that the drug problem is primarily a public health and welfare issue and that risk reduction is its core concept (Leuw and Haen Marshall, 1994). However, in the course of the 1990s, the perspective gradually shifted towards repression and the control element came to play a role in Dutch drug policy almost equal to the health element (Blom, 2006). Several factors played a role in this shift. In terms of drug policy, the 1980s and early 1990s were dominated by the problem of HIV and AIDS among intravenous drug users, and the focus was on harm reduction and low-threshold care for heroin and crack users (Van Laar and Van Ooyen-Houben, 2009). In addition, the late 1980s saw the rapid emergence and spread of ecstasy (MDMA) – and here, too, the emphasis was on harm reduction. However, in the meantime urban "open drug scenes" had evolved (with street dealers selling heroin, cocaine and crack-cocaine, drug-related crime etc.) (Bless, Korf and Freeman, 1995) as well large-scale production of ecstasy for both the national and the international markets (Van Ooyen-Houben and Kleemans, 2016). These problems overshadowed what was happening at the cannabis market, and less attention was paid to coffeeshops. After the Schengen Agreement (1985) the number of coffeeshops rose rapidly, especially in municipalities near the border. This was accompanied by a strong increase in "coffeeshop tourism" of cannabis users from neighboring countries (Korf, Van der Woude, Benschop and Nabben, 2001).

The national government in 1995 published a comprehensive white paper on drug policy entitled *Drug Policy in the Netherlands: Continuity and Change*. It concluded that "… in international terms the situation as regards public health is not unfavorable…," but also that "… the use of drugs and everything that is related to it constitutes an acute, major social and administrative problem in the Netherlands as elsewhere." (Tweede Kamer, 1995, p. 9).[6] Among the problems that needed to be tackled, the white paper referred to nuisance from coffeeshops caused by large numbers of customers, including "coffeeshop tourists"; an increase in organized crime involvement in supply and trafficking of drugs; and criticisms from abroad, the International Narcotics Control Board (INCB) in particular. The white paper concluded that coffeeshops, though "in themselves valuable," had increased "in number and burden" (Tweede Kamer, 1995, p. 37),[7] and supported local initiatives to "rationalize" the coffeeshop policy and decrease their number.

In a critical review of the "Dutch Model" in drug policy, Van Ooyen-Houben and Kleemans (2016) analyzed the evolution of coffeeshop policy in light of the increased focus on control of nuisance and crime since 1995. They argue that this increased control is reflected in administrative and criminal laws and amendments to the Opium Act aiming at improvement and facilitation of the investigation and prosecution of drug offenses. Some of these legal instruments are directly or indirectly related to coffeeshop policy.

Regulating the front door – national and local policy

Both criminal and administrative law apply to coffeeshops. As stated before, Guidelines for Investigation and Prosecution of Opium Act offenses by the public prosecutor set out criteria for non-prosecution of coffeeshops (originally the so-called AHOJ criteria, later AHOJ-G criteria). The first specifications of these criteria date to 1991. Since then, the national criteria have been sharpened and expanded, and re-labelled into AHOJG-I criteria. A short description of these criteria as of 2018 is presented in Box 12.1.

In 1996, both the J- and G-criteria were redefined (Staatscourant, 1996). Access was restricted to persons over age 18 (J-criterion), the maximum transaction per customer per day was reduced from 30 to 5 grams (G-criterion), and the maximum amount of cannabis in stock was limited to 500 grams (G-criterion).

From the mid-1990s onwards, the focus in coffeeshop policy came on tightening the regulation of the front door. This included *curbing the number of coffeeshops*. Since then the number of coffeeshops declined from an estimated 1,100–1,500 in 1995 (Bieleman and Goeree, 2001; Van Ooyen-Houben and Kleemans, 2016) to 813 in 2000, 729 in 2005, 660 in 2010 and 573 in 2016 (Bieleman, Mennes and Sijstra, 2017). There are several reasons for and explanations of this drastic drop in the number of coffeeshops. On the one hand, municipalities were given more national legal instruments for local coffeeshop policy. On the other hand, local communities had to commit to stricter national criteria.

Box 12.1 National AHOJG-I Criteria governing coffeeshops, 2018

(A) No advertising	No advertising, apart from a minor reference (on the shop).
(H) No hard drugs	It is forbidden to have or sell hard drugs in the shop.
(O) No nuisance	Nuisance (in Dutch: *Overlast*) may consist of parking problems around coffeeshops, noise, litter or customers who loiter in front of or in the neighborhood of the coffeeshop.
(J) No young people	No selling to and no access by young people (in Dutch: *Jongeren*) under age 18.
(G) No large quantities	No selling of large quantities (in Dutch: *Grote hoeveelheden*) per transaction, which means quantities larger than suitable for personal use (5 grams). A transaction comprises all buying and selling in one coffeeshop on the same day by one same customer. Maximum selling stock set at 500 grams.
(I) No non-residents	Access to residents (in Dutch: *Ingezetenen*) of the Netherlands only.

Before 1995, municipalities already had the opportunity to take measures against coffeeshops for infringement of the national AHOJ-G criteria. And that is what happened, especially in the case of possession of or trafficking of hard drugs (the H-criterion). Even when only customers are caught for possession of hard drugs, coffeeshops have been closed, sometimes temporarily, but with repeat violation, usually permanently. However, in practice, it turned out that it was often very complicated to objectively define and administratively document "nuisance" in order to close down coffeeshops on legal grounds because of nuisance (the O-criterion).

The latter was one of the reasons why in 1996 the national government provided *local communities* a legal instrument to decide whether they would allow coffeeshops. By the end of 2016, about 70 percent of the Dutch municipalities[8] had opted for a *zero policy* and decided to not allow coffeeshops at all (Bieleman et al. 2017). Consequently, they can close such locations, even if they do not violate the AHOJ-G criteria. Municipalities may also decide to allow one or more coffeeshops and to provide them with a license. Amsterdam was probably the first city to introduce a license system for coffeeshops. This gradually became a more common practice across the country. To date, coffeeshops need a license from the mayor. The decision to condone coffeeshops is made at a municipal level by the mayor, in consultation with the public prosecutor and the police (the so-called "tripartite consultation") and with approval by the city council. Whether a Dutch community has one or more coffeeshops depends in part on its population size, with larger communities being more likely to have coffeeshops.[9] However, it more strongly depends on the political composition of the local council: "The larger the percentage of progressive councilors, the greater the probability that coffeeshops are allowed." (Wouters, Benschop and Korf, 2010, p. 315).

Until 1996, with regard to coffeeshops, there was no nationally uniform definition of "Youth" (the J-criterion). In some municipalities, this had been set at 16 years (at that time the minimum age for alcohol), in others at 18 years (the age to become legally an adult in the Netherlands). In 1996, this was harmonized, and 18 years became the uniform national criterion. Compliance to the J and other national criteria governing coffeeshops is checked periodically (see Box 12.2).

Furthermore, in 1996 at national level, it was decided that coffeeshops had to be *alcohol-free* premises (Staatscourant, 1996). Although at local level this already was common practice in many coffeeshops (whether or not because of additional local criteria), there were coffeeshops serving alcohol. Some of the latter coffeeshops stopped selling alcohol. Other coffeeshops decided to split up their location into an alcohol-free coffeeshop and a physically separated café with alcohol. Some other coffeeshops stopped being a coffeeshop and continued as a café. Thereby the alcohol-free policy contributed to reducing the number of coffeeshops.

Another factor in the declining number of coffeeshops was the introduction *of a minimum distance from school* policy at local level. The city of Rotterdam

Box 12.2 Compliance with national criteria governing coffeeshops and screening owners

If a coffeeshop fails to comply with one of the AHOJ-G criteria, the mayor can apply administrative measures, varying from a fine to closure of the shop for a definite or indefinite period. The public prosecutor can prosecute the coffeeshop owner and staff. The severity of the sanction depends on the violation, i.e. the presence of hard drugs and youths is punished more severely than advertising violations, as are repeated violations (Van Ooyen-Houben and Kleemans 2016). Compliance is checked periodically by municipalities, local police and other agencies such as tax authorities. Customer IDs and the stock of cannabis on the premises are checked. Within a "tripartite consultation model", the mayor, the public prosecutor, and the chief of police agree on enforcement actions. Coffeeshops in general adhere to all these criteria (Bieleman et al., 2017; Van Ooyen-Houben, Bieleman and Korf 2014). One explanation is that coffeeshops are lucrative businesses that their owners do not want to compromise (Van Ooyen-Houben and Kleemans, 2016; Korf, Liebregts and Nabben, 2016).

A different type of instrument to regulate the front door is the BIBOB Act (*Bevordering Integriteitsbeoordelingen door Openbaar Bestuur*; Promoting Integrity Reviews by Public Administration). that was introduced in 2003. This act empowered mayors to check by a screening procedure criminal backgrounds of applicants for licenses. Although this law was not specifically targeted at coffeeshops, it has become quite common to use BIBOB to screen coffeeshop owners (Bieleman et al., 2017).

was probably the first municipality to implement this additional local criterion and in 2009 closed 16 coffeeshops located within 250 meters from schools. In 2011, the national government announced that from January 1, 2014, no coffeeshop should be located within 350 meters of schools for secondary education and secondary vocational education. However, by the end of 2012, the planned national distance criterion of 350 meters was rescinded, and the Minister of Justice decided that this criterion was a matter of local policy. By 2016, four out of five Dutch municipalities with one or more coffeeshops had implemented a distance from school policy, mostly 250 meters or less (Bieleman et al., 2017). One of these municipalities is Amsterdam, where a minimum of 250 meters distance policy was introduced in exchange for not implementing the I-criterion (see below, "Private club and residence criteria for coffeeshops"). Together with the closure of most coffeeshops in the Red Light Area and a rapidly growing tourism, the minimum distance from school policy led to a strong increase in the average number of visitors in remaining coffeeshops (Korf, Liebregts and Nabben, 2016).

In addition to the national criteria for condoning coffeeshops, communities can implement *specific local criteria*, such as the requirement to hire security and/

Box 12.3 Coffeeshops and trends in cannabis use

Trends in the prevalence of cannabis use in the Netherlands more or less paralleled the successive stages in Dutch cannabis policy. The number of users swiftly increased when cannabis was distributed through an underground market (late 1960s and early 1970s). It then decreased as tolerated house dealers superseded the underground market (1970s), went up again after coffeeshops took over the sale of cannabis (1980s), and finally stabilized by the end of the 1990s when the number of coffeeshops was reduced. However, as similar upwards and downwards trends were also observed in other countries that did not decriminalize cannabis, it is questionable whether Dutch coffeeshop policy is causally related to cannabis use prevalence (Korf, 2002; Van Laar and Van Ooyen-Houben, 2009). In 2016, lifetime prevalence among adults (15–64 years) in the Netherlands was 25.2 percent, slightly below the European average (26.3 percent), and the last 12-months rate among young adults (15–34 years) was somewhat above the European average (15.7 percent and 14.1 percent, respectively) (EMCDDA, 2018).

or staff to help reduce nuisance, obligatory staff training and availability of drug prevention information and restricted opening hours. The latter can lead to coffeeshops being busier during the narrower time window, as was the case in recent years for example, in Rotterdam (Korf and Liebregts, 2015).

Private club and residence criteria for coffeeshops

In 2009, a national expert advisory committee on drugs policy (Adviescommissie Drugsbeleid, 2009) concluded that coffeeshops should return to their original purpose of selling small amounts to local consumers, especially in areas along the border. The government acted on this advice with a policy letter, and announced a more restrictive policy toward coffeeshops, with two additional criteria that coffeeshops had to adhere to in order for them to be tolerated:: the private club and the residence criterion (Staatscourant, 2011). From 2012 onwards, the new national policy intended that coffeeshops were only permitted to give access to members (the "private club criterion") and only residents (the I-criterion) of the Netherlands – irrespective of nationality – were permitted to become a member. This tightened policy sought to make coffeeshops smaller and more controllable, to reduce the nuisance associated with coffeeshops and to reduce the number of foreign visitors attracted by the coffeeshops (so-called "coffeeshop tourists").

Enforcement of these new criteria started as a pilot in May 2012 in three provinces in the south of the country (along the German and Belgian border) where the problems of nuisance and drug tourism were defined as most urgent. The remaining provinces were supposed to follow in January 2013.

The introduction of these measures was evaluated in 14 municipalities, 7 in the southern provinces where they were implemented ("experimental group") and 7 in other provinces where they were not ("comparison group"). A baseline assessment (before the implementation in the "experimental group") and follow-ups at 6 and 18 months were performed. A combination of methods was applied: interviews with local experts, surveys with neighborhood residents, coffeeshop visitors and cannabis users, and ethnographic field work. Findings were reported after the first follow-up (Van Ooyen-Houben, Bieleman and Korf, 2013), and after the second follow-up (Van Ooyen-Houben et al., 2014). A short version of the results of the full study was published in English (Van Ooyen-Houben, Bieleman and Korf, 2016). Key findings were:

- in the three southern provinces, drugs tourism to coffeeshops swiftly declined in 2012. Drug tourism decreased, but street dealing flourished. However, 10 of the 14 municipalities in the study sample did not enforce the residence criterion (I-criterion). This criterion remained in force but was adapted: local authorities can decide whether to enforce it (Tweede Kamer, 2012);
- the private club criterion had a number of adverse side effects. After implementation of this criterion in the southern provinces (the "experimental group"), coffeeshops lost a large portion of their local customers, since users did not want to register as a member. Residents turned away

Box 12.4 Rescheduling potent cannabis as a hard drug?

Another proposal made by the Advisory Committee 2009 (p. 11) was to install an expert committee to investigate the pros and cons of the distinction introduced in 1976 between "soft" (Schedule II) and "hard drugs" (Schedule I). The main reason for that advice was the steep increase in potency of domestically cultivated marijuana ("*nederwiet*" [Netherweed]) sold in coffeeshops, from an average of 7.5 percent THC in 1991 to 20 percent THC in 2004. In subsequent years, it fluctuated between 15 percent and 18 percent THC, rather similar to imported hashish.

In 2010, this new expert committee was installed by the Minister of VWS. In its report *Drugs in lijsten* (Expertcommissie Lijstensystematiek Opiumwet, 2011), the committee concluded that the increase in THC went along with growing worries about health consequences of cannabis consumption, risk of cannabis dependence and schizophrenia in particular. As hash oil had already been defined in the 1976 Opium Act as a "hard drug" (List I) because of its high THC percentage, the committee advised accentuating the difference between the two schedules, and placing marijuana and hashish with more than 15 percent THC on List I. Although a draft regulation to amend the Opium Act had been prepared by 2013, the amendment was not agreed upon, and thus not implemented.

from coffeeshops and started buying cannabis on the illegal market, thus fostering nuisance from street dealers. These people did not want to register as a club member. There was a substantial increase in the illegal cannabis consumer market. Young customers aged 18–24 in particular turned away. The growing illegal market attracted young dealers with a vulnerable background;

- the private club criterion was abolished at the end of 2012 (thus never implemented in the "comparison group"). Some resident users returned to coffeeshops (in the southern provinces), but not all. The illegal cannabis market (i.e. cannabis transaction at consumer level sales other than in coffeeshops) decreased but remained bigger than it had been before the policy change.

Controlling the back door

The Dutch policy of tolerance towards coffeeshops does not apply to the "back door." The police turn a blind eye to the purchase of cannabis, as long as this is done discreetly and in small quantities (Van Ooyen-Houben and Kleemans, 2016). This leaves coffeeshops in a complicated interface position between the illegal production market and the condoned sale of cannabis to consumers (Tijhuis, 2006). This paradox and its related problems had been ignored for many years (Van de Bunt, 2006), but this has changed drastically since the early 2000s, and the back door issue gained prominence on the political agenda, not in the least because coffeeshops were increasingly selling domestically-grown marijuana, instead of imported foreign hashish. This product substitution has been characterized as "Green Avalanche" (Jansen, 2002). Domestic marijuana production became more and more associated with criminal organizations (Korf, 2011). For example, Bovenkerk and Hoogewind (2003) concluded that indoor cannabis cultivation was widespread and that criminal networks forced people to become involved, in particular, in socioeconomically vulnerable neighborhoods.

In subsequent years, legislation was enacted to increase and harmonize sanctions on large-scale cannabis cultivation, and to create more room for local policy (Van Ooyen-Houben and Kleemans, 2016). Already in 1999, specifications for "professionalism" of cannabis cultivation were defined in the Opium Act: more severe sanctions for professional cultivation, and higher maximum sanctions for large-scale production and trafficking of drugs, with special emphasis on large-scale cultivation. Also, the "Damocles article" was added to the Opium Act (Article 13b) enabling mayors to close drug-dealing premises in their municipality. In 2007, this article was broadened in scope and from then on, applied to all drug-related premises, including, for example, apartments that had been used to grow marijuana.

A special Hemp Task Force was created, and from 2004 onwards, domestic cultivation has been tackled by a combination of administrative and financial measures (e.g. seizures of criminal proceeds) and criminal law.

Annually, around 5,000 cultivation sites have been dismantled (Van Laar and Van Ooyen-Houben, 2014). Side effects of this intensified policy that have been observed include displacement to other less detectable locations, technological innovation in indoor cultivation, and a transition to professional commercial cultivators and criminal networks (Wouters, Korf and Kroeske, 2007; Emmett and Boers, 2008) and to locations abroad (Jansen, 2012; De Middeleer and De Ruyver, 2017). In 2009, the aforementioned national expert advisory committee on drug policy also advocated more intense and integrated efforts to control organized crime involving cooperation between public and private parties (e.g. housing associations, electricity companies) at a regional level, and administrative, fiscal and criminal law authorities (Adviescommissie Drugsbeleid, 2009). One of the consequences was that in 2015, another article was entered into the Opium Act that criminalized the preparation or facilitation of cannabis cultivation. This new article was specifically intended as a legal instrument against so-called "growshops," as they did not only sell seeds to grow marijuana for personal use, but had been shown to play a crucial role as "facilitator" in commercial indoor cannabis cultivation by selling all kinds of equipment for cultivation sites (e.g. high-tech lamps). More and more growshops came to be understood as important intermediaries in the supply chain to coffee shops, as well as important facilitators and "partner[s] in crime" in marijuana production for illegal export (Emmett and Boers, 2008; Spapens, Van de Bunt and Rastovac, 2007). Is has been estimated that in the Netherlands, more marijuana is grown to be exported than for the domestic market (Van der Giessen, Van Ooyen-Houben and Moolenaar, 2016). It is difficult, if not impossible, to reliably estimate the total cannabis production, as well as what part is grown to supply coffee shops.

Local proposals for regulated supply to coffeeshops

In Dutch cannabis policy, the core of the "back door" problem is that there is not an official authorized system to supply coffeeshops. In recent years, an increasing number of Dutch mayors have voiced their concerns and demanded further regulation. For example, the city of Utrecht suggested a non-commercial social club model that would allow recreational cannabis users to grow up to five marijuana plants per participant/member (Wouters and Korf, 2011).

In the course of 2013 – in response to a letter from the Minister of Justice to the Parliament in February 2013, in which he offered municipalities the opportunity to present plans for cannabis cultivation – Utrecht, as well as other municipalities from all over the country, sent to the national government proposals to regulate cannabis supply to coffeeshops. These proposals varied, among others, in level of detail; level of centralized cannabis cultivation (one cultivator for all local/regional coffeeshops or multiple cultivators); characteristics of cultivation site; safety issues; whether or not to include hashish; legal bodies and the role of coffeeshops in cultivation; reference to quality criteria (e.g. maximum THC percentage) and (type of) quality control; details with regard to financial administration, taxing and control.

The local/regional proposals for regulated supply to coffeeshops were part of a wider strategy, initiated by three municipalities. In the course of 2013, this resulted in a *Manifest Joint Regulation*, in which the municipalities pleaded for a regulation of cannabis cultivation to supply coffeeshops. In short time, this manifest was signed by 23 municipalities/mayors.

In response to the proposals and the manifest, the Minister of Safety and Justice (Mr. Ivo Opstelten, the same minister who had introduced the private club and residence criteria for coffeeshops) refused to give permission to any of the proposed local or regional pilots. Instead, he argued that any type of formal regulation of cannabis cultivation for the recreational user market would violate the international drug treaties or European regulations and would not solve the problem that most domestically cultivated cannabis is exported. According to the minister, the appropriate answer to organized crime would be strong measures against crime and nuisance, not regulation (Tweede Kamer 2013, 2014).

Manifest Joint Regulation and diverging views on international conventions

The Manifest Joint Regulation[10] states that the national cannabis policy needs revision, and calls for the nationwide introduction of certified and regulated cannabis cultivation, in order to (1) better protect the health of cannabis users; (2) improve safety in neighborhoods in their cities; and (3) more effectively control cannabis-related (organized) crime.

As to the health protection of cannabis users, the manifest argues that due to an unregulated supply side of the cannabis market, users are not informed about the content and quality of cannabis (e.g. high percentage THC). With regard to safety problems, the manifest states that many fires are caused by illegal indoor cannabis cultivation in houses and apartments. As to a more effective control of organized crime in domestic cannabis cultivation, the manifest argues that with certified and regulated cultivation, much manpower and money would become available for a better targeted enforcement of remaining criminal actors and organizations involved in unregulated cultivation.

According to the municipalities that signed the manifest, the ministerial conclusion that the international drug conventions do not allow for certified and regulated cannabis cultivation has been based on a one-sided and negative politically biased interpretation of the treaties. In his conclusion, the Minister of Safety and Justice referred to a study commissioned by his ministry (Van Kempen and Federova, 2014). Most interestingly, in a second study, commissioned by three cities with coffeeshops, the same authors took a different legal angle, i.e. human rights conventions regarding health and safety, and concluded that positive human rights obligations could result in allowing, or even obligating, regulated cannabis production and trade (Van Kempen and Federova, 2016).

Turning back to the manifest, it proposes – in case it would not be possible to introduce regulated cannabis cultivation country-wide – to start at local level. In the course of 2017, the number of signatories had amounted to over 60 mayors – mostly from municipalities with coffeeshops. Some simply signed to support the call for regulation, others presented detailed proposals (see previous section). Moreover, in 2017, the Union of Dutch Municipalities (VNG) pleaded for local experiments in regulated cannabis cultivation (VNG, 2017).

Preparing a national experiment with regulated cannabis supply

Dutch governments are constituted by a coalition of two or more political parties; these parties don't necessarily share the same side of the political spectrum. It is not uncommon that the Dutch Parliament (150 members) adopts a proposal that is not supported by one or more political parties in the government. In February 2017, the Dutch Parliament voted for the *Wet Gesloten Coffeeshopketen* (Closed Coffeeshop Circuit Act), a proposal by MP Vera Bergkamp to revise the Opium Act by including a new article by which professional or commercial cannabis growers under strict conditions can be exempted from prosecution (Tweede Kamer, 2017). This proposal was adopted by a slight majority (77 yes vs. 73 no).

In October 2017, a new government took office – a coalition of four political parties with different views on cannabis policy and coffeeshops: MP Bergkamp's "liberal-progressive" party that had taken the initiative to revise the Opium Act, a "liberal-conservative" party with a strong focus on fighting organized crime in cannabis production and trade and two confessional (Christian) anti-coffeeshop parties giving highest priority to prevention of cannabis use. Despite conflicting perspectives, the coalition agreed to an experiment with a "closed coffeeshop circuit" in six to ten municipalities (cities).

In February 2018, the new Minister of (now) Justice and Safety and the Minister of Medical Care and Sports informed parliament that an independent expert committee would be installed to advise the government about the design of the experiment. In the ministerial plans announced in March 2018, the experiment was divided into three stages: (1) *Preparation*: beginning with the implementation of an Experiment Act[11] and the underlying Administrative Decree;[12] (2) *Experiment:* within the legal context of the experiment, cannabis can be produced, delivered to and sold in coffeeshops in the participating municipalities. For this phase, a period of four years was foreseen in the draft version of the Experiment Act; and (3) *Run-down:* within approximately six months, bringing the situation back as it was before the experiment.

In March 2018, the advisory committee – consisting of experts in the field of public health, addiction, surveillance, law enforcement, local administration, criminology and law – was installed. The committee gathered abundant information from scholarly literature and through roundtable discussions with a wide variety of experts and practitioners, including mayors, law enforcers, researchers, scientists, cannabis producers, coffeeshop owners, cannabis users and addiction and prevention experts, among others. By the end of June 2018, the advisory committee had delivered its report (*Adviescommissie Experiment Gesloten Cannabisketen*, 2018).

As to the content of the experiment (the "intervention"), the committee stated that during the preparation phase, it would take much effort to deliver a sufficiently varied range of cannabis to the outlets participating in the experiment. According to the committee, during the experiment, a limited number of reliable and highly qualified growers have to be contracted, who are ready to fulfil the necessary requirements (e.g. no pesticides, information about type of cannabis, THC, CBD, etc.). Over time it could be decided whether it would be desirable and possible to include more cannabis growers in the closed chain. As the committee concluded that variation in cannabis should not be limited to marijuana, it realized that it would be a major challenge to supply participating coffeeshops, not only with various types of domestically cultivated marijuana, but also with a variety of domestically produced hashish. (Approximately 20–30 percent of the cannabis sold in coffeeshops refers to hashish, predominantly imported from Morocco.)

With regard to transportation and trading stock, the committee's recommendations appear to go beyond the G-criterion (a maximum of 500 grams of stock). While not mentioning specific numbers, the committee characterized transport as a vulnerable component in the chain, and concluded that the distribution from grower to seller should take place in the most clear way possible, with minimal risk of mistakes and through prevention of interference by, and "leakage" of, cannabis to the criminal milieu. Therefore, the committee sought to minimize the number of cannabis transport movements as much as possible. It also recommended allowing outlets a maximum trading stock; at least enough for one day.

According to the committee, the retail price of cannabis should be in conformity with the existing market. A surcharge could serve as a buffer against excessive margins between cost price and sales prices and could support a fund for prevention of cannabis use and addiction. Finally, the committee pointed to the potential risk that regulation could lead to cannabis being perceived as safe and not harmful to health, because the government monitors the quality of the product. Also, cannabis users in the Netherlands mostly mix cannabis with tobacco. Therefore, the committee advised prevention measures as part of the "intervention" that address the health damage that cannabis use as well as tobacco smoking can cause.

Concerning the scientific evaluation of the experiment, the committee recommended a mixed method design: a process evaluation to investigate whether the experiment results in a well-functioning closed cannabis chain, and a study of effects. Leading questions in the *process evaluation* are for example: is the chain truly closed and do the coffeeshops succeed in becoming exclusively supplied by legal cannabis growers and producers, and in fully abolishing the sale of illegally produced cannabis in their premises? How do processes within the chain work and evolve? Do cannabis users buy at a legal coffeeshop or do they turn to other outlets? How do users experience the closed chain? Do the "by the government approved" selling points attract more young buyers, and how do they alert them to potential harm to health?

Regarding the *effect study*, the committee pointed out several themes, including cannabis use, combination of cannabis with other substances, cannabis dependence, cannabis-related immediate health effects, driving under the influence of cannabis, criminality, safety and nuisance. To determine certain effects of a closed cannabis chain, the committee noted that possible changes can best be studied comparatively in municipalities where the intervention is implemented and those where it is not. According to the committee, a solid, well-designed comparative study could bring evidence-based findings on short-term effects, yet health effects that are only observable in the longer term are beyond the scope of the effect study, which should be finalized in four years' time. The committee also concluded that the experiment will not allow firm conclusions with regard to general consequences in terms of crime.

As stated previously, the proposed experiment resulted from an agreement between four political parties with different views and preferences with regards to cannabis policy and coffeeshops. This required compromises. One was an experiment limited in terms of size: six to ten municipalities. However, according to the committee, the effect study requires the participation of "considerably more" municipalities. The paradox here seems to be that exactly the additional criteria – and consequently a variety of effect objectives – of the political parties who were less enthusiastic about the experiment and preferred a limited size of it, did lead the committee to advise a larger-scale experiment.

Another sensitive issue concerns the third stage of the experiment: rundown (within six months). This too was a compromise to the political parties in the coalition that preferred not to have coffeeshops. The advisory committee expressed a very clear opinion on this matter.

> The committee finds the experiment to be successful when it has been shown that a closed cannabis chain can be realized and when the measured effects are either favorable or do not show a worsening of the current situation. Such an outcome is in the committee's view an unequivocal result that pleas for regulation of the cannabis chain in the Netherlands. [...] If only the experiment succeeds in creating a closed cannabis chain with negative side effects, the experiment can be understood as successful.
>
> (*Adviescommissie Experiment Gesloten Cannabisketen*, 2018, p. 10)

Moreover, the committee stated that when the experiment succeeds, it would be "illogical and risky" to return to the situation "as it was before the experiment." Instead, the committee advised the government to not start a run-down phase in case of a successful outcome, and to make a clear statement beforehand that it intends to implement the closed cannabis chain nationwide if the experiment succeeds.

In early July 2018, in a letter to the parliament, the Dutch government responded largely positively and in line with the advice of the committee, but disagreed with some proposals and persisted in restricting the experiment to a maximum of ten municipalities.[13] In the next week, a first draft of the Experiment Act was sent to the parliament (Tweede Kamer, 2018a). In the following months, societal discussions and political debates about the experiment continued.[14] The Union of Dutch Municipalities[15] kept pleading for a larger number of cities in the experiment, and against the requirement that all coffeeshops in a municipality should participate, as this would not be realistic for cities like Amsterdam (with around 170 coffeeshops) and Rotterdam (around 40 coffeeshops). Coffeeshops persisted in their concerns about sufficient varieties of marijuana and hashish. Parliament's Permanent Justice Committee extensively discussed the draft Experiment Act. By the end of November 2018, the government published its views (Tweede Kamer, 2018b). In short, the principles and criteria of the experiment and the expected timeline are as follows:

- in the course of 2019, the experiment will be further prepared in consultation with local authorities (including the Union of Dutch Municipalities);
- the experiment formally begins when the Experiment Act and the underlying lower regulations (Administrative Decree) have come into force. This requires that volunteering municipalities have been nominated for participation in the experiment by the Advisory Committee; subsequently six to ten municipalities will have been selected by the government, mentioned in the Administrative Decree, and the decree has been approved by the applicable political and legal authorities and institutions. At that time, the participating coffeeshops will be known as well, and thus mentioned in the decree;
- the next step is the *preparation phase* (expected to last at least one year). At the core is the selection of up to ten growers, who, during this phase, will have to provide proof that they can produce sufficient marijuana and hashish – in size and varieties – that they can structurally supply the participating coffeeshops. Cultivation and production must take place in the Netherlands;
- during the *actual experiment* (i.e. production, supply to coffeeshops and sale of cannabis to consumers), participating coffeeshops may order cannabis from each of the selected growers. In contrast to the national G-criterion (500 grams), maximum stock is set at the average weekly sale rate of each participating coffeeshop;

- the draft Experiment Act provides that the scientific *evaluation* will take place before the end of the experiment phase, in order to enable the then incumbent government to take evidence-based decisions about next steps. In case it is decided to convert the experiment into general legislation, the draft Experiment Act allows for the possibility to extend the experimental phase for up to a year and a half, so that the total duration of the experiment, including the six months run-down phase, may be extended to a maximum of six years.

Summary and conclusion

In the Netherlands, cannabis was statutorily decriminalized in 1976, and cannabis was placed on a separate schedule (List II), with lower sentences than for "hard drugs" (List I). This decriminalization of cannabis resulted from a fundamental national debate on drug policy. Already before 1976, at local level, selling cannabis to consumers had been informally tolerated under certain conditions and in specific settings (so-called house dealers in cultural youth centers). This approach became formalized at national level, and in the course of the 1980s, coffeeshops more and more took over the role of house dealers. From then on, the number of coffeeshops rapidly increased.

Over time, the pendulum in Dutch coffeeshop policy has been shifting between a stronger local and a stronger national orientation – and vice versa. Coffeeshops became more and more regulated. In a dynamic process, local policies towards coffeeshops became formalized, and national criteria governing coffeeshops were defined – and enforced. While on the one hand, the Dutch government provided legal instruments to create more room for local coffeeshop policy, i.e. to define additional criteria/requirements for coffeeshops, on the other hand, municipalities can opt for a zero policy, and thereby not allow coffeeshops at all. To date, there are slightly over 100 municipalities with coffeeshops. This means that around one quarter of Dutch municipalities (a total of 380, with approximately three-quarters of population) has one or more coffeeshops.

Overall, the past decades have resulted in a well-defined set of national criteria to condone coffeeshops and with a transparent enforcement policy. An important lesson to be learned is that restricting (semi-legal) access to cannabis, e.g. registered coffeeshop membership, may give a rapid distortion of the market, with negative consequences such as street dealing.

The policy of "tolerance" only refers to the "front door" of coffeeshops, i.e. the sale of small quantities of cannabis (up to 5 grams per transaction) to consumers. Although the supply of cannabis to coffeeshops – the "back door" – had been under debate for quite some years, calls from local policy-makers and politicians (municipalities) to make a next step, and to also regulate the supply side of the cannabis retail market, did not receive support from the national government. Instead – as one facet of an increased political focus on crime, fueled by, though not limited to the rise of populist parties – a repressive approach towards cannabis cultivation was intensified, thereby unintentionally contributing to an ongoing process of increased involvement of organized crime in the cannabis industry.

Interestingly, the difference between supporters and opponents of regulating cannabis cultivation is not so much in the problem analysis. Both parties recognize the paradox in Dutch cannabis policy (sales tolerated through the front door, no supply via the back door) and are concerned about the role of organized crime in cannabis production. The essential difference is in the advocated political solution: more enforcement in order to fight organized crime versus regulation to steal a march on organized crime.

In response to the continued focus on enforcement, local policymakers and politicians intensified their collaboration with pleas to regulate the "back door," and published a *Manifest Joint Regulation*. While initially the national government refused to create any legal room for regulating supply to coffeeshops, a swift change took place in the course of 2017. The Dutch Parliament voted for a proposal to revise the Opium Act – albeit with a very small majority – that creates legal room for cannabis supply to coffeeshops in a closed circuit from plant to consumer. With the new national government that took office in October 2017, developments came rapidly. An experiment was announced that would allow six to ten municipalities to participate in a trial in which coffeeshops under strict conditions within a regulated, closed circuit would be supplied with cannabis.

As of June 2018, an independent advisory committee of scientists and experts reported their recommendations for the research design and content of the experiment, including: a sufficiently varied range of cannabis in the coffeeshops (both marijuana and hashish); a larger stock of cannabis in coffeeshops and prevention measures. In the course of 2019, the experiment will be further developed in consultation with local authorities as a next step in a complex process to prepare, implement and evaluate the experiment, with the aim of learning evidence-based lessons that in around 2025 will allow the then incumbent government to decide upon future steps in Dutch cannabis policy.

Notes

1 This agreement required the inclusion of Indian hemp in the list of prohibited substances (Krabbe, 1989).
2 In order to exempt cultivation of hemp plants for use as windbreaks in farming and for the manufacture of thread, chicken feed, birdseed and fishing bait (Krabbe, 1989).
3 For a more detailed description, including more specific references, of this and the next section, see De Kort, 1995; Korf, 1995.
4 These guidelines are founded in the expediency principle, which is a guiding principle in Dutch penal law and the opposite of the legality principle. The expediency principle allows authorities to refrain from prosecution of criminalizable behavior without first asking the permission of the courts. Basically, the expediency principle

can be applied in two ways. The first takes prosecution as its starting point but waives it if there are good reasons to do so (negative application: prosecution, unless); this "case directed" approach was common in the Netherlands until the end of the 1960s. The second way is the positive application of the expediency principle; prosecution only takes place if it is expedient by serving the public interest (no, unless).

5 Coffeeshop is the English term for "koffiehuis" – traditionally a very popular kind of neighborhood café serving coffee, tea and other non-alcoholic beverages, and maybe simple meals. In the course of the 1970s, in a growing number of such cafés, cannabis was sold "under the counter," leading to arrests and seizures by the police. To distinguish them from traditional "koffiehuizen," they became known as "coffeeshops."

6 English translation from Van Ooyen-Houben and Kleemans (2016, p. 177).

7 English translation from Van Ooyen-Houben and Kleemans (2016, p. 196).

8 Approximately one quarter of the Dutch population lives in these municipalities.

9 While communities with fewer than 20,000 residents have a coffeeshop, almost all communities with 100,000 or more residents have coffeeshops (Wouters et al., 2010; Bieleman et al., 2017).

10 As published January 31, 2014 by the initiators: Mayor Depla (Heerlen), Deputy Everhardt (Utrecht) and Mayor Van Gijzel (Eindhoven). www.vng.nl. Retrieved January 4, 2018.

11 The aim of the Experiment Act was to regulate that the Opium Act will not apply to the actions that are defined as illegal in this act, but that are necessary for the production of cannabis and for the supply to coffeeshops, in as far as these actions take place within the framework of the experiment.

12 The Administrative Decree (in Dutch: *Algemene Maatregel van Bestuur*, AMvB) formulates the conditions for the experiment.

13 Letter of July 6, 2018 of the Minister of Medical Care and Sport, and the Minister of Justice and Safety. (137242-178738-VGP) "Kabinetsreactie rapport Adviescommissie Experiment gesloten cannabisketen."

14 For example "Oppositie vreest mislukken wietproef"," in newspaper *Trouw*, January 18, 2019 (Barends, 2019).

15 https://vng.nl/onderwerpenindex/veiligheid/softdrugsbeleid/nieuws/aandachtspunten-vng-voor-amvb-wietexperiment. Retrieved January 23, 2019.

References

Adviescommissie Drugsbeleid. (2009). *Geen deuren maar daden: Nieuwe accenten in het Nederlandse drugsbeleid*. Den Haag: Wetenschappelijke Raad voor het Regeringsbeleid (WRR).

Adviescommissie Experiment Gesloten Cannabisketen. (2018). *Een experiment met een gesloten cannabisketen*. Den Haag. Retrieved from www.rijksoverheid.nl/ecg.

Barends, I. (2019, January 19). Oppositie vreest mislukken van wietproef. *Trouw*, 7.

Bieleman, B. and Goeree, P. (2001). *Coffeeshops in Nederland. Aantallen en gemeentelijk beleid 2000*. Groningen: Intraval.

Bieleman, B., Mennes, R. and Sijstra, M. (2017). *Coffeeshops in Nederland 2016. Aantallen coffeeshops en gemeentelijk beleid 1999–2016*. Groningen: Intraval.

Bless, R., Korf, D.J. and Freeman, M. (1995). Open drug scenes: A cross-national comparison of concepts and urban strategies. *European Addiction Research*, 1, 128–138.

Blom, T. (2006) Coffee shops, gedoogbeleid en Europa. *Justitiële Verkenningen,* 32(1), 146–156.

Bovenkerk, F. and Hoogewind, W.I.M. (2003). *Hennepteelt in Nederland: Het probleem van de criminaliteit en haar bestrijding.* Zeist: Uitgeverij Kerckebosch.

Cohen, H. (1975). *Drugs, druggebruikers en drugscene.* Alphen aan den Rijn: Samson Uitgeverij.

De Kort, M. (1995). *Tussen patiënt en delinquent. Geschiedenis van het Nederlandse drugsbeleid.* Hilversum: Verloren.

De Kort, M. and Korf, D.J. (1992). The development of drug trade and drug control in the Netherlands: A historical perspective. *Crime, Law and Social Change,* 17, 123–144.

De Middeleer, F. and De Ruyver, B. (2017). De verschuiving van illegale drugsmarkten van Nederland naar België. Perceptie of realiteit? *Justitiële Verkenningen,* 43(2), 103–123.

EMCDDA. (2018). European Drug Report 2018. Trends and developments. Lisbon: EMCDDA.

Emmett, I. and Boers, R. (2008). *Het groene goud.* Zoetermeer: KLPD.

Expertcommissie Lijstensystematiek Opiumwet. (2011). *Drugs in lijsten.* The Hague: VijfkeerBlauw.

Jansen, A.C.M. (1991). *Cannabis in Amsterdam: A geography of hashish and marihuana.* Muiderberg: Coutinho.

Jansen, A.C.M. (2002). De economie van de cannabissector in beleidsperspectief. *Economisch Statistische Berichten,* 87(4354), 276–278.

Jansen, F. (2012). *Georganiseerde hennepteelt. Criminaliteitsbeeldanalyse 2012.* Woerden: KLPD, Dienst Nationale Recherche.

Korf, D.J. (1995). *Dutch treat: Formal control and illicit drug use in the Netherlands.* Amsterdam: Thesis Publishers.

Korf, D.J. (2002). Dutch coffee shops and trends in cannabis use. *Addictive Behaviors,* 27, 851–866.

Korf, D.K. (2011). Marihuana behind and beyond coffeeshops. In T. Decorte, G.R. Potter and M. Bouchard (Eds.), *World wide weed. Global trends in cannabis cultivation and its control* (pp. 181–195). Farnham: Ashgate.

Korf, D.J. and Liebregts, N. (2015). *Evaluatie terugbrengen sluitingstijden coffeeshops* Rotterdam; Amsterdam: Bonger Instituut.

Korf, D.J., Liebregts, N. and Nabben, T. (2016). *Waterbed, drukte en overlast. Effecten sluitingsbeleid coffeeshops in Amsterdam-Centrum.* Amsterdam: Rozenberg Publishers.

Korf, D.J., van der Woude, M., Benschop, A. and Nabben, T. (2001). *Coffeeshops, jeugd en toerisme.* Amsterdam: Rozenberg Publishers.

Krabbe, H.G.M. (1989). *De Opiumwet. Een strafrechtelijk commentaar.* Alphen aan den Rijn: Samson Tjeenk Willink.

Leuw, E. (1972). Het gebruik van cannabis onder leerlingen van voortgezet onderwijs: Een poging tot interpretatie. *Nederlands Tijdschrift voor Criminologie,* 14, 214–255.

Leuw, E. (1973). Drugsgebruik in het Vondelpark. *Nederlands Tijdschrift voor Criminologie,* 15, 202–218.

Leuw, E. and Haen Marschall, I. (Eds.). (1994). *Between prohibition and legalization. The Dutch experiment in drug policy.* Amsterdam/New York: Kugler Publications.

Spapens, T., Van de Bunt, H.G. and Rastovac, L. (2007). *De wereld achter de wietteelt.* Den Haag: Boom Juridische Uitgevers.

Staatscourant. (1996). *Richtlijnen opsporings – En strafvorderingsbeleid strafbare feiten Opiumwet*. Staatscourant 27 September, nr. 187. Den Haag: Sdu Uitgevers.

Staatcourant. (2011). *Aanwijzing Opiumwet 2015A003*. Staatscourant 27 December, nr. 22936. Den Haag: Sdu Uitgevers.

Tijhuis, A.C.G. (2006). *Transnational crime and the interface between legal and illegal actors: The case of illicit art and antiquities trade*. Institute for the Study of Crime and Law Enforcement. Leiden: The Netherlands.

Tweede Kamer. (1995). *Het Nederlandse drugsbeleid. Continuïteit en verandering*. Tweede Kamer stukken 1994–1995, no. 24007 (3). Den Haag: Sdu Uitgevers.

Tweede Kamer. (2012). *Drugbeleid: Brief van de minister van Veiligheid en Justitie aan de Voorzitter van de Tweede Kamer der Staten-Generaal*. Tweede Kamer stukken 2012–2013, no. 24077 (293). Den Haag: Sdu Uitgevers.

Tweede Kamer. (2013). *Drugbeleid: Brief van de minister van Veiligheid en Justitie aan de Voorzitter van de Tweede Kamer der Staten-Generaal*. Tweede Kamer stukken 2013–2014, no. 24077 (314). Den Haag: Sdu Uitgevers.

Tweede Kamer. (2014). *Drugbeleid: Brief van de minister van Veiligheid en Justitie aan de Voorzitter van de Tweede Kamer der Staten-Generaal*. Tweede Kamer stukken 2013–2014, no. 24077 (315). Den Haag: Sdu Uitgevers.

Tweede Kamer. (2017). *Wet gesloten coffeeshopketen*. Tweede Kamer, vergaderjaar 2016–2017, 34 165, nr. 6.

Tweede Kamer. (2018a). *Voorstel van Wet. (Wet experiment gesloten coffeeshopketen)*. Tweede Kamer, vergaderjaar 2018–2019, 34 997, Nr. 2.

Tweede Kamer. (2018b). *Regels inzake een uniform experiment met teelt en verkoop van hennep en hasjiesj voor recreatief gebruik in een gesloten coffeeshopketen (Wet experiment gesloten coffeeshopketen)*. Tweede Kamer, vergaderjaar 2018–2019, 34 997, Nr. 6.

Van de Bunt, H.G. (2006). Hoe stevig zijn de fundamenten van het cannabisbeleid? *Justitiële Verkenningen*, 32(1), 10–23.

Van der Giessen, M., Van Ooyen-Houben, M. and Moolenaar, D.E.G. (2016). Estimating the production, consumption and export of cannabis: The Dutch case. *International Journal of Drug Policy*, 31, 104–112.

Van Kempen, P.H.P.H.M.C. and Federova, M.I. (2014). *Internationaal recht en cannabis: Een beoordeling op basis van VN-drugsverdragen en de EU-drugsregelgeving van gemeentelijke en buitenlandse opvattingen pro regulering van cannabisteelt voor recreatief gebruik*. Deventer: Kluwer.

Van Kempen, P.H.P.H.M.C. and Federova, M.I. (2016). *Internationaal recht en cannabis. Regulering van cannabisteelt en handel: Positieve mensenrechtenverplichtingen versus VN-drugsverdragen*. Deventer: Kluwer.

Van Laar, M. and Van Ooyen-Houben, M. (2009). *Evaluatie van het Nederlandse drugsbeleid*. Utrecht: Trimbos-Instituut/WODC.

Van Laar, M. and Van Ooyen-Houben, M. (Eds.). (2014). *Nationale drugs monitor, Jaarbericht 2013*. Utrecht: Trimbos-Instituut/WODC.

Van Ooyen-Houben, M.M.J., Bieleman, B. and Korf, D.J. (2013). *Het besloten club – En het ingezetencriterium voor coffeeshops. Evaluatie van de implementatie en de uitkomsten in de periode mei-november 2012*. Cahier 2013–2. Den Haag: Wetenschappelijk Onderzoeks- en Documentatiecentrum.

Van Ooyen-Houben, M.M.J., Bieleman, B. and Korf, D.J. (2014). *Coffeeshops, toeristen en lokale markt: Evaluatie van het Besloten club en ingezetenencriterium voor coffeeshops*.

Cahier 2014–12. Den Haag: Wetenschappelijk Onderzoeks- en Documentatiecentrum.

Van Ooyen-Houben, M.M.J., Bieleman, B. and Korf, D.J. (2016). Tightening the Dutch coffeeshop policy: Evaluation of the private club and the residence criterion. *International Journal of Drug Policy*, 31, 113–120.

Van Ooyen-Houben, M. and Kleemans, E. (2016). Drug policy; The "Dutch model." *Crime and Justice*, 44(1), 165–226.

VNG. (2017). *Position paper cannabisbeleid*. Retrieved from https://vng.nl/onderwerpenindex/veiligheid/softdrugsbeleid.

Wouters, M., Benschop, A. and Korf, D.J. (2010). Local politics and retail cannabis markets: The case of the Dutch coffeeshops. *International Journal of Drug Policy*, 21, 315–320.

Wouters, M. and Korf, D.J. (2011) *De wietpas en het sociaal clubmodel. Meningen en verwachtingen van coffeeshopbezoekers in Utrecht*. Amsterdam: Rozenberg Publishers.

Wouters, M., Korf, D.J. and Kroeske, B. (2007). *Harde aanpak, hete zomer: Een onderzoek naar de ontmanteling van hennepkwekerijen in Nederland*. Amsterdam: Rozenberg Publishers.

13 Cannabis social clubs in Spain

Recent legal developments

Xabier Araña and Òscar Parés

Background

Cannabis social clubs (CSCs) are officially registered non-profit associations that collectively organize the cultivation of cannabis and its distribution among their adult members. Most also offer a space for private consumption (Jansseune, Pardal, Decorte, Parés, 2019; Parés and Bouso, 2015; Barriuso, 2011). By growing their own cannabis, club members are able to control its quality and avoid the dangers of using substances that are obtained illegally. CSCs plan production based on estimates of the consumption of all their members. Members must comply with restrictions on their cannabis intake and their supply of cannabis is guaranteed (Belackova, Tomkova and Zabransky, 2016). CSCs must adopt democratic rules and structures for decision-making. Members have the obligation to participate in decisions, which are to be made during their assemblies. They must hold assemblies at least once a year.

The first CSC was formed in 2001 in Barcelona. This milestone was the culmination of a process initiated in 1994 by anti-prohibitionist activist groups fighting to defend their right to cultivate cannabis in order to avoid having to resort to the illegal market for supplies (Montañés, 2017; Decorte, Pardal, Queirolo, Fernanda, Sánchez and Parés, 2017). This model of CSCs then began to be replicated in Barcelona and in other parts of Spain. Two years later, in 2003, 21 CSCs joined forces to create the Federation of Cannabis Clubs (*Federación de Asociaciones Cannábicas*, or FAC for its acronym in Spanish). The FAC has provided tools on the self-regulation of the CSC model and it represents its members in the process of obtaining legal recognition (Belackova and Wilkins 2018). In 2010, the FAC published its *CSC Guide*, which included the results of a study on a model that would allow groups to grow cannabis without being considered drug traffickers. This favored a rapid expansion of CSCs, but in most cases, the *Codes of Good Practices* or internal operating procedures were reinterpreted, without much control or order. The CSCs affiliated or close to the federation, on the other hand, followed the formulas in the FAC's *CSC Guide* more closely.

From 2011 on, as the CSC phenomenon became more widespread and consolidated, other clubs gradually began to emerge and call themselves

"CSCs." Although their statutes were very similar to those of CSCs, their practices were significantly different: they had more members (close to 10,000 in some cases); their operations were less transparent, and their volume of business indicated that they were making considerable profits. Members of the FAC criticized these clubs for having "devalued the model" and exploiting it for business purposes. However, the FAC's capacity to represent CSCs was very limited, as not even 20 percent of the CSCs that existed at the time belonged to the federation.

Up until the end of the 2000s, the CSC phenomenon was relatively unknown to society as a whole and remained in the hands of growers and activists. At the end of 2018, in Barcelona alone, there were approximately 200 CSCs operating officially (Jansseune et al., 2019). The total number of CSCs in Spain is currently estimated at between 800 and 1,000.

Between 1994 and 2013, numerous police investigations and criminal proceedings were launched against CSC directors or managers. The investigations often focused on cannabis crops – not as part of concrete strategy against CSCs in particular, but rather as part of the more generalized crusade against all cannabis growers in Spain. Even so, up until 2015, the majority of the cases involving CSC members were dismissed and the accused were acquitted (Araña, 2015b). In 2012, the delegate of the National Drug Plan and the Special Anti-drug Prosecutor expressed their opposition to CSCs in public. Then, in 2013, the Attorney General's Office issued Order No. 2/2013, which instructed prosecutors to implement a new way of prosecuting the individuals responsible for CSCs. Not only could CSC directors be accused of committing a crime against public health, but also the offense of unlawful association (belonging to a criminal organization). This change would raise the prison sentences that they faced from two or three years to eight. These actions by state officials were part of what we could call a "strategy of fear" that sought to criminalize the CSC movement and their federations (herein referred to as the cannabis movement) and brought the expansion of CSCs to a halt.

Thus, in Spain, between 2013 and 2018, two opposing approaches to CSCs emerged. On the one hand, one finds the "regulatory approach," which seeks to regulate the activities of CSCs. Changes to city regulations (e.g. municipal permits), popular legislative initiatives (in Navarra and Catalonia), decisions of the parliaments of the autonomous communities in favor of regulation and the non-legislative proposals submitted to the Spanish Congress all belong to this approach. On the other hand, and going in the opposition direction, there is the approach focused on prohibition. This includes the Attorney General's Office's Order mentioned above and important rulings of both the Constitutional Court (CC) and the Supreme Court (SC) of Spain that annulled the laws of autonomous communities on CSCs and the responsibilities of their members, especially those in management positions.

These court rulings are out of step with public opinion in Spain. According to a survey undertaken in 2014:

> Fifty percent of the population is in favor of cannabis associations and clubs, while 26% has not yet formed an opinion. Among those who are in favor, 28% see them as a *positive initiative that allows for controlled and responsible use*; the remaining 22% does not show clear support for them, but says that *"they do not bother me; everyone can do as they please so long as it does not affect me."*
>
> (GEPCA, 2017a)

This chapter discusses the evolution of the CSC phenomenon in Spain based on a social, political and legal analysis of developments in this area. The section below presents the methodology used to obtain the information for this analysis, which took into account the inherent difficulties of conducting research on an unregulated phenomenon. This is followed by an analysis of the recent legislative initiatives of the different levels of government (local, autonomous communities and state) and the rulings of the SC and CC that have affected CSCs in the past three years. Then, we examine the concrete impacts that these legal and judicial developments have had on the activities of CSCs. Finally, we end by discussing how the different initiatives and approaches combine to create a complex situation that is full of uncertainties for CSCs in Spain now and in the future.

Methodology

When we examine the evolution of CSCs over the past 20 years, we can conclude that this is a rapidly evolving phenomenon and, as such, it must continue to be analyzed.[1] This exciting challenge is not without difficulty, such as obtaining up-to-date and reliable information on an unregulated phenomenon. The absence of accurate sources of information on CSCs is largely due to the lack of regulation (Decorte et al., 2017).

To illustrate the challenges involved, let us take the example of the number of officially registered CSCs. According to the Register of Associations of Catalonia, in January 2018, there were 688 entities registered in the region. However, we believe there are no more than 300 that open on a daily basis. The same gap between reality and official numbers exists in the rest of Spain. One way to obtain a more accurate portrait of this reality is by conducting fieldwork and interviews with key informants (KIs).

For the elaboration of this chapter, we conducted an in-depth analysis of the following documents: rulings from CC, SC and provincial hearings, all laws, regulations and bills related to CSCs adopted or proposed in the past five years and the publications of the cannabis movement. Secondly, we interviewed several KIs, who were chosen for their years of experience and insider view on the recent evolution of the CSC phenomenon, their geographic location to ensure coverage of the entire country and their complementary perspectives on the phenomenon. In semi-structured interviews, KIs were asked two questions: (1) What impacts have the recent regulatory changes (municipal bylaws, autonomous community laws and popular legislative initiatives) had on CSCs?; and (2) What impacts have the rulings of the Spanish SC and the CC had on CSCs?

In section 3 below, we present the results of our analysis of the regulations of the autonomous communities and municipalities on CSCs, followed by a discussion of three recent cases brought before the Spanish SC and CC related to CSCs. We then examine the impacts of the changes in regulation and the court rulings on the daily activities of CSCs based on information obtained in the interviews with KIs.

Findings

Spain is a decentralized state in which the governments of different subnational entities (officially called autonomous communities) have gained increasing autonomy and decision-making capacities since the transition to democracy in the late 1970s. This is the case for several drug-related policy areas, notably public health and social welfare issues. However, the national government retains the core decision-making capacity on criminal law, the justice system and public security (except the establishment of regional police forces). This includes the capacity to reform the criminal code, which deals with controlled substances. Also, legislating on pharmaceutical products falls under the jurisdiction of the state (including narcotic and psychotropic substances) (Sánchez and Collins, 2018). Municipalities can also adopt bylaws on issues related to drug use that fall under their jurisdiction, such as public health, public safety, etc. As lower-level regulations, though, municipal authorities must take care to ensure that they do not contain elements that contradict the regulations or laws of higher levels of government.

From 2012 to 2017, numerous reference documents, resolutions and regulations related to CSCs were debated and approved at the municipal, autonomous community and national level in Spain. However, the majority of them – especially the most progressive ones – have not been implemented. This is mainly due to the fact that the proposals came from opposition parties or because the complaints filed by the *Partido Popular* government at the CC led to their suspension or annulment.

Even so, the debate on the proposals is revealing of the regulatory process and it brought the benefits of CSCs to public attention at a time when it was becoming increasingly clear that the policy of prosecuting cannabis use and cultivation criminally had failed. In the cannabis movement's view, the measures taken by the city councils and parliaments of the autonomous communities to spark debate and implement concrete regulations for CSCs were steps in the right direction. These measures are discussed below.

Autonomous communities' regulations on CSCs

The following autonomous communities adopted laws to regulate CSCs: Navarra (Foral Law 24/2014 of December 2, which regulates CSCs); the Basque Country (Law 1/2016 of April 7 on comprehensive care for addictions and drug addictions); and Catalonia (Law 13/2017 of July 6 on CSCs). While the debate on the need for changes to drug policies is not limited to these autonomous communities, they are the only ones to have adopted legislation to regulate cannabis. Each one has taken a different course, advanced at its own pace and has its own particularities (Sánchez and Collins, 2018).

The autonomous community of Navarra

Navarra was the first autonomous community to pass a law to regulate the activities of CSCs within its jurisdiction. The law was the result of a popular legislative initiative promoted by the *Representación Cannábica de Navarra* (RCN-NOK, or Cannabis Representation of Navarra) political group. Its purpose is to establish general rules for the creation of CSCs, their structure and operations (Article 1). It does not go into detail on aspects related to the cultivation of cannabis. To create a CSC, its organizers must comply with the national Organic Law 1/2002 of March 22, which regulates the freedom of association (Article 3) and thus the establishment of any civic association, including CSCs. They must also carry out the process to establish CSCs in accordance with Article 4 of Foral Law 24/2014.

Even though the autonomous community's law was very broad, four months after it was passed, it was suspended when the CC agreed to hear the claim that the then-prime minister Mariano Rajoy submitted to challenge its constitutionality. In December 2017, the CC ruled that the law was unconstitutional, as it impinged upon the state's exclusive power to legislate in the area of criminal law.

After the law was annulled by the CC in February 2018, four of the political parties in the Navarra parliament that also have elected representatives in the Spanish Congress announced that they would send an initiative to the Spanish Congress with the goal of launching the debate at the national level in an attempt to get a law on cannabis use approved.

The autonomous community of the Basque Country

In October 2011, upon the request of members of Cannabis Social Clubs (CSCs) in the Basque Country, the *Ararteko* (Ombudsman of the Basque Country) organized a forum to debate the use, legal security and policies on cannabis. The event brought together legal experts (judges, prosecutors and lawyers), the academic world and CSC representatives. The forum's conclusions emphasized the need to come up with creative ways to ensure that adult PWUDs have access to cannabis without having to resort to the illegal market.

A few months later, in 2012, the Basque Parliament created a parliamentary committee that was to find a solution for the issue of regulating CSCs. Based on the contributions of approximately 30 specialists and the work of the committee members, the committee presented several conclusions and recommendations at the end of its mandate (Araña, 2015b). It called on the Basque Parliament to urge the Basque Government to advance, within its competences, with the development of its own system. It stated that this system should be capable of providing guarantees and legal security for CSCs. It should be based on the principles of harm reduction and a framework that upholds the rights and obligations of PWUDs. Later, it pressed the Basque Government to analyze and adopt, again within its jurisdiction, regulatory developments that could help resolve the problem of regulating CSCs. Finally, it also proposed that in future revisions of the Law on Addictions (Law 1/2016) and its regulations, the government should include rules, programs and protocols to regulate CSCs.

Although Law 1/2016 on comprehensive care for addictions and drug addictions in the Basque Country is not a law adopted to specifically regulate CSCs, it does take into account the recommendations of the Basque parliamentary committee on CSCs. In the interest of protecting public health and reducing harm, Law 1/2016 allows CSCs to be regulated provided that they have been legally registered, are non-profit and only accept adults as members (Article 83.1).

Article 83.1 of Law 1/2016 was challenged in the Spanish CC by the country's prime minister at the time, who argued that the article infringes upon the state's power to legislate in the areas of pharmaceutical products, criminal law and legal security. The CC agreed to hear the case, which led to the immediate suspension of the law as a precautionary measure. On March 18, 2018, the CC ruled to dismiss the challenge. It declared that Article 83 of Law 1/2016 is not unconstitutional, provided that it is interpreted as being limited to establishing the functions that CSCs shall perform in collaboration with the health administration. Thus, on the one hand, the CC's ruling confirms that the Basque Country has the power to legislate on CSCs by adopting its own regulations. On the other, by tying these regulations to CSCs' collaboration with the health system, it puts an enormous straitjacket on the autonomous community and limits its ability to respond to the demands of the cannabis movement.

The autonomous community of Catalonia

In 2012, the Health Department of the Catalan government launched a process that brought together members of parliament, the cannabis federations in Catalonia and a committee created by the Health Department itself. During this collective process, the possibility of elaborating a bill to regulate CSCs emerged. However, due to political differences and the possibility that some of the issues to be included in the future law could infringe upon the powers of the state to legislate in the area of criminal law, it was not drafted. This process culminated in the adoption of Resolution SLT/32/2015, which defined the public health guidelines that CSCs must follow and the conditions that they had to meet to carry out their activities in municipalities in Catalonia.[2] Even though the resolution was not an actual law, it was challenged by the state attorney and was annulled a few months after its adoption. The national government's intervention sparked a citizen's movement in favor of a regulatory solution for CSCs led by *La Rosa Verda* (the Green Rose Group). The movement promoted a popular legislative initiative on the regulation of CSCs, for which it obtained the signatures of 57,000 Catalonians.

After two years of negotiations between organized civil society and the autonomous community government, on July 6, 2017, the Parliament of Catalonia approved Law 13/2017 on CSCs. Of the three laws adopted by the autonomous communities, it is the most complete because it regulates the rights of PWUDs, as well as the cultivation, distribution and transportation of cannabis and its quality. The law was only in effect for a few weeks when the then-Spanish prime minister brought a claim challenging the constitutionality of the law before the CC. In its September 19, 2018 ruling, the CC declared the Catalonian law unconstitutional because in the court's understanding, the Parliament of Catalonia infringed upon the exclusive power of the state to legislate on criminal matters.

A comparative analysis

When one analyzes all three laws, both similarities and differences can be found. One similarity is that all three autonomous communities attempted to use their powers in different areas to pass regulations on CSCs. These areas include public health and social services, the rights of PWUD, risk and harm reduction, legally registered non-profit organizations (created by adults) and the participation of PWUD in the prevention and reduction of risks and harm (Araña, 2018; Sánchez and Collins, 2018).

The fundamental differences lie in the type of legislation proposed. The goal of Law 1/2016 of the Basque Country is to regulate the measures and actions adopted in the areas of health promotion, prevention, supply reduction, social assistance, social inclusion, training and research and institutional organization to provide comprehensive care for addictions, including behavioral addictions. It also contains regulations on actions to protect third parties from harm that may be caused by both drug use or behavioral addictions, which contain special provisions for minors, youth and individuals in particularly vulnerable situations (Article 1). Thus, it is not a law specifically on CSCs, but it does allow for them to be regulated via the adoption of additional regulations (Araña, 2018). The law does not regulate aspects regarding the cultivation, transportation or distribution of cannabis.

Foral Law 24/2014 and Catalonia's Law 13/2017, on the other hand, are laws adopted specifically to regulate CSCs. In their explanatory memorandums, both laws refer to "shared use or consumption" – an issue that is not addressed in the Basque Country's law. The scope of the Catalonian law is much broader and more concrete than that of Navarra. The latter is concentrated more on elements related to the freedom of association and the reduction of risks associated with cannabis use; it does not include provisions on the cultivation, transportation or potential taxes related to cannabis. Catalonia's law regulated all CSC activities by establishing, for example, a monthly limit of 80 grams of cannabis per member, norms for the transportation of cannabis to CSCs and the obligation to carry out quality tests on cannabis samples. It also encouraged CSCs to collaborate with organizations specializing in the implementation of measures for the prevention and reduction of harm related to cannabis use, etc.

All three laws were challenged in the Spanish CC by the then-prime minister Mariano Rajoy, but the cases ended with different results. While the CC declared that the Foral Law (in the ruling handed down on September 17, 2017) and the Catalonian law (the ruling issued on September 19, 2018) were unconstitutional and therefore null because they intervened in the state's jurisdiction, the Basque Country's law was declared constitutional. Therefore, within its competencies in the areas of health and risk and harm reduction, the Basque Country's parliament has the power to regulate CSCs by adopting regulations, provided that they are strictly limited to defining rules on CSCs' collaboration with the government. The goal of this collaboration is to ensure effective compliance with existing regulations, to prevent addictions and to promote the responsible use of cannabis or other substances. In practice, the CC's recognition of this competence strongly limits the Basque Country's room to maneuver and to adopt regulations that meet the expectations of the cannabis movement and other social movements.

Municipal bylaws on CSCs

Several municipal bylaws have also been passed to regulate CSCs on issues that fall under the jurisdiction of the municipalities. These bylaws control registration of this type of association to ensure that they are registered in the appropriate public registry, plus the location of their headquarters. They also establish conditions that the buildings in which CSCs' headquarters are located must meet to ensure that their activities do not cause disturbances in the surrounding neighborhood and that they are in compliance with the safety, sanitation and hygiene regulations in effect.

In the Basque Country, a municipal bylaw in Donostia (San Sebastian) – unanimously approved in November 2014 by all political groups sitting on the city council – regulates the CSCs' locations and operations. This bylaw takes the reality of the CSCs into account and grants them institutional recognition. However, it also demands that they commit to complying with legal requirements and collaborating with the city council on prevention and harm reduction. The bylaw stipulates that all of this is to be framed in a code of good conduct, which is to be elaborated as a binding municipal bylaw by the city council together with CSCs. Its goal would be to ensure transparency in the work of CSCs.

In Catalonia, since 2014, 43 municipal bylaws related to CSCs have been passed.[3] While some existed prior to the approval of Resolution SLT/32/2015 by the Catalonian autonomous community, their numbers have increased significantly since then. Some bylaws have been well-received by the cannabis movement, such as the ones adopted in Barcelona, Badalona and Granollers, whereas others serve as mere instruments of prohibitionism. For example, once the bylaw in Salou was passed, only one of 13 CSCs remained.

Municipal bylaws in Catalonia have been fundamentally based on criteria related to urban planning, safety, hygiene, opening hours, seating capacity, smoke removal and other issues and, in general, they have helped create a more harmonious environment for both CSC members and the residents of the neighborhoods in which they are located. In a few isolated cases, however, these local norms have generated differences between municipalities in terms of regulation. In some municipalities, CSCs have been stigmatized and even expelled, leading to a situation where the rights of PWUD vary from one municipality to the next, even when located only a few kilometers from one another. This confirms that there is a lack of adequate regulation, as the individuals responsible for the CSCs (cannabis growers) are still left to face problems of legal uncertainty. Also, the absence of regulations from higher levels of government (autonomous communities or the state) to frame them is a double-edged sword: on the one hand, these municipal bylaws can be used for the purposes of populist electioneering rather than to defend fundamental rights; on the other, municipalities can take advantage of the lack of higher-level regulations to normalize the situation of CSCs.

In Catalonia, one unintended effect of the municipal bylaws is related to the requirements imposed by certain municipalities: the bigger the municipality, the stricter they are. Barcelona is a case in point. The costs of preparing a venue to open a CSC have increased enormously: as high as 60,000 euro in some cases. CSCs there must now meet a series of environmental, safety and administrative requirements and obtain various permits, which demands sizeable investments. Once a group obtains a permit to operate, if the police intervene in a cultivation site (often located off-site) that can be linked to the CSC (through a contract, for example), it may face criminal charges. This means that it is less risky in legal and economic terms to start growing cannabis than to obtain a municipal permit for a CSC. As we will see below, recent SC rulings favor small CSCs that have no way of assuming such high costs.

Recent legal developments

From the mid-1990s to early 2015, the majority of court rulings involving members of CSCs did not consider their work to be illegal. However, three cases were filed against CSC members at the SC (launched by the Attorney General's Office) even though they had previously been acquitted by provincial courts.[4] The SC convicted the CSC members in all three cases, as it viewed the CSCs as a real and latent risk for an increase in cannabis use (Muñoz Sánchez, 2015). In all three verdicts, the SC considered that the accused had committed an "overcomable or vincible mistake"[5] and condemned them to relatively short prison sentences and large fines. Even though the Attorney General's Office requested that they be prosecuted for belonging to criminal organizations, the SC did not include this in its rulings.

In all three cases, judges submitted individual opinions[6] and the accused presented an appeal to the CC to request protection for their fundamental rights. The CC agreed to hear the appeals. The first case, known as the "Ebers Case," appealed SC ruling 484/2015 of September 2017, which had sentenced one of the three members of the *Asociación de Estudios y Usuarios del Cáñamo Ebers* (Ebers Association of Research on Cannabis and People who use Hemp) to eight months in prison and a fine of 5,000 euro, and the two other members to three months in prison (Miró, 2017). The arguments used to justify the appeal were that there had been a breach of material guarantees inherent to the principle of criminal legality (Article 25.1 of the Spanish Constitution) and that the SC had violated fundamental rights of a procedural nature linked to the right to due process (Article 24.2 of the Spanish Constitution).

With regards to the first argument, the appellants claimed that the reference to the harm that the substance can cause to the protected legal good (public health) is unsubstantiated and that the conduct referred to in Article 368 of the Spanish Criminal Code[7] does not respect the principle of legal clarity, as the article contains undefined legal terms. According to the appellants, the terms "otherwise," "promote, supply or facilitate" and "illegal consumption" lack precision. The CC responded by providing a definition of the crime of illegal drug trafficking that was based much more on the obsolete and ideological principles of the prohibitionist policy originating in the Single Convention on Narcotic Drugs of 1961 than on the principles, rights and freedoms of social and democratic rule of law and on the reality of society in Spain today, as the majority of provincial courts had been doing. The CC rejected the arguments of the appeal and dismissed the claim that Article 368 was unconstitutional because it violates the principle of legality.

However, as for the second argument (Article 24.2 of the Spanish Constitution), the CC recognized that the right to due process and the right to defense had been violated, as the SC did not hear the appellants' defense. Because of this error, the CC referred the proceedings back to the SC so it could rectify the said constitutional challenge. In practical terms, this meant that the convictions in the Ebers Case would be overturned. The arguments used in the Ebers Case were used in the Three Monkeys and Pannagh cases; in all three cases, the members were acquitted of the charges against them.

Overall, the SC and CC rulings generated even greater legal uncertainty for the CSCs, as the CSC members were acquitted for legal technicalities and violations of their right to defense. In the majority of the cases brought before these courts, the courts have reaffirmed that CSCs are illegal. The said rulings also created the need to rethink the model, as they establish that CSCs must restrict their membership and adopt closed circle use to comply with the principle of shared consumption, and accept a series of other controls on their operations. This made the situation worse for larger CSCs. As smaller CSCs have only a small group of members (small crops), are transparent about their finances (their accounts show that there are no "profits" and all costs are shared) and can show that they have functioned this way for several years, they have more arguments to use in their defense. Even so, this is no guarantee that they will not be condemned in court.

While high-level state bodies in favor of prohibition have tried to stifle the cannabis movement and all attempts to start the debate on the legalization of cannabis, since 2016, they have granted up to six permits for research on and growing and exporting medicinal cannabis to companies that have no links to the cannabis movement. The cannabis movement considers the granting of these permits hypocritical and unjust.

The impacts of the changes in regulation and the court rulings on CSCs

The recent developments discussed above have raised a new challenge for CSCs: how to reconcile their official objectives stated in their statutes with the new legal requirements that arose from the SC and CC rulings. CSCs have very little room to maneuver and must use considerable creativity to resolve this issue.

To document how CSCs are responding to this challenge, we interviewed KIs who have accompanied the CSCs throughout this process. The CSCs' responses vary due to several variables, such as affiliation to a federation or political coalition, the criteria used by the law firm that provides them with legal advice, the sociopolitical circumstances of a CSC's location, and the activist and/or business profile of the individuals responsible for the CSCs, among others.

The interviews enabled us to identify four trends: (a) a sudden halt to the expansion of CSCs; (b) more caution among management; (c) closure of some CSCs; and (d) complete indifference. While some trends appear to contradict one another, it is not surprising that they do so for several reasons. One of the main factors is the variation in the attitudes of state actors: police pressure is greater in some parts of the country than in others, and some public prosecutors are more belligerent towards CSCs than others. There are judges who, despite the CC and SC rulings, continue to dismiss charges against CSCs, and lawyers who are more optimistic about the future of the CSC model than others. Some neighborhood communities opposed the opening of a CSC in their area and have forced the municipality to expel it (NIMBY Effect[8]), whereas the large majority of communities coexist peacefully with CSCs.

One example of the measures that CSCs are adopting to reduce risk is the revision of their list of members to eliminate those who are inactive or have not paid their membership fees for a while. This has led to a decrease in CSC membership. Other measures aim to increase CSCs' control over the amount of cannabis being grown, stored or transported to avoid complications with the police and their legal defense (the police consider more than 10kg as a "highly significant amount"). They are also decentralizing cannabis cultivation to go from larger crops to in-house installations with between three and six lamps, as the smaller operations can be justified as cannabis grown for personal use (in case of a police raid). Outdoor crops are also being phased out to avoid the risk of being found and CSCs are seeking ways to reduce the amount of cannabis acquired through group purchases.[9] CSCs have stopped or plan to stop distributing cannabis in small plastic bags and make members bring their own receptacles for storing cannabis to make it appear more like a member is withdrawing a product set aside for him or her than a business transaction. Finally, some CSCs are obliging their members to use cannabis only while on their premises and have established targets to reduce the amount of cannabis distributed daily.

The KIs reported that many CSCs are also working to establish agreements and collaborate with health professionals on monitoring use and providing guidance on risk reduction to PWUD. Some are implementing programs for therapeutic use and establishing alliances with the media or medical clinics. CSCs are also providing their workers with training on the reduction of the risks of cannabis use and on medicinal use, which is conducted by specialized organizations.

Other noteworthy observations are that CSCs are giving more importance to holding formal assemblies with members. In certain CSCs with a more activist profile, whose members identify with CSCs' goals and struggles, when the CSC has been raided by police or faced charges and members of the board expressed their desire to step down from their position, instead of closing the CSC, other members have stepped up to the plate and joined the board of directors to keep the CSC afloat. When more commercial-oriented CSCs find themselves in a similar situation, members tend to simply seek out other CSCs.

With regards to activism, KIs reported that the FAC has realized that it should seek alliances with other civil rights coalitions, such as the #NoSomosDelito (#WeAreNotaCrime) movement. In this movement, the FAC has found the recognition, solidarity and complicity that many people involved in CSCs have denied it. To build this consensus and solidarity, they have put the demands that affect the entire cannabis movement first, such as the repression inherent to the Law on Citizen Safety and the drug tests performed on drivers known as *"DrogoTest."*

The majority of CSCs do not engage in public activism and others have joined numerous organizations or coalitions that have helped enrich the sociopolitical debate on drug policies. Among them, *Plataforma Regulación Responsable* (Responsible Regulation Coalition), the revitalized *CONFAC* (*Confederación de Asociaciones Cannábicas*, or Confederation of Cannabis Social Clubs) or *Círculo Cannábico Podemos* ("*Podemos*" Cannabis Circle) are worth highlighting. Other social actors that are not directly from the cannabis movement have also participated in the debate. One example is the *Grupo de Estudio de Políticas sobre el Cannabis* (*GEPCA*, Cannabis Policy Study Group), which presented a proposal for the regulation of cannabis in Spain (GEPCA, 2017b) that aims to regulate not only CSCs, but also home growing and the market through permits.

Finally, one problematic practice mentioned in the interviews was when CSCs changed the composition of the board of directors to include front men – that is, people who are paid money to assume responsibility for a potential crime in the case of conviction. This practice is clearly illegal. Also, some of the "so-called CSCs" sold their municipal permits for exorbitant amounts of money (over one million euro in a few cases); a few even announced this sale on websites. This type of transaction is also illegal and is only found in cases where the investors' goal is to make profit, which goes against the philosophy and practices adopted when the first CSCs were created.

Discussion and conclusions

Since the founding of the first CSC in Barcelona in 2001, the phenomenon has continued to spread throughout the country, reaching a total of over 800 CSCs in all of Spain. At the same time, and especially from 2013 on, pressure on CSCs from the judicial system has increased. Several cases against CSC members were brought before Spain's highest courts: the SC and the CC. The SC condemned the accused, but shortly after, the CC ruled in favor of the CSCs' appeal, not because of an issue related to fundamental rights (such as the right to personal development, freedom of association or of expression), which was the main underlying issue, but rather to the right to defense – that is, due to a procedural error. The CC sent the case back to the SC, which directly acquitted the accused because it had not respected their right to present their defense in person. Despite the SC and CC's rulings on CSCs, which condemned their operations as illegal, judges in Spain continue to dismiss cases and acquit the accused. This clearly demonstrates the legal insecurity that CSCs face, which varies according to factors such as the autonomous community where the CSC is located, whether the prosecutor in question resolves to enforce the Attorney General's Order 2/2013 or if the Special Anti-drug Prosecutor is involved in the case. This combination of municipal and autonomous community initiatives, civil society interventions and court rulings means that the process of reforming drug policy in the country is often chaotic and difficult to follow from the outside. Drug policy development in Spain can only be understood when analyzed within this context of complex, multi-level political dynamics (Sánchez and Collins, 2018).

If the recent SC rulings on shared consumption were to be strictly applied, only CSCs with much more limited activities would be able to continue operating. In a way, this would confirm that the FAC was right to defend its model, even though not even the CSCs affiliated to the FAC, which tend to be smaller, would be able to meet such strict requirements, as they make collective organizing virtually impossible. Therefore, it would appear that shared consumption is no longer an option and it is not unreasonable to think that, in view of the state's attempt to restrict CSCs' growth and activities, the movement should consider focusing once again on collective cultivation and more horizontal activist organizing.

The path taken by many CSCs that are not affiliated to federations is the result of oscillations that emerge from their interfaces with the informal market or from parts of the "cannabis industry" and some of its nexus. The conflicts and misunderstandings among CSC representatives are directly related to their affinities and antipathies with the "cannabis industry" and its business, legal and other representatives. Spain is a world leader in the seeds sector, towering over the almighty Netherlands in this area. It hosts numerous international fairs every year and is home to more than 1,000 grow shops. The number of conflicting interests, hostile takeovers and opportunists is very high, which directly affects the dynamics of the CSCs.

The SC and CC sentences made it clear to CSCs that their only opportunity to survive legally is if the Congress were to regulate their activities. The courts are no longer a source of hope: contrary to the numerous rulings in their favor issued by lower-level courts, the responses from the country's highest courts were less positive. Thus, changes to legislation are required to respond to the demands of thousands of adults who want to continue using cannabis without having to go to the illegal market for supplies. Even though the new government elected in June 2018 is said to be more progressive than its predecessor, it has explicitly stated that cannabis regulation is not a priority.

Notes

1 For more information on these issues, see: Araña (2015a), Araña (2015b), Araña (2018), Araña and Montañés (2010), Belackova et al., (2016), GEPCA (2017a), GEPCA (2017b), Marín (2010), Martínez and Araña (2015), Montañés (2017), Parés and Bouso (2015), Quintas and Araña (2017) and Regulación Responsable (2017).

2 The Catalan Health Department's guidelines provided information and guidance on how to reduce the risks and harm associated with cannabis consumption, training for the people responsible for dispensing cannabis in the Cannabis Social Clubs, and on early detection, monitoring and prevention of problematic consumption. They also prohibit the use of other drugs and alcoholic beverages on the premises;

restrict the sale of tobacco and reinforce the need to comply with the Spanish tobacco law and establish a minimum distance between CSC locations and schools and healthcare centres. They regulate opening hours (maximum of 8 hours per day; closing time is 10 p.m. during the week and 12 p.m. on weekends). The guidelines also prohibit the use of advertising, emphasize compliance with the sanitation laws and norms and environmental standards and impose measures to prevent disturbances in the surrounding neighborhoods. Members must be 18 years or older and regular cannabis users, belong to only one CSC or obtain the endorsement of another member to join. Also, to avoid cannabis tourism, there is a 15-day waiting period between application submission and membership approval (Parés and Bouso, 2015).

3 Alella, Badalona, Barcelona, Cabrera de Mar, Calella, Cambrils, Castellbisbal, Castelldefels, Cerdanyola del Vallès, El Masnou, Gavà, Girona, Granollers, Gurb, La Jonquera, L'Hospitalet de Llobregat, La Seu d'Urgell, Lleida, Lloret de Mar, Mataró, Montmeló, Olesa de Montserrat, Olot, Pineda de Mar, Prat del Llobregat, Premià de Mar, Ripollet, Sabadell, Salt, Sant Adrià del Besòs, Sant Carles de Ràpita, Sant Cugat del Vallès, Sant Feliu de Llobregat, Sant Just Desvern, Santa Coloma de Gramenet, Sitges, Teià, Terrassa, Tordera, Torredembarra, Vallirana, Vilanova i la Geltrú and Vilassar de Mar.

4 *The Ebers Case*, STS 484/2015, of September 7; the *Three Monkeys Case*, STS 596/2015, of October 5; and the *Pannagh Case*, STS 788/2015, of December 9.

5 The term in Spanish is "*error de prohibición vencible.*"

6 In the first ruling on the Ebers Case, three judges submitted individual opinions: the first argued that there is a need to establish requirements for this type of association; the second considered that the accused had committed an invincible error and thus, they should be acquitted; and the third partially coincided with the first individual opinion, but disagreed with the existence of an invincible error, as proposed in the second individual opinion.

7 Article 368 of the Spanish Criminal Code stipulates the following: individuals who engage in the act of cultivating, producing or trafficking or otherwise promote, encourage or facilitate the illegal consumption of toxic drugs, narcotics or psychotropic substances or who possess them with such objectives shall be sentenced to prison terms of three to six years and a fine that is three times the value of the drug that is the object of the crime in cases involving substances or products that cause serious harm to health, and a prison sentence of one to three years and a fine of up to double the value in all other cases.

8 "Not in My Back Yard" or "Nimby" is a slogan used by residents who oppose the opening of a CSC in their surroundings. It often carries the connotation that such residents are only opposing the development because it is close to them and that they would tolerate or support it if it were built further away.

9 A "group purchase" refers to the acquisition of a certain amount of cannabis on the informal market by CSCs, which does not generate profit because it is distributed among members (closed circle use).

References

Araña, X. (2015a). Código de buenas prácticas para los clubes sociales de cannabis. *Fundación renovatio. Memoria 2013* (pp. 9–37). Gasteiz: Fundación Renovatio.

Araña, X. (2015b). Viabilidad legal de los clubes sociales de cannabis en la comunidad autónoma del País Vasco y propuesta de hoja de ruta. *Fundación Renovatio. Memoria 2014* (pp. 106–155). Gasteiz: Fundación Renovatio.

Araña, X. (2018). Progresiones y regresiones – en materia legislativa y jurisprudencial, y la necesidad de una propuesta sobre un nuevo modelo de regulación del cannabis: El caso español en la presente década. In S. Shecaira, X. Araña, F. Caroso and B. Miranda, *Drogas, desafios contemporâneos* (pp. 431–461). Brazil: Editora D'Plácido.

Araña, X. and Montañés, V. (2010). Cannabis cultivation in Spain. The case of cannabis social clubs. In T. Decorte, G. Potter and M. Bouchard (Eds.), *World wide weed: Global trends in cannabis cultivation and control* (pp. 284–307). UK: Ashgate Publishers.

Barriuso, M. (2011). Cannabis social clubs in Spain. A normalizing alternative underway. *Series on Legislative Reform of Drug Policies,* 2, 1–9.

Belackova, V., Tomkova, A. and Zabransky, T. (2016). Qualitative research in Spanish cannabis social clubs: "The moment you enter the door, you are minimising the risks." *International Journal of Drug Policy,* 34, 49–57.

Belackova, V. and Wilkins, C. (2018). Consumer agency in cannabis supply – Exploring auto-regulatory documents of the cannabis social clubs in Spain. *International Journal of Drug Policy,* 54, 26–34.

Decorte, T., Pardal, M., Queirolo, R., Fernanda, M., Sanchez, C. and Parés, O. (2017). Regulating cannabis social clubs: A comparative analysis of legal and self-regulatory practices in Spain, Belgium and Uruguay. *International Journal of Drug Policy,* 43, 44–56.

GEPCA. (2017a). *Cannabis, de los márgenes a la normalidad. Hacia un nuevo modelo de regulación.* Barcelona: Bellaterra.

GEPCA. (2017b). *Cannabis: Propuesta de un nuevo modelo de regulación.* Barcelona: Bellaterra.

Jansseune, L., Pardal, M., Decorte, T. and Parés, Ò. (2019). Revisiting the birthplace of the cannabis social club model and the role played by cannabis social club federations. *Journal of Drug Issues*, 49(2), 338–354.

Marín, I. (2010). *Cannabis. El movimiento cannábico en España.* Madrid: Ed. Popular.

Martínez Oró, D.P. and Araña, X. (2015). ¿Qué es la normalización en el ámbito de los usos de las drogas? *Revista Española de Drogodependencias,* 40(3), 27–42.

Miró, G. (2017). Organización colectiva de usuarios de cannabis tras la doctrina Ebers. In D.P. Martínez (Ed.), *Las sendas de la regulación del cannabis en España* (pp. 448–464). Barcelona: Edicions Bellaterra.

Montañés, V. (2017). Evolución del activismo cannábico en España. In D.P. Martínez (Ed.), *Las sendas de la regulación del cannabis en España* (pp. 145–159). Barcelona: Edicions Bellaterra.

Muñoz Sánchez, J. (2015). La relevancia penal de los clubes sociales de cannabis. Reflexiones sobre la política de cannabis y análisis jurisprudencial. *Revista Electrónica de Ciencia Penal y Criminología,* 17–22.

Parés, Ò. and Bouso, J.C. (2015). *Innovation born of necessity: Pioneering drug policy in Catalonia.* New York, NY: Open Society Foundations.

Quintas, J. and Araña, X. (2017). Decriminalization: Different models in Portugal and Spain. In E. Savona, M. Kleiman and F. Calderoni (Eds.), *Dual markets. Comparative approaches for regulation* (pp. 121–143). USA: Springer Nature.

Regulación responsable (Ed.). (2017). *Las sendas de la regulación del cannabis en España.* Barcelona: Ed. Bellaterra.

Sánchez, C. and Collins, M. (2018). *Better to ask forgiveness than permission: Spain's subnational approach to drug policy.* Policy brief June 12, 2018. Swansea: Global Drug Policy Observatory.

14 Swiss cannabis policies

Simon Anderfuhren-Biget, Frank Zobel,
Cédric Heeb and Jean-Félix Savary

Introduction

Switzerland is a federalist state with three independent government levels – the confederation, the 26 cantons, and over 2,000 municipalities – each having a defined set of responsibilities and a certain level of freedom regarding the implementation of policies. Their powers and competencies follow the principle of subsidiarity, and the country is considered a model case of power sharing (Ladner, 2010). Switzerland's political institutions also include several instruments of direct democracy. The right of initiative allows citizens to submit new laws/constitutional articles for popular vote, while all laws adopted by legislative bodies can be subject to a referendum if requested by a sufficient number of citizens. Ballot initiatives at the federal level can only modify the Constitution and must have a double majority (voters and cantons) to be adopted (Kriesi, 1998). Overall, the Swiss political system is a paradigmatic case of consensus democracy characterized by strong collaboration among actors within each policy subsystem and consensus-seeking across ideological barriers or interest groups (Lijphart, 2012).

In terms of drug policy, the country is a signatory to the UN drug conventions and its Drugs Law (LStup)[1] pertains to the Confederation, with the Federal Office of Public Health (FOPH) being responsible for overseeing its application. As Health and Law Enforcement are cantonal prerogatives, they (and to a lesser extent municipalities) have a certain latitude in the interpretation of the law, and more critically, the resources and administrative capacity to enforce and implement it (Boggio, Cattacin, Lucas and Cesoni, 1997). In this context, drug policy takes various forms at the local level with some differences in the balance between public health and public order objectives.

Hemp cultivation is historically rooted in the Swiss agricultural landscape (Kessler, 1985) and cannabis policy reform activism can be tracked back to the mid-70s (Arsever, 2010). Personal use of cannabis was not considered an offense until the late 1960s (Zobel, Homberg and Marthaler, 2017) and is nowadays punished with an administrative fine. Legalizing cannabis and regulating its market has been publicly discussed in Switzerland for more than

20 years (CFLD, 1999, 2008) with often intense public debates regarding the results of its prohibition (Nils-Robert, 2016).

This chapter reviews the Swiss cannabis policy debate and the attempts to change that policy over the last 20 years, highlighting institutional and other features that can either help or delay the adaptation of the legal framework to societal changes. The role of consensus building to achieve political change is also discussed, including the time it takes to build such a consensus when issues are divisive and do not require an urgent political response, as is the case for cannabis.

The chapter ends with the presentation of a policy-modelling process that tries to overcome ideological barriers and expertise silos. Through regular meetings, constructive discussion and pragmatic decisions, the authors of this chapter agreed upon ten basic principles to shape a legally regulated cannabis market in Switzerland (GREA and IG-Hanf, 2018). The authors have different backgrounds, positions and interests within the cannabis policy subsystem: academic research, non-governmental organizations active in drugs research and addiction issues and the cannabis industry. Such an opportunity for exchange of ideas allows for the definition of policy agreements that are critical to the formation of effective advocacy coalitions (Ingold, Fischer and Cairney, 2017). For instance, prevention experts had a better understanding of the reality faced by cannabis entrepreneurs, which allowed for the definition of clear, effective and feasible market guidelines. On the other hand, market players regarded the role of advertisement limitations as a critical tool for prevention. All participants had to take a step back from their initial views and positions in order to design a regulatory framework suitable to all sides.

Cannabis policy reform at the federal level: the failed consensus

During the 1990s and early 2000s, cannabis production developed widely in Switzerland, reaching almost industrial dimensions (CFLD, 1999). At the European level, the country was considered one of the largest cannabis producers alongside the Netherlands. Cultivation for personal use flourished on many balconies in urban centers, while "hemp shops" made their revenue by selling "odorous/therapeutic cushions" containing dry cannabis flowers (CFLD, 1999). The Swiss cannabis sector also included grow shops, consumer clubs and cultivators. The actors were often known to the police and enjoyed a certain level of tolerance from cantonal and municipal authorities. In 2004, the number of cannabis retail points was estimated to have reached at least 420 (CFLD, 2008), with many of their owners being members of professional associations like the "Swiss Hemp Coordination" (Reusser, 1997). The cannabis scene also included internationally renowned figures such as Bernard Rappaz (Arsever, 2010).

The relative tolerance towards cannabis and its market in the late 1990s and early 2000s was related to a change of attitudes towards drugs during the 1990s, when harm reduction was adopted both as a set of measures and as a new drug policy paradigm. A proposal from the Swiss government to radically change the country's cannabis policy was also expected (Arsever, 2010; Rappaz, 2013). Several popular votes regarding the national drug policy had already paved the way for such a reform, including two ballot initiatives in 1997 and 1998. The first, "Youth without drugs" came from conservative circles with the goal of restoring a drug policy focusing solely on abstinence and thereby removing harm-reduction measures. The second, "*Droleg*" came from the left as well as from some professionals of the drugs field and required the legalization/regulation of all illicit drugs. The voters considered the initiatives to be too radical and rejected them both. Nonetheless, the process prepared the public opinion for alternative options, and provided the federal government with a middle path in which both the institutionalization of harm-reduction measures and cannabis policy reforms seemed feasible.

In 2001, the Federal Council (executive) sent a proposal for changing the Drugs Law to the parliament. This full revision of the LStup provided a legal basis for harm reduction and the four pillars policy, and also allowed for refraining from prosecuting cannabis users and part of the cannabis trade under the "principle of opportunity." Instead of setting up a legal framework for cannabis market regulation (which was not considered possible under the UN conventions), the Swiss government opted for an approach of limited interference in the existing cannabis market. The proposal acknowledged the existence of a large grey cannabis market and relied on the shift towards public health that the Swiss drug policy had taken during the previous decade.

The proposal was rejected in 2004 by a majority of federal parliamentarians who were strongly opposed to cannabis reforms (Archives fédérales, 2006). The rejection also meant that harm reduction, which was widely implemented by the cantons and part of the federal policy, was still not mentioned in the Drugs Law and that the medical prescription of heroin still needed a legal basis to be continued. In a climate of tension with the parliament, due not only to the rejection of the proposal but also to the absence of any alternative, the Minister of Health announced the withdrawal of the government and left the parliament with the task of reforming the Drugs Law.

Year 2008: a turning point for Swiss drug policy?

In 2006, the parliament came up with a new legislative proposal in order to institutionalize the four pillars policy and harm-reduction interventions. It was prepared by an alliance of the Liberal (center right-wing) and Socialist (center left-wing) parties. To maximize its chances of passing and thereby anchoring the four pillars in the law, the proposal excluded cannabis -related reforms. The National Assembly adopted the partial revision of the Drugs Law in November 2006 but the Federal Democratic Union (conservative right-wing) launched a referendum against the decision and the new law had to be submitted to a popular vote.

Meanwhile, in 2004, a coalition of cannabis entrepreneurs from the Swiss Hemp Coordination launched a ballot initiative entitled: "For a reasonable hemp policy to effectively protect the youth."[2] Its objective was to clarify the cannabis situation, to get rid of existing legal grey zones and to regulate the market. The 100,000 requisite signatures were provided to the Federal Chancellery in January 2006 and the popular vote to add a new article regarding cannabis regulation to the Swiss Constitution was scheduled for 2008. The initiative echoed many of the views advocated by the confederation alongside its 2001 reform proposal. Despite this, both the parliament and the government (Federal Council) recommended its rejection (Archives fédérales, 2006).

The Federal Council decided that Swiss citizens would have to vote on both items the same day, November 30, 2008. A majority (68 percent of voters and all 26 Swiss cantons) supported the parliament's partial revision of the Drugs Law and 66 percent of the voters and all cantons rejected the cannabis ballot initiative.

Back to cannabis repression: the rise of the administrative logic

Following the rejection of the government's proposal in 2004, and of the hemp initiative in 2008, local authorities abandoned their tolerant attitude towards the Swiss cannabis scene and the attention of police forces moved from the heroin problem to the cannabis issue (Reuter and Schnoz, 2009). The "hemp shops" were closed, cannabis fields and cultivation sites were destroyed and several entrepreneurs were arrested and imprisoned (Arsever, 2010; CFLD, 2008; Rappaz, 2013).

Cannabis use peaked in the early years of the new millennium and has remained stable ever since (Reuter and Schnoz, 2009). However, the supply chain changed with domestically produced cannabis, often from relatively small-scale cultivation sites, being partially substituted by imported cannabis involving foreign criminal networks or cannabis grown in large-scale indoor sites managed by Swiss citizens.

The number of cannabis use offenses grew rapidly after 2008 leading to an increasing amount of work for local justice departments. This and the unresolved cannabis debate led the Federal Parliament in 2012 to adopt a reform limited to the decriminalization of adult cannabis use with the introduction of an administrative fine of 100 Swiss francs. The goal was to harmonize the practices between the cantons – who had notoriously different ways of handling cannabis use offenses and sometimes applied the principle of limited opportunity (Albrecht, 2007). In addition, the reform was meant to reduce the amount of work for the justice departments and to introduce a less severe approach towards what was considered benign cannabis use.

The replacement of penal sanctions with administrative fines led to an increase, not only in the likelihood of sanctions for cannabis users, but also in the differences of practices between the cantons (Zobel et al., 2017). The latter is linked to the intrinsic ambiguities of the legal framework regarding the definition of offenses (consumption, consumption and detention, only detention), the exclusion criteria (related offenses) and the context of application (the police forces entitled to give administrative fines) (Zobel et al., 2017). Overall, although the new legal provisions were meant to reduce penalties, their implementation by the cantonal police forces led to a firmer application of the law and an increase in the number of registered offenses.

In a context of increasing legal uncertainty due to multiple provisions regarding drug use and specifically cannabis use, the Federal Court provided a new case law in September 2017. Based on a strict reading of Article 19b of the Drugs Law,[3] the highest jurisdiction of the country stated that possession of less than ten grams of cannabis was in fact not punishable anymore, neither by a fine nor by any other punishment (Tribunal fédéral, 2017). This decision goes against years of law enforcement practices during which people received fines or faced criminal prosecution for cannabis possession for personal use. Police forces in most cantons had to amend internal directives in order to reflect this new interpretation.

Back to experimenting with drug policy: the "pilot-study strategy"

Visible drug markets are a feature of Swiss urban centers. Cities also have to face some of their undesirable features, such as a relatively high demand for psychoactive substances, and a greater percentage of problematic drug use (Schmid, 2001). The development of harm-reduction measures – mainly substitution treatment but also other measures such as drug consumption rooms – led to less harmful and visible heroin markets and forms of use by diverting a part under the control of the authorities. Such changes however did not happen for the cannabis market.

With cannabis reforms at the federal level mostly adding more legal confusion and uncertainty to the situation, local authorities started to discuss the possibility of experimenting with new approaches of cannabis regulation at their level. The idea was not completely new, and it had been discussed by some Swiss cities in the late 1990s and early 2000s. However, as the government's reform proposal of 2001 and the hemp initiative of 2008 were on the agenda, they did not move forward.

After the failure of the popular vote on cannabis in 2008, the political authorities of some of Switzerland's main cities once again started to look for bottom-up solutions for cannabis market regulation. The movement started in 2010 in the German part of Switzerland, when the parliament of the city of Zurich approved a request to explore the feasibility of cannabis sales within a pilot study. The Swiss Drugs Law includes an exception principle that allows for the suspension of the ban on illicit drugs for research purposes (Article 8.5, LStup).[4] Heroin prescription trials carried out in the 1990s were based on this article (Boggio et al., 1997). In 2011, the Parliament of the Canton of Basel City approved a text similar to the one adopted by the city of Zürich. Three years later, the parliament of the city of Bern did the same and commissioned the Institute for Social and Preventive Medicine of the University of Bern to develop a research project to sell and buy cannabis for non-medical purposes in pharmacies.

In the French-speaking part of the country, cases of public nuisance related to the drugs market have triggered several political crises in the city of Lausanne and the canton of Geneva. In the latter, a group of parliamentarians from all political parties convened in 2012, behind closed doors and without an official political mandate, to work on new approaches towards cannabis regulation, with the goal of reducing urban insecurity. The group recommended the development of a research project allowing participants to become members of associations which would supply them with cannabis (Groupe de Réflexion Interpartis, 2013). The group's proposal was taken over by the government that tasked the Sociological Research Institute of the University of Geneva and the Addiction Department of the University Hospital to develop a study design. Other cities such as Biel, Lausanne, Luzern, Thun and Winterthur, as well as the canton of Solothurn, also adopted texts to explore cannabis trials and joined the newly constituted "Interurban working group" on cannabis as observers.

The pilot project led by the city of Bern first submitted a request for a special authorization under Article 8.5 during the summer of 2017. The Federal Office of Public Health (FOPH) narrowly interpreted the law and rejected the request, stating however that pilot projects were of great interest to drug policy development. The federal government's attitude raised leadership concerns and created a phase of parliamentary agitation in order to find a way to allow the pilot projects to proceed. The preferred solution was to develop a new legal provision in the Drugs Law that would allow such experiments. The FOPH drafted a new article that went into a public consultation phase in summer 2018. It limits the trials to the local level and to a maximum of 5,000 participants for each. Other provisions include the amount of cannabis that can be obtained as well as exclusion criteria. The proposal will be discussed in parliament and it will take at least two years until it is adopted, probably with several amendments. The first pilot projects will therefore not start before 2021.

Alongside attempts to reform the so-called recreational market, Switzerland experienced changes in the prescription of cannabinoids for medical purposes and in the developments of a legal low-THC cannabis market.

The medical cannabinoids program overrun by its success

Since 2011, the FOPH can grant exceptional authorizations for the manufacture and marketing of cannabis/cannabinoids, not only for research and the development of new medicines, but also for limited medical applications. The prescription of pharmaceutical products like Sativex® as well as magisterial preparations such as tinctures or infused oils based on herbal cannabis (Frankhauser, 2013) is possible. However, with the exception of the prescription of Sativex® for multiple sclerosis which can be done by any doctor at any time, all other prescriptions require individual authorizations (for each patient and for each pathology) from the federal authorities. While this exceptional licensing system is nowadays well implemented, it involves complex administrative procedures for all parties involved and has both practical and legal limitations. The tedious process delays entrance into therapy and represents an obstacle for treatment access, which is also hindered by the high price of the cannabis products that are often not reimbursed by health insurances. Despite all these barriers, there is a continuous increase in derogatory requests for cannabinoids-based medications (Kilcher, Zwahlen, Ritter, Fenner and Egger, 2017). With 9,177 individual authorizations having been granted over a five-year period, this measure has lost the "exceptional character" assigned to it by the Drugs Law (Conseil fédéral, 2018b). The government therefore recently tasked the FOPH with reducing the obstacles for accessing medical cannabis, with widening the range of authorized products and with examining possible reimbursements by health insurances.

The renewal of the Swiss cannabis sector: the CBD market

Switzerland amended its Drugs Control Ordinance (OCStup)[5] in 2011 and increased the threshold separating licit and illicit cannabis from 0.3 percent to 1 percent THC. This decision was based upon a recommendation from the Swiss Society of Forensic Medicine which argued that the existing cut-off rate didn't take into account natural variations in the THC content of cannabis plants, thus providing legal uncertainty for the legal hemp industry (Conseil fédéral, 2018a).

Meanwhile, the legalization and regulation of medical and later recreational cannabis markets – first in the Americas and later elsewhere – and the increasing interest in the medicinal properties of the cannabis plant (National Academies of Sciences, Engineering, and Medicine, 2017) created new business opportunities (Summers, 2018), including for low-THC/high-CBD cannabis strains and products. The development of cannabinoids extraction (Rosenthal, 2014) and other technological innovations also contributed to greatly diversify the range of products containing cannabinoids. Swiss entrepreneurs followed these international developments and noted that some cannabis products were in fact legal in their country due to the newly established threshold.

The first developments of the new Swiss cannabis market were CBD extractions from industrial hemp allowed by the European catalogue. The first products launched around 2014 were CBD tinctures, oils and e-liquids.

In parallel, companies imported or developed (by selection, crossing or acquisition) other (outside the European catalogue) varieties of cannabis with high levels of CBD with the appearance, taste and fragrance being recognizable by cannabis connoisseurs and consumers.

It was, however, the decision of one company to request (and obtain) a formal approval for the sales of cannabis flowers with less than 1 percent THC as a "tobacco substitute"[6] under the Tobacco Law (LTab) that radically changed the landscape. This entrepreneurial move opened the door, during summer 2016, to the rapid development of a multifaceted market of "legal cannabis."

Facing an increasing number of requests from companies wishing to produce or sell low-THC/high-CBD cannabis products, relevant federal agencies published a set of market guidelines in early 2017 (Confédération Suisse, 2017). The document defines classifications for CBD cannabis products and relative norms of commercialization as tobacco substitutes, cosmetics, food supplements, consumer goods or pharmaceutical products.

By the summer of 2018, more than 600 cannabis companies were officially registered (Jorio and Unterfinger, 2018) and a large number of products containing CBD are currently available on the market. They are sold online, in specialized shops, tobacconists, gas stations or supermarkets. The market divides into several categories. Among them, smokable products under the LTab provision (flowers, manufactured cigarettes, pre-rolled joints, pollens, or shisha tobacco) seem to be the most popular. Around 13 million Swiss francs of tax revenue were collected from the sales of these products in 2017, which represents a sales turnover of about 52 million francs. According to economic projections, the tax revenue could reach 15 million in 2018 and it will be formally included in the next federal budget (Renz, 2018).

Other companies have chosen to make use of Swiss expertise in pharmaceutical preparations and to target the markets with CBD-infused oils and tinctures, and other non-smokable products such as edibles, cosmetics, e-liquids, etc. However, the size of this market remains unknown. Nevertheless, hundreds of entrepreneurs have entered a highly competitive market characterized by product diversification, and now also oversupply and dropping prices. CBD flowers and CBD-containing products are also exported to the newly constituted European markets where demand is high (mainly Italy, France and Austria) (Jorio and Unterfinger, 2018).

Towards a new cannabis policy for Switzerland?

Past and current attempts to reform the country's cannabis policy, as well as recent developments with regard to medical and low-THC cannabis, show that Switzerland is certainly one of the countries in Europe where this issue is most prominent. The fact that both Swiss citizens and Swiss parliamentarians have separately voted on a law allowing for cannabis market regulation may still be unique on the continent. The most recent developments include a parliamentary initiative for cannabis regulation submitted by the Green Party that was rejected in September 2018. The Zürich-based association *Legalize It!* – which has provided legal advice to cannabis users since 1995 – announced its plan in 2016 to launch a new ballot initiative for cannabis legalization and regulation, and it should start collecting the requisite 100,000 signatures in spring 2019. If it succeeds within a period of 18 months, Swiss citizens could soon vote on the subject again. A recent poll indicated that up to two-thirds of the Swiss population could be in favor of such a reform (Umbrich, 2017).

A need for consensus and coalition building

Potential cannabis distribution trials at the local level, combined with a new ballot initiative in the making, a burgeoning low-THC cannabis market, and an official goal to facilitate the access to medicines containing cannabinoids, does not guarantee that a cannabis policy reform similar to those occurring in the US, Uruguay and Canada, will take place in Switzerland. As can be learned from past attempts to reform drug policy in Switzerland and abroad, it remains a major challenge to build a coalition that is large enough to win the necessary votes in parliament or among citizens.

The process that led to the inclusion of the four pillars policy into the Federal Drugs Law was long and tedious, even if the heroin overdoses and HIV crises of the 1990s acted as an "external shock" (Sabatier and Jenkins-Smith, 1993) and sparked a paradigm shift allowing for the birth of the harm reduction coalition that brought to success the four pillars policy (Kübler, 2001; Wenger, Surber, Lanzi, Gantenbein and Kübler, 2014). It included endless debates at city and neighborhood levels, many ballot initiatives and referenda at different governance levels and day-long discussions in parliament. These public discussions contributed to form common core beliefs about the issue and how to solve it with concrete measures, a prerequisite in the formation of advocacy coalitions (Sabatier and Jenkins-Smith, 1993). The debates also fractured the political spectrum by highlighting deeply rooted political cleavages (between the cities and the countryside, between conservative and progressive forces, and between the German, Italian and French-speaking parts of the country). The policy debate staged a long combat between a harm-reduction coalition in the making and a long-standing abstinence movement. The first finally succeeded in reforming the drug policy (Wenger et al., 2014) because an extensive amount of time and effort was put in to progressively build up a common understanding of the drug problem and a coalition of progressive stakeholders strong enough to provide legitimacy to the four pillars policy (Kübler, 2001).

Lessons can also be learned from the successful cannabis ballot initiatives in US states where organizations like the American Civil Liberty Union (ACLU) and the Drug Policy Alliance (DPA) have invested enormous efforts and amounts of time in (re-) framing the cannabis issue. The US initiatives have also shown the importance of bringing stakeholders from various sides together and including a large set of interest groups – such as cannabis users, taxpayers, human rights activists or environmentalist groups – in the coalition leading the reform movement. This was necessary not only to win the popular vote, but also to negotiate the concepts that formed the baseline for the policy-design and implementation phases. These political successes have also shown the need to come up with practical and consensual solutions about how cannabis use and markets should be regulated in order to unify the stakeholders behind a common proposal.

In Switzerland, the legal drug (tobacco and alcohol) policy subsystem includes two opposite traditions and supporting coalitions that often interfere with and oppose each other within the debate: one relates to a relatively strong public health orientation and is connected to a very well-developed health industry. The other is linked to a tradition of a very liberal market regulation allowing a lot of freedom to economic actors, including several tobacco companies that have their headquarters in the country. For alcohol and tobacco, these two coalitions inevitably enter into conflict when addressing regulation issues (Wenger et al., 2014).

Overall, lessons learned from the development of the four pillars drug policy model in Switzerland, from the ballot initiatives in the US and from existing coalitions in the licit drugs field, imply that time and effort are necessary to build up coalitions around a shared view of what cannabis regulation should be.

Building a cannabis regulation model for Switzerland

The authors of this chapter have tried to develop a model for cannabis regulation that could be consensually adopted, or at least a model that provides resources for the ongoing coalition building process. Two of them are working in the field of addiction, one for the GREA *(Groupement Romand d'Études des Addictions)*, an association of professionals which places a strong emphasis on defending human rights; and the other for Addiction Switzerland, a century-old NGO active in the areas of drug research and prevention, which has its roots in the temperance movement and a relatively strong anti-industry stance. Another is working in the cannabis industry and is a key player in IG-Hanf, a newly created association of Swiss cannabis entrepreneurs. Established in 2016, it has the status of an official interlocutor of the FOPH regarding the "CBD market." It also develops several projects aimed at normalizing the branch, for instance with the Swiss Association for Normalization (SNV). Finally, the first author of the chapter is studying cannabis policy reforms and concrete regulations from an academic perspective. Together, this group has tried to bridge the opposition between economic interests and public health priorities (Global Commission on Drug Policy, 2018).

This cannabis regulation model is based on two key areas for action: "controlling and regulating the market" and "protecting the population" (GREA and IG-Hanf, 2018). While there are several overlaps between these areas, it appeared important to acknowledge the new venues for innovative public health measures brought by the legal regulation of psychoactive substances. Learning from examples from abroad and acknowledging the limited political support for cannabis reform in Switzerland, we also opted for a more restrictive model of market regulation. It includes measures such as a clear separation between the medical and non-medical markets, dedicated stores and a thorough tracking of production and sales practices. It is however in the area of "protecting the population" that we may have moved beyond existing models, for instance with the inclusion of harm-related taxation rates, or the prohibition on cannabis shops of selling any smoking paraphernalia. Combustion-free products would be the only ones to have some room for advertisement.

Each of the ten principles was translated into a set of three to five measures that frame its implementation. For instance, market control and licensing and taxation fall under the responsibility of a new national cannabis agency. It would manage a database in which all operators' (including those who produce for themselves), products, tests and transactions would be registered. The agency should also offer training courses for entrepreneurs to help them fulfil their legal obligations.

Area of action 1: to control and regulate the cannabis market

1. separate the medical and non-medical markets;
2. sell cannabis products only in specialized stores;
3. control the production and ensure its traceability;
4. tax cannabis to fund the accompanying measures;
5. limit and control production for personal use.

Area of action 2: protect the population

6. protect the youth;
7. promote lower-risk cannabis use;
8. protect and inform consumers;
9. prevent (and punish) driving and certain types of professional activities under the influence of cannabis;
10. limit the presence of cannabis in the public space and its advertising.

Conclusion

The renewal of the Swiss cannabis debate is characterized by a multitude of policy initiatives that take place in a rapidly changing environment, both nationally and internationally. Such political momentum is not the first in

Switzerland's cannabis policy history, and the opposition towards major policy changes in this area also remains strong. For now, it remains unclear whether change will occur or whether the country is heading for another stalemate in its cannabis policy. However, the number of initiatives and their diversity suggest that change could happen during the next decade.

The process described at the end of this contribution attempts to overcome ideological barriers and expertise silos. It can be understood as a contribution to the building of an advocacy coalition based on pragmatism. It comes from people with different positions within the policy subsystem: academic research, non-governmental organizations active in the field of drugs and the cannabis industry. Through regular meetings, constructive discussions and pragmatic decisions, they agreed upon ten basic principles for the regulation of a future cannabis market in Switzerland. These principles should be disseminated and discussed more widely, with the goal of moving forward with cannabis reforms in Switzerland or elsewhere.

Notes

1 RS 812.121 Loi fédérale sur les stupéfiants et les substances psychotropes (LStup).

2 Text of the initiative: "For a reasonable hemp policy to effectively protect the youth."

- i Use, possession and acquisition of cannabis for personal use is not punishable.
- ii Cultivating cannabis for personal use is not punishable.
- iii The Confederation issues prescriptions for the cultivation, production, import, export and trade of cannabis.
- iv It also takes appropriate measures for youth protection. Advertisement for cannabis or its use is prohibited.

3 RS 812.121 LStup. Art. 19b, (translated by the authors):

- Whoever merely prepares narcotic drugs in small quantities, for his own consumption or to allow third persons over the age of 18 to consume them at the same time after having provided them free of charge, is not punishable.
- Ten grams of drugs with cannabis-like effects are considered a minimal amount.

4 RS 812.121 LStup. Art. 8.5, (translated by the authors):

> If no international convention opposes, the Federal Office of Public Health may grant exceptional authorisations for the cultivation, importation, manufacture and marketing of the narcotic drugs referred to in para. 1 and 3 which are used for research, drug development or limited medical application.

5 RS 812.121.1 Ordonnance sur le contrôle des stupéfiants (OCStup).

6 In Switzerland, products falling into this category are taxed at 25 percent of sale's value (+ the usual VAT rate of 7.7 percent).

References

Albrecht, P. (2007). *Die strafbestimmungen des betäubungsmittelgesetzes (Art. 19–28 BetmG), 2. Auflage*. Bern: Stämpfli verlag.

Archives fédérales. (2006). *Message du conseil fédéral concernant l'initiative populaire: Pour une politique raisonnable en matière de chanvre protégeant efficacement la jeunesse.* Berne: Confédération Suisse.

Arsever, S. (2010). *Cannabis, la grande illusion.* Genève, Lausanne: Le temps.

Boggio, Y., Cattacin, S., Lucas, B. and Cesoni, M.L. (1997). *Apprendre à gérer. La politique Suisse en matière de drogue.* Genève: Georg.

CFLD. (1999). *Rapport sur le cannabis. Commission fédérale pour les questions liées aux drogues (CFLD).* Berne: Confédération Suisse.

CFLD. (2008). Cannabis en 2008. Mise à jour du rapport 1999 sur le cannabis. *Commission fédérale pour les questions liées aux drogues (CFLD).* Berne: Confédération Suisse.

Confédération Suisse. (2017). *Produits contenant du cannabidiol (CBD). Vue d'ensemble et aide à l'execution.* Berne: Confédération Suisse.

Conseil fédéral. (2018a). Réponse du conseil fédéral (interpellation 19.3198).

Conseil fédéral. (2018b). *Traiter les personnes gravement malades avec du cannabis: Rapport du conseil fédéral en réponse à la motion Kessler (14.4164).* Berne: Confédération Suisse.

Frankhauser, M. (2013). Cannabis ist ein vielseitiges heilmittel. *Bulletin des Médecins Suisses,* 94(35), 1321–1323.

Global Commission on Drug Policy. (2018). *Regulation: The responsible control of drugs.* Geneva: Global Commission on Drug Policy.

GREA and IG-Hanf. (2018). *Contrôler et protéger: Un modèle qui concilie contraintes économiques et protection de la population.* Lausanne/Berne: GREA/IG-Hanf.

Groupe de Réflexion Interpartis. (2013). *Pour plus de sécurité dans la ville. Le cannabis social club: Un mode'le efficace de réglementation de l'acce's au cannabis.* Genève: Document de discussion.

Ingold, K., Fischer, M. and Cairney, P. (2017). Drivers for policy agreement in nascent subsystems: An application of the advocacy coalition framework to fracking policy in Switzerland and the UK. *Policy Studies Journal,* 45(3), 442–463.

Jorio, L. and Unterfinger, E. (2018). Trop de cannabis légal: La Suisse devient-elle un pays exportateur? *Swissinfo.ch.*

Kessler, T. (1985). *Cannabis helvetica: Hanf in der Schweiz-hoffnung für die drogenpolitik.* Zürich: Nachtschatten verlag.

Kilcher, G.R., Zwahlen, M., Ritter, C.O., Fenner, L. and Egger, M. (2017). Medical use of cannabis in Switzerland: Analysis of approved exceptional licences. *Swiss Medical Weekly,* 147, w14463.

Kriesi, H. (1998). *Le système politique Suisse.* Paris: Economica.

Kübler, D. (2001). Understanding policy change with the advocacy coalition framework: An application to Swiss drug policy. *Journal of European Public Policy,* 8(4), 623–641.

Ladner, A. (2010). Switzerland: Subsidiarity, power sharing, and direct democracy. In F. Hendriks, A. Lidström and J. Loughlin (Eds.), *The Oxford handbook of local and regional democracy in Europe* (pp. 197–217). Oxford: Oxford University Press.

Lijphart, A. (2012). *Patterns of democracy: Government forms and performance in thirty-six countries*: Yale University Press.

National Academies of Sciences, Engineering, and Medicine. (2017). *The health effects of cannabis and cannabinoids: The current state of evidence and recommendations for research.* Washington: National Academies Press.

Nils-Robert, C. (2016). *Drogues: Un échec annoncé. 40 ans de lutte contre l'ineptie de la prohibition*. Genève: Georg.

Rappaz, B. (2013). *Pionnier!* Lausanne: Favre.

Renz, F. (2018). *Ab sofort zählt der bund auf cannabis*. Zürich: Tages Anzeiger.

Reusser, F. (1997). Le chanvre en Suisse. *Les échos du chanvre, Hiver 96–97* (5), 12.

Reuter, P. and Schnoz, D. (2009). *Assessing drug problems and policies in Switzerland, 1998–2007*. Berne: Office Fédéral de la Santé Publique.

Rosenthal, E. (2014). *Beyond buds: Marijuana extracts: Hash, vaping, dabbing, edibles and medicines*. Piedmont: Quick Trading Company.

Sabatier, P. and Jenkins-Smith, H. (Eds.). (1993). *Policy changes and learning: An advocacy coalition approach*. Boulder CO: Westwiew Press.

Schmid, H. (2001). Cannabis use in Switzerland: The role of attribution of drug use to friends, urbanization and repression. *Swiss Journal of Psychology/Schweizerische Zeitschrift für Psychologie/Revue Suisse de Psychologie*, 60(2), 99–107.

Summers, D.J. (2018). *The business of cannabis: New policies for the new marijuana industry*. Santa-Barbara: Prager.

Tribunal fédéral. (2017). *Jurisprudence du TF 6B_1273/2016. Département de droit pénal*. Berne: Confédération Suisse.

Umbrich, A. (2017). *Telephonische omnibus-befragung zum konsum und handel von cannabis. Quantitative bebragung im auftrag fom fachverbant sucht*. Zürich: Fachverbant sucht/GFS.

Wenger, J., Surber, M., Lanzi, N., Gantenbein, F. and Kübler, D. (2014). *Analyse de la politique en matière des addictions en Suisse: Les coalitions de cause dans les domaines de l'alcool, du tabac et des drogues. Résumé du rapport de recherche*. Zürich: Institut für Politikenwissenschaft.

Zobel, F., Homberg, C. and Marthaler, M. (2017). *Les amendes d'ordre pour consommation de cannabis: Analyse de la mise en oeuvre* (Rapport de recherche Nr. 82). Lausanne: Addiction Suisse.

15 The Australian experience and opportunities for cannabis law reform

Caitlin Elizabeth Hughes

Introduction

Australia is often held up as an exemplar of cannabis law reform, due to it being one of the first countries to adopt a civil penalty scheme for cannabis cultivation and possession for personal use via the 1987 South Australian Cannabis Expiation Notice (CEN) scheme (Babor, Caulkins, Fischer, Foxcroft, Humphreys, Medina-Mora and Room., 2018; Babor, Caulkins, Edwards, Fischer, Foxcroft, Humphreys and Strang., 2010; MacCoun and Reuter, 2001; Room, Fischer, Hall, Lenton and Reuter, 2010). But the trajectory of cannabis law reform since that time remains less well understood. This is a missed opportunity, since Australia has been undergoing a substantial expansion of *de jure* and de facto cannabis law reforms, involving both prohibition with civil penalties and depenalization, and more recently, the legalization of medical cannabis (McDonald and Hughes, 2017). This chapter will thus provide a critical analysis of the Australian trajectory of cannabis law reforms from 1987 until 2018 using legislation, parliamentary Hansard, government inquiries and research.

The chapter proceeds in three parts. First, it outlines the three waves of cannabis law reform that have occurred in Australia. Second, it outlines other key policy developments that have occurred over this period (policy contractions, expansions and shifts in problem framing). Third, it concludes by evaluating the strengths and weaknesses of three different models of cannabis legalization in the Australian context and implications for future Australian cannabis law reform.

Context

Australia is a federated nation comprised of the Commonwealth of Australia and eight states and territories. The main legislative responsibility of the Commonwealth, in relation to drugs, is for border control (Customs Act 1901 (Cth)), and drug trafficking and manufacturing (Commonwealth Criminal Code Act 1995 (Cth); Crimes (Traffic in Narcotic Drugs and Psychotropic Substances) Act 1990 (Cth)),[1] as such responses to illicit drug offenses are largely the remit of states and territories. Nevertheless, in 1967 and 1976, the

Commonwealth prohibited the possession, trafficking and cultivation of cannabis in accordance with the United Nations Conventions, and all states and territories followed suit (Manderson, 1993). While as noted by Manderson (1993) the onset of state/territory drug laws largely preceded cannabis use in Australia, throughout the 1970s, cannabis use grew in Australia (Hall, 2001), and prompted a number of federal and state parliamentary inquiries into cannabis policy. One of note was the Senate Standing Committee on Social Welfare (1977) which called for the reduction of criminal penalties for cannabis use. Such calls were premised on two main reasons. First, that cannabis had lesser harms than alcohol, tobacco and illicit drugs, such as heroin. Second, that the application of criminal penalties for cannabis use and possession often caused more harm than the use of the drug itself.

It was in this context that the first Australian National Drug Strategy (the National Campaign Against Drug Abuse) was adopted in 1985, with the objective of harm minimization: "minimizing the harmful effects of drugs on Australian Society" (Commonwealth Department of Health, 1985, p. 2). As summarized by the then health minister, Neal Blewett (1987, p. 2) such a goal was "moderate and circumscribed. No utopian claims to eliminate drugs, or drug abuse, or remove entirely the harmful effects of drugs, merely 'to minimize' the effects of the abuse of drugs on a society permeated by drugs." This led to a practice, or at least rhetoric, of focusing criminal justice intervention on drug traffickers, rather than people who use drugs. Two years later, the first wave of Australian cannabis law reforms commenced.

The first wave of cannabis reform: prohibition with civil penalties schemes

In 1987, South Australia (SA) introduced a prohibition with civil penalties scheme for minor cannabis offenses, via the Cannabis Expiation Notice (CEN) scheme: Controlled Substances Amendment Act 1986 (SA). The new reform effectively decriminalized the use, possession and cultivation of cannabis for personal use, and enabled infringement notices for simple cannabis offenses defined as possession of up to 100 grams of cannabis, or 20 grams of cannabis resin or cultivation of up to ten plants for personal use. The purpose of the scheme was threefold: to decrease the number of defendants appearing before the courts; to ensure that persons committing simple cannabis offenses did not incur a criminal record or the lasting deleterious impacts of that record; and to strengthen the distinction between private consumers of cannabis and large-scale operators. Following an early evaluation of the CEN scheme (nine months pre and post) that broadly suggested the reform was achieving its intended outcomes (Sarre, Sutton and Pulsford, 1989), the Australian Capital Territory (ACT) and Northern Territory (NT) followed suit, introducing prohibition with civil penalties scheme for cannabis possession and cultivation for personal use in 1992 and 1996 respectively: Drugs of Dependence Amendment Act (No. 2) 1992 (ACT) and Misuse of Drugs Act (NT). Western Australia

Table 15.1 Australian expiation and diversion programs for minor cannabis offences as of 2018

Jurisdiction	*Name of program*	*Program requirement*	*Basis – Law or policy*	*Target group*	*Limit on quantity of cannabis possessed*	*Limit on number of diversion opportunities*
EXPIATION						
Australian Capital Territory	Simple Cannabis Offence Notice (SCON)	Expiation: payment of $100 fine	Law	Youth and adults	≤50 g cannabis or 2 non-hydroponic plants	n/a
Northern Territory	Cannabis Expiation Notice Scheme	Expiation: payment of 2 penalty units = $310 in 2018	Law	Adults or youth 17+	≤50 g cannabis or 2 non-hydroponic plants	n/a
South Australia	Cannabis Expiation Scheme (CEN)	Expiation: payment of $150–$300 fine	Law	Adults only	≤100 g cannabis ≤20 g resin or 1 plant	n/a
DIVERSION						
Australian Capital Territory	Illicit Drug Diversion (IDD)	Diversion with referral for assessment, education, counselling or other treatment as appropriate	Policy	Youth and adults	≤50 g cannabis or 2 non-hydroponic plants	2
New South Wales	NSW Cannabis Cautioning Scheme	Caution with optional/ compulsory (for 2nd offence) referral to an alcohol and drug telephone information service	Policy	Adults only	≤15 g cannabis	2
Northern Territory	Illicit Drug Pre-Court Diversion Program (NTIDPCD)	Diversion with referral for education, counselling and/ or treatment	Policy	Adults and youth 17+	≤50 g cannabis	1

continued

Table 15.1 continued

Jurisdiction	*Name of program*	*Program requirement*	*Basis – Law or policy*	*Target group*	*Limit on quantity of cannabis possessed*	*Limit on number of diversion opportunities*
Queensland	Police Drug Diversion Program (PDDP)	Caution with compulsory referral to a two-hour drug diversion education and assessment program	Law	Adults and youth	≤50 g cannabis	1
Tasmania	Illicit Drug Diversion Initiative (IDDI)	There are three levels: L1: Caution (for 1st cannabis offence) L2: Diversion & brief intervention (for 2nd cannabis offence) L3: Diversion, brief intervention & treatment (for 3rd cannabis offence)	Policy	Adults only	≤50 g cannabis or 2 cannabis plants	3 within 10 years
Western Australia	Cannabis Intervention Requirement (CIR)	Diversion for referral for one-hour therapeutic intervention session	Law	Adults and youth	≤10 g cannabis	Adults: 1 Youth: 2
Victoria	Cannabis Caution Program	Caution and 2.5-hour cannabis education session (Cautious with Cannabis)	Policy	Adults	≤50 g cannabis	2

NB. The ACT IDD, NTIDPCD and Tas IDDI also provide diversion for possession of other illicit drugs.

Source: Hughes, C., Seear, K., Ritter, A. and Mazerolle, L. (2019). *Monograph No. 27: Criminal justice responses relating to personal use and possession of illicit drugs: The reach of Australian drug diversion programs and barriers and facilitators to expansion*. DPMP Monograph Series. Sydney: National Drug and Alcohol Research Centre, UNSW Sydney.

(WA) also introduced a civil penalty scheme for cannabis in 2004, but this was repealed in 2011. This reform differed in one important way in that it included the option for offenders to attend an education session instead of paying an expiation fee. The programs and their key program requirements and eligibility criteria as of 2018 are outlined in Table 15.1.

A large evidence base has arisen from these schemes, much focusing on the SA CEN scheme, and commissioned by the National Drug Strategy Committee and the Commonwealth Department of Health (Ali, Christie, Lenton, Hawks, Sutton, Hall and Allsop, 1999; Donnelly, Hall and Christie, 1999; Lenton, Christie, Humeniuk, Brooks, Bennett and Heale, 1999; McDonald and Atkinson, 1995; Sarre et al., 1989). Such research demonstrated that prohibition with civil penalties reduced the costs associated with a criminal penalty, without generating a much feared increase in the uptake of cannabis, and that it was associated with fewer adverse social consequences, including fewer negative employment problems, such as a loss of a job, less relationship disruption and less adverse accommodation consequences (Lenton et al., 1999).

Three perverse or unintended effects were however observed. First, net-widening, as evidenced by a 2.5-fold increase in expiable cannabis offenses: from 6,231 in 1987 to over 17,170 in 1996 (Christie and Ali, 2000), which was attributed to the greater ease with which a CEN could be issued, compared to an arrest and charge. Second, a low rate of compliance (45 percent) and high level of incarceration for non-payment of expiation notices, which was attributed to financial difficulties of many offenders (Ali et al., 1999). Third, ease of exploitation by organized criminal syndicates to grow commercial quantities under the ten-plant limit and divert cannabis to the black market. Importantly, in spite of the perverse effects, the scheme was found more cost-effective for dealing with minor cannabis offenses, and to have the support of law enforcement and the public as a fairer and more cost-effective approach (Ali et al., 1999).

The second wave of cannabis reform: police cannabis diversion

A second wave of cannabis reforms involved cannabis cautioning or police diversion. Diversion has long been part of Australian police practice, particularly for young offenders, in the goal of lessening youth involvement in the criminal justice system, through the use of warnings, cautions or youth group conferences (Polk, Adler, Muller and Rechtman, 2005). But traditional responses were discretionary and non-therapeutic. Diversion became much more formalized and therapeutic following an adoption of a Council of Australian Government Illicit Drug Diversion Initiative (IDDI) in 1999; a national commitment to divert minor drug offenders away from the criminal justice system and into assessment, education and/or treatment programs (Council Of Australian Governments, 1999). The IDDI was accompanied by a national framework which included principles of best practice for diversion and federal funding amounting to over AU$310 million to enable an expansion of treatment places (Hughes, 2007). A rapid roll-out of police cannabis caution schemes ensued across seven states/territories: Victoria in 1998, NSW, Tasmania and WA in 2000, Queensland and ACT in 2001, and NT in 2002 (and WA again in 2011) (see Table 15.2).

It is important to note that such programs form part of a broader diversionary response in Australia. For example, by 2007 there were more than 52 different diversion programs for drug and drug-related offenders operating across Australia, with most states offering four or five different options: police diversion for use/possession of cannabis; police diversion for use/possession of other illicit drugs; police diversion for young offenders (including for drug offenses); court diversion for minor drug-related offending; and court diversion for serious drug-related offending (Hughes and Ritter, 2008). Nevertheless, the most utilized part of that system has remained the programs targeted at cannabis use/possession, either by prohibition with civil penalties or police diversion.

Under the Australian cannabis diversion schemes, police provide an "on the street" formal caution for offenders using or possessing up to 50 grams of cannabis, as well as a referral to an education session, treatment needs assessment and/or a brief intervention. As summarized in Table 15.1, such programs differ in some important ways to the expiation programs. First, they have an educative or therapeutic mechanism, albeit the intensity and nature of response varies across programs. For example, NSW employs an alcohol and drug telephone information service that is voluntary for anyone other than repeat offenders to contact; WA provides a one-hour therapeutic intervention session for all offenders; and Tasmania provides a hybrid response combining education, assessment and/or brief interventions dependent upon the number of times an offender has been diverted. Second, most cannabis diversion schemes are based in police guidelines rather than law, and hence operate via police discretion. Third, they employ narrower eligibility criteria, i.e. most exclude cultivation and limit the number of times an offender can be diverted. Nevertheless, the net result is that since 2002, some form of expiation programs and/or diversion programs for cannabis use/possession has operated across all Australian states and territories.

The cannabis caution schemes have shown similar benefits to the civil penalty schemes: reduced burden on the criminal justice system and improved social outcomes without increasing offending or drug use. For example, Baker and Goh (2004) found that the NSW Cannabis Cautioning Program led to 2,658 fewer persons convicted with a principal offense of cannabis possession by the local courts in the three years since the introduction of the scheme, compared with the three years prior to the scheme. Moreover, a cost-effectiveness analysis showed that a cannabis caution cost six times less than a criminal charge (Shanahan, Hughes and McSweeney, 2017), and that those diverted were significantly less likely to report a change in employment status such as a termination, as well as disruptive relationships with family and friends. A national evaluation of criminal justice outcomes by Payne, Kwiatkowski and Wundersitz (2008) further showed that the majority of people who were referred by police to illicit drug diversion programs were not detected reoffending in the 12–18 months after their diversion. Specifically, 70–86 percent of first-time offenders diverted were not detected reoffending and 53–66 percent of those with prior offending recorded zero or fewer offenses in the 18 months after diversion. The Australian drug diversion programs have also led to a large increase in assessment and treatment referrals in Australia (Australian Institute of Health and Welfare, 2014), and in some instances, particularly programs with high treatment exposure, reductions in harmful use. For example, amongst participants of the Queensland Police Drug Diversion Program, regular use of cannabis reduced from 95 percent at baseline to 74 percent at the 3-month follow-up, a rate that was sustained at the 6-month follow-up (Hales, Mayne, Swan, Alberti and Ritter, 2004).

The main challenge with such programs is that access through such schemes tends to be more limited than via the civil penalty schemes, on account of both the discretionary basis and tighter eligibility criteria (Hughes, Seear, Ritter and Mazerolle, 2019). This is particularly for programs with very narrow criteria. There can also be geographic variance in diversion provision within a state (NSW Auditor General, 2011).

The third wave of reform: legalization of medical cannabis

The third wave of cannabis reforms involved legalization of medical cannabis. In April 2016, the Victorian government became the first Australian state to legalize medical cannabis for terminally ill people via the Access to Medical Cannabis Act 2016 (Vic), with access to medical cannabis progressively rolled out in other states and territories between 2016 and 2017 (see Table 15.2). The Parliament of Australia passed the Narcotic Drugs Amendment Act 2016 (Cth), allowing for controlled cultivation and supply of cannabis in Australia for medicinal and scientific purposes via a national licensing scheme. The act was assented to in February 2016 and came into effect on October 30, 2016. Key details of the Commonwealth scheme are as follows:

- the Commonwealth has sole responsibility for cultivation and production, and granting of licenses and permits for the cultivation, production and manufacture of medicinal cannabis products via a newly established office of drug control in the Commonwealth Department of Health. Strict rules operate about who can cultivate cannabis, including that licensees must be judged as a "fit and proper person" including having previous business experience, no convictions for a serious offense in the last five years against Commonwealth/State/Territory law and be a person of good repute;

- cannabis was rescheduled in the Narcotic Drugs Act 1967 (Cth) from Schedule 9 (prohibited) to Schedule 8 (controlled) to allow cannabis to be prescribed to patients. Medical cannabis has hence only been prescribed by Australian-registered medical practitioners, and to patients who have been approved to receive the product;
- the Australian Therapeutic Goods Authority (TGA), in conjunction with the states and territories, has responsibility for overseeing patient access and approval of all doctors.

The Australian medical cannabis scheme differs in important ways to many other parts of the world, particularly the USA, evidenced by tight controls over production, product range and patient access. As evidenced by government deliberations, the Australian design is a direct consequence of concerns about diversion to the illicit market and the desirability of ensuring access to only low-risk products.

> We consider that on the present medical evidence, cannabis-based treatments will only be appropriate for a small number of people in specific circumstances, and under the supervision of medical practitioners with suitable expertise. Those patients would necessarily be people with severe and distressing symptoms that are not able to be addressed by existing medications. While we are not convinced that allowing medical use of cannabis will lead to greater non-medical use, we do recognize that government needs to be cautious about the messages it sends to the broader community in such a sensitive area of policy.
>
> NSW Government inquiry on the use of cannabis for medical purposes.
> (Legislative Council, 2013, p. xii)

> This bill, in conjunction with established mechanisms, provides a secure supply chain from "farm to pharmacy," that will give patients access to medicinal cannabis products. The bill is not about the legalization or decriminalization of cannabis for recreational use. Nor is this a discussion about making cannabis products available "over the counter" or outside of a discussion with a qualified doctor. It is important we maintain the same high safety standards for cannabis derived products that we apply to any other medicine. I know many Australians would be concerned if medicinal cannabis products were to be subject to lower safety standards than common prescription painkillers or cholesterol medications. This bill strikes the right balance between patient access, community protection and our international obligations.
>
> Second reading speech on the introduction of the Narcotic Drugs Amendment Bill 2016 by Health Minister Susan Ley.
> (Commonwealth, 2016)

Reflective of the federated system, methods of access and the range of conditions for which access can be provided again differ by state/territory. For example, while some states allow access for any medical condition (e.g. Tasmania), most have a narrower range. Most limit access to people who have failed conventional treatment or for whom the conventional treatment causes intolerable side effects.

Given the recency of adoption, lessons on the medical cannabis schemes are more limited, but one key concern has been large delays in access. For example, as of September 30, 2018, the Australian Therapeutic Goods Administration (2018) had approved a total of 1,442 applications for medicinal cannabis products since access was legalized under the Special Access Scheme. One cause was delay in getting approval, as most states required doctors to obtain both state and Commonwealth approval, which could take many months. In July 2018, a new online single access point has been obtained. Since that time the number of applications approved has increased. For example, there were 469 applications approved between August and September 2018, compared to 97 between January and February 2018. Nevertheless, access to the drug is still severely restricted two years after medicinal use was legalized nationally. That coupled with the strict requirements about entry means many people continue to access cannabis via illegal means. A further concern is that no medical cannabis product is listed on the Pharmaceutical Benefits Scheme which means patients must pay the full costs for treatment, limiting access to those without resources (Parliament of Victoria Law Reform Road and Community Safety Committee, 2018).

Other policy trajectories

Supplementing the three waves of cannabis reform have been a number of other important policy developments. Table 15.2 lists the key cannabis policy events (Hughes, 2018). Three of note are the gradual expansion and mainstreaming of police diversion schemes, policy reversals or contractions in regard to the civil penalties schemes, and a shift in the discourse about the harmfulness of cannabis use in Australia. Each are instructive for understanding current and future cannabis law reform efforts in Australia.

Policy expansions and streamlining of (therapeutic) diversion programs

The period 1999 to 2018 has seen a significant shift in the acceptance about the merits of diversionary responses for use/possession in Australia, particularly therapeutic diversion programs, from a "radical" to a "pragmatic and mainstream" approach (Hughes et al., 2019; Hughes, Shanahan, Ritter, McDonald and Gray-Weale, 2014). This is evidenced by presentations now being given by police about their worth and benefits (Western Australia Police, 2017), and by the inclusion of drug diversion in the National Drug Strategy as a key success from 2004 onwards (Commonwealth Department of Health, 2018a; Ministerial Council on Drug Strategy, 2004, 2011). There

Table 15.2 The Australian cannabis policy timeline, 1985–2018

Year	*Federal*	*State/territory*
1985	First Australian drug strategy – National Campaign Against Drug Abuse (NCADA) – adopted at a special Premiers conference. Campaign heralded as partnership's approach to illicit and licit drugs between federal and state and territory governments and adopted the central aim of harm minimization – minimizing harms caused by alcohol and other drugs.	
1986		SA Cannabis Expiation Notice (CEN) scheme introduced for minor cannabis offenses. Enabled use of infringement notices for simple cannabis offenses including possession and cultivation of up to ten plants for personal use.
1989	Parliamentary Joint Committee on the National Criminal Authority report released: *Drugs, Crime and Society*. Concluded that prohibition had not worked and was associated with considerable costs to users and society. Outlined alternatives, including harsher penalties, decriminalization and regulation, but did not come to a consensus as to what alternative was best.	
1990	Commonwealth Government ratified the *1988 United Nations Convention on Illicit Trafficking in Narcotics and Psychotropic Substances*.	
1991	Evaluation of NCADA chaired by Prof. Ian Webster concluded there was "no quick fix" to the Australian drug problem.	ACT select committee of the ACT Legislative Assembly proposed that the ACT adopt a cannabis expiation scheme and a heroin trial.
1992	The National Drug Strategy Committee convened a National Cannabis Task Force to summarize the state of knowledge about cannabis. Launch of the Australian Parliamentary Group for Drug Law Reform.	ACT Simple Cannabis Offence Notice (SCON) scheme introduced. Enabled minor cannabis offenders possessing ≤25 g of cannabis or ≤5 plants to avoid a criminal conviction by payment of a $100 fine.

1993	The Australian Parliamentary Group for Drug Law Reform launched the *Charter for Drug Law Reform* which called for an end to prohibition.	
1994	National Cannabis Task Force recommended that all Australian jurisdictions should consider removing criminal penalties for personal use/possession of cannabis. Report by Hall et al. (1994) released: *The Health and Psychological Consequences of Cannabis Use*. Concludes there can be acute and chronic effects of cannabis use, including adverse psychological effects e.g. paranoia and impaired driving while intoxicated. Launch of the Australian Drug Law Reform Foundation. Launch of Drug Free Australia.	
1995	Families and Friends for Drug Law Reform was formed.	
1996	The Alcohol and other Drugs Council of Australia held a workshop on drug diversion involving 50 stakeholders from law enforcement, health and attorney general's departments and representatives from drug diversion programs. Workshop led to the identification of best-practice principles of diversion and called for an expansion of diversion programs in Australia (Oct).	NT Cannabis Expiation Notice Scheme adopted (Feb: this entered into force on July 1, 1996). Vic Premier's Drug Advisory Council report recommended cannabis decriminalization and diversion (Mar). Vic cannabis decriminalization failed to win support – liberal backbenchers opposed (Jun).
1997	Prime Minister John Howard launched a "Tough on Drugs" strategy (Nov).	SA Cannabis Expiation Notice scheme modified by the introduction of the 1996 Expiation of Offences Act. This introduced a range of options for payment of expiation fees including payment by instalments and community service (Jan). NSW Woods Royal Commission report concluded that a "war on drugs" approach contributed towards police corruption. Recommended increased attention to alternate approaches such as harm minimization strategies (May). Vic Cannabis Cautioning Program trialled by Victoria Police for use/possession of cannabis (July 1997 to Jan 1998).

continued

Table 15.2 continued

Year	*Federal*	*State/territory*
1998	Launch of the Australian National Council on Drugs (ANCD) to provide independent policy advice to the Prime Minister and Australian Government. Chaired by Major Brian Watters (Mar).	Vic Police Cannabis Cautioning Program rolled out state-wide (Sep). WA Police launched 12-month trial of a Cannabis Cautioning Mandatory Education Session for cannabis possession (Oct 1998 to Sep 1999).
1999	Sixth national household survey on drugs released: *National Drug Strategy Household Survey, 1998*. Illustrated that between 1995 and 1998, recent use of cannabis increased from 13.2% to 17.9% (Sep). Council of Australian Government-Illicit Drug Diversion Initiative (IDDI) signed off including an agreement for a nationally consistent approach to the diversion of minor drug offenders to drug education and treatment. Prime Minister John Howard allocated $110 million to first stage of the IDDI to fund expansion of drug treatment (Nov).	NSW Drug Summit held in NSW Parliament. Summit was attended by 135 NSW Parliamentary delegates; 2 federal parliamentary delegates; 80 non-parliamentary delegates; and 45 associate delegates. 172 recommendations from the summit were adopted, including state-wide trial of a Cannabis Cautioning Scheme (Mar & Jul). National evaluators of the SA CEN scheme concluded (a) expiation was more cost-effective for minor cannabis offenders than a traditional prohibitionist response; (b) that it had the widespread support of criminal justice stakeholders; and (c) that expiation was associated with better social outcomes, e.g. fewer employment and relationship problems. But evaluators also highlighted evidence of net-widening in the scheme and suggested that some people were exploiting the scheme by cultivating and selling cannabis (Jun). SA CEN scheme amended, reducing the number of cannabis plants attracting a civil penalty from ten to three. NSW Working Party on the Use of Cannabis for Medical Purposes established, following calls by the Australian Medical Association (AMA) and the Law Society of New South Wales for people with illnesses to be prescribed cannabis for pain relief (Aug).

2000	NSW report released by Working Party on the Use of Cannabis for Medical Purposes. Concluded THC can be useful in treating nausea and appetite loss in patients with HIV and cancer, but that crude cannabis cannot be prescribed in Australia. Recommended trials into administration of THC via non-oral routes, and that until available, individuals found using cannabis for medical purposes should be exempt from prosecution (Aug). Police drug diversion introduced in three states: NSW Cannabis Caution Program (Apr), Tas Police Drug Diversion Program (for all illicit drugs) (Feb) and WA All Drug Diversion (Oct).
2001	SA CEN Scheme amended, reducing the number of cannabis plants attracting a civil penalty from three to one (Nov). Police drug diversion introduced in two states: Qld Police Diversion for Minor Drug Offences Program introduced (for cannabis possession) (Jun) and ACT Policing and Early Intervention Diversion Program (for cannabis and other drug possession) (Dec). NSW Police Powers (Drug Detection Dogs) Act adopted, giving police the powers to use a drug detection dog (or sniffer dog) in an authorized place (including a pub, sporting event or outdoor festival) (Dec).
2002	NSW Premier Carr announced a draft exposure bill would be introduced at the earliest opportunity to provide for a four-year trial of medical use of cannabis. Had in principle support from Opposition Leader provided supply was tightly regulated (May 20).

continued

Table 15.2 continued

Year	*Federal*	*State/territory*
		SA CEN scheme amended to ban cultivation of hydroponic plants (Sep). NT Illicit Drug Pre-Court Diversion Program (NTIDPCD) introduced for police diversion for use/possession of cannabis and other drugs (Dec).
2003	Report released from House of Representatives, Standing Committee on Family and Community Affairs, chaired by Kay Hull MP: *Road to Recovery: Report on the Inquiry into Substance Abuse in Australian Communities*. Report made 128 recommendations including that the Commonwealth, state and territory governments replace the current focus on harm minimization with a focus on harm prevention, i.e. preventing the uptake of alcohol, tobacco and illicit drugs (Aug).	WA Cannabis Control Act 2003 amended the Misuse of Drugs Act 1981 to allow cannabis infringement notices to be issued for use or possession of up to 30 g of cannabis, possession of a smoking implement or cultivation of up to 2 non-hydroponic cannabis plants. Under the scheme, eligible offenders had the option to avoid a criminal conviction by paying a fine or attending a cannabis education session (Jan).
2004	MCDS endorsed development of the first National Cannabis Strategy (Nov).	WA Cannabis Infringement Notice Scheme commenced (Mar). NSW Premier announced trial of medical use of cannabis had stalled because preferred delivery method – a metered-dose inhaler or spray – was years away from being available and the NSW and federal governments opposed backyard growing (Apr). Vic Police commenced a pilot of roadside drug saliva testing for cannabis and amphetamines – the first such trial in the world (Dec).
2005		ACT Criminal Code (Serious Drug Offences) Amendment Act 2004 came into force, reducing eligibility criteria for the Simple Cannabis Offence Notice (SCON) scheme from a maximum of five to two cannabis plants and excluding all hydroponically-grown plants (May).

2006	National Cannabis Strategy 2006–2009 commenced (May). Report released: *Evidence Based Answers to Cannabis Questions: A Review of the Literature* by the Australian National Council on Drugs provided a review of the health and psychological effects of cannabis use. Concluded that about one in ten people who use cannabis will become dependent, that cannabis use can lead to impaired education attainment and that cannabis use produces minor impairments when driving (May).	NSW Premier Iemma introduced tougher legislation for hydroponic cannabis: five times greater than for non-hydroponic cultivation (Feb). Vic roadside drug testing made permanent following pilot success (Jun). SA introduced roadside drug testing for cannabis and amphetamines (Jul). NSW Ombudsman review of police use of drug detection dogs found that drug dogs were an ineffective tool to target drug suppliers with most detected being people who used drugs in possession of cannabis (Sep).
2007	National Cannabis Prevention and Information Centre (NCPIC) set up with the aim of increasing early intervention and reducing cannabis use (Jun). The House of Representatives Standing Committee on Family and Human Services chaired by the Hon. Bronwyn Bishop released its report into the impact of illicit drug use on families. The report titled *The Winnable War on Drugs* recommended that the Australian government replace the current NDS focus on harm minimization with harm prevention and treatment with the ultimate aim of achieving permanent drug-free status. Other recommendations included that funding be preferentially provided to abstinence-based programs, that takeaway methadone be disallowed for parents, and that welfare payments be linked with child protection concerns (Sep).	WA Police commenced random roadside drug testing for cannabis, amphetamines and ecstasy (May). SA Premier Rann unveiled intention to introduce a comprehensive set of laws designed to make a major dent into organised crime in South Australia. The proposed set of laws covered more coercive powers of investigation, confiscating unexplained wealth, laws against association with criminal members (Jul). WA review of Cannabis Infringement Notice (CIN) scheme tabled in WA Parliament. Review recommended continuing with the CIN scheme,but reducing the quantity of cannabis to which the scheme applied (from 30 to 15 g), removing eligibility for cultivation of any plants, and increasing fines for non-compliance (Nov).

continued

Table 15.2 continued

Year	*Federal*	*State/territory*
2008	Report *Police Drug Diversion: A Study of Criminal Offending Outcomes* released by the Australian Institute of Criminology. The report demonstrated that the majority of offenders were not detected reoffending following diversion. For example, 69–86% of offenders (by state) without records and 31–54% of offenders with records were not detected reoffending within 18 months (Oct).	SA amendments to the Controlled Substances Act 1984 increased penalties against the cultivation of hydroponic cannabis (Jul). WA Liberals elected in coalition with the Nationals and Independents on a mandate to repeal the Cannabis Infringement Notice Scheme and provide a tougher response to cannabis (Sep).
2009	Fifth evaluation of the National Drug Strategy released by Siggins Miller. The evaluators identified a lack of stakeholder support for the term "harm minimization" (Nov).	SA legislation on sale of equipment for hydroponic growth of cannabis adopted (Hydroponics Industry Control Act 2009) with the aim of "preventing criminal infiltration of the hydroponics industry." Required 100 points of ID for every subsequent sale and all transactions recorded and forwarded to the police (Oct). SA Serious and Organised Crime (Unexplained Wealth) Act 2009 adopted (Nov). WA Cannabis Law Reform Bill 2009 tabled. This repealed the Cannabis Infringement Notice Scheme and made cannabis cultivation a criminal offence again. It also established a new legislated cannabis diversion program: the Cannabis Intervention Requirement (CIR), which required first-time offenders (adult and juvenile) in possession of ≤10 g of cannabis to attend a mandatory cannabis intervention session (Dec).
2010		Vic Liberal party were elected under a platform of a zero-tolerance approach to crime, and "banning the bong" to send a clear message to young people about the harmful effects of cannabis (Dec).

2011	The Inter-Governmental Committee on Drugs noted the emergence of new and existing synthetic analog drugs that mimic the effects of illegal drugs, particularly those mimicking the effects of cannabis (May). The TGA scheduled eight synthetic cannabinoids: JWH-018, JWH-073, JWH-122, JWH-200, JWH-250, CP47,497, AM-694 and cannabicyclohexanol. The synthetic cannabinoids, commonly referred to as 'Kronic', 'Spice' and 'Voodoo' etc, were placed on Schedule 9 (prohibited substances), thereby banning from July 8 their use for therapeutic purposes (Jul 6).	NSW Auditor-General released a new report: *Effectiveness of Cautioning for Minor Cannabis Offences*. Concluded those cautioned for cannabis use/possession reoffended less than those charged, and that the caution scheme had saved at least $20 million in court costs over ten years. But it noted large variation in caution rates between police commands (Apr). WA Government became first state to announce a ban on the possession, sale or intent to supply of seven synthetic cannabinoids including Kronic, Spice, Kaos Voodoo, Mango and Northern Lights (Jun). Vic amendment to the Drugs, Poisons and Controlled Substances Act 1981 banned the display, sale and supply of bongs in Victoria (Oct).
2012	Australia21 report released: *The Prohibition of Illicit Drugs is Killing and Criminalising Our Children and We Are All Letting it Happen*. Based on the high-level roundtable discussions involving 24 former senior politicians, law enforcement officers and public health officials (including Former WA Premier Geoff Gallop and Former AFP Commissioner Mick Palmer) the report concluded that the prohibition had failed and that Australia needed to consider alternatives (Apr). Liberal MP Mal Washer, Greens senator Richard Di Natale and independent Rob Oakeshott called on the federal government to ask the Productivity Commission to investigate the current adequacy of Australian drug laws, including "the economic cost of law enforcement around illicit drugs" (Jun).	SA Summary Offences (Drug Paraphernalia) Amendment Act enacted, banning the sale of drug paraphernalia such as cannabis pipes and bongs (Oct). NSW Legislative Council was established to consider the use of cannabis for medical purposes. Key issues included the efficacy and safety of using cannabis for medical purposes and if and how cannabis should be supplied for medical use. A total of 122 submissions were received (Nov).

continued

Table 15.2 continued

Year	*Federal*	*State/territory*
	New Australia21 report launched: *Alternatives to Prohibition: Illicit Drugs, How We Can Stop Killing and Criminalising Young Australians*. Report examined the experiences of four nations (Portugal, Switzerland, the Netherlands and Sweden) and concluded that more effective drug policies are possible (Aug).	
2013		NSW Legislative Council report on the use of cannabis for medical purposes released. Concluded that medical cannabis (either in pharmacotherapies or crude cannabis) had potential as an effective treatment for some medical conditions but noted that access would be dependent on Commonwealth Government approval (May). Vic Police Assistant Commissioner Andrew Crisp argued there had been too much emphasis upon drugs as a law and order issue and that the Victoria Government should treat drugs as a health issue (Jul). NSW Government released response to medical cannabis inquiry. They expressed support for expanding access to approved cannabis pharmacotherapies, and for writing to the Commonwealth to request access, but rejected lawful supply of crude cannabis products for medical purposes "as the potency and safety cannot be guaranteed" (Nov).
2014	Commonwealth Government stated that it would not oppose state or territory moves to decriminalize cannabis for medicinal purposes (Aug). Australian National Council on Drugs released new report: *Medicinal Use of Cannabis: Background and Information Paper* (Aug).	Online petition to the NSW Premier and NSW Health Minister launched by Haslam family calling for the decriminalization of medicinal cannabis in NSW. The campaign was motivated to help their terminally ill son, Daniel Haslam, who was diagnosed with bowel cancer and found medical benefits from using cannabis (Apr).

Prime Minister Tony Abbott backed legalization of medical cannabis and said that "no further testing should be needed on the drug if it is legal in similar jurisdictions" (Sep). Public Health Association of Australia (PHAA) launched position statement strongly supportive of medical cannabis (Sep). Council of Australian Governments meeting led to a national agreement to support a trial of medical cannabis in NSW and "to work collaboratively to share knowledge and information on issues relating to the use of appropriate therapeutic products derived from cannabis for medicinal purposes" (Oct). Regulator of Medicinal Cannabis Bill 2014 introduced by Senator's Di Natale, Macdonald, Leyonhjelm and Urquhart. Proposed to establish an Australian Regulator of Medicinal Cannabis to be responsible for formulating rules and monitoring compliance with those rules for licensing the production, manufacture, supply, use, experimental use and import and export of medicinal cannabis, and provide for a national system to regulate the cultivation, production and use of medicinal cannabis products, and related activities such as research (Nov).	NSW Premier Mike Baird met the Haslam family, announcing he was touched by the plight of Daniel Haslam, and was "sympathetic" to decriminalizing medical cannabis, but wanted issues of supply to be dealt with (Jul). NSW Government announced that it was issuing new guidelines for NSW police that would enable officers to exercize discretion not to charge terminally ill adults (or their carers) who use cannabis to alleviate their symptoms (Sep). ACT Attorney-General Simon Corbell launched a new report: *Evaluation of the ACT Drug Diversion Programs* and announced reforms designed to increase diversion access, including broadening the methods for payment of SCONs and increasing the threshold quantity for the SCON program (from 25 g to 50 g cannabis) (Oct). Tas Legislative Council Sessional Committee Government Administration parliamentary inquiry into "legalized medicinal cannabis" conducted. Concluded current legislation does not reflect the reality that a lot of people use cannabis for medical purposes and that the Government should introduce laws to allow medical cannabis use (Nov). Tas Health Minister ruled out any changes to the cannabis laws (Nov).

continued

Table 15.2 continued

Year	*Federal*	*State/territory*
		Vic Government announced its intention to legalize medical cannabis for individuals with terminal illnesses or life-threatening conditions and asked the Vic Law Reform Commission, under Dr. Ian Freckelton, QC, to review how Victorian laws should change to allow terminally and chronically ill people access to medicinal marijuana (Dec). NSW Premier announced three government-funded trials of medical cannabis would explore the role of medical cannabis in providing relief for patients with a range of debilitating or terminal illnesses, e.g. severe paediatric epilepsy (Dec).
2015	Senate Legal and Constitutional Affairs Legislation Committee commenced an Inquiry into the Regulator of Medicinal Cannabis Bill 2014 which received 261 public submissions. Gave in-principle support for access to products derived from cannabis for particular medical conditions where the use of those products had been proven to be safe and effective, and for passing the bill. Also recommended consulting with state and territory counterparts to ensure a consistent approach to accessing medicinal cannabis (Feb–Aug).	NSW medical cannabis campaigner Daniel Haslam passed away (Feb). NSW Centre for Medicinal Cannabis Research and Innovation launched, funded with $12 million by the NSW government to examine the benefits and treatment options for medicinal cannabis (Jun). Vic Law Reform Commission's *Medicinal Cannabis* report was tabled in Parliament with the government accepting all 42 recommendations, two accepted in principle. It announced that it would legalize access to medicinal cannabis in exceptional circumstances from 2017 (Oct 6). Vic Parliamentary Inquiry into Drug Law Reform established, to look at: (1) the effectiveness of laws, procedures and regulations relating to illicit and synthetic drugs in minimizing drug-related health, social and economic harm; and (2) the practice of other jurisdictions (nationally and internationally) and reforms that could be adopted into Vic law (Nov).

2016	The Office of Drug Control (ODC) established in the Commonwealth Department of Health to regulate and provide advice on the import, export and manufacture of controlled drugs as well as the domestic cultivation of medicinal cannabis. Key roles: to administer the Narcotic Drugs Act 1967 and parts of the Customs (Prohibited Imports) Regulations 1956 and the Customs (Prohibited Exports) Regulations 1958 that relate to drugs (Feb 15). The Federal Parliament of Australia passed landmark legislation, Narcotic Drugs Amendment Act 2016, to allow controlled cultivation of cannabis in Australia for medicinal and related scientific purposes via a national licensing scheme run by the Therapeutic Goods Administration (TGA). Included a detailed regulatory framework on the cultivation, production and manufacture of medicinal cannabis products. Key rules included that licensees must be judged as a "fit and proper person" including having previous business experience, no convictions for a serious offence in the last five years and being a person of good repute (Feb 24, operational as of Oct 30, 2016). Parliamentary Drug Summit held in Canberra, co-hosted by Senator Richard Di Natale (Greens), Sharman Stone MP (LNP) and Melissa Parke MP (ALP). Summit brought together international and Australian representatives with expertise in health, NGO, justice, personal addiction and academia, to share experiences and recommendations around harm minimization and drug law reform. Led to call for Australia to put health and community safety first in illicit drug policy; to remove criminal sanctions for personal drug use; to expand investment in drug treatment and to pursue an open debate on more effective policies (Mar 2).	Vic Access to Medicinal Cannabis Act 2016 adopted. This included a state-based scheme to allow the lawful cultivation and manufacture of medicinal cannabis products for use by a limited cohort of patients, with specific medical conditions. Children with severe intractable epilepsy were the first targeted (Apr). Vic Government announced a new funding package ($28.5 million) to support the roll-out of medical cannabis including the establishment of an Office of Medicinal Cannabis to oversee manufacturing and all clinical aspects of the medicinal cannabis framework and an Independent Medical Advisory Committee (Apr). First medical cannabis treatments were provided to NSW children with severe treatment-resistant epilepsy using Epidiolex® (Jun). Regulatory changes in NSW, Poisons and Therapeutic Goods Amendment (Designated Non-ARTG Products) Regulation 2016, allowed approved doctors to prescribe cannabis-based medicines for people with serious or chronic illnesses who have exhausted standard treatment options (Aug). Tas Premier announced that specialist medical practitioners would be able to prescribe medicinal cannabis for people with serious or chronic illnesses in Tas from 2017, via a Controlled Access Scheme (CAS). Scheme had no limit on diseases treatable and was policy-based – not based on legislative change (Aug).

continued

Table 15.2 continued

Year	*Federal*	*State/territory*
	The Uniting Church in Australia, Synod of NSW and the ACT became the first major Christian denomination in Australia to endorse a policy position to decriminalize the possession and use of small amounts of illicit drugs (Apr).	The Qld Government adopted Public Health (Medicinal Cannabis) Act 2016 to allow medicinal cannabis products to be prescribed and dispensed to patients in Qld for specific medical conditions (Oct). Medical cannabis access provided in four other states: ACT, SA, WA, NT (Nov).
2017	National cost-effectiveness evaluation *Australian Police Diversion for Cannabis Offences: Assessing Program Outcomes and Cost-effectiveness* found that cannabis expiation and cannabis caution were 6 to 15 times cheaper than provision of a traditional criminal justice response (charge) for cannabis use/possession offences, without leading to increased drug use or subsequent offending (Jun). *National Drug Strategy 2017–2026* released: first decade-long drug strategy. Included commitment to expand drug diversion (Jul).	
2018	Bill by Liberal Democratic Party Senator David Leyonhjelm proposed to remove Commonwealth barriers to the legalization and taxation of cannabis, with no restrictions on production of cannabis (May).	Vic Parliamentary Report on Drug Law Reform released, post 231 submissions. Noted the importance of a health response to illicit drugs and ongoing difficulties in accessing medical cannabis, and gaps and inequity in police drug diversion across Victoria due in part to the discretionary nature of programs. The report recommended that the Vic Government work with the Commonwealth to improve patient access to medicinal cannabis products and codify police drug diversion to ensure all offenders are offered a drug diversion. Report also noted the increasing development of cannabis regulatory models for adult use across the globe and recommended continued monitoring of the outcomes of international developments in regulated supply of cannabis (Mar).

Year	*Federal*	*State/territory*
	Australian Greens proposed to legalize cannabis for adult use in a tightly regulated market. Key proposals include: (a) establishment of an Australian Cannabis Agency that would act as a single wholesaler and issue all licenses for production and sale; (b) retail sales outlets with strict age limits, requirements for plain packaging and bans on all advertising; and (c) options for cultivation for personal use (May). New national approval process for medical cannabis unveiled, replacing dual approval process via states and Commonwealth, with single nationally consistent online access pathway via the TGA (Jul).	SA Liberal Government elected on a platform of "winning the war on drugs", including toughening penalties for cannabis possession (Mar). NT government announced it would introduce legislation allowing for the cultivation of industrial hemp and would explore options around growing medical cannabis (May). Vic Government response to drug law reform inquiry released. Concluded that a more healthy approach to illicit drugs was needed and they were working to streamline access to medical cannabis and to "strengthen" the Vic Police drug diversion program (Aug). Bill by ACT Labor backbencher Michael Pettersson proposed legalizing cannabis for personal use, via removing cannabis possession of ≤50 g by an adult as an offence and allowing people to legally grow four non-hydroponic cannabis plants (Sep). WA Government appointed select committee to examine alternate approaches to reducing illicit drug use and its effects on the community, including a comparison of the effectiveness and cost to the community of drug-related laws in other jurisdictions (Oct).

continued

Table 15.2 continued

Year	*Federal*	*State/territory*
		SA Statutes Amendment (Drug Offences) Bill 2018 proposed reintroducing the option of imprisonment for people who did not receive a cannabis expiation notice and increasing the maximum fine from \$200 to \$2000. The option of imprisonment was removed after a public backlash, but not the larger fine (Nov). Vic election proposal by Reason Party MP Fiona Patten proposed to legalise, regulate and tax recreational cannabis for adults aged ≥18 and to introduce strict product safety and product quality requirements. Costings from the Parliamentary Budget Office estimated this could increase the state's budget by \$204.6 million over the forward estimates (Dec).

Source: Hughes, Caitlin. (2018). *Australian illicit drug policy timeline: 1985–2018,* Sydney: Drug Policy Modelling Program.

have also been increased evaluations and internal and external reviews to identify not only what works, but also how to streamline programs (Australian Institute of Health and Welfare, 2008; Payne et al., 2008) and how to remove or modify eligibility criteria that curtail access, such as by increasing threshold limits (Hughes et al., 2014). More generally, there is now a national commitment to expanding police drug diversion for use/possession (Hughes et al., 2019).

Policy reversals and contractions of the prohibition with civil penalty schemes

While acceptance of therapeutic diversion programs has grown, there has been a policy contraction of the prohibition with civil penalty schemes in Australia, with all programs subject to some level of policy contraction or reversal (see Table 15.2). Regarding the SA CEN scheme, the number of cannabis plants attracting an expiation notice was first reduced from ten to three (in 1999), then from three to one (2001), then cultivation of hydroponic plants was banned (2002). More recently there has been a failed attempt in 2018 to reintroduce the option of imprisonment for people who did not receive a CEN (Statutes Amendment (Drug Offences) Bill, 2018, SA). The option of imprisonment was removed following a public backlash, although people remain subject to a larger fine of up to AU$2,000. (The introduction of a larger fine remains a concern, given that failure to pay a fine can lead to prison, particularly amongst people who have lower socioeconomic status, though this is less problematic than automatic imprisonment.) The ACT and NT reforms have been similarly amended over time to exclude hydroponic cultivation and to limit the number of plants that can be possessed. The most noted cannabis policy reversal was however the WA scheme, which, while introduced in 2004, was repealed seven years later (Lenton and Allsop, 2010).

On the face of it, such shifts could be deemed to suggest a movement away from civil penalty schemes, particularly the WA reform which was overturned despite the evidence base and stakeholder support. For example, research showed the reform had shifted the cannabis market towards self-supply and increased the willingness of recent users to seek counselling or other help for cannabis-related problems (Fetherston and Lenton, 2007), and a three-year independent legislative review of the scheme concluded that the reform should be continued on the grounds that it was cost-effective – netting an estimated AU$2.3 million over three years, reduced harms from provision of criminal records, and had the support of police, treatment providers and the public, without increasing recent cannabis use (Drug and Alcohol Office, 2007). Here Lenton and Allsop (2010) attributed the policy reversal to political reasons, as part of a broader law and order agenda following a switch to a more conservative government.

But most of the policy contractions followed evidence and inquiries showing that the schemes were being used to divert cannabis to the black market, counter to the original intent of the scheme. This included the exploitation by organized crime groups of the original SA CEN scheme. Changes were thus in line with the evaluator's recommendations to reduce the number of allowable plants (here from ten to three) (Ali et al., 1999) and/or to prohibit hydroponic cultivation. Importantly, rules surrounding civil penalties for use/possession offenses have remained largely unchanged. The one exception is the ACT, where in 2014, eligibility criteria on the amount of cannabis that was permitted to be possessed under the Simple Cannabis Offence Notice (SCON) scheme was increased from 25 to 50 grams, following evidence that many people purchased cannabis in ounce quantities.

Shifts in the discourse surrounding cannabis in Australia

More generally, Table 15.2 shows that from 1985 to 2018, there has been a sustained shift in how cannabis is viewed and conceptualized by Australian policymakers from seeing cannabis as a "harmless substance" to something that is potentially harmful for some people and where powers to limit harm become increasingly front and center concerns (Ritter and Sotade, 2017). This is exemplified by the 2018 failed policy contraction in SA to reintroduce imprisonment for those who did not receive a CEN, on the premise of the increased health risks of using this drug.

> May I say that, if I were to generally summarize the impetus for the reform in this legislation, it is the recognition that cannabis, amongst all our illicit drugs can no longer, in 2018, be treated as though it is something just a little bit more serious than tobacco.
>
> Second reading speech, Statutes Amendment (Drug Offences) Bill, by Attorney General Vickie Chapman.
> (SA, 2018, p. 2036)

Other important signs of the shift in discourse and conceptualization have been the 2006 establishment of the first *National Cannabis Strategy* (Commonwealth of Australia, 2006), the 2007 establishment of the National Cannabis Information and Prevention Centre (which operated until December 2016), the 2004 introduction and subsequent expansion of zero-tolerance roadside drug testing laws for cannabis (and selected other drugs) across all Australian states/territories (Quilter and McNamara, 2017) and more recently the singling-out of cannabis as a high-priority drug in the *2017–2026 National Drug Strategy* (see Table 15.2).

Some shifts in discourse can be attributed to a conservative shift in Australian drug policy, where harm prevention rather than harm minimization became the focus (Ritter, Lancaster, Grech and Reuter, 2011). See for example the 2003 road to recovery report (House of Representatives Standing Committee on Family and Community Affairs, 2003). But it also reflects increased knowledge about the long-term harms from cannabis within Australia. For example, new knowledge about the harms from cannabis and high-risk priority groups, such as Aboriginal and Torres Strait Islander populations, started to appear in the mid-1990s (Hall, 1994; Hall and Swift, 2000; Hall, Solowij and Lemon, 1994), and by the mid-2000s had become even stronger (Copeland, Gerber and Swift, 2006; McLaren and Mattick, 2007), leading to extended public consultations and ultimately the establishment of the first *National Cannabis Strategy* on the grounds of the

> growing evidence that cannabis use, particularly heavy regular use, has the potential to have a significant negative impact on mental and physical health including mental health problems; respiratory disorders; tobacco dependence; use of other illicit substances; injury from driving under the influence of cannabis; and educational or occupational failure due to adverse motivational and cognitive impacts.
>
> (Commonwealth of Australia, 2006, p. 1)[2]

This reframed discourse can be seen as central to much of the recent Australian debates and reforms, including the preferential expansion of police drug diversion programs offering targeted therapeutic early intervention, as well as the emergence of a tightly regulated Australian medical cannabis market.

Lessons learned and future directions for cannabis legalization in Australia

Australia is now at a point where alternatives to arrest are deemed "mainstream" and where policy endeavors are focused on expanding drug diversion and/or the removal of criminal penalties for the use and possession of all illicit drugs, as well as reducing some of the red tape surrounding medical cannabis access (Parliament of Victoria Law Reform Road and Community Safety Committee, 2018). But as of 2018, there is limited debate about the legalization of cannabis within Australia, with the main view espoused to wait and to learn from the international experiments (Australian Drug Foundation, 2018). Interestingly, such a view is almost consensual, even amongst leading advocacy groups and drug law reform groups (Australia21, 2018). What is shaping this is complex, but appears to reflect a number of factors, including a growing realization that copying the approach taken towards alcohol or tobacco is not the way to go, given the high harms that eventuated from "Big Tobacco." For example, as noted by Dr Alex Wodak, President of the Australian Drug Law Reform Foundation "I think there are a lot of lessons we can learn from the mistakes that were made with the regulation of alcohol and tobacco that we don't want to see repeated with cannabis" (Parliament of Victoria, 2017, p. 95). This marks a direct shift from earlier times where regulation of cannabis was proposed as involving a model like regulation of alcohol or tobacco (Atkinson and McDonald, 1995). More generally it reflects concern that the dominant model today – the US commercialized model – holds few attractions in the Australian context, and that the model of most interest will be the Canadian public health-oriented approach (Parliament of Victoria, 2017). That said, it is likely to be years before the evidence is amassed on the outcomes and lessons from this reform.

More generally, analysis of public opinion data from the National Drug Strategy Household Survey shows that while 84.5 percent of the Australian population in 2016 support the legalization of cannabis for medical purposes (Australian Institute of Health and Welfare, 2017), and 77.5 percent support decriminalization actions for cannabis use, only 31.8 percent support the legalization of cannabis for recreational purposes (Hughes and Ritter, 2018). That said, a number of models of cannabis legalization have been recently discussed in Australia, which provides a useful means to identify the strengths and weaknesses of each approach for the Australian context. This includes free market cannabis legalization, legalization of home-grown cannabis, and a government monopoly.

Model 1: Free market cannabis legalization

The first model is free market cannabis legalization, or "repeal-without-regulation" (Caulkins, Kilmer, Kleiman, MacCoun, Midgette, Oglesby and Reuter, 2015, p. 67) which would remove all prohibitions over the cultivation, supply, acquisition, possession or use of cannabis, without creating any new cannabis-specific regulations. As outlined by Caulkins et al. (2015) there are no existing examples of this model for cannabis, but it was proposed in 2012 in Michigan[3] and it has a broader precedent in the context of overturning of alcohol prohibition in the 1920s in selected states (Room, 2008). In the Australian context, one contemporary operationalization of this model is that proffered by Liberal Democratic Party Senator David Leyonhjelm through the Criminal Code and Other Legislation Amendment (removing Commonwealth restrictions on cannabis) Bill 2018 (Cth). This bill seeks to remove cannabis from the Commonwealth statues, such as the *Commonwealth Criminal Code*, so that cannabis is no longer a "border-controlled drug or plant." It would also repeal the existing regulatory system for medical cannabis, including licensing of people to cultivate, produce or obtain medical cannabis/cannabis products. Senator Leyonhjelm's main argument for this bill is that "adults should be free to make their own choices as long as they do not harm others." In keeping with John Stuart Mill's "harm principle" – that limiting people's liberty is only justifiable to prevent harm to other people – and classical liberal or libertarian principles more generally, Leyonhjelm's bill does not impose any new prohibitions on cannabis. As the bill states:

> nothing in this Act makes it an offence or contravention of a civil penalty provision for any person or body corporate to participate in the cultivation, production, manufacture, extraction, preparation, transportation, distribution, delivery, brokerage, dispatch, trafficking, offering, purchase, sale, trade, exporting, importing, use, consumption or possession of cannabis."

The bill neither restricts the production or advertising of cannabis, nor imposes any excise on the drug, with the only tax being the Australian goods and services tax of 10 percent.

Model 2: Legalization of home-grown cannabis

The second model is to legalize home-grown cannabis for personal use. Such a model is evident in Vermont, USA where since July 2018, adults aged 21 and over have been allowed to possess up to an ounce of cannabis or five grams of hashish and to grow "two mature and four immature marijuana plants" on private property (Caulkins et al., 2015). In the Australian context, one contemporary operationalization of this model is that of ACT Labor backbencher Michael Pettersson. The Drugs of Dependence (Personal Cannabis Use) Amendment Bill 2018 (ACT) would remove the offense of cannabis possession of up to 50 grams for anyone aged 18 and over and allow legal cultivation of up to four cannabis plants by non-hydroponic means. This would also retain the existing SCON prohibition with civil penalties scheme for young offenders (aged under 18) and prohibit public smoking or smoking within 20 meters of a child. While acknowledged to be a smaller shift than a full-scale regulated cannabis market, the stated aims are to reduce criminal convictions for people who use cannabis (particularly for those who currently fail to pay a SCON), reduce the burden on the criminal justice system and the harms from policing people who use cannabis and reduce the exposure of adults to the black market.[4]

Model 3: Government monopoly and public health approach to legalization and regulation

The third model is a government monopoly, whereby the government controls production, retail sales or both, with the goal of increasing oversight (e.g. over prices, products etc.) and reducing potential adverse consequences that may ensue from free market competition (Caulkins et al., 2015). A government monopoly on the legalization and regulation of cannabis is evident in some Canadian provinces, such as Quebec and Ontario (Cox, 2018; Fraser, 2018). For example, since October 17, 2018 adults aged 18 and over in Quebec have been able to consume, possess or purchase cannabis, albeit the sole authorized cannabis distributor and seller has been the Société Québécoise du Cannabis (SQDC). Limits on the quantities that can be purchased and possessed, a ban on advertising, a requirement for plain packaging and other rules also apply.[5] Added to that, many examples of state alcohol monopolies have also operated (Pacula, Kilmer, Wagenaar, Chaloupka and Caulkins, 2014).

In the Australian context, one contemporary operationalization of this model is a proposal by the Australian Green Party to redefine cannabis as a legal substance for adult use in a tightly regulated market (Di Natale, 2018), under the stated goal of reducing harm, increasing protections for vulnerable populations and redirecting resources into treatment. The Greens' model proposes the establishment of an Australian Cannabis Agency that would be responsible for controlling production and sale and would be the only wholesaler for legal cannabis, as well as retail outlets. It seeks to "avoid 'big cannabis' by promoting small scale production" (Di Natale, 2018). The model includes a complete ban on advertising, and a requirement for plain packaging for all cannabis products, with clear information about the strain as well as health warnings and age restrictions (18 and over). All staff in the stores would also be required to undertake a responsible sale of cannabis (similar to a responsible service of alcohol) course, as well as mental health first aid training. Growth of up to six plants would also be allowed at home for personal use only.

This model reflects the belief that drug prohibition has failed to deter use and that treating cannabis use as a criminal rather than a health issue has caused more harm than it has prevented, including through criminal records for people who use drugs, reduced treatment-seeking and increased exposure to the black market and more harmful drugs. The model however, recognizes that cannabis use can be associated with some harms, particularly for people with pre-existing mental health issues, hence legal access to cannabis for recreational purposes would be afforded via a highly regulated model, with money raised through tax revenue invested in drug treatment services, mental health services and drug education programs.

Advantages and disadvantages

Free market legalization (Model 1) offers the potential to reduce law enforcement expenditure on policing of cannabis in Australia and to collect tax from cannabis that could be directed for other purposes. For example, the estimates from the Leyonhjelm bill are that legalizing cannabis would reduce annual Commonwealth law enforcement expenditure by around AU$100 million per year, but that it would also increase cannabis consumption[6] and thus increase GST revenue by around AU$300 million per year. That said, of the set of models, this is the least attractive in the Australian context, as it ignores the proven harms that can be associated with cannabis use (such as dependence, mental health, drug driving or reduced educational attainment) and high risks from a free-market approach of promoting harmful use without any government capacity for controls on product quality or how it is produced, distributed or used (Caulkins et al., 2015). It also ignores the lessons from alcohol or tobacco in Australia and abroad where loose regulation has come at considerable public health costs, particularly amongst minority groups (Bond, Daube and Chikritzhs, 2010; Hall and Kozlowski, 2018; Pacula et al., 2014). Such a model would also repeal the existing medical cannabis scheme, removing the role of doctors in such space which, while currently hamstrung, may create new problems – where there is no capacity for medical advice about the use for medical purposes.

Analysis of public submissions to the Leyonhjelm bill thus show it has earned considerable criticism from almost all Australian stakeholder groups, including government, medical professionals, non-government organizations, researchers and police. Of note, the Commonwealth Department of Health (2018b) raised concerns that the bill would "dismantle the carefully constructed system of regulation of the cultivation, production and manufacture of medicinal cannabis," including product controls on the level of heavy metals, fungal infections and other contaminants permitted in medicinal cannabis in Australia, and thus expose the community to variable or unsafe products. The Western Australia Police (2018) raised concerns that the reform would reduce public safety such as via increased roadside drug driving and increase public health harms. The Australian Medical Association (2018) argued that any potential benefits of reducing civil liberties must be traded off against public health impacts and employ appropriate controls to guard against increased health risks, including to groups at higher risk of the deleterious effects of cannabis, such as Aboriginal and Torres Strait Islander people. As such, it is clear that a free market model is not palatable in the Australian context, and that some form of government controls is vital to mitigate against any potential public health and safety risks.

Model 2 holds attractions in that it mitigates against some of the risks of Model 1. It also has feasibility, given the higher cannabis yields that can be obtained within Australia (Potter, Barratt, Malm, Bouchard, Blok, Christensen and Wouters., 2015). The approach has some useful public health protections including bans on public smoking and retains a diversion option for those aged under 18 in the ACT: a proven cost-effective response.[7] However, a home-grown only model ignores differential access to space to grow cannabis, an issue that affected cultivation under the SA CEN scheme (Sutton, 2000). This is a particular concern in regard to young people aged 18 to 34 (the dominant demographic who use cannabis in Australia, see Australian Institute of Health and Welfare, 2017) and/or those renting or living in apartments in Australia, where there are strict rules around what is permitted, landlord powers for eviction are high and where bans on smoking are becoming common, on the grounds of smoking's public health hazards (Cancer Council NSW, 2017). In such a context, receptivity to cannabis home production, may be limited or unequally distributed. More generally, such a model would afford no government control over mechanisms of cultivation, distribution or use. As such, it leaves out the possibilities of a more public health approach with rules or guidance about how to grow, as well as product labelling and testing and production of lower-harm products.

The final model (Model 3) holds many attractions due to the tight government controls, age limits, ban on advertising, plain packaging, product labelling and taxation and investment in mental health, education and treatment services. In so doing, it accords with many core concerns about how to ensure governments prioritize public health over commercial interests in any new regulatory models (Parliament of Victoria Law Reform Road and Community Safety Committee, 2018), and the explicit recommendations of Dr Alex Wodak, President of the Australian Drug Law Reform Foundation to ban advertising, adopt clear labelling on products and provide evidence-informed health warnings. The model is also broadly in line with an early analysis of the cost-benefits of cannabis legalization in Australia by Shanahan and Ritter (2014). They conducted a cost-benefit analysis of cannabis legalization in NSW versus the status quo (where there is prohibition with cannabis cautioning and youth cautioning), using a hypothetical model of legalization that was similar to that used here. This included a government monopoly, bans on advertising, plain packaging, health warnings, age restrictions and taxation and revenue that was reallocated to government. The main difference is that their model used an age limit of 21, compared to the age limit of 18 in the current model. Shanahan and Ritter (2014) found that the mean net social benefit of cannabis legalization and regulation including government revenue was AU$727.5 million per annum compared to AU$294.6 million per annum for the status quo, taking into account a significant reduction in costs to the criminal justice system, albeit also increased costs from licensing, as well as treatment and healthcare from a likely increase in cannabis use (both prevalence and quantity) and policing drug driving.

Of the models outlined, a government-controlled model along the lines of Model 3 thus has the most appeal for the Australian context, particularly given the complete ban on advertising, but many questions remain unanswered about pricing, purity and product range among others, which US debates have shown are critical to establish (Babor et al., 2018; Caulkins et al., 2015; Kilmer, 2014; Kilmer and Pacula, 2017). For example, if the price is too high, that will perpetuate the black market, but if the price is too low then it may encourage more use. Limits on the maximum THC content, THC/CBD ratios and bans on public smoking as per Model 2 would also appear desirable, as well as requirements to funnel tax to increase treatment access in rural/regional Australia. Similar to debates in Canada with their legalization of cannabis, it would also appear pertinent to consider impacts of legalization of cannabis on indigenous populations, particularly given the heightened harms that can be associated with cannabis use amongst this population. Also important is considering how any policy adoption would play out in a federated system, as the three waves of Australian cannabis law reforms have shown state/territory divergence is common and can have a large impact upon policy outcomes. This is not to say it is necessarily a bad thing, as the state/territory differences have been beneficial for learning about "what works." But this may be a reason that a national approach may have merit, even if it takes time. One final consideration is drug driving laws. Given all Australian states have zero-tolerance roadside drug testing for cannabis and have done so for upwards of 15 years (Quilter and McNamara, 2017), new impairment-based thresholds may be required to ensure that under a legal, regulated cannabis market, it is dangerous driving rather than driving by cannabis consumers that is policed and targeted.

Conclusion

In conclusion, this chapter shows that Australia has a long history of cannabis law reform. It shows that there has been a substantial expansion in *de jure* and de facto cannabis law reform, involving both prohibition with civil penalties and depenalization, and more recently the adoption of the first laws enabling medical cannabis. It shows that both prohibition with civil penalties and depenalization models have led to numerous positive benefits, reducing the burden on the consumer and criminal justice system, and social benefits from avoiding the provision of a criminal conviction. But it also shows that there are clear state/territory differences whereby offenders in some states and territories are much more likely to receive convictions for cannabis use/possession alone, and that over time, there have been some contractions, particularly of the prohibition with civil penalty schemes, as well as an expansion in therapeutic models. That said, while there is a clear appetite and commitment to expand alternatives to sanction for cannabis use/possession, and to increase medical cannabis access (albeit within the realms of a tightly-controlled system), opportunities for legalization of cannabis for recreational purposes appear limited in Australia at the present time. Nevertheless, there is a growing sense of what types of models will have more, or less appeal in the Australian context. Whilst concerns about Big Tobacco mean that laissez-faire approaches or full-scale commercial models like most US cannabis legalization states have low palatability, government monopolies coupled with public health regulations offer much greater appeal.

Notes

1 One exception to this is consumer offenses involving possession of imported substances, although this is seldom used in practice (Hughes, Chalmers and Klimoski, 2018).
2 Arguably, insights from the early cannabis law reforms also played a role in re-shaping the discourse, with the SA CEN scheme evaluators noting the low level of understanding amongst those diverted about the risks of cannabis and the potential benefits of including a health brochure in responding to people who use cannabis (Ali et al., 1999).
3 This proposal ultimately failed to get sufficient votes to be placed on the ballot: see Caulkins et al. (2015) for details.
4 The Drugs of Dependence (Personal Cannabis Use) Amendment Bill 2018 was adopted with amendments in September 2019 and is due to commence in January 2020. This retains the offence of cannabis possession and minor cultivation but removes penalties for adults.
5 In Ontario, the Ontario Cannabis Retail Corp (OCRC) is the sole authorized cannabis wholesaler and distributor, although a private retail model for cannabis

sales has been adopted (set to commence by April 1, 2019). The legal response represents a compromise between the previous government and the new government elected in June 2018, as all retail stores were to have been operated by the OCRC.

6 It is estimated that marijuana consumption would increase from approximately 339 tonnes in 2016–2017 to 381 tonnes in 2017–2018, 388 tonnes in 2018–2019 and 394 tonnes in 2019–2020.

7 That said, it is arguable that a therapeutic diversionary option via the IDD may be preferable to those aged under 18 than the requirement to pay a civil penalty.

References

Ali, R., Christie, P., Lenton, S., Hawks, D., Sutton, A., Hall, W. and Allsop, S. (1999). *The social impacts of the cannabis expiation notice scheme in South Australia.* Canberra: Department of Health and Aged Care.

Atkinson, L. and McDonald, D. (1995). *Cannabis, the law and social impacts in Australia. Trends and Issues in Crime and Criminal Justice No. 45.* Canberra: Australian Institute of Criminology.

Australia21. (2018). *We all pay the price: Our drug laws are tearing apart our social fabric, as well as harming drug users and their families.* Canberra: Australia21.

Australian Drug Foundation. (2018). *Submission to the senate legal and constitutional affairs legislation committee inquiry into the Criminal Code and Other Legislation Amendment (removing Commonwealth restrictions on cannabis) Bill 2018.* (Submission 13). Canberra: Parliament of Australia.

Australian Institute of Health and Welfare. (2008). *The effectiveness of the illicit drug diversion initiative in rural and remote Australia.* Drug Statistics Series No. 19, Cat. No. PHE 96. Canberra: Australian Institute of Health and Welfare.

Australian Institute of Health and Welfare. (2014). *Alcohol and other drug treatment and diversion from the Australian criminal justice system: 2012–13.* Bulletin no. 125. Cat. no. AUS 186. Canberra: Australian Institute of Health and Welfare.

Australian Institute of Health and Welfare. (2017). *2016 National Drug Strategy Household Survey: Detailed findings.* Drug Statistics Series No. 31. Cat. no. PHE 214. Canberra: Australian Institute of Health and Welfare.

Australian Medical Association. (2018). *Submission to the senate legal and constitutional affairs legislation committee inquiry into the Criminal Code and Other Legislation Amendment (removing Commonwealth restrictions on cannabis) Bill 2018.* (Submission 17). Canberra: Parliament of Australia.

Babor, T.F., Caulkins, J.P., Edwards, G., Fischer, B., Foxcroft, D.R., Humphreys, K. and Strang, J. (2010). *Drug policy and the public good.* Oxford: Oxford University Press.

Babor, T., Caulkins, J., Fischer, B., Foxcroft, D., Humphreys, K., Medina-Mora, M.E. and Room, R. (2018). *Drug policy and the public good.* Oxford: Oxford University Press.

Baker, J. and Goh, D. (2004). *The cannabis cautioning scheme three years on: An implementation and outcome evaluation.* Sydney: New South Wales Bureau of Crime Statistics and Research.

Blewett, N. (1987). *National campaign against drug abuse: Assumptions, arguments and aspirations.* NCADA Monograph Series No. 1. Canberra: Australian Government Publishing Service.

Bond, L., Daube, M. and Chikritzhs, T. (2010). Selling addictions: Similarities in approaches between big tobacco and big booze. *Australasian Medical Journal,* 3(6), 325–332.

Cancer Council NSW. (2017). *Smoke-free by-laws: Know your options.* Sydney: Cancer Council NSW.

Caulkins, J.P., Kilmer, B., Kleiman, M.A., MacCoun, R.J., Midgette, G., Oglesby, P. and Reuter, P.H. (2015). *Considering marijuana legalization: Insights for Vermont and other jurisdictions.* Santa Monica: RAND Corporation.

Christie, P. and Ali, R. (2000). Offences under the cannabis expiation notice scheme in South Australia. *Drug and Alcohol Review,* 19(3), 251–256.

Commonwealth. (2016). *Hansard – Narcotic Drugs Amendment Bill 2016 – Second reading speech.* House of Representatives.

Commonwealth Department of Health. (1985). *National campaign against drug abuse.* Canberra: Australian Government Publishing Service.

Commonwealth Department of Health. (2018a). *National Drug Strategy 2017–2026.* Canberra: Commonwealth Department of Health.

Commonwealth Department of Health. (2018b). *Submission to the senate legal and constitutional affairs legislation committee inquiry into the Criminal Code and Other Legislation Amendment (removing Commonwealth restrictions on cannabis) Bill 2018.* (Submission 32). Canberra: Parliament of Australia.

Commonwealth of Australia. (2006). *National Cannabis Strategy 2006–2009.* Canberra: Commonwealth of Australia.

Copeland, J., Gerber, S. and Swift, W. (2006). *Evidence-based answers to cannabis questions: A review of the literature.* Canberra: Australian National Council on Drugs.

Council of Australian Governments. (1999). *Tough on drugs! Diversion programme.* Canberra: COAG.

Cox, C. (2018). The Canadian Cannabis Act legalizes and regulates. *Canadian Medical Association Journal,* 189, 28.

Di Natale, R. (2018). *Cannabis: Just legalise it – Regulating cannabis to reduce harm.* Canberra, ACT: The Australian Greens.

Donnelly, N., Hall, W. and Christie, P. (1999). *Effects of the cannabis expiation notice scheme on levels and patterns of cannabis use in South Australia: Evidence from the national drug strategy household surveys 1985–1995.* Canberra: Department of Health and Aged Care.

Drug and Alcohol Office. (2007). *Statutory review Cannabis Control Act 2003. Report to the Minister for Health: Technical report.* Perth, Western Australia: Drug and Alcohol Office.

Fetherston, J. and Lenton, S. (2007). *Effects of the Western Australian cannabis infringement notice scheme on public attitudes, knowledge and use: Comparison of pre and post change data.* Perth: National Drug Research Institute.

Fraser, T. (2018). *Canadian cannabis legalization highlights by province/territory as of 18th December 2018.* Retrieved from www.dropbox.com/s/r7re1ewe94dxos8/Legalization_Chart%20-Dec.18.18.pdf?dl=0.

Hales, J., Mayne, M., Swan, A., Alberti, S. and Ritter, A. (2004). *Evaluation of Queensland Illicit Drug Diversion Initiative (QIDDI) police diversion program.* Kent

Town, SA: Health Outcomes International Pty Ltd and Turning Point Alcohol and Drug Centre.

Hall, W. (1994). The health and psychological effects of cannabis use. *Current Issues Criminal Justice,* 6, 208.

Hall, W. (2001). Reducing the harms caused by cannabis use: The policy debate in Australia. *Drug and Alcohol Dependence,* 62(3), 163–174.

Hall, W. and Kozlowski, L.T. (2018). The diverging trajectories of cannabis and tobacco policies in the United States: Reasons and possible implications. *Addiction,* 113(4), 595–601.

Hall, W., Solowij, N. and Lemon, J. (1994). *The health and psychological consequences of cannabis use.* Canberra: Australian Government Publishing Service.

Hall, W. and Swift, W. (2000). The THC content of cannabis in Australia: Evidence and implications. *Australian and New Zealand Journal of Public Health,* 24(5), 503–508.

House of Representatives Standing Committee on Family and Community Affairs. (2003). *Road to recovery: Report on the inquiry into substance abuse in Australian communities.* Canberra: House of Representatives Standing Committee on Family and Community Affairs.

Hughes, C.E. (2007). Evidence-based policy or policy-based evidence? The role of evidence in the development of the illicit drug diversion initiative. *Drug and Alcohol Review,* 26(4), 364–368.

Hughes, C. (2018). *Australian (illicit) drug policy timeline: 1985–2018. Sydney: Drug Policy Modelling Program.* Retrieved from https://ndarc.med.unsw.edu.au/resource/australian-illicit-drug-policy-timeline-1985-2015%20.

Hughes, C.E., Chalmers, J. and Klimoski, M. (2018). Assessing concordance between trends in high-level drug trafficking and other serious and organized crimes in Australia, 2005–06 to 2014–15. *Drugs: Education, Prevention and Policy,* 25(3), 217–233.

Hughes, C. and Ritter, A. (2008). *Monograph No. 16: A summary of diversion programs for drug and drug-related offenders in Australia.* DPMP Monograph Series. Sydney: National Drug and Alcohol Research Centre.

Hughes, C. and Ritter, A. (2018). *Bulletin No. 25: What does the research evidence tell us about what Australians think about the legal status of drugs? A 2018 update.* DPMP Bulletin Series. Sydney: National Drug and Alcohol Research Centre and Social Policy Research Centre.

Hughes, C., Seear, K., Ritter, A. and Mazerolle, L. (2019). *Monograph No. 27: Criminal justice responses relating to personal use and possession of illicit drugs: The reach of Australian drug diversion programs and barriers and facilitators to expansion.* DPMP Monograph Series. Sydney: National Drug and Alcohol Research Centre, UNSW Sydney.

Hughes, C., Shanahan, M., Ritter, A., McDonald, D. and Gray-Weale, F. (2014). *Monograph No. 25: Evaluation of Australian Capital Territory drug diversion programs.* DPMP Monograph Series. Sydney: National Drug and Alcohol Research Centre.

Kilmer, B. (2014). Policy designs for cannabis legalization: Starting with the eight Ps. *The American Journal of Drug and Alcohol Abuse,* 40(4), 259–261.

Kilmer, B. and Pacula, R.L. (2017). Understanding and learning from the diversification of cannabis supply laws. *Addiction,* 112, 1128–1135.

Legislative Council. (2013). *NSW Government inquiry on the use of cannabis for medical purposes*. Sydney: New South Wales. Parliament. Legislative Council. General Purpose Standing Committee No. 4.

Lenton, S. and Allsop, S. (2010). A tale of CIN – the Cannabis Infringement Notice scheme in Western Australia. *Addiction,* 105(5), 808–816.

Lenton, S., Christie, P., Humeniuk, R., Brooks, A., Bennett, M. and Heale, P. (1999). *Infringement versus conviction: The social impact of a minor cannabis offence under a civil penalties system and strict prohibition in two Australian states*. National Drug Strategy Monograph No. 36. Canberra: Department of Health and Aged Care.

MacCoun, R. and Reuter, P. (2001). *Drug war heresies: Learning from other vices, times, and places*. Cambridge: Cambridge University Press.

Manderson, D. (1993). *From Mr. Sin to Mr. Big: A history of Australian drug laws*. Melbourne: Oxford University Press.

McDonald, D. and Atkinson, L. (1995). *Social impacts of the legislative options for cannabis in Australia: Phase 1 research*. Report to the National Drug Strategy Committee. Canberra: Australian Institute of Criminology.

McDonald, D. and Hughes, C. (2017). Chapter 11: Drug laws and regulations. In A. Ritter, T. King and N. Lee (Eds.), *Drug use in Australian society* (pp. 223–246). South Melbourne: Oxford University Press.

McLaren, J. and Mattick, R. (2007). *Cannabis in Australia: Use, supply, harms and responses*. Sydney: National Drug and Alcohol Research Centre.

Ministerial Council on Drug Strategy. (2004). *The National Drug Strategy: Australia's integrated framework 2004–2009*. Canberra: Ministerial Council on Drug Strategy.

Ministerial Council on Drug Strategy. (2011). *National Drug Strategy 2010–2015*. Canberra: Ministerial Council on Drug Strategy.

NSW Auditor General. (2011). *The effectiveness of cautioning for minor cannabis offences*. Sydney: NSW Auditor General.

Pacula, R.L., Kilmer, B., Wagenaar, A.C., Chaloupka, F.J. and Caulkins, J.P. (2014). Developing public health regulations for marijuana: Lessons from alcohol and tobacco. *American Journal of Public Health,* 104(6), 1021–1028.

Parliament of Victoria. (2017). *Transcript of hearing – 23 May 2017 – for Victoria Law Reform, Road and Community Safety Committee inquiry into drug law reform with Mick Palmer, Dr Alex Wodak and Paul Bodisco*. Melbourne: Victoria Parliament.

Parliament of Victoria Law Reform Road and Community Safety Committee. (2018). *Inquiry into drug law reform*. Melbourne: Parliament of Victoria Law Reform, Road and Community Safety Committee.

Payne, J., Kwiatkowski, M. and Wundersitz, J. (2008). *Police drug diversion: A study of criminal offending outcomes*. Canberra: Australian Institute of Criminology.

Polk, K., Adler, C., Muller, D. and Rechtman, K. (2005). *Early intervention: Diversion and youth conferencing – A national profile and review of current approaches to diverting juveniles from the criminal justice system*. Canberra: Australian Government Attorney-General's Department.

Potter, G.R., Barratt, M.J., Malm, A., Bouchard, M., Blok, T., Christensen, A.-S. and Wouters, M. (2015). Global patterns of domestic cannabis cultivation: Sample characteristics and patterns of growing across eleven countries. *International Journal of Drug Policy,* 26(3), 226–237.

Quilter, J. and McNamara, L. (2017). "Zero tolerance" drug driving laws in Australia: A gap between rationale and form? *International Journal for Crime, Justice and Social Democracy*, 6(3), 47–71.

Ritter, A., Lancaster, K., Grech, K. and Reuter, P. (2011). *Monograph No. 21: An assessment of illicit drug policy in Australia (1985–2010): Themes and trends*. DPMP Monograph Series. Sydney: National Drug and Alcohol Research Centre.

Ritter, A. and Sotade, O. (2017). Explaining the declining rates of past year cannabis use in Australia: A first pass. *Drug and Alcohol Review*, 36(5), 602–608.

Room, R. (2008). In thinking about cannabis policy, what can be learned from alcohol and tobacco? In S. R. Sznitman, B. Olsson and R. Room (Eds.), *A cannabis reader: Global issues and local experiences* (pp. 119–136). Lisbon: European Monitoring Centre for Drugs and Drug Addiction.

Room, R., Fischer, B., Hall, W., Lenton, S. and Reuter, P. (2010). *Cannabis policy: Moving beyond stalemate*. Oxford: Oxford University Press.

SA. (2018). *Hansard: Statutes Amendment (Drug Offences) Bill – Second reading speech by Attorney General Vickie Chapman*. South Australia Parliament.

Sarre, R., Sutton, A. and Pulsford, T. (1989). *Cannabis – The expiation notice approach*. Adelaide: South Australian Attorney-General's Department.

Senate Standing Committee on Social Welfare. (1977). *Drug problems in Australia: An intoxicated society?* Canberra: Australian Government Publishing Service.

Shanahan, M., Hughes, C. and McSweeney, T. (2017). *Police diversion for cannabis offences: Assessing outcomes and cost-effectiveness*. Trends and issues in crime and criminal justice No. 532. Canberra: Australian Institute of Criminology.

Shanahan, M. and Ritter, A. (2014). Cost benefit analysis of two policy options for cannabis: Status quo and legalization. *PloS One*, 9(4), e95569-e95569.

Sutton, A. (2000). Cannabis law and the young adult user: Reflections on South Australia's cannabis expiation notice system. *International Journal of the Sociology of Law*, 28(2), 147–162.

Therapeutic Goods Administration. (2018). *Access to medicinal cannabis products*. Canberra: Therapeutic Goods Administration.

Western Australia Police. (2017). *Police drug diversion in Australia*. Perth: WA Police.

Western Australia Police. (2018). *Submission to the senate legal and constitutional affairs legislation committee inquiry into the Criminal Code and Other Legislation Amendment (removing Commonwealth restrictions on cannabis) Bill 2018*. (Submission 23). Canberra: Parliament of Australia.

16 Cannabis policy reform

Jamaica's experience

Vicki J. Hanson

Introduction

The policy debate surrounding cannabis regulation in the Caribbean and more specifically Jamaica has been very contentious for several decades. Jamaica has been known to have one of the longest histories of government prohibition of the use of cannabis, (locally called "ganja", and referred to as such throughout this chapter) which dates back as far as the early 1900s (Moyston, 2013). Notwithstanding this official prohibitive approach in policy and regulation of cannabis, the country has had a significantly high cultural use[1] and acceptance of the plant by the general citizenry, especially among traditional communities such as the Rastafarians and the Maroons. This has resulted in cannabis policy and regulation being a main political issue which has often been used as a means of garnering popular support among inner-city youths and rural community youths because this group is a major voting cohort, and both inner-city and rural youths are viewed as the most common users of the cannabis plant. Common use of the cannabis plant had resulted in persistent criminalization for several of these youth and, concomitantly, in increased lobbying from civil society for a new approach to cannabis, as a means of fostering growth and development while still bearing in mind the Government's international responsibilities concerning even domestic drug policy. The following discourse is intended to provide an overview of Jamaica's experience and its relevance to the United Nations General Assembly on drugs (United Nations General Assembly (UNGASS), 2016) sessions.

Jamaica – ganja history

It has been argued that cannabis was first introduced into the Jamaican society by enslaved West Africans and common use of the plant continued for generations as evidenced by current and historical use of the plant for spiritual meditation in certain regions of Africa and simultaneously among African-derived religious practices existent in Jamaica, such as Kumina (Savishinsky, 1998), which is a religious practice that is still maintained by the Maroons and other Afro-Jamaican cultural groups. However, another school of thought posits that the use of cannabis in Caribbean states like Jamaica was influenced primarily by the introduction of indentured workers from India who came to the region with their customs involving the use of cannabis for worship and meditative practices (Rubin and Comitas, 1975; Commissiong, 1978). The influence of the historical Indian roots of cannabis use in Jamaica is also evident in many of the terminologies surrounding the plant, in particular the name "ganja," as is popular in local parlance originated in India and particularly the Sanskrit word for Hemp. Nonetheless, whichever the case of origin, the use of ganja has been embedded in the unique culture and fabric of the Jamaican society.

In addition, the Rastafari movement which began in the 1940s along with its ethos of sustainable development championed by one of its founders, Leonard Howell, saw with it the cultivation and use of ganja not only as sacrament within their religious practices at the Pinnacle Hill commune, but also as a means of economic survival and rebellion (Lepinske, 1955). The cultivation of cannabis in the Rastafari communes still continues to be for the sacramental, cultural and economic benefits of the Rastafarian members. Despite the cultural significance of the plant to the Jamaican Rastafarian community, the group has had to endure an environment of extensive prohibition of the ganja plant and criminalization of the Rastafarian users who were constantly ostracized and abused.

As was previously stated, Jamaican cannabis regulations have had a long history of restriction and prohibition. It is also argued that this prohibition on cannabis is based mainly on social factors and historical prejudices. Rubin and Comitas (1975, p. 21) in their study on ganja in Jamaica, outlined that in 1912, the Evangelical churches in Jamaica raised the concern that cannabis (ganja) smoking was resulting in serious social upheaval because it made persons behave immorally and without any mental control. It was further argued that this type of behavior was mainly from East Indians who were brought to the island as indentured laborers. The urgency and alarming nature of this call by the Evangelicals to the government led to the Legislative Council of Jamaica, which was still under the colonial rule of the British, to pass an ordinance in 1913 against the cultivation, possession and use of ganja. The law (ordinance) was also a ratification of the International Opium Convention which was signed at The Hague the previous year. Failure to obey these rules could have resulted in a fine of £100 or imprisonment of up to 12 months, with or without hard labor (Rubin and Comitas, 1975). The study showed that the laws relating to ganja became severely prohibitive between the years 1913 and 1961.

The severity of the laws prohibiting ganja use and cultivation in Jamaica was also influenced by legislative changes occurring globally in response to the social and economic challenges that were being experienced due to the Great Depression of 1938. This severely restrictive approach to ganja did not consider the social structure of the society and its customs particularly in relation to indigenous cultural communities such as the Rastafarians and the Maroons as was previously mentioned. This, it has been argued, was because the Maroons as well as the Rastafarian communities largely reject European values and culture and as such, the law is intrinsically hostile towards them for their cultural use of the plant.

The Rastafarians viewed the European artefacts and culture as "Babylon" (which is their view of a very oppressive and repressive regime) and they embraced ganja precisely because of its non-western origins (Chevannes, 1988). This resulted in a campaign against the Rastafarian community who were mostly from the lower social strata of the society and had become the main cultivators and users of ganja. As such, the Rastafarian community became the main targets of the 1941 Dangerous Drug Law amendment that instituted a mandatory one-year incarceration for the cultivation, possession and use of the plant.

This draconian approach to ganja and traditional communities who were associated with its cultivation and use was carried over into the post-colonial period. The Jamaican political class emerging during Independence inherited colonial legislation and anxieties, and as such, many of the repressive measures and prohibitions were retained by the ruling political class of the period.

In a study conducted by Rubin and Comitas (1975), it was noted that the two major political parties in Jamaica, the People's National Party (PNP) and the Jamaica Labour Party (JLP), both agreed that more stringent laws were needed to deal with ganja. This consensus saw even further amendments made to the Dangerous Drugs Act in 1964 to grant the police more powers under the law to raid premises used for cultivation of ganja and to seize vehicles used in the transportation of the plant. The 1964 amendments to the Dangerous Drugs Act were not without criticism: even though both political parties thought that ganja was dangerous, there was some difficulty in agreeing on the level of penalty that was to be associated with the cultivation, possession and use of the plant, with the then leader of the opposition PNP noting that "ganja was grown in backyards all over the country and used as medicine" (Rubin and Comitas, 1975, p. 29).

Even though the approach to ganja in Jamaica was discriminatory against the lower class, it was the concern for the impact of the measures on this group that led to another amendment of the Dangerous Drugs Act in 1972, this time to remove mandatory sentencing for the cultivation, trading and possession of ganja. This created a situation in which the courts had the discretion to determine sentences which saw the release of a number of Jamaicans who had been previously convicted under the harsher mandatory laws. This level of inconsistency in the application of the regulation of cannabis in Jamaica was also reflected in the mixed social attitudes that existed towards the plant. This anthropological study of ganja use in Jamaica revealed that the policy governing the use of the plant had often been impacted by the attitudes, reactions, cultural expectations and predispositions commonly found in the society (Rubin and Comitas, 1975). The attitude of the consumers of the ganja plant was that the effect of the plant was mainly based on the situation and underlining reason for which they either consumed or smoked. Therefore, if the individual wanted to meditate, relax, solve a complex problem or just enhance their appetite, it was believed that using ganja could help in each of these situations. The study shows that persons from the upper social classes who consumed the plant were more inclined to use it as teas and tonics, as it was more acceptable in their grouping in that format, while in the low class, the smoking was accepted as a rite of passage and demonstrated affiliation with that group.

In other key literature on cannabis law in the Caribbean, Fraser (1974) sought to discuss how cannabis regulations impacted the lives of persons in the region by highlighting the number of cases that were brought before the courts in the various countries. What was noted in this review was that within Caribbean societies, such as Trinidad & Tobago and Guyana respectively, where a significant proportion of the population is of Indian descent, there were also significant numbers of community members who did not view the use of ganja as a major social problem. However, despite these progressive social views toward the use of cannabis at the grassroots level, the continued debate at the international policy level resulted in a number of Caribbean countries like Guyana, Trinidad & Tobago and Jamaica changing their approach to ganja during the early 1960s by becoming more prohibitive in the regulation of the plant, despite general cultural acceptance among the citizenry. Indeed, this widespread cultural acceptance of cannabis in many Caribbean societies certainly also influenced the political and social discourse surrounding the production and use of the plant in the late 1960s and the 1970s.

Jamaica's motivation for change

Some of the earliest social agitators for a change in the thinking and approach to regulating cannabis in Jamaica have been the Rastafarian community and particularly outspoken Rastafarian musicians like Bob Marley and Peter Tosh. In 1976, Peter Tosh released an album titled "Legalize It," in which the title song bluntly advocated for the legalization of cannabis. This popular form of advocacy led in turn to a proliferation of youths protesting and campaigning for the "herb" during that time (Chevannes, 1988, p. 13). The advocacy for legalization of ganja was given further support in 1979 when Bob Marley gave a controversial interview on New Zealand television where he stated that "herb" (cannabis) was a plant that was "good for everything" and when used, results in persons becoming more conscious to the injustices of society (Dailyalternativenews.co.uk, 2013).

This type of social commentary on cannabis policy and regulations continued in Jamaican music and popular culture through several decades and into the present. These social commentaries on cannabis even became a part of the political discourse in Jamaica.

The issues relating to the amendment of the Dangerous Drugs Act and regulating the cultivation and use of cannabis in Jamaica are as much about achieving political success for those in leadership as they are about recognizing cultural rights of the Jamaican people. The process of addressing the issue was initiated by the People's National Party (PNP), who then formed the governing administration, at their 62nd annual conference in 2000, where a public call was made for a review of the country's ganja laws.

In 2000, Party Leader and Prime Minister Percival James 'PJ' Patterson stated: "Countries all over the world are being forced to give consideration to the complex but delicate issues of social, economic, cultural and security policies which relate to the issue of ganja," and as such he announced the formation of the National Commission on Ganja.

The announcement was welcomed by many ganja lobbyists including the very powerful PNP Region Three Chairman, Paul Burke. Despite initial enthusiasm, the composition of the National Commission on Ganja was not without controversy (see Figures 16.1 and 16.2). Several prominent lobbyists argued that the Commission did not reflect the participation of groups and members in the society such as Rastafarians, small traditional ganja cultivators and traditional medicine practitioners, who were mainly affected by prohibitionist regulations. The composition of the National Commission on Ganja was an important political issue because it was believed that the groups disproportionately affected by the laws relating to ganja were among the very poor in society and made up the majority of the voting population.

Additionally, in Jamaica, social concerns which have been highly moralized carry major political consequences, and similarly this is the case with ganja, where the negative stigma has significantly influenced the debate on establishing a legal ganja industry or decriminalizing the possession of ganja for personal use. The report submitted to Jamaican Parliament in 2001 stated

Figure 16.1 Cartoon from the *Jamaica Observer* (2000).

Figure 16.2 Cartoon from the *Jamaica Gleaner* (2000).

that even though the use of ganja can have some side effects (as with any other substance) it was not justifiable for the use to be criminalized because a significant number of citizens used ganja due to the practice being deeply rooted in the country's culture.

The National Commission on Ganja Report in Jamaica (Chevannes, Edwards, Freckleton, Linton, McDowell, Standard-Goldson and Smith, 2001) also noted with interest the many changes in attitudes and regulatory structures that were happening in more developed countries such as Canada and the United States, which at the time were both respectively moving to a more liberal approach to cannabis use and trade. It was viewed by the Commission Committee that the changes in these North American territories would critically impact whatever discussions were occurring in the Jamaican milieu (Chevannes et al., 2001). This discourse continued quietly in the years following the submission of the Commission's Report. However, the Commission's report during this period did not lead to any action in relation to a change in the country's draconian ganja policy. This is because there remained internationally, and more specifically in our region of the Americas, a strong prohibitionist stance towards cannabis largely emanating from the United States during that early 2000s period.

However, the political motivation for change to Jamaica's cannabis regulations was brought more forcibly to the political directorate and the Government of Jamaica in 2014 after the gruesome death of Mario Deane, a young man who was killed in jail after being arrested for possession of a "ganja spliff" (cannabis joint). The death of a promising young man for what was viewed by many Jamaicans as a petty offense resulted in tremendous public pressure for a change in the attitude and laws governing the regulation of ganja (Nationwide Newsnet, 2014).

In response to this incident and the subsequent mounting political pressure, the Minister of National Security issued a press release in August 2014 advising the police to "ease" the arrest of persons for possession of a small quantity of cannabis (Walker, 2014). The increased public interest in ganja regulation also led to a resurgence of several civil society organizations supportive of the decriminalization and regulation of ganja and initiated a debate in the House of Parliament in January 2015, resulting in the Dangerous Drug (Amendment) Act 2015 in Jamaica. The DD(A)A 2015 was passed in the Houses of Parliament also with the support of the then opposition, Jamaica Labour Party (JLP). One opposition member, Senator Tom Tavares-Finson expressed support for the amendment because it meant that a number of young persons who were previously criminalized for possession of small quantities of ganja would now be able to have their records expunged, and likewise access several opportunities for personal development (CEEN TV, 2015). This level of political support was influenced by the growing agitation in wider society, as was evident in the ganja civil society groups, with several groups of ganja growers, lobbyists, community organizers and academics making public their views of support for more liberal ganja laws in Jamaica.

The most recent wave of support for the development of a Jamaican cannabis industry has been brought about by the emergence of several interest groups in the last four years, including the Ganja Growers and Producers Association (GGPA), the National Coalition of Ganja (NCG) as well as the Cannabis Commercial and Medicinal Research Task Force (CCMRT). These civil society organizations have played a significant role in the debate on regulation of the industry. Their existence has been buoyed by increased discussion on the issue of a regulated cannabis industry, not just in the local sphere, but also at the regional and international levels. In fact it has been argued that it was the participation of these various civil society groups, including members of the traditional ganja cultivators, Rastafarians, the Maroons and other private sector interests like the Women Business Owners (WBO) that energized the movement and successfully led to the 2015 amendment in the Dangerous Drug Act (DDA).

The Jamaican DDA created a reformed approach to the regulation of cannabis that was in keeping with the stipulations of the United Nations Conventions governing the cultivation and medicinal use of illicit plants. However, the later DD(A)A 2015 was also mindful of the cultural and historical relationship between Jamaicans and the cannabis plant. This was evident in the amendment that allowed the traditional Rastafarian communities to legally use ganja as a sacrament in adherence with their faith, and further granted permission to host events in celebration of that faith where ganja can be transported to and also used at these events.

The traditional use of the plant in home-made medicine for various illnesses such as asthma, fever and ailments also led to an amendment that allowed each household the right to cultivate five plants for personal use. Another critical amendment to the DDA was the establishment of a Cannabis Licensing Authority (CLA) to issue licenses and regulate the use of cannabis for medicinal, therapeutic and scientific research. These reforms to Jamaica's cannabis policy have had a significant influence on the country's discourse at the United Nations, as well as the Government of Jamaica's recent policy position in regulating the cannabis market.

Jamaica takes on the United Nations to change the cannabis discourse

Jamaica's bipartisan and multi-sectoral approach to local reform was very evident in the delegation that attended the UNGASS 2016 and the accompanying side events in April 2016.

The delegation consisted of:

- former Minister of Justice, Mark Golding who piloted the bill for the DD(A) A in the House of Parliament in Jamaica;
- Minister of Foreign Affairs, Senator Kamina Johnson-Smith from the current JLP administration;
- a Deputy Solicitor General from the Attorney General's Office;
- a representative of the Rastafarian community;
- a representative from Jamaica's business community; and
- a public policy analyst who was also a member of the GGPA.

This group's representation at the UNGASS 2016 was very important because of the limited opportunities for representation afforded to Jamaica (and all other Caribbean countries) at the global drug policy discussions at the United Nations. The lack of discussions and lack of opportunities to influence discussions about the Caribbean on cannabis policy is concerning and is also noticeable in other spaces such as the Commission on Narcotic Drugs in Vienna where very few Caribbean states even have a representative.

Notwithstanding the above-mentioned constraints, the civil society representatives on the Jamaican delegation to the UNGASS 2016 received very crucial advice and support from international lobby organizations such as the Transnational Institute (TNI) and Amanda Feilding's Beckley Foundation that gave credibility to their collective stance, particularly in facilitating their preparation and participation in the various side events for civil society groups at the conference. This provided the key opportunity for discussion about the unique perspective of those for whom the traditional use of cannabis represents part of their cultural identity, such as Rastafarians and the traditional cultivators.[2]

In a presentation at a summit held at the City University of New York (CUNY) preceding the UNGASS 2016, one civil society representative from the GGPA highlighted that the civil society groups in Jamaica wanted to have a cannabis policy and regulatory framework taking into consideration the socio-cultural realities of the society (Hanson, 2016). This, it was hoped, would result in a reduction in the restrictions on growth for local communities and also improve the inclusion of persons previously victimized by those formerly prohibitive regulations. It was this thrust of the various national civil society groups and traditional communities such as the Rastafarian movement that urged the Government of Jamaica to push forward on progressive reform, despite pressure and international opposition, in order to reform the country's cannabis policy and regulations.

The move to approach cannabis policy in a different way in Jamaica was openly expressed by Jamaica's government representative to the UNGASS in 2016. In her presentation to the General Assembly, Minister of Foreign Affairs, Senator Kamina Johnson-Smith clearly outlined Jamaica's reasons for wanting to reform. Senator Johnson-Smith stated:

> We are cognizant that one size does not fit all. In Jamaica, cannabis has traditionally been used as a folk medicine and as a religious sacrament by practitioners of our indigenous faith, Rastafari. Such specific uses are not associated with illicit large-scale cultivation for trade.
>
> (United Nations General Assembly UNGASS, 2016)

Jamaica advanced the position that there needed to be a more comprehensive approach to the international policy on crops such as cannabis, which would also include reform at the International Narcotics Control Board (INCB), the World Health Organization (WHO), the United Nations Human Rights Council (UNHRC) and the United Nations Development Programme (UNDP). In all the presentations, both from the General Assembly and the side events, the country's delegation highlighted that the focus of Jamaica's reformed cannabis policy and approach would be centered on a healthy society and sustainable human development, inclusive of the indigenous communities that are dependent on cannabis cultivation for their traditional use.

Jamaica's current dilemma

In an effort to remain diligent to its signature on United Nations drug conventions, Jamaica has embarked on a path to regulate cannabis for medicinal, therapeutic and scientific purposes only, with one exception; that is, the sacramental use of the plant by an indigenous cultural group, the Rastafari. Jamaica's latest policy position towards ganja was brought about through the Dangerous Drugs (Amendment) Act 2015, which was passed on April 15, 2015 (Government of Jamaica, 2015). This amended law also resulted in the establishment of a government agency, the Cannabis Licensing Authority

(CLA), to issue and regulate licenses, permits and authorizations for the "handling of hemp; and ganja for medical, therapeutic, and scientific purposes" (Government of Jamaica, 2015). The establishment of the CLA was in compliance with the Single Convention on Narcotic Drugs of 1961 which outlines in Articles 23 and 28 that there should be a "national agency" for the control of the production of the cannabis plant and to prevent its inappropriate use and diversion into the illicit trade (United Nations, 1961).

Under the amended policy approach, the CLA has the authority to accept applications from individuals, companies, and cooperatives to operate within the scope of the law in relation to cannabis in Jamaica (Cannabis Licensing Authority, 2016). There are five types of licenses that can be applied for in the Jamaican medicinal, therapeutic and scientific regulated system, which includes a cultivator's license, processing license, transport license, retail license and research and development license. In the case of an application for a cultivator's license, this can be made within one of three categories: Tier 1 – for applicants wanting to cultivate land of one acre or less; Tier 2 – for applicants wanting to cultivate between one to five acres of land; Tier 3 – for applicants to cultivate over five acres. The processor's license can also be applied for in two categories, such as Tier 1 for a facility of up to 200 square meters, and Tier 2 for a facility of over 200 square meters. In relation to the

Table 16.1 Schedule of Fees (extracted from *The Jamaica Gazette Supplement*, The Dangerous Drugs (Cannabis Licensing) (Interim) Regulations, 2016

Type of fee	*Type of license*		*Annual license fee*
Application Processing Fees	Individual		US$300 (Fee per application)
	Company, Business or Cooperative		US$500 (Fee per application)
Licence Fees	Cultivator's Licence	Tier 1	US$2,000
		Tier 2	US$2,500 per acre
		Tier 3	US$3,000 per acre
	Processing Licence	Tier 1	US$3,500
		Tier 2	US$10,000
	Transport Licence	-	US$10,000 for the first vehicle and US$1,000 for each additional vehicle
	Retail Licence	Herb House	US$2,500
		Therapeutic	US$2,500
	Research and Development Licence	Experimental	US$5,000
		Analytical Services	US$5,000
Security Bond (Refundable)	Cultivator's Licence	Tier 1	US$1,000
		Tiers 2 and 3	US$2,000 per acre
	Processing Licence	-	US$3,000
	Research and Development Licence	-	US$3,000

retailer's license, these can be applied for in the categories of herb house, herb house with consumption facility and therapeutic center.

The costs to apply for and obtain a license in Jamaica's regulated medicinal system are quoted by the CLA in United States dollars (US$) and are listed for the public on the CLA's official website (see Table 16.1). This cost is often seen as prohibitive to potential local applicants given the fluctuating value of the Jamaican dollar relative to the US$ and the relatively low per capita income of the populace (Jamaica's GDP per capita is US$5,109. World Bank 2017).

In addition to the cost of the applications for licenses, there is the requirement that the persons applying for the license should have legal access to the property proposed to be licensed for use in the system, and further that these persons should not have had previous criminal records. In order to ensure that these basic criteria are met by each applicant, the CLA conducts very rigorous due diligence and background checks for each application received.

In addition, the Jamaican amended regulation also included a recognition of the religious rights of one specific cultural group; the Rastafarians. The new Sections 7D (6), 7D (8), and 7D (9), address the Rastafarian religious rights, stating that the Minister of Justice authorizes that:

> a [A] Person who has attained the age of eighteen years and who the Minister is satisfied is an adherent of the Rastafarian faith or any group of such persons; or
>
> b [An] Organization that the Minister is satisfied is comprised of such persons,
>
> [may] cultivate, on lands designated by the Minister in the order and in accordance with such regulations as the Minister may prescribe for that purpose, ganja for use for religious purposes as a sacrament in adherence to the Rastafarian faith.
>
> (Government of Jamaica, 2015)

This amended section of the DDA also gives the Minister of Justice the authority to declare an event as an "exempt event," that would allow members of the Rastafarian faith to possess, use and consume in "celebration and observance" of their faith.

Another important adjustment that was made to Jamaica's policy approach to ganja regulation is the allowance of the private cultivation of five plants or less for medicinal, therapeutic, or horticultural purposes in households, and the possession and smoking of two ounces or less in private spaces.

This new policy approach to the production and use of ganja in Jamaica represents a shift from total prohibition to one of a highly regulated and strict medicinal cannabis framework, and an acceptance of Rastafarian religious rites, as well as the right to private use of cannabis. Though progressive, the novel policy approach is not without its challenges.

The first and most important dilemma relates to the restrictive nature of a medicinal, therapeutic and scientific framework in the Jamaican milieu. As highlighted from Jamaica's historical relations with ganja, it should be noted that for the most part, the communities and individuals that participated in the illicit ganja trade were from sociocultural and economic segments in society that could not satisfy the requirements for obtaining a license from the authority. Historically, these communities and individuals participated in the illegal trade as a means of obtaining subsistence income by producing ganja in a system that did not require an application licensing fee of US$300 (approximately J$39,000) or more. Many simply lack the technical capacity to even be considered under the new regulatory guidelines.

Second, a number of previous participants in what was historically the traditional Jamaican ganja industry would still remain outside of the newly-created medicinal, therapeutic and scientific framework as they would have been cultivating on lands that belonged to the state (Crown lands) or other privately-held property illegally, and the new regulatory structure requires permission for land use which is often challenging to acquire. The third important dilemma faced by traditional cultivators and participants in Jamaica's ganja industry under this new policy approach, is that of being determined "fit and proper" to participate in the industry. The challenge here is that a number of traditional participants would have been previously viewed as being participants in an illegal ganja industry, and by virtue of this designation would not qualify to participate in the newly-created medicinal industry, as many would have had encounters with the law pursuant to their attempts to farm or attempt to export a so-called "dangerous drug".

Another critical set of dilemmas came into being with the amendment to recognize the sacramental use of ganja by one group or sect within the Jamaican society, and that is Rastafarians. This dilemma is duly noted in both the 2016 and 2017 INCB reports in which it is stated that: "the recent regulatory developments in Jamaica are not in accordance with the 1961 Convention, which limits the use of cannabis for medical and scientific purposes" and that "use for any other purposes, including religious, is not permitted" (International Narcotics Control Board 2017, p. 55; 2018, p. 36).

Another element to this dilemma is that the religious and cultural use of ganja in Jamaica is not limited only to the Rastafarians, but there are other groups and cultural practices, such as the Maroons and the Kumina observances, which have been previously stated as a traditional African celebration embedded in the Jamaican culture and consistently practiced throughout the island.

The Jamaican amendment is further complicated by the fact that in addition to not taking into account the traditional use of ganja by other cultural groups beyond Rastafari, the regulations and laws do not identify a system outside of the Minister of Justice to regulate the sacramental, traditional and cultural use of ganja, as in the case of the medicinal framework that has already been established.

It can therefore be argued that Jamaica's current medicinal, therapeutic and scientific regime for cannabis does not present a longer positive sustainable development framework for ganja in Jamaica, and by extension other Caribbean jurisdictions with similar sociocultural characteristics.

Jamaica's way forward with cannabis

Since the DD(A) Act 2015, the government of Jamaica has continued to implement its reform program through the engagement of important civil society organizations and traditional communities, such as the Rastafarians and the Maroons. The Government of Jamaica (within the legally regulated framework for cannabis) should seek to be inclusive of the traditional cultivating communities. The CLA and the Ministry of Industry, Commerce, Agriculture and Fisheries (MICAF) should aim to develop a sustainable alternative development program centered on cannabis in partnership with representatives of several civil society groups. The full implementation of such a program would provide a model for other Caribbean countries and can be a basis for comparison with other states, such as Bolivia, that have implemented a social control model for the coca plant. The objective of this type of sustainable alternative development model is to remove these plants from the illicit markets, while creating a legal avenue for their use in development projects for the communities that depend on their cultivation. Additionally, this sustainable alternative development program would provide much needed access to government-owned land, such as those previously used by large sugar plantations, to assist traditional ganja cultivators, many of which now illegally occupy private properties and government holdings.

Additionally, as Jamaica's sole regulating agency, the CLA approaches its second full year of operation and as a high-level review at the United Nations nears, the country is in a very advantageous position to provide important data on the sustainability of taking a traditional and cultural approach to the use and cultivation of crops deemed illicit. The intention of such an approach to cannabis is to demonstrate to the UN, agencies such as the INCB, UNDP and UNHRC that the cultivation of crops such as cannabis in a socially-controlled environment can be beneficial to the achievement of the sustainable development goals (SDGs) in developing states and removing the label of being a narcotic state. However, as clearly stated before, and outlined in Jamaica's experience, there has to be political will at the local and international levels and there needs to be a strong partnership and involvement of the communities that are considered cultivating areas.

Therefore, a recommended path for Jamaica's cannabis regulation is one that would include a fully legal but regulated production of cannabis and its byproducts, which is community-based and built on the cultural rights and use of the product. This would require a full recognition of the uniqueness of Jamaica's cultural right and historic relation to the cannabis plant, allowing the country to cultivate, trade and use cannabis as it would any cultural product, such as its rum and ackee. It is precisely because of this historic cultural relationship that Jamaica and other Caribbean countries have had with cannabis that a recent report by the CARICOM Regional Commission on Marijuana stated that countries should "proceed with a responsible, controlled regime that will depend on focused and adequate institutional resources to achieve the desirable objectives" (CARICOM Regional Commission on Marijuana 2018, p. 5). This report is reflective of the human rights, people-centered approach to cannabis that is currently pervasive in the Caribbean.

We can therefore conclude that the way forward for Jamaica in regulating a successful and all-inclusive cannabis industry is to ensure that the policy framework chosen is culturally relevant and people-centered, leading to more sustainable development goals.

Notes

1 In Jamaica's case, the cultural use of ganja is referenced to the common use of the plant along with other products, such as rum and pimento, to treat cold symptoms and body pains, as well as the use of the plant by construction workers and fishermen to assist them while working. This practice has existed for several generations.

2 It should be noted that there is often no distinction between the traditional farmers who grow ganja for traditional use and for the traditional unregulated market, because in most cases these are small community-based farmers.

References

Cannabis Licensing Authority (2016). *Cannabis Licensing Authority*. Retrieved from http://cla.org.jm/.

CARICOM Regional Commission on Marijuana (2018). *Report of the CARICOM Regional Commission on Marijuana 2018: Waiting to exhale – Safeguarding our future through responsible socio-legal policy on marijuana*. Georgetown, Guyana: Caribbean Community (CARICOM) Secretariat. Retrieved from https://caricom.org/documents/16434/marijuana_report_final_3_aug_18.pdf.

CEEN TV (2015). Jamaica Senate debates ganja reform. *CEEN News*, CEEN TV.

Chevannes, B. (1988). *Background to drug use in Jamaica* (Vol. 34). An ISER working paper. Mona, Jamaica: Institute of Social and Economic Research, University of the West Indies.

Chevannes, B., Edwards, W., Freckleton, A., Linton, N., McDowell, D., Standard-Goldson, A. and Smith, B. (2001). *A report of The National Commission on Ganja To Rt. Hon. P.J. Patterson, Q.C., M.P. Prime Minister of Jamaica*. Retrieved from www.cannabis-med.org/science/Jamaica.htm.

Commissiong, J.W. (1978). *Ganja (marijuana)*. Mona, Jamaica: Department of Extra-Mural Studies, University of the West Indies.

Dailyalternativenews.co.uk (2013). Bob Marley New Zealand Interview 1979. In *Alternative News for the People*, YouTube.

Fraser, H.A. (1974). The law and cannabis in the West Indies. *Social and Economic Studies*, 23(3), 361–385.

Government of Jamaica (2015). *An Act to amend the Dangerous Drugs Act.* Jamaica Parliament. Jamaica: Houses of Parliament.

Hanson, V.J. (2016). *First movers: Uruguay and Jamaica, charting new paths.* The Cannabis Science & Policy Summit, The Graduate Center, 34th Street & 5th Avenue, New York City, April 17, 2016.

International Narcotics Control Board (2017). *Report of the International Narcotics Control Board for 2016.* New York: International Narcotics Control Board.

International Narcotics Control Board (2018). *Report of the International Narcotics Control Board for 2017.* Vienna: International Narcotics Control Board.

Jamaica Gleaner. (2000, September 15). Commission to review use of ganja. *Jamaica Gleaner.* Retrieved from http://cifas.us/news/gj_jg_20000915_1.html#index

Jamaica Observer. (2000, November 6). Call for boycott of Ganja Commission. *Jamaica Observer.* Retrieved from http://cifas.us/news/gj_jo_20001106_1.html

Lepinske, H.C. (1955). *Jamaican ganja: A report on the marihuana problem.* New York: Exposition Press.

Moyston, L. (2013). The ganja law of 1913: 100 years of oppressive injustice. *Jamaica Observer,* Columns. Accessed October 9, 2016. www.jamaicaobserver.com/columns/The-ganja-law-of-1913-100-years-of-oppressive-injustice_15548584

Nationwide Newsnet. (2014). Police high command denies constabulary involvement in Mario Dean's death. *Nationwide Radio.* Retrieved from http://nationwideradiojm.com/police-high-command-denies-constabulary-involvment-in-mario-deans-death/.

Rubin, V. and Comitas, L. (1975). *Ganja in Jamaica: A medical anthropological study of chronic marihuana use.* The Hague: New Babylon.

Savishinsky, N.J. (1998). African dimension of the Jamaican Rastafarian movement. In *Chanting down Babylon: The Rastafari reader.* Philadelphia, USA: Temple University Press.

United Nations (1961). *Single convention on narcotic drugs, 1961.* The Economic and Social Council of the United Nations. New York: United Nations.

United Nations General Assembly (UNGASS) (2016). *General Assembly thirtieth special session.* United Nations. New York: United Nations.

Walker, K. (2014). Ganja law ease. *Jamaica Observer.* Retrieved from www.jamaicaobserver.com/news/Ganja-law-ease.

Part V

New cannabis legalization proposals

17 The risks of cannabis industry funding of community and drug treatment services

Insights from gambling

Chris Wilkins and Marta Rychert

Introduction

There is a growing appetite around the world for policy approaches to cannabis other than the long-standing prohibition with criminal penalties (Caulkins, Kilmer and Kleiman, 2016). This has manifested most dramatically with the full legalization of cannabis use and supply in ten states in the United States, Uruguay and, most recently, Canada (Authier, 2017; Caulkins and Kilmer, 2016b; Cerdá and Kilmer, 2017; Hall and Lynskey, 2016; Hunt and Pacula, 2017; Subritzky, Pettigrew and Lenton, 2016). In New Zealand, the coalition government has recently announced there will be a national referendum on the legalization of cannabis for personal use at the next general election in 2020, signaling the potential for a major change in policy direction (Radio New Zealand, 2018).

Policy commentators have raised a number of concerns about the commercial markets for cannabis that have recently been established in a number of US states. These include declining cannabis prices, the sale of high-potency THC cannabis products, unintentional poisoning from cannabis products, the use of unregulated pesticides in growing operations, proliferation of cannabis retail outlets, aggressive marketing of cannabis products, cannabis-related vehicle crashes and cannabis industry influence over regulation making (Caulkins, Bao, Davenport, Fahli, Guo, Kinnard and Kilmer, 2018; Caulkins and Kilmer, 2016b; Fiala, Dilley, Firth and Maher, 2018; Hall and Lynskey, 2016; Hunt and Pacula, 2017; Smart, Caulkins, Kilmer, Davenport and Midgette, 2017; Subritzky, Pettigrew, et al., 2016). Drug policy researchers have responded by pointing out there are potentially a range of alternative "middle ground" regulatory approaches to commercial markets, including home cannabis cultivation, cannabis social clubs, "for benefit" cannabis companies, and cannabis community trusts (Caulkins and Kilmer, 2016a).

In New Zealand, community alcohol licensing trusts and gaming machine (i.e. slot machines) gambling trusts have operated for many decades, distributing significant funding to the local "not-for-profit" community sector, including sports, arts, education, culture, health and emergency rescue organizations. It has been proposed that a similar community trust approach could be developed to sell legal cannabis, with the revenue from sales used to fund local community services, including drug prevention and drug treatment services (Wilkins, 2018). However, real-world experience of gambling industry funding of community groups has raised important concerns about inappropriate industry practices related to the allocation of community grants, industry influence over policy and regulatory responses and related research priorities, and the general undermining of community groups concerned with the social problems created by gambling (Livingstone and Adams, 2015a).

Some leading gambling researchers have argued that any gambling industry funding is inherently tainted and so not desirable (Livingstone and Adams, 2015b), as independent community funding from the gambling industry is difficult to achieve in practice. Large amounts of gambling industry funding have created a community sector financially dependent on the ongoing success of the gambling industry, and most of the money provided by the gambling industry comes from problem gamblers who experience serious negative consequences, including harms imposed on their partners, family, friends and employers (Adams and Rossen, 2012; Livingstone and Adams, 2015b). In New Zealand, the Salvation Army charitable group has refused to accept money from the gaming industry in recognition of these community harms. Instead, these researchers recommend that the community sector be funded directly from the consolidated tax fund (Livingstone and Adams, 2015b).

Other researchers, while clearly acknowledging the need to avoid direct industry funding and industry partnership models, and ensure transparency with regard to any conflict of interest, argue that independent, indirect funding from gambling industry sources is practicable and can be done with integrity (Daube and Stoneham, 2015; Hancock, 2015; Room, 2015). Indeed, Room describes gambling industry funding to counter the social problems created by the industry as a "logical connection," and one that is "politically saleable" (Room, 2015). These researchers offer a number of examples of successful independent health funding agencies supported by gambling industry money, including the health promotion organization in the Australian State of Victoria (i.e. VicHealth), the Gambling Research Panel in Victoria, and Thai Health in Thailand (Daube and Stoneham, 2015; Hancock, 2015; Room, 2015). Key to the success of these models is the establishment of independent funding committees with no industry members or input, administration of the system by a health or social government agency, and evaluation of funding proposals on the basis of "scientific quality" and "societal relevance" (Room, 2015).

When entering this debate, it is important to reflect on why industry funding of the community sector is considered in the first place. Firstly, because of the health and social harm caused by high-risk addictive products, it seems reasonable that on principle, the industry should be made to compensate the community for the costs imposed and also support public services that mitigate these harms. Secondly, there is often limited alternative funding available to support these high-demand community services. Both charitable donations and government funding can vary depending on economic and political conditions and priorities (Berdahl and Azmier, 1999). In New Zealand, the shortage of funding for the drug treatment sector is reflected in the long waiting lists to enter treatment services in many regions (Nationwide Service Framework Library, 2018). While funding from the consolidated general tax fund would provide the most indirect form of funding, in reality there is an almost insatiable demand for this tax revenue to address a wide range of government and public priorities, and the drug treatment sector has been repeatedly overlooked in this highly-contested process.

The aims of this chapter are therefore to provide an overview of the alcohol and gaming machine community trusts currently operating in New Zealand, briefly outline how this community trust model could be adapted to provide a financial and regulatory structure to support legal cannabis sales, identify the issues experienced with gambling industry funding of community groups and explore regulatory design features that could be employed to address these concerns under a community cannabis trust regime.

The gaming machine gambling trust regulatory regime in New Zealand

The New Zealand Gambling Act 2003 was a response to the rapid growth in expenditure on gaming machine ("slot machine") gambling in New Zealand through the 1990s (Department of Internal Affairs, 2016). Gaming machine gambling had been identified as a particularly high-risk form of gambling associated with addictive problem gambling (Department of Internal Affairs, 2016). The intended public health focus of the new regime was made clear in the aims of the Act, which include to "control the growth of gambling" and "prevent and minimize harm from gambling, including problem gambling" (Department of Internal Affairs, 2016). There was also a clear intent in the new legislation to "facilitate community involvement in decisions about the provision of gambling" and "ensure that money from gambling benefits the community" (Department of Internal Affairs, 2016).

Under the Gambling Act, gaming machines can be provided by either "clubs" which operate machines only from their own clubrooms and apply net proceeds to club purposes, or gaming machine societies[1] which provide gaming machines to separately-owned pubs and bars and distribute "net proceeds"[2] to authorized community purposes (Department of Internal Affairs, 2014). Gaming machine societies are required to distribute a *minimum* of 40 percent of their "gross proceeds"[3] to authorized community purposes (Department of Internal Affairs, 2016). In 2015, gaming machine societies distributed NZ$262 million in funding to the community sector, including sports, community, health, education, arts and emergency services (Figure 17.1). Gaming societies are also required to pay 23 percent of their gross proceeds to

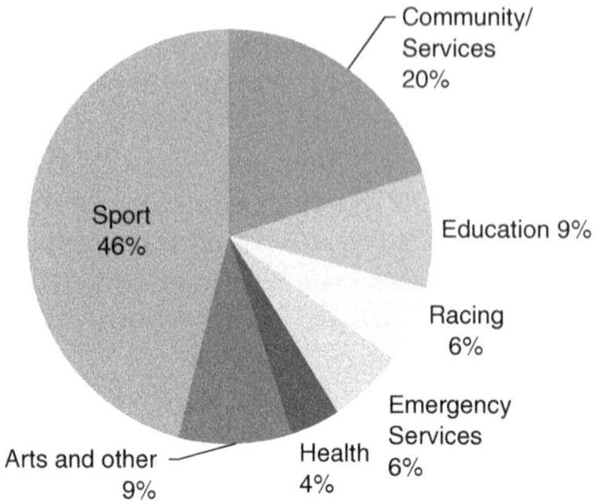

Figure 17.1 2004 to 2012 Class 4 Gambling Grant Recipients.

Source: Cabinet Economic Growth and Infrastructure Committee, 2016.

the government as levies and licensing fees, 3 percent to fund the regulatory agency that administers the regulatory regime, and 1.5 percent to support specific responses to problem gambling. Gaming machine societies also have explicit obligations to minimize the harm from gambling, including by identifying problem gamblers, and, where necessary, issuing exclusion orders from venues (Department of Internal Affairs, 2016).

Each gaming machine society is required to establish their own "net proceeds committee" to determine which community groups receive funding (Department of Internal Affairs, 2015). Local government authorities (i.e. councils) are required to develop a local gaming machine gambling venue policy that specifies whether gaming machine gambling can be situated in their territory and where venues may be located, with consideration given to the social impact of gambling on local communities (Department of Internal Affairs, 2016). The local policy can include a cap on the number of gambling venues and/or gaming machines in a territory but does not include the power to reduce the number of venues and gaming machines (Department of Internal Affairs, 2016).

Alcohol licensing trust regulatory regime in New Zealand

Alcohol licensing trusts are community-owned entities that operate alcohol retail outlets and related hospitality-related services (e.g. hotels) in a defined local territory (Auditor General, 2014; Stewart and Casswell, 1987). They undertake to return a portion of the profits from alcohol sales back to the local community in the form of grants, loans and donations. An alcohol licensing trust's primary responsibility, as outlined in the original legislation, is to "enhance the well-being of their communities" (Auditor General, 2014). There are currently 18 alcohol licensing trusts in New Zealand, four of which have a near monopoly right to sell alcohol in their local territories (i.e. restaurants are still permitted to sell alcohol) (Teahan, 2017).

An underlying principle of alcohol licensing trusts is the concept of "disinterested ownership and management" based on the absence of a commercial incentive to maximize financial returns to private owners and share owners (Licensing Trusts Act 1949 (1949 No 43); Teahan, 2017). Decisions about the distribution of community grants are largely made by community-elected trustees. Community trustees are elected to the Alcohol Trust Board in triennial local elections. Licensing trusts are only involved in the retail sale of alcohol and must purchase their alcohol supplies from private alcohol companies.

Alcohol trusts distribute the net profits from alcohol sales for "education, science, literature, art, physical welfare and other cultural and recreational purposes" or philanthropic activities in their territories (SSAA, s 307, s 350). Over the past ten years, the licensing trusts have made substantial donations to their communities, including direct gifts to households (e.g. smoke alarms, fire extinguishers), sports activities (e.g. "Kids Learn to Swim" program), educational projects (e.g. funding interactive whiteboards in local schools, tertiary scholarships) and investments in major cultural and sports infrastructure (e.g. sponsorship of a stadium) (Figure 17.2). Grants are allocated to community groups in various ways. For example, the West Auckland Licensing Trusts divide their grant budgets proportionally based on support received via a web-based public vote.

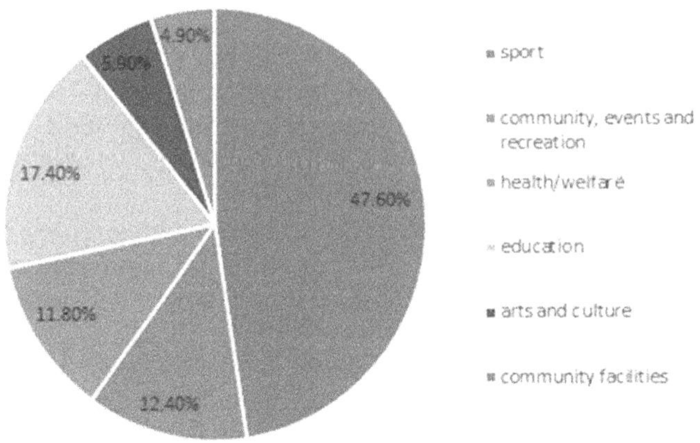

Figure 17.2 Community grant allocation by the Invercargill Licensing Trust (ILT) and ILT Foundation, 2018.

Source: Invercargill Licensing Trust Annual Report, 2018.

The alcohol licensing trusts argue the monopoly power they have over alcohol sales has restricted the availability of alcohol, for example, by not allowing sales from supermarkets, and has also contributed to reducing alcohol-related harm in trust districts, although the latter claim has been challenged by opponents. There are also anecdotal claims by opponents that alcohol prices are higher in trust areas.

Communities can vote to restore private alcohol sales in their territory through a "competition poll." A competition poll can be called at the request of at least 15 percent of the voters from a territory (SSAA, s 349). Sixteen competition polls have been held to date, and in most cases, communities have voted in favor of restoring private alcohol sales. As a result, 14 alcohol trusts now compete with private enterprise in a fully competitive commercial market.

Alcohol trusts are not under government control (although the Auditor General has oversight over their financial performance) but are accountable to the local community via competition polls and triennial elections of community trustees (SSAA, ss 309–314) (Auditor General, 2016). Conflict of interest policies in the legislation prohibit board members from any involvement with the alcohol industry (SSAA, s 322). However, licensing trusts themselves have been found to have close relationships with the alcohol industry via alcohol supply relationships (e.g. alcohol producers sponsoring an annual community grants celebration gala, and some trusts hold shares in breweries).

General features of the community trust model

The gaming machine and alcohol community trusts share a number of core features. First, they are purposely designed to suppress market expansion. Instead, they are expected to focus on philanthropic goals, such as promoting sports or supporting emergency rescue services. Second, there is an expectation that some of the revenue they generate from their operations is used to fund local community services, such as sport, culture and education. Third, there is an implicit expectation that they will be more accountable to the local community than profit-driven private businesses.

However, there are important differences in the weight given to these core features in each model, largely reflecting the legalization used to set them up. For example, gaming machine trusts are required by legislation to distribute a minimum of 40 percent of their revenue for community purposes, i.e. while alcohol licensing trusts have no such specific legislative requirement. As a consequence, critics have questioned whether some alcohol licensing trusts have met their community obligations based on level of donations. Conversely, alcohol licensing trusts are directly accountable to their communities via elected community trust members and community polls, while gaming machine trusts have no defined territories. One implication of this that has raised concerns is that gaming machine revenue is earned in poor neighborhoods and spent on community services in more affluent neighborhoods (New Zealand Parliament, 2010).

A community trust regulatory regime for recreational cannabis

The development of a similar community trust regime for legal recreational cannabis would begin with a purpose-written "Cannabis Act." This new legislation would clearly state the public health aims of the new cannabis regime; the most important one being to "prevent and minimize the health and social harms from cannabis use, including cannabis dependency." The new Cannabis Act should also include clear community aims, such as to "facilitate community involvement in decisions concerning the sale of cannabis" and "ensure money from cannabis sales benefits the community, including by supporting drug treatment and prevention services." The legislation should make it clear that the cannabis industry is required to make financial payments to drug prevention, drug treatment and other community services as part of an obligation to compensate and mitigate the harms caused by their products. This legislative provision is important to frame the subsequent understanding of cannabis industry payments to community services as financial compensation for the health and social costs of cannabis use, not philanthropic donations based on industry benevolence.

The principal purpose of community cannabis licensing trusts would be to operate retail cannabis dispensaries, and this could be extended to the operation of premises for cannabis consumption in the future, for example Netherlands-style coffeeshops. The cannabis trusts would purchase cannabis from government-licensed private cannabis producers. It is possible that cannabis trusts could become involved in producing cannabis, much like some alcohol trusts have joint commercial ventures with alcohol companies, but their principal focus will be the retail sale of cannabis. Just as different gaming machine trusts are involved with venues in the same territory, a number of different cannabis trusts could operate in the same territory to ensure competition in terms of the variety and quality of cannabis products available.

Community cannabis trusts would be required to pay a minimum 20 percent of the gross revenue from retail cannabis sales to support publicly available local drug treatment services, with a further 20 percent to be transferred to support authorized community purposes, including drug prevention, health services, sports, arts and cultural activities. A further requirement would be that 80 percent of the community grants be spent in the territory where they are collected to ensure the money from cannabis sales is spent in the local communities where it is generated. The government would receive 25 percent of gross cannabis sales revenue for licensing, enforcement and levies to support health services to address the wider health and social impacts of cannabis use.

Local government authorities would be required to develop a local cannabis policy that specifies where cannabis retail outlets can be located in their territories relative to sensitive sites such as schools, playgrounds, sports grounds and churches, and detailed regulation of retail outlets, including opening hours. The local cannabis policy should include a cap on the maximum number of cannabis retail outlets permitted in a territory. To avoid any potential for conflict of interest, the legislation should include provisions preventing local government members from being involved in the management of cannabis trusts or standing as cannabis community trustees. Cannabis trusts would be required to develop a policy for identifying dependent cannabis users and providing information concerning accessing local treatment services.

Communities would elect trust board members to serve on the cannabis trust and ensure the trust is meeting its community obligations. To prevent conflicts of interest, the legislation would ban cannabis trust members (and employees of the trust) from involvement in the alcohol or tobacco sector. Cannabis trusts would also be banned from any commercial partnerships with the alcohol and tobacco industry.

The ongoing operation of a cannabis licensing trust would rely on the continued support of the local community. Should a community be dissatisfied with a trust's performance, they could request a "prohibition poll" (through a petition signed by 15 percent of eligible voters), following which a negative majority vote would result in the closure of the trust's retail outlets for a set number of weeks until the concerns are addressed. The trust could then request a restoration of business community poll where they demonstrate how they have addressed issues.

Risks of cannabis industry funding of community groups

Both the gaming machine gambling trusts and alcohol licensing trusts that operate in New Zealand have direct control over the funding of community groups from their commercial activities. Community groups receive funding directly from these trusts based on each trust's internal distribution process. In the case of alcohol licensing trusts, even the total amount of money to be allocated to the community sector is at the licensing trusts' discretion, and, as previously noted, some critics have argued that licensing trusts have failed to distribute enough funding back to the community (du Fresne, 2017).

Gaming machine societies have faced ongoing allegations of inappropriate community funding practices, some of which have resulted in prosecutions (New Zealand Parliament, 2010). These include "kick-backs" where a gaming machine society agrees to provide an applicant with a community grant in exchange for some pecuniary or non-pecuniary benefit (Cabinet Economic Growth and Infrastructure Committee, 2016; Department of Internal Affairs, 2013). Gaming machine societies have also been found to compete for entertainment venues that generate high returns for gaming machines by paying for venue renovations, overstating venue operating payments and providing grants to community groups associated with a venue (Department of Internal Affairs, 2013).

Researchers with experience of gambling industry funding of the community sector have identified seven types of risk with these arrangements, namely ethical, contributory, reputational, relationship, governance, neutrality and wider democratic risks (Adams and Rossen, 2006). Ethical risk refers to the ethical dilemma faced by a community group whose principal purpose is to serve the community when they accept money from an industry known to harm people in that same community (Adams and Rossen, 2006). Visible relationships with community groups can boost the public image of the gambling industry and downplay the harm caused by their products (Adams and Rossen, 2006). The public may even come to associate the gambling industry with the philanthropic activities of the community sector (Adams and Rossen, 2006). This positive public image can then be incorporated in the industry's marketing strategies, to the extent they promote the buying of their products as a means to support worthy community causes (Adams and Rossen, 2006). As a parallel, a cannabis company may promote the buying of their products as a means to fund local drug prevention and drug treatment services.

Contributory risk occurs when, by accepting money from the industry, the community group indirectly or directly contributes to sales of the harmful product (Adams, 2016). This can occur indirectly when a company uses their donations to improve their public image and thereby elevate their standing in policy-making circles (Adams, 2016). For example, cannabis companies may argue that their donations to drug treatment justify being consulted about government drug prevention strategies and other regulatory responses. It can also occur directly when consumers buy a product with the understanding that some of the money they pay is going to a worthy cause (Adams, 2016). Cannabis companies may market their products to promote this expectation; that is, as a way to support local drug treatment services. The cannabis industry may even seek to include the logos of drug treatment organizations on their packaging and advertisements to highlight their financial support of these services.

Reputational risk refers to the implications of accepting industry funding for the community group's relationships with other stakeholders, such as other community groups, potential collaborators, researchers and the wider public (Adams and Rossen, 2006). For example, if a sports club accepts money from a cannabis business, some parents may not want their children to play for the club and local government may no longer be comfortable providing them with community-funded sports fields. Similarly, if a drug treatment provider accepts funding from a cannabis company, publicly-funded health providers (e.g. mental health services) may refuse to work with them through fear of being tainted by association.

Governance risk refers to the threat to organizational independence of having to rely on industry funding (Adams and Rossen, 2006). The community and drug treatment sectors are traditionally underfunded and consequently, the cannabis industry may come to contribute a substantial proportion of total funding to these sectors. This may lead to some community groups and drug treatment facilities becoming financially dependent on ongoing cannabis industry funding. Berdahl and Azmier (1999) found 20 percent of Canadian not-for-profit organizations received over half their revenue from the gambling industry, and 50 percent reported gambling grants as a top-three source of funding (28 percent reported gambling money as their top funding source). Eighty-four percent of the non-profits surveyed "agreed" or "strongly agreed" that without gaming grants, they would not have the necessary funds to run their programs (Berdahl and Azmier, 1999). This reliance on gambling industry funding makes it difficult for community groups to speak out about the harms of gambling activity and campaign for stricter gambling controls (Adams and Rossen, 2006). This may not only lead to self-censorship by a community group, but also discourage dissenting voices within the organization (Adams and Rossen, 2006). For example, if a drug treatment center takes money from a cannabis company, they may be reluctant to publicly raise the role cannabis use plays in drug dependency and mental illness and may censure individual staff within the organization who wish to raise these issues.

The reluctance of gambling industry-funded community groups to speak up concerning the harms of gambling can even develop into a public role of defending the gambling industry through fear of reducing overall levels of community funding (Adams and Rossen, 2006). In New Zealand, community groups receiving money from gaming machine societies have publicly defended the societies when the issue of the harm from gaming machines has been raised (Adams and Rossen, 2006, 2012). The likelihood of a community group defending the industry is higher when the community group is not directly involved in addressing social problems created by industry products. For example, Berdahl and Azmier (1999) found that 23 percent of social, health and education not-for-profits compared to only 4 percent of sports and recreation not-for-profits "agreed" or "strongly agreed" that their boards oppose the use of funding from the gambling industry. The industry may therefore strategically direct funding to community groups more likely to act as public defenders. Consistent with this understanding, Berdahl and Azmier (1999) found that 29 percent of sports groups compared to 9 percent of social, health and education groups received over half their funding from gaming grants. In the long term, industry funding of community groups can shape the public view of the industry as a whole and present the industry as a responsible community benefactor and corporate citizen (Adams and Rossen, 2006, 2012). In New Zealand, this can be seen with the national lottery (Lotto), where marketing promotes the lottery as a means to support worthwhile community services.

Neutrality risk occurs when, due to increasing contact with the industry, members of a community group inadvertently modify their perceptions of the industry and their products (Adams, 2016). Receiving industry money, and establishing convivial relationships with industry representatives, perhaps via mutual attendance at charity events, influences members of community groups to soften their views on the behavior of the industry and the risks of their products.

Risk to democracy can emerge over time as government bodies, political parties, media and the community sector become corrupted by the scale of industry funding (Adams, 2016). Central and local government agencies can become dependent on the tax revenue from industry sales and see this tax revenue as essential to the continuation of public programs and services. For example, the contribution of gambling to state tax revenue in Australia has risen to 13 percent in Victoria and 11 percent in South Australia and Queensland (Adams, 2016). Government sector reliance on industry funding has a silencing effect on criticism of industry products and a perceived financial stake in protecting the sales of industry products. This reliance can manifest in weak policy responses to the social harm created by industry products, including the funding of research that does not threaten industry sales (Adams, 2016).

Minimizing the risks of cannabis industry funding of the community sector

We propose here a number of strategies to minimize the risks described above. The first is to employ a low-risk funding arrangement. Direct industry funding of community groups, where companies fully control the distribution of funding via an internal process, is the least desirable approach as the contribution is not anonymous and the industry has complete control over who does and does not receive grants (Adams and Rossen, 2006; Daube and Stoneham, 2015; Room, 2015). Direct funding allows the industry to target community funding to maximize strategic marketing, public relations and political lobbying advantage, as discussed above (Adams and Rossen, 2006; Daube and Stoneham, 2015). Consequently, we recommend that financial payments from the cannabis industry be anonymously distributed by an independent national grant allocation committee based on objective social need criteria and service effectiveness. The grant committee process needs to be completely independent from the industry and potential recipients of community grants, and from political and government agency influence that can also taint the process (Berdahl and Azmier, 1999). The allocation of grants should be anonymous in the sense that individual cannabis companies will not be identified as the source of funding.

A second important means to minimize the risk of cannabis industry funding of the community sector could be to ban all industry involvement in the allocation of community funding (Adams and Rossen, 2012; Room, 2015). There is often industry and political pressure to include industry representatives on grant allocation committees as part of a so-called "partnership approach" (Adams and Rossen, 2012). Industry partnership engagement creates opportunities for the industry to block effective intervention initiatives that reduce product consumption and reward supporters who align with the industry (Adams and Rossen, 2012). For example, in New Zealand, gambling industry executives make up half of the Problem Gambling Committee, and, according to one researcher who served on the committee for five years, this ensured that "activities that might threaten the consumption of gambling were unlikely to receive significant funding" (Adams and Rossen, 2006, p. 9). Consequently, we propose a ban on any consultation and partnership with the cannabis industry in the grant allocation process. This separation of the industry from the community grant funding process would extend to a ban on including cannabis company branding on community products and services, or alternatively, cannabis companies including community recipients of their grants in their marketing campaigns.

The pressure to adopt a "partnership approach" is likely to be particularly strong in the case of the cannabis industry as, based on previous activist and counterculture associations with cannabis, there may be a perception that the cannabis industry is more altruistically motivated. There may also be a belief that the nascent legal cannabis industry needs to be nurtured to supplant the cannabis black market, and that the novel nature of a legal cannabis sector requires cannabis industry technical expertise in order to develop effective regulation. The latter was the rationale for cannabis industry membership on regulatory bodies in Colorado (Subritzky, Lenton and Pettigrew, 2016; Subritzky, Pettigrew, et al., 2016). One consequence of this in Colorado was the blocking of pesticide regulation, which the cannabis industry viewed as imposing too high a financial burden on the industry (Subritzky, Lenton, et al., 2016; Subritzky, Pettigrew, et al., 2016).

A third means of mitigating the risk of cannabis industry funding of the community sector could be to have the whole cannabis trust regime administered by *one* central government agency, with health as their key responsibility (Adams and Rossen, 2012; Room, 2015). The first stipulation could avoid the slowing of progress on regulation and enforcement caused by the involvement of a number of government agencies with different priorities (Adams and Rossen, 2012). The second stipulation requiring health as a key focus acknowledges that some government agencies have responsibilities to promote commercial activity as a means to promote economic growth, employment, regional development and tourism (Adams and Rossen, 2012). These agencies may view the cannabis industry in largely economic terms as an important business, employer, entertainment and tourist provider that generates substantial taxes. The levies, license fees and taxes from the cannabis industry can then come to be viewed as an important source of agency and wider government revenue that requires protection (Livingstone and Adams, 2015a). To some extent, this was an issue in Colorado with the regulatory powers for the recreational cannabis scheme being given to the Colorado Department of Revenue, rather than to the Health or Human Services Department (Subritzky et al., this volume). We recommend that the cannabis trust regime is managed by the Ministry of Health rather than a government agency with a commercial focus.

A fourth means of addressing the risk of cannabis industry funding is by raising awareness within community organizations concerning the risks of direct funding and partnership arrangements with industry (Adams and Rossen, 2006). This could involve educational packages, discussion workshops and educational booklets discussing the need for transparency concerning funding, declaring conflicts of interest and avoiding direct funding and influence from industry groups (Adams and Rossen, 2006). Employees and volunteers in community groups can act as important "whistle-blowers" concerning industry influence if appropriately educated and externally supported. We therefore propose that central government provide ongoing education and training to community groups with regard to the risks of cannabis industry influence and direct funding.

Conclusions

There is little reason to believe that direct community funding from a commercial cannabis industry would be any different to the experience of direct community funding from the gambling or alcohol industry. The maximizing of financial returns to private owners and shareholders demands a relentless pursuit of profit, and, in this context, cannabis businesses would aim to co-opt their community funding to gain strategic marketing, public relations and political lobbying advantage.

The community cannabis trust model proposed in this chapter is purposely designed to suppress the profit motivation by removing private owners and shareholders, and by establishing a requirement that financial payments be made to community services that mitigate the harms from cannabis products, such as drug prevention and treatment. It also introduces local community governance and oversight via the election of community board members and the power to call a community poll to vote on the future of a cannabis trust.

However, it is likely that cannabis trusts would seek public and political influence, and even indirect pecuniary reward, if allowed to directly fund community groups of their choosing, as has been the experience with gaming machine societies' funding of the community sector in New Zealand (Wilkins, 2018). Consequently, we have proposed four specific mechanisms to address the risks of cannabis trust funding of the community and drug treatment sector: (1) anonymous distribution of community grants by an independent national committee based on objective social need and service effectiveness criteria; (2) a ban on cannabis trust partnerships with government and/or community groups in regard to the allocation of community grants, and a ban on direct sponsorship of community groups; (3) central administration of the cannabis community trust regime by the Ministry of Health according to a harm minimization and health agenda; and (4) ongoing provision of education and training to community workers concerning the risks of direct cannabis industry funding and partnership. These specific mechanisms may well be challenged by the cannabis sellers over time, as has been the experience with gambling and alcohol, as they will directly reduce profit and reduce industry influence over the regulatory, governance and research sectors. Government agencies and political parties may also challenge these structures as they impact tax revenue, business opportunities and inhibit tourism. Consequently, it is important that provisions are included in the Cannabis Act that clearly state that the financial payments of the cannabis industry to the community sector are compensation for the health and social costs of cannabis products, rather than the benevolent donations of a socially responsible industry.

Notes

1 Under New Zealand law, a corporate society is incorporated under the Incorporated Societies Act 1908, or incorporated as a board under the Charitable Trust Act 1957, or is a company incorporated under the Companies Act 1993 that does not have the power to make a profit and is incorporated solely for authorized purposes (Department of Internal Affairs, 2014, p. 2).

2 "'Net Proceeds' is the dollar amount available to be distributed to authorized purposes after costs, levies and taxes have been deducted from a society's gambling turnover and any interest or earnings from investment or sale of assets" (Department of Internal Affairs, 2014, p. 2).

3 "'Gross Proceeds' are the turnover of gambling plus interest or other investment return on that turnover plus proceeds from the sale of fittings, chattels, and gambling equipment purchased from that turnover or investment return, less prizes" (Department of Internal Affairs, 2014, p. 2).

References

Adams, P. (2016). *Moral jeopardy: Risks of accepting money from the alcohol, tobacco and gambling industries*. Cambridge, UK: Cambridge University Press.

Adams, P. and Rossen, F. (2006). Reducing the moral jeopardy associated with receiving funds from the proceeds of gambling. *Journal of Gambling Issues,* 17. http://jgi.camh.net/index.php/jgi/article/view/3738/3698.

Adams, P. and Rossen, F. (2012). A tale of missed opportunities: Pursuit of a public health approach to gambling in New Zealand. *Addiction,* 107, 1051–1056.

Auditor General. (2014). *Challenges facing licensing trusts*. Retrieved from www.oag.govt.nz/2014/licensing-trusts/docs/licensing-trusts.pdf.

Auditor General. (2016). *Challenges facing licensing trusts: An update (17 November 2016)*. Retrieved from www.parliament.nz/resource/en-NZ/51SCJE_EVI_00DBSCH_OTH_59483_1_A539155/81affa8a67351f01afc26967f6391ee3a87a9661.

Authier, P. (2017, November 16). *Quebec cannabis: Strict marijuana law leaves sales to new arm of SAQ*. Retrieved from https://montrealgazette.com/news/quebec/quebec-cannabis-provinces-strict-marijuana-law-leaves-sales-to-saq.

Berdahl, N. and Azmier, J. (1999). *Summary report: The impacts of gaming upon Canadian non-profits: A 1999 survey of gaming grant recipients*. Retrieved from https://

prism.ucalgary.ca/bitstream/handle/1880/314/Impact_of_Gambling_Upon_Non_Profits_Summary.pdf?sequence=2.

Cabinet Economic Growth and Infrastructure Committee. (2016). *Gambling Act 2003: Review of Class 4 gambling*. Retrieved from www.dia.govt.nz/diawebsite.nsf/Files/RIS_Gambling/$file/C4-review-Cab-paper_7-April-2016.pdf.

Caulkins, J., Bao, Y., Davenport, S., Fahli, I., Guo, Y., Kinnard, K., Kilmer, B. (2018). Big data on a big new market: Insights from Washington State's legal cannabis market. *International Journal of Drug Policy,* 57, 86–94.

Caulkins, J. and Kilmer, B. (2016a). Considering marijuana legalization carefully: Insights for other jurisdictions from analysis for Vermont. *Addiction,* 111(12), 2082–2089.

Caulkins, J. and Kilmer, B. (2016b). The US as an example of how not to legalize marijuana? *Addiction,* 111(12), 2095–2096.

Caulkins, J., Kilmer, B. and Kleiman, M. (2016). *Marijuana legalization. What everyone needs to know* (2nd ed.). New York: Oxford University Press.

Cerdá, M. and Kilmer, B. (2017). Uruguay's middle-ground approach to cannabis legalization. *International Journal of Drug Policy,* 42, 118–120.

Daube, M. and Stoneham, M. (2015). Gambling with interests [Commentary]. *Addiction,* 111(12–13).

Department of Internal Affairs. (2013). *Regulatory impact statement: Government position on the Gambling (Gambling Harm Reduction) Amendment Bill.* Retrieved from www.dia.govt.nz/diawebsite.nsf/Files/Class4GamblingReforms/$file/Class4GamblingReforms_Doc32RIS-April2013.pdf.

Department of Internal Affairs. (2014). *Regulatory impact statement: Increasing the proportion of Class 4 gambling proceeds returned to local authorized purposes*. Retrieved from www.dia.govt.nz/diawebsite.nsf/Files/RIS-Class-4-regulatory-reform-Aug-2014/$file/RIS-Class-4-regulatory-reform-Aug-2014.pdf.

Department of Internal Affairs. (2015). *Guide: Pokies in New Zealand – A guide to how the system works*. Retrieved from www.google.co.nz/url?sa=t&rct=j&q=&esrc=s&source=web&cd=1&cad=rja&uact=8&ved=0ahUKEwju0ZXnm4rWAhXGjJQKHRTiBxkQFgglMAA&url=https%3A%2F%2Fwww.dia.govt.nz%2Fdiawebsite.nsf%2FFiles%2FPokie-system-101-untracked-10-2016%2F%24file%2FPokie-system-101-untracked-10-2016.docx&usg=AFQjCNGhko0giZMI1qqroBPZAiUqR857Kg.

Department of Internal Affairs. (2016). *Discussion document: Review of Class 4 gambling*. Retrieved from www.dia.govt.nz/diawebsite.nsf/Files/Class-4-Gambling-review-2016/$file/Class4-review-discussion-document2016.pdf.

du Fresne, K. (2017, October 18). *Licensing trusts set unrealistically ambitious goals*. Retrieved from www.stuff.co.nz/manawatu-standard/opinion/97942141/licensing-trusts-set-unrealistically-ambitious-goals.

Fiala, S., Dilley, J., Firth, C. and Maher, J. (2018). Exposure to marijuana marketing after legalization of retail sales: Oregonians' experiences, 2015–2016. *American Journal of Public Health,* 108(1), 120–127.

Hall, W. and Lynskey, M. (2016). Evaluating the public health impacts of legalising recreational cannabis use in the United States. *Addiction,* 111, 1764–1773.

Hancock, L. (2015). Fine-tuning Livingstone and Adams' ethical principles for integrity in gambling research. *Addiction,* 111, 13–15.

Hunt, P. and Pacula, R. (2017). Early impacts of marijuana legalization: An evaluation of prices in Colorado and Washington. *Journal of Primary Prevention,* 38(3), 221–248.

Licensing Trusts Act 1949. (1949 No 43). Retrieved from www.nzlii.org/nz/legis/hist_act/lta19491949n43242/.

Livingstone, C. and Adams, P. (2015a). Clear principles are needed for integrity in gambling research. *Addiction,* 111, 5–10.

Livingstone, C. and Adams, J. (2015b). Response to commentaries – Clear principles for gambling research. *Addiction,* 111, 16–17.

Nationwide Service Framework Library. (2018, September 7). *Mental health, alcohol and drug addiction sector performance monitoring and improvement.* Retrieved from https://nsfl.health.govt.nz/accountability/performance-and-monitoring/mental-health-alcohol-and-drug-addiction-sector.

New Zealand Parliament. (2010). *Gambling (Gambling Harm Reduction) Amendment Bill.* Retrieved from www.parliament.nz/en/pb/bills-and-laws/bills-digests/document/50PLLaw20771/gambling-gambling-harm-reduction-amendment-bill-2010.

Radio New Zealand. (2018, December 18). *Binding referendum on legalising cannabis for personal use to be held at 2020 election.* Retrieved from www.radionz.co.nz/news/political/378523/binding-referendum-on-legalising-cannabis-for-personal-use-to-be-held-at-2020-election.

Room, R. (2015). Integrity without extinction: Paths forward for gambling research [Commentary]. *Addiction,* 111, 11–12.

Smart, R., Caulkins, J., Kilmer, B., Davenport, S. and Midgette, G. (2017). Variation in cannabis potency and prices in a newly legal market: Evidence from 30 million cannabis sales in Washington State. *Addiction,* 112(12), 2167–2177.

Stewart, L. I. Z. and Casswell, S. (1987). Public control of alcohol: Licensing trusts in New Zealand. *British Journal of Addiction,* 82(6), 643–647.

Subritzky, T., Lenton, S. and Pettigrew, S. (2016). Legal cannabis industry adopting strategies of the tobacco industry. *Drug and Alcohol Review,* 35(5), 511–513.

Subritzky, T., Pettigrew, S. and Lenton, S. (2016). Issues in the implementation and evolution of the commercial recreational cannabis market in Colorado. *International Journal of Drug Policy,* 27, 1–12.

Teahan, B. (2017). *A great social experiment: The story of licensing trusts in New Zealand.* New Zealand: Fraser Books.

Wilkins, C. (2018). A "not-for-profit" regulatory model for legal recreational cannabis: Insights from the regulation of gaming machine gambling in New Zealand. *International Journal of Drug Policy,* 53, 115–122.

18 Insights for the design of Cannabis Social Club regulation

Tom Decorte and Mafalda Pardal

Introduction

With the legalization of recreational cannabis markets in Uruguay, Canada, and a number of US states, a breakthrough in the prohibitionist status quo may be emerging. A fundamental question for these jurisdictions as well as for other countries considering legalization is what types of organizations should be granted the right to produce and/or distribute the formerly prohibited good? In the US, the preference has been to establish profit-driven markets, resembling those for alcohol (Pardo, 2018). This is despite mounting evidence that the alcohol and tobacco industries have sought to maximize profits by promoting use targeting heavy and young users, investing in advertisement and downplaying the health risks of their products, while actively lobbying for industry-friendly regulatory frameworks (Adams, 2013; Caulkins, 2016; Hall, 2016; Subritzky, Lenton and Pettigrew, 2016; Wilkins, 2018). It is likely that a profit-driven commercial market for cannabis will develop similar features. Furthermore, moving directly from prohibition to commercial legalization is a leap from one extreme to the other, and once a multi-billion-dollar industry is in place, it may prove too difficult to reverse it.

At the same time, a fully commercial market is just one of the many possible architectures for legalization, one at the far end of a broad spectrum of options. As the research in this area has pointed out, there are other regulatory options for cannabis supply, including home cultivation or grow-your-own schemes (see Chapter 7 in this book by Belackova et al.), Cannabis Social Clubs and other not-for-profit options, or a government monopoly (Caulkins, Kilmer, Kleiman, MacCoun, Midgette, Oglesby, Pacula and Reuter, 2015; Caulkins and Kilmer, 2016; Kilmer, 2014; Paoli, Decorte, Kersten, Coutteel, De Grauwe, Panzavolta, Pardal, Peuskens, Royer, Tytgat, Van den Broeck, Vankrunkelsven, Verbruggen, Verslype and Verstraete, 2018; Rychert and Wilkins, 2019). These mid-range models constitute alternative options for policies in this area, without necessitating a giant leap to full commercialization of cannabis. This chapter focuses on one particular middle-ground regulatory option: the Cannabis Social Club. A Cannabis Social Club (hereinafter CSC or Club) is a legally constituted non-profit association of cannabis consumers. CSCs collectively cultivate cannabis plants for their adult members' personal consumption (Barriuso, 2011; Belackova, Tomkova and Zabransky, 2016; Pardal, 2018a).

The CSC model has historically been the product of grassroots movements of users (Araña and Montañés, 2011; Blickman, 2014; Pardal, 2016). Although CSCs can be found in many countries, the label is often applied broadly to cover very different on-the-ground realities (Pardal, 2018a). In most jurisdictions today, the way CSCs function and develop their activities also remains primarily the result of their own self-regulatory efforts (Decorte and Pardal, 2017; Belackova and Wilkins, 2018; Pardal, 2018a). In the absence of a clear legal framework in European countries, these organizations continue to operate, at best, in a regulatory "grey zone" of opportunistic workarounds. Uruguay is the clear exception in that it adopted a nationwide legal framework for CSCs in 2013 (Queirolo, Boidi and Cruz, 2016).

Unsurprisingly, a critique raised in relation to some of these middle-ground options is that they remain too vague, lacking a detailed outline or concrete examples from actual regulation, which reduces the likelihood that they are taken seriously by policymakers considering the development of new legal frameworks for cannabis. However, there have been a few instances where the CSC model has been adapted to specific jurisdictions (e.g. in Uruguay and in Spain, at the regional level). In addition, some researchers have developed comprehensive regulatory scenarios for CSCs and other non-profit models (Decorte, 2018; Wilkins, 2016, 2018; Rychert and Wilkins, 2019). In this chapter, we focus on those efforts and analyze the specific ways in which CSC legislation or scenarios for such legislation have been designed to date. In doing so, we hope to contribute to a more nuanced view of this middle-ground model and stimulate the debate beyond the fallacious binary frame of prohibition vs. commercialization.

Regulatory pathways for the CSC model

Previous research has offered in-depth analyses of the core practices and self-regulations developed by CSCs and by the federations representing some of them (especially in Spain and Belgium) (Belackova and Wilkins, 2018; Decorte, Pardal, Queirolo, Fernanda, Sanchez and Parés, 2017; Jansseune, Pardal, Decorte and Parés, 2019; Marín, 2008; Pardal, 2018a). While we acknowledge the contribution made by those self-regulatory codes,[1] in this chapter we seek to offer a complementary view by focusing on other regulatory proposals drafted either by academics or by the legislature.

Legal frameworks for CSCs in Uruguay and Spain

There have only been a few instances where the CSC model has been formally acknowledged and regulated by legislators at the national or regional levels. More specifically, Uruguay remains the only nationwide jurisdiction to have introduced a comprehensive legislative framework with regards to CSCs (see Chapter 5 by Queirolo in this volume). This regulation, particularly with regards to CSCs, has been implemented since October 2014. Currently, under the Uruguayan scheme, about 110 CSCs have completed registration and are operating within this new legal framework (IRCCA, 2018a). The Uruguayan legal reform introduced also two other supply channels (for recreational use) that coexist with the CSC model: home cultivation and sales through pharmacies. In addition, at least three autonomous regions in Spain have also passed legislation concerning the functioning of CSCs: Navarre, the Basque Country and Catalonia. These regulatory efforts of the Spanish regional legislature focused exclusively on the CSC model, but were rather short-lived as they were suspended by the competent domestic courts soon after being approved (for more on this see Chapter 13 by Araña and Páres in this volume). Thus the first difference that emerges in this regard relates to the level of legislative support for CSCs: in Uruguay the CSC were legislatively approved at the national level, while in Spain the laws were passed at the sub-national level, without the support of the central government (Sanchéz and Collins, 2018).

Beyond these examples of actual legislation of the CSC model, a number of proposals have been brought forward at national and regional parliaments elsewhere but were not approved. For instance, this has been the case in Belgium (with a bill drafted by Onkelinx and other members of the Socialist Party in 2017, see Onkelinx, Di Rupo, Demeyer, Lalieux, Fernandez, Ozen, Massin and Frédéric, 2017) and in Portugal (with a bill promoted by left-wing party *Bloco de Esquerda* on at least two occasions: in 2013 and later in 2015) (Bloco de Esquerda, 2013, 2015; Kilmer, Kruithof, Pardal, Caulkins and Rubin, 2013). Mexico is currently debating a legislative reform in this area, and a recent bill includes also the creation of "cooperatives of production" – which to some extent resemble the CSC model, allowing the annual production of 480 grams per member for up to 150 members (Grupo Parlamentario Morena, 2018).

We will focus here on the rationale, goals and specific regime of the CSC legislation from Uruguay, Catalonia and Navarre. While the Ley 1/2016 of the Autonomous Region of the Basque Country on Addictions and Drug Dependence included a few provisions concerning CSCs, under a broader range of social initiatives, this legislative piece did not outline a particular framework for the functioning of CSCs but invited the introduction of subsequent legislation that would fill that void. For instance, in Article 83 of that legislation, it is noted that with the goal of protecting public health and reducing risks, the associations of cannabis users (legally registered and non-profits) would be regulated in future legislation.[2]

The stated goals of CSC legislation

The Uruguayan cannabis legislation has three stated core goals (Articles 1–4): (1) enhancing public security by "protecting the inhabitants of the country

Table 18.1 Legal requirements for the functioning of CSCs in Uruguay and in two autonomous Spanish regions

	Uruguay (Ley 19.172)	*Autonomous region of Catalonia (Ley 13/2017)*	*Autonomous region of Navarre (Ley Foral 24/2014)*
Registration	Yes	Yes	Yes
	Non-profit	Non-profit	Non-profit
	National registry, managed by national control agency IRCCA[1]	Regional registry (for Associations of Catalonia)	Regional registry (for Associations of Navarre)
		Local registries (depending on local regulation)	
		Founding members must be at least 18 years old and cannabis users	Founding members must be regular cannabis users, prior to setting up CSC
	CSC must appoint a technical manager[2]		
Membership	15–45 members		
	At least 18 years old	At least 18 years old	At least 18 years old
	Nationals or permanent residents	Extant cannabis consumers	Extant cannabis consumers (but possible for non-users to join as honorary members or activist members)
		Vouched by another member (except for medical users)	
		Complete registration form	
	Registered in national registry[3]	Registered in CSC records	Registered in CSC records
Cultivation	Maximum of 99 plants	Agricultural engineer to assess number of plants needed to supply CSC members but cannot exceed 150 kg annually	
	Crop and distribution plan[4]	Self-supply register[5]	Organic cultivation is recommended
		Transport from the grow site to the CSC to be authorized by local authorities	
			Testing to be regulated in future legislation

	Uruguay (Ley 19.172)	*Autonomous region of Catalonia (Ley 13/2017)*	*Autonomous region of Navarre (Ley Foral 24/2014)*
Distribution	Each member may receive up to 40 g per month	Each member may receive up to 60 g per month (does not apply to medical users) Members aged 18–21 years old may receive only up to 20 g/month Waiting period of 15 days between enrolment and first collection of cannabis by member (does not apply to medical users) Staff to follow specialized training	Quantity to be distributed is to be determined by the association (in accordance with measures of prevention of risks and international standards)
Social	Social area for members	Social area for members	Spaces open to public or non-members must be physically separated from the spaces dedicated to consumption
	Only members are allowed to enter CSC premises (exceptions may be granted by IRCCA)	Only members are allowed to enter CSC premises	Access to the consumption space is only open to CSC members
		Consumption of alcohol or food products containing cannabis are not allowed	
		Information and professional counselling with regards to risk prevention and harm reduction should be offered by the CSCs to their staff and members. A specific program for 18–21 year-old members should be implemented. CSCs should collaborate with the health department and specialized organizations to provide information about harm reduction. They should also inform members about such organizations	All members should receive education in risk and harm reduction. CSCs should encourage "responsible use" of cannabis and organize activities to reduce problematic use

continued

Table 18.1 continued

	Uruguay (Ley 19.172)	*Autonomous region of Catalonia (Ley 13/2017)*	*Autonomous region of Navarre (Ley Foral 24/2014)*
Other	No advertisement	No advertisement	Members should avoid advertising or promoting the consumption of cannabis among non-CSC members
	No exterior signs or boards at CSC premises	Exterior sign at CSC premises may only include the name of the association, and its registration number, indicating that it is a private, members-only space	
	Security system (video surveillance, alarm, smoke sensors, filters, fire extinguishers)		
	Location restrictions (e.g. in relation to education or treatment centers, other CSCs, etc.) and premises exclusively dedicated to the CSC (members and staff are not allowed to live at the CSC)	Location restrictions to be determined in complementary legislation (e.g. in relation to education centers, health facilities, etc.)	Must adhere to local rules with regards to location, structure and hygiene conditions
	CSCs to function in accordance with defined opening days/hours (proposed by the CSC during registration). No activities to take place beyond that schedule (except maintenance and cleaning)	Further regulation will introduce limitations to the opening days/schedule of CSCs	

Sources: The following regulation or complementary guidance was consulted: Resolución 29/2014, Resolución 32/2014, Resolución JD/9/2018, Ley 13/2017, Ley Foral 24/2014.

Notes

1 IRCCA (Instituto de Regulación y Control del Cannabis) is the national agency set up by Law 19.172 to further regulate and oversee the cannabis market in Uruguay.

2 The technical manager is responsible for compliance with the regulation on cultivation and distribution and liaises with IRCCA on technical matters.

3 Cannabis users can choose to register for one of the three supply channels (i.e. home cultivation, CSC, sales through pharmacies) but can only register for one channel at a time (although switching from one supply channel to another is possible).

4 This plan should include detailed information with regards to: infra-structure of the grow site, cultivation process, register of plants, products used for nourishment of the plants or to tackle pests, harvest, storage, handling of materials and documentation and traceability. For a comprehensive overview, please see: https://ircca.gub.uy/plan-de-produccion/ (last accessed March 2019).

5 This register includes information on: (1) the members accessing cannabis through the CSC (and the quantities acquired by them); (2) the cultivation process (cultivation techniques, quantities produced, etc.); (3) the transport of the cannabis to the CSC location; and (4) the distribution of cannabis to the members.

from the risks associated with the illegal trade and narcotrafficking" and "reducing the incidence of drug trafficking and organized crime"; (2) enhancing public health through education, prevention and risk minimization; and (3) recognizing and protecting the rights of cannabis users. In Catalonia, the legislature focused also on the protection of public health, explicitly noting as a goal of the legislation to "protect, promote and improve the public health of the population through a policy aimed at raising awareness of the risks and harms of cannabis use and minimizing them" (Article 2). In addition, ensuring the rights of cannabis users was also a general stated goal of this legislation. The Navarre legislation focused on providing legal security to both the members of CSCs as well as to larger society, and also referred to the protection of public health as a goal.

The legal definition of CSC

The legislation issued by the autonomous region of Catalonia offers a broad definition of what should be understood as CSCs within that framework, i.e.

> non-profit associations, legally constituted, that self-supply and distribute cannabis among their members, all of them of legal age, who use this substance in a private environment, either recreationally or for therapeutic purposes, and thus reducing the social and health harms associated with the illicit market and certain uses of cannabis.
>
> (Article 4)

In addition, the Navarre legislation lists a set of minimum goals that CSCs should pursue. These include offering training in risk prevention associated with cannabis consumption, informing members about their use and contributing to reducing illicit sales of cannabis (Article 8). The scope and functioning of these associations is established in more detail in all three legal instruments. We provide a comparative overview of those legal requirements in Table 18.1.

Decorte's "detailed scenario for a non-profit cannabis market"

In 2018, one of the authors of this chapter developed a comprehensive hypothetical scenario for a non-profit cannabis market with a view to contributing to the debate on cannabis policy reform. Decorte (2018) included three legally regulated channels (in a first phase): (1) a grow-your-own scheme; (2) Cannabis Social Clubs; and (3) supply of cannabis for medical use (through pharmacies). The introduction of these three models would be preceded by some fine-tuning and adjustments of the scenario to the specific context(s) in which it would be introduced. In addition, the author recommended the launch of an education campaign, informing the public at large about the new regulation. Preparatory scientific research would also be conducted prior to the introduction of the three supply models. The key features of this scenario are presented in Table 18.2.

Table 18.2 Key aspects of a regulatory scenario for CSCs (by Decorte, 2018)

Registration	Yes Non-profit Licensed by Federal Agency for the Regulation and Control of Cannabis (FARCC) Founding members (at least three) must be permanent residents, at least 21 years old, with no previous conviction for membership of criminal organization, money laundering, extortion, corruption, serious violent crimes and drug production on a large scale. Previous convictions for cannabis possession or small-scale cultivation are not sufficient reason for exclusion
Membership	Up to 250 members At least 18 years old Permanent residents Registered in CSC records (which may be consulted by the FARCC) Members can only join one CSC
Cultivation	Maximum of 1,500 plants (250 members × 6 plants per member) Growing procedures according to organic farming standards and regulations CSC can only produce a limited range of herbal cannabis and hash products (no concentrates such as cannabis oil, tinctures or edibles) Growing location: non-publicly accessible (only for plant caretakers[1] and other CSC staff), closed, discretely designed, fire-proofed and with ventilation systems (to avoid nuisance) Every plant must have a proof of ownership of a registered club member
Distribution	Each member may receive up to 60 g per month Mandatory information leaflets must accompany the cannabis supplied (including information about THC and CBD content, major effects and possible side-effects, references to where to find help or advice, etc.) Packaging to follow specific requirements (e.g. childproof, non-transparent, no branding or design, include information about potency, etc.)
Social	CSCs can decide on whether to have consumption facilities[2] CSCs are responsible for promoting the least harmful methods of cannabis use
Other	No advertisement No promotion of cannabis use Security system

Source: Decorte, 2018.

Notes

1 Decorte sets out also a number of requirements for the role of CSC cannabis grower or "plant caretaker."

2 Decorte proposes an additional set of requirements for those CSCs which opt to have consumption space (e.g. no sale of tobacco, alcohol, no display of promotions or advertisement of cannabis products, etc.).

Discussion

A comparative analysis of CSC regulation

The analysis of the few pieces of CSC legislation which have been introduced so far provide an interesting perspective on what have been the stated priorities and detailed design of the model across different settings. CSC legislation in Uruguay and in the Spanish Autonomous Regions of Catalonia and Navarre seems to be associated with the aim of strengthening public health protection. Public security concerns (associated with drug-related violence) are specific (and central) to the Uruguayan context only (Queirolo, Rossel, Álvarez and Repetto, 2018; Repetto, 2014) but may also be relevant to other jurisdictions where CSCs are being discussed, if not yet proposed. Generally, the sub-national Spanish legal frameworks seem to have indeed placed more attention on ensuring that the CSCs develop a risk and harm reduction program, as well as educational activities and training of staff and members than the Uruguayan model. We are of course only considering here the approach taken by the legislature at face value and not analyzing CSCs' actual implementation of it.

There are a number of commonalities across the three legislations and Decorte's proposal (2018), which also seem to reflect what have been practices historically associated with the CSC model (Belackova et al., 2016; Decorte et al., 2017; Marín, 2008; Pardal, 2018a; Parés and Bouso, 2015). For instance, CSCs should operate as not-for-profits, with no advertisement or marketing being allowed, and these associations must register in some form of regional or national database. In this regard, the Uruguayan legislation is particular in that it also foresees individual members' registration in a national database (while the Spanish laws leave users' registration to be managed internally by the CSCs). It will need to be tested whether cannabis users are willing to be registered as such on a government-controlled list, or whether simply being registered with the CSC would be more acceptable. A national agency overseeing cannabis regulation and implementation has also been created in Uruguay and is one of the measures included in Decorte's regulatory scenario (2018).

Access to CSCs is limited to adults (18 or older) in all the jurisdictions considered, and the Catalonian law actually sets up a specific category for the younger members (18–21 years old), establishing a lower-quantity threshold and inviting the CSCs to organize educational activities tailored to this age group. This may be an interesting particularity for the consideration of other jurisdictions especially given the concerns about the impact of heavy regular cannabis use on the developing brain and which may continue until the early 20s (Lubman, Yucel and Hall, 2007). Access to CSCs in the two Spanish autonomous regions is possible for candidate members who were already using cannabis prior to joining the club – a criterion which may be difficult to enforce in practice. Only the Uruguayan legislator attempted to limit the size of the CSCs by setting a cap at 45 members (and a minimum of 15). Decorte (2018) suggests a larger CSC size by permitting CSCs to register up to 250 members. In both Uruguay and Decorte's scenario, a residency criterion is applied to limit entry to CSCs, in an attempt to avoid or curb "cannabis tourism."

With regards to cultivation, two approaches emerged: in Uruguay, the legislator established a limit in terms of the number of plants a CSC is allowed to grow – an approach followed also by Decorte (2018); in Catalonia, the threshold corresponds to the quantity (in kilograms) of dry cannabis produced. No legislation introduced any restrictions to the potency of the cannabis produced, and in fact, only the Navarre legislator did explicitly note that cultivation should adhere to organic cultivation standards and be subject to testing (which would be defined in future legislation). Nevertheless, the legislations under analysis have included clear requirements to ensure some degree of traceability and documentation of the cultivation process (see for instance the provisions around the development of a crop and distribution plan in Uruguay or the so-called self-supply register in the case of Catalonia).

Decisions about price and/or other financial contributions (for instance, in the form of an entry or regular membership fee) to the functioning of the CSCs seem to have been left to the CSCs themselves, across the three jurisdictions. Both in Uruguay and Catalonia, limits to the quantities the CSCs can distribute to their members were legally defined. This was also the case in Decorte's scenario (2018), who also proposes specific packaging requirements as well as that the cannabis supplied is accompanied by informative leaflets. All three actual legislations invite CSCs to have a social area for members. In Decorte's scenario the decision to have a space for the consumption of cannabis is left to the CSCs (2018). The Catalonian legislation includes restrictions to the use of other substances (e.g. alcohol) or other cannabis food products (also, Decorte limits product availability to herbal cannabis and hashish).

What can we learn from the implementation of CSC legislation and CSCs' self-regulatory practices?

Our understanding of the implementation of CSC legislation is still very limited. As we have seen here, despite growing interest in the model, there have only been a few instances where a regulatory framework specific to CSCs has been put in place. The sub-national legislative efforts in Spain have furthermore been brought to a halt by national courts (see Chapter 13 by Araña and Páres in this volume). These were short-lived experiments that, to our knowledge, have not been evaluated. Differently, the nationwide legislation introduced in Uruguay continues to be implemented today and some preliminary analyses have been carried into the impacts of cannabis legalization on public health, crime and the illicit market, among other aspects.[3] Also the implementation of the CSC model more specifically has become a subject of study (Queirolo et al., 2016; Pardal, Queirolo, Álvarez and Repetto, 2019).

Given that there are some commonalities between a number of legal prescriptions and CSCs' own self-regulated practices, we can also draw on the body of research examining CSCs experiences in unregulated contexts (Belackova et al., 2016; Decorte et al., 2017; Jansseune et al., 2019; Pardal, 2018a; Parés and Bouso, 2015).

An aspect of CSC legislation that warrants further reflection is the introduction of registers of users, either at the national level or by the CSCs themselves. An earlier attempt to introduce this type of practice within coffeeshops in the Netherlands proved to be of difficult implementation, as many users distrusted the registry (Korf, Doekhie and Wouters, 2011; Wouters and Korf, 2011; Ooyen-Houben, Bieleman, Korf and De Witte, 2017). With regards to Uruguay, there seem to be somewhat mixed results. Initially, the registration process for CSCs was described as being lengthy and possibly over-bureaucratic, managed by a new and under-staffed/under-resourced IRCCA (Queirolo et al., 2016). At the individual level (i.e. for the registration as users), in a 2014 survey among frequent consumers in the capital Montevideo, 39 percent of the enquired reported "probably" or "certainly not willing" to complete registration – but the majority indicated some degree of willingness to do it (58 percent) (Boidi, Cruz, Queirolo and Bello-Pardo, 2015). Nevertheless, the underlying issue, i.e. some users may prefer to avoid registration altogether, remains to some extent unresolved. According to IRCCA's own estimates, one CSC member is typically sharing the cannabis received from the CSC with two other unregistered users (IRCCA, 2018c). This helps partially explain[4] why the relatively low limit introduced by law regarding the maximum number of members allowed per CSC (N = 45) does not seem to have become problematic to date – the (national) average number of members per CSC amounts to 25 only (IRCCA, 2018b).

Research into CSCs in Catalonia (particularly in Barcelona) has identified CSCs that are open to (and even proactively recruiting) tourists and which supply them immediately upon enrolment (Jansseune et al., 2019; Martínez, 2015; Parés and Bouso, 2015).[5] While it is not clear how widespread these practices are, they suggest that legislators may want to consider ways to restrain them (to avoid de facto commercialization). Some of the CSC legislation analyzed in this chapter seems to attempt to do so: for instance, by introducing registration and membership criteria (including residency or nationality requirements) or setting up limits to the quantity supplied per month. It is interesting to note that the Catalonian regulation actually introduces a waiting period of 15 days between the enrolment of a member and their first cannabis collection – which seems precisely to be aimed at reducing the attraction of CSCs among tourists. It will be important to examine how such legislation is implemented (and enforced) in practice.

The perceived quality of the cannabis produced and supplied by CSCs has been repeatedly noted in research into CSCs as one of the key strengths of the model (Belackova et al., 2016; Decorte et al., 2017; Pardal, 2018a). The legislative pieces and Decorte's scenario introduce additional requirements with regards to the cultivation process: the focus seems to be on traceability (with the requirement to have detailed records of production). While research in this area has mostly described CSCs as cooperatives of production and distribution, there is also evidence that some CSCs may be distributing cannabis bought from the illicit market (Barriuso, 2012a, 2012b; Decorte et al., 2017; Jansseune et al., 2019; Pardal, 2018a). The Navarre legislation explicitly demands the adoption of organic cultivation practices and indicates that cannabis testing is to be regulated in subsequent legislation. This is an important point as formal quality control has not been widely nor regularly introduced (in either regulated or unregulated contexts) (Decorte et al., 2017; Lenton, Frank, Barratt, Potter and Decorte, 2018; Pardal, 2018a). The type of product delivered by CSCs is primarily herbal cannabis (Pardal and Decorte, 2018; Pardal, 2018a), although there may be exceptions to this (Jansseune et al., 2019). CSC legislation seems to intend to maintain limits on the types of products CSCs can produce or distribute to their members. As we noted elsewhere (Pardal and Decorte, 2018), the relatively limited assortment of cannabis products could be a strength of the model from a public health perspective – in the sense that CSCs would not be promoting innovative, high-THC cannabis products and derivatives (as it has been reported in relation to for-profit models, see Carlini, Garrett and Harwick, 2017; Smart, Caulkins, Kilmer, Davenport and Midgette, 2017). But it could also constitute a weakness as users may want to have access to other types of cannabis products too (Boidi, Queirolo and Cruz, 2016).

Another important aspect from which we can learn relates to CSCs' ability or willingness to implement a social and/or health-oriented program, including harm-reduction initiatives for their members and training for staff, for instance. The CSC model has often been associated with a harm-reduction perspective (Belackova et al., 2016), but the data from CSC studies has offered a somewhat mixed picture in this regard. While there are CSCs that have established collaborations with harm-reduction organizations and offer a number of activities to their members to better inform them about, for instance, alternative or less harmful consumption methods, other CSCs have not – and may in practice function almost as a vending point for members only, with little interaction among members or between the CSC (and staff) and the members (Jansseune et al., 2019; Pardal, 2018a; Pardal et al., 2019). Some of the legislation presented here, particularly from the autonomous Spanish regions, seeks to enshrine the development of harm-reduction activities, for instance, by requiring the CSCs to collaborate with the state Health Department and specialized organizations to provide information about harm reduction.

The difficulty of finding the right balance: regulating while granting sufficient space for self-regulation

As the previous paragraphs already suggest, there may be tensions or divergences in the types of practices CSCs adhere to. One of this chapter's authors has tried to identify and capture these differences – drawing on empirical data, in a first CSC typology (Pardal, 2018a). It suffices to say that large, commercial CSCs constitute a very different proposition than smaller, cooperative CSCs. This is perhaps an extreme example, but the variations in the CSC model abound. In part, this can be explained by the fact that in most jurisdictions, CSCs have been self-regulating their own activities, and thus different approaches and different types of CSCs have emerged. CSC Federations – umbrella organizations representing groups of CSCs – have attempted to bring some consistency to CSC practices and developed overarching codes of conduct that the CSCs they represent are expected to follow. However, there are limitations to the extent CSC Federations can guarantee adherence of CSCs to those voluntary codes of conduct (Jansseune et al., 2019).

An important challenge for academics and policymakers is whether and how the weaknesses of and threats to the CSC model can be converted into strengths and opportunities through governmental regulation. Government regulation can offer CSCs legal protection and stimulate the stability and sustainability of the model, in adherence to its core ethos as a cooperative, closed supply, non-profit and harm-reduction-driven model. At the same time, such a regulatory framework should also grant sufficient autonomy to CSCs in order to make the model attractive enough for users (and so avoid that they return to the illicit market). As Belackova and Wilkins (2018) note, there are clear advantages in engaging with CSCs and users in the development of legislation in this area, enhancing "consumer agency and responsibility" (p. 32). Furthermore, legislative efforts in this area should also pay attention to the extent to which their citizens, civil society and wider society are used to experiencing state regulation or intervention in other aspects of their life and activities. For instance, a mandatory national registry for cannabis users may be perceived as a less intimidating measure in jurisdictions where general state intervention is higher (e.g. Uruguay), than in contexts where the state does not necessarily play such a role (e.g. US).

Finally, we should (re-)emphasize that while the focus of our analysis lies on the design of CSC regulation, we recognize that its actual enforcement will have significant impacts as to how CSCs will turn out to function in practice. This is to say that, in both a scenario where a detailed, state-led regulatory framework is introduced or in a context where self-regulatory guidelines are allowed, the way those sets of rules are enforced will be of crucial importance. For example, it can be the case that in a jurisdiction relying primarily on CSCs' own regulations, but with close state oversight (for instance, through regular inspections or contact between authorities and CSC representatives), the CSCs will generally comply with those self-regulatory codes. On the contrary, it may well be that in a jurisdiction with a stricter, formal CSC regulation, but without proper enforcement, CSCs will deviate from the set requirements and boundaries, for instance, evolving into commercial outlets. This may be of particular relevance for jurisdictions with diluted or destabilized state capacity that may be considering regulating this (or other) cannabis supply model(s).

Conclusion

A key goal of this chapter was to counter the idea that non-profit models for the supply of cannabis remain vague proposals. Although there are only a few cases of actual implementation of legislation specific to CSCs, these offer a rather detailed overview of the key aspects of the model and how the legislator intends to shape them. Lessons can be drawn from the design of legislative pieces regulating CSCs, from academic proposals, as well as from what we already know about the self-enacted CSC practices. Uruguay, as the only national jurisdiction with CSC legislation still in place to date, offers a unique learning opportunity and we encourage future research efforts in that country.

Notes

1 We are aware that at least some CSCs or their representatives have also put forward their own proposals for regulation, based on their views of what a cannabis market should look like, including the CSC model in those scenarios. See for instance a 2016 proposal by two Belgian CSCs: www.cannabis-social-clubs.be/csc/IMG/pdf/2016_-_blauwdruk_tup_mambo-3.pdf (last accessed March 2019).
2 The article further indicated that such forthcoming legislation would determine the conditions of admission, introduce guarantees with regards to the dissemination by the CSCs of information about responsible use, and would define the control and inspection mechanisms by the competent local authorities.
3 See for instance the research reports by Monitor Cannabis and by the Latin American Marijuana Research Initiative.
4 Multiple factors may be contributing to the small size of CSCs in Uruguay. We reflect on other possible explanatory elements in Pardal et al., 2019.
5 Data from Belgium did not offer examples of such practices (Pardal, 2018a). This could arguably be explained by the more stringent law enforcement control applied in that country, as well as the relatively small volume of CSCs (Pardal, 2018b) if compared to the Spanish context.

References

Adams, P.J. (2013). Addiction industry studies: Understanding how proconsumption influences block effective interventions. *American Journal of Public Health*, 103(4), 35–38.

Araña, X. and Montañés, V. (2011). Cannabis cultivation in Spain – The case of Cannabis Social Clubs. In T. Decorte, G.R. Potter and M. Bouchard (Eds.), *World wide weed: Global trends in cannabis cultivation and its control* (pp. 163–177). Surrey, UK: Ashgate.

Barriuso, M. (2011). Cannabis social clubs in Spain: A normalizing alternative underway. *Series on Legislative Reform of Drug Policies*, 2, 1–9.

Barriuso, M. (2012a). *Los Clubes Sociales de Cannabis en la encrucijada: Entre la autogestión y la mercantilización* [Between collective organization and commercialisation: the Cannabis Social Clubs at a crossroads]. Retrieved from www.tni.org/en/node/11903.

Barriuso, M. (2012b). *Ni prohibición ni mercantilización: Buscando el equilibrio en la regulación legal del cannabis* [Neither prohibition nor commercialisation: Seeking the balance in the legal regulation of cannabis]. Cannabis: Usos, seguridad juridica y politicas (pp. 167–181). Victoria-Gasteiz: Ararteko,

Belackova, V., Tomkova, A. and Zabransky, T. (2016). Qualitative research in Spanish cannabis social clubs: "The moment you enter the door, you are minimising the risks." *International Journal of Drug Policy*, 34, 49–57.

Belackova, V. and Wilkins, C. (2018). Consumer agency in cannabis supply – Exploring auto-regulatory documents of the cannabis social clubs in Spain. *International Journal of Drug Policy*, 54, 26–34.

Blickman, T. (2014). Cannabis policy reform in Europe: Bottom up rather than top down. *Series on Legislative Reform of Drug Policies*, 28, 1–24.

Bloco de Esquerda (2013). *Projeto de lei nr. 403/XII/2: Legaliza o cultivo de canábis para consumo pessoal e cria o enquadramento legal para os clubes sociais de canábis* [Law bill nr. 403/XII/2: Legalizing cannabis cultivation for personal use and introducing a legal framework for cannabis social clubs]. Retrieved from: www.parlamento.pt/ActividadeParlamentar/Paginas/DetalheIniciativa.aspx?BID=37667.

Bloco de Esquerda (2015). *Projeto de lei nr. 880/XII/4: Legaliza o cultivo de canábis para consumo pessoal e cria o enquadramento legal para os clubes sociais de canábis* [Law bill nr. 880/XII/4: Legalizing cannabis cultivation for personal use and introducing a legal framework for cannabis social clubs]. Retrieved from: www.parlamento.pt/ActividadeParlamentar/Paginas/DetalheIniciativa.aspx?BID=39363.

Boidi, M.F., Cruz, J.M., Queirolo, R. and Bello-Pardo, E. (2015). *Regulación del mercado de marihuana. Evidencia desde Uruguay a las Américas* [Regulation of the cannabis market. Evidence from Uruguay to the Americas]. Montevideo: Universidad Católica del Uruguay.

Boidi, M.F., Queirolo, R. and Cruz, J.M. (2016). Marijuana consumption patterns among frequent consumers in Uruguay. *International Journal of Drug Policy*, 34, 34–40.

Carlini, B.H., Garrett, S.B. and Harwick, R.M. (2017). Beyond joints and brownies: Marijuana concentrates in the legal landscape of WA State. *International Journal of Drug Policy*, 42, 26–29.

Caulkins, J. (2016). Legalising drugs prudently: The importance of incentives and values. In J. Collins and A. Soderholm (Eds.), *After the drug wars: Report of the LSE expert group on the economics of drug policy* (pp. 40–50). London: London School of Economics and Political Science.

Caulkins, J.P. and Kilmer, B. (2016). Considering marijuana legalization carefully: Insights for other jurisdictions from analysis for Vermont. *Addiction*, 111(12), 2082–2089.

Caulkins, J.P., Kilmer, B., Kleiman, M.A.R., MacCoun, R.J., Midgette, G., Oglesby, P., Pacula, R.L. and Reuter, P. (2015). *Considering marijuana legalization: Insights for Vermont and other jurisdictions*. Santa Monica: RAND Corporation.

Decorte, T. (2018). *Regulating cannabis: A detailed scenario for a nonprofit cannabis market.* Bloomington: Archway Publishing.

Decorte, T. and Pardal, M. (2017). Cannabis Social Clubs in Europe: Prospects and limits. In R. Colson and H. Bergeron (Eds.), *European drug policies: The ways of reform* (pp. 285–299). New York, NY: Routledge.

Decorte, T., Pardal, M., Queirolo, R., Fernanda, M., Sanchez, C. and Parés, O. (2017). Regulating Cannabis Social Clubs: A comparative analysis of legal and self-regulatory practices in Spain, Belgium and Uruguay. *International Journal of Drug Policy*, 43, 44–56.

Grupo Parlamentario Morena (2018). *Proyecto de decreto por el que se expide la ley general para la regulación y control de cannabis* [Decree Project to introduce general law for the regulation and control of cannabis]. Retrieved from http://infosen.senado.gob.mx/sgsp/gaceta/64/1/2018-11-08-1/assets/documentos/Inic_Morena_Control-Cannabis_081118.pdf.

Hall, W. (2016). Alcohol and cannabis: Comparing their adverse health effects and regulatory regimes. *International Journal of Drug Policy*, 42, 57–62.

IRCCA (2018a). *Clubes de membresia con licencia aprobada al 21/11/2018* [Cannabis social clubs with approved license by 21/11/2018]. Retrieved from www.ircca.gub.uy/clubesaprobados/.

IRCCA (2018b). *Mercado regulado de cannabis: Informe al 30/09/2018* [Regulated cannabis market: Report from 30/09/2018]. Montevideo. Retrieved from www.ircca.gub.uy/wpcontent/uploads/2018/11/InformeMercadoReguladoCannabis-30set2018.pdf.

IRCCA (2018c). *Mercado regulado de cannabis. Informe al 05/06/2018.* [Regulated cannabis market: Report from 05/06/2018] Montevideo. Retrieved from www.ircca.gub.uy/wpcontent/uploads/2018/06/InformeMercadoReguladoCannabis-05jun2018.pdf.

Jansseune, L., Pardal, M., Decorte, T. and Parés, Ò. (2019). Revisiting the birthplace of the Cannabis Social Club model and the role played by Cannabis Social Club Federations. *Journal of Drug Issues*, 49(2), 338–354.

Kilmer, B. (2014). Policy designs for cannabis legalization: Starting with the eight Ps. *American Journal of Drug and Alcohol Abuse*, 40(4), 259–261.

Kilmer, B., Kruithof, K., Pardal, M., Caulkins, J.P. and Rubin, J. (2013). *Multi-national overview of cannabis production regimes*. Santa Monica: RAND Corporation.

Korf, D., Doekhie, J. and Wouters, M. (2011). *Amsterdamse coffeeshops en hun bezoekers* [Amsterdam's coffeeshops and their visitors]. Amsterdam: Rozenberg Publishers.

Lenton, S., Frank, V.A., Barratt, M.J., Potter, G.R. and Decorte, T. (2018). Growing practices and the use of potentially harmful chemical additives among a sample of small-scale cannabis growers in three countries. *Drug and Alcohol Dependence*, 192, 250–256.

Lubman, D.I., Yucel, M. and Hall, W.D. (2007). Substance use and the adolescent brain: A toxic combination? *Journal of Psychopharmacology*, 21, 792–794.

Marín, I. (2008). *La cultura "cannabica" en España (1991–2007)* [The "cannabis" culture in Spain (1991–2007)]. Granada, Spain: Universidad de Granada.

Martínez, D.P. (2015). Clubs sociales de cannabis: Normalización, neoliberalismo, oportunidades politicas y prohibicionismo [Cannabis Social Clubs: Normalisation, neoliberalism, political opportunities and prohibition]. *CLIVATGE*, 3, 92–112.

Onkelinx, L., Di Rupo, E., Demeyer, W., Lalieux, K, Fernandez, J., Ozen, O., Massin, E., Frédéric, A. (2017). *Voorstel van kaderwet tot instelling van een gereglementeerde cannabismarkt* [Proposal of legal framework for the introduction of a regulated cannabis market]. Retrieved from www.dekamer.be/FLWB/PDF/54/2660/54K2660001.pdf.

Ooyen-Houben, M. v., Bieleman, B., Korf, D. and de Witte, K. (2017). Het besloten club – En het ingezetenencriterium voor coffeeshops: Een natuurlijk experiment [The closed club and residency criterium for coffeeshops: A natural experiment]. *Tijdschrift voor Criminologie*, 59(1–2), 10–29.

Paoli, L., Decorte, T., Kersten, L., Coutteel, E., De Grauwe, P., Panzavolta, M., Pardal, M., Peuskens, H., Royer, S., Tytgat, J., Van den Broeck, A., Vankrunkelsven, P.,

Verbruggen, F., Verslype, C. and Verstraete, C. (2018). *Tijd voor een nieuw Belgisch cannabisbeleid? Evaluaties, opties en aanbevelingen* [Time for a new cannabis policy? Evaluations, options and recommendations]. Leuven: KU Leuven.

Pardal, M. (2016). Cannabis Social Clubs through the lens of the drug user movement. *Tijdschrift over Cultuur and Criminaliteit*, 2, 47–58.

Pardal, M. (2018a). Belgian Cannabis Social Clubs' supply practices: A shapeshifting model? *International Journal of Drug Policy*, 57, 32–41.

Pardal, M. (2018b). The Belgian Cannabis Social Club landscape. *Drugs and Alcohol Today*, 18(2), 80–89.

Pardal, M. and Decorte, T. (2018). Cannabis use and supply patterns among Belgian Cannabis Social Club members. *Journal of Drug Issues*, 48(4), 689–709.

Pardal, M., Queirolo, R., Álvarez, E., Repetto, L. (2019). Uruguayan Cannabis Social Clubs: From activism to dispensaries? *International Journal of Drug Policy*, 73, 49–57.

Pardo, B. (2018) American exceptionalism and the failure to learn from mistakes of the past. *Addiction*, 113, 602–603.

Parés, O. and Bouso, J. (2015). *Innovation born of necessity: Pioneering drug policy in Catalonia.* New York, NY: Open Society Foundations.

Queirolo, R., Boidi, M. F. and Cruz, J. M. (2016). Cannabis clubs in Uruguay: The challenges of regulation. *International Journal of Drug Policy,* 34, 41–48.

Queirolo, R., Rossel, C., Álvarez, E., Repetto, L. (2018). Why Uruguay legalized marijuana? The open window of public insecurity. *Addiction*, 114(7), 1313–1321.

Repetto, L. (2014). Regulación del cannabis: ¿Un asunto de seguridad? Entrada y mantenimiento en agenda de un problema de política pública [Regulation of cannabis: A security issue? Entry and maintenance on the agenda of a public policy problem]. *Revista Uruguaya de Ciencia Política*, 23(1), 119–141.

Rychert, M. and Wilkins, C. (2019). A "community enterprise" model for recreational cannabis: Lessons from alcohol licensing trusts in New Zealand. *International Journal of Drug Policy,* 67, 72–78.

Sanchéz, C. and Collins, M. (2018). Better to ask forgiveness than permission: Spain's sub-national approach to drug policy. *Global Drug Policy Observatory*, Policy Brief 12, June 2018.

Smart, R., Caulkins, J.P., Kilmer, B., Davenport, S. and Midgette, G. (2017). Variation in cannabis potency and prices in a newly legal market: Evidence from 30 million cannabis sales in Washington State. *Addiction*, 112, 2167–2177.

Subritzky, T., Lenton, S. and Pettigrew, S. (2016). Legal cannabis industry adopting strategies of the tobacco industry. *Drug and Alcohol Review*, 35, 511–513.

Wilkins, C. (2016). After the legalisation of cannabis: The Cannabis Incorporated Society (CIS) regulatory model for recreational cannabis in New Zealand. *New Zealand Medical Journal*, 129(1433), 17–20.

Wilkins, C. (2018). A "not-for-profit" regulatory model for legal recreational cannabis: Insights from the regulation of gaming machine gambling in New Zealand. *International Journal of Drug Policy,* 53, 115–122.

Wouters, M. and Korf, D. J. (2011). *De wietpas en het sociaal clubmodel: Meningen en verwachtingen van coffeeshopbezoekers in Utrecht* [The weedpass and the social club model: Opinions and expectations of coffeeshop visitors in Utrecht]. Amsterdam: Rozenberg Publishers.

Conclusion

Chris Wilkins, Simon Lenton and Tom Decorte

The overall aim of this book has been to inform socially beneficial cannabis policy reform by identifying the learnings from jurisdictions that have already legalized cannabis or implemented earlier cannabis law reforms, and by reviewing the findings from decades of research into the effective regulation of alcohol, tobacco and "legal highs."

The new legal cannabis markets

The obvious place to start this journey of exploring cannabis regulation was to investigate the outcomes from jurisdictions that have already fully legalized the use and supply of cannabis. The authors of all these case studies agree that the relative newness of these reforms means that many of the public health consequences of legal cannabis markets are yet to clearly manifest themselves, including the impact on youth, mental illness, drug dependency, vehicle accidents and emergency department admissions (Subritzky et al., this volume; Mosher and Akins, this volume; Fischer et al., this volume). However, these case studies clearly illustrate the complexities and challenges of regulating legal cannabis markets and identify some of the social and health risks related to a commercial approach to legal cannabis sales. The collective wisdom emerging from these chapters is that, given these regulatory complexities and the unintended negative outcomes from commercialization, there is a strong case for conservative regulatory frameworks and related implementation that seeks to limit the size and scope of the new market and related industry power.

Pardo (this volume) characterizes the legal cannabis reforms enacted in 11 US states as largely establishing for-profit commercial cannabis markets that are broadly regulated similarly to alcohol. These reforms were predominately established via citizen-initiated referenda, and the brevity and rigidness of these initiatives has led to the commercial alcohol-style approach and, inadvertently, prevented the development of more nuanced, public health oriented regimes and regulation (Pardo, 2019, this volume, Subritzky et al., this volume).

Subritzky et al. (this volume) confirm that a minority of people with problematic cannabis use constitute the majority of the legal cannabis market in

Colorado, and these people have been targeted by cannabis businesses who exploit regulatory loopholes to promote products. The authors lament that more has not been done in Colorado to protect vulnerable people from the new commercial cannabis industry, such as requiring prominent product health warnings, raising prices, strengthening and widening marketing restrictions and mandating plain packaging. Regulating the quality of legal cannabis products is identified as a key regulatory challenge owing to the variability in potency due to different testing procedures, lack of proficiency standards for cannabis cultivation and difficulties in regulating and enforcing restrictions on chemical pesticides and other additives.

Both in Colorado (Subritzky et al., this volume) and Washington State (Mosher and Akins, this volume), the state governments have earned substantial tax revenue from legal cannabis sales. For example, Mosher and Akins (this volume) report that Washington State collected US$314.8 million in tax revenue from cannabis sales in 2017, 26 percent more than projected. As expected, there have also been reductions in cannabis arrests and convictions, and related criminal justice costs. Mosher and Akins (this volume) point out the number of cannabis related low-level court filings in Washington State decreased from 6,879 in 2011 (the year prior to the passage of legalization) to only 120 in 2015, and the number of cannabis convictions decreased from 7,303 to 1,723 over the same period. The new streams of cannabis tax revenue appear to have been spent in the health and social sector, including on services specifically responding to drug harm. In Washington State, cannabis tax revenue has been used to fund substance abuse education and treatment programs, with the largest proportion allocated to the state's share of Medicaid (Mosher and Akins, this volume). In Colorado, tax revenue has been used to increase funding for the Department of Education and Department of Human Services, including US$12 million on substance disorder services (Subritzky et al., this volume). However, over time, there will likely be numerous competing demands on this tax revenue, and, depending on the political party in power, health services for cannabis users may or may not be deemed a high priority. Furthermore, the impressive tax income earned from legal cannabis sales must be offset against the potential and often hidden extra costs due to cannabis-related harms, for example increasing emergency department admissions and mental health admissions, along with the additional spending required for general health and social services to address harms.

Subritzky et al. (this volume) argue that the negative outcomes and unintended impacts of the Colorado commercial cannabis market support the case for a conservative roll-out of new legal cannabis markets. This includes limiting product types and allowing time for regulator rules to be developed. In addition, key public health initiatives, such as youth education, roadside driver impairment training and evaluation surveys, should be operational *before* the new legal market commences, rather than waiting to belatedly fund these from tax revenue from cannabis sales.

Fischer et al. (this volume) describe how the Canadian government characterized their framework to legalize cannabis as "public health" focused with "strict regulation" to distance their approach from the commercial regimes established in the US. The resulting Canadian legislation restricts retail distribution to approved sources, establishes an online distribution system, limits personal production to up to four plants per household, introduces strict controls over promotion and limits product types to dried cannabis plant and oils. Significant regulatory powers are delegated to the territories and provinces, including setting the legal age of use, rules concerning public consumption, home production and retail distribution. Based on the plans released to date, this devolution will result in considerable heterogeneity in cannabis regulatory frameworks between territories and provinces (e.g. government shops in Quebec, private retail outlets in Alberta, and a hybrid of public and private outlets in British Columbia) (Fischer et al., this volume). Fischer et al. (this volume) conclude that due to the newness of the reforms, many key questions about the Canadian model remain unanswered. These include: Can heavily regulated legal outlets compete with the numerous unregulated ones? What will be the impact of legal cannabis on health and social harm, and levels of use by youth under the legal purchase age? And, what will be the outcome of the marketing tactics employed by commercial cannabis companies, some of which have already been subject to financial take-over and investment by alcohol and tobacco companies?

The final case study of a legal cannabis market is the often-overlooked Uruguay cannabis reforms. It is important to consider the Uruguayan cannabis regime due to the emphasis placed on making provision for non-commercial legal means of cannabis supply. Cannabis is legally available via three sources: home cultivation, Cannabis Social Clubs (CSCs) and via retail purchase from pharmacies. Despite the controversial user registration requirement, both home cultivation and CSCs have proven popular supply options. As of September 2019, there are 7,286 current registered home cannabis growers and 126 CSCs. It is the retail sale of cannabis via pharmacies that has experienced the greatest implementation issues, including the small number pharmacies wanting to sell cannabis, shortfalls in the amount of cannabis commissioned by government to meet demand, and government-approved cultivators producing cannabis that did not meet the required standards. Queirolo and colleagues (this volume) argue that a key measure of the success of the Uruguay reforms is that over half of cannabis users now obtain their cannabis from legal sources, rather than financially supporting the illegal drugs trade and related criminal organizations.

Re-evaluating decriminalization and depenalization approaches

We acknowledge that while the recent examples of cannabis legalization have grabbed considerable global attention, there are many examples of earlier cannabis law reforms that have been in place for decades. These can offer alternative "middle ground" approaches to cannabis policy reform that do not entail the establishment of a fully commercial cannabis market. Before the wave of legal cannabis market reforms began, these approaches were often considered smart, pragmatic responses to cannabis use that both significantly reduced the number of arrests and convictions for cannabis, and the related criminal justice costs, and established tolerance of cannabis use. Many were local responses in the face of national policy inertia, and this "local customization" contributed to policies that particularly fitted local communities. Some of these early reforms suffered initial implementation problems that were only addressed over time. Many were considered highly controversial at the time, and hence attracted political opposition that led to some policy retrenchment and some case reversals. Yet, by and large, these decriminalization and depenalization approaches have remained in place. Given the recent emergence of fully commercial cannabis markets, it seems timely to re-evaluate these pragmatic policy responses to see if they can be reinvigorated and expanded to provide an acceptable compromise between criminal penalties on the one hand and a fully commercial cannabis sector on the other.

Eastwood (this volume) summarizes the numerous examples of cannabis decriminalization, including instances where laws have been specifically passed to remove criminal penalties for minor cannabis offending (i.e. *de jure* reform), and examples where minor cannabis offenses have been given a low priority for arrest and prosecution (i.e. de facto reform). Eastwood (this volume) cautions that while there is a wealth of evidence on cannabis decriminalization, it is difficult to assess the actual impact on cannabis consumption levels due to the many confounding factors and drivers of cannabis use. Nevertheless, she concludes it is safe to say based on the assessment of the many examples of decriminalization, that the ending of criminal penalties for personal cannabis use has not led to an explosion in use.

Eastwood (this volume) points out that cannabis decriminalization can result in significant criminal justice savings (i.e. police, courts, probation and prison services) and improve employment opportunities for people who would otherwise be criminalized. Eastwood (this volume) also notes that police often come to support decriminalization, as this approach improves relationships with the public. However, decriminalization can fail to deliver these benefits if the policy is poorly implemented and people are not actually diverted away from the criminal justice system due to the net-widening activity of police, high administrative sanctions, low thresholds for eligibility and ongoing racial profiling (Eastwood, this volume).

Hughes (this volume) recounts that Australia was an early reformer of cannabis laws with four states/territories introducing *de jure* decriminalization involving prohibition with civil penalties. A second wave of seven states/territories introduced de facto decriminalization involving police diversion and cannabis cautioning programs. Although these reforms were seen to reduce criminal justice costs without generating any increase in the use of cannabis, a number of unintended effects emerged including net-widening, non-compliance and exploitation of the schemes by organized crime. In the context of widening societal awareness that cannabis use could be associated with serious health risks, these perverse outcomes fueled opposition and retrenchment of the civil penalty schemes. Hughes (this volume) summarizes the current mood for further reform in Australia as one of "wait and learn" from the international examples of legalization, and a growing recognition that repeating the approach taken with alcohol and tobacco would be a mistake.

Belackova and colleagues (this volume) explore an important aspect of cannabis policy reform that tolerates or explicitly permits small-scale home cultivation of cannabis. This can occur within wider depenalization, decriminalization or legalization of cannabis, and can stipulate no commercial sales (i.e. gifting only). The variability in provisions for home cultivation, as well as the availability of alternative options for supply (e.g. cafes and retail outlets), complicates the evaluation of home-cultivation policies. Home cultivation could potentially reduce enforcement costs by permitting self-supply, shift demand away from the black market, and – in cases of full legalization – provide a non-commercial source of supply. Questions remain as to whether home cultivation stimulates use by increasing availability (even though there are officially no legal sales), and whether growers will actively engage with information on safer pesticide and fertilizer use, and other safe growing techniques. Belackova and colleagues (this volume) suggest an important step for evaluating home cultivation policies is to include questions in data collection systems about all the different ways users obtain their cannabis (i.e. home-grow, purchase from black market, purchase from legal outlet).

Lessons from local pragmatic responses

Blickman and Sandwell (this volume) detail how local government authorities have played important roles in developing creative local policy responses to drug problems, notably in the Netherlands (cannabis "coffeeshops") (see also Korf, this volume), Denmark, Germany and Switzerland (see also Anderfuhren-Biget et al., this volume). Local customization has also played an important part in US states that have legalized cannabis by allowing counties to opt out of some regulation, for example in relation to retail cannabis outlets. Subritzky (this volume) notes that in Colorado, local government has played an important role in introducing public health regulation of the legal cannabis market, including with respect to external signage, opening hours, outlet density and the application of chemical pesticides during the cultivation stage. Blickman and Sandwell (this volume) argue that this "local customization" can soften opposition to reform and allow for more nuanced reform responses for localities with different demographic make-ups, histories and political visions. At the same time, these local experiments are ultimately restrained by national law and policy and this can impede further development of such regimes to address outstanding problems. In addition, unless local regulatory responses to cannabis use are reflected in national laws and regulations, they are at increased risk of reversal by policy changes at national or other local levels.

Anderfuhren-Biget et al. (this volume) describe how in Switzerland, the absence of a political consensus about how to address cannabis use led to piecemeal reforms and localized initiatives. In 2012, criminal sanctions for adult cannabis use were replaced with administrative fines. A subsequent 2017 federal judicial review concluded that possession of less than ten grams of cannabis should not be punishable by either a fine or other penalty. Meanwhile, Swiss entrepreneurs had become involved in the medicinal cannabis industry, including producing and selling low-THC/high-CBD cannabis products. This led to the rapid development of a multifaceted market for legal cannabis with less than 1 percent THC, including the introduction of federal market guidelines in early 2017. By the summer of 2018, more than 600 cannabis companies were officially registered, and a large number of products are currently available on the market.

Anderfuhren-Biget et al. (this volume) note the contrast between the US experience of legalization, which was characterized by the bringing together of a range of stakeholders to support the reforms, and the lack of political consensus on cannabis in Switzerland. As a result, they propose a model that would establish a restrictive model of cannabis market regulation, including separating the medical from the non-medical market, establishing dedicated stores and thorough tracking of production and sales practices. The model includes enhanced public health protections for consumers, such as harm-related taxation rates and a prohibition on sales of smoking paraphernalia from cannabis shops.

Perhaps the most well-known of the early cannabis law reforms is the Dutch cannabis "coffeeshop" regime that emerged locally during the late 1970s. The Dutch approach took decriminalization a step further by permitting users to buy and use small amounts of cannabis in "coffeeshops." Korf (this volume) explains that over the subsequent decades, control of the coffeeshop policy vacillated between local municipalities and national government. The eventual result is a well-defined set of national regulations and enforcement policies, including a minimum age and maximum amount of cannabis per transaction, as well as provisions for local arrangements, including a zero coffeeshop option. In more recent times, there has been some retrenchment of the system with the introduction of a residents-only criterion to prevent cannabis tourism, and private club criterion requiring patrons to register as members. The unintended impact of the increased restrictions on cannabis coffeeshops has been a tendency for people to return to purchasing cannabis from street drug dealers, resulting in associated problems. A long-standing problem has been that while the retail side of the cannabis market is regulated via the coffeeshops, the supply of cannabis from the black market continues, with the related problems of organized crime involvement and no safety regulation of cannabis products. In 2017, after pressure from municipal authorities and the election of a new government, a policy trial was announced that would enable up to ten municipalities to organize the regulated supply of cannabis to coffeeshops in "a closed circuit from plant to consumer."

Cannabis Social Clubs (CSCs) are another well-known example of a pragmatic grassroots response that developed in the context of cannabis decriminalization, whereby users self-organize to combine their permitted individual plant cultivation quotas into one larger collective crop and then share the resulting harvest among club members. Araña and Parés (this volume) describe that while over 800 CSCs are currently operating in Spain, with some in operation for over 15 years, there is still no national framework in place to regulate them. As a result, the clubs have been left to self-regulate, leading to different approaches and different types of social clubs, with some larger clubs pursuing commercial activities by providing cannabis to tourists. Recent unfavorable Spanish court rulings suggest CSCs will be required to return to their original civil club origins to survive, including by reducing their membership numbers, demonstrating genuine club participation, and restraining the scale of cannabis production.

Jamaica also offers a unique local response to cannabis influenced by long-standing societal debate concerning the use of cannabis for "sacramental purposes" by Rastafarians and Maroons, incidents of police brutality related to cannabis law enforcement and the lobbying of civil society organizations and traditional local ganja growers. In 2015, the Dangerous Drug (Amendment) Act decriminalized cannabis use, allowed use by Rastafarians in the context of their religious faith (as a religious sacrament) and allowed home cultivation of up to five plants for folk medicinal use. The Jamaican reforms had both social equity and economic objectives, including stimulating rural economic development, ending the exclusion of people previously discriminated against via cannabis law enforcement and supporting traditional communities involved in cannabis cultivation.

Lessons from alcohol, tobacco and legal highs

Part III of the book investigates the learnings that can be drawn for legal cannabis regulation from decades of research into effective regulation of alcohol, tobacco and legal highs. This substantial body of research suggests that while cannabis has some unique psychoactive, health, social and production characteristics, many of the key findings from research into the regulation of alcohol and tobacco is highly relevant to developing an effective regulatory framework for cannabis. An important implication is that politicians and policymakers need to familiarize themselves with this body of research when designing regulatory frameworks for legal cannabis, rather than treating cannabis as a largely novel regulatory exercise.

Stockwell et al. (this volume) explain that decades of alcohol research show that public health outcomes improve when alcohol is less affordable, less available and less marketed. Particularly effective regulatory tools include a minimum price for alcohol and restricting the density of alcohol outlets. Government monopolies over the sale of alcohol have been found to be effective for applying these two key policy levers, as well as for enforcing point-of-sale checks on sales to intoxicated and underage customers. Product labelling and point-of-sale messaging can also make valuable contributions in raising awareness of health risks and safe consumption guidelines and help create public support for evidence-based regulations. Finally, Stockwell et al. (this volume) recommend ongoing monitoring of policy implementation and related health outcomes against objective criteria to support the achievement of public health outcomes.

Gartner and Hall (this volume) similarly identify a range of lessons from tobacco control that could be effectively translated to cannabis regulation, such as substantial product taxes, age restrictions on sales, smoke-free policies, restrictions on promotional activities, track and trace programs to identify black market supply and plain packaging. Based on tobacco research, high taxes on legal cannabis products can be expected to limit youth use and discourage heavy consumption among both youth and adult users. Gartner and Hall (this volume) recommend that a proportion of cannabis tax revenue be specifically dedicated to funding cannabis-related regulation, including controlling the black market, drug treatment programs and cannabis research. Gartner and Hall (this volume) argue that as there is no established legal cannabis industry or cannabis consumer base, regulators should take the opportunity to pursue ambitious regulatory controls, including limiting the number of retail licenses to control the size of the cannabis market, establishing state or not-for-profit monopolies over sales, mandating limits on the level of THC in products and requiring user licenses.

Rychert and Wilkins (this volume) revisit the ultimately unsuccessful attempt to regulate "legal highs" in New Zealand to identify key mistakes that should be avoided when developing a legal cannabis regime. The Psychoactive Substances Act 2013 was a world-first attempt to regulate the out of control grey market for "legal highs." It was passed with great fanfare in 2013 and an interim regulated market immediately established. Yet, this interim market was effectively ended by legislative amendment after only nine months due to concerns about health impacts and growing public opposition. Rychert and Wilkins (this volume) identify a number of key issues that led to this failure, including insufficient time for planning; not allocating sufficient budget and expertise to the regulatory authority; lack of regulation of price, product type, product potency, outlet density and opening hours; gaps in the system with regard to monitoring adverse events from products; lack of ongoing engagement with health stakeholders and failure to communicate with the public about the policy aims. There are also important questions about the role the legal high industry played in instigating policy change and developing the regulatory regime.

New cannabis legalization proposals

The final section of the book provides two new proposals to advance middle-ground approaches to cannabis law reform. These proposals provide alternative approaches to commercial models and attempt to address key outstanding issues in these new models.

The first new model comes from New Zealand and proposes that the community trusts currently utilized to sell alcohol and operate gambling gaming machines could be adapted to sell cannabis. Wilkins and Rychert (this volume) explain that community trusts have been purposively designed to suppress market expansion and, instead, are expected to focus on philanthropic goals, such as promoting sports, education or cultural activities. A proportion of the revenue from the commercial activities of the community trust is allocated to local "not-for-profit" community services. There is an implicit expectation that community trusts will be more accountable to their local community than profit-driven businesses, via community-elected board members and community polls of the ongoing operation of a trust. To avoid ethical risks associated with direct industry funding of the community sector, Wilkins and Rychert (this volume) propose the inclusion of four mechanisms in the trust model framework: allocation of community grants via an independent national committee based on objective social need; banning of direct funding and sponsorship of community groups; central administration by a health agency; and providing ongoing education to "not-for-profit" community organizations concerning the risks of direct industry funding and partnership.

Decorte and Pardal (this volume) return to the Cannabis Social Club model and discuss the regulatory infrastructure required to make CSCs more viable. The lack of central government regulation has been identified as a key limitation in the Spanish CSC movement. Such a regulatory framework is needed to support social clubs to be more stable and sustainable, but also to stop them drifting towards commercial operations, such as selling cannabis to tourists. Decorte and Pardal (this volume) recommend that CSCs should operate as "not-for-profits," with no advertising or marketing, and register in some form of regional or national database. A national agency is required to oversee their regulation and implementation. They discuss a range of regulatory requirements for CSCs, including: a residency criteria for membership to avoid tourism and related commercialization; limits on the maximum number of members; limits on the number of plants a CSC is allowed to grow; a system for traceability and documentation of the cultivation process; limits on the quantities the CSCs can distribute to their members; and restricting the product to herbal cannabis and hashish. Regulations should also require CSCs to collaborate with local health departments and non-government drug organizations to provide information to club members about health risks, harm reduction strategies and drug treatment services. It is also important that the regulatory framework protects the autonomy of CSCs in order to ensure the model remains attractive to users and avoids them returning to the black market.

Overall conclusions

Seventeen key conclusions emerge from the chapters authored for this book:

1. The existing legal cannabis markets have not been in operation long enough for their social and health impacts to fully manifest;
2. Experience of cannabis legislation to date has demonstrated the complexities of developing regulatory frameworks for cannabis production and products;
3. Existing legal cannabis markets confirm that problematic cannabis users are responsible for the majority of legal cannabis sales;
4. Successful reform movements to date demonstrate the importance of consensual solutions concerning the regulation of cannabis use and markets in order to unify as many stakeholders as possible behind a common proposal;
5. Early experience of cannabis legalization demonstrates that legal cannabis markets can attract substantial demand away from the black market, but some level of black market activity persists, reflecting the need for regulatory controls such as purchase-age restrictions, bans on particularly high-risk product types, absence of legal retail outlets and shortfalls in legal supply;
6. Given the complexities of regulating legal cannabis markets and the risk that vulnerable cannabis users will be exploited by commercial cannabis sellers, there is a strong case for an initially restrictive regulatory framework and conservative implementation of a legal cannabis market;
7. Regulatory rules are required to prevent the cannabis industry from directly funding the community sector to enhance their public image and political influence, including: the banning of direct funding and sponsorship of community groups, central administration of cannabis regulation by a health agency and providing ongoing education to the community sector concerning the ethical risks of direct industry funding;
8. While cannabis has some unique psychoactive, health, social and production characteristics, many of the key findings from studies of effective alcohol and tobacco regulation are highly relevant to the regulation of cannabis, including high product taxation, minimum pricing, restrictions on the density of retail outlets, plain packaging, smoke-free policies, age restrictions on sales, restrictions on advertising and promotion and track and trace programs to identify black market supply;
9. Based on the experience of trying to regulate a legal high market in New Zealand, it is likely that the establishment of a regulated legal cannabis market can be undermined by a lack of forward planning, inadequate

resourcing of the regulatory agency, lack of detailed regulation of the retail market, lack of engagement with key health stakeholders, poor communication of policy aims to the general public and a flawed system for monitoring adverse events from use and products;

10 The legalization of cannabis provides opportunities to address social equity issues related to cannabis enforcement, including discrimination against minorities, disproportionate penalties and inhibiting rural economic development, via the expungement of previous convictions, providing support to enter the cannabis industry and by specifically allocating cannabis licenses to affected communities;

11 Many of the earlier cannabis law reform approaches were local responses, and this "local customization" has allowed them to be adapted to the characteristics of their communities. At the same time, local experiments are ultimately restrained by national law and policy, and there is a need for alignment between local, regional (state) and national policies to avoid the risk of policy reversal and to allow further development of such regimes to address outstanding problems;

12 There are a range of early examples of pragmatic "middle ground" cannabis law reforms that have established legal tolerance of cannabis use while avoiding a commercial cannabis market, such as decriminalization, cannabis coffeeshops and CSCs, which – despite some incidences of retrenchment – have largely been accepted and could now be revitalized and further extended;

13 It is recommended that "decriminalization" options include provisions for home cultivation and social clubs in order to provide an alternative means of supply to the black market and its related harms. However, the extent to which home cultivation can address the supply side of the market and reduce harms associated with the illegal trade remains an issue;

14 CSCs require central regulation to ensure their stability and sustainability, and to allow them to realize their full public health and wider policy potential;

15 Non-commercial modes of legal cannabis supply, such as home cultivation and CSCs, have proven to be popular among cannabis users in legal cannabis markets, but questions remain about their capacity to meet the needs of all types of consumers, some of whom will not be interested in home cultivation or joining a cannabis club;

16 State or not-for-profit monopolies for alcohol have been found to be most effective at applying key policy levers to achieve public health outcomes, and hence are worthy of consideration for legal cannabis sales;

17 Community trusts in the New Zealand example may offer an approach to selling cannabis that aims to reduce commercial incentives for market expansion, introduce community oversight into the local cannabis retail environment and provide significant funding for local community services.

Index

Page numbers in **bold** denote tables, those in *italics* denote figures.

For Product Safety Concerns and Information please contact our EU representative GPSR@taylorandfrancis.com
Taylor & Francis Verlag GmbH, Kaufingerstraße 24, 80331 München, Germany

www.ingramcontent.com/pod-product-compliance
Ingram Content Group UK Ltd.
Pitfield, Milton Keynes, MK11 3LW, UK
UKHW020024200926
475702UK00014B/2049

* 9 7 8 1 0 3 2 1 7 4 0 4 4 *